WORLD AFFAIRS
National and International Viewpoints

WORLD AFFAIRS
National and International Viewpoints

The titles in this collection were selected
from the Council on Foreign Relations' publication:
The Foreign Affairs 50-Year Bibliography

Advisory Editor
RONALD STEEL

THE IRISH FREE STATE
AND ITS SENATE

A Study in Contemporary Politics

by

DONAL O'SULLIVAN

ARNO PRESS
A NEW YORK TIMES COMPANY
New York • 1972

Reprint Edition 1972 by Arno Press Inc.

Reprinted by permission of Faber and Faber Ltd.

Reprinted from a copy in The University of Illinois
Library

World Affairs: National and International Viewpoints
ISBN for complete set: 0-405-04560-3
See last pages of this volume for titles.

Manufactured in the United States of America

∞∾∽∾∽∾∽∾∽∾∽∾∽∾∽∾∽

Library of Congress Cataloging in Publication Data

O'Sullivan, Donal Joseph, 1893–
    The Irish Free State and its senate.

    (World affairs: national and international
viewpoints)
    Reprint of the 1940 ed.
    Includes bibliographical references.
    1. Irish Free State. Parliament. Senate.
2. Ireland--Politics and government--1922-1949.
I. Title. II. Series.
JN1415.O74 1972   320.9'415'09   72-4286
ISBN 0-405-04579-4

THE IRISH FREE STATE
AND ITS SENATE

THE IRISH FREE STATE
AND ITS SENATE

THE IRISH FREE STATE
AND ITS SENATE

A Study in Contemporary Politics

by

DONAL O'SULLIVAN

FABER AND FABER LIMITED
24 Russell Square
London

FIRST PUBLISHED IN SEPTEMBER MCMXL
BY FABER AND FABER LIMITED
24 RUSSELL SQUARE, LONDON, W.C.1
PRINTED IN GREAT BRITAIN BY
WESTERN PRINTING SERVICES LTD., BRISTOL

TO
MY WIFE

'Whether we are of an ancient Irish descent, or of later Irish birth, we are united in one people, and we are bound by one lofty obligation to complete the building of our common nation.'

ALICE STOPFORD GREEN, 'Message to the Senate'.

'Quis nescit primam esse historiae legem, ne quid falsi dicere audeat? deinde ne quid veri non audeat?'

CICERO, *De Oratore*, II, 15.

PREFACE

Although the Irish Free State as such lasted for only fifteen years, the period is one more filled with incident than any other comparable period of Irish history. For almost the whole of that time it was governed under a bicameral system, in which the Senate played a not inconsiderable part; and as the Clerk of that House I was privileged to view the political arena from a position of intimate detachment. When, therefore, both the original Senate and the Irish Free State were successively brought to an end, I decided to compile a record in which the history of the Second Chamber and of the State itself should be combined, to serve as a chronicle of the past, and also, it may be, as a guide for the future. This book is the result.

A word is called for regarding the general plan. After an introduction to the period, the general history and the history of the Senate are dealt with, so far as possible, *pari passu*, the Senate triennial periods being adopted for this purpose as a convenient, if arbitrary, division. There follows a review of the constitutional changes brought about after the legislature had been reduced to a single chamber, and some chapters dealing with subjects of special interest to the student of parliamentary institutions. Finally, some account is given of the principal events from the promulgation of the Constitution of 1937 down to the outbreak of the present European War.

The path of any writer of contemporary history is beset by pitfalls, all of which I can hardly hope to have avoided. But it has been my endeavour throughout to produce an objective record, based exclusively on documentary materials, such as the published debates of both Houses of the legislature, Parliamentary Reports of various kinds, and contemporary newspapers. I have not thought it either necessary or desirable wholly to suppress my personal opinions, which are, indeed, strongly held; but neither do I desire to obtrude them on the reader, who can judge for himself whether or not they are sustained by the evidence.

As the subject breaks virtually new ground, my obligations are naturally few. I have, however, derived much profit from a study of the quarterly articles in which the Irish correspondent of the *Round Table* has, for the last fifteen years, presented a vivid, accurate, and impartial account of the contemporary Irish scene.

In conclusion, I wish to tender my sincere thanks to Mr. J. C. Jennett, of the staff of Messrs. Faber & Faber, for the care with which he has seen the book through the press.

DONAL O'SULLIVAN

Cairn Hill
Foxrock
County Dublin
Saint Patrick's Day, 1940

CONTENTS

Chapter III. DRAFTING THE CONSTITUTION

Chapter IV. THE ESTABLISHMENT OF THE SENATE

for the improvement of agriculture, fisheries, and housing—Defence of the State and of society—The Republican Government and Army—Repudiation of the National Loan—Statistics of lawlessness—The Cove outrage—Remedial measures and their success—Statesmanship of Kevin O'Higgins—The Government's internal troubles—Ministerial changes—The stillborn National Party—Restoration of stable conditions.

b

PART V. THE FOURTH TRIENNIAL PERIOD
6TH DECEMBER 1931 TO 5TH DECEMBER 1934

Chapter XVII. MR. DE VALERA TAKES OFFICE *page* 281

Chapter XVIII. THE SENATE AND THE PARLIAMENTARY OATH *page* 301

Chapter XXI. THE BILL TO ABOLISH THE SENATE
page 363

Chapter XXII. MR. DE VALERA'S HISTORICAL
AUTHORITIES *page* 390

CONTENTS

PART VI. THE FIFTH TRIENNIAL PERIOD
6TH DECEMBER 1934 TO 29TH MAY 1936

PART VIII. CHAPTERS ON SPECIAL SUBJECTS

PART IX. EPILOGUE

APPENDICES

INTRODUCTION

For the adequate presentation of the political and constitutional history of a country an abundance of documented fact and of apposite quotation is doubtless essential. But even if the piling of phenomena upon phenomena be accompanied by a continuous attempt at interpretation, one is left with the feeling that, in the absence of an epitome, the result may well have been to produce a series of fugitive silhouettes rather than a picture bearing some resemblance to reality and to artistic truth. Moreover, when a writer of contemporary history is dealing, not with some foreign country, but with his own land, the patriotic duty is imposed on him of examining its perplexities with insight and sympathy, and, if possible, of suggesting (however diffidently) a solution of its discontents.

If the operation of the Home Rule Act of 1914 had not been frustrated by the *non possumus* attitude of the Ulster Unionists, there can be no doubt that the subsequent history of Ireland would have been very different. The contacts which would have been made by the Unionists with men of the calibre of the Redmonds, John Dillon, T. M. Healy, and William O'Brien would have removed prejudices and allayed suspicions. The joint task of solving the problems of their common country would, in time, have produced an identity of interest. The limited status conferred by the Act would inevitably have been outgrown by consent, and by this time a united Ireland would probably have been as independent as South Africa. In short, there would have been evolution instead of revolution. The creation of a distinctive Irish way of life in the modern world, while maintaining the links with our ancient past, the preservation of the Irish language —these and other fruitful tasks could have been attempted in conditions of tranquillity; and they are the only conditions in which such attempts are likely to succeed.

The fact that Nationalists and Unionists fought side by side in the Great War would undoubtedly have conduced to a more propitious atmosphere but for the march of events at home. The Insurrection of

Easter, 1916, is now looked upon as the beginning of a new era, but it is an historical fact that it was condemned at the time by almost every public body in Ireland. What subsequently swayed public opinion in the opposite direction was the execution one by one of the heroic leaders who took part in it, and national sentiment was further aroused by the senseless (and, in the circumstances, quite futile) attempt to impose conscription in April 1918. It was this attempt that finally broke the Irish Parliamentary Party and ensured the supremacy of Sinn Féin and the Irish Volunteers. Just before the conscription issue was raised the Ulster Unionists selfishly sabotaged the considered proposals of the Irish Convention for a parliament for the whole of Ireland.

The seventy-three Sinn Féin members (out of a total of 105) returned at the general election of December 1918 made the mistake of pitching their demands too high. They met as the first Dáil, issued a Declaration of Independence, and set up a Government of the Irish Republic. These were noble and inspiring gestures, but they had obviously no prospect of being realized in full. Great Britain had just emerged victorious from a struggle with the greatest military power in the world, and the Irish Volunteers, who had now become the Army of the Irish Republic, could not possibly hope to defeat her in the field. After the inevitable clash there would be negotiations, and the Irish negotiators would have to accept something less than the Republic. If all other obstacles had been surmounted, there still remained the hard fact that one-quarter of the total representation, from the north-east area of the country, was solid for the maintenance of the union with Great Britain.

In December 1920, in the middle of the Anglo-Irish war, the British Government attempted to cut the Gordian knot by establishing *two* legislatures in Ireland, one for the six counties of north-east Ulster and the other for the remaining twenty-six counties. In other words, the country was partitioned, but provision was made for contact through a Council of Ireland and for unification by mutual agreement. Only four of the Ulster counties contained a majority of Unionists, and even in them there were considerable areas in which the Nationalists were in a very substantial majority. The other two counties (Tyrone and Fermanagh) were added in order to make 'Northern Ireland', as it was called, a viable area. The result was that a part of Ireland in which the Catholic Nationalists numbered more than one-third of the population was placed under a government of Protestant Unionists who had never given any evidence of capacity for governmental functions—none of them had held office at Westminster—nor of any regard for the rights of the minority. In the remaining twenty-six counties, somewhat humorously designated 'Southern Ireland', partition was ignored and the guerrilla war continued.

Viewed in retrospect, the Anglo-Irish Treaty of 1921 possesses a quality of inevitability. The Irish were not prepared to take less than what was then called dominion status. The British were not prepared to concede more. In their final dispatch leading up to the negotiations, the British Government had made it clear that on the question of the recognition of the Republic they were adamant; and, as the Irish were not in the position of dictating terms, it must have been obvious to the Dáil Cabinet, when consenting to nominate plenipotentiaries, that no progress could be made on that basis. Also, as the Belfast Government were not represented, it must have appeared unlikely, to say the least, that the *status quo* in Northern Ireland would be seriously disturbed. The partition difficulty was met by the boundary provisions, which later, of course, proved to be nugatory in practice. Against the undoubted benefits conferred by the Treaty must be set two facts. The British had conceded to physical force what they had consistently refused to constitutional agitation—a portent that was not lost upon many of our people; and large numbers of Irish Volunteers had spent their formative years in activities which, however patriotic, ill fitted them for their return to the humdrum life of the Irish countryside.

It is only to be expected that the leaders of the opposition to the Treaty should continue vehemently to assert that the Provisional Government established thereunder was the result of a *coup d'état*, the authors of which were accordingly responsible for the Civil War. But a statement which has no basis in fact does not become true by constant repetition, and the facts have never been in doubt. The Treaty was approved by a majority of the people's representatives in the Dáil. Two days later Mr. De Valera said that the resolution of approval was not the same thing as an Act of Ratification, though he had not adverted to the point before the decision had been taken. Pursuant to the Treaty, a Provisional Government was set up, and it functioned alongside the existing Dáil Cabinet and in harmony with it. Mr. De Valera held that the Provisional Government was illegal and said that it would not be obeyed. In March, at Dungarvan, although he was then only a private member of the Dáil, holding no office either civil or military, he used words, quoted in the text, which might be construed as advising the resumption of hostilities against the British forces, which were then engaged in evacuating the country. The justifiability or otherwise of homicide is, in the highest degree, a moral issue; and it is the doctrine of the Catholic Church that the teaching of the bishops on moral questions must be obeyed. The united Catholic Hierarchy issued a joint statement in April in which they said that, whatever speculative views might be held on the subject, in practice there could be no doubt where the supreme authority lay so long as the Dáil and the Provisional Government continued to act in unison; and they stated that the participants in the military revolt, when they shot their brothers on the opposite side, were murderers. A few days afterwards Mr. De Valera said that it would be a terrible thing if the taunt that these men were murderers should be upheld by the common people; he did not, however, attribute the 'taunt' to the bishops, but to 'the English'.

The general election fought on the issue of the Treaty resulted in its acceptance by an overwhelming majority of the people. As the outrages continued the Hierarchy, in October, issued a Joint Pastoral, in which they again expounded the moral law and condemned what the irregular forces called a war as morally only a system of murder and assassination. They also referred to the possibility that vanity and self-conceit might have blinded some who thought that they, and not the nation, must dictate the national policy. A few weeks later the anti-Treaty minority of the Dáil appointed Mr. De Valera to be 'President of the Republic', established a government to function in co-operation with the irregular forces, and rescinded the resolution approving the Treaty. The truth is that the actions, throughout 1922, of the dissident minority both in the Dáil and among the Irish Volunteers had rendered civil war inevitable. There was no *coup d'état*, unless it be a *coup d'état* to oppose force with force in order to uphold the plainly expressed decision of the majority.

Mention need be made of only one further matter in this connection, and that is desirable because of Mr. De Valera's own frequent references to it, even at the present time. In March 1922 he made three speeches in which he predicted the shedding of Irish blood if the Treaty was ratified at a general election, and his explanation has always been that his words merely constituted a solemn warning against ratification, on the ground that the methods hitherto adopted in the struggle for the Republic would be impossible, since those methods would involve the shedding by the Irish Volunteers of the blood of their fellow countrymen. The passages in question are quoted in the text of this book, and it will be seen that the wording of two of them renders this explanation impossible. Mr. De Valera said at Carrick-on-Suir that, if the Treaty was accepted, *the fight for freedom would still go on*, and that the Irish people, instead of fighting foreign soldiers, would have to fight the Irish soldiers of an Irish government. At Killarney he said that if the Treaty was ratified and if the Volunteers continued, *and he hoped they would continue until the goal was reached*, then, in order to achieve freedom, they would have to wade through Irish blood. It will be seen that the words which I have placed in italics forbid any explanation except the obvious one. Indeed, from the beginning to the end of these speeches there is no suggestion that 'slaughter fratricidal' was a horror to be avoided at all costs.

The Civil War has cast an enduring and malign shadow over Irish public life. It has poisoned, and to some extent continues to poison, the relations between the two principal political parties. It is not improbable that it barred, soon after the Treaty was signed, a peaceful solution of the problem of partition; and it has provided the excuse for the continued existence of the Irish Republican Army, which has the same objects and uses the same slogans as did the irregular forces in 1922.

The Civil War has also had the effect, insufficiently noticed, of retarding our political development, just as the partition issue has had a similar effect in north-east Ulster. For several decades before 1921, while Ireland was part of the United Kingdom, the political education of the people of Great Britain progressed, under a gradually extending franchise, by means of the programmes expounded to them by the various political parties—Liberal, Conservative, and, later, Labour. The British elector had an opportunity of assessing the merits of each, of making his choice, and of revising it later if he thought fit. The case in Ireland was far otherwise. Inevitably, the only subject of secular interest (apart from the land question) was the subject of Home Rule. On this there was unanimity. General elections came and went, but, except in Ulster, the candidates were either unopposed or else contested the seats on largely personal issues. In Ulster, the issue in the contested constituencies was Nationalism versus Unionism, just as it is in the Six Counties to-day.

Thus the political education of the Irish people in 1921 was, through no fault of our own, far below that of the people in the neighbouring island. The self-government achieved under the Treaty gave us an opportunity to remedy this position, but the Civil War intervened to prevent it by substituting the Treaty issue for the Home Rule issue. The refusal of those who led the country into civil war to accept the

Treaty position made the growth of normal political parties, on social or economic lines, impossible. Even to-day, when the differences between the two major political parties are tending to become obliterated—largely through the Government's adoption of the policy of the Opposition—the average elector still sees the issue as, 'Having regard to their past record, whom do you favour, Mr. Cosgrave or Mr. De Valera?'

The first five years of the Irish Free State were the formative years. The attempt to overthrow the State was successfully resisted, and foundations were laid which, in spite of shocks, endure substantially until this day. Friendly relations were maintained with Great Britain, and by presenting their case in an unprovocative manner our representatives at the Imperial Conference of 1926 did their full share in clearing away much of the dead wood that hampered the free development of the independent nations of the Commonwealth. With no sacrifice of the essentials of Irish nationality, the co-operation of the former Unionist element was welcomed and obtained.

Gratitude in politics is a fleeting thing, but it is right to give due credit to Mr. Cosgrave, as head of the Government, for the achievements of this early period. He was the idol of the people at that time, but he was never betrayed into demagogy, or into refraining from unpopular acts for the sake of retaining his hold on the electors. As to his Cabinet, *il savait bien s'entourer*, as the French say. Such Ministers as O'Higgins, Hogan, Mulcahy, O'Sullivan, and McGilligan were all highly educated men, with their feet firmly on the ground, who knew their jobs before they started, or were not slow to learn. All were of strong—in some cases, even dominant—personality, but Mr. Cosgrave held them together. He was never more than a leader among equals, which is precisely as it should be in a democratic State; and if he had retired or been removed from the political arena the régime would have continued, for there were others to succeed him.

For the successful working of parliamentary institutions a strong government is not enough. A strong opposition is also essential, and until August 1927 the Dáil was a mere truncated assembly, since upwards of one-third of the members did not attend. In their absence it was extremely fortunate that the small Labour Party was able to produce a leader of the calibre of Mr. Thomas Johnson, a politician of great ability and integrity, of undoubted patriotism, and of tireless energy in opposition. His colleagues included some capable men, but the empty benches often seemed more eloquent than the speeches in the House. Mr. De Valera apparently remained 'President of the Republic' until near the end of 1925, when the 'Government of the Republic' was repudiated by the Irish Republican Army. Thereafter he proposed to Sinn Féin that Republicans should enter the Dáil, provided that the parliamentary Oath was removed. Sinn Féin rejected this proposal, and in May 1926 he founded the Fianna Fáil Party. But Fianna Fáil still stood for the establishment (or, as Sinn Féin and the Irish Republican Army would have put it, the maintenance) of the Irish Republic; and it continued to boycott the Dáil because of the Oath.

In these early years the Senate proved to be of very great value to the State. It is true that its powers were limited, and that the attitude to it of both the Government and the Dáil left much to be desired. But in personnel it was probably the equal of any Second Chamber then existing, and it exercised a considerable and wholly beneficial influence on legislation. Its principal achievement, however, lay in the proof it afforded that Nationalists and Unionists could work harmoniously together in Parliament for the good of their common country. It would be less than the truth to say that each side met the other half-way, because, in general, they never gave the impression of taking sides at all in a Nationalist or Unionist sense. Much of the credit is due to the Nationalists (including, of course, the Labour Party), because they were in the majority and so could, if they had been so minded, have created an opposition and then have overridden it. But that was never their way. The former Unionists have had their detractors, and so it is fitting that I, as a Catholic and a Nationalist who was intimately acquainted with them individually, should place on record my informed opinion. Of the Protestants and former Unionists who were at one time or another members of the Senate, an extremely high percentage were capable men, and not a few were men of quite exceptional ability. They unreservedly accepted the new order, and I never found that they held corporate views which ran counter to the national interest. I never knew one who was not, in the most genuine sense, a lover of Ireland, or who regarded Ireland as other than his own country. I never knew one who, at any time, put the interests of England before those of Ireland. And (except for one solitary incident, duly chronicled, which merely served to prove the rule) I never knew one who showed a trace of bigotry in the religious sense.

The murder of Kevin O'Higgins in the summer of 1927 marked a turning-point in the history of the State, of which he had been the strongest pillar. The Government passed legislation to end abstentionism, and Mr. De Valera was forced either to modify his principles or to abandon politics. He chose the former course, subscribed the parliamentary Oath, and entered the Dáil with his followers, thus completing the membership of the House. He was destined to spend four and a half years as Leader of the Opposition, but his ultimate return to power was now inevitable, since the force of his personality had kept the Treaty issue in the foreground and prevented the development of political parties on rational lines. Entry into the Dáil did not involve recognition of its legality, however. The Fianna Fáil newspaper described the party's action, editorially, as sheer expediency. The Dáil, it said, was a faked parliament, a Dáil of usurpers, which they believed in their hearts to be illegitimate; and the Cosgrave Government was not the *de jure* government, but a junta. Mr. De Valera stated that those who remained on in the organization which he had left could claim the same continuity that he had claimed up to 1925— in other words, that the 'Government of the Republic', which still pursued a shadowy existence, was the real government of the country. This was not an isolated instance. Mr. O'Kelly referred to the Minister for Defence as 'the so-called Minister for Defence', the implication being that the real Minister for Defence was the one in the 'Government of the Republic'; and Mr. Lemass described Fianna Fáil as 'a slightly constitutional party', which would not necessarily confine itself to constitutional methods if those methods did not promote its object, which was the establishment of a Republican government.

The fact that the Opposition held these views was naturally of incalculable value to the Irish Republican Army. Every attempt by the Government to suppress intimidation and outrage was fought by Fianna Fáil as bitterly as a rearguard action in the field. Mr. De Valera held that the Cosgrave Administration was merely continuing the British policy of coercion. The right way of dealing with the situation, he maintained, was to abolish the parliamentary Oath, though it had not proved to be a barrier in his own case and he should have known from personal experience that it was not a factor in the calculations of those who placed their faith in physical force. In 1931, after some particularly atrocious murders, he stated that the members of the Irish Republican Army were misguided, but still they were brave men, and he enjoined for them the respect that is due to the brave. Fortunately, the Government were not deflected from their obvious duty to the people, and the insertion in the Constitution, a few months before they left office, of an article authorizing the establishment of military tribunals gave them, and any government that might succeed them, adequate powers for the suppression of disorder. There was a certain irony about this drastic legislation. The whole of the unpopularity which resulted from its enactment was incurred by the Cosgrave Administration, and practically the whole of the benefit of its provisions accrued to their successors. In view of the vehement denunciations of the Opposition, nobody could have supposed that they would operate the Military Tribunal Article when they became a government. Indeed, Mr. De Valera promised to repeal the article in full, and there can be no doubt that his attitude towards it contributed very largely to his success at the general election of 1932.

There was a like irony in the advance to complete independence, within the Commonwealth, which was achieved by the Cosgrave Administration on the basis of the Treaty. The general principles laid down at the Imperial Conference of 1926 were worked out in detail at the Conferences of 1929 and 1930. The Reports of these Conferences were denounced by Fianna Fáil with no less vigour than the Military Tribunal Article, and they were approved in the teeth of their opposition. The results were embodied in the Statute of Westminster, 1931, which gave the Irish Free State unfettered legislative freedom, enabled her to repeal any existing laws of the United Kingdom Parliament in so far as they applied to her, and prohibited that Parliament from enacting such laws in future without her express consent. Two months after this crowning achievement had reached the Statute Book the Cosgrave Government were voted out of office and their successors were enabled, pursuant to the Statute, to repeal the Treaty; but, of course, its validity as an international instrument remains unaffected unless and until it is denounced by either of the parties to it or else abrogated by mutual consent.

The last years of the Cosgrave Administration saw the influx of the Fianna Fáil Party into the Senate, and consequently the rudiments of a party system. This was not on very pronounced lines, but, if the Senate had not been abolished, the decision to constitute the two Houses as the electorate would have produced in the long run a completely political Second Chamber, in which independent men of distinction would have found no place. The ceaseless attacks made upon the Senate by leaders of the Opposition helped to discredit it in the eyes of the public, who were not in a position to know the facts; and their aim was admittedly to transform it into a body so nearly a reflex of the Dáil as to render it useless and so to facilitate its abolition.

Mr. De Valera's advent to office ushered in the expected period of unrest. He had been given a mandate to retain the Land Annuities hitherto paid over, by agreement, to the British Government acting on behalf of the bond-holders; and he claimed a mandate to abolish the parliamentary Oath on the alleged ground that its removal would not be a breach of the Treaty. He now announced his intentions on these matters *urbi et orbi*, leaving the British Government to make the first move in the inevitable dispute. As in private life he is the most courteous of men, this action is probably to be explained by his fanatical belief that he is right, and that there is no other side to any question on which he has decided views. Indeed, it is not unlikely that he did not foresee any dispute, since, in the election programme containing these two items, he stressed the fact that Ireland and Great Britain are each other's best customer and looked forward to getting a preference for Irish agricultural products. The Senate suspended the Bill to abolish the Oath, thereby putting a nail in its own coffin; but the British Government regarded the proposal as a breach of the Treaty and declined to negotiate any trade agreement with the Irish Free State at the Ottawa Conference. When Mr. De Valera withheld the Land Annuities the British collected them by levying customs duties on Irish imports. The Irish Free State retaliated, and the result was the economic war. Anglo-Irish relations were not improved by the treatment accorded to the Governor-General. He was insulted by Ministers on a number of occasions, and, being refused an apology by Mr. De Valera, published the correspondence against the formal advice of the Government. He was accordingly dismissed, and the choice of his successor made it clear that the office itself was unlikely to be of long duration.

The Irish Republican Army had played an important part in Mr. De Valera's election success, and as soon as he had formed his Government the prisoners were released post-haste and the ban was removed. No obstacle was placed in the way of its members' marching openly in military formation, and the Minister for Justice defended the issuing of military words of command on such occasions. Intimidation became rife, and the right of free speech was seriously threatened. Unofficial action of an intimidatory character was taken in the prosecution of the economic war, and while the Minister for Justice promised protection from unwarrantable interference the Minister for Finance said that all traders must bear in mind the consequences of flouting public opinion. In these conditions of impending anarchy the Army Comrades Association, later to be known as the Blue Shirts, extended its membership to all who stood for the freedom of speech, of the Press, and of elections. A new party, called the National Centre Party and led by Mr. Frank MacDermot and Mr. James Dillon, was formed about the same time, with the object of giving the farmers and the ratepayers their just share in the political life of the country. The possibility of amalgamating this new party with the Cosgrave Party was canvassed, and, with the object of forestalling any such movement and of making himself independent of the Labour vote in the Dáil, Mr. De Valera decided on a dissolution. His first Administration had lasted less than ten months, during which time the whole Treaty position had been called in question, a bitter struggle had been entered upon with Great Britain, and the Irish Republican Army had acquired a power greater than it had enjoyed since the days of the Civil War.

During the election campaign free speech and freedom from intimidation were secured with difficulty by the Army Comrades Association. Mr. De Valera was again returned to power, with a party numbering just half the House, but with a minority of the total first preference votes cast. The Bill to abolish the parliamentary Oath was duly enacted over the head of the Senate, and so was brought to the test Mr. De Valera's professed belief that the Oath had been the barrier to unified action and the cause of extremism. The Irish Republican Army was by this time a heavily armed body, and it went from strength to strength, its principal victims being the supporters of the parliamentary Opposition and the unarmed Blue Shirts, now reorganized under General O'Duffy, who had been relieved of his post as Chief of Police. There had been a pre-election promise that all citizens would be treated as equal before the law, but Mr. De Valera regarded the Irish Republican Army as a body which had its roots in the past and one which might be said to have a national objective, and he made no attempt to disarm it. He considered the unarmed Blue Shirts to be a cause of provocation to the Irish Republican Army, and his method of pacification consisted in suppressing the Blue Shirts while allowing immunity to their opponents. The Blue Shirt organization was accordingly banned, the Military Tribunal was set up for the trial of its members, and a body of armed men was recruited into the police force, mainly consisting of ex-members of the Irish Republican Army. Impelled by the stress of events, the Cosgrave Party and the National Centre Party joined forces with the Blue Shirts to form the United Ireland Party, but the union was ill-starred. At intervals of twelve months General O'Duffy resigned, Mr. MacDermot resigned, and the Blue Shirts gradually came to an end.

I regard the years 1932 to 1936 as the most sombre period in recent Irish history. The Irish Republican Army was for the most part tolerated, occasionally cajoled, and seldom seriously threatened, while the constitutional Opposition was almost continuously harassed. The Government's security of tenure was facilitated in other ways. The men who had sought to destroy the State during the Civil War, and who had been condemned at the time by public opinion and by the Catholic Church, were pensioned on the same terms as the officers and men of the regular army, and, if their property had been damaged or destroyed during that period, they were compensated. Besides the recruiting of ex-members of the Irish Republican Army into the police, others were placed in key-positions in the Army Volunteer Reserve. The parliamentary constituencies were rearranged in such a manner as to reduce still further the chances of election of independent members; and the abolition of university representation not only deprived the Dáil of a much-needed leavening of educated men but also removed some potential opponents of the Government. Speaking in the Senate in 1934, Mr. Andrew Jameson made a prophecy which came very near to fulfilment. He referred to the electoral changes and said that they had seen the powers of the law strained to the limit for the purpose of putting the representatives of the Opposition, if possible, into gaol, or at any rate preventing them getting a free method of stating their case; and he predicted that, in two years' time (when the Senate would have been abolished), the country would be dominated by one party, 'and one man at the head of that party, with all that party bowing in acquiescence'. Though he could not have known it, the country was being made ripe for the new Constitution.

The Blue Shirts had, in Mr. De Valera's phrase, used the machinery of the law to defeat and prevent their own suppression, and so a Bill was introduced to prohibit the wearing of political uniforms. Its provisions did not apply to the Irish Republican Army, the members of which do not wear uniform. The Senate rejected the Bill, and a Bill to abolish the Senate was introduced on the following day.

The Senate's action merely provided the occasion for the proposal to abolish it, as Mr. De Valera stated that it was due to be abolished in any case. It is now known that his object was to facilitate the subversion of the Constitution. At that time (1934) no specific mention of any such intention had been made in Ireland, though early in 1930 Mr. De Valera is reported to have predicted in the United States that his party would obtain a majority at the general election of 1932 and that they would then be able to overthrow the Constitution. His election manifesto of that year asked for a mandate to abolish the Oath and retain the Land Annuities, and he pledged himself not to exceed that mandate without again consulting the people. All through the debates on the abolition of the Senate, while adducing familiar and unfamiliar arguments in favour of single chamber government, he always left himself a loophole by proclaiming that, if anyone could succeed where he had failed in devising a satisfactory Second Chamber, he would preserve an open mind. He was adamant, however, on the necessity for 'a period of transition', during which the Dáil was to be the sole House of the legislature, though the reason for this was never made clear. When his purpose had been accomplished without a fresh appeal to the people, he gave the reason for the first time. With the national objectives which he had in front of him, he said, he wanted to get rid of a Second House, and in particular he wanted to get rid of the existing Second House while an important piece of constitutional work had to be done. His new Constitution made provision for a Senate, and electors were urged to vote for the Constitution and the restoration of the bicameral system.

While the Senate was still in being measures were passed to deprive the Governor-General of certain of his formal functions and to terminate the right of appeal to the Privy Council. This right of appeal had long been a dead letter and its existence was, of course, incompatible with co-equality; and in general this legislation is of interest merely as affording further evidence of reluctance to observe the customary Commonwealth forms. The same could not be said of the two Acts dealing with citizenship and alienage, which purported to deprive Irish Free State citizens of their status of British subject, Mr. De Valera stating that so to describe them would be an impertinence. Conversely, the citizens, subjects, or nationals of the other member-States of the Commonwealth were made aliens under our law, but were saved from the consequences of alien status by a revocable ministerial order. Further advances towards the Republican ideal without reference to the people had to await the abolition of the Senate.

The changes in the Constitution and the pensioning and admission of their ex-members into the Army and the police had no more effect upon the attitude of the Irish Republican Army than had the abolition of the parliamentary Oath. But it was not until the spring of 1935 that the organization became a serious menace to the Government, which had for years allowed it a reasonably free hand against the Opposition. Its members were increasingly arraigned before the Military Tribunal, although Mr. De Valera waited till June 1936 before taking the extreme step of re-imposing the ban which had been revoked when Mr. Cosgrave left office more than four years earlier.

It was not until the disappearance of the Senate was imminent that Mr. De Valera made the definite announcement that there was to be a new Constitution. At a later date he mentioned that the British Government had been notified, but that the notification had been informal, 'because they have no right to interfere'. Normally, the issue at the plebiscite would have been the existing Constitution, based on the Treaty and including the King, against a new Constitution in which neither appeared. If the issue had been put to the people in this net form it is not at all unlikely that the result would have been the same as in 1922, 1923, and twice in 1927 (the Treaty was not made an issue in 1932 and 1933). But the abdication of King Edward VIII gave Mr. De Valera an opportunity of putting his policy into force without an appeal to the electors. In the space of little over twenty-four hours the Single Chamber removed the King from the Constitution and abolished the Governor-General, the connection with the Commonwealth being retained for external purposes in an ordinary statute, which Mr. De Valera has recently indicated may be repealed.

After this revolution had been effected the new Constitution came somewhat as an anti-climax. The issue was the old Constitution, now incorporating 'external association' and a single chamber, versus the new Constitution, also incorporating 'external association' but providing for a bicameral system. The new instrument creates a President (who is not, however, designated the head of the State), changes the name of the State to Éire, and asserts *de jure* authority over Northern Ireland. It contains a number of 'Directive Principles of Social Policy' which make the document superficially attractive, but as these are expressly stated not to be cognizable by any court their appropriateness is not obvious.

The draft was 'approved' by the existing Dáil, then nearing the end of its statutory term, and it was approved by the people, by a narrow majority, at a plebiscite held on the same day as a general election, the number of non-voters forming 31 per cent of the electorate. Whatever may be our constitutional status, now or in the future, the need for a high standard of truth in political life remains paramount. In the issue for December 1937 of the *Fianna Fáil Bulletin* the passing of the old order was greeted as follows: 'On December 29th we enter a new phase of national history. The old Constitution, drafted in Westminster, amended and excoriated by successive Fianna Fáil amendments until it is an empty symbol of imperial domination, will become a scrap of paper.'

So ends our epitome. Let us now assess our gains and losses over nineteen years. On the credit side, the march of events has proved the wisdom of those who held that the Treaty of 1921 gave us 'freedom to achieve freedom'. At that time it might have seemed that 'dominion status' was a misnomer and a misfit, since Ireland, like Great Britain, is a mother-country of the British Commonwealth and Empire. But the successive advances in status which culminated in the Statute of Westminster placed all the States of the Commonwealth on terms of absolute equality, theoretical and practical, the sole link being the Crown, which in the case of the Irish Free State was to function solely on the advice of Irish Ministers. Though the fact is not generally realized, the term 'dominion status' has itself become outmoded. The present Prime Minister of Canada (Mr. Mackenzie King) has put the position accurately. Speaking in the Canadian House of Commons on the 24th May 1938, he said: 'The time has come to cease speaking of "the Dominions" as if they were some peculiar, half-fledged type of community, and all alike in their interests and views. Such a usage leads to confusion. . . . South Africa is South Africa, New Zealand is New Zealand, Australia is Australia, and Canada is Canada, and it will help to good understanding if that elementary fact is borne in mind.'[1]

No other member-State has put the fact of complete independence to such proof as we have, since we have reduced the link of the Crown to the tenuity of a spider's filament, and nobody doubts that if the oft-threatened Republic were to be proclaimed to-morrow its declaration would be received with regret but without retaliation by the other members. The supreme test of a nation's freedom is its right to neutrality in war. This right has never been questioned in our case, and our exercise of it has occasioned neither protest nor surprise. Indeed, our Ministers have testified to the cordial and helpful attitude adopted by the British Government since the outbreak of the present conflict.

On the debit side there are two grievous items, which by reacting on each other bedevil the whole political situation. The first is the continued existence of the Irish Republican Army and the second is partition. For the former, history will assign the responsibility. Its aim is the establishment of a Republic for the whole of Ireland, and its principles and methods have not altered since 1922, though its leadership has changed. It is now an unlawful organization, but it may well be

[1] *House of Commons Debates (Canada)*, ccxvi, 3189–90.

questioned whether it would be in existence at all but for the encouragement afforded to it by Mr. De Valera and his supporters during the Cosgrave régime and the toleration which it enjoyed during the first four years of the Fianna Fáil Administration. The members of the present Government are sometimes at pains to show that the position now is radically different from what it was in 1922, and their anxiety on the point is intelligible enough. They say that we now have a Constitution chosen freely by the people at a plebiscite, whereas the Constitution of 1922 was not submitted to the people for approval or rejection. It is as well to recall the facts. The Provisional Government offered an election in June 1922 on the issue of the Treaty and the Constitution, asking for a guarantee against intimidation. This proposal having been refused by Mr. De Valera, they offered an election on the single issue of the Treaty, the body so elected to devise the Constitution and then to dissolve, so that the electors might give their verdict. This suggestion was also rejected. Actually, the Constitution was published in the newspapers on the morning of the general election, but nobody can doubt that, if there had been a separate plebiscite, the result would have been the same. After more than a year's experience of the Constitution the Government which had sponsored it was returned to power. In such cases, it is not a question of 'the nicely calculated less or more', but it is pertinent to point out that, of those who voted in the general election of 1922, 78 per cent were in favour of the Treaty and 22 per cent were against it; of those who voted in the plebiscite of 1937, 57 per cent were in favour of the new Constitution and 43 per cent were against it.

No terrorist organization can long exist in defiance of public opinion, and I do not believe that there is a strong public opinion behind the Irish Republican Army. But, our history and traditions being what they are, there is no doubt that our people, encouraged by the utterances of a few brittle intellectuals, do readily respond to an emotional appeal, especially on the subject of the partition of Ireland. The Church has laid down the moral law for those who are not deaf to its teaching, and it must and will be heard. The Catholic individual —still more the Catholic nation—who flouts the Church's doctrine must remain unblest. If I were the head of the Government, while allowing the fullest freedom to preach a republican policy, I should make it my object to ensure that an unlicensed firearm was as rare as a snowflake in summer. That this is not impracticable is shown by the sequel to the magazine raid in the Phoenix Park a few days before Christmas 1939. About two million rounds of ammunition were stolen, and as a result of intense activity by the forces of the State practically the whole of it was recovered within a few weeks. But until we have a government which is in a position to condemn terrorism not only on the grounds of illegality and expediency but on the moral ground as well, it is to be feared that it will continue to vex us. For the moral ground transcends and includes all others. As John Morley said, 'Those who would treat politics and morality apart will never understand the one or the other.'

Before we consider the question of partition it is desirable to say something of the Irish language, since it is the keystone of the arch in Mr. De Valera's conception of nationality, and also in that of numerous others, by no means confined to his political party, who think as he does. Its connection with partition is made clear by the following quotation from one of Mr. De Valera's speeches in the Senate (7th February 1939):

'If I were told to-morrow: "You can have a united Ireland if you give up your idea of restoring the national language to be the spoken language of the majority of the people," I would, for myself, say no. . . . I would say it for this reason: that I believe that as long as the language remains you have a distinguishing characteristic of nationality which will enable the nation to persist. If you lose the language the danger is that there would be absorption.'[1]

This puts the issue in a net form.

It would be a good thing if everyone who discusses this highly controversial subject were to state his qualifications before doing so. I do not regard my own as very considerable. I am not a native speaker of Irish, although it was the language of my immediate forebears; but I have loved it since boyhood with a passion that has been only deepened by time. Over a period of twenty years I have published, annotated, and translated some thousands of lines of the poetry of the people, from manuscripts and from oral tradition—of which work it can, of course, be said that it would have been better done if its author had been better equipped. Hardly a day passes that I do not read or write some Irish; and its folk songs, stored in my memory, are always my invisible companions.

At the least, then, I have no prejudice against the Irish language. But I am a realist, and I say, firstly, that language is not an essential hall-mark of nationality, and, secondly, that I rejoice that it is not. For the attempt to make the Irish language the spoken tongue of the majority of the people cannot, in my opinion, possibly succeed. In-

[1] *Senate Debates*, xxii, 1522–3.

C

deed, I hold it to have already failed; but, as Matthew Arnold said, we are eternal rebels against the despotism of fact, and if a fact is unpleasant we close our eyes to it. In the Senate speech from which I have just quoted, Mr. De Valera came as near to admitting failure as one could fairly expect, for he continued: 'One of the sad things for me all the time is that there has not been a fuller appreciation of that fact amongst the young people of the country,' that is to say, the alleged danger of absorption if the language is lost.

The Irish language volume of the 1936 census has not yet been published, but the figures for 1926 reveal the fact that the number of persons who spoke Irish only was then 12,460 out of a total population of 2,971,992—or less than one-half of one per cent. It will now be much less still, because the majority of these were elderly people fourteen years ago. Apart from this figure, the most valuable information that the census could have afforded would have been (a) the number of native speakers, and (b) the number of persons whose Irish is acquired. The questionnaire was designed on this basis, but the project had to be abandoned because the answers were so often obviously erroneous. For example, native speakers were returned as 50 per cent more numerous between the ages of ten and fourteen than between the ages of five and nine! However, the number of 'Irish speakers' (of both kinds) was returned as 18·3 per cent of the total population.

This is little enough, but personally—and I wish I could say otherwise—I do not believe that the percentage was, or is, anything like so high. As the Director of Statistics points out, personal judgement entered so largely into the replies as to render the numbers insusceptible of exact measurement. It is certain that many persons, from mistaken motives of patriotism, claim to 'know Irish' when their acquaintance with it falls far short of knowledge—even if, sometimes, they cannot do much more than write their names in that language. A literate person may fairly claim to know a language other than his mother tongue only if he can read it with ease, converse fluently in it, and, without the aid of a dictionary, translate a passage of ordinary difficulty into his native tongue, and vice versa. Judged by this test, I greatly doubt whether 5 per cent of the population could be said to know Irish. Even a modest 5 per cent would mean 150,000 persons—a public quite large enough to justify the publication, on a commercial basis, of at least one weekly newspaper of general interest, and we have not a single one.

The truth is that when the politicians took control of the language movement, ousting Dr. Douglas Hyde from the presidency of the

Gaelic League, they again pitched their claims too high. The slogan 'Up the Republic' was paralleled by the slogan, *Gan teanga, gan tír*, which means 'No language, no country', and Mr. De Valera is even more tied to the one than to the other. Not only is the teaching of Irish compulsory in the schools, but other subjects are taught, or rather attempted to be taught, by teachers who have themselves had to learn the language and who often know it only imperfectly. The result may well be, as has been said, to make the children illiterate in two languages. Protests are made by parents, by the teachers themselves, and by responsible educationalists, but these are unlikely to have any effect while the present theory of nationality is predominant.

The policy of compulsory Irish exercises an influence in spheres other than that of education, and the general position may be given in Mr. De Valera's own words. Speaking in the Dáil on the 23rd May 1939 he said: 'It is one of the most difficult tasks that we could possibly tackle, this task of trying to make Irish the spoken language. You cannot do it without making sacrifices. It is not alone here that I have spoken of the sacrifices we have had to make in order to get Irish put into a position of prominence. You have frequently to take the second best. We have, in regard to certain appointments that have been made, appointments of a technical character, said that where a person has a competent knowledge of Irish, if he is otherwise qualified, he has to take precedence over those who may have even a better technical knowledge. If you do not do that, you make no progress.'[1]

This is not progress but retrogression, and it may easily lead to jobbery. The sacrifices referred to have to be made not by the politicians but by the poor. If the poor are ill, it is small consolation to them to know that their 'second best' dispensary doctor has 'a competent knowledge of Irish'—a singularly elastic term, by the way—while men with superior qualifications have, quite probably, departed to practise their profession in England or elsewhere. And similarly in the case of midwives, sanitary engineers, veterinary surgeons, and a host of others.

Our natural resentment at folly of this kind should not blind us to the fact that we have in the Irish language a heritage of great price, and that we should do everything in our power to preserve and to propagate it. The policy of compulsion is now eighteen years old, and so those of the population who are in their twenties or early thirties have had the benefit of it or otherwise. The time has come to make a searching examination of the position in the light of experience, and,

[1] *Dáil Debates*, lxxvi, 97.

if I were in control, I would have such an investigation conducted by a representative, independent commission. Its task would be (*a*) to discover how far the policy of compulsion has justified the expectation of making Irish the spoken language of the majority of the people, and (*b*) to assess the effect of that policy upon education in general. In view of these terms of reference I would not confine the membership of the commission to persons who know Irish, but I would rigidly exclude politicians and persons whose knowledge of the language amounts to no more than a smattering. If the Report of the Commission were unfavourable to the policy I would scrap the policy without hesitation.

On the other hand, I would spare no effort to rekindle the enthusiasm which gave such satisfactory results under the voluntary system and which compulsion has turned into apathy or active dislike. I look forward to the time when a sound knowledge of Irish may be regarded as not unexceptional among the educated classes, but I should not look for it among those who have no special aptitude for languages nor regard it, *per se*, as a title to preferment. The genuinely Irish-speaking areas constitute a special problem. They are the only repositories of the living language, and the most strenuous efforts are needed to arrest the decay which has been in progress for a century. In these areas not only education but all the administrative and social services should continue to be conducted through the medium of Irish and more money ought to be spent on the indigenous industries. Modern industries should be kept away from them, since the language which has its roots in these relatively primitive districts is not in a position to survive modern industrial development.

The Six Counties of Northern Ireland contain very few native speakers of Irish, and so, even if no other obstacle existed to Irish unity, the language question would constitute an effective barrier so long as Mr. De Valera remains a force to be reckoned with. His policy in this and other matters is the result of a constrictive national philosophy which should have no place in the modern world and which would have been unintelligible to any of the great men who preceded him in the leadership of the Irish people. He seems to envisage the Irish nation as it was before the several conquests, and takes small account of the place in that nation of the descendants of the English and Scottish settlers who reached our shores on the successive waves of invasion centuries ago. A passage from a recent book by two distinguished scientists is here in point, though the authors do not refer specifically to Ireland.

'All the movements towards national unity that were so character-istic of the nineteenth century present certain features in common. Among these we would especially note the rise of a myth, so similar in all these cases that we must suppose that it is a natural way of thinking for peoples in like circumstances. Among all the newer and almost all the older nationalities a state of freedom from external political domination has been projected into the past and associated with a hypothetical ancient unity, itself considered as derived from a common inheritance. The implications of this unity were usually left vague; sometimes they were conceived in a legal and historical sense, but often also they were grafted on to a conception of kinship re-garded as a matter of physical transmission. . . . A "nation" has been cynically but not inaptly defined as "a society united by a common error as to its origin and a common aversion to its neighbours".'[1]

On this, as on so many other matters, my views are at direct vari-ance with those of Mr. De Valera. Paying no heed to alleged racial origins, I am content to regard any man as Irish who claims Ireland as his home and who, instinctively or by habit of mind, does not place the interests of any other country before his own. We are of diverse origin, but we are one people, and the exuberance of the Republican and of the Orangeman are but the obverse and the reverse of the same medal. If an Irishman feels a special loyalty to the King (as do most Protestants and some Catholics), I say that he is quite entitled to do so, and that he is not thereby deprived of his title-deeds of nationality. If a man whose ancestors were of English stock feels no special en-thusiasm for the Irish language, I regret the fact but regard it as natural enough, though I remind him that some of the greatest of our living scholars of Irish are also of English stock. A northern acquain-tance recently asked me, in all sincerity, whether there was any room for Protestantism in a united Ireland. My answer is that our national history and our national principles alike forbid the exclusion of Irish Protestants from our common heritage. In the past they have often been the spearhead of Irish nationalism. In the future they have much to contribute to our national life. The nature and extent of that con-tribution must, however, depend on themselves. It can only be given on a basis of freedom and equality. In short, to me at all events, we are neither Gael nor Gall, but Irishmen finding our inspiration in the tradition of our race—a sea which is fed by many streams. Our coun-try is not Éire, the Irish Free State, Northern Ireland, or any of the other aliases with which the politicians have sought to camouflage

[1] Julian S. Huxley and A. C. Haddon, *We Europeans* (1935), pp. 15, 16.

their mistakes, but Ireland, the common mother of Gael and Gall, of Protestant and Catholic. Anything superadded to the name of Irishman is but the leather and prunella of nationality.

There can, however, be no adequate appreciation of the injustice of partition, of its danger to the Commonwealth, and of the difficulties surrounding its removal, unless the fact is fully realized that the Government of Northern Ireland is on a politico-religious basis. The General Report of the census taken on the 28th February 1937 is not yet available, but the following figures and percentages have been compiled from the County Books issued in connection therewith.

Catholics	428,290	33·5
Presbyterians	390,931	30·5
Church of Ireland	345,474	27·0
Methodists	55,135	4·3
All others	59,915	4·7
	1,279,745	100

Thus, the Catholics are the largest single religious denomination, but the government is in the hands of the Orange Order, a society established in 1795 for the maintenance of Protestant ascendancy in Ireland. Dozens of examples could be adduced in proof of this fact, but the following should prove sufficient. They are taken from typical 'Twelfth of July' orations delivered in 1933, though any other year would do as well. The Prime Minister, Lord Craigavon, said, 'I am an Orangeman to the heart, and always an Orangeman.'[1] Captain H. Dixon, Chief Government Whip, since elevated to the peerage as Lord Glentoran, gave point to this statement by referring to the Church of Rome as the 'old hereditary enemy' of the Orange Order.[2] Sir Basil Brooke, baronet and Minister of Agriculture, who lives in County Fermanagh, where Catholics are in a majority, expressed himself as follows: 'Many of his audience employed Roman Catholics, but he had not one about his place. Catholics were out to destroy Ulster with all their might and power. They wanted to nullify the Protestant vote and take all they could out of Ulster and then see it go to hell.'[3] The Rt. Hon. J. M. Andrews, Minister of Labour, refuted an allegation that, of thirty-one porters employed at Stormont (the seat of the Belfast Government and Parliament), twenty-eight were Catholics. 'I have investigated the matter and I have found that there are thirty Protestants and only one Roman Catholic—there

[1] *Belfast News-Letter*, 13 July 1933.   [2] Ibid.   [3] Ibid.

only temporarily.'[1] On another occasion Sir E. M. Archdale, also a member of the Cabinet, dealt with Catholics of a higher social status and actually apologized for even the exiguous number of them employed in his Department of State. 'I have 109 officials, and, so far as I know, there are four Roman Catholics. Three of these were Civil Servants turned over to me, whom I had to take when we began.'[2]

It is safe to say that this condition of affairs, if allowed to develop indefinitely, might easily provoke a revolution, since more than one-third of the population is relegated to a permanent state of inferiority; moreover, this minority is part of the majority of the whole island, with which it longs for reunion. The claim of Northern Ministers to speak for Ulster should be exploded for good. Ulster consists of nine counties, and if the Partition Act of 1920 had placed Ulster under the Belfast Government the domination of the Orange Order would have ended many years ago. Lord Craigavon (then Captain James Craig) himself admitted the fact when the Bill was before the House of Commons. He said: 'We had to take the decision a few days ago as to whether we should call upon the Government to include the nine counties or be satisfied with the six. . . . The majority of Unionists in the nine counties' Parliament is very small indeed. . . . We quite frankly admit that we cannot hold the nine counties. . . . Therefore, we have decided that, in the interests of the greater part of Ulster, it is better that we should give up those three counties.'[3] In other words, the British Government gave the Orangemen whatever they decided to take, and they took the largest possible area that would give them a perpetual, impregnable majority.

Tragedy, in Hegel's words, is the conflict not of right with wrong, but of right with right; and this philosophic truth is here exemplified. The Irish nation has an inalienable and sacred right to territorial unity. The Northern Protestants have a right to be continued in that allegiance which has been theirs for centuries. Until these two rights are acknowledged and reconciled we shall make no progress.

Each side has been driven along the road of extremism by the extravagances of the other. Lord Craigavon claims 'Ulster' as 'an outpost of Empire' which only wishes to know how best it can serve 'the mother country'. Thus he is back nearly as far as some of the politicians on the other side of the border, regarding himself and his co-religionists in much the same light as the defenders of Derry in 1689.

[1] *Belfast News-Letter*, 13 July 1933.   [2] *Irish News*, 2 April 1925.
[3] *House of Commons Debates*, cxxvii, 991.

I do not believe that his better-educated followers look upon themselves as colonists, or upon England as their mother country; and I am glad to acknowledge, from my own experience, that the more thoughtful Northern Protestants have scant sympathy with such an attitude. A community which ceases to develop culturally and spiritually, drawing its inspiration from the soil in which it has its roots, is ready to be measured for its shroud. History has shown that an English or Scottish colony cannot continue to thrive as a sort of enclave in Ireland, taking its culture from elsewhere.

Instant as is the need for a settlement, I see no prospect of one while the official policies in Dublin and Belfast remain what they are. Mr. De Valera's inconsistencies need not be overstressed, but they do denote the absence of any definite plan. Some of his utterances will be found quoted in the Epilogue. In June 1938 he said that he was certain that, when there was a majority in the North for unity, there would be no interference by Great Britain; the following November he held Britain responsible, on the ground that partition could not continue if British support were withdrawn. On the 7th February 1939, in the Senate, he said that he 'would feel perfectly justified in using force to prevent the coercion of the people of South Down, South Armagh, Tyrone, Fermanagh, and Derry City';[1] and on the following 26th July, again in the Senate, he said that there were people in the country who, whenever they wanted it, were both Irish and English and that it would pay to put it up to them to decide which they were. 'If they were to say they were English it would pay both countries to contribute to buy them out, and let them go to the country of their own allegiance.'[2] Against these foolish statements may be set some words of wisdom which occur in an interview which he gave to a special correspondent of the New York *Herald-Tribune*, reproduced in the Dublin newspapers of the 28th February 1940: 'Apart altogether from the fact that force would be met by force, you must remember that, even if force were successful, we would have in our midst an embittered minority, who in heart would be more separated from us than ever. We never forget that many of these people, who with their forebears have been here for hundreds of years, though they differ from us, are proud of being Irish, and we want to have them fully and completely one with us. We are confident that on the basis of that bond of common love for Ireland reunion can hardly be other than inevitable.'

Mr. De Valera's only concrete proposal is that published in the

---

[1] *Senate Debates*, xxii, 1514.   [2] Ibid., xxiii, 1002–3.

London *Evening Standard* on the 17th October 1938 and reproduced in the Epilogue. Belfast is to retain its present local Parliament, provided that fair play is guaranteed to the minority, and the powers now reserved to the Imperial Parliament are to be transferred to an all-Ireland Parliament. This seems vague enough, since it makes no mention of the numerous complex questions—such as defence and tariff policy—which would have to be decided before such a plan could be seriously considered. But the whole proposal is vitiated by the fact, since made clear on numerous occasions, that the Constitution of 1937 is to be accepted as a *sine qua non* of union. The author of a constitution frequently regards his creation as an inspired evangel, but, on every democratic principle, Mr. De Valera's Constitution would have to go into the melting-pot if any approach were to be made to unity. Not only is its basic principle of 'external association' known to be inacceptable to the majority in the North, but it has never been submitted to the electors in any part of Ireland, since it was already a *fait accompli* at the time of the plebiscite. Apart from the question of 'external association', Northern Ireland is told, in effect, that it must accept a constitution on which it has had no opportunity of expressing an opinion and which, at the plebiscite, received only a small minority of the total votes, if we consider them on an all-Ireland basis. The voting at the plebiscite was: for the Constitution, 26 per cent; against the Constitution, 20 per cent; eligible to vote but did not vote, 22 per cent; ineligible to vote (Northern Ireland), 32 per cent. Before a constitution comes to be framed for the whole of Ireland, it will have to be preceded by a round-table conference of delegates representative of every substantial interest in the country, who will endeavour to reach agreement on the main lines on which such a constitution should be drafted.

What, then, shall we say of the problem of partition? Obviously, no immediate solution is possible, because, even if there was no other obstacle, the war would stand in the way. The abolition of partition would involve either the Twenty-six Counties' becoming belligerent or the Six Counties' renouncing their belligerency, and I do not regard either of these possibilities as practical politics. Looking beyond the war, I see no royal road to unity, but I am certain that there is no republican road. When I reflect on the manifest difficulties, that pregnant saying of Thiers keeps recurring to my mind, '*Le régime qui nous divise le moins.*' Now, what is the régime which divides us the least? There can be only one answer. Some of us (I speak of the whole of Ireland) have a republic as their objective, by force of arms if necessary. Others would oppose a republic by force of arms. 'External association', which is Mr. De Valera's peculiar invention, is rejected out of hand by at least a quarter of our people and it makes for permanent instability, since, as he has so often pointed out, it enables a republic to be declared to-morrow. In any case, 'external association' has no existence in international law, and it ill consorts with the national dignity. The régime which divides us the least is, beyond all question, the complete independence which is conferred by full membership of the Commonwealth, with all its rights and privileges and its few remaining obligations. I know that such a policy will be assailed by the ignorant and unscrupulous as 'Imperialist domination' and 'a betrayal of the Republic', but that should not deter us from advocating it. Personally, I am not interested in names and symbols, but I am tremendously interested in things and ideas, in feelings and points of view; and I dislike a priori reasoning in politics.

But before we can make any headway in removing partition, we must remove the psychological barriers of which it is merely the outward manifestation. In other words, a campaign of political education is overdue on both sides of the border. We must, for the time being, agree to differ, but that is no reason why we should not try to see each other's point of view, to dispel prejudices by personal contact, and to provide the ordinary people with the information about the other side which they so sadly lack. Good work is already being done in this field by the recently formed Irish Association, and it will doubtless fructify. While not contemning the loyalty of the Orange and Protestant minority, we should seek to rationalize it by reference to the dynamism of the Commonwealth and Empire, of which they know little or nothing. Equally, the majority need to be convinced that the Commonwealth is not the old Empire, but is, indeed, sui generis, that membership of it does not injure or inhibit one single national ideal, and that, on the contrary, it would provide the sole guarantee of the unity and territorial integrity of Ireland. The deplorable situation of the Northern Catholics would be greatly ameliorated if there existed in Dublin a government in a position to renounce, finally and for ever, the use of force against the North; for fear is the stepmother of oppression. Better still if the agreement of December 1925 to hold joint meetings of the two Cabinets could now be taken up and carried through; but this presupposes on both sides a change of heart and probably also a change of Government. Above all, Irish men and women, whatever their political or religious belief, must be made to realize their interdependence, that their common interests are greater and more important than the things which divide them, and that they must subordinate passion and prejudice to patriotism if their country is to survive.

The life of any nation is not a continuous progression. There must be loss and gain, ebb and flow. Looking back on the last twenty years of Irish history, I see no grounds for pessimism, but rather the reverse. Inevitably, mistakes have been made, but they are in general recognized to have been mistakes, even though it is not in human nature that they should always be openly acknowledged. The principle of majority rule is now virtually of universal recognition. We have demonstrated to ourselves and to the world that our legislative freedom is absolute, and we are beginning to realize that freedom has its duties and responsibilities as well as its rights. While partition remains, our political institutions will continue in a state of flux, but the flow is now in the right direction. Our principal need is for more and more men of knowledge, experience, and education in both Houses of our Parliament; for I am convinced that, if given the opportunity, our people will respond in the future, as they have in the past, to the leadership of patriotic Irishmen, informed with high purpose and preaching with conviction and courage the faith that is in them.

PART I

THE YEARS
PRIOR TO THE ESTABLISHMENT
OF THE
IRISH FREE STATE

'*Now we celebrate an independent Government, an original Constitution, an independent Legislature.*'

Pennsylvania Packet, 9th July 1789.

'*Better far, if brothers' war be destined for us,*
  (God avert that horrid day, I pray!),
That ere our hands be stained with slaughter fratricidal
  Thy warm heart should be cold in clay.'

SIR SAMUEL FERGUSON, *Lament for Thomas Davis*.

CHAPTER I

THE PRELUDE TO THE ANGLO-IRISH TREATY OF 1921

Constitutional agitation for self-government—Government of Ireland Bill, 1912—Limited powers thereunder—Proposals for a Senate—Gaelic League and Gaelic Athletic Association—Arthur Griffith and Sinn Féin—Irish Republican Brotherhood—Hostility of Ulster to Bill of 1912—Ulster Volunteers—Irish Volunteers—Danger of civil war—Outbreak of Great War—John Redmond's declaration—Postponement of Government of Ireland Act—Split in Irish Volunteers—Irish Republican Brotherhood decide on insurrection—Easter Week, 1916—Executions and aftermath—Casement's speech from the dock—Irish Convention set up—Mr. De Valera's victory in Clare election and attitude to Ulster—Elected President of Sinn Féin and of Irish Volunteers—Death of Redmond—Report of Irish Convention—Composition and powers of proposed Senate—Threat of conscription—Ruin of parliamentarianism —'German Plot'—General election of December 1918—Triumph of Sinn Féin—Establishment of Dáil Éireann and Declaration of Independence—Irish Republican Army—Anglo-Irish War—Government of Ireland Act, 1920, and Partition—General elections of May 1921—Truce of July 1921—Correspondence between Mr. De Valera and Mr. Lloyd George—Signature of Anglo-Irish Treaty.

The history of Ireland during the years immediately before the establishment of the Irish Free State has been dealt with in detail, and from various aspects, by several writers. No more than a bare outline of that history need be given as the prelude to the main theme of this book, and many facts of importance must necessarily be omitted. Reference will, however, be made to the abortive proposals put forward at one time or another for the constitution of a Second Chamber in a self-governed Ireland.

For many decades before the Great War the age-old aspiration of the Irish nation for legislative independence had found expression in constitutional agitation through its Members of Parliament at Westminster. The last insurrection against English rule had occurred so long ago as 1867; it had been organized by the Irish Republican Brotherhood (a secret society popularly known as the Fenians), and, like its numerous predecessors, it had been a failure. The Irish Parliamentarians had undoubtedly secured great material benefits for the people, for which too little credit is now given to them. But they had failed to achieve the purpose for which they were elected, owing to the veto of the House of Lords. The general election of December 1910 was fought on the issue of this veto, and the Liberal Government was returned to power. By the Parliament Act, 1911, the veto was swept away and a mere power of delay was substituted for it. The following year a Government of Ireland Bill was introduced in the House of Commons, and it was passed by that House early in 1913, by a comfortable majority and independently of the Irish Nationalist vote. It was rejected by the House of Lords by an overwhelming majority, but such rejection was no longer fatal to it, and the Bill was due to become law under the Parliament Act in the summer of 1914.

This Bill made provision for a parliament for the whole of Ireland, but the powers of that parliament were to be extremely limited. Foreign affairs and fiscal control were excluded from its purview, it had only a restricted control over finance, and none at all over the police force during the first six years. Ireland was to have no army or navy, and the Irish connection with Westminster was not severed, as 42 members were to be elected to the Imperial Parliament instead of the 103 returned under the Act of Union of 1800. Of the 103 Irish members elected at the general election of December 1910, 84 were Nationalists and 19 were Unionists. All but a few of the Nationalists were followers of the late John Redmond. Apart from the two members for Dublin University and one from a Dublin constituency, the Unionists all came from the north-eastern area of the province of Ulster.

The Parliament under the Bill was to consist of a Senate and a House of Commons. The number of Senators was fixed at forty, to be nominated in the first instance by the Lord-Lieutenant, and afterwards to be elected by the four provinces of Ireland, as separate constituencies, in the following proportions: Ulster, 14; Leinster, 11; Munster, 9; Connaught, 6. The election was to be held on the single transferable vote system of proportional representation, and the term of office was to be five years. The Senate could reject or otherwise hold up a Bill, but if it again did so in the next session the differences between the two Houses were to be resolved by a vote taken at a joint sitting.

Though the fact may now seem surprising, the Bill of 1912, with its severely restricted powers, commanded the overwhelming support of the people. There were some who had a wider and deeper conception of Irish nationality, but their numbers were quite negligible. In 1893 Dr. Douglas Hyde, Mr. (afterwards Professor) John MacNeill, and others had founded the Gaelic League, a purely non-political body, which had for its primary purpose the preservation and spread of the Irish language, but which also brought Irish history, music, and dancing within its ambit, as well as the fostering of native industries. The Gaelic League never had anything of a popular appeal, but those who joined it came under a spell which is not easy to describe. They were mostly young, and the nascent patriotism which had brought them within the circle grew and flourished in an Irish-Ireland atmosphere very different from that to which their elders had been accustomed. Probably the bulk of them never obtained any real mastery over Irish, which is a difficult language; and it is a curious but little-known fact that, of those who did, comparatively few became extremists in the political sense after 1921. But the Gaelic League marks a real national renaissance, and many of the leading political figures of the present day were members of it àt one time or another. Complementary to the Gaelic League was the Gaelic Athletic Association, founded in 1884, which fostered national games and pastimes.

Inevitably, most of the members of the Gaelic League became followers of the political gospel which began to be preached by Arthur Griffith early in the twentieth century. Intellectually, Griffith stood head and shoulders over the political figures of his time. He was a man imbued with an intense love of his country, utterly unselfish, and having in him nothing of the fanaticism or insincerity of the demagogue. His policy was one of national self-reliance, expressed in the political sphere by abstention from the British Parliament. Inspired by what had been accomplished in Hungary by Francis Deák, he believed that Irish independence could be achieved if the people elected members who would turn their backs on Westminster and meet in Dublin as a parliament, adopting a policy of passive resistance to English rule. He was not an advocate of physical force. For the furtherance of the abstentionist policy, Griffith founded

D

in 1905 the organization known as Sinn Féin. This means 'Ourselves', and not, as sometimes stated, 'Ourselves alone'; it is the exact equivalent of the French 'nous-mêmes'. In his weekly journals, *United Ireland* and later *Sinn Féin*, Griffith preached this doctrine in a polemical English the like of which had not been written in Ireland since the days of Swift. They had a very small circulation, however, and if Griffith had stood for Parliament it is unlikely that he would have received more than a few hundred votes in any constituency. Even his name would have been unknown to most of the electors.

Operating in the background, in conditions of the profoundest secrecy, was the Irish Republican Brotherhood, having for its object the overthrow of the British Government in Ireland by force of arms. At the time of the introduction of the Home Rule Bill in 1912, this organization was extremely weak, and had been so for many years. The British Empire was at the height of its power, and a policy of violence against it seemed ridiculous. English rule in Ireland had ceased to be oppressive, the people were contented, and, on the whole, prosperous, and they placed their faith in the Parliamentary Party. Moreover, the members of the Brotherhood came under the general ban of the Catholic Church against secret societies.

If the enthusiasm of the Nationalists for such an anaemic form of self-government as the Bill of 1912 seems surprising, the lengths to which the Orange and Protestant minority in Ulster were prepared to go in resisting it must appear even more so. In 1912 the Ulster Covenant had been extensively signed in the province, pledging resistance to the death. In 1913 there were frequent armed parades of Ulster Volunteers, and a provisional government was set up in Belfast, with Sir Edward Carson, K.C., a Dublin man, at its head. Leading English soldiers and politicians, including Sir F. E. Smith, K.C., crossed over to take a hand in the military preparations. Threats were made to kick the King's Crown into the Boyne if any attempt were made to coerce Ulster.

The Ulster Volunteers were armed to resist a prospective Act of Parliament. On the 25th November 1913 the Irish Volunteers, then unarmed, were formed in Dublin to uphold it. The British Government immediately imposed a ban on the importation of arms into Ireland. On the 24th April 1914 a cargo of rifles from the Continent for the Ulster Volunteers was landed at Larne, north of Belfast, in open defiance of the ban, with the police looking on. On the 26th July a similar cargo was run in to Howth, County Dublin, for the Irish Volunteers. A company of British soldiers was sent out from the capital to meet the returning Volunteers, and attempted unsuccessfully to disarm them. There were no serious casualties. When the soldiers arrived back in Dublin, stones were thrown at them in Bachelors' Walk. The troops fired on the crowd and four civilians were killed and thirty-seven wounded.

It was in this tense atmosphere of impending civil war that the Great War broke out. Indeed, it is now generally believed that the Kaiser was considerably influenced by the feeling that the British Government had its hands full in Ireland.[1] In the previous June Mr. John Redmond, who had held aloof from the Volunteer movement at the beginning, obtained virtual control of it by the addition of his nominees to the Provisional Committee, and the accession of the Irish Parliamentary Party was welcomed in a manifesto to the Volunteers signed by Mr. John MacNeill and published in the *Irish Review* of that month. The war enthusiasm in Ireland was intense, and Mr. Redmond at once promised the Irish Volunteers for the defence of Ireland, whereby the British Army stationed in Ireland would be released for active service. 'For this purpose', he said, 'armed Nationalist Catholics in the South will be only too glad to join arms with the armed Protestant Ulstermen in the North.'[2] Ulster had won, however. The Government of Ireland Act received the King's Assent on the 18th September 1914, but on the same date there reached the Statute Book the Suspensory Act, 1914, which suspended its operation (and also the operation of the Welsh Church Act) until twelve months from the date of enactment, or, if the War was not then ended, until such later date (not being later than the end of the War) as might be fixed by His Majesty by Order-in-Council.

Mr. Redmond's declaration was, of course, anathema to those who had originally founded the Irish Volunteers. None of them had any sympathy with parliamentarianism, and the members of the original executive were mostly also members of the Irish Republican Brotherhood. By November 1914 the movement had split into two, the vast majority following Mr. Redmond, with the title of the National Volunteers, and the old nucleus maintaining a separate existence with the original title. Thousands of Irish Nationalists, both National Volunteers and others, joined the Irish regiments in the British Army and fought gallantly in France, Gallipoli, and elsewhere; but Redmond's request that a special Irish division should

[1] For extracts from speeches by Orangemen and English Conservative politicians, and their effect on German opinion, see *The Complete Grammar of Anarchy*, compiled by J. J. Horgan (Nisbet, 1919).
[2] *House of Commons Debates*, lxv, 1829.

be recruited under Irish officers for service in Europe was refused by Lord Kitchener and the War Office. It was evident that any concessions to Ireland's distinctive nationality were taboo.

As soon as war broke out the Irish Republican Brotherhood decided upon an insurrection, using the Irish Volunteers as their instrument. In 1915 envoys were sent to the United States to get in touch with the allied Irish-American organization, known as Clan-na-Gael, and to collect funds. In the same year Sir Roger Casement, an Ulster Protestant of profound Nationalist sympathies, endeavoured without much success to recruit an Irish Brigade from among the prisoners of war in Germany. At home, the Irish Volunteers continued their week-end route marches in the Dublin mountains and elsewhere, and one of the songs they sang on the march was 'A Soldier's Song', which afterwards became the national anthem of the Irish Free State.

Early in 1916 the Rising was timed for Easter week of that year. There never was any expectation that it would succeed in the material sense, but Patrick Pearse, one of the leaders of the Volunteers, and James Connolly, a Labour leader and internationalist, who was head of a smaller band of Dublin men called the Citizen Army, were both convinced that a 'blood sacrifice' was necessary if the Irish nation was to survive. Parades and manœuvres of the Irish Volunteers were publicly announced for Easter Sunday, the 23rd April, but only those in the Irish Republican Brotherhood knew that an insurrection was to take place. There were two miscarriages in Holy Week. Sir Roger Casement landed from a German submarine on the Kerry coast, with the object of trying to prevent the Rising on the ground that no substantial help could be expected from Germany;[1] he was arrested by the police and taken to London. The German auxiliary cruiser *Libau*, disguised as a Norwegian tramp steamer and renamed the *Aud*, carrying a cargo of arms and ammunition, was escorted by a British cruiser towards Cork Harbour, but just outside that port her crew hoisted the German flag and blew her up. Professor MacNeill, the head of the Volunteers, did not know until the middle of the week that an insurrection was planned. He regarded it as a blunder, and on the Saturday he issued an order cancelling the parades. For this reason the Rising was virtually confined to Dublin.

At noon on Easter Monday the General Post Office was occupied as the headquarters of the insurgents, the tricolour flag of green, white, and orange was run up, and a proclamation was issued,

[1] Gwynn, *The Life and Death of Roger Casement* (1930), Part IV.

couched in strangely moving terms, declaring an Irish Republic 'in the name of God and of the dead generations'. There were seven signatories, each one of whom knew that he was signing his death warrant. Other buildings were occupied at strategic points, and heavy fighting took place between the insurgents and the British troops in various parts of the city, with casualties on both sides. The courage of these few hundred men can only be described as sublime. They held out for six days until, surrounded and hopelessly outnumbered, they surrendered unconditionally on the Saturday afternoon.

The insurrection was at first regarded with lively detestation by the citizens of Dublin and in the country generally. Then came the aftermath. The seven signatories of the proclamation, and eight others, were shot at intervals between the 3rd and the 12th May, by order of British Courts Martial. Before the shots of the last firing-squad rang out, public opinion had turned completely round. Any Irishman with a spark of national feeling in him regarded these executions as the murder in cold blood of gallant, chivalrous men who had borne themselves as heroes.

The same sentiment was awakened by the execution of Roger Casement in Pentonville Prison on the following 3rd August. His prosecution on a charge of treason was conducted by the Attorney-General (the Rt. Hon. F. E. Smith, K.C., afterwards Lord Chancellor), who had taken a leading part in the fomenting of armed opposition to the Home Rule Act. Casement alluded to the fact in the remarkable speech which he delivered from the dock after his conviction (29th June 1916):

'If, as the right honourable gentleman, the present Attorney-General, asserted in a speech at Manchester, Nationalists would neither fight for Home Rule nor pay for it, it was our duty to show him that we knew how to do both. . . . The difference between us was that the Unionist champions chose a path they felt would lead to the Woolsack, while I went a road that I knew must lead to the dock. And the event proves both were right. The difference between us was that my "treason" was based on a ruthless sincerity that forced me to attempt in time and season to carry out in action what I said in word—whereas their treason lay in verbal incitements that they knew need never be made good in their bodies.'[1]

Mr. De Valera took part in the Rising as a battalion commander, showing as great courage as any and more tactical ability than most. He was condemned to death and would have been shot but for the

---

[1] Gwynn, *The Life and Death of Roger Casement*, pp. 417, 418.

fact that he was an American citizen, having been born in New York. Mr. Cosgrave was also in the fight and was among a batch who were sentenced to death but reprieved. They, and scores of others, were deported to penal servitude in England. Hundreds more were interned in Wales. Arthur Griffith, who had not been in favour of the Rising, was arrested and lodged in Reading Gaol.

In February 1917 Count Plunkett, one of whose sons had been executed, stood as an abstentionist candidate at a by-election in Roscommon and defeated the nominee of the Parliamentary Party. The following May another abstentionist, who was in gaol, scored a similar victory in Longford. It looked as if the tide was beginning to turn against Mr. Redmond. On the 21st May the Prime Minister (Mr. Lloyd George) announced in the House of Commons that the Government had decided to summon immediately a convention of representative Irishmen in Ireland to submit to the British Government and Parliament a constitution for the future government of Ireland within the Empire. He mentioned the fact that similar schemes had succeeded in Canada, Australia, and South Africa, and said that the time had come for Ireland to try her own hand at hammering out an instrument of government for her own people. He added that the Government accepted responsibility for giving legislative effect to the report of the convention, provided that there was substantial agreement. Mr. Redmond declared that for the first time in her history Ireland had been asked to settle these problems for herself.[1] Sinn Féin, on the other hand, declined participation on the grounds that the convention was not elected by the people of Ireland and that it was not free to declare for absolute independence.

The Irish Convention, as it is called, met on the 25th July 1917 in Dublin and elected the late Sir Horace Plunkett as its chairman. It was fully representative of Unionist and moderate Nationalist opinion, North and South, and the late George Russell (AE) and Mr. E. MacLysaght held what might be called an unofficial watching brief for Sinn Féin. They both resigned shortly before the Convention submitted its Report. It is fashionable nowadays to deride the Convention, but it had the support of the Catholic Church, and its ablest member on the Nationalist side—perhaps the most statesmanlike member of all—was the Most Rev. Dr. O'Donnell, Bishop of Raphoe and subsequently Cardinal Archbishop of Armagh. 'If the Convention fails', said Cardinal Logue, 'all is chaos.' He was to prove a true prophet.

[1] *House of Commons Debates*, xciii, 1995–2025.

In order that the Convention might meet in an atmosphere of peace and goodwill the men imprisoned in England since the Rising of 1916 were released, and arrived back in Ireland on the 18th June. The gesture had exactly the opposite effect. There was a triumphal procession from Kingstown (later named Dún Laoghaire, and popularly called Dunleary), headed by Mr. De Valera, who was now the hero of the populace. On the 11th July there was a by-election in Clare, caused by the death of Major William Redmond (brother of John Redmond), who had been killed in action in France. Mr. De Valera was the Sinn Féin candidate, and his Nationalist opponent was Mr. Patrick Lynch, K.C., who was later to become Attorney-General in Mr. De Valera's Government. In this campaign the Irish Volunteers appeared in public for the first time since the Rising.

Mr. De Valera triumphed in Clare, polling 5,010 votes as against 2,035 cast for Mr. Lynch. The country was moving faster than the capital, however, for only a week earlier a Nationalist was returned unopposed in South County Dublin, where Sinn Féin did not even put up a candidate. Close on Mr. De Valera's victory came a similar success in Kilkenny, where Mr. Cosgrave easily defeated his Nationalist opponent (10th August). In Mr. De Valera's speeches both before and after the Clare election we can discern signs of that intransigence which was later to be so marked a feature of his political career. Thus, in a victory speech in Dublin on the 12th July, he said he 'did not believe in mincing matters, and if Ulster stood in the way of the attainment of Irish freedom Ulster should be coerced'.[1] One may well imagine that the effect of such utterances upon the Ulster Unionist members of the Irish Convention would be merely to stiffen their resistance to any form of Home Rule.

Sinn Féin was obviously becoming a force to be reckoned with, and so its Annual Convention, held in public on the 25th October, was regarded with a good deal of interest. Arthur Griffith had been president of the organization since the beginning, but on this occasion there were rival candidates in the persons of Mr. De Valera and Count Plunkett, the former being put forward by the extreme element. Griffith at once announced that he retired in favour of Mr. De Valera, whereupon Count Plunkett did likewise; and Mr. De Valera was unanimously elected president of Sinn Féin. If, as is said to have been the case, Griffith was certain of election in case of a contest, he showed extraordinary magnanimity in thus handing over to another the headship of an organization which he had founded

[1] *Irish Independent*, 13 July 1917.

and which, after years of obscurity, was now nearing its hour of triumph.

A few days later, at a secret convention of the Irish Volunteers, Mr. De Valera was elected president of that body also. These two events, taken together, tended to show that if Sinn Féin succeeded in ousting the parliamentarians its policy would not be Griffith's old policy of abstention from Westminster plus passive resistance. Mr. De Valera was not, however, a member of the Irish Republican Brotherhood, which was contrary to his religious principles.

At the beginning of 1918 there was still a reasonable chance that the Nationalist Party would put up a successful resistance to Sinn Féin, which had no practical policy. On the 6th March John Redmond died; he was a great leader and a great gentleman, to whom history will in time accord his due. At the resulting by-election in Waterford his son Captain William Redmond, a serving officer in France, easily defeated the Sinn Féin candidate. Two other by-elections occurred about this time, in Armagh (February) and Tyrone (April), and Sinn Féin was worsted in both.

Meantime, the Irish Convention had completed its labours, and its Report was signed on the 8th April 1918.[1] It is a voluminous document, and the chairman (Sir Horace Plunkett) could claim with truth that 'a larger measure of agreement has been reached upon the principle and details of Irish self-government than has ever yet been attained'. It is true that there were numerous reservations and separate minority reports. At the same time, there is no doubt whatever that a practicable scheme for Irish autonomy, under a single parliament, could have been evolved from the recommendations of the Convention—but for one factor, the uncompromising hostility of the Ulster Unionist members. At that time the British Empire was probably in greater peril than at any time else during the War. Ludendorff had broken through in the west, and on the 13th April Haig issued his historic 'backs to the wall' message to the troops. By joining with the Nationalists and the Southern Unionists in accepting, with proper safeguards, an all-Ireland parliament, the Ulstermen would have removed an outstanding threat to the Empire. But they refused to do so.

The powers of the Senate proposed by the Irish Convention were similar to those contained in the Act of 1914. As regards the personnel, there were to be sixty-four members, made up as follows:

[1] Cd. 9019 (1918) (vol. x, p. 697).

The Lord Chancellor of Ireland	1
Archbishops or bishops of the Catholic Church	4
Archbishops or bishops of the Church of Ireland	2
Representative of the General Assembly (Presbyterian)	1
Lord Mayor of Dublin	1
Lord Mayor of Belfast	1
Lord Mayor of Cork	1
Resident Irish Peers elected by their fellow Peers	15
Nominated by the Lord Lieutenant:	
Irish Privy Councillors	4
Representatives of learned institutions	3
Other persons	4
Representatives of commerce and industry	15
Representatives of Labour (one for each province)	4
Representatives of county councils (two for each province)	8
	64

Mr. Lloyd George at once announced that the British Government would introduce legislation to implement the Report of the Convention. At the same time he introduced on the 9th April, and passed through the House of Commons in seven days, a Bill to apply conscription to Ireland. Conscription had been in force for more than a year in Great Britain, but the military situation now made it necessary to extend the age limit to fifty. The point of view of the British Government was that this proposal could not be carried if recruiting in Ireland remained on a voluntary basis. Moreover, large numbers of men of military age, contemptuously termed 'fly boys' by the Irish, had crossed over from the neighbouring island for the purpose of avoiding conscription. On the other hand, the Irish are as fond of fighting as most people, and the Nationalists had volunteered in at least equal proportions to the Orangemen of Ulster. Some who were pro-Ally but would not fight for England had enlisted under the French flag. But the proposal to conscribe Irishmen for service in the British Army was as fantastic as any that could be imagined. Even before Easter Week, 1916, it would have been impracticable, but by 1918 it was sheer lunacy. It could never have been enforced and the view held in Ireland was that it was put forward only for the purpose of side-tracking the Report of the Irish Convention.

Mr. John Dillon, the veteran Irish statesman, had been elected to the chairmanship of the Parliamentary Party following the death of Mr. Redmond. The Conscription Bill having been carried in the teeth of Nationalist opposition, he and his followers abandoned Westminster and returned to Ireland to carry on the fight at home. The Catholic Hierarchy, the Nationalists, Sinn Féin, the Irish Volunteers and Labour joined together in a nation-wide campaign of resistance.

At one blow Mr. Lloyd George had achieved the ruin of the Nationalist Party. On the 19th April, only three days after the passage of the Conscription Bill by the Commons, a by-election was held in the King's County. Dr. Patrick MacCartan, one of the ablest and most high-minded of Irish Republicans, was returned unopposed. Mr. Lloyd George had also ensured the success of the policy of physical force. Conscription was equivalent to a declaration of war, and the only men in a position to take up the challenge were the Irish Volunteers.

To clear the way for the conscription drive, the police and military conducted a midnight round-up of the leaders on the 17th May, and Messrs. Griffith, De Valera, Cosgrave, and close on a hundred others were transported to England, where they were interned. The pretext was that they were plotting with Germany, and the Viceroy (Lord French) issued a proclamation calling on 'loyal subjects of His Majesty' to 'suppress this treasonable conspiracy and to defeat the treacherous attempt of the Germans to defame the honour of Irishmen for their own ends'. This alleged German plot was a pure fabrication. The Commander-in-Chief of the British Forces in Ireland at that time was the late General Sir Bryan Mahon, and if anyone was fully informed on the subject it would be he. Sir Bryan once told me in conversation that he did not believe a word of it, and was satisfied that it was a myth.

The threat of conscription persisted, but the British Government was powerless to enforce it, and the result was to strengthen Sinn Féin and to swell the ranks of the Irish Volunteers. On the 20th June Arthur Griffith, then in gaol, easily defeated the Nationalist candidate at a by-election in East Cavan. Sinn Féin, the Irish Volunteers, the Gaelic League, and other organizations were 'suppressed' in July, and went from strength to strength. Other leaders, chief of whom was the redoubtable Michael Collins, stepped into the gap to carry on the work of those arrested and interned.

Then came the end of the War and the general election of December 1918, when Sinn Féin reaped its reward and the British Government got its deserts. In England, this was the 'coupon' election and the chief slogan was 'Hang the Kaiser'. In Ireland, the issue was national resurgence, and nothing less. The number of constituencies had been increased by two under the Redistribution of Seats (Ireland) Act, 1918. In many of them Sinn Féin was unopposed. The result was as follows:

Sinn Féin	73
Nationalists	6
Unionists	26
	105

Outside of Ulster, the Nationalists held only one seat (Waterford: Captain Redmond) and the Unionists had only three seats (Rathmines, County Dublin: Sir Maurice Dockrell; and Dublin University: Mr. Samuels and Sir Robert Woods). (Actually, Sir Robert Woods was returned as an Independent; he was a distinguished surgeon, unconnected with politics.) On the one hand, the Nationalist Party and constitutional methods were dead beyond hope of resurrection; on the other, one-fourth of the entire representation, concentrated in one area of the country, had declared once more for union with England. Nationalist Ireland had not, of course, declared for a republic. What the people had done was to give their reply to English repression. It 'was not a victory of conviction, but of emotion'.[1]

On the 21st January 1919 such of the Sinn Féin members as were not in prison or evading arrest met publicly in Dublin as Dáil Éireann (which means 'the Assembly of Ireland'). The roll was called of the whole 105 members, including the Unionists (Sir Edward Carson, Sir James Craig, and others) and the six Nationalists. All these were, of course, absent. A declaration of independence was then read in Irish, French, and English, containing the following: 'We, the elected Representatives of the ancient Irish people in National Parliament assembled, do, in the name of the Irish nation, ratify the establishment of the Irish Republic and pledge ourselves and our people to make this declaration effective by every means at our command.'[2]

At a private session of the Dáil on the 1st April Mr. De Valera (who had escaped from Lincoln Prison) was elected President of the Dáil—not President of the Republic, which never seems to have had a president—and a Cabinet was constituted. Shortly afterwards, Mr. De Valera left for the United States, where he engaged in propaganda, not arriving back in Ireland till the end of 1920.

[1] P. S. O'Hegarty, *The Victory of Sinn Féin* (1924), p. 31.
[2] *Proceedings of First Dáil*, pp. 14–17.

Arthur Griffith's policy of Sinn Féin had meant abstention from Westminster and passive resistance. Whether such a policy was now practicable may be open to question. At all events the policy adopted was something very different. A republic had been declared, and the Irish Volunteers became the army of that republic or, in the popular phrase, the Irish Republican Army. The new situation was emphasized by Cathal Brugha (Charles Burgess), the Secretary for Defence in the Dáil Cabinet:

'He pointed out that the Volunteers had now become the Army of a lawfully constituted Government, elected by the people, and were entitled morally and legally, when on the execution of their duty, to slay the officials and agents of the foreign invader who was waging war upon our native Government. He also declared that we were entitled to put to death all spies, informers, and all Irishmen who acted as agents of the foreigners in the warfare against us.'[1]

So began the Anglo–Irish war, which endured at a gradually increasing tempo until the Truce of the 11th July 1921. It was a campaign of an unusual type, with, on the one side, soldiers and police well equipped with arms, and, on the other, flying columns of men, ill-armed and not in uniform, who attacked and burnt police barracks and engaged in ambushes and other forms of guerrilla activity. Great heroism, and sometimes great chivalry, were shown by the Irish Republican Army, but there were ugly incidents as well. In the early summer of 1920 the Royal Irish Constabulary (nearly all the original members of which were Irishmen) was reinforced by the Auxiliary Police, nicknamed the Black and Tans. Their record of outrage, arson, and murder is well known.

The following autumn, Mr. Lloyd George's Government introduced the Government of Ireland Bill, which became law on the 23rd December 1920, and which partitioned Ireland into Northern Ireland (the six counties of north-east Ulster) and Southern Ireland (the remaining twenty-six counties). 'Southern' Ireland contained the most northerly county of all (Donegal), but the nomenclature helped to foster the belief that Ireland is split into two roughly equal halves of Orangemen and Nationalists. Two of the six counties (Tyrone and Fermanagh) contained substantial Nationalist majorities and could never have been included in Northern Ireland if a plebiscite had been taken. The Senate of Southern Ireland (sixty-four members) was substantially that recommended by the Irish Convention for the whole of Ireland. The Senate of Northern Ireland was to consist of

[1] Béaslaí, *Michael Collins*, vol. i, p. 270.

the Lord Mayor of Belfast and the Mayor of Derry, *ex officio*, and twenty-four other members, elected by the House of Commons of Northern Ireland. The Act made provision for the possible unification of the country by agreement between the two parts of it; but as the Orangemen had been prepared to fight sooner than go into a parliament with John Redmond it did not seem likely that they would voluntarily go into another with Mr. De Valera. Northern Ireland consented, more or less under protest, to work the Act. The rest of the country—Sinn Féin, Nationalist, and Unionist—was unanimously against partition, and the Act became a dead letter in the twenty-six counties.

A general election for Southern Ireland and another for Northern Ireland were held in May 1921. In Southern Ireland Sinn Féin was everywhere unopposed, the only other members being the four returned for Dublin University. In Northern Ireland, out of a total of fifty-two seats, the Unionists obtained forty (including the four University seats) and the Nationalists and Sinn Féin each obtained six. The Nationalists returned one member in each of the six constituencies (Belfast, Antrim, Derry, Armagh, Down, and Tyrone-Fermanagh) and Sinn Féin obtained one seat in Derry, Armagh, and Down and three seats in Tyrone-Fermanagh. Thus, apart from the University, the anti-partition *bloc* had one-third of the representation.

By this time the struggle was drawing towards its close. Each side had had about enough, and English public opinion was becoming increasingly vocal against the excesses of the Black and Tans. When opening the Northern Ireland Parliament in Belfast on the 22nd June the King made a strong appeal for peace in a speech now known to have been drafted by General Smuts. This was followed up two days later by a letter from Mr. Lloyd George to Mr. De Valera, requesting a conference. The latter accepted on the 8th July, and on the 10th July a truce was signed between representatives of the Irish and British armies, to come into force at noon the next day. The news was received with intense enthusiasm, for everyone knew that, though it might be called a truce, the war with England was at an end.

The conference between Mr. De Valera and Mr. Lloyd George took place in London (14th–21st July), and came to nothing. A long and inconclusive correspondence followed. At length, on the 29th September, Mr. Lloyd George sent to Mr. De Valera an invitation to a conference in London, in the course of which he said:

'In spite of their sincere desire for peace, and in spite of the more conciliatory tone of your last communication, they [the British Government] cannot enter a conference upon the basis of this correspondence. Notwithstanding your personal assurance to the contrary, which they much appreciate, it might be argued in future that the acceptance of a conference on this basis had involved them in a recognition which no British Government can accord [i.e. the recognition of the Irish delegates as the representatives of a sovereign and independent State]. On this point they must guard themselves against any possible doubt. . . . The position taken up by His Majesty's Government is fundamental to the existence of the British Empire, and they cannot alter it. . . . We feel that conference, not correspondence, is the most practical and hopeful way to an understanding such as we ardently desire to achieve. We therefore send herewith a fresh invitation to a conference in London on the 11th October, where we can meet your delegates as spokesmen of the people whom you represent, with a view to ascertaining how the association of Ireland with the community of nations known as the British Empire may best be reconciled with Irish national aspirations.'

Mr. De Valera replied on the following day: 'Our respective positions have been stated and are understood, and we agree that conference, not correspondence, is the most practical and hopeful way to an understanding. We accept the invitation and our delegates will meet you in London on the date mentioned "to explore every possibility of settlement by personal discussion".'[1]

The following were accordingly nominated as Envoys Plenipotentiary 'to negotiate and conclude on behalf of Ireland, with the representatives of His Britannic Majesty George V, a treaty or treaties of settlement, association and accommodation between Ireland and the community of nations known as the British Commonwealth':

Arthur Griffith, Minister for Foreign Affairs (chairman)
Michael Collins, Minister for Finance
Robert C. Barton, Minister for Economic Affairs
Edmund J. Duggan
George Gavan Duffy.

After protracted negotiations, 'Articles of Agreement for a Treaty between Great Britain and Ireland' were signed on the 6th December 1921 between these five plenipotentiaries and seven members of the British Cabinet, headed by the Prime Minister (Mr. Lloyd George). Ireland received the status of a Dominion within the British Com-

[1] Cmd. 1470, 1502, and 1539 (1921) (vol. xxix, pp. 401-15).

monwealth of Nations, with the title of the Irish Free State, and she had the right to maintain her own army. On the debit side, it was provided that Northern Ireland could opt out within a specified period, the Irish Free State was made liable for its proportionate share of the public debt of the United Kingdom, and the British Government was accorded certain harbour and other facilities which it deemed necessary for purposes of defence.

CHAPTER II

THE FIGHT FOR THE TREATY

Popular enthusiasm for the Treaty—Attitude of Catholic Hierarchy —Procedure for establishment of Provisional Government—Mr. De Valera declares against the Treaty—The Treaty before the Dáil— 'Document No. 2'—Griffith's declaration—The Dáil approves the Treaty—Mr. De Valera's resignation and subsequent attitude—Provisional Government set up—Telegrams from the Pope—The British begin evacuation—Outbreaks of violence—Mr. De Valera's efforts to avoid an appeal to the people—His speeches in Munster—Repudiation of the Dáil by a section of the Irish Republican Army—Seizure of the Four Courts—Pronouncement of the Catholic Hierarchy—Mr. De Valera's contrary view—Continued efforts to prevent a decision by the people—The Collins–De Valera Pact—The general election of June 1922—The people declare for the Treaty—Civil War—Death of Griffith and Collins—Stern condemnation of the Irregulars by the Hierarchy—Mr. De Valera appointed 'President of the Republic'— Resolution of approval of the Treaty purported to be rescinded—Decision not to appeal to Rome against the Hierarchy—The Pope's message to the Governor-General.

The circumstances which surrounded the signing of the Treaty, and the tragic events which succeeded it, have been dealt with in considerable detail in volumes which have appeared in recent years; but certain facts of vital importance have too often been either insufficiently emphasized or ignored altogether. The first is the fact—for which the evidence is overwhelming—that the vast majority of the people were enthusiastically in favour of the Agreement which had been secured by the plenipotentiaries. The second, which follows from the first, is that Arthur Griffith and Michael Collins were never, except in a secondary sense, protagonists of the Treaty; their position was that they were determined that no subtlety, casuistry, or threat of force should deprive the people of their clear right to say by whom, and under what instrument, they wished to be governed. The third fact is that the Catholic Hierarchy were unanimously in favour of acceptance; they had no concern with politics as such, but they were, and are, the appointed custodians of Catholic faith and morals, and they knew only too well that a continuance of the anarchic conditions of the previous three years would result in a moral degeneration of their flocks from which it would take generations to recover.

Provision for the approval of the Treaty and for the bridging of the interregnum was made by the instrument itself, the last two Articles of which read as follows:

'17. By way of provisional arrangement for the administration of Southern Ireland during the interval which must elapse between the date hereof and the constitution of a Parliament and Government of the Irish Free State in accordance therewith, steps shall be taken forthwith for summoning a meeting of members of Parliament elected for constituencies in Southern Ireland since the passing of the Government of Ireland Act, 1920, and for constituting a provisional Government, and the British Government shall take the steps necessary to transfer to such provisional Government the powers and machinery requisite for the discharge of its duties, provided that every member of such provisional Government shall have signified in writing his or her acceptance of this instrument. But this arrangement shall not continue in force beyond the expiration of twelve months from the date hereof.

'18. This instrument shall be submitted forthwith by His Majesty's Government for the approval of Parliament and by the Irish signatories to a meeting summoned for the purpose of the members elected to sit in the House of Commons of Southern Ireland, and if approved shall be ratified by the necessary legislation.'

There is no mention here, or elsewhere in the Treaty, of the Dáil, which claimed to be the Parliament of the Republic of the whole of Ireland. There was no serious difference of personnel, however, between the Dáil and the Parliament of Southern Ireland. At the general elections held in Northern Ireland and Southern Ireland in May 1921 the members elected in Southern Ireland had all belonged to the Sinn Féin Party, except the four members for Dublin University, who did not attend the Dáil. None of the Unionists and Nationalists elected in Northern Ireland recognized the Dáil, and, of the six Sinn Féin members, all except one (Mr. John O'Mahony) were also elected for

E

constituencies in Southern Ireland. Hence the effective representation
of the Dáil at the time of the Treaty was virtually the same as that of
the Parliament of Southern Ireland minus the four members for
Dublin University: that is to say, 124 members, all of whom belonged
to Sinn Féin.

A meeting of the Dáil was summoned for the 14th December. Instead of waiting for it, Mr. De Valera, the President of the Dáil,
issued a *pronunciamento* on the 8th, addressed 'To the Irish People',
in the course of which he said:

'The terms of this Agreement are in violent conflict with the wishes
of the majority of this nation as expressed freely in successive elections during the past three years.

'I feel it my duty to inform you immediately that I cannot recommend the acceptance of this Treaty, either to Dáil Éireann or the
country. In this attitude I am supported by the Ministers of Home
Affairs and Defence [Messrs. Stack and Brugha]. . . .

'The great test of our people has come. Let us face it worthily
without bitterness and, above all, without recriminations. There is a
definite constitutional way of resolving our political differences—let
us not depart from it, and let the conduct of the Cabinet in this
matter be an example to the whole nation.'[1]

This has been likened to throwing a torch into a powder magazine.
Certainly nobody could have so far suggested a method other than
the constitutional method for resolving political differences, for the
Treaty was as yet but two days old and this was the first public intimation that such differences existed.

For the decision on a question of such grave national import, a
parliament less suitable than the Dáil could hardly be imagined. It
was anything but a microcosm of the country, since Nationalists,
Farmers, Labour, and Southern Unionists were completely unrepresented in it. Its members, who were all of one party, had been elected
unopposed as a gesture of defiance to England and of hostility to
partition at the height of the Black and Tan régime. Most of them
were fighting men, or youths, and the lists had been scrutinized at
Sinn Féin headquarters for the purpose of ensuring that none but
politically 'safe' candidates should be adopted.[2] Moreover, some
may have had scruples about the oath which they had taken to the
Republic.

The public debate began on the 14th December, and the first to

[1] *Irish Independent*, 9 December 1921.
[2] P. S. O'Hegarty, *The Victory of Sinn Féin* (1924), p. 75.

speak was Mr. De Valera. A small detail in his opening sentences was revealing. Speaking in Irish he said: 'My Irish is not as good as I should like it to be. I am better able to express my thoughts in English, and so I think that I had better speak wholly in English.' He continued in English: 'Some of the members do not know Irish, I think, and consequently what I shall say will be in English.'[1] He had a great deal to say, alleging that the plenipotentiaries had exceeded their instructions. Arthur Griffith and Michael Collins indignantly controverted this charge, and, after an acrimonious discussion, during which no attention appears to have been paid to the rules of order, the Dáil went into private session.

In the private session Mr. De Valera propounded his now famous 'Document No. 2' as an alternative to the Treaty. Except that the Irish Free State is called Ireland and the term 'association' and its cognates are used, there does not appear to be a great deal of difference between the two instruments. Mr. Béaslaí, who was a member of the Dáil, published it as an Appendix to his *Michael Collins*, and comments on it as follows: 'The majority of the paragraphs are identical, word for word, with those of the Treaty, and . . . where they differ it is only a difference of phraseology. The British Empire, the English King, liability for the English National Debt and for pensions to English officials and police in Ireland, Partition, the granting of English naval bases in Ireland—all are swallowed. Mr. De Valera asked us to reject the Treaty, and agree unanimously to publish this as our offered alternative to England.'[2]

There was no parliamentary oath in 'Document No. 2', but the same writer states that Mr. De Valera had dictated the following oath which he would be willing to take: 'I do swear to bear true faith and allegiance to the Constitution of Ireland, and the Treaty of Association of Ireland with the British Commonwealth of Nations, and to recognize the King of Great Britain as Head of the Associated States.'[3]

After three days in private session the Dáil resumed in public on the 19th December, and the Speaker immediately informed the House that Mr. De Valera had now withdrawn 'Document No. 2' and that it 'must be regarded as confidential until he brings his own proposal forward formally'. Arthur Griffith said: 'Are my hands to be tied by this document being withheld after we were discussing it for two days?' And Michael Collins added: 'I as a public representative cannot consent, if I am in a minority of one, in withholding

---

[1] *Treaty Debates*, p. 7.   [2] Vol. ii, p. 317.   [3] Ibid., p. 316.

from the Irish people my knowledge of what the alternative is.'[1] Mr. De Valera's contention was that he had been prepared to stand on the secret document, but that it would cease to be of value in the absence of virtual unanimity. But he is precluded from this line of argument by his subsequent conduct. In February 1923, when faced with defeat in the Civil War, he resurrected 'Document No. 2' in a statement to the Press Association,[2] and his Constitution of 1937 embodies the principle of 'external association'.

After this preliminary skirmishing, Arthur Griffith formally moved: 'That Dáil Éireann approves of the Treaty between Great Britain and Ireland, signed in London on December 6th, 1921.' In a supremely able speech, stripped of rhetoric and meretricious argument, he commended to the Parliament the document which he had signed.

'. . . By that Treaty I am going to stand, and every man with a scrap of honour who signed it is going to stand. It is for the Irish people—who are our masters, not our servants, as some think—it is for the Irish people to say whether it is good enough. I hold that it is, and that the Irish people—that ninety-five per cent of them believe it to be good enough. . . .

'The gentlemen on the other side are prepared to recognize the King of England as head of the British Commonwealth. They are prepared to go half in the Empire and half out. They are prepared to go into the Empire for war and peace and treaties, and to keep out for other matters, and that is what the Irish people have got to know is the difference. Does all this quibble of words—because it is merely a quibble of words—mean that Ireland is asked to throw away this Treaty and go back to war? So far as my power or voice extends, not one young Irishman's life shall be lost on that quibble. We owe responsibility to the Irish people. . . .

'Thomas Davis said: "Peace with England, alliance with England to some extent, and, under certain circumstances, confederation with England; but an Irish ambition, Irish hopes, strength, virtue and rewards for the Irish."

'That is what we have brought back, peace with England, alliance with England, confederation with England, an Ireland developing her own life, carving out her own way of existence, and rebuilding the Gaelic civilization broken down at the battle of Kinsale. I say we have brought you that. I say we have translated Thomas Davis into the practical politics of the day. I ask then this Dáil to pass this resolution, and I ask the people of Ireland, and the Irish people

[1] *Treaty Debates*, pp. 19, 20.   [2] *Irish Independent*, 17 February 1923.

everywhere, to ratify this Treaty, to end this bitter conflict of centuries, to end it for ever, to take away that poison that has been rankling in the two countries and ruining the relationship of good neighbours. Let us stand as free partners, equal with England, and make after seven hundred years the greatest revolution that has ever been made in the history of the world—a revolution of seeing the two countries standing, not apart as enemies, but standing together as equals and as friends. I ask you, therefore, to pass this resolution.'[1]

After the motion had been seconded by General MacKeon, one of the bravest and most chivalrous soldiers in the Anglo-Irish war, Mr. De Valera followed with an impassioned speech. 'Document No. 2' had served its purpose in the private session, and he returned to the Republic: 'Did the Irish people think we were liars when we said that we meant to uphold the Republic, which was ratified by the vote of the people three years ago, and was further ratified—expressly ratified —by the vote of the people at the elections last May?'[2]

The debate seemed interminable. On the 22nd December the Dáil adjourned over Christmas and resumed on the 3rd January. Next day Mr. De Valera at last produced 'Document No. 2', but Arthur Griffith protested that it showed material changes and it was referred to as 'Document No. 3'. When the session opened on the 6th January Mr. De Valera, speaking at great length, announced his resignation of the Presidency of the Dáil, and said that his resignation involved that of the whole Cabinet. Having referred to his Irish upbringing, he said: 'I know what I am talking about; and whenever I wanted to know what the Irish people wanted I had only to examine my own heart and it told me straight off what the Irish people wanted.' He continued: 'I stand definitely for the Irish Republic as it was established—as it was proclaimed in 1916—as it was constitutionally established by the Irish nation in 1919, and I stand for that definitely; and I will stand by no policy whatever that is not consistent with that. Now if you re-elect me [cries of "We will!"]—steady for a moment—I will have to have the right to get a Cabinet that thinks with me so that we can be a unified body. Next, I will have to have the full use of all the resources of the Republic to defend the Republic—every resource and all the material that is in the nation to defend it. If you elect me and you do it by a majority I will throw out that Treaty—if we have a majority, if this Cabinet goes down. Next, I will bring from our Cabinet a document such as that [Document No. 2] and we will offer it to the British people as a genuine peace Treaty—to the British peoples, not merely

[1] *Treaty Debates*, pp. 20–3. [2] Ibid., p. 24.

Lloyd George and his Government, but to all the States of the British Commonwealth—of the British Empire.'[1]

If this strategy had succeeded, Mr. De Valera's personality, and not the Treaty, would have been made the issue. After much argument, Griffith remarked: 'Why we should be stopped in the middle of this discussion and a vote taken on the personality of President De Valera I don't understand; and I don't think my countrymen will understand it.' Mr. De Valera replied: 'I am sick and tired of politics—so sick that no matter what happens I would go back to private life. . . . If this House wants to take a vote on a straight issue I don't want to draw any red herring across. It is because I am straight that I meet crookedness with straight dealing always.'[2]

The debate on the Treaty proceeded, and on the 7th January 1922 the vote was taken and the Treaty was approved by 64 votes to 57. As a result, Mr. De Valera announced that he would resign the Presidency of the Dáil, and he then broke down.

At the next meeting, two days later, he allowed himself to be proposed as 'President of the Republic', and he made it plain that, if he were elected, his Cabinet 'would be composed for the time being of those who stood definitely by the Republic'.[3] He said: 'We are finished with that Treaty as far as we are concerned. It has nothing further to do with this House. We have not passed any Act of Ratification of that Treaty. We have simply passed a resolution of approval, which means that the Government of the Republic is not going actively to interfere with those who are to complete that Treaty. When they have completed that Treaty then they will have a definite issue before the Irish people, and not till then, and I challenge them on that.'[4]

There would thus have been (1) a provisional government, composed of Ministers who had accepted the Treaty and responsible to the Dáil which had approved the Treaty; (2) a government of the Republic, headed by Mr. De Valera and composed of men bitterly opposed to the Treaty. It speaks volumes for Mr. De Valera's ascendancy over men of the type of which the Dáil was composed that this proposal was defeated by only two votes (60 to 58). The following day, Arthur Griffith was elected President of the Dáil, but before the division was taken Mr. De Valera withdrew from the House with his supporters. The new President then nominated his Cabinet, which was approved.

---

[1] *Treaty Debates*, pp. 274, 275.   [2] Ibid., p. 281.
[3] Ibid., p. 356.   [4] Ibid., p. 353.

The anti-Treaty party returned for the afternoon session, and General Mulcahy, the new Minister for Defence, gave an assurance that the Army would continue to be the Army of the Republic. This meant, of course, pending the acceptance or rejection by the people of the Treaty at a general election.

The Treaty had been confirmed and ratified by both Houses of Parliament at Westminster on the 16th December 1921; it now remained for the strict letter of Articles 17 and 18 to be fulfilled on the Irish side. On the 14th January 1922 a meeting was held of 'the members elected to sit in the House of Commons of Southern Ireland'. It was attended by the pro-Treaty members of the Dáil and the four members for Dublin University, and resolutions were passed (1) approving the Treaty and (2) setting up a Provisional Government under the chairmanship of General Michael Collins.

The new régime was thus launched, and it started with the blessing of the Catholic Church, Pope Benedict XV dispatching two congratulatory telegrams, one to King George V and the other to the President of the Dáil.[1]

The British now began to keep their part of the bargain by evacuating the country. On the 16th January Dublin Castle, for centuries the nerve-centre of British Government in Ireland, was formally handed over by the Viceroy (Lord FitzAlan) to General Collins and his colleagues of the Provisional Government. The British soldiers marched out of the military barracks throughout the twenty-six county area and the Irish soldiers marched in; the Union Jack was lowered and the tricolour was hoisted in its stead. During one of his numerous visits to London Collins signed a *modus vivendi* with Sir James Craig (now Lord Craigavon) which might, in happier circumstances, have paved the way to the ultimate unity of Ireland.[2]

But the dark shadow of impending anarchy already loomed over the country and it was deepened by what Kevin O'Higgins (a member of both the Dáil Cabinet and the Provisional Government) characterized as 'the concurrent lack of jurisdiction of Dáil Éireann, the Provisional Government and the British Government'. The impasse could have been solved only by an early general election, and it was the object of the opponents of the Treaty (who well knew what the result would be) at all costs to prevent it. Also, if the British evacuation could be stopped, the British Government might hold the Treaty to be at an end. Accordingly, departing members of the British

---

[1] *Irish Times*, 13 January 1922, and *Treaty Debates*, p. 391.
[2] Béaslaí, *Michael Collins*, vol. ii, p. 358.

forces had their arms seized and some of them were shot dead; there
was bloodshed on the Northern Ireland border and the beginning of
a religious war in Belfast. At a monster anti-Treaty meeting held in
O'Connell Street, Dublin, on the 12th February Mr. De Valera was
introduced by the chairman as 'the President of the Republic'.[1] This
was an indication that the decision of the majority in the Dáil was
not recognized.

On the 22nd February Griffith and Collins, hard pressed and anxious for peace, agreed that there should be no general election for
three months, and that the new Constitution, as well as the Treaty,
should then be submitted to the people. By this concession they
doubtless hoped to satisfy Mr. De Valera to some extent, to secure the
Provisional Government from open attack, and to stave off mutiny in
the Army. In the first week of March there were murderous outrages
in Waterford, Tipperary, and Limerick. On the 6th March the city of
Limerick was occupied by anti-Treaty forces; next day, troops loyal
to the Provisional Government arrived and a clash was averted only
by a hair's breadth, the city being evacuated by both sides some days
later. On the 12th March Michael Collins addressed a public meeting
in Cork, and there was intimidatory shooting all round the platform.
'If the incidents attendant upon to-day's Treaty demonstration are a
foretaste of the election campaign,' said a newspaper correspondent,
'then Heaven help the country.'[2]

Having obtained a postponement of the election, Mr. De Valera
next proposed that it ought to be held on a new register. On the 16th
March Arthur Griffith replied:

'Were a new register begun now, an election would be impossible
for the next six months. This would suit the game of those who desire
to muzzle the Irish electorate, but I cannot be a party to any muzzling
order.

'I agreed with you to place the Constitution simultaneously before the electorate with the Treaty. I agreed with you to postpone
the election for three months. Now you attempt to raise a
new and false issue intended to further postpone or prevent an
election.'[3]

On the 15th March the dissident minority of the Dáil founded
Cumann na Poblachta (League of the Republic), the announcement
being signed by Mr. De Valera as President. He then left for a tour
of the south, where excitement was already at fever pitch. The fol-

[1] *Irish Times*, 13 February 1922.   [2] Ibid., 13 March 1922.
[3] *Irish Independent*, 17 March 1922.

lowing extracts from his speeches on this tour are quoted from contemporary newspaper reports.

At Dungarvan, County Waterford, on the 16th March: 'The Treaty . . . barred the way to independence with the blood of fellow-Irishmen. It was only by Civil War after this that they could get their independence. . . . If you don't fight to-day, you will have to fight to-morrow; and I say, when you are in a good fighting position, then fight on.'[1]

At Carrick-on-Suir, County Tipperary, on the 17th March (Saint Patrick's Day), to a crowd which included seven hundred men of the Irish Republican Army: 'If the Treaty was accepted the fight for freedom would still go on; and the Irish people, instead of fighting foreign soldiers, would have to fight the Irish soldiers of an Irish Government set up by Irishmen. If the Treaty was not rejected, perhaps it was over the bodies of the young men he saw around him that day that the fight for Irish freedom may be fought.'[2]

At Thurles, County Tipperary, on the same day, at a meeting largely composed of Volunteers, about two hundred of whom carried rifles: 'If they accepted the Treaty, and if the Volunteers of the future tried to complete the work the Volunteers of the last four years had been attempting, they would have to complete it, not over the bodies of foreign soldiers, but over the dead bodies of their own countrymen. They would have to wade through Irish blood, through the blood of the soldiers of the Irish Government, and through, perhaps, the blood of some of the members of the Government in order to get Irish freedom.'[3]

At Killarney, County Kerry, on the 18th March, again in the presence of armed men: 'In order to achieve freedom, if our Volunteers continue, and I hope they will continue until the goal is reached, if we continue on that movement which was begun when the Volunteers were started, and we suppose this Treaty is ratified by your votes, then these men, in order to achieve freedom, will have, I said yesterday, to march over the dead bodies of their own brothers. They will have to wade through Irish blood.'[4]

Incidentally, it was in the Killarney speech that Mr. De Valera uttered the aphorism: 'The people have never a right to do wrong.'

Even in a country by now inured to horrors, these four speeches caused a shudder of dismay. At this time the Sinn Féin Executive was still in being, in spite of the split, and Arthur Griffith and Mr. De

---

[1] *Irish Independent*, 17 March 1922. [2] Ibid., 18 March 1922.
[3] Ibid., 18 March 1922. [4] Ibid., 20 March 1922.

Valera were members of it. According to Griffith's friend Mr. Seán Milroy (afterwards Senator Milroy) Griffith said to him: 'I shall not sit in the same room with that man until he withdraws his incitement to assassination.'[1] The *Irish Independent* published two condemnatory editorials on these speeches, and on the 23rd March it printed a letter from Mr. De Valera, dated the previous day, in which they were characterized as 'villainous' and 'criminal malice'. He had been misrepresented.

'My argument was an answer to those who said that the London Agreement gave us "freedom to achieve freedom". I showed that, instead of opening the way, it erected in the nation's path two almost impassable barriers:

'(1) the nation's own pledged word, and

'(2) a native Government, bound to act in accordance with and to secure, even by force, respect for that pledged word.'

In a footnote the editor defended the construction which had been placed on Mr. De Valera's words: 'We believe it is the construction which would be placed on them by thousands of others. . . . We hope that in view of the above letter Mr. De Valera will use his best efforts to discountenance any attempt at civil war in the future.'

Towards the end of March the mutinous section of the Army definitely repudiated the authority of the Dáil, one of the ringleaders being one Rory O'Connor, who termed himself Commandant-General.[2] Mr. De Valera did not condemn this secession. In a letter dated the 13th September 1922, captured by the Government and alleged to have been written by Mr. De Valera (the attribution to whom has never been disavowed), the writer states that 'Rory O'Connor's unfortunate repudiation of the Dáil which I was so foolish as to defend, even to a straining of my own views, in order to avoid the appearance of a split, is now the greatest barrier that we have.' The further comment is made: 'We cannot, as in the time of the war with the British, point to authority derived from the vote of the majority of the people. We will be turned down definitely by the electorate in a few months' time in any case.'[3]

On the 6th April, at Dunleary, Mr. De Valera repudiated the Provisional Government: 'When Dáil Éireann took its rightful place as the Government of the nation, then they would have a stable Government; but if they attempted to do that which they legally could not do, to set up a Provisional Government as the Government of the

[1] *Senate Debates*, xvii, 1186.   [2] *Irish Times*, 29 March 1922.
[3] *Irish Independent*, 16 August 1923.

country, that Government would not be obeyed. That Government would not function.'[1]

Shortly after midnight on the 13th April the Four Courts (the Courts of Justice in Dublin) were seized by Rory O'Connor and the Irregulars, as they were now called. This was in Holy Week. On Good Friday members of the Labour Party, among them Mr. J. T. O'Farrell (afterwards Senator O'Farrell), interviewed Mr. De Valera. Senator O'Farrell subsequently recalled the occasion in a speech in the Senate.

'We spent two hours pleading with him then, with a view to averting the impending calamity of the civil war, and the only statement he made that has abided with me since as to what his views were was this: "The majority have no right to do wrong." He repeated that at least a dozen times in the course of the interview, in response to statements made to him to the effect that the Treaty had been accepted by a majority, and that, consequently, it was his duty to observe the decision of the majority until it was reversed. He refused to accept it on the ground that the majority had no right to do wrong.'[2]

Intimidation, sabotage, and murder grew in volume, and the Church, always reluctant to interfere in a political or quasi-political issue, could no longer remain silent. On the 26th April Cardinal Logue and all the members of the Hierarchy issued a joint statement, from which the following extracts are taken. Perhaps one needs to be a Catholic to realize the immense importance which is, or should be, attached to such a pronouncement in a Catholic country.

'The great national question of the Treaty is a legitimate question for national discussion and debate. On that big question every Irishman is entitled to his own opinion, subject, of course, to truth and responsibility to God. We, too, hold very definite and decided views upon that important issue, but we do not mean to obtrude them on anybody, founded though they are on a disinterested and conscious love of Ireland's welfare.

'Like the great bulk of the nation, we think that the best and wisest course for Ireland is to accept the Treaty and make the most of the freedom it undoubtedly brings us. . . . But we recognize that this is a national question, to be settled by the national will, ascertained by an election carried out in the ordinary constitutional way. . . .

'The cause of all our present scandals and turmoil is the unconstitutional policy of certain leaders who think themselves entitled to force their views upon the nation, not by reason but by firearms. . . .

[1] *Irish Independent*, 7 April 1922.   [2] *Senate Debates*, xx, 1876.

'As to the organ of supreme authority in this country at present, whatever speculative views may be held upon the subject, in practice there can be no doubt as long as the Dáil and the Provisional Government act in unison, as they have hitherto done.

'We beg the young men connected with this military revolt to consider religiously our solemn teaching on this fundamental maxim of social morality. . . . When they shoot their brothers on the opposite side they are murderers. When they injure public and private property they are robbers and brigands bound to restitution—all sins and crimes of the most heinous guilt. . . .

'We appeal, in the name of God, of Ireland and of national dignity, to the leaders on both sides, civil and military, to meet again . . . and, if they cannot agree upon the main question, to agree upon two things at all events, and publish their agreement authoritatively to the world—that the use of the revolver must cease and the elections, the national expression of self-determination, be allowed to be held, free from all violence.

'The man who fails to hearken to this appeal, made not so much by us as by Ireland, will carry with him to the grave an odious and a dreadful responsibility.'[1]

On the 30th April Mr. De Valera made a speech in Longford. He said: 'It would be a terrible thing if the taunt of the English that they were criminals, murderers, and rebels should appear to have been upheld by the common people of any constituency in Ireland. . . .

'It would be good-bye to stable conditions if they accepted the Articles of Agreement, because there were men in Ireland who were determined that if it was necessary for them again to offer another sacrifice such as was done in Easter Week they would do it before they allowed that nation to dishonour itself.'[2]

Longford is remote from the capital, and Mr. De Valera's audience would probably know little and care less about 'the taunt of the English'. But even the humblest of them could hardly be unaware of the fact that, only four days previously, the united Hierarchy of Ireland, invoking the moral law, had condemned the acts of the Irregulars as those of murderers, robbers, and brigands.

This speech by Mr. De Valera was made the day after the breakdown of a conference which had been sitting under the chairmanship of the Catholic Archbishop of Dublin (Most Rev. Dr. Byrne). Griffith and Collins offered a general election in June on the issue of the Treaty and the Constitution, asking for a guarantee against in-

[1] *Irish Independent*, 27 April 1922.   [2] Ibid., 1 May 1922.

timidation. This offer was refused. They next offered a general election in June on the single issue of the Treaty; the body so elected to devise the Constitution and to dissolve, giving the people an opportunity of accepting or rejecting it. This offer was also refused. 'To meet specious objections raised as to the state of the Register', they finally offered (a) no general election for three months, and (b) a plebiscite on the Treaty, within one month, of all adults, whether on the register or not. This, too, was rejected, 'both in principle and detail'.

Mr. De Valera justified his refusal in a long statement to the Press, in which he said, *inter alia*, that 'Republicans maintain . . . that there are rights which a minority may justly uphold, even by arms, against a majority.' He had proposed that the issue of the Treaty should not be referred to the people for at least six months. 'Time would be secured for the present passions to subside, for personalities to disappear, and the fundamental differences between the two sides to be appreciated—time during which Ireland's reputation could be vindicated, the work of national reconstruction begun, and normal conditions restored.'[1]

On the day before these words appeared, the Irregulars raided branches of the Bank of Ireland all over the country and stole more than a quarter of a million sterling. Arthur Griffith put the position bluntly: 'I say that whatever quibble, whatever force, whatever juggling or intrigue they attempt to use to prevent an election, we will meet that intrigue, that juggling or that force, because we are determined to assert the sovereign right of the Irish people to say whether they will or will not have the Treaty.'[2]

But Collins was willing to go further than Griffith in an attempt to secure unity, and on the 20th May he signed an agreement with Mr. De Valera which is known not to have had Griffith's approval. This provided for what was called a 'National Coalition Panel' of candidates for the general election, the Treaty party and the anti-Treaty party being represented on this panel by their existing strength. An 'election' conducted on this basis would have violated every principle of democracy, but the Agreement contained a saving clause as follows: 'Every and any interest is free to go up and contest the election equally with the National-Sinn Féin Panel.'[3] The agreement was approved by the Sinn Féin Convention, and the General Election was held on the 16th June. The Draft Constitution was issued for

[1] *Irish Independent*, 2 May 1922.   [2] Ibid., 1 May 1922.
[3] Ibid., 22 May 1922.

publication on the previous evening—the day after the successful termination of the London negotiations, which are recounted in the next chapter. But as the issue was clearly the acceptance or rejection of the Treaty its belated appearance, inevitable in the circumstances, was of no great importance.

The election campaign was marked by appalling intimidation on the part of the Irregulars, and candidates other than those on the Panel were 'discouraged'. As polling day approached Collins virtually disregarded the agreement, which by this time he probably regretted having signed. It was, however, partially effective, as out of a total of 128 seats no less than 37 were unopposed. Of these, 16 belonged to the anti-Treaty part of the panel, 17 to the pro-Treaty part, and the remaining 4 were the members for Dublin University. By coming forward in sufficient numbers, however, the members of the Labour Party, the Farmers, and the Independents vindicated the right of the electors to say whether or not they wanted the Treaty. The result was as follows:

Party	Number of candidates	Elected unopposed	Total elected
Pro-Treaty Panel	65	17	58
Anti-Treaty Panel	57	16	35
On both panels	1		
Labour	18		17
Independents	17		7
Farmers	12		7
Dublin University	4	4	4
	174	37	128

In so far as it had been allowed to express its wishes, the country had declared decisively for the Treaty. The valid votes cast in the contested constituencies were:

Pro-Treaty Panel	239,193
Anti-Treaty Panel	130,716
On both panels	3,148
Labour	132,511
Independents	63,641
Farmers	51,074
	620,283[1]

[1] *Irish Independent*, 26 June 1922.

If we include in the anti-Treaty vote the votes given to Mr. Daniel Breen, whose name was on both panels, the result in summary form is:

| Total vote for the Treaty | 486,419 |
| Total vote against the Treaty | 133,864 |

Thus the anti-Treaty vote was less than 22 per cent. of the whole. It must be emphasized that, on the Treaty side, this was a perfectly free election, in the sense that the members elected were not required to take any parliamentary oath. Mr. De Valera has always contended that it was not free, inasmuch as the Treaty was signed under a threat from Mr. Lloyd George of 'immediate and terrible war'. But this seems counterbalanced by Mr. De Valera's own plain intimations of what would inevitably happen if the Treaty was ratified by the votes of the people. They had, indeed, had a foretaste of it for months prior to the election.

At midnight on the 27th June the Forces of the Provisional Government served a four-hour ultimatum on the Irregular garrison in occupation of the Four Courts, where one of their officers, who had been kidnapped, was detained as a hostage. The ultimatum was ignored and hostilities began. This was not, as is so often supposed, the beginning of the Civil War. Civil war had been in progress ever since the repudiation of the Dáil by the Irregulars under Rory O'Connor on the 28th March; but hitherto it had been all on one side. Fortified by the result of the general election, the Provisional Government at last felt itself in a position to discharge its elementary duty to the citizens. It so happened that, just prior to the attack on the Four Courts, the British Government, alarmed by the Collins-De Valera Pact and the growing anarchy, was itself preparing to take action against the Irregulars if the Provisional Government failed to do so. In view of this fact, Mr. De Valera's followers allege that the attack was made on British orders. Arthur Griffith denied that this was so, but his denial is unnecessary. It is obvious that no government worthy of the name could tolerate indefinitely the occupation of the Courts of Justice and other principal buildings by armed men who acknowledged no civil authority whatever.

There is no need here to follow the course of the military operations. The Irregulars in the Four Courts surrendered after three days and blew the place up, including the Public Record Office, with its irreplaceable historical documents. Street fighting took place in the streets of Dublin until the 5th July, the principal thoroughfare,

O'Connell Street, being partially demolished. The rebels were gradually cleared out of Waterford, Limerick, Cork, Clonmel, and other centres which they had occupied, leaving a trail of destruction behind them. By the end of August field operations were virtually at an end, but a guerrilla campaign continued for some months, as will be explained in a subsequent chapter.

On the 12th August Arthur Griffith died, his great heart broken by the ruin of his dreams. Michael Collins said that he had 'no shadow of doubt but that his death was hastened by the mental anguish he has endured because of the actions of those who . . . have acted as they have done and as they are doing still. . . . Even so, it is not too late for De Valera and those who are with him to honour the passing of a great patriot by now achieving what that patriot has given his life for —a united Ireland, an Irish nation.'[1] Ten days later Collins was himself a corpse, slain while fighting his way out of an ambush into which he had fallen while on a tour of inspection in his native county of Cork. Thus within the space of a few days Ireland had lost the two principal architects of the Treaty, one the President of the Dáil, and the other the Chairman of the Provisional Government and Commander-in-Chief of the Army. A more grievous blow at such a time could scarcely be imagined; but the nation's government had to be carried on, and two brave men stepped into the shoes of the dead leaders, Mr. William T. Cosgrave becoming President and General Richard Mulcahy Commander-in-Chief.

The appeal issued by Cardinal Logue and the archbishops and bishops of Ireland on the 26th April had fallen on deaf ears. Since then the people had declared their will, but anarchy had grown. On the 10th October the Hierarchy, again headed by the aged Cardinal, issued a Joint Pastoral, in which they spoke even more sternly.

'. . . A section of the community, refusing to acknowledge the Government set up by the nation, have chosen to attack their own country as if she were a foreign power. Forgetting, apparently, that a dead nation cannot be free, they have deliberately set out to make our motherland, so far as they could, a heap of ruins. They have wrecked Ireland from end to end, burning and destroying national property of enormous value, breaking roads, bridges and railways, seeking by this insensate blockade to starve the people or bury them in social stagnation. . . . They carry on what they call a war, but which, in the absence of any legitimate authority to justify it, is mor-

[1] *Freeman's Journal*, 14 August 1922.

ally only a system of murder and assassination of the National forces, for it must not be forgotten that killing in an unjust war is as much murder before God as if there were no war. . . .

'In spite of all this sin and crime they claim to be good Catholics and demand at the hands of the Church her most sacred privileges, like the Sacraments, reserved for her worthy members. . . .

'Vanity, perhaps self-conceit, may have blinded some who think that they, and not the nation, must dictate the national policy. Greed for land, love of loot and anarchy have affected others, and they, we regret to say, are not a few; but the main cause of this demoralisation is to be found in false notions on social morality.'

The Hierarchy then laid down the teaching of the Church, from Saint Paul onwards, on obedience to authority as a divine duty as well as a social necessity, and the Pastoral continued:

'No Republican can evade this teaching by asserting that the legitimate authority in Ireland is not the present Dáil or Provisional Government. There is no other and cannot be, outside the body of the people. A Republic without popular recognition behind it is a contradiction in terms. Such being Divine Law, the guerrilla warfare now being carried on by the Irregulars is without moral sanction, and, therefore, the killing of National soldiers in the course of it is murder before God, the seizing of public and private property is robbery, the breaking of roads, bridges and railways is criminal destruction, the invasion of homes and the molestation of citizens a grievous crime.

'All those who in contravention of this teaching participate in such crimes are guilty of grievous sins and may not be absolved in Confession nor admitted to Holy Communion if they persist in such evil courses. . . .

'Our people will observe that in all this there is no question of mere politics, but of what is morally right or wrong according to the Divine Law. . . . What we condemn is the armed campaign now being carried on against the Government set up by the nation. If any section of the community . . . disapprove of the National Government, they have the elections to fall back upon and such constitutional action as is recognized by God and civilized society. If their political views are founded on wisdom they will succeed sooner or later, but one thing is certain: the hand of Providence will not be forced, nor their cause advanced by irreligion and crime.

'It may, perhaps, be said that in this our teaching we wound the strong feelings of many of our people. That we know, and the

F

thought is agony to us. But we must teach Truth in such a grave crisis, no matter what the consequences. . . .

'With all earnestness we appeal to the leaders in this saddest revolt to rise above their own feelings, to remember the claim of God and the sufferings of the people in their conscience, and to abandon methods which they now know beyond the shadow of a doubt are unCatholic and immoral, and look to the realisation of their ideals along lines sanctioned by Divine Law and society. . . .'[1]

Up to this point the Irregulars had been operating independently of even a pretended civil authority. On the 26th October 1922—that is to say, just sixteen days after the date of the Joint Pastoral of the Hierarchy—there was published a sheet entitled *Poblacht na h-Éireann: War News No. 78*. Under the headlines 'Stop Press. Dáil Éireann. Official Communiqué' it stated that 'Dáil Éireann, the Parliament and Government of the Republic, met yesterday in secret session' and had passed certain resolutions. Prefixed to the resolutions was a preamble, in which the 'traitorous conspiracy and armed revolt' against the Republic are recited. The resolutions are:

'1. We, the faithful Deputies of Dáil Éireann, assembled to maintain the Republic and to secure the continuity of independent Government for the whole of Ireland, in the name of all loyal citizens of the Republic and by the express wish of the soldiers fighting in its defence, call upon the former President, Éamon De Valera, to resume the Presidency and to nominate a Council of State and Executive Ministers, to assist him in carrying on the government until such time as the Parliament of the Republic is allowed freely to assemble or the people are allowed by a free election to decide how they shall be governed.

'2. That Éamon De Valera be hereby appointed President of the Republic and Chief Executive of the State.

'3. That the following, nominated by the President, be hereby appointed the Council of State.' (Here follow certain names.)

So that the Government of the Republic professed to be re-established by the anti-Treaty party of the Dáil, with Mr. De Valera as President of the Republic and the Irish Republican Army as its military arm. A subsequent issue of this sheet (*Poblacht na h-Éireann: War News No. 97*), dated the 21st November 1922, contains the text of a resolution passed by this 'Dáil' formally rescinding the resolution of approval of the Treaty passed on the 7th January 1922. The proclamation containing it is signed by Mr. De Valera as 'President

[1] *Irish Independent*, 11 October 1922.

of the Republic' and by Mr. Ruttledge as 'Minister for Home Affairs'.

In the course of their Joint Pastoral, the Hierarchy had referred to their previous pronouncement of the 26th April, and had continued: 'We now again authoritatively renew that teaching, and warn our Catholic people that they are conscientiously bound to abide by it, subject, of course, to an appeal to the Holy See.' In view of this last phrase, it was rumoured in the newspapers that Mr. De Valera and his colleagues intended to appeal to the Vatican. An 'Official Communiqué', dated Thursday, 9th November 1922 and published in *Poblacht na h-Éireann: War News No. 88*, made it clear that this was not so. The 'Communiqué' is as follows:

'The Government of the Republic does not intend to enter an "Appeal" at Rome against the pronouncement of the Hierarchy, as is suggested by the Press. The constitutional question at issue is not one for the Hierarchy, but rather for the Supreme Court of the Republic. The terms of the Resolution passed by Dáil Éireann are:

' "That we ask the President to make representations to the Vatican, formally and emphatically protesting as Head of the State against the unwarrantable action of the Irish Hierarchy in presuming and pretending to pronounce an authoritative judgment upon the question of constitutional and political fact now at issue in Ireland, viz., whether the so-called Provisional (Partition) Parliament, set up under threat of unjust war and by a *coup d'état*, was the rightful legislature and government of the country or not—and in using the sanction of religion to enforce their own political views and compel acquiescence by Irish Republicans in an usurpation that entails no less consequences than the partition of the ancient territory of our Nation, the loss of its sovereignty and independence, and the imposition of a test oath that amounts to the disfranchisement of Republicans who have regard for the sacred bond of an oath and will not take it without meaning to keep it. . . ." '

So there was to be no appeal, but merely a protest. The view of the Vatican was sufficiently indicated by the message sent a month later by His Holiness Pope Pius XI to His Excellency Timothy Michael Healy, K.C., cordially welcoming his appointment as the first Governor-General of the Irish Free State.

'The Holy Father prays that a happy era of peace and prosperity may now set in for the beloved people of Ireland, and from his heart sends you the Apostolic Benediction.'[1]

---

[1] *Freeman's Journal*, 12 December 1922.

CHAPTER III

DRAFTING THE CONSTITUTION

Appointment of the Constitution Committee—Its personnel—Three separate Drafts—Unanimity on question of bicameral system—Powers of Second Chamber—Negotiations with the British Government on the draft proposals—Views of Kevin O'Higgins and others on the subsequent agreement—Arthur Griffith and the minority—Problem of the Southern Unionists—Griffith's interview with representatives of the minority—Their character and standing—Their subsequent interviews with Mr. Lloyd George and Griffith—Undertakings given—Formal negotiations begun—Griffith's identity of view with Kevin O'Higgins—Main points of contention—The Heads of Agreement—Unionist dissatisfaction with character of Senate—Circumstances precluding further concessions—Publication of the Draft Constitution.

It was assumed from the beginning that the new State was to be provided with a written Constitution, based, of course, upon the Treaty, which, taken by itself, was clearly inadequate as an instrument of government; and reference to this project has already been made in connection with the discussions which took place between the pro-Treaty and the anti-Treaty parties regarding a general election. It is proposed here to examine the genesis of the Draft Constitution which was subsequently presented to the Constituent Assembly, and the subject falls under three heads: (1) the work of the Constitution Committee; (2) the negotiations with the British Government; and (3) the negotiations with the Southern Unionists. We shall consider these in turn.

In January 1922 the Provisional Government appointed a committee to draw up a draft constitution. The Committee held its first meeting on the 30th of the same month,[1] and its members were as follows:

[1] *Irish Times*, 31 January 1922.

General Michael Collins, chairman
James G. Douglas
Darrell Figgis
C. J. France
Hugh Kennedy, K.C.
James Murnaghan
James McNeill
John O'Byrne
Alfred O'Rahilly.

Michael Collins's chairmanship can hardly have been other than nominal, as his time was fully occupied by his duties as Chairman of the Provisional Government, and the acting chairmanship devolved on Darrell Figgis, a close friend of Arthur Griffith. Figgis was a man of letters of undoubted genius, and during the Anglo–Irish struggle he had proved his patriotism in a number of ways, having been imprisoned on several occasions by the British. He had, however, in some degree, the instability and egotism which so often accompany genius. He afterwards became the senior member of the Dáil for County Dublin, and died tragically in London some years later.

Mr. Douglas was a Dublin business man and a member of the Society of Friends. During the Anglo-Irish struggle he had done valuable humanitarian work as honorary treasurer and trustee of the Irish White Cross Funds—a form of activity which had brought him into touch with Michael Collins. He later became a member of the Senate, of which he was the first Vice-Chairman. Mr. C. J. France was a United States lawyer who had been sent to Ireland during the Anglo-Irish War by the American Committee for Relief in Ireland. Mr. Hugh Kennedy, K.C., at the time of his appointment to the committee held the post of Legal Adviser to the Provisional Government. He subsequently became the first Attorney-General of the Irish Free State, and, following the establishment of the new courts, its first Chief Justice—a position which he held until his death in 1936. Mr. Murnaghan, a barrister, was Professor of Jurisprudence in University College, Dublin, and afterwards was appointed to be a Judge of the Supreme Court. Mr. McNeill had had a distinguished career in the Indian Civil Service, and on his retirement had become chairman of the Dublin County Council. He was subsequently the first High Commissioner of the Irish Free State in London and its second Governor-General. Mr. O'Byrne, a prominent barrister, afterwards became Attorney-General on Mr. Kennedy's elevation to the

Bench. He was a Judge of the High Court from 1926 to 1940, when he was elevated to the Supreme Court. Mr. O'Rahilly was then, as now, Professor of Mathematical Physics in University College, Cork, and a prolific writer on political and social questions.

It will be apparent that the Constitution Committee was in no sense a political body. It was a group of distinguished men in which commerce, administration, the theory and practice of law, and what might be termed the professorial outlook were all represented. The absence of any spokesman of those who opposed the Anglo-Irish Treaty was regrettable, but inevitable in the circumstances. The Southern Unionists were also unrepresented, but the extent to which they were consulted will be detailed later. The Committee had an able and experienced secretariat of three (Messrs. R. J. P. Mortishead, P. A. O'Toole, and E. M. Stephens), and after a period of intensive work extending over two months it had discharged the task entrusted to it.

The members of the Committee were unable to agree upon a single draft and three were sent to the Government.[1] Other copies of these drafts are known to exist besides those in the Government archives; Mr. De Valera, for instance, when Leader of the Opposition, told the Dáil that he had seen them and mentioned the names of some of the signatories, as well as giving other details.[2] In the circumstances, it is to be regretted that the Government has never published them, more especially as they are documents of great historical interest.

Article 2 of the Treaty provided that 'the position of the Irish Free State in relation to the Imperial Parliament and Government and otherwise shall be that of the Dominion of Canada'. The question arose whether these words implied that the Irish Free State was necessarily tied to the bicameral system, and the point was cleared up in a letter written by the Prime Minister (Mr. Lloyd George) to Arthur Griffith, to the effect that the analogy thus drawn with Canada did not in any way imply that a Second Chamber should be formed on the Canadian model, or, indeed, that there should necessarily be any Second Chamber at all.[3] The Constitution Committee was therefore quite free to recommend a unicameral system if it so chose; but it is noteworthy that all three drafts contained provisions for a senate.

Two of the drafts agreed on the type and powers of the second

---

[1] *Senate Debates*, xvii, 20.   [2] *Dáil Debates*, xxiii, 1502, 1503.
[3] Letter quoted in full in *Treaty Debates*, pp. 21, 22.

chamber.[1] The number of senators was apparently to be forty,[2] and the suspensory power was for a period of 180 days. Actually, the period was longer, for the senate, by a majority, could suspend a Bill, after it had been passed, for a further period of ninety days, during which it was to be submitted to a referendum.[3] Both these drafts contained provisions for the initiation of legislation by the people.[4]

The third draft, signed by two members, laid great emphasis on the initiative and on the referendum, and it included detailed proposals for both.[5] The authors of this draft were prepared to give much wider powers to the upper house than were the authors of the other two, as the following Article will show:

'(1) All Bills passed by the House shall be presented to the Senate for approval. If within one month, being time of session, after such presentation, the Senate does not express disapproval, it shall be taken to have approved.

'(2) In case the Senate amends or rejects the Bill, it shall be brought before the House for further consideration. Should the House and Senate not arrive at an agreement within three months, being time of session, the Bill, if it appropriates revenue or imposes taxation, shall become law as finally passed by the House, save as provided in the preceding Article. If the Bill does not appropriate revenue or impose taxation it shall become inoperative unless within that interval a Referendum is demanded by 50,000 voters or by a majority of the House or Senate, in which case the law as finally passed by the House shall be submitted to a vote of the people for acceptance or rejection.

'(3) If the House by a two-thirds majority declare that the measure is of extreme urgency the period of three months provided in the preceding section shall be reduced to one month.'[6]

If this Article had been incorporated in the Constitution, it would have placed the Senate in a dominant position in regard to all legislation except finance.

The foregoing is all the information that has so far been made public regarding the work of the Constitution Committee. But it is not unreasonable to assume that the Draft Constitution introduced in the Constituent Assembly embodied in substance the proposals contained in one or more of the three drafts, apart from those

---

[1] *Senate Debates*, xvii, 20.
[3] *Senate Debates*, xvii, 20, 21.
[5] *Senate Debates*, xvii, 21.

[2] *Dáil Debates*, i, 1154.
[4] *Dáil Debates*, xxiii, 1502.
[6] Ibid.

Articles which were the subject of the negotiations that we are now about to consider.

Arthur Griffith went to London on the 25th May 1922, taking with him the Provisional Government's draft proposals for a constitution,[1] and the conversations with the British Government and the representatives of the Southern Unionists proceeded *pari passu*. At these and subsequent meetings, Griffith was accompanied by his able young lieutenant, Kevin O'Higgins, and by the Law Officer of the Government (Hugh Kennedy, K.C.). The purpose of the negotiations with the British Government was to arrive at an agreed interpretation of those portions of the Draft Constitution which dealt with the relations between the two countries. The original draft has never been published, but there seems to be no doubt that it did not embody the constitutional forms common to the constitutions of the overseas nations of the Commonwealth. Mr. Ernest Blythe, who was Minister for Local Government and a member of the Cabinet at the time, said of it later:

'For my part, I never had any belief whatever that the British would agree to all that was in the draft that was taken over to London, and, for my part, I believe the draft went outside the terms of the Treaty, and was such as we had no right to expect would be agreed to. I agreed to it as the first draft because it left room for bargaining.'[2]

When the Draft Constitution was before the Constituent Assembly, Kevin O'Higgins enumerated fifteen Articles (out of a total of seventy-nine) on which the Government were prepared to stand as a matter of Treaty obligation,[3] and we may assume that these, and these only, had been either inserted or modified as a result of the inter-governmental negotiations in London. They include Article 1, which states that 'the Irish Free State is a co-equal member of the Community of Nations forming the British Commonwealth of Nations'; Articles 17, 55, and 77, which deal with the parliamentary Oath; Article 40, which provides for the withholding of the King's assent to Bills; and Article 65, which contains the provision for appeals to the Privy Council. All the remaining Articles are merely those which contain references to the King, the Crown, and the Governor-General as part of the formal governmental machinery through which South Africa and other Commonwealth countries continue to operate in conditions of complete legislative freedom.

The negotiations came to a successful conclusion in the month of

---

[1] *Irish Times*, 26 May 1922.   [2] *Dáil Debates*, i, 383.   [3] Ibid., i, 578.

June, and Kevin O'Higgins described the agreed draft as 'a strict but fair interpretation of the Treaty'.[1] It must be remembered that, at the time of the conversations, the Civil War was raging, and Darrell Figgis recalled that Michael Collins had stated 'that if the first draft of the Constitution had been taken over two or three months before it was taken over, he believed that substantially it would have passed and would not have come back in the form in which it did come back: the change having been wrought because of the action of certain men in this country who had created disturbance from one end of the nation to the other, and who had spoken threateningly against the obligation that this nation had incurred, and whose action, therefore, had weakened the hand of our negotiators in London.'[2] Mr. Gavan Duffy (now the Hon. Mr. Justice Gavan Duffy, of the High Court), who had been a signatory of the Treaty, was dissatisfied with the form of the Draft Constitution, but he agreed that there was something to be said for this view: 'I sympathise with the Minister who said that, because it is true that Mr. De Valera and his friends have forgotten the day when they promised that there was a constitutional way of settling our differences, and they have forgotten the day when they promised us that if we were up against England they would be behind us as an auxiliary army. Yes, there is some truth in the fact that the deplorable performances of that party have made the Government position difficult.'[3] It is interesting to speculate what the form of the agreed Constitution of 1922 would have been if the country had not been split on the issue of the Treaty and if there had been no Civil War.

We now come to the negotiations with the Southern Unionists, but before dealing with them we must describe Arthur Griffith's general outlook on the minority problem. Griffith was a man of statesmanlike breadth of vision, who realized quite clearly that there was no future for a self-governing Ireland except through the full and willing co-operation of all classes and creeds within its shores. As Gambetta refused to inquire the date at which any Frenchman became a Republican, so Griffith intended that, once the struggle for autonomy had been won, the memory of old wrongs and recent differences should be gradually effaced in the joint effort to rebuild the nation. There was to be a place in the new Ireland for Irishmen whatever their origin—Gael, Norman, Jacobite, Cromwellian, Williamite—and work to do for all. This, of course, is the doctrine of Wolfe Tone and the United Irishmen, of O'Connell, of Thomas Davis and Young

---

[1] *Dáil Debates*, i, 358.   [2] Ibid., i, 498, 499.   [3] Ibid., i, 536.

Ireland, of Parnell and of Redmond: in short, of all the great leaders of the Irish people in modern times. Though Griffith did sterling work for the revival of the native language, the notion (which gathered force only after his death) that the unity of the country is to be achieved through the intensive Gaelicization of English-speaking Ireland, with the hegemony of the Gael as the ultimate ideal, would have seemed as fantastic to him as it would have been inconceivable to them.

The kernel of Griffith's problem in this matter was the position of the Southern Unionists, that is to say, of those who, in the past, had been in favour of the maintenance of the legislative union with Great Britain. Mostly Protestant by religion, they were but a tiny fraction of the total population, but the course of history had endowed them with wealth, influence, and prestige far disproportionate to their numbers. Their forebears were for the most part Englishmen and Scotsmen who had settled in Ireland after one or other of our old wars; but it would be a cardinal mistake to suppose that these people were a sort of *uitlander* in the country. Centuries of environment, accompanied in many cases by intermarriage, had evolved an Anglo-Irish type that was just as distinctly Irish as the Catholic Nationalist majority, but imbued with a loyalty to the Crown and the British connection which the majority, being a conquered people, could not feel. The atrocities perpetrated during the Black and Tan period had alienated the sympathies of many of the Southern Unionists; they recognized that the days of the British régime were numbered; and their responsible leaders were concerned to secure that, in whatever scheme of self-government might be decided upon, there should be adequate safeguards for the minority. At the time, it might have been thought that their nervousness was not justified, and was in fact an unwarranted reflection on their fellow countrymen; but the manner in which their persons and property were singled out for attack by Mr. De Valera's supporters during the Civil War of 1922–3 proved their fears not to have been groundless.

The negotiations actually began before the Treaty was signed, as is shown by the following document, which was quoted in full in the Senate (doubtless from the original in the Government archives) by Senator William Quirke (a member of the Fianna Fáil Party) on the 16th January 1936:[1]

---

[1] *Senate Debates*, xx, 1896.

AGREEMENTS WITH SOUTHERN UNIONISTS

'On the 16th November, 1921, Mr. Arthur Griffith met Lord Midleton, Dr. Bernard (Provost of Trinity College) and Mr. Andrew Jameson in London, and discussed with them the question of safeguards for the interests of the Unionist minority. He reported this meeting in a letter to the President [Mr. De Valera] of the same date. In this letter he made the following statement regarding the discussion on a Senate and the understandings reached:

'"They strongly argued there should be a Senate. I said I was in favour of a Second Chamber and I believed my colleagues would be. If it comes to a point, when we were erecting the machinery I would propose that they be consulted as to the constitution of the Senate. They said they were satisfied with this."

'Replying to a letter from Mr. Lloyd George on the 1st December, 1921, Mr. Arthur Griffith referred to his agreement with the Southern Unionists, "to provide safeguards for the representation of minorities and the general protection of their interests." He added: "Similar safeguards we shall expect in the case of the minority in the North-East area of Ireland."'

At the time that these discussions took place, Griffith was in London, engaged as chairman of the Irish Plenipotentiaries in the negotiations with the British Government which resulted in the Treaty. The three gentlemen on the other side were not in any sense, and would not have claimed to be, accredited representatives of the Southern Unionists; for the Southern Unionists were not organized in a political sense. Numerically, they were too small to return members to the House of Commons, but political representation was immaterial to their interests under the British régime, since they were of the 'ascendancy class', as it was called, and preferment of all kinds was open to them. It is for this reason that Kevin O'Higgins later referred to these negotiators as 'representative Southern Unionists . . . rather than representatives of the Southern Unionists.'[1] Their suitability as spokesmen for the minority could scarcely be questioned, however. All three had been members of the Irish Convention of 1917–18. The Most Rev. Dr. Bernard was Archbishop of Dublin from 1915 to 1919 and represented the Church of Ireland on the Convention; in the latter year he became Provost of Trinity College, an office which he held at the time the Treaty was signed. The other two negotiators had formed part of the Southern Unionist

[1] *Dáil Debates*, i, 1725.

delegation to the Convention. Mr. Andrew Jameson was a distinguished figure in the financial and business life of the City of Dublin; he was a member of the Irish Privy Council and a Director and former Governor of the Bank of Ireland. The Earl of Midleton, as Mr. St. John Brodrick, M.P., had been Secretary of State for War during the Boer War and shortly afterwards (1901–3); he was an extensive landowner, and might therefore be regarded as fairly representative of political Unionism and of the landlord class.

With regard to Griffith's letter to Mr. Lloyd George, two points are to be noted. The promise of safeguards for the Southern Unionists was not conditional on the provision of similar safeguards for the Northern Nationalists; and the request for the latter (which was not acceded to) was made to the British Prime Minister and not to the Southern Unionists, who have small contact or influence with the ruling class in Belfast and who have never been characterized by the same circumscribed rigidity of outlook.

The Treaty had been signed on the 6th December 1921, in the small hours of the morning. Mr. Andrew Jameson has informed me that in the forenoon of that day the Prime Minister (Mr. Lloyd George) sent for him, Dr. Bernard and Lord Midleton, told them the details of the Treaty, heard their views upon it, and stated that it was with the new rulers of the country, and not with the British Government, that any consultation must take place with regard to the future of the minority. The same afternoon, they had an interview with Arthur Griffith and it was on this occasion, apparently, that Griffith promised (a) the adoption of Proportional Representation in elections for the Dáil and (b) due representation for the Southern Unionists in the Senate. These undertakings were specified in a letter written by Griffith to Mr. Lloyd George.[1]

We are now in a position to consider the formal negotiations which, as has been said, began in London towards the end of May 1922. At that time, the Dominions Office had not been established, and the invitation to the conference was issued by the Secretary of State for the Colonies, Mr. Winston Churchill, who was a signatory of the Treaty.[2] The Provisional Government was represented by Arthur Griffith and Kevin O'Higgins, and the three Unionist negotiators were joined by the Earl of Donoughmore, who was Chairman of Committees and Deputy Speaker of the House of Lords.

Griffith's general attitude to the problem of the Unionist minority has already been described. He saw clearly that the Anglo-Irish

[1] *Dáil Debates*, i, 355, 1153.   [2] Ibid., i, 1153, 1455.

tradition is an essential element in the life of the nation, and he was prepared to welcome the co-operation of his erstwhile opponents in shaping the destiny of their common country. His death a few months later, at the height of the Civil War, was a tragedy for Ireland; but it was some consolation that there was between him and Kevin O'Higgins, who survived him, a complete identity of view on this question. Speaking in the Dáil on the minority problem shortly after Griffith's death, O'Higgins said:

'We now know no political party. We have taken quite definitely a step forward in our evolution towards completion of nationhood. These people are part and parcel of the nation, and we being the majority and strength of the country . . . it comes well from us to make a generous adjustment to show that these people were regarded, not as alien enemies, not as planters, but that we regard them as part and parcel of this nation, and that we wish them to take their share of its responsibilities.'[1]

No memoranda of the conference were published, but it is a matter of common knowledge that the discussions centred on the constitution and powers of the Second Chamber, this being the subject on which Griffith had promised to consult the Southern Unionists. The main points of contention are readily deducible from statements which were subsequently made by Kevin O'Higgins when the Constitution Bill was before the Dáil, and which are quoted below.

The Irish Convention had proposed a Senate of a nominated type, but by 1922 public opinion would no longer have tolerated a Second Chamber of that kind. Hence the Unionists now urged that the electorate for the Senate should be on a restricted franchise, based on a high rateable qualification. 'There was a certain pressure over what we all felt would be a very unpopular thing, a certain pressure over the property qualification, and in the negotiations which took place we were rather firm in our refusal to consider anything of the kind.'[2] It was agreed, however, that the Senate should not be elected like the Dáil, under universal adult suffrage, but by persons of thirty years and upwards.

The Unionists also considered it important that the number of Senators should be in a reasonably high proportion to the number of members of the other House, which at that time stood at 128. The original proposal of the Provisional Government was for a Senate of forty members,[3] but this figure was increased to sixty by agree-

---

[1] *Dáil Debates*, i, 482.   [2] Ibid., i, 483–4.
[3] Ibid., i, 1154.

ment. 'We wish it to be sixty, because some stress was laid on the total membership by the people whom we met in London.'[1]

The importance of the higher number, from the Unionists' point of view, is explained by the fact that it was coupled with a proposal that, in case of disagreement between the two Houses, the dispute should be resolved by a joint sitting, at which there would be joint voting. 'There was pressure for joint voting, but that particular request was not conceded.'[2] Nevertheless, the suggestion was a valuable one. This device for the removal of deadlock was incorporated in the Constitution of South Africa (Section 63 of the South Africa Act, 1909) and the experience of more than a quarter of a century has confirmed its value in that country.

The chief remaining point in dispute concerned the suspensory power to be accorded to the Upper House. The Unionists desired a power of delay of twelve months and the Provisional Government proposed one of six months. Finally, a period of 270 days, or roughly nine months, was agreed upon as a compromise. 'It was a deal between six months, which some thought to be too short, and twelve months, which some thought to be too long, and then there was the middle course.'[3]

Heads of Agreement were drawn up jointly by the Law Officer (the late Hugh Kennedy, K.C.) on behalf of the Provisional Government and by Sir Francis Greer, Parliamentary Counsel to the Irish Office, and Sir Frederick Liddell, First Parliamentary Counsel to the Treasury on behalf of the British Government and the Southern Unionists; and the two sides held their final meeting in the Colonial Office on the 14th June 1922, under the Chairmanship of Mr. Winston Churchill.[4] The representatives of the Provisional Government were Arthur Griffith and Kevin O'Higgins. In reply to a Parliamentary Question on the following 3rd October, O'Higgins said: 'The Agreement in question was made about the 10th June last [the actual date appears to have been the 14th], and the people who represented the Southern Unionists were as follows: Most Rev. Dr. Bernard (Provost of Trinity), Lord Donoughmore, Lord Midleton, Mr. Andrew Jameson.' Asked, further, whether the Agreement was written or verbal, he replied: 'In a sense, both; there were certain negotiations and certain arguments across the table, and, finally, the draft Agreement was written.'[5]

The matters agreed upon were later detailed in the following

[1] *Dáil Debates*, i, 1798. [2] Ibid., i, 484, 1163. [3] Ibid.
[4] *Irish Times*, 15 June 1922. [5] *Dáil Debates*, i, 1024.

memorandum, published by the Provisional Government and dated the 26th September 1922. The references to 'the Draft' are to the Draft Constitution, then before the Dáil. Speaking in the Dáil, Kevin O'Higgins made it clear that the text is not that of the actual Agreement, but merely some notes upon it.[1]

HEADS OF AGREEMENT

'1. The Senate to consist of 60 members, of whom two are to be elected by the National University of Ireland and two by the Dublin University. If the Six Counties remain in the Free State, there would also be two members added from the University of Belfast.

'2. The remaining 56 members of the Senate to be elected from a panel consisting of three times the number of members to be elected, of whom two-thirds are to be nominated by the Dáil and one-third by the Senate, in each case voting according to principles of Proportional Representation; and also of persons who have at any time been members of the Senate and indicate their desire to be included on the panel.

'3. The electorate for the Senate to be persons of 30 years and upwards.

'4. The period between the first presentation of a Bill to the Senate and the date upon which it shall be deemed to be passed, whether the Senate agree or not, to be 270 days, as provided by Article 37 of the Draft.

'5. Power to be given to three-fifths of the members of the Senate to require a referendum during the 90-day period mentioned in Article 46, without a petition being signed as there provided, that is to say, a three-fifths majority of the Senate in session and voting may call for a referendum, or, in the alternative, the petition there mentioned to remain.

'6. Provision to be made for joint debate of the two Houses in cases of disagreement, but not for joint voting (see end of Article 37). This provision not to be applied to a Money Bill.

'7. Decision on a referendum to be final, without further delay. Voting at the referendum to be by ballot.

'8. The question whether any particular Bill is or is not a Money Bill to be certified by the Speaker of the Dáil, subject to appeal to a Committee of Privileges, drawn equally from both Houses, presided over by a Judge of the Supreme Court, who shall have a casting vote but no other vote.

[1] *Dáil Debates*, i, 1156.

'9. The first Senate to be one half nominated and the other half elected by the Dáil: the whole to be divided into four classes, of whom one half of the nominated members retire from office at the end of twelve years, half of the elected members at the end of nine years, the remaining half of the nominated members at the end of six years, and the remaining half of the elected members at the end of three years. The nominated members to be nominated by the President in manner calculated to represent minorities or interests not represented adequately in the Dáil, and such nomination to be made on the advice of the following bodies:

  Chambers of Commerce

  College of Physicians and College of Surgeons

  Benchers of King's Inns and Incorporated Law Society

  The Corporations of Dublin and Cork

The stipulation as to consultation not to be embodied in the Constitution, but to be contained in an undertaking to be embodied in a resolution of the new Parliament. The text of the resolution to be submitted to the Provisional Government was agreed between President Griffith, the Southern Unionists and the British Government, and will be properly submitted when that portion of the Constitution is dealt with.

'10. A matter which gave rise to considerable difference of opinion, and was ultimately, after much debate, agreed to was that the constituency for the election of Senators should be the Irish Free State, taken as a whole.

'11. It was also agreed that the term of office of a Senator should be twelve years, and that no person should be eligible for election who had not reached the age of 35 years.

'12. The clauses in which these various headings of agreement are set out were first settled by the Law Officer on behalf of the Provisional Government and by Sir F. Greer and Sir F. Liddell on behalf of the British Government and the Southern Unionists, and the texts were submitted at a Conference and agreed to as they are now contained in the Draft Constitution.

'13. All these matters are the subject of deliberate agreement between the Irish Government representatives and the Southern Unionists and the British Government; and the Irish Government is accordingly bound 'to pass all these provisions as Government provisions.'

This Agreement was far indeed from satisfying the four Unionist negotiators, who had pressed unsuccessfully for the precedent in the abortive Government of Ireland Act, 1920, to be followed. In particular, they regarded the nine months' power of delay as hopelessly inadequate, and they felt that the system of popular election adopted for the Second Chamber afforded no real safeguard for the protection of minorities. On the 14th June 1922 they addressed the following communication to the Secretary of State for the Colonies:

'We, the undersigned, wish to place it on record that although, according to the pledge of His Majesty's Government and the Provisional Government, we have been given the opportunity of seeing and discussing those articles of the Irish Constitution which affect the composition and relations of the two Houses, the other articles of the Constitution have not been submitted to us. Our advice and suggestions have been limited to the composition of the Senate and its relation to the Lower House.

'We fully recognise the desire to meet our views, and the concessions which have been made during the prolonged discussions which have taken place on the scheme as originally submitted to us.

'Nevertheless, we regret that the precedent of the Senate now in existence for Southern Ireland under the Act of 1920 has not been followed, and we are not satisfied that any Senate constituted, as proposed, by popular election, and with powers so strictly limited, can afford a genuine protection to minorities in Ireland.

> (*signed*) Midleton.
> J. H. Bernard, Bp.
> Donoughmore.
> Andrew Jameson.'[1]

There is, however, another side to the question. It is inconceivable that, in the circumstances then existing, Griffith and O'Higgins could have advanced further than they did in the way of concessions to the minority's point of view without jeopardy to the whole Treaty position—the upsetting of which would have been at least as bad for the Southern Unionists as for anyone else. The Constitution had to be piloted through the Constituent Assembly, many members of which had accepted the Treaty with reluctance and some of whom were not slow to allege that the draft presented for their acceptance represented a whittling-down of the Treaty. Here again, the Civil War had its effect. 'Every time we crossed to England', said Kevin O'Higgins, 'to negotiate points consequential on the Treaty, things happened here that were meant to be mines under our feet. There

---

[1] *Irish Times*, 16 June 1922.

was never a time we sat down at the table with the British that wires did not come pouring in of soldiers shot in College Green, or raids across the Six-County border, or some such incidents that were not calculated to smooth our path and create a better atmosphere.'[1]

In the long run, no government can successfully move far in advance of public opinion; and it is as true to-day as it was eighteen years ago that Ireland differs from most of the countries that still enjoy free institutions in that no substantial body of public opinion holds the view that a strong Second Chamber is a vital necessity, not so much as a safeguard for minorities as for the protection of democracy itself.

Having thus obtained agreement with the British Government and the Southern Unionists, the Provisional Government lost no time in publishing the Draft Constitution. It was issued to the Press on the night of the 15th June 1922—the eve of the general election—and was printed in full in the Dublin newspapers of the following morning.

[1] *Dáil Debates*, i, 358, 359.

CHAPTER IV

THE ESTABLISHMENT OF THE SENATE

The Dáil as Constituent Assembly—Mr. Cosgrave's classification of the Articles of the Constitution—Amendments to the Senate provisions —Transfer of university representation from Senate to Dáil—Minor amendments—Composition of Senate in Constitution as finally enacted —Qualifications of Senators—Special provisions for first Senate— Terms of office of nominated and elected members—Casual vacancies— Triennial elections—Powers of the Senate—Money Bills—Suspensory power—Joint sitting—Referendum—Initiation of Bills—Senators excluded from Executive Council—Extern Ministers—Miscellaneous provisions—The thirty nominated members—Analysis and commentary —Lack of legal representation—The thirty elected members—Circumstances of the election—Commentary on personnel—Representative character of first Senate—Number of Catholics and non-Catholics.

The Dáil, sitting as a Constituent Assembly, met on the 9th September 1922. The date originally fixed was the 1st July, and there were several postponements by successive proclamations owing to the Civil War. The Bill to enact the Constitution was formally read a first time on the 18th September. In his introductory speech, the President of the Dáil (Mr. Cosgrave) adopted the classification which logically followed from the London negotiations, viz.:

(*a*) those Articles which were the subject of agreement with the British Government;

(*b*) those which implemented the Agreement with the Southern Unionists, the heads of which he read;

(*c*) the remaining Articles.

He stated that the Government stood absolutely upon class (*a*) as a matter of Treaty obligation; they stood upon class (*b*) as an obligation of honour; and in regard to class (*c*) the Dáil would have a free hand.[1] He added that, with the consent of the Cabinet, he had asked the Minister for Home Affairs to take charge of the Bill in its passage through the Dáil—a task which Kevin O'Higgins, then just turned thirty years of age, discharged with consummate ability.

The Second Reading of the Bill was carried on the 21st September 1922, after a two-day debate, by 47 votes to 16. The minority consisted of the members of the Labour Party, but their dissent did not extend to the Senate provisions. In fact, their action seems largely to have been conducted on the principle that it is the duty of an opposition to oppose.

Eight days were given to the Committee Stage of the Bill and two to the Report Stage; and the Bill was finally passed by the Constituent Assembly, without a division, on the 25th October 1922. Numerous amendments were inserted during the Bill's progress, but only a few of them affected the Senate. These touched the question of university representation, the period given to the Second Chamber to consider Money Bills, and the right of audience of Ministers. When these three points have been considered the Senate provisions of the Constitution as finally enacted can be summarized.

It will be recalled that the Agreement with the Southern Unionists provided for a Senate of sixty members, two of whom were to be selected by the National University of Ireland and two by Dublin University (Trinity College). During the Committee Stage of the Bill Deputy William Magennis, Professor of Metaphysics in the former university, and one of its four representatives in the Dáil, tabled a motion to the effect that the Dáil approved the principle of university representation in the Popular Chamber (4th October 1922). The weight of opinion was in favour of the proposal, which was accepted without a division, and the necessary changes were made in the Constitution. Each of the two universities was given three seats in the Dáil; and, as it was clearly not intended that there should be university representation in both Houses, the relative Senate provisions were deleted.

Under the old régime the Members of Parliament representing Dublin University at Westminster had almost invariably been Unionists. Hence the remarks of the spokesmen of the university in the Dáil on this subject of university representation are worthy of being quoted, as indicative of their unqualified acceptance of the new order. Deputy Gerald Fitzgibbon (afterwards the Hon. Mr. Justice Fitzgibbon, of the Supreme Court) said:

[1] *Dáil Debates*, i, 354–7.

'The people who purported to represent Southern Unionists when they were discussing certain matters with the Irish representatives in London—I do not consider them as representing me. I represent the constituency that sent me here, and I am satisfied and take on my own shoulders the responsibility of deleting University representation . . . in consideration of the great concession this House has made in placing University representatives in the Dáil, to assist in the legislation, instead of being put into a cooling chamber. So far as I and those who represent the University here are concerned, we will, as far as we can, absolve the Government of a charge of breach of faith with these people with whom they made arrangements.'[1]

Mr. O'Higgins, in fairness to the signatories of the London Agreement, here intervened to say that they had stated 'quite clearly that they had no definite mandate from any particular body, and were simply there as fairly representative of a class'; and then Deputy William Thrift (now Provost of Trinity College) followed his colleague on the same side:

'I should like to associate myself with what Deputy Fitzgibbon has said. I represent the University and it has no connection with Southern Unionists. On behalf of that University, I associate myself with him in saying that I am prepared to accept the withdrawal of this clause . . . in consideration of the concession made giving university representation in the Dáil.'[2]

The resultant change left a Senate of fifty-six members; but on the Report Stage of the Bill the total was restored to sixty, Mr. O'Higgins stating that the number agreed on with the Southern Unionists ought, in his opinion, to be adhered to.[3]

In the Bill as introduced, the Senate was given only fourteen days in which to consider Money Bills. On the Committee Stage, Deputy Darrell Figgis moved to substitute one calendar month, but withdrew his amendment, the Government undertaking to consider the matter. On the Report Stage, Mr. O'Higgins proposed a period of twenty-one days as a compromise, and this was adopted.

The only other amendment of substance, so far as the Second Chamber was concerned, was also effected on the Report Stage. A new Article (57) was inserted, conferring on Ministers the right of audience in the Senate.

We are now in a position to review the constitution and powers of the Upper House as embodied in the Bill as finally passed by the Constituent Assembly. The Senate was created as a constituent

[1] *Dáil Debates*, i, 1152.   [2] Ibid., i, 1153.   [3] Ibid., i, 1726.

House of the legislature (Article 12); and it was to 'be composed of citizens who shall be proposed on the grounds that they have done honour to the Nation by reason of useful public service or that, because of special qualifications or attainments, they represent important aspects of the Nation's life' (Article 30). It was recognized from the beginning that this Article represented no more than, in Mr. O'Higgins's words, 'a useful headline'. As a result of it, the Proposal Paper of every candidate for election to the Senate contained a column in which the nature of his useful public service or special qualifications had to be set out. Some of these statements make curious reading. They were limited by the Electoral Rules to forty words; and the more unsuitable the candidate, the greater the likelihood that he would approach the limit, or even seek to exceed it. Few would-be candidates can have been refused nomination on the ground that they did not come within the scope of the Article.

The test of eligibility for membership of the Senate was the same as that for membership of the Dáil, that is to say, it was subject to the usual statutory disqualifications; the minimum age was thirty-five years; and the normal term of office was twelve years (Article 31).

Special provision for the constitution of the first Senate was made by Article 82. Thirty members (that is, one-half of the House) were to be nominated by the President of the Executive Council, with special regard to the providing of representation for groups or parties not then adequately represented in the Dáil. Of these, fifteen, to be selected by lot, were to hold office for the full term of twelve years, and the remaining fifteen for six years.

The other thirty members were to be elected by the Dáil, voting on principles of proportional representation. The first fifteen elected were to hold office for nine years, and the second fifteen for three years.

Casual vacancies (caused by death, resignation, or disqualification, were to be filled by a vote of the Senate itself, and the member so co-opted was to retire at the end of the current Triennial Period (Article 34).

Apart from casual vacancies, one-fourth of the Senate would thus be renewable every three years. For the purpose of the Senate Triennial Elections the whole country was to form a single electoral area, and the elections were to be held on principles of proportional representation (Article 32). The electorate was to consist of all citizens over thirty years of age who complied with the provisions of the prevailing electoral laws. There was no property qualification of any sort (Article 14).

Each Triennial Election was to be from a panel composed of three times as many qualified persons as there were members to be elected, of whom two-thirds were to be nominated by the Dáil and one-third by the Senate: plus such former Senators as desired to be included in the panel. The method of proposal and selection for nomination to the Dáil and Senate portions of the panel was to be decided by the respective Houses, 'with special reference to the necessity for arranging for the representation of important interests and institutions in the country', and each House was to vote according to principles of proportional representation (Article 33).

It will be appreciated that the system was an extremely cumbrous one, and so it proved in actual practice, as we shall see when we come to consider the first Triennial Election, held in 1925. As a result of that unfortunate experience, the method of election was changed.

The powers of the new Senate were severely restricted as compared with those of Second Chambers elsewhere. The Dáil was given exclusive legislative authority over Money Bills as defined in Article 35; but every Money Bill was to be sent to the Senate for its recommendations. The Senate was obliged to return the Bill to the Dáil within twenty-one days, and the Dáil might accept or reject all or any of the Senate's recommendations (Article 38). The subject of Money Bills is discussed at length in Chapter XXXII.

With regard to Bills, other than Money Bills, received from the Dáil, the Senate was given a power of suspension of 270 days. The Senate had a full power of amendment over such Bills, but if it exercised this power in a manner not acceptable to the Dáil, or if it rejected or failed to pass any such Bill, the Bill, after the expiration of nine months from the time it left the Dáil, was to be deemed to have been passed by both Houses in the form in which it had been passed by the Dáil (Article 38). No resolution or other action of the Dáil was necessary before the Bill could be sent to the Governor-General for his signification of the King's Assent. This nine months' period was a compromise between the six months desired by the Provisional Government and the minimum of one year urged by the Southern Unionists.

There was a provision that a Joint Sitting of both Houses might be convened at the request of the Senate, for the purpose of debating, but not of voting upon, the proposals of any non-Money Bill received from the Dáil, or any amendment thereof (Article 38). In the absence of the power of joint voting (which had been pressed for by the Southern Unionists but not conceded), this was an entirely useless provision for the removal of deadlock. No attempt was ever made to operate it, and it was deleted from the Constitution in 1928.

A much greater power than the power of suspension was the right given to the Senate by Article 47 to force a referendum. A Bill passed, or deemed to have been passed, by both Houses might be suspended for ninety days on the written demand of two-fifths of the members of the Dáil or of a majority of the members of the Senate, presented to the President of the Executive Council within seven days after the Bill had been passed or deemed to have been passed. The Bill had to be submitted to a referendum if such was demanded within the period of ninety days (a) by a resolution of the Senate assented to by three-fifths of its members, or (b) by a petition signed by not less than one-twentieth of the voters on the register. Apart from the right to demand a referendum, it will be seen that Article 47 operated indirectly to increase the Senate's power of suspension from nine months to twelve. For, when a Bill had been suspended for 270 days, it could be suspended for a further period of ninety days on the written demand of a majority of the members of the Senate. Even if the further steps necessary for a referendum were not proceeded with, the Bill could not become law until the ninety-day period within which such steps could be taken had expired. These referendum provisions did not apply to Money Bills, or to Bills declared by both Houses to be necessary for the immediate preservation of the public peace, health, or safety.

Article 47 was undoubtedly a valuable safeguard; but, until its deletion from the Constitution in 1928 (in circumstances which will be recounted in their place) no occasion arose for the exercise by the Senate of the right to demand a referendum, and it never was in fact exercised.

The Senate had the right to initiate Bills (Article 39) and the manner in and extent to which this power was exercised are discussed in Chapter XXX.

Senators were excluded from membership of the Executive Council (i.e. the Cabinet). The Executive Council was to consist of not more than seven nor less than five Ministers (Article 51), all of whom had to be members of the Dáil (Article 52). Under Article 55, Ministers who were not members of the Executive Council might be appointed by the Representative of the Crown on the nomination of the Dáil, the total number of Ministers (including members of the Executive Council) not to exceed twelve. Such 'Extern' Ministers, as they came to be called, were to be responsible solely to the Dáil for the administration of the Departments of which they were the head (Article 56).

In the absence of any restriction in the Constitution, the Extern Ministers could have been members of either House, or of neither; but in the short period during which this constitutional novelty was tried no member of the Senate was appointed. All Ministers were, however, given a right of audience in the Senate (Article 57).

Three Extern Ministers were appointed during Mr. Cosgrave's first Administration (December 1922), and all three—Messrs. Patrick Hogan, J. J. Walsh, and Finian Lynch—were members of the Dáil, holding respectively the portfolios of Agriculture, Posts and Telegraphs, and Fisheries. The experiment was not a success. Mr. Hogan, who was a man of outstanding ability, was in charge of one of the most important Departments of State, and it was politically and administratively inconvenient that he should be outside the Cabinet. Mr. Walsh freely availed himself of his undoubted constitutional right to criticize the Executive Council on major matters of policy, and this did not make for cohesion. For these and other reasons the experiment was discontinued. Though the Articles relating to Extern Ministers remained in the Constitution, no such Ministers were appointed after the dissolution of May 1927, and thenceforward the Executive Council assumed full collective responsibility for all the Departments of State.

The remaining Articles of the Constitution affecting the Senate can be shortly summarized. There were the usual provisions regarding parliamentary privilege (Articles 18 and 19) and against dual membership (Article 16). The Chairman of the House was given a casting vote, but not an originating vote (Article 22). The payment of members was mandatory and the provision of free travelling facilities optional (Article 23). Finally, there was to be one parliamentary session in each year and the sessions of the Senate were not to be concluded without its consent (Article 24).

It will be recalled that thirty members of the first Senate were to be nominated by the President of the Executive Council and that the remaining thirty were to be elected by the Dáil; also, that it had been agreed with the Southern Unionists that the President's nominations were to be made 'in manner calculated to represent minorities or interests not represented adequately in the Dáil' and on the advice of certain named bodies: 'the stipulation as to consultation not to be embodied in the Constitution, but to be contained in an undertaking to be embodied in a resolution of the new Parliament'.

Pursuant to this agreement, the following resolution was passed by the Dáil on the 25th October 1922, on the motion of Mr. Cosgrave: 'That it is expedient that the President of the Executive Council, in nominating the nominated members of the Senate, should, with a view to the providing of representation for groups of all parties [sic] not adequately represented in the Chamber, consult with representative persons and bodies, including the following:

'Chamber of Commerce, the Royal College of Physicians of Ireland, the Royal College of Surgeons in Ireland, the Benchers of the Honourable Society of King's Inns, Dublin, the Incorporated Law Society of Ireland, Councils of the County Boroughs of the Irish Free State.'

The new Constitution came into force on the 6th December 1922. At the meeting of the Dáil held on that day Mr. Cosgrave was elected President of the Executive Council without opposition. On the same day he announced to the House his nominations for the Senate in alphabetical order, as follows:

John Bagwell	Benjamin Haughton
Rt. Hon. H. G. Burgess	The Marquess of Headfort
The Countess Dowager of Desart	Arthur Jackson
J. C. Dowdall	Rt. Hon. Andrew Jameson
The Earl of Dunraven	Sir John Keane, Bart.
Sir Thomas H. Grattan Esmonde, Bart.	The Earl of Kerry
	General Sir Bryan Mahon
Sir Nugent Talbot Everard, Bart.	The Earl of Mayo
Edmund W. Eyre	James Moran
Martin Fitzgerald	Sir Horace Plunkett
Rt. Hon. Baron Glenavy	Sir William Hutcheson Poë,
Dr. Oliver St. John Gogarty	Bart.
James Perry Goodbody	Mrs. J. Wyse Power
The Earl of Granard	Dr. George Sigerson
Captain J. H. Greer	The Earl of Wicklow
Henry S. Guinness	W. B. Yeats

Anyone with a knowledge of Ireland must agree that this was a remarkable list. Sixteen of the thirty might be described as belonging to the class formerly known as Southern Unionists, and among these sixteen were men who had given distinguished service to their country in various ways. Lord Dunraven, Lord Mayo, and Sir Hutcheson

Poë had been members of the Irish Landlords' Convention of 1903, which had paved the way for the beneficent Wyndham Act, 1903, in relation to land purchase. Mr. Jameson was a leader of the Southern Unionists, and he and Mr. Guinness were directors of the Bank of Ireland. Sir Nugent Everard was closely associated with projects for industrial development and a pioneer of tobacco-growing in Ireland. Sir Horace Plunkett had been chairman of the Irish Convention, and his name was a household word in connection with the co-operative movement in agriculture. Lady Desart had founded the Kilkenny Woollen Mills, and was noted for her social and philanthropic activities in that county. Captain Greer was the director of the National Stud at the Curragh and a recognized authority on blood stock. Practically all of the sixteen had some special quality which they could bring to the deliberations of the new Second Chamber.

Among the remaining fourteen commerce and administration were well represented, as well as regional interests. Mr. Burgess had been Director-General of Transport in Ireland during the Great War, and at the time of his nomination to the Senate he was the general manager of the London, Midland and Scottish Railway. Messrs. Dowdall and Haughton were well-known figures in commercial circles in the south of Ireland, where they were directors of numerous companies. The old nationalism, which had no spokesman in the Dáil, was to be represented in the Senate by men like Sir Thomas Esmonde, who had been a Member of Parliament continuously from 1885 to 1919, and Mr. Martin Fitzgerald, the proprietor of the *Freeman's Journal*. The Earl of Granard, unlike his fellow peers in the new House, had never been a Unionist. He was the King's Master of the Horse and a life-long supporter of the Home Rule movement, holding the post of Assistant Postmaster-General in Sir Henry Campbell Bannerman's Liberal Administration of 1906. Sir Bryan Mahon was a distinguished Irish soldier whose tenure of office as Commander-in-Chief of the British Forces in Ireland from 1916 to 1918 had been marked by an insight and a sympathy with Irish life not commonly associated with the holder of that post. Mr. W. B. Yeats's nomination was a deserved recognition of the honour he had brought to his native land as the greatest living poet in the English-speaking world.

Though this list is of a quality that silences criticism, it seems worth noting that it did not contain the name of a single solicitor or practising barrister. The omission is curious in view of the fact that the Benchers of the King's Inns and the Incorporated Law Society were mentioned in the formal resolution of the Dáil among the bodies which it was expedient for the President to consult when making his nominations. Lord Glenavy, as a former Lord Chief Justice and Lord Chancellor, was an automatic choice, and did not owe his nomination to the Benchers. The legal element proved to be entirely absent from the elected half of the new House; and for the first year of its existence, until the co-option of the late Mr. S. L. Brown, K.C., the acknowledged leader of the Bar, the Senate was to some extent handicapped by the lack of legal knowledge among its members.

For the thirty members to be elected by the Dáil, the system of proportional representation adopted was that of the single transferable vote, with certain modifications rendered necessary by reason of the electorate being so small and the number to be elected correspondingly large. The Rules were approved by the Dáil on the 1st November 1922, and nominations opened on that day and closed at 12 noon on the 7th December following. Voting papers were distributed at 3 p.m. on the 7th December and the poll closed two hours later.[1]

The election contained many elements of farce, and the blame for this is attributable not to the system but to the circumstances of the time. In the first place, of a total Dáil membership of 128, only eighty-six had taken their seats; most of the rest were anti-Treaty followers of Mr. De Valera, but some had been killed on both sides in the Civil War. Of the eighty-six who attended the Dáil, five, for one reason or another, did not vote in the election. Thus the effective electorate was reduced to eighty-one. Next, it must be remembered that, with the exception of the Labour Party, there were no political parties in any strict sense in the Dáil. The main body consisted of upwards of fifty Griffith-Collins supporters who gave general support to Mr. Cosgrave now that the other two leaders were dead; but no Ministerial party had as yet been evolved from them. There were seventeen members of the Labour Party and the balance was made up of farmers, Independents, and the four representatives of Dublin University. Normally, a political party will not put forward at an election many candidates in excess of the numbers it can hope to return; but this rather amorphous condition of the Dáil resulted in a plethora of candidates. Further, the right of an individual mem-

[1] The Rules, Result Sheet, and Report on the conduct of the election were published as a White Paper in February 1923 (P. Pro. 3/1923).

ber of the Dáil to propose candidates was not limited by the rules, and this fact led to a curious situation. Mr. Cosgrave, in consulting county councils, chambers of commerce, and other representative bodies with regard to the nominated half of the Senate, had received names far in excess of the number for whom he could provide in that half. So he took the course of proposing these for the elected half, thus giving the Dáil the opportunity of choosing them if it so wished; and he explained the situation to the members immediately after the conclusion of the sitting on the 4th December, in a short statement which was not published in the Official Report.[1]

The interaction of these factors made the election one of the most remarkable that can ever have been held under proportional representation. The electors numbered only eighty-one, and there were 113 candidates for the thirty seats. The first preferences were distributed as follows:

Candidates with 4 first preferences	1
Candidates with 3 first preferences	17
Candidates with 2 first preferences	11
Candidates with 1 first preference	4

Thus thirty-three candidates exhausted the eighty-one first preferences between them, and the remaining eighty candidates received no first preferences at all. Of these eighty candidates, no less than seventy-two got no votes whatever in any of the thirty-five counts which were necessary before the final result was ascertained. As the quota was 2·6, any candidate with three or more first preferences was certain of election; actually, any candidate who obtained two first preferences was elected, and the last five successful candidates were elected although they failed to reach the quota.

Among the defeated candidates were a number of men who would have made admirable Senators, such as Mr. James McNeill, who afterwards succeeded Mr. T. M. Healy as Governor-General; Major Bryan Cooper, who later, as a member of the Dáil, did more than any other man to reconcile the old order and the new; Lord Monteagle, who had spent a lifetime in the service of his country; and Dr. Lombard Murphy, who occupied, as he does to-day, an outstanding position in the commercial life of the city of Dublin.

The result of the election was announced in the Dáil on the 8th December 1922, as follows:

[1] *Irish Independent*, 5 December 1922.

1. Mrs. Alice Stopford Green	16. Thomas Linehan
2. Sir John Purser Griffith	17. John T. O'Farrell
3. James G. Douglas	18. Richard A. Butler
4. Brian O'Rourke	19. Thomas W. Westropp Bennett
5. Colonel Maurice Moore	20. Dr. Henry L. Barniville
6. William J. Molloy	21. Peter De Loughry
7. James MacKean	22. Cornelius J. Irwin
8. Mrs. E. Costello	23. Edward Mansfield
9. Dr. William O'Sullivan	24. Edward MacLysaght
10. John MacLoughlin	25. Edward MacEvoy
11. Patrick W. Kenny	26. George Nesbitt
12. William Barrington	27. Joseph C. Love
13. Michael Duffy	28. James J. Parkinson
14. Thomas MacPartlin	29. John J. Counihan
15. Thomas Farren	30. Michael O'Dea

The first fifteen were to sit for nine years and the second fifteen for three years.

In view of all the circumstances, the result was better than might have been expected. Spectacular results were not to be looked for, but the list contained such names as Alice Stopford Green, who was Ireland's most distinguished historian; Sir John Purser Griffith, Ireland's most celebrated engineer, as well as the Maecenas of the arts in Dublin; and Colonel Maurice Moore, a distinguished soldier in whose family a patriotic activity in Irish politics had been something of a tradition. None of the thirty had previous legislative experience, but Mr. Douglas had been a prominent member of the committee which drafted the Constitution, and had given much thought to constitutional problems. Commercial interests were represented by such men as Mr. Moran, a past chairman of the Dublin Port and Docks Board, and Mr. O'Dea, the head of a large business in Dublin. There were two members of the medical profession, and the horse-breeding industry had its spokesman in Mr. Parkinson, the noted owner and trainer. But the list is chiefly noteworthy for the fact that two classes were represented in it which are essential to the composition of a balanced Second Chamber but which found no place in the nominated list. These are the farmers (as distinct from the large landowners) and organized labour. The farmers had some eight or nine elected members, including Mr. Butler, the chairman of the Irish Farmers' Union, and Mr. Counihan, a member of the Executive of the Irish Cattle Traders' Association. The Labour Party had five members, one of whom resigned without taking his seat; the remaining four, Messrs. Duffy, Farren, MacPartlin, and O'Farrell, were all first-class men, whose activities in the Senate greatly enhanced its prestige.

Taking the Senate as a whole, and apart from the absence of adequate legal representation, we see it as a body admirably qualified for the task of expert revision which was to be its main function under the Constitution. It was much more truly a microcosm of the country as a whole than was the Dáil, comprising as it did representatives of the professions, commerce, agriculture, letters, organized labour, banking, and the landlord interest. The danger of over-centralization was avoided, for of the total of sixty members only twenty-four lived in or near the capital. The remaining thirty-six lived or had residences elsewhere in the country, though some few, such as Lord Kerry and Lord Dunraven, resided for the most part in England. Of the twenty-six counties forming the Irish Free State only five (Carlow, Cavan, Leitrim, Mayo, and Westmeath) had no representative in the first Senate. By provinces, Leinster (exclusive of the City of Dublin) had eighteen Senators, Munster had thirteen, Connacht three, and Ulster two.

Throughout the thirteen years' history of the Senate, allegations were dishonestly made by some, and ignorantly repeated by others, to the effect that it was predominantly a Protestant and Freemason body. It is distasteful to take cognizance of such matters, but in view of the widespread character of these allegations it is desirable that the facts should be put on record. The first Senate consisted of thirty-six Catholics and twenty-four non-Catholics. Not all of the non-Catholics were Protestants; Lady Desart, for example, was a Jewess, and no less than three Senators were members of the Religious Society of Friends. The proportion of non-Catholics to Catholics decreased as time went on, so that the largest number of non-Catholics ever present in the Senate was twenty-four out of a total of sixty.

PART II

THE FIRST TRIENNIAL PERIOD
6th DECEMBER 1922 TO 5th DECEMBER 1925

H

'*Choosing each stone and poising every weight,*
Trying the measures of the breadth and height;
Here pulling down, and there erecting new,
Founding a firm State by proportions true.'
                    ANDREW MARVELL, *The First Anniversary.*

'*The main need for which a Senate is constructed is that all legis-*
lative measures may receive a second consideration by a body different
in quality from the primary representative assembly and, if possible,
superior or supplementary in intellectual qualifications.'
                    HENRY SIDGWICK, *The Elements of Politics*
                    (1891), p. 445.

CHAPTER V

THE END OF THE CIVIL WAR

Tactics of the Irregulars—Mr. De Valera's association with them—Outrages against members of the Dáil—Execution of imprisoned Irregular leaders—Mr. De Valera's Christmas Message—Campaign of intimidation, kidnapping, and arson against Senators—Sabotage and murder—Condemnation by Cardinal Logue and the Hierarchy—The beginning of the end—The Leader of the Parliamentary Opposition denounces the attack upon society—The 'Cease Fire' order—Senators Jameson and Douglas as intermediaries—The Government's peace conditions—Rejection of Mr. De Valera's alternative proposals—The end of the Civil War.

Months before the first meeting of the Senate, the Irregular rebel forces had lost all hope of overthrowing, by victory in the field, the Government established by the will of the people. Their tactics were then directed to the following ends: (1) by intimidation, arson, and assassination, to prevent the legislature and the Judiciary from functioning; (2) by arson and plunder on a colossal scale, to drive the land-owning class, principally Protestant, out of the country; (3) by fire, mine, and bomb, wrecking of railway trains and stations, destruction of the lighting and water supply of towns and other means, to reduce the economic life of the country to ruin, and so to render government impossible. They would make a desert and call it a republic.

On the 13th November 1922 'President' De Valera addressed a letter[1] to each member of the 'Army Council', in which he gave the names of the men whom he had nominated to form his 'Cabinet' and requested formal approval for these nominations. In this letter

[1] This and other documents quoted or referred to in this paragraph were cited by General Mulcahy in the debate on the Army Pensions Bill, 1932 (*Dáil Debates*, xliv, 222–43).

he stated that 'in regard to Defence, the Chief of Staff agrees that for the present the best plan would be that his name and mine should appear on any official document relating to the Department of Defence'. On the 30th November following, the 'Chief of Staff' (Liam Lynch), with whom 'President' De Valera was thus associated, sent to 'O.C.s all Battalions' instructions for operations against the 'enemy'. There were no less than fourteen categories of persons who were directed to be 'shot at sight', including all members of the Provisional Parliament who had voted in favour of the Army Emergency Powers Resolution (27th–28th September 1922), which had set up Military Courts empowered to inflict the death penalty; 'members of Senate in List A'; High Court judges; 'proprietors, directors, editors, sub-editors and leader-writers of hostile press in Ireland'; and even 'aggressive Free State supporters'. The residences 'and, where mentioned, the offices' of all persons in these categories were to be destroyed, as well as the residences of all Senators; and included in the proposed holocaust were the residences of 'Imperialists (ex-D.L. type)'. These Deputy Lieutenants of counties were mostly Protestants.

It is proposed here to recount the result of these instructions in the case of members of the Senate; but it is important to remember that Senators were by no means the only, or even the worst, sufferers. A complete list of outrages committed by the Irregulars against persons and property, with brief details of each, would fill a volume the size of this book. So far as members of the Dáil were concerned, a very few examples must suffice. On the 7th December 1922, just after leaving their hotel to attend a meeting of the House, Deputy Seán Hales was shot dead on the Dublin Quays and his companion Pádraic O Máille, the Deputy-Chairman of the Dáil, was gravely wounded, the assassins making good their escape. On the 28th December a land-mine was exploded in Deputy McCullough's music warehouse in one of the principal thoroughfares in Dublin, blowing out the whole front of the premises on to the street. On the 10th December Deputy McGarry's house in Dublin was destroyed by fire and his little son, aged seven, died of his burns within a week, the jury at the inquest returning a verdict of 'wilful murder'. On the 13th January Mr. Cosgrave's house was reduced to ashes. On the 11th February Dr. T. F. O'Higgins, the father of Kevin O'Higgins, was murdered in his house at Stradbally, Queen's County, his body being riddled with bullets in the presence of his wife and seventeen years old daughter.

As a reprisal for the assassination of Deputy Hales and the attempted assassination of the Deputy-Chairman of the Dáil, four of the Irregular leaders (Rory O'Connor, Liam Mellowes, Joseph McKelvey, and Richard Barrett), who were at that time imprisoned in Mountjoy Gaol, were executed on the following morning by order of the Executive Council. This stern action was, of course, entirely illegal, and caused much misgiving in the minds of many, both in the Dáil and outside it, whose support for the Government in all legitimate measures against the Irregulars, however drastic, was not in doubt. 'While the existence of this nation is at stake', said Mr. O'Higgins, 'there can be but one code—though it sounds a grim code—whereby to judge the actions of those who have been made responsible for the restoration of order here, and that is the code, *Salus populi suprema lex*.' But the doubts of others were well expressed by Deputy Fitzgibbon:

'Let them [the Executive Council] come here and get authority for any form of drastic action that they please against the people who have been concerned in the rebellion against organized Government here. I confess that it seems to me that the men who suffered this morning were treated with extraordinary leniency in being allowed to live so long. I do not seek . . . to voice any passion or sympathy with them at all. They, so far as one could form an opinion from what one has read and heard, particularly deserved their fate as much as any men who have been executed in this country during the last fortnight or so, but they deserved their fate for something they did not do yesterday, but something they did weeks—or it may be months—ago. . . . I do appeal to them not to continue the policy that appears to have been commenced to-day.'[1]

However this action of the Executive may be regarded from the ethical standpoint, it proved to be an effective deterrent, for no other member of the legislature was assassinated during the progress of the Irregular campaign.

The list of outrages against the persons and property of members of the Senate, which will be given in chronological order, may be suitably prefaced by a 'Christmas Message' issued over the name of 'President' De Valera, less than three months after the issue of the Joint Pastoral by the Hierarchy.[2]

[1] *Dáil Debates*, ii, 66.
[2] Published in a sheet entitled *Poblacht na h-Éireann: War News No. 122*, dated 28 December 1922.

Government of the Republic.

Greetings to every Soldier and Citizen of the Republic. As we consecrate ourselves anew to the achievement of the Independence of our country, and pray for our comrades who have fallen in the fight, let us humbly beg Almighty God so to enlighten and direct us that we may do His Will and obtain His Blessing in all our efforts to bring to our harrassed [*sic*] people the liberty, the peace and the happiness which they need and desire.

On behalf of the Government and Army Command.

(*signed*) ÉAMON DE VALERA.

Christmas, 1922.

The Constitution came into force on the 6th December 1922, and from that date until the 'Cease Fire Order' issued by 'President' De Valera on the 27th April 1923 the following is the tale of outrage against Senators. Most of the occurrences were literally, as well as figuratively, deeds of darkness, and mere shootings at residences are omitted, as being too numerous to be recorded.

6th December 1922. Senator Martin Fitzgerald, the proprietor of the *Freeman's Journal*, received the following communication from 'the Acting O.C., Dublin Brigade':

'In spite of repeated warnings, you have refused to obey Orders issued to you on several occasions by Command H.Q. and G.H.Q., I.R.A. You were clearly told either to (*a*) hand your paper over to Free State Provisional Government to be run by them as a Free State organ or (*b*) to be a free Press. You have refused to do either and have instead persisted in your campaign of misrepresentation against the I.R.A.

'You are therefore ordered to leave Ireland before 12 o'clock noon on the 8th December, 1922. The penalty for refusal to obey this order, or for being found in Ireland after 12 o'clock noon on the 8th December, is death.'

Beyond publishing this communication in facsimile in his newspaper on the 9th December (in the place of the usual leading article), Senator Fitzgerald ignored this threat to murder him. He attended the first meeting of the Senate two days later, and died in his bed some years afterwards.

10th December. Three bombs were hurled through the plate-glass window of Senator Mrs. Wyse Power's business premises in Camden Street, Dublin. Fortunately, two of them failed to explode, but, even so, considerable damage was done. Mrs. Wyse Power had been an executive member of the Ladies' Land League in Mr. Parnell's time, a member of the Gaelic League since its inception, and one of the founders of Sinn Féin.

26th December. Senator Sir William Hutcheson Poë, who was then seventy-four years of age, was held up at midnight by the Irregulars while driving in his motor-car some distance from his home in the Queen's County. He was ordered to stand by the hedge, and, thinking he was about to be murdered, he asked for time to write to his wife. He was not shot, however, but his watch and money were stolen and his car was sprinkled with petrol and burned before his eyes. He was then ordered to walk home, but he replied that this was impossible, owing to his age and his physical disability (he had lost a leg in the Sudan so long ago as 1884). Ultimately, he had to wait in the chill December air until his chauffeur could procure a second car to take him home. The Irregulars succeeded in driving this aged and soldierly figure from the country in which he had his roots and which he loved; for shortly afterwards he took up his residence in England, although he continued to attend meetings of the Senate until his resignation in 1924.

9th January 1923. Half an hour after midnight a band of armed incendiaries arrived outside Marlfield, Clonmel, County Tipperary, the ancestral home of Senator John Bagwell. They roused Senator Bagwell and his family, and stated that 'they had orders to burn the house, as Mr. Bagwell was a member of the Free State Senate'. The place contained valuable collections of china and works of art, and also one of the finest private libraries in the country, amassed by the Senator's father, Richard Bagwell, the historian. Within a short time the petrol had done its work, and the premises were gutted.

12th January. At about 8 p.m. a motor-car, containing three men and one woman, drove up to the Dublin residence of Senator Oliver Gogarty, a well-known surgeon and man of letters who had been Arthur Griffith's medical adviser. The occupants requested Dr. Gogarty to accompany them to an urgent case. In view of the suspicious circumstances, he demurred, whereupon the men, dropping all pretence, forced him into the car at the point of the revolver and drove him, blindfolded, to a house on the outskirts of Dublin, on the banks of the river Liffey. While there, he managed to escape and ran for his life to the river. Though a fusillade of shots was fired after him, he was not hit. He jumped into the river, which was in flood, and after swimming in the icy waters for a quarter of an hour he

pulled himself up on the opposite bank and escaped. He was suc-
coured at a near-by house and obtained a change of clothing at a Civic
Guard Barracks, after which he was able to return home. Thereafter,
his house was given an armed guard by the Government.

29th January. Palmerstown, the home of Senator the Earl of
Mayo, and one of the most beautiful mansions in the County Kildare,
was entered by armed men after dark. The Earl and his Countess
were given a short time in which to leave, and then the rooms, except
the servants' wing, were sprinkled with petrol and set alight. In a
short time nothing remained but the gaping, blackened walls. Of the
numerous old masters, only three—all by Sir Joshua Reynolds—
were carried out in time to save them from the flames. When asked
if he would make a new home in England or elsewhere, Lord Mayo,
who was seventy-one years old, replied, 'No! I will not be driven
from my own country.' He added that he would not even leave his
ruined home and demesne, but would live in the servants' quarters.

29th January. At 1 a.m. armed Irregulars broke into Kilteragh, Foxrock, County Dublin, the home of Senator Sir Horace Plunkett. Sir
Horace was absent in the United States, but his secretary and chauffeur, who were sleeping on the premises, were told peremptorily to
clear out. A powerful land-mine was placed in the fire grate of the
main hall, and the resultant explosion wrecked practically the whole
building. There was a slight outbreak of fire, but it was extinguished.
Sir Horace's comment was 'It is not so sad as if it had been a poor
man's one-roomed house.'

The Government placed a guard upon the premises, but at 2.15
a.m. on the following morning (30th January), supposing the danger
hour to be past, the men returned to their barracks. The raiders, who
had been watching for their opportunity, immediately swooped down
with tins of petrol and completed the work of destruction. Half an
hour later the place was a blazing furnace. Sir Horace's secretary,
who was sleeping in the only habitable room, was roused by the
chauffeur and brought by means of a life-line to the ground, and so
escaped being burnt to death. The hose which had been used to ex-
tinguish the small outbreak on the previous night had been rendered
useless by the incendiaries. The mansion and its whole contents, including many thousands of pounds' worth of pictures, were destroyed.

29th January. While walking with his wife, after dark, near his
home at Howth, County Dublin, Senator John Bagwell (whose place
near Clonmel had been destroyed three weeks earlier) was stopped by
armed men, forced into a waiting motor-car at the point of the re-

volver, and driven away. Stern action was taken by the military as soon as the kidnapping became known. A proclamation was posted all over Dublin, bearing the date and time '31st January, 1923. 9 a.m.' and signed by Major-General Hogan, G.O.C., Dublin Command. It recited the circumstances, and concluded: 'Warning is hereby given that, in the event of the said Senator John Bagwell not being set, unharmed, at liberty, and permitted to return to his own home, within 48 hours of the date and hour of this Proclamation, punitive action will be taken against several associates in this conspiracy, now in custody or otherwise.'

After a two hours' drive, Senator Bagwell was brought to a farmhouse in north County Dublin, where he was kept under guard. He was moved the next night to another commandeered house in the vicinity; and from this he escaped at 11 a.m. on the following day (1st February), by climbing through a window while his captors were at breakfast. He ran for a considerable distance, and eventually obtained a lift from a passing motorist, who drove him back to the city. But for the proclamation, and its warning of further reprisals, it is possible that he might not have escaped so easily.

1st February. Moore Hall, the beautiful ancestral home of Senator Colonel Maurice Moore, overlooking Lough Carra, County Mayo, was totally destroyed. Moore Hall, which was the property of the Colonel's elder brother, the late George Moore, the novelist, was an historic landmark, for it was from there that the colonel's grandfather John Moore marched with his men to join General Humbert after the French landing at Killala in September 1798; and it was in Moore Hall that the Independence of Connacht was signed. Many irreplaceable treasures of historic interest to Ireland were destroyed in this fire.

1st February. At 10 p.m. the residence of Senator Thomas Linehan at Whitechurch, County Cork, was visited by incendiaries. The whole place was sprinkled with petrol, which was set alight, and the house and its contents were destroyed.

3rd February. About 7 p.m. a party of ten or twelve young men casually entered a restaurant owned by Senator Mrs. Wyse Power in Henry Street, Dublin, sat at separate tables and ordered tea, there being nothing in their manner to excite suspicion. When tea was about to be served, however, they produced bottles of petrol, which they sprinkled on the table-cloths and carpets. But the hysterical screams of the women in the restaurant so alarmed the miscreants that they were unable to get the place well alight, and they escaped into the crowd which had collected. The fire was extinguished without a great deal of damage being done.

4th February. The summer residence of Senator Dr. O'Sullivan at Dooks, Glenbeigh, County Kerry, was burnt to the ground, the house being first looted.

5th February. Senator Dr. George Sigerson, who, at eighty-four years of age, was the most venerable figure in Irish public life, wrote to the President of the Executive Council resigning his seat in the Senate, owing to intimidation. In an interview with the Press, he stated that he had received written notice that, if he continued his membership, his house (in Clare Street, Dublin) would be burnt. 'I attended the Senate every day, taking the same risk as my colleagues; but if I continue to act my house is to be burnt.' It contained a magnificent collection of books, manuscripts, paintings, and miniatures, and he probably regarded these as more valuable than his life. He had been the intimate friend of Irish patriots for more than half a century, from the time of Smith O'Brien, John Martin, Charles Kickham, and others of the Young Ireland movement; and he was the father of the Irish language, having published a book of Irish poetry so long ago as 1860. He recalled the fact that, after the insurrection of Easter Week, 1916, many of the leaders had taken refuge in his house. 'And now,' he said, 'this is the new generation.'

As Dr. Sigerson's resignation had been wrongly sent to the President of the Executive Council instead of to the Chairman of the Senate, it was ineffective. Mr. Cosgrave persuaded him that his resignation might set a bad example; and so, though the threat to him was not withdrawn, he continued with great courage to attend the Senate, of which he remained a member until his death in 1925. Happily, his house escaped destruction.

16th February. Mullaboden, Ballymore Eustace, County Kildare, a stately mansion which was the home of Senator Sir Bryan Mahon and Lady Mahon, was burnt down in daylight, with all its contents. Sir Bryan and Lady Mahon were absent at the time. The incendiaries arrived in a stolen motor-lorry, with seventy tins of petrol. The windows were broken to ensure a good supply of air. The servants, who were unarmed, were compelled to pile the furniture in the middle of the rooms, to facilitate the holocaust. The petrol was then applied, with the usual result. A gramophone, a pair of field-glasses, and Sir Bryan's military uniform (he had been G.O.C. at Salonika and elsewhere) were taken as trophies. As the lorry drove away, one of the raiders was seen to don the uniform.

19th February. Senator Sir John Keane's mansion, Belmont, Cappoquin, County Waterford, was burnt to the ground.

22nd February. Desart Court, County Kilkenny, was so effectively fired that nothing remained but the bare walls, though a quantity of furniture was saved from the flames. This was one of the finest mansions in the south of Ireland, and was the home of the Earl of Desart, whose sister-in-law, the Countess Dowager of Desart, was a member of the Senate.

23rd February. Senator Oliver Gogarty's house in the west of Ireland, Renvyle, Connemara, was burnt to ashes, with valuable modern paintings by Orpen, Augustus John, and others.

26th February. At 11.30 p.m. raiders arrived at Castle Forbes, County Longford, the Irish seat of Senator the Earl of Granard, and one of the most magnificent inhabited castles in the British Isles. Lord and Lady Granard were away in London. A land-mine was placed in the hall and another in one of the rooms. Fortunately, the one in the hall failed to explode. The other was so powerful that the explosion was distinctly heard seven miles away, and all the windows in the neighbouring village of Newtown Forbes were shattered. Very great damage was done, but if both mines had detonated the castle might have been wrecked beyond repair.

9th March. A party of about fifty incendiaries descended upon Ballynastragh, County Wexford, the country seat of Senator Sir Thomas Esmonde. Sir Thomas had had the foresight to remove some of his heirlooms and treasures to the National Museum for safe keeping, but a number of his possessions of very great value remained. Petrol was sprayed over everything, and the mansion and its contents were totally destroyed. Ballynastragh was one of the beauty spots of Wexford. The original building dated from 1300, and part of the modern building was four hundred years old. It had been burnt down once before—by the soldiers of Oliver Cromwell.

24th March. Burton Hall, Stillorgan, County Dublin, the seat of Senator Henry Seymour Guinness, was visited by a band of armed men. They broke into the mansion and turned out Senator Guinness and his family. They placed a large tin of gelignite in the basement. They then sprinkled the upper part of the house with petrol and set it alight. A match was applied to the fuse of the gelignite, and the miscreants beat a retreat. The centre portion of the house was burnt, but the gelignite failed to explode, and so Burton Hall escaped total destruction. In anticipation of an attack, Senator Guinness had re-

moved much of the furniture, and also priceless old manuscripts and
Irish pamphlets of the Restoration period.

26th March. A pantechnicon and a four-ton lorry, both loaded with
furniture that had been rescued from Desart Court (burnt on the 22nd
February), were stopped by Irregulars on the road between Desart
Court and Cuffe's Grange, County Kilkenny. Both vehicles were
sprayed with petrol, set alight, and destroyed with their contents.

It says much for the courage and steadfastness of Senators that,
throughout this appalling period, when no man knew on whom the
blow might next fall, they did not blench or flinch, but discharged
their duties as legislators as though the atmosphere had been one of
serenity. In the nature of things, the situation could not last, for if it
had gone on much longer the economic life of the country would
have been throttled beyond retrieval. When murder and sabotage
were of daily occurrence, it is difficult to particularize, but the following may be given as typical outrages. In the month of February the
gas-works at Tralee (a town of over 10,000 inhabitants) were smashed
with sledges, and the town deprived of its lighting supply; the water-
works at Athlone (7,500 inhabitants) and Maryborough (over 3,000
inhabitants) were destroyed by mine and bomb, and the citizens had
to have recourse to pumps and wells; and a descent was made by
about fifty Irregulars on the little town of Ballyconnell, County
Cavan, who shot two of the inhabitants dead, looted the shops of
quantities of goods, stole two motor-cars, blew up and burnt a
garage, raided the post office, held up a train, and then fled to their
fastness in the Arigna Mountains. The case of Sligo is typical of
what happened on the railways. Sligo station, one of the most substantial buildings of its kind in Ireland, was laid in ruins; steam was
got up on one of the engines, six others were coupled to it, and all
seven were sent to their destruction, some falling through the retaining wall into the sea. But the campaign against the railways went
beyond mere sabotage; there were also what the Railway Unions
characterized as 'murderous attacks on defenceless and inoffensive
railwaymen'.[1] Only one example need be given. The death of an
engine-driver named Daly, in respect of which the coroner's jury
brought in a verdict of 'wilful murder', was thus referred to by Dean
O'Leary, of Tralee, speaking from the altar:

'On his way to worship his Creator, Daniel Daly was attacked by
lurking assassins, and a bullet was fired into his body, because he had
shrunk from, and refused to obey, a wrong and wholly unauthorised

[1] *Irish Times*, 26 January 1923.

command that would involve the destruction of thousands of pounds' worth of the property of his employers.'[1]

The Catholic Hierarchy, who had, in the previous October, formally condemned all such attacks as murder but whose words had been disregarded, returned to the subject in their Lenten Pastorals, read in the churches of their several dioceses. Excerpts from those of the four archbishops are sufficiently indicative of the tenour of the whole.

The Archbishop of Armagh (His Eminence Cardinal Logue) dealt with Mr. De Valera's 'external association' policy and hinted at other factors, such as pride and ambition.

'Never before in the world's history did such a wild and destructive hurricane spring from such a thin, intangible, unsubstantial vapour. The difference between some equivocal words in an oath; the difference between internal and external connection with the British Commonwealth: this is the only foundation I have ever seen alleged. Men versed in the subtleties of the schools may understand them; men of good, sound, practical common sense shall hardly succeed. There may be other foundations—pride, jealousy, ambition, self-interest, even mere sentimentality; but, if they exist, they are kept in the background. . . . It seems as if the powers of darkness were, from day to day, inspiring with fresh ingenuity the agents of destruction. The torch has been added to the revolver, the bomb and the road mine. Before, in some cities and towns no peaceful person could go for a walk or to transact business without the danger of being killed or seriously wounded; now, no quiet family can retire to rest without the dread of being called out in the night to fly from exploded or blazing home.'[2]

The Archbishop of Dublin (Most Rev. Dr. Byrne): 'Unfortunately, the counsel which the Bishops of Ireland, acting in discharge of their office as Shepherds of God's flock, gave their people some months ago has fallen on many unheeding ears. Acts which were declared to be grave sins are still being committed with appalling frequency.'[3]

The Archbishop of Cashel (Most Rev. Dr. Harty): 'We see around us many things that bring shame on our motherland. Banks and post offices are raided; roads and railways are broken; private houses are pillaged and burned to the ground; the sacredness of human life is set at naught; even women and children are done to death by men guilty of a most grave crime against God and society.'

---

[1] *Irish Times*, 30 January 1923.
[2] *Irish Independent*, 12 February 1923.   [3] Ibid.

Having referred to the declaration of the bishops in the previous October on fundamental points of social morality, Dr. Harty continued: 'The Bishops of Ireland were not content with deciding the moral question; they also issued an appeal to the young men of Ireland who were taking part in the sad revolt to return to their homes and to spare the country further ruin. If my words could reach them, I would appeal to the young men of the Archdiocese, who are engaged in this rebellion against our Irish Government, to act in harmony with the teaching of the Bishops.'[1]

The Archbishop of Tuam (Most Rev. Dr. Gilmartin): 'It is the clear teaching of Saint Paul that all power, including the power to govern, comes from God. The people, according to the common opinion of theologians, have the right to nominate their rulers. Once a definite form of government is duly set up by the people, they are bound to accept it as having come from God. The majority of the people's representatives accepted what we call the Treaty. As a result of that acceptance, a certain form of government has been set up. A minority were opposed to the acceptance of that Treaty. Instead, however, of forming a constitutional opposition, they have had recourse to methods of violence, which include the destruction of life and property. . . . For the gun, the revolver, the bomb and the mine, substitute argument. For terrorism, substitute an appeal to the dignity and intelligence of the voter.'[2]

'President' De Valera's views on the subject were, however, clear and definite. In an interview given to the *Daily Mail* a few days before these Pastorals were read he expressed himself as follows: 'In so far as we are concerned, we are in arms against and resisting now exactly what the whole nation resisted in the period 1919–21. The only difference is that in the earlier period England was maintaining her claims directly; now she is maintaining them indirectly through Irishmen. This is a continuance of the former war.'[3]

But the fabric of the 'Republic' was beginning to crack. On the 29th January Mr. Liam Deasy, styled 'Deputy Chief of Staff', who had been captured and sentenced to death but reprieved, accepted immediate and unconditional surrender of all arms and men, and issued an appeal to the other Irregular leaders, including Messrs. De Valera, Ruttledge, Derrig, and Aiken, to do likewise. The appeal was made public by the Government, and in a proclamation dated the

[1] *Cork Examiner*, 19 February 1923.
[2] *Irish Independent*, 12 February 1923.
[3] Quoted in the *Irish Times*, 3 February 1923.

8th February an amnesty was offered to all surrendering with their arms on or before the 18th February. There was no response from the leaders, but a certain amount from the rank and file. However, it was the beginning of the end.

On the 9th March, in the Dáil, Mr. Thomas Johnson, the Leader of the Opposition, made it clear that he and his colleagues of the Labour Party ranged themselves with the Government in resisting the attack upon the foundations of the State.

'I believe it is true to say that a large section of those who are inspiring the Irregular campaign hold that by a sufficient attack upon the material resources the State cannot maintain itself. . . . The present attack is, in reality, an attack upon the social fabric itself. . . . I think it well to say that in the opinion of the Dáil, in the opinion of those of us on these benches at any rate, and, I am sure, in the opinion of the Dáil as a whole, the attempt to break up the social fabric, once it is seized upon by the people, will mean that, at any cost and at any sacrifice, the country will rally to the defence of the State. . . . I think it well to send it out from the Dáil that, despite any increase in Estimates that may be called for, even though it is an increase multiplied one hundred times, even though the private resources of the people are going to be brought to nothing, still for the sake of maintaining society in this country the opposition to society must be resisted and overthrown.'[1]

On the 10th April Lynch, the Irregular 'Chief of Staff', was captured in an engagement in the Knockmealdown Mountains, in County Waterford, and died later of his wounds. He was a brave but fanatical man. Four days later Mr. Austin Stack, 'Minister for Finance' in Mr. De Valera's 'Cabinet', was captured in the same region. In his possession was a draft memorandum, in his own handwriting, calling for a general laying down of arms. On the 17th April Mr. Daniel Breen, another leader, was taken. With most of the leaders gone, the campaign could not profitably be pursued further; and so, on the 27th April 1923, a long proclamation was issued by 'President' De Valera from 'Irish Republican Army, G.H.Q., Dublin', which was in effect a cease fire order. Concurrently with this proclamation, there was issued by Mr. Frank Aiken, who had succeeded Lynch as 'Chief of Staff', an Order addressed to 'O.C.s, Commands and Independent Brigades', ordering a suspension of all offensive operations from noon on the 30th April, 'in order to give effect to decision of the Government and Army Council'.

[1] *Dáil Debates*, ii, 2279–81.

The Senate now·comes into the picture again.[1] On the 30th April Senator Jameson and Senator Douglas both received letters, marked 'Confidential', from Mr. De Valera, requesting them to meet him with a view to discussing practical steps for the conclusion of an immediate peace. (Eight years later, he stated that he did not send for them;[2] but this statement is not in accordance with fact.) The selection of these two members of the Senate was peculiar, the more so as Senator Jameson was Number 1 on 'List A' of Senators who were to be shot at sight. They replied that, if they met, they could not discuss peace conditions, but could act as intermediaries only. He answered that that was his intention.

They saw Mr. De Valera on the 1st May, and he requested them to endeavour to arrange a conference between members of the Government and himself, either alone or accompanied by other leaders associated with him, with a view to the discussion of peace conditions based on his proclamation. Two days later Senator Jameson saw Mr. Cosgrave, who was accompanied by two other Ministers, and they authorized him to inform Mr. De Valera that it was not considered advisable by them that personal negotiations should take place. They handed Senator Jameson a document, to be shown to Mr. De Valera, the fundamental conditions of which would have to be included in any agreement that might be arranged. This document is as follows:

'All political action within the country should be based on a recognition by every party in the State of the following principles of order:

'(a) that all political issues, whether now existing or in the future arising, shall be decided by the majority vote of the elected representatives of the people:

'(b) as a corollary to (a) that the people are entitled to have all lethal weapons within the country in the effective custody or control of the Executive Government responsible to the people through their representatives.

'The acceptance of these principles and practical compliance with (b) by the surrender of arms to be the preliminary condition for the release of prisoners, who shall be required to subscribe individually to (a) and (b).'

---

[1] The whole of what follows regarding these negotiations is summarized from a statement read by Senator Douglas in the Senate on the 9th May 1923. (*Senate Debates*, i, 1018–26.)
[2] *Dáil Debates*, xl, 360.

Messrs. Jameson and Douglas were further authorized to inform Mr. De Valera that:

'(1) military action against him and his followers would cease when the arms held by them were delivered into the effectual custody of the Free State Executive authorities. The arrangements for the delivery of the arms and the place of their deposit would be made with as much consideration as possible for the feelings of those concerned:

'(2) prisoners to be released on the satisfactory fulfilment of (1) and the signature of each prisoner before release to the conditions of the document above mentioned:

'(3) the Free State Government would keep a clear field for Mr. De Valera and his followers to enable them to canvass for the votes of the people at the next election, provided they undertook to adhere strictly to constitutional action.'

The two Senators were also requested to ask Mr. De Valera to give the names of the leaders on whose behalf he could speak, and to state his opinion as to what proportion of the rank and file would agree to be bound by his decision and also as to what amount of acceptance the proposals, when approved by him, would receive from the prisoners.

The terms offered would seem to be the maximum that could safely be granted by any government having a due regard for its responsibilities to the people; and the language in which they were couched indicated a desire to avoid bitterness or harsh feelings. They were not, however, acceptable to Mr. De Valera. Messrs. Jameson and Douglas saw him three times in six days, at the end of which (7th May) he produced an alternative draft of his own. In contrast to Mr. Cosgrave's, which was short and unambiguous, this was, in the latter's words, 'a long and wordy document, inviting debate where none is possible'. It contained sounding phrases about 'the sovereign rights of this nation', which were already, in principle, enshrined in the Constitution, and one of its conditions stipulated that no citizen should be debarred from Parliament by any political oath. Acceptance of this condition would, of course, have abrogated the Treaty of 1921, which had been accepted by an overwhelming majority of the votes of the people. Mr. De Valera's counter-proposals with regard to the lethal weapons in the possession of the Irregulars were so extraordinary as to merit quotation in full:

'Assigning to the Republican forces at least one suitable building in each province, to be used by them as barracks and arsenals, where

I

Republican arms shall be stored, sealed up and defended by a specially pledged Republican guard—these arms to be disposed of after the elections by re-issue to their present holders, or in such other manner as may secure the consent of the Government then elected.'

Needless to say, Mr. De Valera's alternative draft was not accepted by the Government. To use a phrase of Mr. O'Higgins, 'This is not going to be a draw, with a re-play in the autumn.' Senators Jameson and Douglas conveyed Mr. Cosgrave's letter of refusal to Mr. De Valera, from whom they received a courteous acknowledgement, with thanks for their good offices; and there the matter ended.

The episode produced one result of value, for it established Mr. De Valera's acceptance of direct, personal responsibility for the orders given to the Irregulars and for the acts done thereunder. 'With regard to the condition of the Government that prisoners should individually sign acceptance of the principles proposed, Mr. De Valera stated that he did not consider this necessary. When he will sign he will do so on behalf of all Republican forces, including prisoners, and will assure himself before signing that prisoners when released will act in the spirit of the agreement. Mr. De Valera stated that he spoke on behalf of the combined Republican Government and Army Council, who, with the exception of one member not available at the moment, were aware of the proposals made.'

The approach to Senators Jameson and Douglas had been a despairing effort to avoid the consequences of defeat. Very shortly afterwards, on the 24th May, a proclamation was issued, beginning:

'To all ranks, from the President.

'Soldiers of liberty! Legion of the rearguard! The Republic can no longer be defended successfully by your arms. Further sacrifices on your part would now be in vain, and continuance of the struggle in arms unwise in the national interest. Military victory must be allowed to rest for the moment with those who have destroyed the Republic.' And more to similar effect.

Concurrently, an Order was issued 'To all ranks' by Mr. Frank Aiken, the 'Chief of Staff' of the Irregulars.

'Comrades! the arms with which we have fought the enemies of our country are to be dumped. The foreign and domestic enemies of the Republic have for the moment prevailed.'[1]

In less flamboyant but more accurate language, it was not the voice of the Church that had prevailed, nor yet that of right reason,

[1] *Irish Times*, 29 May 1923.

but the resistance of the people, standing firmly behind their elected representatives and their lawful government, to an organized attack upon society by men whose actions had been characterized by the Catholic archbishops and bishops of Ireland in the terms which have already been quoted. The arms so hidden were not again used by that section of the Republicans which followed Mr. De Valera. It was the end of the so-called Civil War. On the Irregular side, seventy-three men had been executed under the powers conferred on the military by the Army Emergency Powers Resolution, passed by the Dáil on the 28th September 1922; and, as has been stated, four others were shot as a reprisal for the murder of a member of the Dáil. Among those executed was Erskine Childers (24th November 1922), whose great ability was as unquestioned as his deep sincerity in the cause he had espoused. The number of soldiers and civilians, including women and children, killed during the progress of the hostilities must have been very much larger. The material damage exceeded thirty millions sterling.

CHAPTER VI

RELATIONS OF SENATE AND DÁIL

The Senate's first meeting—Election of Chairman and Vice-Chairman—Absence of party system—The Senate's conception of its duties—Irish language and cultural activities—Relations with Government and Dáil—No leader of the House—Administrative difficulties—No Parliamentary Questions—Legislative congestion—Defence Forces Bill—Land Bill—Suspension of the Intoxicating Liquor Bill—A flaw in the Constitution—Public Safety Bill—Attitude of the Senate—Habeas corpus case—Constitutional difficulty over referendum provision—De Valera and titles to land—The dissolution—Mr. Cosgrave's tribute to the Senate—The general election of August 1923.

The Senate met on the 11th December 1922, and the Oath was administered in public by Mr. E. J. Duggan, Minister without Portfolio, who was one of the signatories of the Treaty. The occasion was an historic one. For the first time representative Irishmen, irrespective of racial origin or religious belief, were assembled together in a Second Chamber to enact laws for their common country. When Thomas Davis wrote:

> *Filled with hate, our Senate sate*
> *To weld anew each fetter's flaw,*

he was speaking of an older and an unhappier day. This new Senate was in a position to realize, in microcosm, Davis's dream of a united Ireland wherein all men of goodwill would work together in a self-respecting, self-governing motherland: and, given the conditions, a spirit of co-operation there engendered and fostered might in time infuse the whole polity. The growth of such a spirit might be expected to be slow, for *natura nihil facit per saltum*, and the suspicions begotten of generations of aloofness are not to be dispelled

116

overnight. But a beginning must be made somewhere, and it was made on the 11th December 1922 in the Senate.

A possible line of cleavage arose at once, over the important question of the election of a chairman. If the only criterion was to be suitability for the office, Lord Glenavy was the obvious choice. He was the only lawyer in the Senate, he had had many years' parliamentary experience at Westminster, and he had held the highest judicial posts in the country. On the other hand, the majority of the Senators were Nationalists, and Lord Glenavy's preferment was due to the fact that he was of the ascendancy class. He had been a lifelong Unionist, and was Edward Carson's right-hand man in the campaign of opposition to Home Rule. The Nationalists at once made it clear that these things belonged to the dead past. Lord Glenavy's election was proposed by Senator John MacLoughlin, an Ulsterman and a Nationalist. 'We are prepared', he said, 'to treat every man as a brother Irishman, irrespective of what his politics were in the past or his religion is in the present.' Sir Thomas Esmonde, a former Nationalist Member of Parliament, took the same view. 'Whatever has happened in the past, however much we may have differed, there is only one thing before us now, and that is our common country.' The opinion of the Labour Party, as expressed by Senator MacPartlin in homely and rugged phraseology, was not dissimilar. 'What we are interested in is the ability of the man whom we select and for whom we are going to vote. . . . We will vote for the best man, and we do not want to know whether he is a Colonel or a Lord or a road worker.' Though, in the nature of things, they could not make it manifest on this occasion, the attitude of the ex-Unionists was the same, and their subsequent actions afforded manifold proof of their sincerity. 'The past is dead,' said one of them, 'not only for us but for this country. We are assembled here no longer in a Nationalist or Unionist sense, but merely as members of the Senate.' In the result, Lord Glenavy was elected to the Chair with only two dissentients; and Senator Douglas, who had been a member of the Constitution Committee, was unanimously elected Vice-Chairman. A good beginning had been made with the spirit of co-operation.[1]

The fostering of this spirit was made easier by the fact that there were no organized political parties, save for the small but influential Labour Party of five members, whose special position was generally appreciated. Indeed, a rigid alignment of parties can hardly be said to have taken place until December 1928, when the election of a

[1] *Senate Debates*, i, 8–20.

number of Mr. De Valera's supporters, new to the Senate and its traditions, made that course inevitable. As Senator Jameson said, 'We have our own individual opinion about things. I do not believe there is any member of the Senate . . . who is belonging to a party, or in any way shaping his actions or votes in the interest of any party.'[1] The truth of this statement is exemplified by the division lists of the early days. Senators who by tradition and habit of mind might have been supposed to be in agreement frequently voted on opposite sides.

The general view of the Senate held by members of the Dáil was that it was a cooling chamber of a conservative type. Questions of national honour, and such matters as the propagation of the Irish language, were regarded as the prerogative of the popular Chamber. The refusal of the Senate to accept the role prepared for it occasioned a good deal of surprised annoyance. Among the first Bills sent by the Dáil to the Senate was one to indemnify members of the British military and police in respect of acts done during the Black and Tan period and earlier. The Senate refused to pass the Bill, on the ground of lack of reciprocity, since some Irish soldiers in the British Army, who had mutinied out of sympathy with the struggle of their fellow countrymen, were still in prison in Great Britain. The Senate reconsidered the matter some time later, as the result of an eloquent appeal made by the head of the Government in person. But Mr. Cosgrave's suggestion that such an objection would come more properly 'from the House in which popular feeling is more generously represented' was warmly repudiated from all quarters of the Senate. The comment of Senator W. B. Yeats was typical. 'I think it is . . . very important to this Senate,' he said, 'because of the very nature of its constitution, that we should show ourselves as interested as the Dáil is in every person in this country. We do not represent constituencies; we are drawn together to represent certain forms of special knowledge, certain special interests, but we are just as much passionately concerned in these great questions as the Dáil.'[2]

In regard to the Irish language, on the 19th April 1923 the Senate set up a committee to submit to the Government a scheme for the editing, indexing, and publication of the Irish manuscripts in the Royal Irish Academy and elsewhere, for the scientific investigation of the living dialects, and for the compiling and publication of an adequate dictionary of the older language. The authors of this project were Senators W. B. Yeats and Alice Stopford Green. The Committee heard evidence from the greatest living scholars of the lan-

[1] *Senate Debates*, i, 155.   [2] Ibid., i, 167, 168.

guage, and issued a long Report containing detailed recommendations. The tenour of the Report is sufficiently indicated by its opening
paragraph:
'Your Committee is gravely impressed by the responsibility now
laid upon the Saorstát [Irish Free State] towards the Irish people.
For the first time in many centuries our country, free and independent, is
charged with the pious duty of preserving and making accessible to
Irishmen the mass of learning and tradition which forms the basis of
our national history—a body of manuscript tradition bequeathed to
us by a noble succession of scholars and scribes throughout a thousand years of labour, and further enriched by folk-lore, folk-song and
music, and the important study of topography.'[1]
No action was taken on the Report by the Government. Some of its
recommendations were implemented many years later by the establishment of the Irish Manuscripts Commission and the Irish Folk-
lore Institute; others, such as those relating to a systematic survey of
the antiquities of the country and the collection and publication of
its folk-music, remain in abeyance. The Senate kept a close watch on
the subject of ancient monuments, however, and when the Shannon
Electricity Bill was before the House in 1925 Senators Brown and
Yeats obtained the insertion of a new section which, in effect, secured
the preservation of any such monument that might be endangered
through the raising of the level of the Shannon by providing for its
safe removal and re-erection elsewhere. It was pursuant to the provisions of this Senate section that the beautiful seventh-century church
on an island in the lower Shannon was removed and re-erected in the
churchyard at Killaloe.
The much-criticized policy of introducing the Irish language, by
methods of compulsion, into the ordinary life of the country also had
its advocates in the Senate. Early in 1923 a Bill to establish a new
police force (in place of the disbanded Royal Irish Constabulary) was
introduced in the Dáil, and the name given to the new force was the
Civic Guard. By an amendment introduced and passed in the Senate,
the title was changed to 'Gárda Síochána', which is the Irish, in-
accurately spelled, for 'Guard of Peace', and this has been the legal
title ever since. A year later, when the Bill to amalgamate the railways
was passing through the Senate, two amendments dealing with the
same subject were inserted. The first made Irish an obligatory subject
for all examinations for clerkships in the reconstituted Great Southern
Railways Company. The second made it mandatory on the company

[1] *Senate Debates*, iii, 162.

to replace all public notices and signs, including names of stations (all of which were wholly in English) by notices and signs in Irish and English, and also to print the railway tickets in both languages. It is one of the contrasts of Irish life that the strongest supporters of the noble projects envisaged by the Report of the Senate Committee on Irish Manuscripts (which was not given effect to) were among the stoutest opponents of these amendments (which became law immediately). But, whatever one's private opinion of amendments of this character, the fact that they were proposed and passed in the Senate at least goes to prove that the Senate was not reactionary, and that in such matters as compulsory Irish it was in advance of the Dáil.

It is necessary in the interests of historical truth to state that the attitude of the Government and the Dáil towards the Senate was, from the outset, one of imperfect sympathy. The reasons for this are not difficult to understand. The country had but lately won its legislative freedom, after a bitter struggle in which every member of the Government had been a protagonist and probably a majority of the other members of the Dáil had been active participants. The Senate, on the other hand, was largely composed of men whose attitude during the national struggle was supposed, rightly or wrongly, to have been one of apathy or even of passive hostility. The Dáil, moreover, was a product of universal suffrage and regarded itself as the real repository of the sovereign rights of the people; and, in respect of law-making, it intended to share those rights as little as possible with an 'unrepresentative' Second Chamber. Further, the Dáil had been in existence, in one form or another, for four years, and the Senate was regarded to some extent as an interloper. It was a situation which could be remedied only by the experience which time brings, and, above all, by the experience of a change of government.

For these or other reasons, the Senate was never admitted to full co-partnership in the legislative scheme, in the same sense as, for example, the Senate of South Africa. Under the Constitution there was nothing to prevent the appointment of a Senator to ministerial rank, membership of the Dáil being a pre-requisite only in the case of those Ministers who formed the Executive Council or Cabinet. But no such appointment was made. Three 'Extern' Ministers were appointed in Mr. Cosgrave's first Administration (December 1922) and four in his second (September 1923); but they were all members of the Dáil. Under the Ministers and Secretaries Act, 1924, power was given to the Executive Council to appoint Parliamentary

Secretaries to Ministers, up to a maximum of seven. It might have been expected that at least one such post would be allotted to the Senate, if only for the purpose of providing a Leader of the House who could speak officially for the Government. Three Parliamentary Secretaries were at once appointed, the number being increased later to five; but they were always members of the Dáil. It should be said that there were at all times several members of the Senate, holding the same political opinions as the Government, who were eminently qualified to hold office.

This absence of any nexus with the Government placed the Senate in a position of isolation hardly to be found in the case of any other Second Chamber. It was also the occasion of much administrative difficulty. The numerous day-to-day matters dealt with in a normal Chamber by the Leader of the House had to be settled by the officials, in consultation with the Government. The Government's views and intentions were transmitted to the Chairman, who in turn communicated them to the House. If any question arose out of them, there was no one in a position to give an authoritative answer.

Under the Constitution, Ministers had the right of audience in the Senate; though Parliamentary Secretaries had no such right, when their presence was desirable permission was specially accorded from the Chair. The two Houses generally sat at the same hour, and it frequently happened that the Minister or Parliamentary Secretary in charge of a Bill before the Senate was unable to attend, as his presence was required in the Dáil. In such cases the debate had to be postponed or the measure proceeded with in the absence of its sponsor. It was not until 1930 that something like normality was reached, by the adoption of a Standing Order which provided that the debate on the Second Reading of a Bill should be opened by the Minister or Parliamentary Secretary in charge of it.

The system of parliamentary questions never existed in the Senate. The desirability of framing Standing Orders for this purpose was discussed on more than one occasion.[1] It was common ground that questions dealing with individual interests or grievances ought not to be allowed; Senators represented no constituencies, and the proper place for questions of that character was the Dáil. But it did seem desirable that parliamentary questions on matters of broad public policy, affecting the country as a whole, should be permitted in the Senate. However, the fact that there was no power to compel the attendance of Ministers for the purpose of answering such questions

[1] *Senate Debates*, i, 502, 507; ii, 210–14.

proved to be an insuperable barrier. Ministers showed no desire to co-operate, and the matter had to be dropped.

Another grievance of the Senate was the manner in which large blocks of Bills were sent to it periodically, especially before the Christmas and summer recesses, and required by the Government to be passed at short notice, on grounds of administrative urgency. This may have been excusable in the very early period, when the Government was engaged in meeting the armed challenge to the State; but the habit persisted after all reason for it had disappeared. Lord Glenavy made frequent protests in the name of the House, but they somehow lacked sincerity, and one felt that the sausage-machine method of enacting legislation did not greatly disturb his serenity. Before the summer recess of 1924 he blandly informed the Senate that 'there are nineteen Bills for our consideration when we meet to-morrow. Twelve months ago it would have occurred to me that that would mean two days' protracted sitting of the Senate. But seeing that we have despatched fifteen Bills to-day in the space of an hour I see no limit to the speed and the powers of this House. Therefore I think we will be quite able to dispose of these nineteen Bills to-morrow.'[1] One obvious remedy was for the Government to initiate in the Senate a number of their complex but largely uncontroversial Bills; the expert criticism which they would have received there would have put them into something like their final shape; the Senate would have been kept continuously busy, and the pressure on the Dáil would have been correspondingly relieved. This course was urged upon the Government, and on one occasion Mr. Cosgrave informed the Senate that it was intended to adopt it.[2] But because the anti-Senate bias proved too strong, or for some other reason not disclosed, it was never in fact adopted. Eventually, the Senate took matters into its own hands by refusing to hurry legislation, and the Standing Orders were amended so as to provide that there should be an interval of three days between the receipt of a Bill (other than a Money Bill) from the Dáil and its appearance on the Order Paper, and also so as to prevent more than one stage of a Bill being taken on the same day.

Other instances might be given of what might be called the Dáil's policy of non-co-operation, but one example will suffice. In May 1924 a motion was proposed in the Senate by Senator Douglas to the effect that a Joint Standing Committee should be set up, consisting of five members from each House, to consider the position of the

[1] *Senate Debates*, iii, 894.   [2] Ibid., iii, 139.

Irish Free State in relation to foreign affairs. He expounded this proposal in a well-informed speech, and the motion was cordially supported in all quarters of the House, only one member speaking against it.[1] There can be no doubt that the proposal was an admirable one, and a Joint Standing Committee on Foreign Affairs would have had great educative value. A message was duly sent to the Dáil, embodying the resolution and requesting concurrence. The message was not considered, and the Senate never even received the courtesy of a reply.

Leaving aside these general considerations which have so far occupied our attention, we shall now review the legislative work done, and the Senate's part in that work, from the beginning until the dissolution of August 1923. Article 81 of the Constitution provided that the Dáil elected as a Constituent Assembly on the 16th June 1922 might, for a period not exceeding one year from the date of the coming into operation of the Constitution (6th December 1922), exercise all the powers conferred on the Dáil by the Constitution: and that the first election for the Dáil under the Constitution should take place as soon as possible after (*sic*) the expiration of such period. These provisions necessitated a general election within a comparatively short time. Actually, it took place in the early autumn of 1923, before the year had expired.

The period was one of very great legislative activity. In eight months no less than forty-seven Acts were passed, covering almost every aspect of the national life. In the sphere of public order and administration temporary Acts were passed establishing an army, a police force, and a paid magistracy called District Justices, and regulating the Civil Service. The system of local government was recast by another temporary Act, and the Unemployment Insurance and National Health Insurance codes were amended. An Electoral Act and a Prevention of Electoral Abuses Act were also passed, and the ruined buildings and the state of general lawlessness which were the *sequelae* of the revolutionary period were dealt with in a Damage to Property (Compensation) Act and an Enforcement of Law (Occasional Powers) Act. Most of these benefited—some very considerably —by the critical attention which they received in the Senate and by the amendments inserted in them as a consequence.

All the temporary Acts were replaced in the following year by permanent measures, with one very important exception—the Defence Forces (Temporary Provisions) Act, 1923. This Act, which

[1] *Senate Debates*, iii, 29–44.

contains no less than 246 sections and eight Schedules, and is the basis in law of the Army, was introduced avowedly to make purely temporary provision for the armed forces of the State. That being the case, very few amendments were offered in the Dáil. When the Bill came before the Senate, the Minister for Defence (General Mulcahy) assured the House—of course, in perfect good faith—that it was intended to bring in a permanent measure in the course of six months or so. The Senate accordingly agreed to take all the successive stages of the Bill at once, without attempting to scrutinize it in any detail or to amend it; though the occasion did not pass without a wise and statesmanlike warning from Senator Jameson (which proved afterwards to have been sadly needed) on the subject of Army accountancy and finance.[1] But though more than sixteen years have elapsed since then, and the State has experienced two administrations, this 'temporary' Act is still the law governing the Army, being renewed annually.

One of the most valuable services rendered by the Senate during this period was in connection with the Land Bill, 1923, the main object of which was the completion of land purchase, that is to say, to enable Irish agricultural tenants to become the owners of their holdings. This measure was conceived and carried through by the late Mr. Patrick Hogan, one of the most brilliant and realistic of Mr. Cosgrave's Ministers, whose untimely death in 1936, as the result of a motor-car accident, was an irreparable loss to Irish political life. The Bill reached the Senate towards the end of the session, when only six consecutive days remained for its discussion. But the House sat on five of those days and devoted more than twenty-four hours of parliamentary time to the Bill. Two questions arose: what would be the attitude of the ex-Unionist, landlord class in the Senate towards the proposals of a native government in regard to the land question, which had been a secular subject of controversy in Ireland; and to what extent was the Senate as a whole capable, even in so short a time, of improving a Bill which had been in the possession of the Dáil for six weeks and had been subjected to a most careful scrutiny in that House? The manner in which these questions were answered could give nothing but encouragement to those whose hopes were set upon a new era of co-operation, in which the Second Chamber would exercise a distinctive function of the highest utility. Senator Sir John Keane was the protagonist of the landlords, but his numerous amendments received scant support from other ex-Unionists, who were

[1] *Senate Debates*, i, 1993, 1994.

generally found ranged against him in the division lobby. The value of the Senate's work on the Bill, in which it inserted no less than twenty-seven amendments, evoked a generous tribute from Mr. Hogan.

'I have no intention of wearying the Senate by answering the various points raised for the fifth time by Sir John Keane and answered for the seventh or eighth. I am extremely sorry that the Bill should have to be discussed in the Senate under such unfavourable circumstances, that it should be rushed in this fashion and that the Senate should not have had an opportunity of discussing it at more leisure. I want to say that I realize that the Bill leaves the Senate really improved, especially in a very important section—section 24— and really improved in regard to the points which Senator Jameson and Senator Guinness raised at an earlier stage. I think the Senate realized that the Bill did need improvement in that direction. I think it is a big improvement. I have only to thank the Senate for the invariable consideration they have shown to me during the discussions.'[1]

A point of some constitutional interest arose in connection with the Intoxicating Liquor Bill, 1923, which did not come before the Senate until the day before the conclusion of the session. It was intended to be a temporary measure, and its purpose was to extend the hours within which alcoholic drink might not be sold. The Minister in charge of the Bill (Kevin O'Higgins) pressed the Senate to pass it, but the Bill was not a popular one and, there being obviously no urgency about it, the House refused. Instead, a resolution was carried postponing further consideration of the Bill 'until the re-assembly of the Oireachtas'. Senators took this step in the full assurance that a dissolution of the Oireachtas would have the effect of killing the Bill, and when the House re-assembled after the general election it was not restored to the Order Paper.

The Government were at that time also of the same opinion, and on the 30th May 1924 they introduced into the Dáil a new Intoxicating Liquor Bill, which included the provisions of the Bill believed to be dead. But, later, the Attorney-General advised that the Bill passed by the Dáil in 1923 was caught by the provisions of Article 38 of the Constitution, which stated that a Bill passed by the Dáil and considered by the Senate shall, not later than two hundred and seventy days after it shall have been first sent to the Senate, be deemed to be passed by both Houses. This suspensory period had expired on the 29th April 1924, and, in accordance with the Attorney-General's

[1] *Senate Debates*, i, 2175, 2176.

view, it was the duty of the Executive Council, under Article 41 of the Constitution, to send the Bill to the Governor-General for the signification of the Royal Assent.[1] The Bill was accordingly signed by the Governor-General on the 23rd July 1924. The Government did not then require it, and the whole Act was repealed by an amendment introduced into the second Bill, which became law later in the same year. The affair had disclosed an undoubted flaw in the Article of the Constitution which dealt with the suspensory power of the Senate: and when this Article was amended in 1928 machinery was devised which provided that, after the suspensory period had elapsed, a positive resolution of the Dáil was required before formal enactment.

During the period of armed rebellion against the State, very large numbers of persons had been interned under the inherent powers possessed by the military, re-inforced by the Army Emergency Powers Resolution passed by the Dáil on the 28th September 1922. Mr. De Valera's 'Cease Fire Order' of the 27th April 1923 created a new situation, however. A short time later a writ of *habeas corpus* was applied for, this 'Cease Fire Order' being impleaded. The application was refused by the Master of the Rolls on the 15th June, on the ground that 'the Irish Republican Army Proclamation did not state that a state of war had ceased to exist. It meant nothing more than that a rest stage had been reached.' Similar applications were refused on the 18th and 21st June; but it was becoming clear that the time was approaching when the courts would hold that a state of war had ceased to exist and a writ of *habeas corpus* would be granted. This would be tantamount to a judicial declaration that all the internees were thereafter illegally detained. They would all, therefore, have had to be released; and, as their arms had not been surrendered but only dumped, their release involved a risk which society could not afford to take. Moreover, action could no longer be taken against the Irregulars who were still at liberty, since the army's powers of arrest and detention would be at an end. In these circumstances, the Government introduced in the Dáil on the 15th June 1923 (the day of the decision of the Master of the Rolls) the Public Safety (Emergency Powers) Bill. This Bill was duly passed by the Dáil and sent to the Senate on the 23rd July.

It is proposed here' to examine in some detail the amendments inserted by the Senate in the Bill (often against the wishes of the Government), since they well exemplify the general attitude of the

---

[1] *Dáil Debates*, viii, 1109–11.

Second Chamber towards measures of this type. This attitude was the same in all cases: to accord to the Government the powers deemed necessary by them in the grave situation with which they were confronted, but at the same time to examine the proposed legislation in a critical spirit, with a view to ensuring that the ordinary processes of law should be followed so far as possible, that the civic rights even of persons in arms against the Government should be safeguarded, and that nothing should be done to retard an ultimate appeasement.

The Bill provided for the continued internment of the Irregulars who had been taken prisoner, and for the arrest and detention of any person in respect of whom a report had been received from the Civic Guard or the military authorities that he was suspected of certain scheduled offences or that the public safety was endangered by his being allowed to remain at liberty. Senator Douglas moved to delete the reference to a report from the Civic Guard or the military authorities, and to substitute for it the written certificate of the Minister.

'What I want to avoid if possible,' he said, 'is bringing in these new Forces, particularly the Civic Guard, and mixing them up with this Bill in the eyes of the public. I should like it to be made quite clear that, if an officer of the Civic Guard arrests a man, he brings him forward in the ordinary Courts for trial. But if, in the meantime, under the Bill, the Minister interferes and interns him, the public cannot blame the Civic Guard officer. This . . . amendment . . . would have the effect . . . of placing the full responsibility on the Minister.'

Senator W. B. Yeats concurred: 'The principle is that the Minister can be changed if he does an unpopular act. He can go away, taking the bitterness he has raised with him. But the Civic Guard cannot be changed.'

The amendment was supported by Senators Jameson and O'Farrell and was carried, in spite of the opposition of the Minister (Kevin O'Higgins).[1]

The Bill made provision for the establishment of Appeal Councils, to investigate, at the request of individual internees, the question of their continued detention, and it specified that one member of each such council should be certified by the Attorney-General to have legal knowledge or experience. The Senate did not deem this safeguard sufficient, and it inserted an amendment to the effect that the legal member should be a practising barrister or solicitor of not less than five years' standing. Further, if an appeal council reported that there were no reasonable grounds for suspicion against an internee,

[1] *Senate Debates*, i, 1576–81.

the Senate made it mandatory on the Government either to refer back the case to the council, or to put the internee on his trial before a regular court in the ordinary way, or to release him within one month of the receipt of the report.[1]

The well-being of the internees was the especial interest of Senator Sir Hutcheson Poë, in spite of the fact that the Irregulars had spared neither his age nor his physical disability. He pressed upon the Government an amendment providing for the inspection of the internment camps and the visitation of the prisoners by persons of recognized status and independent position. He spoke of the natural concern of the relatives and friends of 'these unfortunate people', and concluded: 'Liberty is . . . a subject which is dearest to men's hearts, and I hope that some means may be found . . . of releasing a considerable number of these men and women . . . before very long, and that in any case, long before the expiry of this Bill, the whole of these persons may be restored to their homes. In the meantime, I think that, if the Minister can see his way to obtain the services of three men or women who will fulfil the condition laid down, their very presence and their association with the Government in the administration of the prison camps and so on will inspire confidence and allay any anxiety that may still be felt on behalf of the internees.' The principle was supported from the Labour benches and by Senator W. B. Yeats and others, and an amendment embodying it was incorporated in the Bill.[2]

A number of offences, greatly varying in their degrees of gravity, were grouped together in the schedule to the measure, e.g. arson, robbery under arms, wrongful entry on land, and illicit distillation; and all judicial discretion was taken away by the provision that any person found guilty of any of these offences *shall* be sentenced to three years' penal servitude. This flat-rate, mandatory system was thoroughly bad in principle, and Senator Douglas sought to delete it from the Bill by means of an amendment altering 'shall' to 'may'. Speaking on this amendment, Senator Mrs. Stopford Green attacked the principle in one of the most striking speeches ever delivered in the Senate.

'The mandatory system in fact appoints that it is with the Minister, not with the Judge, that lies the punishment of crime. I urge that, so far as the nation consents to weaken the responsibility of Judges and Magistrates, it lowers their virtue. . . . We can thus, in this critical moment, lower the non-political authority of law, and fashion it into

---

[1] *Senate Debates*, i, 1623–32.   [2] Ibid., i, 1633–42, 1723, 1724.

a tool of this State, degrade its dignity, and once more make it the object of popular distrust, and even presently of contempt.' The Minister (Kevin O'Higgins) had urged that the responsibility in these critical decisions rested with the Government. But the ultimate authority of Parliament *vis à vis* the Executive can seldom have been stated with greater cogency than by Alice Stopford Green: 'Our responsibility is as great as that of the Minister. Where he sees danger ahead if we do not accept his mandate, we have on our part rightly to measure his demands and balance them against other dangers, deeper and more persistent, which might follow any lack in us of foresight and responsibility.' Senator Douglas's amendment was carried, the mandatory principle being thus excised from the Bill by the alteration of 'shall' to 'may', and the flat-rate sentence of three years giving place to a variable term not exceeding five years.[1]

The Bill, with all the Senate's amendments, thirteen in number, was passed into law on the 1st August 1923. It was only just in time. From documents captured from the Irregulars it had looked as though the period of quiescence was still, as the Master of the Rolls had called it, merely a rest stage. For instance, in a letter dated the 27th June, written by Mr. Frank Aiken, the Irregular 'Chief of Staff', to another leader who was in prison, the writer had stated that 'with regard to the future, I believe the rifle and revolver is [*sic*] out of date as an offensive weapon. . . . The use of explosives, gas and fire may be concentrated on, also small trench mortars. . . . If we have to fight another war with the Staters, it will have to be short and sweet.'[2] But a month later Mr. De Valera stated in an interview with the Associated Press that 'it is not the intention of the Republican Government or the Army Executive to renew the war in the autumn or after the elections. The war, so far as we are concerned, is finished.'[3] A further application was made for a writ of *habeas corpus*, in this case on behalf of an internee named Mrs. Connolly O'Brien. The Court of Appeal held that the state of war had come to an end, and, on the 31st July 1923, granted the application and ordered the release of the prisoner.[4]

This decision meant, of course, that the further detention of all the internees was illegal. The State claimed the right to make a return to the writ of *habeas corpus*, and in the return, made on the 2nd August, it relied on an Order detaining Mrs. Connolly O'Brien made

[1] *Senate Debates*, i, 1660–70.
[2] Quoted by Mr. O'Higgins in the Senate: *Debates*, i, 1584, 1585.
[3] *Irish Times*, 23 July 1923.
[4] Rex (O'Brien) *v.* the Minister for Defence, [1924] 1 I.R. 32.

K

under the provisions of the Public Safety Act, passed on the previous day. An extraordinary constitutional point then arose, which it is necessary to refer to here, on account of its connection with the history of Parliament. It was submitted on behalf of Mrs. Connolly O'Brien that the State's return to the writ was bad, and for this reason. Article 47 of the Constitution provided that, not later than seven days after a Bill had been passed by both Houses, two-fifths of the members of the Dáil or a majority of members of the Senate might demand the suspension of the Bill for ninety days, during which period a referendum might be demanded. This provision was not to apply to Money Bills, or to such other Bills as might be declared by both Houses to be necessary for the immediate preservation of the public peace, health, or safety. There had been no such declaration in the case of the Public Safety (Emergency Powers) Bill, and it was contended that the Act was *ultra vires* the Constitution, inasmuch as it had received the Royal Assent on the day on which it had been actually passed, instead of after a due interval of seven days during which its suspension might have been demanded under Article 47. The Court of Appeal upheld this contention, and decided that the State's return to the writ of *habeas corpus* was bad.

The Government's method of dealing with this constitutional difficulty was ingenious and effective. On the day following this decision (3rd August 1923) a fresh Bill was passed by both Houses, entitled the Public Safety (Emergency Powers) (No. 2) Bill. The abortive Act was scheduled to it in its entirety, and Section 1 of the Bill provided that the schedule should have the force of law. Section 2 declared that it was necessary for the immediate preservation of the public peace and safety; and, to make assurance double sure, separate declarations in the same sense were passed by both Houses. The Bill was signed by the Governor-General the same day, and it became law immediately, all constitutional requirements having been complied with.

Being thus made aware of the implications of Article 47, the Government sought and obtained similar declarations from both Houses in the case of the Defence Forces Act, the Indemnity Act (which indemnified the armed forces in respect of acts done during the continuance of the state of war), and the Land Act. That such declarations were desirable in the case of the first two is obvious; but that this course was expedient in the case of the Land Act requires some explanation. It was, in fact, equally necessary. Agrarian trouble was prevalent over a large part of the country, trespass and outrage were frequent, and in the County Waterford a land war had been in progress for months. Mr. Hogan's Land Act went to the root of the matter, and if the rule of law was to prevail it was essential that there should be no delay or possible hitch in its operation.

Shortly before the Hogan Act was passed, Mr. De Valera, who was then in hiding, sent a message to be read at a meeting of his party held in the Dublin Mansion House on the 17th July. In this he said that the principle they meant to stand upon was that of Fintan Lalor, his faith and theirs: 'That the entire ownership of Ireland, moral and material, up to the sun and down to the centre, is vested of right in the people of Ireland; that they, and none but they, are the land-owners and law-makers of this island; that all laws are null and void not made by them, and all titles to land invalid not conferred or con-firmed by them, and that this full right of ownership may and ought to be asserted by any and all means which God has put in the power of man.'[1] The habit of quoting the utterances of Irish patriots of former days, without regard to circumstance and the passage of time, is a common one, and greatly to be deprecated. Fintan Lalor wrote these flaming words in the forties of the last century, imme-diately after the Great Famine, when the whole of Ireland groaned under a tyranny of landlordism which had few parallels in Europe. From 1870 to 1909 six Land Acts had been passed, whereby 400,000 holdings had become the property of the tenants; a rental of £7,000,000 had been purchased by the State, and about 130,000,000 pounds' worth of Land Stock had been issued to the vendors in payment. It was the purpose of Mr. Hogan's Act to complete this vast revolution. But the Oireachtas, like the British Parliament, was not, in Mr. De Valera's view, a body entitled to confer or to confirm titles to Irish land; and so, by reasserting Fintan Lalor's words as a principle on which he and his friends intended to stand, Mr. De Valera told the land-hungry Irish labourer, in effect, that all titles to land derived under these Acts were invalid, and that the full right of ownership 'ought to be asserted by any and all means which God has put in the power of man'. In these circumstances, the need becomes apparent for declarations under Article 47 of the Constitution in respect of the Land Act, and also in respect of the Public Safety Act, which imposed severe penalties for trespass.

The Oireachtas was dissolved on the 9th August 1923. On the afternoon of that day, prior to the dissolution, Mr. Cosgrave attended the Senate and, as head of the Government, expressed the very deep

[1] *Irish Independent*, 18 July 1923.

appreciation of himself and his colleagues for the co-operation and assistance of the Second Chamber, and for the useful and constructive criticism given by it to the legislative proposals of the Ministry. He also paid a tribute to 'the extraordinary courage and perseverance of the Senators who were marked out for special attention during the past six or eight months, and to the fine exhibition of citizenship shown by them during that period.'[1]

Mr. De Valera and his friends contested the general election under the name of the Sinn Féin Party. Sinn Féin had been the name of Arthur Griffith's movement, which was, of course, one of national regeneration, and had nothing to do with physical force. In an appeal to the electors, it was stated that 'Sinn Féin will abolish the murder gangs and secure the life, liberty and property of the people. Sinn Féin will take immediate steps to end unemployment by undertaking remunerative works of reconstruction.'[2] But these strange promises from men who, a few months earlier, had been engaged in an attempt to wreck the economic and social life of the nation could hardly be taken seriously. This appeal, which was published in the Dublin newspapers, was accompanied by a manifesto signed by Mr. De Valera, which showed that the issue was again to be Free State versus Republic: 'Shall it be said that this generation has turned renegade to the national faith and outdone the disastrous submission of the princes and prelates to Henry II, which brought us centuries of shame and sorrow?'[3] The reference to the prelates of 1172 is noteworthy, in view of Mr. De Valera's disagreement with their successors seven and a half centuries later.

Mr. De Valera stood as a candidate for County Clare, and was elected by an enormous majority, in spite of, or perhaps because of, the fact that he was arrested on his appearance in the constituency (15th August 1923). His supporters do not seem to have seen anything illogical or peculiar in the president of a republic, who had rejected the will of the people as a criterion, offering himself as an ordinary candidate for election to a parliament which he did not recognize.

The election was held on the 27th August 1923, and the result was as follows:

---

[1] *Senate Debates*, i, 2207–8.
[2] *Irish Independent*, 24 August 1923.
[3] Ibid., 25 August 1923.

Party	Candidates nominated	Members elected
Cumann na nGaedheal (Cosgrave)	109	63
Sinn Féin (De Valera)	85	44
Labour	44	14
Farmers	64	15
Independents	71	16
Independent Labour	4	1
	377	153

The people had declared for the Treaty again.

CHAPTER VII

BUILDING THE NEW STATE

The new Parliament—Composition of the Administration—Three main classes of legislation—Laying the foundations—The Ministers and Secretaries Act and other measures—Erection of a stable polity—Laws for the improvement of agriculture, fisheries, and housing—Defence of the State and of society—The Republican Government and Army—Repudiation of the National Loan—Statistics of lawlessness—The Cove outrage—Remedial measures and their success—Statesmanship of Kevin O'Higgins—The Government's internal troubles—Ministerial changes—The stillborn National Party—Restoration of stable conditions.

The new Parliament assembled on the 19th September 1923. None of the forty-four members of Mr. De Valera's Sinn Féin Party took their seats, and so the Cosgrave party, with sixty-three members out of 109, had a clear majority in the Dáil. All the other Deputies were, of course, pro-Treaty, and the Opposition was provided by the Labour Party of fourteen members, led with very great ability by Mr. Thomas Johnson.

The Administration was composed as follows:

Members of the Executive Council

President: W. T. Cosgrave.

Vice-President and Minister for Home Affairs: Kevin O'Higgins.

Minister for Finance: Ernest Blythe.

Minister for Industry and Commerce: Joseph McGrath.

Minister for Education: John MacNeill.

Minister for External Affairs: Desmond Fitzgerald.

Minister for Defence: General Richard Mulcahy.

Ministers not Members of the Executive Council
Minister for Agriculture: Patrick Hogan.
Minister for Local Government: James A. Burke.
Postmaster-General: James J. Walsh.
Minister for Fisheries: Finian Lynch.

The period was one of reconstruction and nation-building on the one hand, and of revolutionary aftermath on the other. The legislation may accordingly be divided broadly into three main classes: first, the laying of the foundations; second, the erection upon those foundations of a stable polity and a national well-being; third, the restoration of the rule of law, and the safeguarding of that polity and that well-being from destruction at the hands of those who still refused to accept the verdict of the people or to seek to alter that verdict by methods other than those of violence. The Senate's contribution to this legislation will be examined in the chapter which follows.

As to the first class, at the apex of the political pyramid the functions of the several Departments had hitherto been largely a matter of unwritten convention. By the Ministers and Secretaries Act, 1924, all politico-administrative functions were crystallized in eleven separate Departments of State, with a Minister as the responsible head of each, viz. President, Finance, Justice, Local Government and Public Health, Education, Lands and Agriculture, Industry and Commerce, Fisheries, Posts and Telegraphs, Defence, and External Affairs. For the service of these Departments there was enacted the Civil Service Regulation Act, 1924, replacing the temporary Act passed in the previous year. The Gárda Síochána Act, 1924, established an unarmed civic guard or police force, to serve the needs of the whole country, also replacing a temporary Act of 1923. And the whole judicial system of the country was recast by the Courts of Justice Act, 1924, the provisions of which will be considered more particularly later.

In the second class, comprehensive measures introduced by Mr. Hogan, the Minister for Lands and Agriculture, gradually raised the standard of Irish agricultural exports—the economic mainstay of the country—to heights which they had never reached before. By the Agricultural Produce (Eggs) Act, 1924, the marketing of eggs was subjected to strict regulation, and penalties were inflicted for the sale of dirty or unfit eggs. By the Dairy Produce Act, 1924, a similar standard was set for the marketing of butter; and under the Live Stock

Breeding Act, 1925, all bulls had to be licensed, with a view to the elimination of the unfit and the improvement of the breed and quality of cattle. This type of legislation gradually restored Irish products to their rightful place in the British market, and so improved the status of the farmers, many of whom also benefited by the Arterial Drainage Act, 1925, whereby provision was made to cope with the many thousands of acres of lands subject to flooding. Moreover, by the Beet Sugar (Subsidy) Act, 1925, under which a factory for the manufacture of sugar from beet was established in Carlow, the farmers were given a new crop and Ireland a new industry. The inland fisheries were another valuable asset, but control had broken down during the revolutionary period, to the great detriment of the tourist industry. Under the Fisheries Act, 1925, new Boards of Conservators were organized and provided with adequate funds, and licensed retailers were required to keep registers of all purchases of salmon and trout, by which means the disposal of poached fish was rendered extremely difficult.

A like energy was displayed in other fields. An attack was made on the slum problem by the Housing (Building Facilities) Act, 1924, whereby grants of £250,000 were made available for the erection of small houses and £50,000 for reconstructed houses, followed up by the Housing Act, 1925, whereby the Minister for Local Government was empowered to make grants up to £300,000 for the same purposes. The Local Government Act, 1925, amended the whole law relating to this subject. The railway system, which had been on the down grade ever since the Great War, was reorganized by the Railways Act, 1924, which amalgamated the four companies operating wholly within the area of the Irish Free State and established a railway tribunal to regulate charges. The drink evil was tackled by the Intoxicating Liquor (General) Act, 1924, which severely restricted the hours of sale of alcoholic drink and virtually prohibited its sale altogether on Christmas Day, Good Friday, and Saint Patrick's Day. Most courageous of all, Mr. Patrick McGilligan (who had succeeded Mr. McGrath as Minister for Industry) made a beginning, in the Shannon Electricity Act, 1925, with a gigantic project of making a supply of electric light, heat, and power available throughout the country by harnessing the waters of the River Shannon.

Constructive work of this kind may not be spectacular, but it is directed to making the nation prosperous and happy; and the daily grappling with complex problems which it entailed enabled the statesmen engaged in it to integrate their personalities, unlike those who held aloof on the issue of the Republic, destroyed much and learnt nothing.

This brings us to the third class of legislation during this period, namely, the measures necessary for the defence of the State and of society. But, before considering these measures, we must first review the conditions with which they were designed to cope. There existed at this time the Government of the Irish Republic, with the Irish Republican Army allegedly responsible to it. This Government claimed jurisdiction over the whole of Ireland, but it had no *de jure* authority from God or man, and no *de facto* authority except where the writ of the gunman still ran. Logically, it might have been expected that, as Mr. De Valera and his friends had contested the general election, they would have been content to abide by the result; but such was not the case. The position was one which no government could tolerate. As Mr. O'Higgins said: 'We will not have two Governments in this country, and we will not have two armies in this country. If people have a creed to preach, a message to expound, they can go before their fellow-citizens and preach and expound it. But let the appeal be to the mind, to reason rather than to physical fear. They cannot have it both ways. They cannot have the platform and the bomb.'[1] Letters were addressed to private individuals from persons styling themselves 'Minister for Agriculture' and so on which were in fact from Ministers of this pretended Government.[2] In December 1923 the Government issued a loan for ten millions sterling, for purposes of reconstruction, and a special appeal was made to the small investor. In the absence in prison of the 'President of the Republic' (Mr. De Valera), a statement was issued by the 'Vice-President' (Mr. Patrick Ruttledge) with the object of wrecking the loan.

'The Free State Executive are engaged in attempting to raise a loan in portions of this country. This loan is of the utmost importance to them because of the use they intend to make of its success. The Government has already issued a proclamation refusing to accept any responsibility for this or any other liability contracted by such a body. In view of the attempts being made to stampede the small investors, particularly, to participate in this loan, all members of Sinn Féin should endeavour to save such people from sinking their savings in such an unauthorised flotation and thereby incurring subsequent loss.'[3]

[1] *Dáil Debates*, v, 1944.   [2] Ibid., x, 280.
[3] Quoted by Mr. O'Higgins in *Dáil Debates*, v, 1944, 1945.

The threat was unsuccessful. The loan was quickly over-subscribed, and the support given to it by the small investor is sufficiently indicated by the fact that the average subscription was only slightly over £500.[1]

One of the results of these pretended claims to governmental authority, and of the fact that the arms of the Irregulars had not been surrendered but only dumped, was a reign of lawlessness in many parts of the country.[2] For the month of January 1924 there were 545 indictable offences reported to the Civic Guard.[3] During the period August 1923 to February 1924 there were no fewer than 738 cases of arson and robbery under arms. Though this is a terrifying total, the Government were gradually getting the upper hand, for the number of such cases during the comparable period of 1922–3 was 1,502.[4] But as late as the 21st February 1924 Mr. O'Higgins informed the Dáil that, in some counties, there were certain persons elected to the Dáil 'but who have not, so far, taken advantage of the honour, leading armed gangs of robbers'.[5] On the 21st March 1924 there occurred perhaps the most horrible outrage of all. A number of unarmed British soldiers, who were proceeding on shore leave from the garrison at Spike Island, arrived at the landing-stage at Cove (Queenstown), County Cork, accompanied by some civilian friends. These soldiers were there by virtue of the Treaty of 1921, which placed the harbour defences of Queenstown under British care and maintenance parties. Immediately these defenceless people disembarked from their launch, fire was opened upon them from two machine-guns concealed in a powerful touring car, which, occupied by four men, had pulled up near the landing-stage a few minutes prior to the arrival of the launch. One soldier was mortally wounded, an officer and seventeen soldiers were wounded, some dangerously, and five civilians, including two women, were among the casualties. The miscreants then drove away rapidly towards Cork. When the Dáil met four days later it adjourned at once, in Mr. Cosgrave's words, 'as an expression of the sympathy of the Irish Nation in this wanton and murderous outrage and as an evidence to the British Nation and to the civilized world of the regret and humiliation which we feel that such a crime should be committed in our country.'[6] A similar resolution was passed by the Senate.[7] Though a reward of £10,000 was offered by the Government for the apprehension of the assassins, and

---

[1] *Dáil Debates*, v, 1619, 1620.
[2] Ibid., v, 1942.   [3] Ibid., vi, 1216.   [4] Ibid., vi, 1172.
[5] Ibid., vi, 1257, 1258.   [6] Ibid., vi, 2291–4.
[7] *Senate Debates*, ii, 1257–60.

their detection engaged the personal attention of the highest officers of the State, the attempt to bring them to justice was unsuccessful. Another of the results of the prevailing unrest was the threatened collapse of legal process for the recovery of debt. This is, of course, the vindication of the legal right of the individual citizen against his neighbour; and this right must be upheld if commerce is to thrive and the springs of credit are to be prevented from drying up—a condition of things which would ultimately fall more heavily on the poor than on anyone else. For reasons of history, the bailiff had not been a popular figure in Ireland, and the recognition that a native government and native courts brought changed conditions was slow in coming. But, as Kevin O'Higgins said, 'the ceasing of the bailiff to function is the first sign of a crumbling civilization'.[1] The courts were not recognized as legal courts by Mr. De Valera's followers, and intimidation was rife. Moreover, there are always, in any community, numbers of persons only too ready to take advantage of such a situation as this by refusing to pay their lawful debts. The figures of the period speak for themselves. On the 11th March 1924 there were roughly 7,000 decrees outstanding, representing approximately £170,000. Of these decrees, some 2,000, representing £17,000, were for public debts, and 5,100, representing £150,000, were for private debts.[2] On the 31st July 1924 the number of unexecuted judgements was 7,063, representing a sum of £126,538; and on the 31st March 1925 the number was 5,712, representing £107,790.[3] The threat to the social fabric represented by such figures as these, though not so obtrusive, was none the less real than the revolver, the petrol can, the bomb, and the mine.

From the foregoing summary we can now see the directions in which legislative action was called for in the interests of the public safety during the period covered by this chapter. At the beginning of the period hundreds of men who had been captured during the Irregular campaign were still in custody. The Government's policy was one of release as quickly as considerations of public safety admitted,[4] but obviously that course could not be adopted while the events were taking place which have just been recounted; and on the 2nd April 1924 the total number of political prisoners was 941, of whom 314 had been sentenced and the rest were interned.[5] The provisions as to internment contained in the temporary Public Safety Act which had been passed before the general election were

---

[1] *Dáil Debates*, vi, 1928.   [2] Ibid., vi, 1926, 1927.   [3] Ibid., xi, 418.
[4] Ibid., v, 1943.   [5] Ibid., vi, 2736.

accordingly re-enacted in the Public Safety (Powers of Arrest and Detention) Temporary Act, 1924, which had a duration of one year. This, of course, entailed the suspension of *habeas corpus*, but Kevin O'Higgins hesitated as little about it as did Abraham Lincoln in similar circumstances in Maryland in 1861. By the time the Act expired, on the 31st January 1925, the Government's policy of firmness mingled with clemency had so far succeeded that there was no need to renew it. On the 21st May 1924 there were only 616 political prisoners, of whom 302 were sentenced and 314 were internees.[1] By the 1st July the numbers had fallen to eighty-six sentenced prisoners and 123 internees.[2] Mr. De Valera was released on the 16th July, and most of the others were set free before Christmas.

The menace from arson, robbery under arms, and similar crimes was met by the re-enactment, in a separate but temporary Act, of those sections of the temporary Act of 1923 which had prescribed the punishment (including flogging) for such offences. This new Act expired on the 20th April 1925, and by that time the threat to society had been successfully resisted and the circumstances did not call for its renewal.

A third set of provisions contained in the temporary Act of 1923, namely, those relating to the possession, sale, and licensing of firearms and the control of lethal weapons generally, were in substance continued until the 31st July 1925 by the Firearms (Temporary Provisions) Act, 1924 and the Firearms (Temporary Provisions) (Continuance) Act, 1925.

The obstruction of legal remedies for debt was countered by the Enforcement of Law (Occasional Powers) Act, 1924, which substantially re-enacted the provisions of a similar Act of 1923 and which was itself extended by a Continuance Act of 1925 until the 31st March 1926. These Acts greatly strengthened the powers of the sheriffs. There was naturally a time-lag in the suppression of this kind of more or less passive disorder, but recovery was none the less sure. It will be recalled that, on the 11th March 1924, there were 7,000 decrees outstanding, representing £170,000. On the 31st January 1926 there were only 3,434 such decrees, representing £69,910.[3] This was still, of course, a far from normal position, but the figures did indicate a substantial degree of recovery; and a permanent measure, entitled the Enforcement of Court Orders Act, 1926, which was passed into law on the 29th May 1926, achieved normality within a comparatively short time.

[1] *Dáil Debates*, vii, 1119.   [2] Ibid., viii, 88.   [3] Ibid., xiv, 890.

By the middle of the previous year (1925) the condition of the country was such that the temporary Public Safety Acts, which were then due to expire, could be replaced by permanent measures. The release of the internees had led, in some places, to a renewal of the disorders in connection with which they had been detained;[1] but it was a time of comparative peace, and it was thought better to eschew emergency legislation and to bring in measures which would give permanent powers to the Executive, no matter what government was in power, for dealing with an attack upon the State. Hence the Treasonable Offences Act, 1925, was passed, inflicting the death penalty for levying war against the State and imposing varying sentences of imprisonment for such offences as misprision of treason (which was statutorily defined) and the intimidation of judges and Ministers. The usurpation of executive authority or of parliamentary functions, and the formation of a pretended military or police force, were made misdemeanours punishable by fine or imprisonment or both. As a corollary to this measure, a permanent Firearms Act, 1925, was also passed.

All these measures for the public safety, for the suppression of disorder, and for the restoration of self-respect, dignity, and honour among the Irish people were carried upon the shoulders of one young man, the late Kevin O'Higgins, Minister for Justice. Courageous in thought as in action, resolute without being vindictive, his lodestar throughout was the guiding principle proclaimed by Lincoln at Gettysburg, that government of the people, by the people, for the people, should not perish. On the 20th April 1932 Mr. De Valera, in one of his first speeches in the Dáil as head of the Government of that Irish Free State which he had sought unsuccessfully to destroy, read out a list of these Acts and classed them with the Coercion Acts passed against Ireland by the British Government.[2] But by that time Kevin O'Higgins had been in his grave nearly five years, slain by the bullets of assassins.

The Government and the State also surmounted troubles of a different kind during this period. In March 1924 there was a mutiny among certain Army officers, due partly to dissatisfaction with the rate of advance in national status and partly to alleged grievances in regard to demobilization. General O'Duffy, the head of the Civic Guard, was appointed Commander-in-Chief and Inspector-General of the Forces to deal with the emergency, and the affair was settled without bloodshed. As a consequence, but for opposite reasons, two

---

[1] *Dáil Debates*, x, 273.　　　　[2] Ibid., xli, 193, 194.

members of the Executive Council resigned : the Minister for Industry and Commerce (Mr. Joseph McGrath) on the 7th March 1924 and the Minister for Defence (General Mulcahy) on the 19th of the same month. Mr. Cosgrave took over the portfolio of Defence for the time being (20th March), handing it over to Mr. Peter Hughes on the 21st November; and Mr. Patrick McGilligan was appointed Minister for Industry and Commerce on the 3rd April 1924, holding the post until the Cosgrave Administration went out of office in 1932.

Shortly afterwards, Mr. McGrath, Mr. Seán Milroy, and seven other members of Mr. Cosgrave's party became recalcitrant and formed a sort of Cave of Adullam. At the end of October 1924 they resigned from the Dáil in a body and offered themselves for re-election, seeking support for the foundation of a new National Party. In the words of a contemporary writer, the new party 'had no real policy save vague denunciations of the Government for not using the Free State as a stepping-stone to a Republic, and for being in the grip of the Freemasons, an organization which in Ireland is endowed with all the powers of the unknown'.[1] The miniature general election which resulted (February 1925) was contested by the Government party, by the new National Party, and by Mr. De Valera's Sinn Féin Party of abstentionists; and, as the nine seats were spread over seven counties and three out of the four provinces, it afforded an excellent test of public opinion. During the progress of the campaign, Kevin O'Higgins, speaking at Boyle, County Roscommon, on the 8th February, said : 'We have got to face the facts. Mr. De Valera hates facts like a cat hates water, and we have got to rub these facts into him during the next few weeks. It is time we grew up and recognized that we cannot just live in a world of make-believe. If we denounce the Treaty and tear up the Constitution, it does not mean that by the mere act of doing that you will get international recognition of the sovereign and independent Republic. It is more likely to mean a Crown Colony, and it is certain to mean the loss of the North-east, as well as the economic ruin of the State.'[2] The result was a striking vindication of the Government's policy. It won seven of the nine seats, Sinn Féin won the remaining two, and the only mandate received by the new National Party was a mandate to efface itself.

The local government elections which were held later in the same year provided another test. The Government party held aloof from them, its view being that party politics have no place in local affairs

[1] *The Round Table*, September 1925, p. 751.
[2] *Irish Independent*, 9 February 1925.

and that the most suitable men should be chosen for the work of county councils and similar bodies, irrespective of their political beliefs. But Mr. De Valera's party held a different view, and contested these elections on the issue of the Republic. The Republicans were everywhere overwhelmed by the Farmers' and Independent candidates, who obtained a substantial majority on all the local bodies.

Thus by the end of the year 1925, which roughly coincides with the end of the First Triennial Period of the Senate, a great change had come over the country. The foundations had been well laid, the superstructure was in process of erection, and the armed menace had been successfully resisted. The national finances had been managed with the strictest orthodoxy, and income-tax had been reduced by a shilling in the pound. The Government established pursuant to the Treaty, and based upon the will of the people, was firmly in the saddle; and, by a seeming miracle in so short a time, Ireland had become one of the most peaceful countries in Europe.

CHAPTER VIII

THE WORK OF THE SENATE, 1923-5

*Re-election of Chairman and Vice-Chairman—Co-option of Mr.
S. L. Brown, K.C.—Value of Senate's work of revision—Attitude to
measures for restoration of order—Continuance of unsatisfactory relations with the Dáil—New procedure for removal of deadlock by conference—Instances of its application—Money amendments in non-
Money Bills—Salaries of the District Justices—Decision on the
Senate's power of amendment—The First Triennial Election—Defects
of the system—Minor constitutional amendments—Conduct of the
Triennial Election—Analysis of the result—Work done in First Triennial period.*

Following the general election the Senate reassembled on the 19th
September 1923, pursuant to the Proclamation of the Governor-
General. As a result of the policy of the Executive not to initiate
Bills in the Upper House, there was little to be done for a considerable time, during which the Dáil was working at high pressure.
On the 12th December 1923 Lord Glenavy and Senator Douglas,
who had in the first instance been elected Chairman and Vice-Chairman for one year only, were unanimously re-elected for the remainder
of the Triennial Period. On the same day the Senate received an invaluable accession to its personnel by the co-option of Mr. Samuel
Lombard Brown, K.C., in the room of Senator Sir Horace Plunkett,
who had resigned.[1] The new Senator had been the leader of the Irish
Bar, and was one of the most brilliant lawyers of his time. Devoid of
any political bias or ambition, and utterly lacking in any forensic
insincerity, he proved a tower of strength to the Senate, to which he
devoted the whole of his time and of which, save for an interval of
two months, he remained a member until its abolition. It might be

[1] *Senate Debates*, ii, 169–86.

said of Samuel Brown, as was said of John Stuart Mill during his three years in the House of Commons, that he did only work that needed to be done and that nobody else seemed equally able or willing to do, and that he spoke only when he had something to say; and Mr. Speaker Denison's remark about Mill is true of him also, that his presence in Parliament elevated the tone of the debates.

In the previous chapter the legislation of the period was divided into three classes, covering the laying of the foundations of a national polity, the erection of a superstructure, and the suppression of internal disorder. The Senate's work of revision in all three classes was very notable. In the first class ten amendments were inserted in the Ministers and Secretaries Bill, seven in the Civil Service Regulation Bill, six in the Gárda Síochána Bill, and forty-four in the Courts of Justice Bill. The vast majority of these amendments were agreed to by the Dáil. Those made to the Courts of Justice Bill were particularly important; most of them were due to the expert criticism and skill in draftsmanship of Senator Brown, and his principal achievement in regard to this measure will be examined later in the chapter on Delegated Legislation (Chapter XXXI). But it seems worth while noticing that it was on the initiative of the Senate that a section was inserted providing that, so far as practicable, a District Justice assigned to an Irish-speaking area should have a competent knowledge of Irish. In Irish-speaking areas the poor are in a majority, and, as the District Court is the poor man's court, this was a sensible amendment.

In regard to Bills of the second class, the fact that the various proposals could be discussed in a non-party atmosphere by men having an intimate knowledge of the subject-matter had a wholly beneficial effect on the measures brought before the House. Mr. Hogan's three comprehensive Bills, dealing respectively with the marketing of eggs, the marketing of butter, and the improvement of livestock, had the benefit of criticism from such practical farmers as Senator Butler (the chairman of the Farmers' Union), Senator Sir John Keane, and Senator Counihan, with the result that a total of seventy-four amendments was inserted in them, all of which were accepted by the Dáil. To the Railways Bill twenty-eight amendments were made—many of them of far-reaching importance. But all these figures are outstripped by the case of the Local Government Bill, to which no less than 212 amendments were tabled by Senators. Of these, 109 were carried, all except six being agreed to by the other House. Statistics such as these show the industry of the Second Chamber in its work of revision, and

L

also the benefit to the country's laws which resulted from it; and they are a sufficient answer to the charge so frequently made by Mr. De Valera's followers in later years that the Senate was little more than a sleeping partner in the legislative scheme until Mr. Cosgrave went out of office.

The general attitude of the Senate towards Bills of the third class, namely, those dealing with the public safety, has already been described in Chapter VI and need not be repeated here in any detail. A few examples may, however, be given of the efforts made, even at such a time of national danger, to guard against a possible abuse of the exceptional powers which it was necessary to accord to the Executive and to the Army. The Public Safety (Powers of Arrest and Detention) Bill, 1924, gave certain powers of arrest to the military. With a view to ensuring, so far as possible, the supremacy of the civil arm, the Senate inserted an amendment providing that no dwelling-house should be entered for the purpose of effecting such an arrest unless, if it was practicable, the military were accompanied by a member of the Dublin Metropolitan Police or of the Civic Guard.[1] The Public Safety (Punishment of Offenders) Temporary Bill, 1924, contained a schedule of offences of varying degrees of gravity, such as arson, robbery under arms, trespass to land, and the selling of illicit spirits; and Section 1 of the Bill proposed that a person convicted of any of these offences by a court of summary jurisdiction might be sentenced to a term of imprisonment not exceeding twelve months. The accused might be indicted before a superior court, in which case he would, if convicted, suffer a severer penalty, but there was a possibility that the Executive might choose the court of first instance even for the graver offences, and so deprive the prisoner of his constitutional right to trial by a jury. This possibility was removed by an amendment inserted by the Senate, whereby such cases were removed from the jurisdiction of a court of summary jurisdiction, unless in the opinion of the court the offence was a minor one fit to be tried summarily.[2] Under the Treasonable Offences Bill, which made permanent provision for the public safety and which came before the Senate in the following year, it was made a felony to harbour, protect, or comfort persons committing certain offences against the State, and, in the Bill as it left the Dáil, the offence would be complete the moment that the fact of harbouring and so on was proved. The Senate made two amendments, under which the liability to conviction of a person so accused was removed if he satisfied the

---

[1] *Senate Debates*, ii, 552-7, 582, 583.   [2] Ibid., ii, 1170-5, 1187.

court that he did not know, and had no reason to believe, that the person so harboured, comforted, or protected was engaged in offences against the State. The same Bill made it an offence to incite members of the military and police forces to refuse to obey the orders of their superior officers. The Senate inserted the word 'lawful' before the word 'orders'.[1] All these amendments and a number of others made by the Senate to Bills of this class were agreed to by the Dáil.

The somewhat unsatisfactory relations between the Senate on the one hand and the Government and the Dáil on the other have already been noticed; and the two instances which follow are specially mentioned merely because the first of them resulted in a very desirable change in procedure and the second raised a point of some constitutional importance.

On the 20th December 1923 the Senate returned to the Dáil a Bill entitled the Local Government Electors Registration Bill, in which it had inserted an amendment of a contentious character but of which the purport does not otherwise concern us. In moving the rejection of the amendment in the Dáil on the following 11th January, the Minister in charge of the Bill (Mr. J. A. Burke) was severely critical of the Senate; the Chairman of the Dáil made it clear that if the amendment had originally been moved in that House he would have been obliged to rule it out of order, and the President of the Executive Council used words which seemed to imply that it was unfair for the Senate to insert a contentious amendment in a Bill which had been passed by the Dáil in a non-contentious atmosphere.[2] The Dáil did not disagree with the amendment immediately, but, on the 16th January, sent a message to the Senate requesting the setting up of a Joint Committee to consider procedure in regard to Senate amendments to Bills.[3] When the message came before the Senate a week later, the proposal was agreed to; but Lord Glenavy took occasion to recount the whole circumstances at great length and to vindicate the rights and privileges of the House of which he was Chairman.[4]

In its Report the Joint Committee expressed the opinion that, on the disagreement by either House to an amendment of the other House, the reason assigned for the disagreement should be one other than a reason involving a question of order, and it suggested that the Standing Orders of both Houses should be amended so as to allow of a conference being set up to discuss the points at issue in cases of

[1] *Senate Debates*, v, 112–14, 159–65, 238–40.
[2] *Dáil Debates*, vi, 131–43.   [3] Ibid., vi, 230, 231.
[4] *Senate Debates*, ii, 470–81.

disagreement.[1] The Report was adopted by both Houses, and the Standing Orders were amended accordingly.

This new procedure for the removal of deadlock through conference was far more likely to effect its object than the provision in Article 38 of the Constitution for the convening of a joint sitting, which was useless without the power of joint voting and which was in fact never used. The conference method had the advantage that the request for it could come from either House, whereas a joint sitting could be demanded only by the Senate.

No conference was requested over the Local Government Electors Registration Bill; the Dáil disagreed with the amendment and the Senate did not insist on it. The conference machinery was in fact operated in only three cases, and it will be convenient to set them forth here, even though two of them occurred outside the period covered by this chapter.

Intoxicating Liquor (General) Bill, 1924. Two of the Senate amendments prohibited the sale of alcoholic drink on Saint Patrick's Day (which is a public holiday in Ireland); a third provided that, in any licensed premises where another business was carried on, the place where drink was sold should be structurally separated from the rest of the premises. The Dáil disagreed with these three amendments and requested a conference. The conference recommended the acceptance of the first two (i.e. that Saint Patrick's Day should be 'dry') and the non-acceptance of the third. Both Houses agreed.

Shop Hours (Drapery Trades, Dublin and Districts) Bill, 1926. The closing hour for drapers' shops was fixed in the Bill at 9 p.m. The Senate altered the time to 7.30 p.m., and, the Dáil having disagreed, requested a conference. The conference recommended 8.30 p.m. as a compromise, and this was accepted by both Houses.

Game Preservation Bill, 1929. One of the Senate amendments to this Bill consisted of a section empowering the Minister for Justice to establish a consultative council to assist him in framing regulations thereunder, and a sub-section of this section provided that payment out of public funds might be made to the members of such council in respect of travelling expenses and subsistence allowance. On the 12th February 1930 the Minister for Justice proposed the agreement of the Dáil to the whole new section, but the Chairman of the Dáil intervened with a query as to whether the Minister had adverted to the sub-section referred to. This intervention could only mean that, in the opinion of the Chairman of the Dáil, the Senate had not the

---

[1] *Reports of Committees*, vol. i, p. 533.

power to insert an amendment involving the appropriation, actual or potential, of public money. As such it was a clear violation of the spirit of the agreement embodied in the Joint Committee's Report of 1924, to which reference has already been made and of which the Chairman of the Dáil had been a signatory; for it was stated in that Report that, on the disagreement by either House to an amendment of the other House, the reason assigned for the disagreement should be one other than a reason involving a question of order. In the circumstances the Minister for Justice asked to have the matter postponed.[1] On the 20th February, the Minister proposed the acceptance of the section minus this particular sub-section, and the only reason he gave was that it was a money clause. The proposal was accepted by the Dáil.[2]

In the resultant message to the Senate no reason was assigned for the rejection of the sub-section; but in the debate on the message the Minister informed the House that 'that was possibly one of the underlying reasons—that it was a money clause'. It was, in fact, the only reason that had been given. The Senate insisted on the amendment and requested a conference.[3] The conference reported that in its opinion the payment of travelling expenses and subsistence allowances to members of the Consultative Council could be effected under another section of the Bill, and that, in these circumstances, the constitutional question did not arise. Accordingly, the Senate did not insist on the sub-section.[4]

The constitutional question had, in fact, been decided years earlier; and this brings us to the second point of disagreement between the Senate and the Government which occurred during the period covered by this chapter and with which it is proposed to deal here. Under the Constitution the Senate's power of amending Bills was the same as that of the Dáil, except in regard to Bills certified by the Chairman of the Dáil to be Money Bills. In the case of any Bill which would, if passed, entail the appropriation of money, regard had to be had to Article 37 of the Constitution, which read as follows: 'Money shall not be appropriated by vote, resolution or law, unless the purpose of the appropriation has in the same session been recommended by a message from the Representative of the Crown acting on the advice of the Executive Council.'

This provision is, of course, more or less common form in all the Constitutions of the Dominions. What happened in practice was that

[1] *Dáil Debates*, xxxiii, 34, 35. [2] Ibid., xxxiii, 675–7.
[3] *Senate Debates*, xiii, 571–86. [4] Ibid., xiii, 1162, 1163.

a motion, in the terms of the message from the Representative of the Crown, was tabled in the Dáil in the case of every such Bill and passed before the Committee Stage of the Bill was taken. Under the Standing Orders of the Dáil, any such motion, or any amendment thereto proposing to increase the amount mentioned therein, could be moved only by a member of the Executive Council. Further, any amendment to the Bill itself which, if passed, would increase or extend the scope of the appropriation mentioned in the message could be moved only by a member of the Executive.

These restrictions on the rights of members of the other House were purely domestic and self-imposed. Though they did not derive from the Constitution, they were perfectly proper. The Executive Council was responsible to the Dáil, and the Standing Orders of that House were a matter for itself. The Senate was in different case. The Executive Council was not responsible to it, and therefore any legislative action carried by the Senate against the Government involved no question of confidence. Moreover, there was nothing in the Constitution which restricted the right of the Senate as to the character or class of amendments which it might insert in non-Money Bills. Yet on more than one occasion attempts had been made by the Government to place Senators on the same footing as private members of the Dáil.

The matter came to an issue in 1924, in connection with an amendment inserted by the Senate in the Courts of Justice Bill. This Bill recast the whole judicial system of the country. It set up a Supreme Court, a High Court, Circuit Courts (which corresponded to the old County Courts, but with an enlarged area and an enlarged jurisdiction), and District Courts, which replaced the old Petty Sessions Courts and were also given an enlarged jurisdiction. The District Courts were to be presided over by paid District Justices, sitting alone. These District Justices had to be practising barristers or solicitors of six years' standing, and they had, of course, to give their whole time to their duties. The Bill, as passed by the Dáil, drew a distinction between the method of payment of the judges and that of the District Justices. The salaries of the judges were to be a charge on the Central Fund (which is the same as the Consolidated Fund in England), and this meant that the judges would be immune from parliamentary criticism; but the salaries of the District Justices were to be provided annually by Parliament, by means of the ordinary Appropriation Act. This would have rendered them liable individually to parliamentary criticism. The Senate took the view, which seems unquestionably correct, that the District Justices should be just as independent in the exercise of their functions as the judges of the Superior Courts, and, on the motion of Senator O'Farrell, it passed an amendment the effect of which was to place the salaries of these Justices on the Central Fund. The Attorney-General of the day (afterwards Chief Justice Kennedy) took exception to the amendment on the ground that it was one which it was not within the competence of the Senate to insert.[1] The constitutional question involved was referred to a Committee of the Senate, presided over by Lord Glenavy, and the point which fell to be decided was, Could the Senate amend an appropriation clause in a Bill other than a Money Bill? After reviewing the whole circumstances, the Committee concluded as follows:

'The answer is to be found in the Constitution, which by Article 38 provides that every Bill initiated and passed by the Dáil may, unless it be a Money Bill, be amended in the Senate, and the Dáil shall consider any such amendment. The sole and only restriction to be found in the Constitution upon this unlimited right on the part of the Senate to amend any Bill other than a Money Bill is in the case of an amendment which involves the appropriation of any part of the revenues of the Free State, as no such amendment can be made unless and until the purpose of such appropriation has been recommended by a message from the Governor-General under Article 37, a condition precedent which is equally binding upon both Houses of the Oireachtas. As this condition was admittedly fulfilled by the message in the case of the particular amendment which has given rise to this question, we have no hesitation in answering it in the affirmative.'[2]

The Report was formally adopted by the Senate, after Lord Glenavy had explained its implications (20th March 1924).[3] The amendment was insisted on, and the Dáil agreed to it with a slight modification as to the point of time when it would commence to operate.[4] An important principle affecting the constitutional rights of the Second Chamber had thus been vindicated once and for all.

By the summer of 1925 preparation had to be made for the first Triennial Election to the Senate. It will be recalled that, under the Constitution, fifteen original members were due to retire, and added to their number were four others who had been co-opted to fill casual

---

[1] *Senate Debates*, ii, 792–802, 918–24.
[2] *Reports of Committees*, vol. i, p. 357.   [3] *Senate Debates*, ii, 1138–46.
[4] *Dáil Debates*, vi, 2784–8 and 2812–17.

vacancies. These nineteen seats were to be filled by an electorate consisting of all citizens of the Irish Free State, duly qualified, who had
reached the age of thirty years, voting according to the principles of
proportional representation on a panel composed of three times as
many qualified persons as there were members to be elected, of
whom two-thirds were to be nominated by the Dáil and one-third by
the Senate: plus such former Senators as desired to be included in
the panel. Thus, in the circumstances then existing, the Senate had
to select nineteen candidates and the Dáil thirty-eight candidates,
and to these fifty-seven names had to be added those of the nineteen
retiring Senators, all of whom intimated their desire to offer themselves for re-election. The result was a ballot paper several feet long,
containing seventy-six names arranged in alphabetical order, from
which nineteen new Senators had to be elected.

We can see now that this was ridiculous. The original proposal
that the electorate should be the whole country was coupled with a
provision for a Senate of forty members.[1] As a result of the Agreement with the Southern Unionists, the number had been increased
to sixty, but the system of election was retained, without regard to
the changed conditions. Obviously, the election of ten Senators from
a panel of twenty was a not unreasonable proposal, and it was at any
rate very different from the election of nineteen from a panel of
seventy-six. The difficulty brought about by the increased numbers
had been clearly foreseen by Deputy Darrell Figgis, who had been
Acting Chairman of the Constitution Committee. He spoke at some
length on the subject while the Constitution Bill was being considered by the Dáil (4th October 1922) and in the course of his speech
he said: 'Every three years all the voters in Ireland will receive, not
a convenient list of candidates, which they can study at a glance, and
of whom they may know something, but they will receive something
like a small book of candidates' names against whom they will have
to vote. It has been the experience in Proportional Representation
that when you get much beyond the tenth or eleventh candidate you
are increasing the difficulties very considerably.'[2] Unfortunately, no
attention was paid to these criticisms, and the Senate election scheme
was unaltered.

Before the first Triennial Election could be held it was necessary
to remedy certain defects, and this was done by the Constitution
(Amendment No. 1) Act, 1925, which became law on the 11th July
1925. First, it was necessary to define the duration of the Triennial

[1] *Dáil Debates*, i, 1154.   [2] Ibid., i, 1155.

CONSTITUTIONAL AMENDMENTS 153

Periods. The Senate had first met on the 11th December 1922, but the Constitution had come into operation five days earlier. The Act provided that the periods should be reckoned from the 6th December 1922, and from the appropriate triennial anniversary of that day (Article 31A). Second, Article 32A provided that a Triennial Election might be held at any time not earlier than three months before nor later than three months after the conclusion of a Triennial Period; and it made provision for the contingency of a casual vacancy occurring after the electoral panel had been formed. Third, Article 34 was amended to meet an unforeseen difficulty. As the Article stood, the sixteenth member elected was to fill the casual vacancy first created in order of time, and so on. This would have meant that No. 16 would fill Senator MacPartlin's vacancy and so sit for six years, while Nos. 17, 18, and 19 would fill those of Senators Sir Horace Plunkett, Sir Hutcheson Poë, and Dr. Sigerson and so sit for nine years. The Article was amended so as to provide that the sixteenth member should be deemed to have filled the vacancy created by the death or resignation of the Senator the unexpired period of whose term of office was greatest at the time of the election, and so on.

This Act was the first of a series of non-controversial Acts amending either the Constitution or the electoral laws in relation to the Senate. In the circumstances, it might have been expected that these measures would have been introduced first in the Senate by the Government; but they were all initiated in the Dáil.

The Rules for the selection by the Senate and the Dáil of their respective portions of the panel were duly approved by each House.[1] They were similar to each other, and provided for personal voting by secret ballot, within each Chamber, on principles of Proportional Representation.

The selection of the Senate portion of the panel took place on the 1st July 1925. There were twenty-nine candidates for the nineteen places. Voting papers were distributed to forty-seven Senators (out of a possible sixty), the same number of valid votes was returned, and the names of the successful candidates will be found recorded in the Senate's *Journal of Proceedings* for that day.[2] The result can only be described as a very great disappointment. It is true that there were a few distinguished names among the successful, but the list as a whole could not compare with the list of the ten rejected. These were:[3]

[1] *Senate Debates*, v, 611–56; *Dáil Debates*, xii, 1313–46.
[2] *Journal*, 1925, p. 218.   [3] *Irish Independent*, 2 July 1925.

David Barry   John McCann
L. Grattan Esmonde   The McGillycuddy of the Reeks
Lady Gregory   Dr. Lombard Murphy
John J. Horgan   Sir J. H. Scott
Hugh A. Law   J. J. Stafford

Nobody who is acquainted with the public life of Ireland can doubt that all of these persons had either done useful public service or represented important aspects of the nation's life, and so had the qualification laid down for Senators. The same could by no means be said of all the successful candidates. The rejection of Lady Gregory, who was world famous as the founder of the Abbey Theatre, was the most astonishing of all. Of the nineteen retiring Senators, eighteen were present and voted; and it is perhaps not cynical to assume that some of them might not be over-anxious that candidates should be returned who would prove formidable rivals at the election. The result was the subject of caustic comment by Senator Dr. Gogarty, who expressed the fear that 'the Senate might become a refuge and an asylum for pensioners'.[1]

The Dáil made its selection on the 8th July 1925. For the thirty-eight places on the panel there were fifty-seven candidates. While the voting was in progress the Leader of the Opposition (Deputy Johnson) entered a vigorous protest against the 'candidates on whose behalf there has been a great deal of canvassing, telegraph-sending, letter-writing and personal importuning'.[2] We may be sure that, in some cases, these activities were motived by the desire to obtain an assured income of £360 a year for twelve years; and it is a fact of some significance in this connection that among the fifty-seven candidates there were eight former members of the Dáil, three of whom had been rejected by the electors.[3] The number of Deputies who voted was 101 and there were 100 valid votes, one ballot paper being rejected as invalid. The list of the thirty-eight successful candidates is printed in the Dáil Journal of the day.[4] Though it is not specially distinguished, it is on the whole superior to the Senate list. The voting was on strict party lines, and the thirty-eight candidates were made up as follows: Government party, 21; Independents, 9; Farmers' Party, 5; and Labour Party, 3.

The polling day was Thursday, 17th September. The electorate numbered approximately 1,300,000, and they were expected to make

[1] Senate Debates, v, 865, 866.   [2] Dáil Debates, xii, 2161.
[3] Irish Independent, 9 July 1925.
[4] Journal, 1925, p. 453; Dáil Debates, xii, 2163.

an intelligent choice of nineteen persons from a list containing seventy-six names, most of which they had never seen or heard of before. The Republicans, of course, boycotted the election, and the day was wet in most parts of the country. As might have been expected, the result was a fiasco. Only about 25 per cent of the electors troubled to record their votes, except in County Monaghan, where a poll of 80 per cent brought the Chairman of the County Council, Mr. Thomas Toal, into second place. The quota was only 15,286, but more than half the successful candidates failed to obtain it and were elected without a quota. The counting of the votes took sixteen days, and the result was as follows:

1. Sir William B. Hickie
2. Thomas Toal
*3. John T. O'Farrell
*4. William Cummins
5. Cornelius Kennedy
6. Michael F. O'Hanlon
7. James Dillon
*8. Thomas Foran
9. Sir Edward Bellingham
*10. Dr. Henry L. Barniville
11. Michael Fanning
*12. James J. Parkinson
13. Stephen O'Mara
*14. Thomas Linehan
15. Joseph O'Connor
16. Sir Edward Coey Bigger
17. Francis McGuinness
*18. T. W. Westropp Bennett
*19. John J. Counihan

Of the nineteen outgoing senators, eight were re-elected, including all three members of the Labour Party. Dr. Douglas Hyde, who had been co-opted to the Senate in the previous February, was not far from the bottom of the list with a miserable 1,721 first preferences, and Mr. S. L. Brown did little better with 2,787. It was too much to expect that Mr. Brown's qualities would be appreciated by the electorate at large; but Dr. Hyde was in different case. Famous as the protagonist of the Irish language, he was the father of the intellectual renaissance in Ireland, and, though he was never a politician, his work and influence were such that it is probably not too much to say that but for him there would have been no Treaty and no Irish Free State. Recognition of his work came later, however, when he was elected unopposed as the first President under the Constitution of 1937. Attempts have been made to explain Dr. Hyde's defeat on grounds other than the indifference of the people to the Irish language, but these ignore, or are unaware of, the fact that there were three other candidates who are justly celebrated for their work in this field (Professors Henry and O'Brien of Galway and Mr. R. A. Foley of

* Outgoing Senator.

Dublin) and that all three were near the bottom of the poll. The lamentable truth is that, whatever the politicians may say or think, the vast majority of the people of Ireland care little or nothing about Irish.

Of the eleven new Senators, all except two were from the Dáil portion of the panel. It was generally understood that the return of Major-General Sir William Hickie and of Brigadier-General Sir Edward Bellingham was due to the votes of ex-service men of the British Army, and that Messrs. Kennedy and Fanning owed their success to the licensed trade. This, coupled with the success of all three Labour candidates, suggests that such a system of election favours the return of those who have the backing of organized groups. The election had at any rate one good result. Not a single candidate of the 'professional politician' type was successful, and none of the new Senators could be described as an extreme party man.[1]

The election had taken place in the middle of the summer recess, and the Senate met on only one occasion before the end of the First Triennial Period. The members could look back with justifiable pride on a record of good work well done. They had considered about 130 Bills, of which more than one-third had been amended. The number of amendments totalled over 500, all but about a dozen being accepted by the Dáil. If the chief function of the Second Chamber was to be in the field of revision, it had made an excellent beginning.

---

[1] For a discussion of the election from the expert point of view, see *Representation*, No. 43 (December 1925), and the *American Political Science Review* (February 1926), vol. xx, pp. 117–20.

CHAPTER IX

THE SENATE CASKET

Alice Stopford Green—Nature and purpose of her gift—The remarkable message which accompanied it—Acceptance by the Senate—Strict fulfilment of the conditions prescribed—Ultimate destination of the Casket and its contents.

On the 26th November 1924 Senator Mrs. Alice Stopford Green, the distinguished historian, who was the senior elected member of the Senate and who was then approaching seventy years of age, presented to the Senate an exquisitely wrought casket of metalwork, which had been executed to her order by Miss Mia Cranwill, a noted Irish artist in that medium. As Mrs. Green was ill at the time, the communication in which she offered the gift was read to the House on her behalf by Senator Brown.

'Very early after my generous and unexpected election I formed the desire to offer to the Seanad some effective service, as it was plain that my working days were slipping away.

'When the plan of the casket came into my heart I hoped to be able to present it before our summer separation.

'But, as you will see, the work was long and difficult, and could by no means have been finished until now.

'My request to the Seanad is that they will find it possible to accept the offering I lay before them.

'My purpose was that the shrine should contain a vellum roll, on which every member of the first Irish Seanad elected up to this date should sign his name. And that the shrine should be placed on the table at the opening of every meeting of the Seanad—now and in the future—to be a perpetual memorial of the foundation of this body, and a witness in later times of its increasing service to the country.

'If the Senators do me the honour of accepting this gift, with these

157

conditions, I will then proceed to do what could not be done without their consent—to inscribe on the shrine my name as donor, and that of the artist, and to place in it the vellum roll.'[1]

The speech which Mrs. Green had intended to deliver on the occasion of the presentation was also read, in the form of a message to the Senate. There have been many Irish patriots who were also masters of the English tongue; but the lofty ideals for Ireland expressed in this message, and the passionate love of country which inspired them, can seldom have found expression in language at once so moving and so beautiful. As it is not fitting that this message should lie buried in the limbo of forgotten parliamentary records, it shall be reproduced here in full.

'I ask leave to send a few words as to the casket which I offer to the Seanad.

'Senators will agree that we should place no emblem before us in this Assembly that is not of Ireland, in spirit and in workmanship, carrying in it the faith both of the Old Irish world and of the New. I have insisted, therefore, that the form of the casket should go back in direct descent to the "shrines" designed by the Irish over a thousand years ago. The artist has magnificently proved the power of that spiritual inheritance which has been bequeathed to us from an Old Ireland; and has shown that a really living art has no need to copy in slavish routine, and can to-day be as free and original and distinguished as in the times of ancient renown, supposed to have been lost.

'Thus the shrine in its intense vitality carries to us its own message. That if we want to revive here an Irish nation we must dig our roots deep into its soil, and be nourished by that ancient earth. In Old Ireland, a land of many peoples, it was not privileges of race that united Irishmen in one country and under one law. It was a common loyalty to the land that bore them. "This then is my foster-mother, the island in which ye are, even Ireland. Moreover, it is the mast and the produce, the flower and the food of this island that have sustained me from the Deluge until to-day." This feeling was the refrain of Irish nationality, the loyalty of a people made one by their sonship to the land that bore them, an early and passionate conception of nationality. A sudden and brief outburst by an Irish poet of the old time has no parallel in European mediaeval history—"The counsels of God concerning virgin Eriú are greater than can be told."

[1] *Journal of Proceedings*, 1924, p. 297.

'From the beginning, Ireland has been rich in her hospitality to men of good-will coming within her borders. And at all times there have been incomers who have honourably responded to that generosity, and have become faithful members of her people. She has had her reward among the strangers who under her wide skies have felt the wonder of the land, and the quality of its people, and have entered into her commonwealth.

'Through the long record of wars and assaults, in every generation in turn, men who came as warriors, even the roughest of them, remained as men of Ireland. They took their share in defence of their new home, and endured, if need were, in evil times outrage, ruin and death in the cause of Irish freedom and independence. No real history of Ireland has yet been written. When the true story is finally worked out—one not wholly occupied with the many and insatiable plunderers—it will give us a noble and reconciling vision of Irish nationality. Silence and neglect will no longer hide the fame of honourable men. We shall learn the ties which did in fact ever bind the dwellers in Ireland together. Whether we are of an ancient Irish descent, or of later Irish birth, we are united in one people, and we are bound by one lofty obligation to complete the building of our common nation. We have lived under the breadth of her skies, we have been fed by the fatness of her fields, and nourished by the civilization of her dead. Our people lie in her earth, and we ourselves must in that earth await our doom. We have shared our country's sorrows, and we expect her joys. "The mother that has nursed us is she, and when you have looked on her she is not unlovely." To Ireland we have given our faith. In Ireland is our hope.'[1]

By formal resolution, the Senate gratefully accepted the gift of the Casket on the conditions named by the donor; and it further resolved that, in addition to the vellum roll containing the names of the members, the message of Alice Stopford Green which is printed above should also be inscribed on vellum and enclosed within the Casket.[2] The engrossment was executed, with illuminated capitals, by George Atkinson, esq., R.H.A., the head of the Dublin Metropolitan School of Art; and an ornamental silver band of Irish design was made by the same school, wherewith to enclose the vellums.

Alice Stopford Green died on the 28th May 1929, and so did not live to see the end of the Senate on which she had set such high hopes.

---

[1] *Journal of Proceedings*, 1924, pp. 298, 299.
[2] *Senate Debates*, iii, 1140–5.

The conditions attached to the gift were strictly fulfilled. From the date of presentation until the final sitting of the House on the 19th May 1936 the Casket was placed on the Chairman's desk in the Chamber immediately prior to every meeting; and one of the last formal acts of the Senate before its abolition was to offer the Casket and its contents to the Council of the Royal Irish Academy as a gift for preservation.

CHAPTER X

THE DIVORCE CONTROVERSY

The law prior to the establishment of the Irish Free State—Limited jurisdiction of the Irish Courts—Contrast with English law—Procedure for divorce by promotion of Private Bill—The changed position caused by the Treaty and Constitution—Joint Standing Orders for Private Bills—The procedure summarized—Lodgement of Divorce Bills—Absence of special provision in Standing Orders and reasons therefor—Report of Joint Committee—An unsatisfactory position—Mr. Cosgrave's motion in the Dáil—Lord Glenavy's adverse ruling in the Senate—Senator Douglas's motion for removal of deadlock—Senator W. B. Yeats's unfortunate speech—Senator Douglas's position explained—The Dáil rejects the Senate's proposal—Mr. Cosgrave's reasons—The Senate resolution rescinded—The problem unsolved—Misrepresentation of the Senate's attitude—Effect on the First Triennial Election.

The spirit of close co-operation between men of different religious and political beliefs which had hitherto characterized the proceedings of the Senate received a severe, though temporary, set-back by the divorce controversy which broke out in 1925. In view of its intrinsic importance, and of the effect which its repercussions in the country had on the Triennial Election held in September of that year, it is as well that the facts should be set out here.

Before the establishment of the Irish Free State, jurisdiction in regard to matrimonial causes and matters was exercised, in the case of persons domiciled in Ireland, under the Matrimonial Causes Marriage Law (Ireland) Amendment Act, 1870, by the King's Bench Division of the High Court of Justice, sitting in Dublin: such jurisdiction having been transferred thereto from the former Court for Matrimonial Causes and Matters by the joint operation of the Judicature

(Ireland) Acts, 1877 and 1897. The jurisdiction was the same as that of the ancient jurisdiction of the Ecclesiastical Courts prior to 1871, i.e. it was limited to (*a*) the granting of decrees for divorce *a mensa et thoro* on the statutory grounds of adultery, cruelty, and unnatural practices, and (*b*) the granting of declarations of nullity of marriage for causes existing at the date of the marriage, e.g. impotence. A divorce *a mensa et thoro* is, in effect, a judicial separation. The relationship of husband and wife ceases, from the point of view of legal rights and obligations, to exist; but the parties are not free to remarry. The power to grant a full divorce *a vinculo matrimonii*, which severs the marriage bond for all purposes and leaves the parties free to remarry, never resided in the Irish courts.

The position in Ireland was thus in sharp contrast to that in England, where, under the Matrimonial Causes Act, 1857, the Probate and Matrimonial Division of the High Court of Justice has power to grant decrees of divorce *a vinculo matrimonii* in cases in which the husband is domiciled in England or Wales. The English court has the further powers, not possessed by the Irish matrimonial court, to vary a settlement made on the marriage, to deal with the custody of the children of the marriage, and to give damages against a co-respondent.

A person of Irish domicile desirous of obtaining a divorce *a vinculo matrimonii* had to invoke the sovereign power of Parliament and to proceed by way of *ad hoc* legislation. Prior to the Union in 1800 a number of such Bills were passed by the Irish Parliament (Grattan's Parliament). Thereafter, the jurisdiction of the Irish Parliament was transferred to the Imperial Parliament at Westminster. In the years immediately before the Treaty what occurred in actual practice was that a petitioner obtained his or her decree of divorce *a mensa et thoro* from the Court of King's Bench in Dublin, and then promoted a Private Bill for divorce *a vinculo matrimonii* in the Imperial Parliament. Special Standing Orders were framed to deal with such Bills, the record of the proceedings in the King's Bench and the judgement of the court had to be produced, and the most stringent precautions were taken against collusion or fraud.

As a result of the Treaty and the Constitution, the sovereign power in this, as in every other legislative matter, passed from the Imperial Parliament to the Parliament in Dublin, so far as concerned that part of Ireland comprised in the area of the Irish Free State.

In November 1923 Standing Orders for Private Bills in general were jointly adopted by the Senate and the Dáil. These Standing Orders were based on those of the British House of Commons, but as much as possible of the procedure governing the passage of such Bills through the two Houses was made joint, so as to save expense to the promoters. It is desirable to present this procedure in outline, as it is necessary to a proper understanding of the divorce controversy.

In accordance with the Standing Orders, the Vice-Chairman of the Senate had charge of Private Bills in his House, and the Deputy Chairman of the Dáil had charge of them in the Dáil; that is to say, they moved the requisite motions in their respective Houses, but they moved them *pro forma*, and had no concern with the merits or otherwise of a particular Bill. Any person, or group of persons, desiring to introduce a Private Bill had to lodge an application in the Private Bill Office in conformity with prescribed conditions. After the expiry of one month the Examiner of Private Bills (a permanent official) publicly examined the Bill, and reported to both Houses whether or not the Bill had complied with the Standing Orders. There was an appeal from his decision to a Joint Committee on Standing Orders, which consisted of three members from each House and a chairman appointed jointly by the Chairman of the Senate and the Chairman of the Dáil. The Vice-Chairman of the Senate for the time being was always appointed to this position.

In normal cases, i.e. those in which the Examiner reported that the Standing Orders had been complied with and no appeal from his decision had been received, the Bill was *deemed to have been read a first time in the Senate*. After a prescribed interval, it received a Second Reading in the Senate, and thereupon stood referred to a Joint Committee of both Houses, appointed *ad hoc*. After the Joint Committee had considered the Bill, it was returned, with or without amendment, to the Senate, where the Fourth and Fifth Stages took place (these correspond to the Report Stage and Third Reading in England). It then came before the Dáil for its Fourth and Fifth Stages, the previous stages being deemed to have been passed. On the conclusion of the Fifth Stage in the Dáil, the Bill was sent to the Governor-General for the signification of the Royal Assent.

It should be pointed out that each House had power to reject a Bill at any stage after the First Stage, or to take such other action as would bring the proceedings in regard to it to an end. For example, in 1927 the Dáil declined to set up a Joint Committee to consider the Merrion Square (Dublin) Bill, the purpose of which was to erect a War Memorial in one of the principal Dublin squares; and the Bill had to be withdrawn by the promoters.[1] In 1931 the Senate rejected two Private Bills on Second Reading; one for the registration of hairdressers[2] and the other for the conferring of Irish Free State citizenship on a Czechoslovak national.[3]

We now come to the question of Private Bills for Divorce. Before the end of February 1924, i.e. very shortly after the establishment of the Private Bill Office, no less than three such Bills were lodged with the Examiner. No special provision had been made in the Standing Orders for dealing with Bills of this kind. The reason for the omission is obvious. The population of the Irish Free State is overwhelmingly Catholic; and the doctrine of the Catholic Church regarding the indissolubility of marriage is well known. It is hardly too much to say that every Irish Catholic regards the subject of divorce with abhorrence. In the circumstances, the only Standing Order which could apply to the three Bills in question was No. 1, which read as follows: 'Every Bill promoted for the particular interest or benefit of any person, or that interferes with the private property of any person, otherwise than in the interests of the public generally and as a measure of public policy, shall be treated as a Private Bill.' The Examiner of Private Bills informed the Joint Committee on Standing Orders (as stated in its subsequent Report) that this Standing Order was the only one applicable, and that if no further Standing Orders were prepared dealing with Bills of this character he would have no option but to report that the Standing Orders had been complied with, and the three Bills would then be deemed to be read a first time.

The personnel of the Committee was: Senator Douglas (chairman), Senators Barrington, S. L. Brown, K.C., and Farren, Deputies Bryan Cooper, Professor Magennis, and O Máille. In the circumstances, the Committee considered the position and presented a Report to both Houses, dated the 11th July 1924, in which the whole problem was posed but no solution was propounded.[4] They stated that 'whilst the Committee do not desire to prejudge the decision to be reached by the Oireachtas, they consider it proper to point out that the present position is unsatisfactory from every point of view, as under Standing Order No. 1 unrestricted power is given to introduce Divorce Bills into the Oireachtas even in cases where a judgment of a court of law has not been previously obtained'.

The question was shelved for a considerable time until at length,

---

[1] *Dáil Debates*, xix, 395–438.   [2] *Senate Debates*, xiv, 693–728.
[3] Ibid., xiv, 2058, 2059.   [4] *Reports of Committees*, vol. i, p. 637.

on the 11th February 1925, Mr. Cosgrave proposed the following motion in the Dail:

'That the Joint Committee on Standing Orders relative to Private Business be requested to submit additional Standing Orders regulating the procedure to be adopted in connection with Private Bills relating to Matrimonial matters other than Bills of Divorce *a vinculo matrimonii*, and to propose such alterations in the Standing Orders as will prevent the introduction of Bills of Divorce *a vinculo matrimonii*; and that a Message be sent to the Senate requesting its concurrence in this Resolution.'

The motion was seconded by Kevin O'Higgins, the Vice-President, and the debate upon it, which was short, was throughout on a high level and of a temperate character. The Catholic point of view was clearly expounded by the proposer and seconder, and the spokesmen of the small Protestant minority in the Dáil, while expressing their personal dislike of divorce, stated their objections to the motion on the ground of principle. The motion was carried without a division, and the appropriate message was sent to the Senate.[1]

The message came before the Senate on the 5th March following, when the Chairman (Lord Glenavy) ruled that no parallel motion could be moved in that House, on the ground that any such motion would be out of order, as being a violation of the Constitution and of the Standing Orders. He gave the reasons for his ruling at considerable length, but, put shortly, they were as follows. The right of a citizen to petition Parliament by way of a Private Bill (not, of course, the right to have such a Bill passed) was an existing *legal* right, at Common Law. As such, it came within the ambit of Article 73 of the Constitution, which provides that the laws in force at the date on which the Constitution came into operation shall continue to be of full force and effect until repealed or amended by *enactment* of the Oireachtas. Hence the extinction of an existing legal right could be achieved only by statute, not by resolution. Article 65 enabled the High Court to decide upon the validity of any *law* having regard to the provisions of the Constitution, but this power did not extend to the constitutionality or otherwise of a *resolution*. Lastly, the Senate Standing Orders specified the matters which might be dealt with by resolution, but expressly provided that 'the matters which shall be dealt with by Bills shall include all legislation'.[2]

There can be no doubt that Lord Glenavy's ruling was correct, and the manner of its delivery was certainly unexceptionable, since he

[1] *Dáil Debates*, x, 155–82.   [2] *Senate Debates*, iv, 929–45.

dealt purely with the general principles of law involved, and stated expressly that he had no interest in the question of facilities for divorce. In the nature of things, however, his action was bound to result in considerable ill feeling against the Senate, both in the Dáil and in the country. The reasons for his ruling were not such as could be readily apprehended by the non-legal mind. It was, in fact, called in question in a debate in the Senate on the 30th April 1925, in which some Senators obviously found it difficult to distinguish the general legal principle involved from its special application to the subject of divorce.[1] If the motion was out of order in the Senate, it was equally so in the Dáil, and so there was an implied (but unavoidable) censure on the Government for proposing it and on the Chairman of the Dáil for permitting it to be moved. Non-Catholics, though always a minority in the Senate, were much more numerous than they were in the other House, and there was the equally irrelevant (and entirely fortuitous) circumstance that the Chairman of the Senate was himself a Protestant. In view of these facts, it is perhaps not surprising that his ruling was misunderstood and that the Senate became the object of misrepresentation.

With the object of resolving the deadlock caused by the ruling, Senator Douglas (who, it will be remembered, was chairman of the Joint Committee on Private Business) tabled the following motion in the Senate:

'That in the opinion of the Senate the object desired by the Dáil in its Message of the 12th February would be best achieved by the adoption by both Houses of the Oireachtas of the following resolution: "That the Joint Committee on Standing Orders relative to Private Business be requested to submit additional Standing Orders regulating the procedure to be adopted in connection with Private Bills relating to matrimonial matters, including a Standing Order or Orders which will prevent Bills of Divorce *a vinculo matrimonii* from being deemed to have been introduced under Standing Order 55 and which will provide that such Bills must be read a first time in each House before they are further proceeded with in the Senate."

'That a Message be sent to the Dáil requesting its concurrence in this Resolution in place of that proposed in its Message of the 12th February.'

This motion was moved by Senator Douglas on the 11th June 1925. He explained the reasons for it in a speech which, one would have thought, was hardly capable of being misunderstood. The purport of

[1] *Senate Debates*, v, 38–72.

the motion, was, of course, obvious. Short of actual legislation prohibiting divorce (which, apparently, the Government was unwilling
to contemplate), the method proposed was the only one which, in
view of Lord Glenavy's ruling, was capable of achieving the result
desired by the Government, the Dáil, and the country. There would
no longer be any question of a Divorce Bill being 'deemed' to have
been read a first time in the Senate. Before any such Bill could be
said to be properly started on its legislative career, it would have to
receive the approval of both Houses by means of a First Reading in
each House. This was a plain impossibility, since there was a Catholic
majority in the Senate and an overwhelming Catholic majority in the
Dáil. In the circumstances, no individual would be likely to waste
time and money in promoting such a Bill.

The course which the debate took was unfortunate. The two items
before the House were the Report of the Joint Committee and
Senator Douglas's motion. As the former was purely expository and
did noi ask the House to take any specific action, any debate on it
was out of order; and, in accordance with the rules of parliamentary
procedure, the terms of the motion did not permit of a general discussion on the question of divorce or no divorce. Yet the Chairman
took the Report first and allowed the late Senator W. B. Yeats, the
distinguished poet, to open a debate on it. His speech was nothing
less than an envenomed attack on the religion of the majority of his
fellow countrymen. He attacked the Catholic Church in general, and
in Ireland in particular. He joined issue, on the subject of divorce,
with Cardinal O'Donnell, perhaps the most statesmanlike ecclesiastic
Ireland had produced for generations. He lashed with invective the
Protestant Bishop of Meath, who a short time previously had made
a striking pronouncement against divorce. He ridiculed the authen-
ticity of the Gospels. He dilated on the moral delinquencies, real or
alleged, of Nelson, O'Connell, and Parnell, whose statues adorn
Dublin's principal street. ('Do you not think we might leave the dead
alone?' asked Lord Glenavy. 'I would hate to leave the dead alone,'
retorted Senator Yeats.) And he concluded by bombastic references
to the superiority of the ascendancy class.

This extraordinary speech was happily unique in the history of the
Senate. Its author was not provoked into unwisdom by the utterances
of previous speakers, for he opened the debate. Nor was he carried
away by the self-engendered heat of the moment, since his speech was
delivered from a manuscript which had obviously been carefully prepared. It has been necessary to refer to it because it poisoned the

atmosphere that surrounded the question of divorce, and to some extent explains, though it does not excuse, the ridiculous charges subsequently made in the country against Senator Douglas and those Senators, Catholic and non-Catholic, who voted for his motion.

Lord Glenavy, in the course of his brilliant career at the Bar, had acquired the reputation of coming into court with his brief unread, and of mastering it in all its details within a few minutes. He imported this habit into the Senate, but the Chair of a House of Parliament is no place for the display of such virtuosity. During Senator Yeats's speech, he had been engaged in reading the Report for the first time, looking up occasionally to rebuke the speaker for his grosser breaches of good taste, and when Senator Yeats sat down he announced to the House, with considerable *naïveté*, his discovery that the Report was a colourless document which did not commit the House to anything, and deprecated a discussion on the lines initiated by Senator Yeats. Not unnaturally, there was a chorus of protest; but a good-humoured, statesmanlike speech by Senator Colonel Moore on the one side and a temperate exposition by Senator Bagwell of the Protestant point of view on the other did much to raise the tone of the debate, and when the Vice-Chairman rose to move his motion he did so in a calmer atmosphere.

Senator Douglas (who is a member of the Religious Society of Friends, in which divorce is practically unknown) made it clear at the outset that his personal views on the sanctity and indissolubility of the marriage tie are in substance those of the Catholic Church. He explained that his connection with the subject was fortuitous, and that if he had known beforehand that the Joint Standing Committee would have had to deal with the question of divorce he would not have accepted the chairmanship of it. In regard to the proposal before the House, which he put forward entirely on his own responsibility, he stated that it was the duty of the Senate to recognize the fact 'that the vast majority of the people are not prepared to accord divorce facilities to a small minority', and showed that the method suggested in his motion was, in the circumstances, the only practicable method of giving effect to such recognition.

A desultory debate followed, in which the outstanding contribution was a speech by Senator O'Farrell, who supported the motion, and, treating divorce as a social question, attacked it on that ground. The motion was carried on a division by fifteen votes to thirteen; ten Senators were present at the sitting but did not vote—eight Catholics and two non-Catholics.[1]

[1] *Senate Debates*, v, 426–82.

The resultant message came before the Dáil on the 25th June 1925, when the following motion was proposed by Mr. Cosgrave: 'That in the opinion of the Dáil the object intended by the Dáil in the Resolution of the 11th February 1925 would not be achieved by the Resolution adopted by the Senate on the 12th June 1925, and that a Message to this effect be sent to the Senate.' Mr. Cosgrave stated his case with his habitual moderation; but he somehow failed to touch the kernel of the difficulty. He reaffirmed his belief in the course originally proposed by the Dáil—that of preventing by Standing Order the introduction of Bills for divorce, ignoring the fact that the ruling of the Chairman of the Senate had rendered such a course impossible. He had two objections to the Senate's proposal. One was that it did make provision for divorce Bills, and to that extent implied that such Bills might be dealt with and relief granted. This objection was theoretical rather than practical, since it was common ground that no such Bill had the slightest chance of receiving a First Reading even in one House, let alone in both. His second objection, which he said was more serious, was that, if the Senate method were adopted, it would involve the discussion by Parliament 'of the particular facts of each individual case, with all its unsavoury details'. In making this objection he can hardly have adverted to the fact that in the Senate no debate was allowed on the First Reading of a Bill; and that, in the Dáil, the Standing Orders enabled the Speaker to put the question after hearing a short explanatory statement from the member introducing the Bill and another from a member opposed to it. In the course of his speech, Mr. Cosgrave foreshadowed the introduction of legislation to confer upon the courts, when granting decrees of divorce *a mensa et thoro*, power to make provision for the children of the marriage and to vary settlements made on the marriage. The only other speaker on the motion was Deputy Johnson. It was carried without a division, and the appropriate message was sent to the Senate.[1]

The final episode in the parliamentary history of this unhappy affair took place in the Senate on the 7th July 1925, when the Senate Resolution to which the Dáil had objected was formally rescinded, on the motion of Senator John O'Neill. In strictness, the step was unnecessary, since the Resolution had already been rendered inoperative by the non-concurrence of the Dáil; just as the Dáil Resolution had been rendered inoperative by Lord Glenavy's ruling that a motion for a parallel resolution could not be proposed in the Senate. After

[1] *Dáil Debates*, xii, 1563–72.

the formal recission had been effected, Lord Glenavy referred to the matter in words which are worth quoting:

'If in the interval between now and the time we meet again [i.e. the following November] any Senator can bring forward any proposal or suggestion that will provide an honourable way out of the *impasse*, no one will be better pleased than I will. When I was first confronted with the question in March last, I ransacked the Constitution and the Standing Orders, and I came to a conclusion from which I have never wavered and which has never been challenged: that, having regard to my oath as a Senator and having regard to the Constitution, it was impossible that this matter could be disposed of except in one or other of two ways: either to let it alone, in which case I think we all agree it would have died a natural death long before now, and Divorce Bills *a vinculo* would have disappeared for ever from the Free State; or to bring in a short Act of Parliament, which has not been done. . . . If any Senator could succeed where I failed, and find an alternative course, no one would be better pleased than I would be.'[1]

There was, in fact, no *via media*, and the position remained as it was until the enactment of the Constitution of 1937, which provides (Article 41) that 'no law shall be enacted providing for the grant of a dissolution of marriage.' Divorce was not formally prohibited, and any person domiciled in the Irish Free State possessed the theoretical right, at common law, to petition Parliament by means of a Private Bill for divorce *a vinculo matrimonii*. No person did so, however, in view of the certainty that such a Bill would be rejected. The three divorce Bills which had been the immediate cause of the controversy were withdrawn by the promoters, and, in Lord Glenavy's phrase, divorce died a natural death. The projected legislation referred to by Mr. Cosgrave was never introduced, and the Irish matrimonial courts, when granting a decree of divorce *a mensa et thoro*, still lack the power to award damages against a co-respondent, to vary the trusts of a settlement made on the marriage, and to deal with the custody of the children of the marriage.

It remains to refer briefly to the aftermath in connection with the Triennial Election, which took place in September 1925, shortly after the events recorded had taken place. A campaign of vilification was begun against the Senate which, in view of the honest efforts made to solve this difficult problem, seems hard to understand. That Senator Yeats's deplorable speech should evoke popular indignation was only to be expected; but the matter went much further than that. Senator

---

[1] *Senate Debates*, v, 933–8.

Douglas's position has been made amply clear; but his motion was characterized by responsible men, in journals with a considerable circulation, as 'an insidious move in the divorce game', and he himself was described as a man 'whose name must always be prominently associated with the artful attempt to introduce divorce'. And much more to the same effect. Senators Foran and O'Farrell, two Catholic members of the Labour Party who had voted for the motion, were represented as having voted for divorce. In regard to the Senators whose term of office was expiring and who offered themselves for re-election, a black list was published, on which appeared the names of these two Senators and also the names of five 'defaulters', who had been present at the sitting at which the motion was passed but had not taken part in the division. At the same time, the outgoing Senators who had voted against the motion were specially commended to the electors.

In view of the unusual nature of the election (which has already been dealt with in Chapter VIII), it is difficult to say what effect this campaign had on the fortunes of the candidates. Messrs. Foran and O'Farrell, in regard to whom the public had been told that 'the Catholic's duty is plain', easily secured re-election. Of the eight retiring Senators who voted against Senator Douglas's motion, no less than five lost their seats. The five 'defaulters' fared worst of all, for of these only one was re-elected, and he was near the bottom of the list of successful candidates.

PART III

THE SECOND TRIENNIAL PERIOD
6th DECEMBER 1925 TO 5th DECEMBER 1928

The ship is anchored safe and sound, its voyage closed and done;
From fearful trip the victor ship comes in with object won:
Exult, O shores, and ring, O bells!
But I, with mournful tread,
Walk the deck my Captain lies,
Fallen cold and dead.

WALT WHITMAN, *On the Assassination of President Lincoln.*

You malign our senators for that
They are not such as you.

SHAKESPEARE, *Coriolanus,* I, i, 119.

CHAPTER XI

POLITICAL DEVELOPMENTS, 1925-7

---

*Boundary provisions of the Treaty—The Boundary Commission—
The* Morning Post *forecast—Crisis precipitated—Resignation of Dr.
MacNeill—Tripartite agreement signed in London—Its provisions—
The Council of Ireland—Mr. Cosgrave's attitude—Fruitful personal
contact between leaders of North and South—A hopeful augury unful-
filled—Mr. De Valera's views—Political groupings—Elements of impermanence—Formation of Clann Éireann—Dissensions between Ministers on tariff issue—Captain Redmond founds the National League—
The Irish Republican Army repudiates the Republican Government—
Mr. De Valera's proposal to Sinn Féin—His attitude to the parliamentary Oath—Sinn Féin votes against his policy—Formation of Fianna
Fáil—Legislative activity—The Government's external policy—Diplomatic status—The League of Nations—The Imperial Conference of
1926—Outrages by the Irish Republican Army—Public Safety Bill—
Kevin O'Higgins and the licensed trade—The general election cam-
paign—Political parties—The proposals of the Irish Republican Army
—The parties of the Right—Issues before the electors—The parliamentary Oath—Ambiguous attitude of Fianna Fáil—Result of the
general election of June 1927—Mr. De Valera's legal opinion on the
Oath—Fianna Fáil members attempt to take their seats—Mr. De
Valera's pledge not to take the Oath—Mr. Cosgrave on the sanctity of
international agreements—The new Administration—Assassination of
Kevin O'Higgins.*

The Second Triennial Period of the Senate opened in the midst of a
political crisis of the first magnitude. The demarcation of the boundary between the Irish Free State and the six counties of Northern
Ireland, which had been in abeyance for three years, had at last come
sharply to an issue. The Treaty of 1921 was so framed as to apply to

the whole of Ireland, but under Article 12 of that instrument it was provided that 'the powers of the Parliament and Government of the Irish Free State shall no longer extend to Northern Ireland' if an Address to that effect was presented to His Majesty by both Houses of the Parliament of Northern Ireland within one month of the passing of the (British) Act of Parliament for the ratification of the Treaty. In such a case, a commission of three persons, consisting of an appointee of each of the two Irish governments and a chairman to be appointed by the British Government, was to be set up to 'determine in accordance with the wishes of the inhabitants, so far as may be compatible with economic and geographic conditions, the boundaries between Northern Ireland and the rest of Ireland'.

The British Act entitled the Constitution of the Irish Free State (Saorstát Éireann) Act, 1922, was signed by the King on the 5th December 1922 and came into force on the following day. On the 7th December an address in the sense of Article 12 was duly presented to His Majesty by the Belfast Parliament, and the boundary provisions of the Treaty thus came into operation. But the Government of Northern Ireland refused to appoint a representative to the Commission, and matters hung fire until, by an Agreement dated the 4th August 1924 and signed by Mr. Cosgrave and Mr. Ramsay MacDonald, the Treaty was amended to permit of the British Government appointing a representative for Northern Ireland. This Agreement was duly ratified by the Parliaments at Westminster and Dublin, and the Boundary Commission was set up. The chairman, appointed by the British Government, was Mr. Justice Feetham, of South Africa; the representative of Northern Ireland, also appointed by the British Government, was Mr. J. R. Fisher, a prominent Orangeman and a former editor of the *Northern Whig*; and the representative appointed by the Irish Free State Government was Dr. John MacNeill, an Ulsterman, the distinguished historian and Irish scholar, who was Minister for Education in that government.

During the spring and early summer of 1925 the Commission took evidence on the spot, but no clue was forthcoming as to the interpretation which it proposed to place upon its terms of reference, and for months there was complete silence. This was broken on the 7th November 1925 by the publication in the *Morning Post* of a detailed forecast of the Commission's findings, according to which the new boundary line was to be a mere minor rectification of the existing one, and an important strip of Irish Free State territory in County Donegal was to be transferred to Northern Ireland. This forecast was regarded by the general public as being substantially correct, and Mr. Cosgrave's Administration found itself facing perhaps the worst crisis of its career. Dr. MacNeill resigned from the Commission on the 21st November, on the ground that there was no likelihood that the work of the Commission would result in a report based upon the terms of reference, and that the award would be one which he could not defend. There was a feeling, however, that he ought to have broken sooner with his fellow Commissioners, and three days later he resigned his seat on the Executive Council.

It seems clear now that one of two things had happened: either the British signatories of the Treaty had deliberately tricked the Irish by offering them what Lord Birkenhead, who was one of the parties to it, later described as 'a certain consideration for their signatures'[1] in the shape of a boundary commission which they intended should be nugatory; or, more probably, the British Government had altered its position (as it had done in 1914) in face of the intransigence of the Orange minority of north-east Ulster—an intransigence which had been deepened by the circumstances of the Civil War and by Mr. De Valera's threats that the Ulster Unionists 'should be coerced'. The only satisfactory method by which the Commission could have fulfilled its terms of reference would have been first to ascertain the wishes of the inhabitants on the border by means of a plebiscite, and then to determine how far these wishes could be given effect to, due regard being paid to economic and geographic conditions. But the holding of a plebiscite would have required special legislation to be introduced by the British Government and passed by the Imperial Parliament, and no such legislation was forthcoming, for the very good reason that, whatever the unit of the plebiscite, very large areas of Northern Ireland would have voted for inclusion in the Irish Free State and there were no valid economic or geographic conditions which could fairly have precluded their transfer. If the county were the unit, two of the six counties (Tyrone and Fermanagh) would have so voted by large majorities; and if a smaller unit had been taken, such as the Poor Law area or the parish, there would also have been portions of two of the remaining four counties (Down and Armagh).

Four days after the publication of the forecast in the *Morning Post*, questions were asked in the Dáil, to which, in the circumstances, no very reassuring answer could be given by the Government;[2] and on the following day in the Senate the matter was raised on the

---

[1] *Life of Lord Birkenhead*, by his son, vol. ii (1935), p. 238.
[2] *Dáil Debates*, xiii, 113, 114.

adjournment by Senator MacLoughlin of Donegal, who described the boundary clause as the corner-stone of the Treaty, 'inserted specifically to ensure the application of the principles of self-determination and non-coercion to that section of the majority of the Irish people residing in the Six Counties'.[1] On the other side of the border, Sir James Craig, the Prime Minister of Northern Ireland, stated that he would no more hesitate than he did in 1914 'to fight in the open against our enemies who would take away the loved soil of Ulster from any of the loyalists who would want to remain there'; and another member of the Northern Parliament boasted that 'if certain things happen . . . the Prime Minister and the members of the Government will hand in their resignations and take the field'.[2]

The findings of the Boundary Commission were not invalidated by the resignation of the Irish Free State member, and once its decision was promulgated the new boundary would be binding on all parties. In such a tense atmosphere rapid action was necessary if bloodshed was to be avoided. The leaders met in London, and on the 3rd December 1925 a tripartite Agreement was signed, amending and supplementing the Treaty of 1921. The signatories to this Agreement were: for the British Government, the Prime Minister (Mr. Stanley Baldwin) and four members of his Cabinet; for the Irish Free State Government, the President of the Executive Council (Mr. Cosgrave), the Vice-President (Mr. O'Higgins), and the Minister for Finance (Mr. Blythe); for the Government of Northern Ireland, the Prime Minister (Sir James Craig) and the Secretary to the Cabinet (Mr. C. H. Blackmore). The Agreement recited that the three governments were 'resolved mutually to aid one another in a spirit of neighbourly comradeship', and its main provisions were (1) the boundary to remain unaltered; (2) the Irish Free State to be released from any liability under Article 5 of the Treaty for its share of the Public Debt of the United Kingdom and for the payment of war pensions; (3) the powers of the Council of Ireland in relation to Northern Ireland under the Government of Ireland Act, 1920, to be transferred to the Government of Northern Ireland, and that 'the Governments of the Irish Free State and of Northern Ireland shall meet together as and when necessary for the purpose of considering matters of common interest arising out of or connected with the exercise and administration of the said powers .

This third provision requires some explanation. Under the Act of 1920 a Council of Ireland was established, consisting of an equal

[1] *Senate Debates*, v, 955-60.   [2] *Belfast News-Letter*, 16 November 1925.

number of representatives from the Free State (then 'Southern Ireland') and Northern Ireland, with powers to deal with certain common services, including railways and fisheries. Such a council would have helped to destroy the psychological barriers to Irish unity, and so it contained the germ of ultimate union. Under Article 14 of the Treaty of 1921 the Parliament and Government of the Irish Free State retained these powers in relation to Northern Ireland; that is to say, the Free State had a 50 per cent representation in Northern Ireland so far as the services in question were concerned, but Northern Ireland had no such representation as regards the Free State, to which the powers of the Council of Ireland did not apply. In 1922, owing to the Civil War and the circumstances of the time, the Free State Government agreed to postpone the operation of these provisions for five years, but in 1927 they would have come into effect. By transferring these powers to the Government of Northern Ireland, the new Agreement put an end to the Council of Ireland, and to that extent favoured the Northern Government. This was more than counterbalanced, however, by the arrangement that the two governments should meet for consultation from time to time; for an agreement to meet, freely entered into, was of much greater value than a cold power contained in a statute. Mr. Baldwin informed the House of Commons that these words were inserted not only with the consent of Mr. Cosgrave and Sir James Craig, but at their desire.[1] And Mr. Cosgrave was very sanguine that good results would follow.

'We have arranged that for the purpose of dealing with certain matters of common concern the two Cabinets should meet together. These meetings must inevitably tend to remove prejudices and allay anxieties and to promote better understanding. Every step in this direction between North and South will react, through the development of a better spirit, in a favourable manner upon the position of the Nationalists in the North, and the Nationalists of the Six Counties can assist in this development by becoming a connecting link instead of a wall of partition between Dublin and Belfast....

'On the Council, half the representatives would have been drawn from the Free State, and Northern Ireland could not have looked on its operation as anything but irritating interference. No real unification, even of the services under its control, could have been achieved in this way. We made the arrangement contained in the Agreement with the intention, which actuated all parties, of removing every outstanding cause of difference, in order to allow for the development, in

---

[1] *House of Commons Debates*, clxxxix, 319.

future, of the best relations. In abandoning the Council of Ireland, the Free State will lose nothing. It will gain good will.'[1]

If ever we are to learn wisdom for the future, we shall do well to pause here and consider the events of these days. On the 27th November 1925 the relationship between the two Irish governments, North and South, was undoubtedly one of enormous strain. One week later the leaders met across a table in London, and by that personal contact the atmosphere was miraculously changed to one not merely of mutual respect but of cordiality, informed by the common desire to co-operate for the good of Ireland in a spirit of neighbourliness and goodwill. Unhappily for their common country, Mr. Cosgrave and Sir James Craig never saw each other again, nor was this hopeful augury followed up by a single joint meeting of their Cabinets. They did not hold apart on any punctilio, and probably the dead weight of extremism on both sides, of Orangism in the North and of Republicanism in the South, made them averse from a policy of conciliation which would have been fruitful for the country but which might have been politically fatal to both.

The Boundary Agreement was duly given the force of law by corresponding Acts passed at Dublin and Westminster. Taken as a whole, it was a grave disappointment to Irish Nationalists, and more particularly to those in Northern Ireland who had cherished just expectations of being included in the area of the Irish Free State. But any boundary in Ireland is an evil thing, and the greater the area of the Free State the less chance there would be of achieving unity with the remainder, since the proportion of uncompromising Unionists in Northern Ireland would be much greater. Politics is the science of the second best, and Mr. Cosgrave's Government secured the best terms possible short of tearing up the Treaty, which was the only alternative propounded by his opponents. The abolition of the Free State's financial obligations under Article 5 of the Treaty, in regard to the Public Debt of the United Kingdom, was a substantial achievement; for this unascertained and unliquidated commitment had told heavily against the credit of the State and might have proved a crippling burden in the future.

Mr. De Valera was still President of a Republic claiming jurisdiction over the whole of Ireland, and his attitude both before and after the settlement was directed towards inflaming public opinion against the Treaty. In a statement issued on the 24th November 1925, when the crisis was at its height, he referred to the financial provisions of

[1] *Dáil Debates*, xiii, 1307, 1313.

Article 5: 'If there are any people left who still believe in the Treaty policy and the professions of those who carried it, they will be finally disillusioned when that other Commission provided for in the Treaty—the Financial Commission—is set up and comes to deliver its award. As a warning in advance, I inform all these that the demand of the British at the time of the negotiations was for a yearly sum of over nineteen million pounds.'[1] Less than a fortnight later (6th December 1925), after the Boundary Agreement had been signed and the Irish liability under Article 5 had been completely wiped out, he told a public meeting in Dublin: 'The papers were full of the glorious victory and the generosity of the British, just as they were full of similar stories about the original Treaty. Ireland had gained by the Treaty of last week, but the gain lay solely in being relieved from the possibility of being cheated further. . . . [Ireland's counter-claim] would, at the time of the Treaty, be something like three thousand millions.'[2] As Goldsmith said of Johnson, 'when his pistol misses fire he knocks you down with the butt end of it'.

The Boundary Settlement was one of the factors in the disintegration of political groups and the formation of new ones, which were characteristics of the period covered by this chapter. Before we review these changes, it is desirable to state briefly the position at the end of 1925. In a complete Dáil of 153 members, there were 109 who had accepted the Treaty and had taken the Oath and their seats; the remaining forty-four, under the leadership of Mr. De Valera, were members of the Sinn Féin Party, who had not accepted the Treaty and who regarded the Republic declared in 1919 as still established. The principal party in the Dáil was Cumann na nGaedheal (League of Gaels), consisting of sixty-three members led by Mr. Cosgrave. This was the Government party, and most of its leaders and many of the rank and file had taken a prominent part in the Anglo-Irish struggle; but other elements, such as farmers, professional and business men, were well represented in it, and it had the more or less tacit support of the Catholic Church, without which it could not have hoped to carry the Boundary Settlement. When this party was being formed in the spring of 1923 it appears to have been the object of the leaders to found an organization without definite policy or class interest, and Mr. Cosgrave urged the first delegate convention to bring into the party all the best elements of the country, irrespective of class or creed.[3] These highly unusual views must, of course, be read in the

---

[1] *Irish Times*, 25 November 1925.   [2] Ibid., 7 December 1925.
[3] *Freeman's Journal*, 28 April 1923.

light of the circumstances of the time. If there had been no anti-Treaty party and no Civil War, the party politics of the country would have had a chance to develop along normal lines. But it was necessary to marshal the pro-Treaty forces so far as possible under one banner, and so the Cosgrave party embraced men of all shades of opinion, those who were satisfied with Commonwealth status and those who wished to use the Treaty as a stepping-stone to a republic, protectionists and free-traders, and so on. It thus contained within itself the seeds of its own disruption, and that disruption might be expected to manifest itself as soon as, if not before, the Treaty position had become stabilized.

The only two other organized parties, the Farmers' Party and the Labour Party, had only fifteen members each, and neither could ever hope to form an alternative administration. The Farmers' Party, which was sponsored by the Irish Farmers' Union, was led by the late D. J. Gorey, and was representative only of the larger farmers. It was by no means united on the question of protection versus free trade, and it did not accept the Government Whip, though it in general supported the Government against Labour, which, under Mr. Thomas Johnson, formed the official Opposition. In a non-industrial country of peasant proprietors, Labour could never hope to do more than secure the balance of power as between two major parties. The remaining sixteen members were Independents of various types: three members for Dublin University, a few former Nationalists of the old school like Captain Redmond (the son of John Redmond), and some business men and others of the ex-Unionist type from Cork, Dublin, and the three Ulster counties.

This, then, was substantially the position at the end of 1925, and we can see now that it contained elements that make for impermanence. What was required for political stability was that the Government party should be homogeneous, having a clear-cut policy, to which all its members adhered, over the whole range of governmental activity; and that a strong Opposition should arise, also with a well-defined but different policy (albeit one which agreed on fundamentals), and sufficiently numerous to form an alternative administration. In this way the attention of the electorate would be diverted from barren and sterile controversy about the Treaty into more profitable and educative channels. Of course, conditions such as these can hardly be created artificially; they arise either naturally or not at all. But if no such change came over the Irish scene the result was easily predictable. There is no gratitude in politics, and as soon as prosperity and stability returned Mr. Cosgrave would be put out of office. The man in the street would vote against him, much on the same principle as the Athenian citizen who voted for the ostracism of Aristeides, 'because he was tired of hearing him called "the just". In such a case, the only alternative would be Mr. De Valera, who, with a party already nearly as large as Mr. Cosgrave's, remained outside the Dáil; and this process would be expedited if Mr. De Valera were astute enough to make a clean break with methods of violence, to drop the Republic without formally abandoning it, to put forward an attractive internal programme, and, above all, to allay the fears entertained by the Catholic Church of all revolutionary movements. Once returned to power, he could claim that the people had at last undone the great wrong they had committed when they rejected him and his policy in 1922.

There was a secession from the Cosgrave party as a result of the Boundary Settlement. Professor Magennis, a distinguished Professor of Metaphysics who sat for the National University, broke away and formed a new party called Clann Éireann (the Children of Ireland). He was able to recruit only two other members of the Dáil and one member of the Senate (Colonel Moore), but to some extent he obtained support from the earlier National Party of nine members, who had seceded in October 1924 and who had all been defeated at the polls when they sought re-election. Under capable leadership and with a well-considered policy, Clann Éireann might well have appealed to moderate Republicans and supporters of Labour. But Professor Magennis's eminence in other fields did not extend to politics. He attacked the Government over the boundary, the Treaty Oath, and numerous other matters, but his own programme was nebulous, and it never at any time seemed likely that Clann Éireann would be a numerous family.

Another cleavage arose over the question of protection, but in this case it did not lead to the formation of a new party. Two of the 'Extern' Ministers, who were not members of the Executive Council, held opposing views on the subject of tariffs. The Minister for Agriculture (Mr. Patrick Hogan) was a free-trader, while the Minister for Posts and Telegraphs (Mr. J. J. Walsh) was a strong protectionist. The Government as a whole regarded agriculture as the economic mainstay of the country but favoured a cautious policy of selective tariffs, and, by the Tariff Commission Act, passed in 1926, a permanent commission was set up to examine all claims for tariffs and to advise the Government after a thorough sifting of the evidence for and against. This was a sound method, but it had the defect that it was necessarily slow in operation. The spectacle of two Ministers perpetually disagreeing in public on a fundamental issue seems to have decided the Government against the system of 'Extern' Ministers, and to deal with the matter they introduced legislation which is dealt with in detail in the chapter which follows. The differences between Mr. Walsh and his colleagues grew wider, and he left the Dáil for business in the autumn of 1927.

In September 1926 Captain William Redmond launched a new party, the National League, in his constituency of Waterford—always a Redmondite stronghold. This was an attempt on his part to resuscitate the old Nationalist Parliamentary Party, which had been led by his father and which came to grief in 1918. Wisely led, such a movement would doubtless have attracted support from many people of middle age or over, whose loyalty to the Redmond name and to the Home Rule tradition was still strong; and a policy of full and frank co-operation with Great Britain and Northern Ireland in the spirit of the Boundary Agreement would have commended itself to large numbers. But Captain Redmond dissipated his energies in stentorian attacks on the Government without having any definite programme of his own, except to propose that Messrs. Cosgrave and De Valera should retire with their respective followers and leave the government of the country to men who had taken no part in the Civil War. In the circumstances, this proposal was a mere chimaera, and the National League seemed hardly more likely to thrive than did Clann Éireann.

Hence the various activities of Professor Magennis, Mr. J. J. Walsh, and Captain Redmond held out no hope to those who were looking within the Dáil for a new alignment of parties on rational lines. We must now see what had been happening meanwhile to Mr. De Valera and his Republicans outside the Dáil. It will be recalled that, on the 25th October 1922, Mr. De Valera was appointed 'President of the Republic' and that the 'Government' of which he was the head made itself responsible, through its 'Department of Defence', for the control of the Irregular forces known as the Irish Republican Army; that, on the 24th May 1923, he issued a proclamation to these forces, which was in effect a cease fire order, stating that 'military victory must be allowed to rest for the moment with those who have destroyed the Republic': and that on the following 22nd July he made a statement to the Associated Press that it was 'not the intention of the Republican Government or the Army Executive to renew the war'. Mr. De Valera was arrested at Ennis on the 15th August 1923 and released on the 16th July 1924. The Republic was still in being, he was President of it, and during his internment the duties of the office were discharged by the Vice-President, Mr. Patrick Ruttledge. Since the area of the Republic was the whole of Ireland, the activities of the Irish Republican Army extended to Northern Ireland, a Belfast battalion being in existence.

Throughout 1924 and most of 1925 the 'army' remained, at least nominally, under the control of the 'Government', the 'Minister for Defence' being Mr. Seán Lemass and the 'Chief of Staff' Mr. Frank Aiken. How far this control was effectively exercised it is, of course, impossible to say; but it became more and more shadowy, and at an Irish Republican Army Convention held on the 14th November 1925 the organization was completely altered. 'The Army withdrew its allegiance from the Government (the Government meant Mr. De Valera and his confrères), and an Army Council with supreme authority and dictatorial powers was set up. At this stage, therefore, the Irregular army which had carried on the Civil War under Mr. De Valera's direction, and had remained nominally under his direction up to the end of 1925, now cut itself adrift completely from all control of anybody who pretended to represent politically any section of the electorate.'[1]

Mr. De Valera's position at this date may therefore be summarized as follows: he was President of a notional Republic which had twice been rejected by the people; the army of the Republic had been decisively defeated, and finally it had repudiated him. In these circumstances he did not take long to make up his mind as to the best course for him to follow. He could not continue *bombinans in vacuo*; so he would put the Republic in cold storage, and concentrate on the abolition of the Oath. On this basis, in the absence in the Dáil of any possible alternative government to Mr. Cosgrave's, his ultimate return to power would be a virtual certainty. Accordingly, at a meeting of the General Council of Sinn Féin (the Republican Organization) held in Dublin on the 13th January 1926, the matter was brought forward for discussion. In the absence of agreement, it was decided to call a general meeting of the organization for the 9th March to decide the question at issue. This, according to a communication given to the Press by Mr. De Valera, was as follows: 'Whether with a view to massing the people of Ireland against the oath of allegiance,

[1] Statement by Mr. Cosgrave in the Dáil, 26 July 1927 (*Dáil Debates*, xx, 830).

which is a national humiliation and a barrier to unified national action, it could be promised officially on behalf of the organization at any time that if the oath were removed the Republican members would sit with the other representatives of the people in the Free State assembly, regarding that assembly frankly as a non-sovereign, subordinate, twenty-six county institution, but one which in fact was in a position to control the lives of a large section of our people.'[1] Why the Irish Free State Parliament was not sovereign, and to what it was subordinate—whether to the Irish Republic or to the Imperial Parliament—was not made clear. Otherwise, the only interest of this singular conundrum is that it shows the direction in which Mr. De Valera's mind was working. It undoubtedly marked an advance on the attitude which he had maintained twelve months earlier, for on the 25th January 1925 he had said at Cavan: 'No matter what the newspapers said, no decent Republican would ever enter the present Dáil.'[2]

The General Meeting of the Republican Organization was duly held in Dublin on the 9th March. It had before it a long and wordy motion proposed by Mr. De Valera, the gist of which is contained in its opening paragraph: 'That once the admission oaths of the 26-County and 6-County Assemblies are removed, it becomes a question not of principle but of policy whether or not Republican representatives should attend these Assemblies.'[3] A principle is a fundamental truth or a general law as a guide to conduct or action, and it is not dependent on contingencies. Of its very nature it cannot, like a method, be altered or abandoned to suit changed circumstances. In a proclamation dated the 18th November 1922, and signed by Mr. De Valera as President of the Republic, Mr. Cosgrave and his colleagues were characterized as men who had 'entered into a conspiracy with other enemies of the Republic to divide this ancient nation and dismember its territory and to subvert the Republic which they were sworn to defend'.[4] The Proclamation contains no word about 'admission oaths', and there can be no question that the entire illegality of the two Irish parliaments was held by Mr. De Valera as a basic principle.

In the circumstances, it is not surprising that the motion met with considerable opposition, and on the 10th March the following amendment to it was carried by 223 votes to 218: 'That it is incompatible with the fundamental principles of Sinn Féin to send repre-

---

[1] *Irish Independent*, 15 January 1926.   [2] *Irish Times*, 26 January 1925.
[3] *Irish Independent*, 12 February 1926.   [4] *Dáil Debates*, xliv, 229.

sentatives into any usurping legislature set up by English law in Ireland.' When this amendment was put as a substantive motion, however, it was rejected by 179 votes to 177.[1] There had been 85 abstentions, and the whole question was left in the air. Mr. De Valera did not wait for further developments, and on the following day he resigned, stating that he 'was compelled to regard the vote as one against his policy'.[2]

On Sunday, 16th May 1926, Mr. De Valera's new party was formally inaugurated at a public meeting held in the Scala Theatre, Dublin. He told his audience that 'he came there as President of nothing; he came there simply as a private and a Republican. It was because he had not lost faith in Republicanism he had suggested the present movement; it was because he felt he would not be doing his duty to the rank and file of Republicans, or the Irish nation, if he were to allow Republicanism to be put into the position in which it would appear to be merely a nominalistic formalism.'[3]

The name chosen for the new party was Fianna Fáil, meaning Warriors of Fál. According to legend, the Fianna were a semi-military, semi-hunting body of men, organized to help the ancient Kings of Ireland; owing to their excesses, two joint kings combined against them in the sixth century and practically exterminated them at the Battle of Gowra, in Meath. *Fál* is a poetical name for Ireland, derived from *Lia Fáil*, the *Saxum Fatale* or Stone of Destiny which was supposed to cry aloud under the rightful sovereign when the men of Ireland were assembled on the Hill of Tara to choose a king; but, as Dr. Keating says, it has not cried since pagan times, 'óir do balbhuigheadh bréig-dhealbha an domhain an tan rugadh Críost'[4] ('for the false images of the world were struck dumb when Christ was born'). For the title of a modern Republican political party, Mr. De Valera could hardly have gone further back, or have chosen one more associated with kingship.

Amid all this political activity, inside and outside the Dáil, Mr. Cosgrave and his colleagues, with their eyes on the future and their backs turned to the past, steadily pursued their policy of 'keeping to the middle of the road', erecting a stable structure on the foundations already so well laid and getting the best out of the Treaty position. At home, coinage and currency Acts were passed, and a coinage was issued which is one of the most artistic in Europe; land purchase was expedited; the Shannon electricity works were nearing completion,

[1] *Irish Independent*, 11 March 1926.   [2] Ibid., 12 March 1926.
[3] Ibid., 17 May 1926.   [4] Keating, *Foras Feasa*, vol. i, p. 101.

an Electricity (Supply) Act was passed to market the current, and all over the country the steel pylons were going up as symbols of a new era; the Agricultural Credit Corporation was set up, with a capital of half a million sterling, to supply loans to farmers; intensive efforts were being made in every direction for the prosperity, happiness, comfort, and education of the people. Abroad, the Irish Free State had already, in 1924, appointed a Minister to Washington, and so was the first member of the Commonwealth to break through the diplomatic unity of the British Empire. It is right to say that this step was taken with the cordial co-operation of the British Government, and it was followed up by similar action in regard to Paris, Berlin, and the Vatican. In 1926 the Minister for External Affairs (Mr. Desmond Fitzgerald) established another precedent by putting forward his country as a candidate for the Council of the League of Nations. He was not successful on that occasion, and the Irish Free State had to wait until 1930, when it succeeded Canada on the Council; but Mr. Fitzgerald's application provided an opportunity for the principal Canadian delegate (Sir George Foster) to vindicate the right of the Dominions to co-equality with Great Britain and the other member States. 'We consider that we have equal rights to representation on the Council and otherwise with every one of the fifty-six members of the League of Nations, and we do not propose to waive that right.'[1] In the same year (1926) the Government sent the strongest possible delegation to the Imperial Conference, and it is now generally accepted that the Report of the Inter-Imperial Relations Committee of that Conference owed much to the skill with which Messrs. O'Higgins, Fitzgerald, and the other Irish delegates prepared their case and to the pertinacity with which they presented it. The Report defined the members of the Commonwealth, in the words of the now famous Balfour Declaration, as 'autonomous communities within the British Empire, equal in status, in no way subordinate one to another in any aspect of their domestic or external affairs, though united by a common allegiance to the Crown, and freely associated as members of the British Commonwealth of Nations'. Mr. De Valera's belated decision to recognize the Irish Free State Parliament as 'frankly, a non-sovereign, subordinate twenty-six county institution' was being made to look more and more ridiculous.

A general election was due in 1927, but the Cosgrave Administration did not go out of its way to court popularity in preparation for

---

[1] Keith, *Sovereignty of the British Dominions* (1929), p. 330.

it. On the night of the 14th November 1926 the Irish Republican Army conducted a series of attacks on twelve Civic Guard barracks, as a result of which two unarmed policemen were killed. The Government immediately met this challenge to its authority by introducing a Public Safety Bill, which was quickly passed by both Houses. Political capital was made out of this drastic step by the Labour Opposition, but Mr. Cosgrave said: 'I would much prefer to go before the electorate and say that after my four or five years' administration it was never necessary to introduce such a measure as this. I would feel far easier and I would feel far more confident in making an appeal for my return, but I am not ashamed to stand behind the measure, to defend it and say to the people, "No steps did we neglect to take to ensure that your lives, your liberties and your property were secure".'[1] Similar courage was shown by Kevin O'Higgins, but in a different field. As late as February 1927 he introduced an Intoxicating Liquor Bill, which, as he said himself, was 'ushered in in the customary journalistic setting of war and rumours of war'.[2] The licensed trade has always exercised great power in Irish politics; and though this Bill followed the lines of the unanimous Report of an impartial commission, presided over by Mr. John J. Horgan, the well-known Cork solicitor and publicist, it was anything but welcome to the publicans, since it proposed to reduce the number of public-houses and the hours of opening. The Bill caused more commotion in the country than did Mr. De Valera's agitation about the Oath, but Mr. O'Higgins got most of his proposals through intact, though he could not expect much quarter from the trade at the general election.

By the end of April, the election campaign was in full swing. The parties and policies were:

1. *The Government Party.* This went to the country on its record.

2. *Fianna Fáil.* The principal plank in this party's programme was the removal of the Oath; the Cosgrave party was a British Empire party which insisted on the retention of the Oath merely for the purpose of keeping Mr. De Valera and his friends out of public life. The Government was responsible for partition and had bungled the Boundary Settlement. Emigration, unemployment, and the decline in trade were due to its policy, and these evils could and would be cured by the imposition of protective tariffs, the withholding of the Land Annuities paid to Great Britain, and the effecting of economies in the public services, including a reduction in the size of the Army.

[1] *Dáil Debates*, xvii, 157, 158.   [2] Ibid., xviii, 522.

3. *Labour*. This came out with a good constructive programme on Socialist lines. The Cosgrave party was the party of the wealthy; it had no real cure for unemployment, and the wages paid on the Shannon Scheme and elsewhere were scandalously low. On the other hand, Fianna Fáil knew nothing of economic affairs, and its proposal to issue an employment loan while repudiating the Financial Agreement with Great Britain was ridiculous. A strong Labour Party was necessary to focus attention on economic issues and to get away from the dog-fight about the Treaty.

4. *Farmers' Party*. The members of this party mostly supported the Government, but a minority, chiefly of barley-growers, were attracted by the tariff policy of Fianna Fáil. In the end, the Farmers' Party fell between two stools.

5. *National League*. Like everyone else, Captain Redmond favoured 'economy'. He strove to rekindle the dead embers of the old Parliamentary Party, but his appeals were chiefly to sectional interests, such as the liquor trade, the ex-soldiers of the Great War, and the Town Tenants.

6. *Clann Éireann*. Professor Magennis's party stood for the abolition of the Oath, the revision of the Boundary Settlement, and the imposition of tariffs. On these issues it was a mere echo of Fianna Fáil, the sole difference being that the latter was not (apparently) willing to enter the Dáil.

7. *Sinn Féin*. This party, led by Miss Mary MacSwiney, consisted of what was left of the Republican Party after Mr. De Valera and his followers had broken away. It held the Republic established in 1919 to be inviolate and would not in any circumstances recognize the Parliaments of the Free State and of Northern Ireland, which it regarded as usurping legislatures set up by English law.

All except the two principal parties suffered from lack of funds. Fianna Fáil had obtained inadequate financial support in Ireland, but Mr. De Valera had remedied this defect by going on a mission to the United States, whence he returned with ample supplies for the election. Negotiations for a *modus vivendi* went on between the various groups, but these largely came to nothing. As to the parties of the Left, Clann Éireann would have welcomed an understanding with Fianna Fáil, but Mr. De Valera had nothing to learn in the way of political strategy from a professor of metaphysics, whom he probably suspected of wishing to catch him bathing for the purpose of stealing his clothes. The Irish Republican Army took upon itself the role of peacemaker between Sinn Féin and Fianna Fáil, and on the

20th May it issued a statement of the result of its efforts. It had suggested a three-party delegate conference, on the basis of proposals which it put forward. All parties were to agree to the restoration of the Republic; the Treaty, the Boundary Settlement, and all other agreements with Great Britain were to be repudiated; all arms were to be placed under the control of the Irish Republican Army, and the 'removal' was to be effected from Dublin and its vicinity of all enemy forces (that is to say, the Free State Army), after which they were to be disarmed and demobilized; 'to prevent clashing and overlapping', a panel of candidates was to be approved by a National Board, and the board was to select the Cabinet *before* the election. The Standing Committee of Sinn Féin agreed to a conference, provided that Fianna Fáil would give a guarantee that they would 'not enter any foreign-controlled Parliament as a minority or majority, with or without an oath or other formal declaration'. The National Executive of Fianna Fáil decided unanimously that the proposals were not acceptable as a basis for discussion.[1]

With regard to the parties of the Right, union with Captain Redmond's National League had been proposed by certain members of the Farmers' Party in November 1926, but nothing had come of it. In the spring of 1927 Mr. Gorey, the leader of the party, and Mr. M. F. O'Hanlon, its secretary (afterwards Vice-Chairman of the Senate), discussed fusion with leaders of the Cosgrave party. The results were satisfactory to both sides, and the Farmers' Party recommended amalgamation to the Farmers' Union Congress. But the Congress rejected the scheme, and Messrs. Gorey and O'Hanlon resigned from the Farmers' Party, which faced the election without any prominent leaders.

So far as the Fianna Fáil Party were concerned, the main issue before the electors was the abolition of the Oath. A Bill had been introduced in the Dáil for this purpose on the 6th April 1927 by Mr. Daniel Breen, a daring Irregular leader who had taken the Oath and his seat in the previous January; and Mr. Cosgrave, in moving the rejection of the Bill, had made the Government's position clear on the subject. The Treaty (of which the Oath was an integral part) had been approved by an overwhelming majority of the people at the general elections of June 1922 and August 1923. Since the latter date there had been twenty-one by-elections, and the result of these had been seventeen for the Treaty and four against. 'We believe in honouring our bond, we believe in the sanctity of international agreements. . . . Our

[1] *Dáil Debates*, xx, 831–6.

honour as the representatives of a nation which has approved of that Treaty is bound to the carrying out of our part of the transaction.'[1] This is the exact point made by Mr. De Valera in March 1922 in explanation of his 'wading through blood' speeches, when he referred to 'the nation's own pledged word' as 'an almost impassable barrier'. Kevin O'Higgins dealt with the matter more trenchantly when, referring to Mr. De Valera, he said that 'the man who did his damnedest to cut his country's throat now invited it to commit political *hara-kiri* in order to save his face'.[2]

In speech after speech delivered prior to the election Mr. De Valera used language which left no room for doubt that the question was for him one of immutable principle, and that he would never enter the Dáil until the Oath was abolished. It had been suggested from time to time that the Oath differed from ordinary oaths, and was not morally binding; but Mr. De Valera dismissed all subtlety of this kind at the inaugural meeting of Fianna Fáil. 'As to the theological aspect of the Oath, it was enough for him that it was called an official oath and began, "I do solemnly swear". Why go through mockery of that sort if it were not an oath?'[3]

Towards the close of the campaign the Catholic Dean of Cashel (Monsignor Ryan) said that a sincere Republican had asked him whether the Oath could be consistently taken by him in view of the Oath which he had already taken to the Republic. He had replied that a man was bound to his wife by the vow he took to her while she was alive, but when she was dead he was perfectly free to make a vow to a second wife.[4] But Mr. De Valera revels in this sort of dialectic, and he answered Monsignor Ryan the very next day. 'Would the Dean tell them that they were free to take a vow to a second wife with the intention of proving unfaithful to her, or with a view of compassing her death? The people who told them now to take the Oath lightly, and that it meant nothing, would be just the people to tell them they had them in the trap, that they had taken an oath and must keep it.'[5] Nevertheless, in view of the circumstances surrounding Mr. De Valera's disruption of Sinn Féin, many people felt that this principle, however clearly enunciated and with whatever passionate insistence reiterated, would never be allowed to stand in his way if he found it politically expedient to disregard it. Colour was given to this belief by his party's use of ambiguous posters and newspaper advertise-

[1] *Dáil Debates*, xix, 992.
[2] Quoted in *The Round Table*, September 1926, p. 810.
[3] *Irish Times*, 17 May 1926.
[4] *Irish Independent*, 7 June 1927.   [5] Ibid., 8 June 1927.

ments with the slogan 'Fianna Fáil is going in'; and there is no doubt that many thousands of electors voted for Fianna Fáil in the belief that they would take their seats, Oath or no Oath.

The general election took place on the 9th June 1927, and the result was as follows:

Party	Candidates nominated	Members elected
Cumann na nGaedheal (Cosgrave)	97	47
Fianna Fáil (De Valera)	87	44
Labour	50	22
Independents	57	14
Farmers	38	11
National League	30	8
Sinn Féin	15	5
Independent Republicans	2	2
Clann Éireann	7	0
	383	153

This result was, of course, entirely inconclusive. The Government party had dropped from 57 to 46 (excluding the Chairman of the Dáil) and no longer had a majority in the House, though it was still the largest party. Professor Magennis and his Clann Éireann had been wiped out, and so the Children of Ireland had become Orphans of the Storm; but none of the other constitutional parties had done at all well, and their unmeasured attacks on the Government had merely served Mr. De Valera's purposes. As they had nothing else in common with each other, they could not hope to form an alternative coalition government. The position was one of stalemate, with everything depending on the attitude of Fianna Fáil.

The new Parliament assembled on the 23rd June 1927 and the Dublin morning newspapers of that day contained Mr. De Valera's big surprise. He had obtained a legal opinion, dated the 21st June 1927, from three members of the Irish Bar, that there was no authority in anyone under the Treaty or the Constitution or the Dáil Standing Orders to exclude any member of that House from any part of the House before the House had been duly constituted and the Chairman thereof duly elected. Any member might be proposed and elected as Chairman without taking any oath; and if any member were excluded the Chairman would not have been validly elected.[1]

[1] *Irish Independent*, 23 June 1927.

Fortified by this strange 'open sesame', Mr. De Valera led his entire party to the Parliament Building on the same afternoon, and what occurred there was recounted in the Dublin newspapers on the following day. They were conducted to a committee room, and Mr. O'Kelly, the deputy leader of the party, informed the Clerk of the Dáil that they wished to proceed to the Chamber. The Clerk said he had a 'little formality' for them to comply with, and, on being asked to state it, he read Article 17 of the Constitution, which contains the text of the Oath and stipulates that it 'shall be taken and subscribed by every member of the Oireachtas before taking his seat therein'. Mr. O'Kelly retorted that he would not take the Oath, but would proceed to the Chamber, adding that there was nothing in the Constitution to prevent his doing so. Mr. De Valera conducted an exchange with the Clerk on similar lines. The Clerk ordered the doors leading to the Chamber to be locked, and the party withdrew to the Fianna Fáil headquarters, from which Mr. De Valera addressed the expectant crowd. 'They pledged themselves to the people that as long as they were the representatives of the people they would never take an oath of allegiance to a foreign king. They had been prevented because they would neither take a false oath nor prove recreant to the aspirations of the Irish people and renounce their principles.'[1] But, if he was still not willing to cross the Rubicon, he had at least arrived at the water's edge; and the pressure of his followers behind him on the bank seemed likely soon to push him across.

> *Stabant orantes primi transmittere cursum,*
> *Tendebantque manus ripae ulterioris amore.*

While these singular occurrences were taking place, Mr. Cosgrave was nominated for the Presidency of the Executive Council. He made it clear that he did not seek office, and would accept it only if the Opposition parties were unable or unwilling to do so, and then only if he was to receive sufficient support to carry out his programme. His position with regard to the Oath was as follows.

'As long as the Treaty remains, neither this House nor any other assembly can remove the obligation which the Treaty imposes upon elected representatives of subscribing to the Oath prescribed in Article 4 of the Treaty. The Irish people, through their representatives, can denounce the Treaty. They cannot alter it except by agreement with Great Britain, ratified by legislation on both sides. But until it is either denounced or altered the Oath must remain, because

[1] *Irish Independent*, 24 June 1927.

the international obligations of any country override its internal laws.

'We have neither sought nor received any mandate for the denunciation of the Treaty, and we do not intend to take any steps in the matter. Nor have we sought any mandate for its alteration. The Party which asked for that mandate did not obtain it, notwithstanding the fact that they enshrined their request in a bower of rosy promises. They dangled before the people visions of bread and work for all, smaller taxes, no Land Commission annuities, no emigration, no partition. Now they have taken up the position that unless some other Party saves their faces in the matter of the difference between the oath in the Treaty and the oath which their leader himself drafted, with an annual tribute to His Majesty superimposed, they cannot put their promises to the test of performance. We have no intention of imperilling our good relations with Great Britain to secure a dishonest saving of faces, or to acquiesce in a national deception.'[1]

There being no other nomination for the Presidency, Mr. Cosgrave was re-elected, the only opposition to him in the division lobby being the twenty-two members of the Labour Party. He thereupon obtained the assent of the Dáil to the following Executive Council:

Vice-President, Minister for Justice and Minister for External
    Affairs: Kevin O'Higgins
Minister for Finance: Ernest Blythe
Minister for Defence: Desmond Fitzgerald
Minister for Industry and Commerce: Patrick McGilligan
Minister for Education: John M. O'Sullivan
Minister for Lands and Agriculture: Patrick Hogan
Minister for Fisheries: Finian Lynch
Minister for Local Government and Public Health: Richard
    Mulcahy
Minister for Posts and Telegraphs: James J. Walsh

On the following Sunday fortnight, the 10th July 1927, as Kevin O'Higgins was walking alone, unarmed and unguarded, to twelve o'clock Mass from his home in Blackrock, County Dublin, he was fired upon by three assassins who had been lying in wait for him in a motor-car with the engine running. He ran a short distance, but fell wounded, and they stood over him and fired bullets into his prostrate body, driving off in the car when their fell work was done. Dr. John MacNeill, his friend and former colleague in the Government, who

[1] *Dáil Debates*, xx, 11–15.

was going to the same Mass, was the first to reach his side, and had the agonizing experience of finding that the man whom he had hastened to succour was Kevin O'Higgins. He knelt beside him, and the first words spoken to him by the stricken man were, 'I forgive my murderers.' His poor wounded body was removed to his house three hundred yards away, where his young wife had heard the shots and feared the worst. He had eight wounds, of which all save one were sufficient to cause death; and yet he lingered for nearly five hours, during most of which time he was perfectly conscious. He spoke to his grief-stricken friends and colleagues who had gathered round his death-bed, said to General O'Duffy that they had done good work and should continue on the same lines, sent his eternal love to his wife, and went to meet his God with serenity.

Kevin O'Higgins was a steadfast and heroic figure, a statesman of vision and an enemy of shams and knavery. He had much in common with Abraham Lincoln, to whom, in his modest, shy way, he liked to be compared. He had brought his country safely through the horrors of a civil war and had vindicated the principle that the will of the people shall prevail. He was scrupulously fair in controversy, scorning all tricks and subterfuges. But, unlike Lincoln, he was struck down, not by a madman, but by assassins who saw him for what he was, the strongest bulwark of the State against its enemies, and who had decided that for that reason his life was forfeit. If he had lived, it is certain that the subsequent history of his country would have been very different. For he had a clear and reconciling conception of Irish nationality, his plans for the future were well laid and informed by high purpose, and he had the capacity and the strength of character to carry them out.

CHAPTER XII

THE GOVERNMENT AND THE SENATE

Contested elections for the Chair and Vice-Chair—Rushing of Bill to confirm Boundary Agreement—Senators' opinions on the Agreement —Lord Glenavy's acceptance of the closure—Continued hasty legislation—Ineffective protests—The Ultimate Financial Settlement—Attitude of Minister for Finance to the Senate—Virtual abolition of Extern Ministers—Effort to abolish Senatorial disqualification for Executive Council—The question considered in Select Committee—Views of Kevin O'Higgins—Request for a Joint Committee—Refusal of the Government—Continued opposition of Kevin O'Higgins—Major Bryan Cooper states the practice elsewhere—The Senate's reaction to the refusal—The Juries Bill—Senator Brown and the case for women jurors—The Intoxicating Liquor Bill—The work of revision summarized —Tributes to the dead Vice-President—His funeral.

The Second Triennial Period did not open with the same degree of harmony as the first. The memories of the divorce controversy still lingered, and they had their effect on the elections to the Chair and the Vice-Chair. Senator T. W. Westropp Bennett was proposed for the Chairmanship in opposition to Lord Glenavy, but was defeated by thirty-four votes to eighteen. The same Senator was thereupon proposed for the Vice-Chairmanship in opposition to Senator Douglas, and this time he was successful by one vote, twenty-six votes being cast for Senator Bennett and twenty-five for Senator Douglas. The affair can perhaps best be described as a partial revolt of Catholics, to some extent against Lord Glenavy and to a greater extent against Senator Douglas, re-inforced in the case of the latter by the feeling that to allot both these posts to non-Catholics exceeded what might reasonably be required in the way of toleration. The vote of thirty-four for Lord Glenavy was made up of eighteen non-Catholics and sixteen Catholics; and the vote of twenty-five for Senator Douglas was made up of seventeen non-Catholics and eight Catholics. The non-Catholic vote was not split, as no non-Catholic voted for Senator Bennett in either division.[1]

The Government's treatment of the Senate in the matter of rushing legislation was exemplified at the very beginning of the period by what occurred in connection with the Treaty (Confirmation of Amending Agreement) Bill, 1925. This was the Bill to give effect to the Boundary Agreement, and it was, of course, of the highest public interest and importance. It was passed by the Dáil on the 15th December 1925, at ten minutes before midnight. Under the Standing Orders of the Senate, an interval of three days had to elapse before that House could take the Second Stage of a Bill received from the Dáil; but, when the Senate met at 11 a.m. on the very next morning, one of the supporters of the Government proposed, without notice, a motion to suspend the Standing Orders to enable not only the Second Stage but all the remaining stages to be taken on that day. Lord Glenavy accepted the motion and, in spite of a Labour protest, it was carried.

Though the President, the Vice-President, and the Minister for Industry and Commerce were all present, none of them expounded the Bill, and the debate on it was opened by Senator Farren of the Labour Party, who was opposed to it. The case against the boundary settlement was capably put by Senators O'Farrell and Colonel Moore, and, in a maiden speech, by Senator Toal, one of the three Ulster members. His two colleagues from that province, Senators MacLoughlin and O'Rourke, supported the Bill however, the latter stating that, having considered all the arguments put forward for its rejection, he considered acceptance of the agreement to be the only statesmanlike policy. Mr. De Valera's allegation that the country had been sold was dealt with by speakers of such different view-points as Senators Douglas, Dowdall, and MacLoughlin. Senator Douglas said:

'Those who were responsible for civil war in the South and for the many things that happened in this country, in my opinion—and I challenge anyone to deny it—are the persons most responsible of all for the continuance of partition since then.'

Senator Dowdall was of the same opinion: 'When the civil trouble broke out here in 1921, partition, so far as it has ever been stereotyped,

---

[1] *Senate Debates*, vi, 1–17.

was stereotyped, and the only chance that the then Government had was taken away from it by the people who now accuse the Government and the Oireachtas of selling the country. All I can say is, that it was better to sell the country than to burn it.'

Senator MacLoughlin placed the responsibility directly on the shoulders of Mr. De Valera: 'Instead of coming to the rescue of the Nationalists of the Six Counties, with all the resources of the victorious young manhood of a united Ireland, and with all the friendliness and power of the Coalition Government in England, which had passed the Treaty and, I might add, in spite of intense provocation stood by it, he deliberately split the country and plunged it into an inferno of civil war, in which the houses of Protestants were burned in the name of the Irish Republic, and in the name of the great Protestant patriot Wolfe Tone, whose life's aim was to do away with sectarianism and unite all Irishmen in a common fold. That was De Valera's contribution to a united Ireland. That was his invitation to the Protestants of the North to join their Southern fellow-countrymen for the common good of their native land. . . . When I hear people talking about the betrayal of the Nationalists in the Six Counties and of the Catholics of the North being sold, I reply that the time they were betrayed was when De Valera first launched his first thunderbolt against the Treaty and the time they were sold was when he lit the torch of civil war in Ireland. And now this architect of their misfortunes is again attempting to exploit the plight of these Nationalists and use them as pawns in his game to bring about the downfall of the Free State.'

After the debate on the Second Stage had been in progress only four hours, the closure was moved by a supporter of the Government; and, although only thirteen Senators had spoken, Lord Glenavy accepted the motion. Such an action as this made many people doubt the sincerity of his frequent remonstrations with the Government for rushing legislation. The closure motion and the successive stages of the Bill were all passed by substantial majorities, and then, again without notice, a motion was allowed to be moved declaring that the Bill was necessary for the immediate preservation of the public peace and safety, and that accordingly the provisions of Article 47 of the Constitution should not apply to it. This Article, it will be recalled, stipulated for a delay of seven days between the passage of a Bill and its enactment, to permit of the machinery for a referendum being set in motion. This declaratory motion was duly passed, amid protests, although it did not seem likely that the public peace and safety would be endangered by a mere week's delay in stabilizing a boundary which had existed for more than five years.[1]

The day after these summary proceedings (17th December 1925) the Minister for Justice (Mr. O'Higgins) wrote a letter to the Chairman of the Senate, referring to the Courts of Justice Bill (which had been passed by the Dáil only the previous night) and giving reasons why, in his opinion, it was necessary for the Bill to be passed by both Houses not later than the 10th January. The letter was read to the House from the Chair, and strong exception was taken to this method of communicating the Government's wishes in regard to the legislative programme. Senator Sir John Keane said: 'It is not desirable that the reading of letters from Ministers, or from anybody else, should be made a precedent by the Senate. It never happened before, and in my opinion it would be a dangerous precedent. I know that Ministers find it inconvenient often to attend here, but I do not think that inconvenience can in any way be met by our receiving written communications like this.'[2]

The remedy, of course, lay in the Senate's own hands; because, however inconvenient Ministers might find it to attend the House, they would have found it still more inconvenient if Senators had refused to expedite Bills in accordance with their wishes, on the ground that Ministers had not taken steps to bring such Bills before the Senate in due time for their proper consideration. This particular Bill had been before the Dáil for more than a month; but the Senate passed it through all its stages in one day, three days before the latest date mentioned by Mr. O'Higgins.

One of the consequences of the rushing of Bills was that the Chairman was obliged in many cases to waive the rule that amendments for the Committee Stage should be received before 11 a.m. on the previous day. The result was that amendments often had to be hastily drafted, the Government experts had not time to examine their implications, and the Minister in charge of the Bill opposed them as a measure of precaution: whereas, if time had permitted, he might have accepted some of them as improvements. Such a bad practice is liable to spread, and in some instances Senators were themselves at fault in sending in their amendments late. Such occasions were rare, however, and it might have been expected that Ministers would be the last to complain. But on one such occasion (28th April 1926) Mr.

---

[1] For the whole debate, from which the foregoing extracts have been quoted, see *Senate Debates*, vi, 122–242.
[2] *Senate Debates*, vi, 271–4.

O'Higgins entered a strong protest in the case of his Enforcement of Court Orders Bill, though the amendments in question numbered only five. Senator O'Farrell replied: 'Bills have come very often in heaps from the other House to us and we were asked to deal with them hurriedly, even more important Bills than this. We have perhaps spoiled the Government in that respect, and if we do make a mistake they are responsible for the bad example.'[1]

This bad example was continued a few months later, when the annual rush began before the summer recess. There being no leader of the House, nor any spokesman for the Government, Lord Glenavy occupied five columns of the Official Report in detailing the order of the business (30th June 1926). He classified the Bills which the Government wished to be passed into law before the adjournment, and which, he said, had been furnished in a minute received from the Executive Council. A number of these Bills had not then reached the Senate. Lord Glenavy further explained the provisional time-table which he had sketched out, and 'I can tell the House', he said, 'it will mean hard work if they are to put all this mass of legislation through this week'. But he made no suggestion that the Senate should refuse to facilitate the Government and should insist on being given adequate time for the due consideration and revision of the Bills submitted to it. He did, however, again refer to the question of the initiation in the Upper House of Government Bills:

'I have only to say that I express my regret that the Executive Council has not seen its way to introduce some of those Bills into this House. I see no reason why some of those Bills should not have been introduced into this House weeks ago, and by this they would have been passed into law. I have thrown out that suggestion already to the Executive Council, but evidently this House has been divorced, so far as the Government is concerned, from the initiation of Government Bills. That, of course, may be their policy. I think, myself, it would be more in the interests of, certainly the efficiency of, this House, and also the dispatch of public business, if many of those not very contentious Bills were originated and passed in their first stages here. I have nothing more to say in that matter.'[2]

The Government by this time doubtless knew that, however he might complain, they had really nothing to fear from the Chairman of the Senate. But any doubts there may have been must have been removed by an episode which occurred at the end of the year. On the 16th March 1926 Mr. Ernest Blythe, the Minister for Finance, and

[1] *Senate Debates*, vii, 28–30.   [2] Ibid., vii, 551–6.

Mr. Winston Churchill, the British Secretary of State for the Colonies, signed the Heads of the Ultimate Financial Settlement between the two governments. (This is the Agreement which was subsequently repudiated by Mr. De Valera.) The document was laid on the table of the Senate on the 19th November 1926, and on the following 15th December Senator Colonel Moore proposed a motion on the subject, expressive of the opinion that the settlement was prejudicial to the financial stability of the country. It is quite certain that the great majority of Senators did not agree with this view, but an amendment was offered to the motion by Senator Bennett, the purport of which was to refer the matter to a Special Committee of the Senate, 'to consider and report whether such settlement is prejudicial to the financial stability of the Irish Free State, and will, if carried out, be an excessive burden on Irish taxpayers'.

The right of a House of Parliament to set up such a committee can scarcely be questioned; and that right is unaffected by the merits or otherwise of the particular case. If the Senate, in its wisdom or unwisdom, decided by a majority that the ultimate financial settlement was a proper subject for investigation by a Special Committee of the House, its right to take such action could not be gainsaid. Moreover, the proceedings of the committee would have been conducted in private, its report would have had to be submitted to the Senate, which could accept or reject it, and, in the unlikely event of an adverse report being approved by the Senate, the validity of the Agreement would not have been affected, since it did not require ratification by Parliament.

The Minister for Finance, who took part in the debate, adopted an attitude in regard to the amendment which seems difficult to justify on any view of the rights and privileges of Parliament. He said: 'I would not attend at the Committee if it had been appointed, especially with the terms of reference which are attached to the setting up of the Committee, and which aim at repudiation. No papers would be submitted by the Government and no information would be given to the Committee. When it became a substantive motion I would deal with it in that way. . . . If such a Committee were appointed I would not appear before it. I would give no facilities.' The acceptance by the Senate of such an attitude would affect any committee that might afterwards be appointed, with power to send for persons, papers, and records; for the precedent might bar the committee and the House from dealing with a refusal, even if such refusal were impertinent or contumacious. The Senate could, if necessary for the upholding of its privileges, have threatened to suspend all but essential Bills; but a mere caveat from the Chair would probably have sufficed to bring about a change of tone. Lord Glenavy dealt with the matter as follows:

'I am very sensitive about the position and the dignity of this House, and I would suggest to the Senate, not touching on the merits of this particular controversy at all, that they should think very long before they proceed to set up a Committee under the conditions mentioned here to-day, a Committee that will have no powers, a Committee which the Government will refuse to recognize, and which will, therefore, not be in a position to extract the information they want. They will simply report this to us, and leave the position where it is to-day. I am suggesting to the Senator that he should not put the House in this very undignified position. If this were a Committee that had powers of its own and that could investigate these particular matters, I, for one, would not have intervened at all. They can only act on information which they can only obtain through Government channels, and these channels have been closed by the declaration made by the Minister. I put it to the House whether they are consulting their own dignity in appointing a Special Committee.'

Those in favour of the proposal to set up a committee were not convinced by this line of reasoning. A division was demanded, the voting was equal, and Lord Glenavy gave his casting vote against the proposal. There had been a surrender to truculence.[1]

Early in 1927 an effort was made to end the Senate's position of isolation by a removal of the bar which prevented Senators from being appointed members of the Executive Council. The position at that time was as follows. Under Article 51 of the Constitution, membership of the Executive Council was limited to a maximum of seven, all of whom (Article 52) had to be members of the Dáil. Under Article 55, 'Extern' Ministers might be appointed by the Representative of the Crown on the nomination of the Dáil, and these could be members of either House or of neither; but the total number of Ministers, of both kinds, was not to exceed twelve. Under Section 7 of the Ministers and Secretaries Act, 1924, the Executive Council might appoint Parliamentary Secretaries up to the number of seven. These had to be members of either the Senate or the Dáil, and the total number of persons in receipt of salaries either as Ministers or as Parliamentary Secretaries at any one time was not to exceed fifteen. At the beginning of 1927, there were seven members of the Execu-

[1] *Senate Debates*, viii, 12–62.

tive Council, four 'Extern' Ministers and three Parliamentary Secretaries—a total of fourteen. All were members of the Dáil, and, as the Government party numbered less than seventy, one member of the party in every five held office.

The system of 'Extern' Ministers having proved unsatisfactory, the Government introduced the Constitution (Amendment No. 5) Bill, 1926, whereby it was proposed to amend Article 51 of the Constitution by increasing the maximum membership of the Executive Council from seven to twelve. If the Bill was passed, and if the President availed himself of it to have an Executive Council of twelve, no 'Extern' Ministers could be appointed, since, under Article 55, twelve was still an overriding maximum for Ministers of both kinds. In such a case, the Senate would be deprived of the possibility of having even an 'Extern' Minister, though this was, of course, a deprivation that was shared in theory by every individual citizen.

At all events, when the Bill came before the Senate (2nd February 1927) this theoretical point was used by Senator P. W. Kenny as a basis for the plea that Article 51 should be further amended so as to permit of Senators being members of the Executive Council. As might be expected, the proposal received general support. Senator Colonel Moore said:

'I have felt from the very beginning the great embarrassment of not having some party leader in this House. As matters stand, no one knows exactly what a particular Minister wants. There is no one to decide. Ministers themselves are obliged to leave their other duties to come to this House and sit here in a very awkward position in order to give their views occasionally as to what they mean. I do not think such a course is dignified or is very suitable for Ministers themselves.

'I think it would be very much better if we had a leader in this House. The result of not having such a leader is just as I prophesied, that the Chairman of this Assembly is in two positions whether he likes it or not. He is in the position of an ordinary Chairman and he is also a sort of leader of the House, giving advice and doing things which an ordinary Chairman would not do because there is nobody else to do them. I do not think it is convenient; I think it would be better if the Minister could take his place in this House, as is done in the other Dominions and in every country that I know of.'[1]

Senator Sir John Keane made the same point about the Dominions: 'The fact that the Senate cannot have several members on the Executive Council, or that the President or Minister for Finance can-

[1] *Senate Debates*, viii, 153.

not be a member of the Senate, does not affect the principle. That should be kept clearly in view. . . . I do strongly feel that we should come into line with our sister Dominions, all of whom, I think, have the power to choose Ministers from their Senate or Upper House.'[1]

And Senator Douglas was substantially of the same opinion as Colonel Moore: 'I think the Senate suffers considerably by not having either a Minister or a Parliamentary Secretary in this House. I think that the Government ought to look in the future to having one person who would be in a real sense a representative of the Government and, consequently, the leader of the House. It is not satisfactory as it is at present, and I think a good deal of misunderstanding and difficulty with regard to the stages of Bills are due to the fact that there is no authoritative person, as there is in most Second Chambers, representing the Government of the day. Whether that Government has a majority in the Senate or not has nothing to do with it; they should have a representative.'[2]

Mr. O'Higgins, who was the Minister in charge of the Bill, did not reply to any of these arguments, but merely gave the reasons why the Government wished to extend the permitted maximum membership of the Executive Council. In these circumstances the Senate, after giving the Bill a Second Reading, referred it to a Select Committee for a detailed examination of its implications.

This Select Committee met on the 10th February 1927, and it was attended by Mr. O'Higgins. The sole question discussed was whether or not membership of the Executive Council should be open to Senators. Mr. O'Higgins's arguments against the proposal were three. First, he doubted 'whether it is wise to call into collective responsibility to the major administration and legislation, and matters affecting the electors, persons who have never been elected, persons who are not conscious, and who cannot be conscious, of a feeling of direct political responsibility to the electors'. Second, in a mixed Executive Council, 'they are not all in the same position. The reaction of defeat is not the same for all of them, because whereas in the event of defeat in the Dáil some members of the Executive Council would probably find themselves facing the electorate and battling for their seats, the Senate members would retire to the Senate, with, perhaps, eight or ten years of office and with no obligations to face the electorate.' Third, there was a lack of uniformity in the Senate. 'Some have been nominated, some have been co-opted and some elected. That is a patchwork position.'

[1] *Senate Debates*, viii, 152.   [2] Ibid., viii, 151.

Lord Glenavy asked, 'Are not these arguments all applicable, not only to the British Constitution to-day, but to the Constitutions of South Africa and Canada?' and Senator Douglas added, 'To every other country except the United States.' Mr. O'Higgins replied, 'No doubt, but we must examine our affairs here.'

In the end, Mr. O'Higgins stated that he 'would be prepared to ask the Dáil to co-operate in extending the eligibility of members of the Executive Council to the entire Oireachtas', but he deprecated the holding up of his Bill pending a decision on the question. The Select Committee returned the Bill to the Senate with a unanimous recommendation that the further consideration of the Bill should be postponed and that the Dáil should be asked to agree to set up a Joint Committee to consider and report on the question of the eligibility of Senators for membership of the Executive Council.[1]

The Senate adopted the recommendation of the Select Committee (23rd February 1927), and the appropriate message was sent to the Dáil, requesting the concurrence of that House in the appointment of a Joint Committee. Mr. O'Higgins appears to have been nettled by the fact that the Senate had meantime postponed further consideration of the Bill, and when the Senate message came before the Dáil (2nd March 1927) he met the request for a Joint Committee with a blank refusal. He stated that he did so on two grounds: first, because the Government objected to what he called its 'bargaining complexion' and an alleged 'underlying threat', and second, on the merits. His arguments on the merits were the same as those which he adduced before the Select Committee of the Senate, with the additional reason that, when the Constitution was being enacted, it was not the intention that members of the Second Chamber should be eligible for Ministerial office.

'The Provisional Parliament enacted this Constitution. Only after its enactment did the Senate come into existence at all. It came into existence with certain prescribed functions, functions of revision, of criticism, of suggestion, and, as its maximum power, the function of imposing a certain delay to measures of which it disapproved. Now we are asked to take the view that it is desirable to explore, at any rate, the possibility that some members of that Assembly so constituted, constituted for this purpose, to those ends, should be made suddenly and gratuitously eligible for quite other functions.'[2]

The only other notable contribution to a comparatively short

---

[1] *Committee Debates*, vol. i, pp. 279–89.
[2] *Dáil Debates*, xviii, 1167.

debate was that made by Major Bryan Cooper, who spoke on the other side.

'There is no doubt whatever that the present position of the Senate is unique and, I think, anomalous. It is not in the same position as any other Second Chamber in the world that I know of. Ministers without portfolio sit in the Canadian Senate. Ministers sit in the Senate of New Zealand; the Vice-President of the Executive Council and the Minister for Home Intelligence sit in the Senate of Australia. In France the Prime Minister, Monsieur Poincaré, is a member of the Senate. In every Second Chamber in the world, except that of the United States, where the Executive is entirely divorced from the Legislature and where members of the Executive are not members of either House, members are eligible for office, and by the fact that there are Ministers in those particular Chambers they derive a great advantage, because they get guidance . . . of which the Senate has very often stood in need. . . . One practical effect of adhering to the present position and refusing to discuss any change at all will be, in the end, to exclude men of ability from the Senate. No man of ability and ambition will be willing to go to the Senate if he is aware . . . that under no circumstances could a member of the Senate go for a Ministerial position.'[1]

Such arguments as these, however, carried no weight with Mr. O'Higgins and the Government, and the motion refusing the Senate's request for a Joint Committee was carried without a division.

When the Dáil message of refusal came before the Senate (9th March 1927) considerable surprise was expressed at Mr. O'Higgins's belief that the Senate's postponement of the Bill had had a 'bargaining complexion'. The members of the Select Committee disclaimed any such intention. Senator Kenny, who had been the protagonist, stated that 'there was not in the Committee Stage, or in any discussion in this House, any suggestion of a threat to the Ministers or to the Dáil'. Senator Jameson said: 'The decision we came to was a unanimous decision to do a certain thing which we thought we had the approval of the Minister for, and the last thing in our minds was that we were doing anything to hold out a threat to the Dáil. I never was so astonished as when I read the remarks which the Minister made in opposing our proposal in the Dáil.'

And Senator Douglas also added his testimony: 'I very much regret that the Minister for Justice, whom we all respect so much, should have been misled in that matter. I think his memory must

1 *Dáil Debates*, xviii, 1158.

have failed him. I do not think that a statement like that will help the good relationship that should exist between the two Houses.'

The sincerity of these utterances is proved by the fact that, in spite of the curt refusal of the Dáil, it was not suggested in any quarter of the Senate that the Bill should be held up.[1]

On the Committee Stage (7th April 1927), Mr. O'Higgins, who was always an honourable controversialist, said, apropos of the 'threat': 'I want to say, if I have done the Senate less than justice, I regret that very much.' But the most he would concede was that, if the Senate passed the Bill, the Government would not oppose the setting up of a Joint Committee to consider the eligibility of Senators for membership of the Executive Council; it would not itself propose such a committee. Of course, in view of the strong views already expressed by Mr. O'Higgins, and of his personal prestige in the Dáil, such a concession was entirely useless, even though he promised that the question of setting up a Joint Committee would be left to a free vote of the Dáil. The Senate bowed to the inevitable, and passed the Bill without amendment.[2]

This whole episode well exemplifies the general attitude of the Government and the Dáil towards the Senate at that time and also conveys some idea of the frigid atmosphere of isolation in which the functions of the Second Chamber were discharged. It seems useless unduly to blame Mr. O'Higgins, the Ministry, or the Dáil. As a result of past history, the country was then, and is still, passing through an ultra-democratic phase which forbids the concession of any but minimum powers to the members of an Upper House.

In spite of the manifest handicaps, Senators continued to apply themselves to their duties conscientiously and with zeal. One Government Bill was suspended during this period—the Civil Service Regulation (Amendment) Bill, 1925, sponsored by the Minister for Finance. This Bill proposed to confer power on the Civil Service Commissioners to restrict admission to examinations held by them to members of one sex. Objection was taken to this proposal from all quarters of the House on the ground that it was directed against women, and the Bill was rejected on Second Reading by a large majority (17th December 1925).[3] It remained in abeyance for the suspensory period of 270 days prescribed by the Constitution and reached the Statute Book on the 22nd September 1926.

The feminist question was also the principal subject of controversy in the case of the Juries Bill, 1927. This was a comprehensive measure

[1] *Senate Debates*, viii, 463–72.   [2] Ibid., viii, 748–80.   [3] Ibid., vi, 244–66.

of seventy-two sections, codifying the existing law in regard to the liability for service of jurors, their registration, the preparation of jurors' lists and books, and procedure to secure their attendance in court. Under the law then in force, women were liable to serve on the same terms as men, but Ireland is a conservative country so far as women's rights are concerned, and the law in this respect was practically a dead letter. Most of the women summoned to serve on juries were excused for business or domestic reasons, and the few who were called on the panel were almost always challenged by one or other of the parties, or by the accused in a criminal case. In view of these facts, Mr. O'Higgins in his Juries Bill proposed to exclude women altogether from jury service. The Senate's opposition to this proposal was very pronounced, and Senator Brown opened the case against it on the Second Reading. He characterized the proposed exclusion as not only unconstitutional but illogical.

'You have given the franchise to every woman of twenty-one in this country whether she has the property qualification or not, and you are denying to a woman, who is bound to have the property qualification for the purpose, the right or the obligation of serving on a jury. In my opinion the average woman knows far more about the question which will come before her when sitting on a jury than she knows about the political issues involved, say, in the next general election. . . . I am not here to make a case for women jurors that does not exist. I think up to the present they have, to a large extent, been a failure, but that is not altogether, or indeed to any great extent, their own fault. They have never had a chance before. That kind of job is not one which comes to you by nature, and especially it is not one which comes to people whose lives have been more or less in domestic retirement; but, with time, better education, and wider experience of life, I have no doubt that the average woman will be just as good a juror as the average man at present.'[1]

The speakers who followed were nearly all on the same side; and on the Committee Stage an amendment restoring the liability of women was proposed in a convincing speech by Senator Sir Edward Coey Bigger and carried against the Government by a large majority. Ultimately, a rather amusing compromise was reached whereby women were placed in a Special Schedule of 'persons exempted but entitled to serve on application', along with doctors, dentists, veterinary surgeons, licensed pilots, and others.

When the Intoxicating Liquor Bill, 1927, came before the House,

[1] *Senate Debates*, viii, 668, 669.

Senator Farren, of the Labour Party, was not afraid to espouse what might be an unpopular cause, and he led the opposition to a proposal in the Bill that the public-houses should again be allowed to open on Saint Patrick's Day. He referred to the struggle which had taken place between the Senate and the Dáil on this question in 1924.

'We had a real stand-up fight on the question. . . . The Senate on that occasion decided to insist on St. Patrick's Day being treated the same as Christmas Day and Good Friday. The matter went back to the Dáil, and the Dáil disagreed with our amendment. It came back to the Senate, and, like good men and true, Senators insisted on their amendment . . . and we carried the day. . . . If St. Patrick came to earth again and saw the manner in which some people drown the shamrock he would be prepared to drown the people who drown the shamrock.'[1]

Senator Farren's amendment was carried against the Government, and this time it was accepted by the Dáil. It is not unlikely that Mr. O'Higgins, who was in charge of the Bill, was secretly in favour of it; and this was probably one of the many cases in which the Ministry avoided the unpopularity of a decision with which they agreed by allowing the onus to fall upon the Senate. This is, of course, quite a usual and a perfectly legitimate use of a Second Chamber.

The energy with which the Senate discharged its function of revision over the whole field of legislation is sufficiently indicated by some specimen figures. Agriculturalists, members of the Labour Party, bankers, business men, and lawyers all co-operated in improving the measures submitted to the House. To the Court Officers Bill, twenty-four amendments were made, and thirty-two to the Agricultural Credit Bill. In the case of the Electricity (Supply) Bill and the Industrial and Commercial Property Bill—two very complex measures—the figures were fifty-four and seventy respectively. During this short period of just over a year and a half, more than sixty non-Money Bills were passed, of which about one-third were amended. The number of amendments fell just short of 300, and of this huge total all except two were agreed to by the Dáil.

Even after the lapse of twelve years it is difficult for anyone who enjoyed the friendship of Kevin O'Higgins to write without emotion concerning his death. Two days after the assassination (Tuesday, 12th July 1927) the Senate and Dáil met specially at three o'clock in the afternoon, and in both Houses moving tributes were paid to the

1 *Senate Debates*, viii, 916, 917.

dead Vice-President. In the Senate there was practically a full attendance, and Lord Glenavy addressed the House as follows from the
Chair.

'We meet to-day under the shadow of a great national catastrophe.
We mourn the loss, under cruel and tragic circumstances, of one who
was perhaps the great outstanding Irishman of his day and generation,
a man who in his duties as a Minister of the State, with an unparal-
leled fearlessness and lion-hearted courage acting up to a conscientious sense of duty, left himself without a moment of leisure to devote
himself exclusively to the work of the regeneration of his country. In
these efforts he had succeeded beyond, I think, perhaps even his own
hopes or expectations, and beyond the expectations of most of us. In
the course of his work he had commanded the confidence and gained
the affection of all his colleagues and of all his countrymen. He had
asserted the position of our Free State with a dignity, ability and
efficiency in the councils of the Empire and the councils of Europe,
where his transparent honesty, unselfish patriotism and devotion to
duty had earned him a reputation in a few brief years that few others
in a lifetime have succeeded in gaining. We are each and all of us the
poorer for his death, but, on the other hand, his country is rich, enriched by the example he has set each of us of devotion to duty and
of unselfish and loyal work for his country. I do not think there
could be any more noble epitaph placed upon the grave of any one
of us than what he himself recorded in his dying words, when he said,
"We have done good work; continue on the same lines." That
should be an inspiration to each and all of us, and I am sure that I
was only acting in accordance with the sentiments of Senators in asking each and every one of you to assemble here to-day, for the purpose of considering how best you could pay your tribute to the
memory of this great man at his funeral obsequies to-morrow.'

The Minister for Finance (Mr. Ernest Blythe) followed Lord
Glenavy in a short speech, in the course of which he said :

'Other countries have had statesmen whose names were more
widely known throughout the world, but I do not believe that any
nation has ever had a servant who, in purity of purpose or powers of
mind, excelled this man who is now dead in his thirty-fifth year. He
was struck down by assassins, not because of anything he had done in
the past, but because of the work they knew him to be capable of
doing in the future, because he was the strongest pillar of the State.
The best tribute we can pay to his memory is, solemnly to resolve
that we shall preserve and strengthen the fabric of this State, which

he laboured to build up and for which he died, and that we shall
guard it against all enemies within and without.'

Then, one by one, the spokesmen of the different groups and sections in the House added their tributes to the dead leader in solemn
language that fitted well the tragic occasion. That from Senator
Jameson was particularly touching. He referred to his first meeting
with Kevin O'Higgins at the time of the negotiations with the
Southern Unionists in London.

'I happened to be associated with him at the very beginning of the
Irish Free State. With some of my colleagues I met him and discussed
the conditions under which the Free State was to be started. We
formed a great opinion then of Mr. O'Higgins. We saw that his
vision of the future was clear and just. We saw his great statesmanship, his great moral bravery, and we recognized above all things that
what he said he would do he would do no matter what it cost when
it came to the doing. I have had the good fortune, because of making
his acquaintance at that time, to become a great friend of his, and I
can speak both as a personal friend and as an ordinary citizen of the
Free State as to the great man we have lost. Since those early days
we who have worked with him to try and establish our country on a
sound political and governmental basis have seen him follow the same
line of conduct that he pursued at that time. He has never flinched.
He has always acted up to his own ideal.' Mr. Jameson went on to
say that O'Higgins's ideal was the ordered government of the
country, with security for its citizens. 'That was Kevin O'Higgins's
ideal, and it was because it was his ideal, and because he worked for
it, that they killed him. Mr. Blythe said quite truly that they knew the
man they had to deal with, and that they knew how he meant to carry
on the country. The forces of disruption and disorder feared him,
and with good reason. Now, we citizens who are left have to take
care to carry on the record, and wherever the Government asks us to
support them in their defence of law and order we should act and
give them every support. I hope when we go to meet Mr. O'Higgins
on the other side of the Great Divide, that we, one and all of us, will
be able to look him fearlessly in the face and say: "We have done
our best to follow the great standard of conduct you set, and we feel
glad and honoured to be in your company once more." '

The Vice-Chairman (Senator T. W. Westropp Bennett), adding his
own tribute, formally moved 'That Seanad Éireann attend the funeral
ceremonies of the late Vice-President, Minister for Justice and
Minister for External Affairs, Deputy Kevin O'Higgins, on Wednes-

day, 13th July 1927.' The motion was seconded by Senator Brown and passed in silence, all the members standing.

On the following morning the members of both Houses assembled in their respective Chambers and marched in processional order to the church of Saint Andrew, Westland Row, Dublin; and having assisted there at a solemn Requiem Mass, presided over by His Grace the Archbishop of Dublin, they walked in the State funeral procession to Glasnevin Cemetery, where the body of Kevin O'Higgins was laid to rest.[1]

[1] *Senate Debates*, ix, 5–16.

CHAPTER XIII

MR. DE VALERA ENTERS THE DÁIL

Emergency legislation demanded by the assassination—The Public Safety Bill—The Electoral Amendment Bill—Amendment of Constitution regarding referendum and initiative—Mr. De Valera's dilemma— Fianna Fáil enter the Dáil and subscribe the Oath—Preparations for referendum on Electoral Amendment Bill not proceeded with—Mr. De Valera's arrangement with Labour Party and National League—The motion of no confidence—Revolt of Mr. Vincent Rice, K.C.—The Jinks episode—The motion defeated by casting vote of the Chair—The dissolution—The election campaign—Rival policies—Mr. De Valera's moderation—Major Bryan Cooper joins the Government party—Result of the general election of September 1927—The new Administration —Fianna Fáil and the legitimacy of the State—Mr. De Valera and the right of the Republican Government and Army to claim continuity— The Leader of the Labour Party on Mr. De Valera's attitude—Attempted presentation of a petition for a referendum to abolish the Oath —The Government replies with a Bill to abolish the referendum and the initiative—Criticism of the Government's action—Passage of the Bill by the Dáil.

Following the assassination of Kevin O'Higgins, Mr. Cosgrave took over for the time being the portfolios of Justice and External Affairs, and Mr. Blythe, the Minister for Finance, was appointed Vice-President. The Government's proposals for dealing with the emergency were contained in three Bills, all introduced in the Dáil on the 20th July. The first, a Public Safety Bill, gave power to the Executive Council to declare as unlawful any association which had for its object the overthrow by force of the Government of the Irish Free State or pursued similar treasonable or seditious activities; and membership of such associations, and the possession of documents relating to them, were made offences punishable by penal servitude. Drastic powers of search were conferred by the Bill, and the Executive Council was authorized to establish special courts for the trial of offences named in the Bill. One member of each such court had to be a person certified by the Attorney-General as having legal knowledge and experience, and the others were to be Army officers. A special court had power to inflict the penalty of death or penal servitude for life for the offence of unlawful possession of firearms.

This Bill was quickly passed into law, no amendment being carried to it in the Senate. It was clearly a case of desperate diseases needing desperate remedies, and the Labour opposition was re-inforced only by Senators Colonel Moore and Mrs. Wyse Power, who had been members of the Senate from the beginning and who both subsequently joined Mr. De Valera's party. Joint Resolutions were passed by both Houses, declaring that the Bill was immediately necessary for the preservation of the public peace and safety, thus removing it from the referendum provisions of the Constitution; and it became law on the 11th August 1927. Some of its provisions clearly infringed the constitutional guarantees of the liberty of the subject and trial by jury, and this difficulty was surmounted by the insertion of a section to the effect that 'every provision of this Act which is in contravention of any provision of the Constitution shall . . . operate and have effect as an amendment' thereof. It seems extremely doubtful whether such general words as these could operate to effect a valid amendment of the Constitution within the meaning of Article 50; but this particular Public Safety Act had a short life, being repealed on the 26th December 1928, and its constitutionality was never tested in the courts.

The second of the Government's three measures, an Electoral Amendment Bill, was designed to meet the abstentionist policy of Fianna Fáil and Sinn Féin, which was a prime cause of unrest in the country. The Bill provided that every candidate for election to either House should, on nomination, swear an affidavit that he would, if elected, take the Oath prescribed by the Constitution. Every member elected who failed to do so within the time prescribed by the Bill would be disqualified and his seat vacated. This Bill was passed by the Senate on the same day as the Public Safety Bill (10th August 1927), but its formal enactment was suspended in circumstances which will be referred to later.

The third Bill proposed to amend the Constitution in two respects: first, the right of members to demand a referendum under Article 47 of the Constitution was to be restricted to members who had taken the Oath; and second, the provisions were to be deleted which permitted of the initiation by the people of proposals for laws or constitutional amendments. This Bill received a Second Reading in the Dáil, but was killed by the dissolution of the 25th August.

Mr. De Valera was placed in a cruel dilemma by the Electoral Amendment Bill. For the second time within less than two years he was called upon either to sacrifice his principles or to face political extinction. In the spring of 1926, after having been repudiated by the Irish Republican Army, he had seceded from Sinn Féin, recognized the Irish Free State Parliament, and thereby abandoned the all-Ireland Republic of which he had been President. In his new organization, Fianna Fáil, he had concentrated on the abolition of the Oath and, as we have seen, had made it clear in speeches innumerable that in no circumstances would he subscribe it. As recently as the 29th May, at Athlone, he had stated that 'they had those taking it who did not mean to keep it, and those were nothing more or less than perjurers who had abjured their nationality'.[1] There was now little doubt that, in face of the certain passage of the Electoral Amendment Bill, a number of his followers, perhaps the majority, would take the Oath and their seats. Already, one of them, Mr. Daniel Breen, had done so the previous January. On the 26th July Mr. Patrick Belton, a man of considerable force of character, had broken with Fianna Fáil and done likewise. If the majority of the party should decide to follow suit, Mr. De Valera would either have to go with them or retire from politics. The only abstentionist party in the State would then be Sinn Féin; but he had already broken with Sinn Féin on the issue of the Republic, and there was small likelihood that he would be received back into its ranks as a leader.

A conference of the Fianna Fáil members was held on the 10th August 1927 to discuss the question. It will be recalled that, on that date, none of the three Bills referred to had yet been passed into law. The discussion was prolonged, and it was not until after midnight that a decision was arrived at. This decision was embodied in a long communication to the Press, which published it the next morning. Reference was made to the three Bills, and the communication continued:

'They recognize that this legislation may imperil the general peace and cause widespread suffering; that it disfranchises, and precludes from engaging in any effective peaceful political movement towards independence, all Irish Republicans who will not acknowledge that any allegiance is due to the English Crown. Nevertheless, they have

[1] *Irish Independent*, 30 May 1927.

come unanimously to the decision that even under these circumstances it is not competent for them, as pledged Republicans, and as elected representatives of the Republican section of the community, to transfer their allegiance.

'It has, however, been repeatedly stated, and it is not uncommonly believed, that the required declaration is not an oath, that the signing of it implies no contractual obligation, and that it has no binding significance in conscience or in law; that, in short, it is merely an empty political formula which deputies could conscientiously sign without becoming involved, or without involving their nation, in obligations of loyalty to the English Crown.'

The communication ended with an intimation that, on this basis, the members of Fianna Fáil proposed to attend at the Parliament buildings and comply with Article 17 of the Constitution by subscribing their names in the book kept for the purpose.[1]

Mr. De Valera had again apparently sacrificed principle to expediency, and there is a curious similarity between the two cases. When he decided to recognize the Free State Parliament, he held it up to odium as 'frankly, a non-sovereign, subordinate, twenty-six county institution'. When he decided to subscribe the Oath, it was characterized as 'merely an empty political formula'.

On the following day (11th August 1927), Mr. De Valera and his forty-two followers subscribed the Oath. This *volte face* must have been unexpected even to his intimates, for the copy of the weekly paper of Mr. De Valera's own party, *The Nation*, which is dated two days later (but which must have gone to press earlier), contains the following: 'If all the Fianna Fáil deputies published to-morrow a signed declaration that in their opinion the oath in the Free State Constitution is an unsworn undertaking, the oath would still remain an oath and to swear it falsely would still continue to be perjury.'[2] Nearly five years later, after Mr. De Valera had achieved power, he told the Dáil what happened when he subscribed the Oath.

'Believing that "I swear" would mean an oath, I said, in my opinion, it was an oath. My view was that it was an oath. But the Deputies opposite had said quite differently. They said that it was not, that it was a mere formality—they used the words long before I used them—and had no binding significance whatever, that anyone could take it, and that it meant nothing. I asked myself whether in a crisis like that I would be justified in staying outside if it were, in fact, true that this thing was a mere formality. I could only find out in one way.

[1] *Irish Times*, 11 August 1927.   [2] *The Nation*, 13 August 1927.

In order that the people's attention should not be attracted to it, instead of taking the oath—as they would have done, if they dared to stand over it as a thing the Irish people would stand for—publicly, as in other Parliaments, they hid it away in a back room, hid it away out of sight, so that the public could not know what it was. I said that at least we were entitled to find out. We published a declaration and here is the original document, signed by every member, in which we stated our attitude. The attitude was in fact this: the majority party of that time held that this was no oath at all; we are going to put it to the test. In order that our coming in here might not be misrepresented we made a public declaration as to what our intentions were. When we came to take this so-called oath I presented this document to the officer in charge and told him that that was our attitude—there were witnesses present for every word—that this was our attitude; that we were not prepared to take an oath. I have here the original document written in pencil, and in Irish, of the statement I made to the officer who was supposed to administer the oath. I said, "I am not prepared to take an oath. I am not going to take an oath. I am prepared to put my name down in this book in order to get permission to go into the Dáil, but it has no other significance." There was a Testament on the table and in order that there could be no misunderstanding I went and I took the Testament and put it over and said, "You must remember I am taking no oath." '

A Deputy having here interrupted to ask whether he did not sign the declaration, Mr. De Valera replied: 'I signed it in the same way as I would sign an autograph in a newspaper. If you ask me whether I had an idea what was there, I say "Yes." It was neither read to me nor was I asked to read it.'[1]

Put more precisely and in unemotional language, what this explanation amounts to is this. Mr. De Valera believed that the Oath was an oath. His political opponents said it was a mere formality. There was only one way in which he could ascertain which contention was correct, and that was to go and see. He did so on the 11th August, found that it was a formality, and, as such, he complied with it for the purpose of obtaining admission to the Dáil. But this explanation must be read in the light of what had occurred on the previous 23rd June. On that date, as we have seen, he had already gone to see for himself, he had been shown into the 'back room', and the 'officer in charge' had characterized the oath as a 'formality'. But Mr. De Valera had then refused compliance and had retired to his party

---

[1] *Dáil Debates*, xli, 1101, 1102.

headquarters, from which he informed his audience that 'they pledged themselves to the people that as long as they were the representatives of the people they would never take an oath of allegiance to a foreign king. They had been prevented because they would neither take a false oath nor prove recreant to the aspirations of the Irish people and renounce their principles.' What had been a matter of high principle on the 23rd June had become an 'empty political formula' on the following 11th August. The reason was that the passage of the Electoral Amendment Bill would stand between Mr. De Valera and power.

The forty-three members of the Fianna Fáil Party took their seats in the Dáil on the 12th August 1927; and they at once combined with the members of the Labour Party to furnish the sixty-two signatures (being two-fifths of the entire House) necessary for a written demand to suspend the Electoral Amendment Bill for ninety days, preparatory to a referendum. This should' have been followed up by a petition signed by not less than one-twentieth of the voters on the register; but no such petition was presented, and the Bill became law after the period of ninety days had elapsed (9th November 1927). But it had fully succeeded of its purpose long before its formal enactment, and in this way it must be unique among Acts of Parliament.

By combining with the Labour Party (twenty-two votes) and the National League (eight votes), Mr. De Valera was now in a position, on a full muster of all parties, to overtop by a few votes the united strength of the Government, Farmers, and Independents. Negotiations took place and an arrangement was concluded on the basis, apparently, that the Government was to be put out of office and that Mr. Johnson and Captain Redmond should form a coalition government which would be kept in power by Mr. De Valera. From the Labour point of view, this was a legitimate move enough; but it is not easy to understand how men who still called themselves Republicans were prepared to keep Captain Redmond in office, or how Captain Redmond could be prepared to accept office from them. The matter was put to the test immediately. On the 16th August Mr. Johnson moved 'That the Executive Council has ceased to retain the support of a majority in Dáil Éireann'. But the result was not in accordance with expectations. Mr. Vincent Rice, K.C., by a long way the ablest member of the National League, denounced his leader's flagitious bargain in unmeasured terms.

'Does Deputy Redmond think that a child would be deceived as to who is to control the new Government? Does he imagine that

Deputy De Valera and his party will waste their time keeping him in power if they are not advancing his policy? I do not think that Deputy De Valera has ever disguised that his aim is to get rid of the Treaty and the Constitution, and, if he is not serving that purpose by keeping Deputy Redmond in office, how many hours will he keep him there? Let us get back to the plain facts of the case and recognize that this Government will not last one hour except, and so long as, it obeys the behest of Deputy De Valera and his party.'[1]

While the debate was in progress Major Bryan Cooper, a Sligo man who was an Independent deputy for County Dublin, had a conversation with Alderman John Jinks, National League member for Sligo. Major Cooper pointed out to Mr. Jinks that the ex-servicemen of Sligo had certainly never sent him to the Dáil for the purpose of putting Mr. Cosgrave out of office and of helping Mr. De Valera. Mr. Jinks replied that in that case perhaps the best thing for him to do would be to take the next train back to Sligo; which he did. As a result of his abstention, and of the transfer of Mr. Vincent Rice's vote to the other side, the division on the 'No Confidence' motion resulted in a tie, seventy-one members voting for the motion and seventy-one against. The Chairman gave his casting vote against the motion, which was declared lost. For the time being, Mr. Jinks was the laughing stock of the English-speaking world, and, *more Hibernico*, a celebrated racehorse was named after him. Captain Redmond's National League was doomed; and Mr. De Valera gained nothing but a reputation for willingness to play a purely political game to suit his own ends. There were two by-elections pending, and the Dáil adjourned until the 11th October, Mr. Cosgrave undertaking to summon it immediately if the Government did not win them both. It did so by substantial majorities, Mr. Cosgrave advised a dissolution, and on the 25th August the Dáil was dissolved, after a short life of only two months.

The election campaign which ensued was brief but bitter. All parties were short of funds, and the number of candidates was only 261, as compared with 383 in the previous June. Sinn Féin dropped out altogether, and there was a fissure in the Labour ranks between the moderate and the extreme elements. The Farmers were virtually allied with the Cosgrave party, and the struggle once more resolved itself into one between the Government and Fianna Fáil. With power so near his grasp, Mr. De Valera was studiously moderate in tone. The Republic was kept in the background, and he emphasized in a

1 *Dáil Debates*, xx, 1708.

manifesto addressed to 'The People of Ireland' that 'the sinister design of aiming at bringing about a sudden revolutionary upheaval with which our opponents choose to credit us is altogether foreign to our purpose and programme. We do not believe in attempting to practise sleight-of-hand on the electorate. We shall proceed as a responsible constitutional Government, acknowledging without reserve that all authority comes through the sovereign people, and that before any important step likely to involve their safety is taken the people are entitled to be taken into the fullest consultation. The stubborn political and economic facts are of necessity the base from which any successful advance must be made. To ignore them would be to court defeat.'[1] These words might have been culled from the speeches of Kevin O'Higgins, Patrick Hogan, or any of the pro-Treaty leaders during the previous five years. But the impossibility, from the Fianna Fáil point of view, of any real union of hearts, such as was prayed for by Thomas Davis and other Irish patriots, became apparent during the campaign. Major Bryan Cooper, a Protestant and a former Unionist Member of Parliament, had sat in the Dáil as an Independent since 1923. He had done more than any other private individual to reconcile the old régime with the new; and after the dissolution of August 1927 he joined the Cosgrave party and stood as a Government candidate. The greatest use was made of this fact by Mr. De Valera's followers to inflame nationalist opinion against the Government by throwing the mantle of Unionism over it, and dead walls were plastered with the offensive slogan, 'Cooper's Dip for Free State Sheep'.

Polling took place on the 15th September 1927, and the result was as follows:

Party	Candidates nominated	Members elected
Cumann na nGaedheal (Cosgrave)	88	62
Fianna Fáil (De Valera)	88	57
Labour	28	13
Independents	30	12
Farmers	20	6
National League	6	2
Independent Labour	1	1
	261	153

[1] *Irish Independent*, 12 September 1927.

Both the major parties had increased their strength at the expense of the smaller ones, and a neck-and-neck race had just been won by Mr. Cosgrave. Captain Redmond's National League had been practically wiped out, the only survivors being the leader and Mr. Coburn, of Dundalk. The Farmers had fared little better. The Labour Party had been nearly halved, and its able chairman, Mr. Thomas Johnson, paid the penalty of his moderation by losing his seat in County Dublin. Thus, after five years, despite the encouragement given by proportional representation to small parties and groups, the electors seemed to have made up their minds that there were to be only two main parties in the State, with Labour and Independents holding the balance of power between them. Other parties, founded at different times, had all disappeared or virtually disappeared: Sinn Féin (1918), the Farmers' Party (1922), the National Party (1925), Clann Éireann (1926), and the National League (1926). And, as Mr. De Valera's political education progressed and the Republic receded further into the background, the difference between the two main parties seemed likely to diminish.

The Cosgrave party was still the largest in the Dáil and it was the only one in a position to form a government. It came to an understanding with the Farmers' Party, as a result of which the new leader of that party (Mr. M. R. Heffernan) was given a Parliamentary Secretaryship and so associated with the Administration. When Parliament reassembled on the 11th October Mr. Cosgrave was elected President of the Executive Council by seventy-six votes to seventy. There was no other candidate for the office, and the opposition consisted of the combined strength of Fianna Fáil and Labour. The two members of the National League took no part in the division.[1] On the following day, after a long and tedious debate, the Dáil assented by the same majority to Mr. Cosgrave's nominations to his Executive Council, as follows:

Vice-President, Minister for Finance and Minister for Posts and
    Telegraphs: Ernest Blythe
Minister for Defence: Desmond Fitzgerald
Minister for Industry and Commerce and Minister for External
    Affairs: Patrick McGilligan
Minister for Education: John M. O'Sullivan
Minister for Lands and Agriculture: Patrick Hogan
Minister for Local Government and Public Health: Richard
    Mulcahy

[1] *Dáil Debates*, xxi, 18-58.

Minister for Fisheries: Finian Lynch
Minister for Justice: James Fitzgerald-Kenney, K.C.

As compared with the previous June, the only changes were those necessitated by the assassination of Kevin O'Higgins and the retirement from the Dáil of Mr. J. J. Walsh. The portfolio of Posts and Telegraphs was combined with that of Finance, Mr. McGilligan assumed responsibility for External Affairs as well as for his old Ministry of Industry and Commerce, and the sole newcomer to the Cabinet was Mr. Fitzgerald-Kenney, a member of the Inner Bar of high professional standing, who became Minister for Justice.

The result of the election was a blessing in disguise for Mr. De Valera. At that time neither he nor any member of his Shadow Cabinet had had any experience of government, and they could not have assumed office with any prospect of success. Mr. De Valera seemed not even to know the meaning of the collective responsibility of the Cabinet, for when the Chairman of the Dáil followed the usual practice of putting the Executive Council to the House for approval *en bloc*, he protested angrily that the Dáil should have the right of veto over each individual Minister. He told the Chairman that if there was someone else in the Chair his ruling might be different, and suggested that the Constitution was being overridden.[1] But when he became President in 1932, the former precedents were followed under a new Chairman, and the Council was approved as a single entity without debate.[2] Nor did Mr. De Valera appear to have any clear appreciation of the respective functions of the Executive and the Legislature, for when the second portion of the National Loan was about to be issued in November 1927 he was astonished that the Dáil was not to be allowed to discuss its terms.[3] In these and numerous other ways it was necessary for Fianna Fáil to serve an apprenticeship before they could with any confidence take over the administration.

In external affairs, also, the four and a half years spent by him in opposition were to prove invaluable to Mr. De Valera. In 1927 he could hardly have put his policy into operation without a formal repudiation of the Treaty, and this was a step which perhaps he would have hesitated to take. He could not have solved the Anglo-Irish problem by negotiation, because his point of view at that time, as expressed by his spokesman Mr. P. J. Little, was that 'an invitation to London is an invitation to the fly into the spider's web'.[4] Mean-

[1] *Dáil Debates*, xxi, 68–71.   [2] Ibid., xli, 37,38.
[3] Ibid., xxi, 1922, 1923.   [4] Ibid., xli, 1043.

time, Ministers of the Cosgrave Government were meeting the British in London as equals. Their participation in the Conference on the Operation of Dominion Legislation, 1929, and in the Imperial Conference, 1930, led up to the enactment of the Statute of Westminster in 1931. Thus, in their last year of office they cleared the path for Mr. De Valera and rendered it possible for him to implement his policy.

The end of abstentionism ought to have meant the beginning of a stable polity, but this was retarded by the unhappy fact that the recognition by Fianna Fáil of the Government and Parliament of the Irish Free State was neither whole-hearted nor unequivocal. Mr. Seán Lemass, who had been 'Minister for Defence' in the Government of the 'Republic', defined his party's position in a speech in the Dáil on the 21st March 1928.

'Fianna Fáil is a slightly constitutional party. We are perhaps open to the definition of a constitutional party, but before anything we are a Republican party. We have adopted the method of political agitation to achieve our end because we believe, in the present circumstances, that method is best in the interests of the nation and of the Republican movement, and for no other reason. Five years ago the methods we adopted were not the methods we have adopted now. Five years ago we were on the defensive, and perhaps in time we may recoup our strength sufficiently to go on the offensive. Our object is to establish a Republican Government in Ireland. If that can be done by the present methods we have, we will be very pleased, but, if not, we would not confine ourselves to them.'[1]

On the 27th February 1929 Mr. Seán T. O'Kelly referred to the Minister for Defence in public debate as 'the so-called Minister for Defence';[2] and on the 14th March following Mr. De Valera gave his views on the legitimacy of the State in a long speech.

'I still hold that our right to be regarded as the legitimate Government of this country is faulty, that this House itself is faulty. You have secured a *de facto* position. Very well. There must be some body in charge to keep order in the community, and by virtue of your *de facto* position you are the only people who are in a position to do it. But as to whether you have come by that position legitimately or not, I say you have not come by that position legitimately. You brought off a *coup d'état* in the summer of 1922. . . .

'If you are not getting the support from all sections of the com-

---

[1] *Dáil Debates*, xxii, 1615, 1616.   [2] Ibid., xxviii, 460.

munity that is necessary for any Executive if it is going to dispense with a large police force, it is because there is a moral handicap in your case. We are all morally handicapped because of the circumstances in which the whole thing came about. The setting up of this State put a moral handicap on every one of us here. We came in here because we thought that a practical rule could be evolved in which order could be maintained; and we said that it was necessary to have some assembly in which the representatives of the people by a majority vote should be able to decide national policy. As we were not able to get a majority to meet outside this House, we had to come here if there was to be a majority at all of the people's representatives in any one assembly. . . .

'As a practical rule, and not because there is anything sacred in it, I am prepared to accept majority rule as settling matters of national policy, and therefore as deciding who it is that shall be in charge of order. . . .

'I for one, when the flag of the Republic was run up against an Executive that was bringing off a *coup d'état*, stood by the flag of the Republic, and I will do it again. As long as there was a hope of maintaining that Republic, either by force against those who were bringing off that *coup d'état* or afterwards, as long as there was an opportunity of getting the people of this country to vote again for the Republic, I stood for it.

'My proposition that the representatives of the people should come in here and unify control so that we would have one Government and one Army was defeated, and for that reason I resigned. Those who continued on in that organization which we have left can claim exactly the same continuity that we claimed up to 1925. They can do it. . . .

'You have achieved a certain *de facto* position, and the proper thing for you to do with those who do not agree that this State was established legitimately, and who believe that as a matter of fact there was a definite betrayal of everything that was aimed at from 1916 to 1922, is to give those people the opportunity of working, and without in any way forswearing their views, to get the Irish people as a whole again behind them. They have the right to it. You have no right to debar them from going to the Irish people and asking them to support the re-establishment, or if they so wish to put it, to support the continuance of the Republic. . . .

'The Executive have been trying to use force, and have been using it all the time. If they are going to meet force by force, then they can-

Q

not expect the co-operation of citizens who wish that there should not be force.'[1]

It has been necessary to give these extended extracts because of their importance for the understanding of the attitude to the State of Mr. De Valera and his party. The most serious fallacy is in the assumption that if the genuine Republicans were given an opportunity of entering Parliament 'without in any way forswearing their views' (that is, if the Oath were abolished) they would take it. But the genuine Republicans had not broken with Mr. De Valera on the question of the Oath, but because they held, as against him, 'that it is incompatible with the fundamental principles of Sinn Féin to send representatives into any usurping legislature set up by English law in Ireland'. He had asked Sinn Féin to say that the question of entering the Dáil, *if the Oath were removed*, was not a question of principle but of policy; and Sinn Féin had refused.

For Mr. De Valera to state that 'those who continued on in that organization which we have left [Sinn Féin] can claim exactly the same continuity that we claimed up to 1925' was a declaration of the utmost gravity. It could mean nothing less than that, in his opinion, the Government of the Republic was still the *de jure* government of the whole of Ireland, and that the Irish Republican Army was still the *de jure* army. The mere abolition of the Oath would not affect this position. Mr. De Valera might, in course of time, succeed Mr. Cosgrave as head of the Government. He might remove the Oath without formally repudiating the Treaty. But, even so, he could hardly expect that his moral right 'to meet force by force' would not be questioned by the Irish Republican Army.

Mr. T. J. O'Connell, who had succeeded Mr. Thomas Johnson in the leadership of the Labour Party, immediately took up this point.

'I want to know where we stand here. I want to know from the leader of the chief Opposition Party, who may be the President of the Executive Council of this State in a very short time, and who might possibly look to receive support from our Party to put him into that position, where we stand? Have we a Government in this country? Who is the Government of this country if those people who have been voted in by the majority of this House are not the Government of the country? I do not agree with the policy of the present Government; I am in opposition to the present Government; but I am forced to recognize that while they are there they are the custodians of law and order in this country until we put somebody else in their place,

[1] *Dáil Debates*, xxviii, 1398–1405.

and it is the duty of all right-thinking men to obey the laws while those laws are there. It is our duty to make the laws; it is our duty to see that, in so far as we can—we may not always be able to do it—the laws are equitable. But as responsible citizens it is also our duty, once the law is made, to obey that law and to do our best to see that it is obeyed until it is changed in this House. That is a fundamental principle that must be, I think, accepted by everybody—by any of us who has any respect for law.

'Now, who is the Government of this country? Where are they if they are not the Party that is sitting there? If they are not, who is the legitimate Government of this State? Deputy De Valera made what to me sounded as an extraordinary statement when he said that those who now claim to be what I took him to mean the legitimate Government of the country are people who are outside this House, who are not represented in this House. That was the conclusion I drew from what he said; I may be wrong, but that was the clear inference when he said that they could claim the same continuity and authority as they themselves claimed when they were in that position, and we know what they claimed when they were in that position. And he has come in here, has taken part in the work of this Assembly, taken part in the making of laws for this Assembly, while he now says that this is not a legitimate Assembly, that the legitimate authority and Government of this country reside in some body outside this House. That to me is certainly a most extraordinary statement, and I think it is a statement that will not serve the interests of this country and will not serve the interests of the community as a whole.'[1]

All this seems so true as to be axiomatic, but it evoked no modification of his attitude from Mr. De Valera; and it was clear that little help could be expected by the Government from Fianna Fáil in its efforts to suppress disorder. The matter had, in fact, been put to the test much earlier. On the 28th March 1928 the Minister for Defence stated that it would be 'a very important and useful assurance' if members of Fianna Fáil would undertake to convey to the police any information that might come into their possession which might lead to the apprehension of the murderers of Kevin O'Higgins. No such assurance was forthcoming. Mr. P. J. Little stated that 'it is absurd to say to any Party that they are to act as if they were officers of the police of the Government', and when the question was again raised he said: 'My answer to that was that to undertake to do that—there might be circumstances when one could undertake to do a thing like

---

[1] *Dáil Debates*, xxviii, 1406, 1407.

that—would put one into a position of odium altogether. It is really a matter for one's personal conscience as a citizen as to what he would do if circumstances like those arose. But it is very unfair to try to put a whole Party in a position in which they are required to give a certain undertaking. It would be unfair to impose that on the Labour Party, for instance. What the individual conscience would do on a question like that would be quite a different matter.' Mr. McGilligan retorted, 'I did not understand the Deputy's statement, but he does not admit it is his duty as a citizen to give information,' whereupon another Fianna Fáil member (Mr. Cooney) interjected, 'To become an informer.'[1]

At the Fianna Fáil Party Convention in November 1927 Mr. De Valera announced his intention of invoking Article 48 of the Constitution in order to get rid of the Oath. The relevant portion of this Article stated that 'The Oireachtas may provide for the Initiation by the people of proposals for laws or constitutional amendments. Should the Oireachtas fail to make such provision within two years, it shall on the petition of not less than seventy-five thousand voters on the register, of whom not more than fifteen thousand shall be voters in any one constituency, either make such provisions or submit the question to the people for decision in accordance with the ordinary regulations governing the Referendum.' No provision had been made to enable the people to exercise the Initiative, and so Fianna Fáil set about preparing a petition to compel this to be done. Tacked on to the petition was an indication of the immediate object, namely, the deletion from the Constitution of the Article which contained the Oath.[2] By the end of April 1928 the petition was ready for presentation, and on the 3rd May an attempt was made to present it. Mr. Cosgrave lodged a formal objection, and Mr. De Valera tabled a motion that leave be given to present the petition. A protracted debate took place on this motion, extending over four days, and ultimately an amendment was carried to it, proposed by Professor Thrift (an Independent) that the matter be not further considered until the Oireachtas had prescribed the procedure for the presentation of such petitions (1st June 1928). Professor Thrift put down a consequential motion to refer the question of procedure to a Joint Committee of both Houses; but the discussion on this was forestalled by the Government. Six days later (7th June 1928) they introduced a Bill to amend the Constitution by deleting the provisions regarding the Referendum and the Initiative.

---

[1] *Dáil Debates*, xxii, 1960, 1966, 1973, 1974.
[2] Full text in *Dáil Debates*, xxiii, 1499, 1500.

Mr. Cosgrave had undoubtedly been wrong in opposing Mr. De Valera's motion for the presentation of the petition, for the latter was technically within his rights under the Constitution. On the other hand, the Initiative had been inserted in the Constitution for the purpose of inculcating a sense of political responsibility among the people, and this first attempt at its use was as irresponsible as it could well have been. The Oath was, and is, an integral part of the Treaty. The Treaty had been made the sole issue by Mr. De Valera at the general elections of 1922 and 1923, and he had been heavily defeated. He had made the Oath an issue at the two general elections held in 1927, and he had been defeated again. Moreover, the petition could never have achieved its object. Section 2 of the Constitution Act (to which the Constitution and the Treaty are scheduled) states that if any amendment of the Constitution 'is in any respect repugnant to any of the provisions of the Scheduled Treaty, it shall, to the extent only of such repugnancy, be absolutely void and inoperative'. Mr. De Valera had accordingly been engaged in a political manœuvre to gain an end which he had failed to reach by other means, and to amend the Constitution in a respect which the Constituent Assembly had decreed should be void and inoperative.

But the Government's method of dealing with the situation by abolishing both the Referendum and the Initiative seems in retrospect to have been too drastic. No tears need have been shed over the disappearance of the Initiative, which is a constitutional device quite unsuited to Ireland in its present stage of political development; but the abolition of the Referendum was quite another matter. The Referendum applied not only to ordinary Bills, but also to Bills amending the Constitution passed within an experimental period of eight years, i.e. up to the 5th December 1930. In the case of all such Bills, a Referendum could be demanded by three-fifths of the members of the Senate or by a petition signed by not less than one-twentieth of the voters on the register. This was a valuable safeguard, especially in regard to constitutional amendments. After the period of eight years had expired the Referendum was automatic for Bills amending the Constitution, and this provision was left intact. But for all other purposes the Referendum was abolished, including constitutional amendments passed within the eight years. At the time the Bill abolishing the Referendum was enacted (12th July 1928), the eight years' period had only eighteen months more to run, and it probably did not seem worth while to retain the Referendum for constitutional amendments for such a short time, especially as no revolutionary changes were contemplated by the Cosgrave Government. The whole situation was transformed, however, by the action of the same Government in the following year (1929), when a Bill was passed extending the eight years' period to sixteen years. As a result, if Mr. De Valera became the head of the Government, he could amend the Constitution by ordinary legislation up to the 5th December 1938, and neither the Senate nor the people could force a Referendum on his proposals.

The Bill to abolish the Referendum and the Initiative was finally passed by the Dáil on the 28th June 1928, and its passage was marked by a scene in which a prominent member of Mr. De Valera's party was suspended.[1] The Government thereupon took the further step of getting the Dáil to declare that the Bill was necessary for the immediate preservation of the public peace and safety, and so forestalled the possibility of a Referendum being demanded in regard to it. It seems impossible to justify the application of this procedure to such a Bill. This particular provision was inserted in the Constitution so that Bills urgently required in times of crisis might be passed into law without any delay whatever, and it required a declaration of both Houses. The Dáil declaration was passed on the 28th June, but the parallel declaration in the Senate was not moved until the following 12th July. This fact alone is sufficient to show that the Bill was not required for the immediate preservation of the public peace. One would have supposed that if ever there was a constitutional amendment on which a Referendum might properly have been demanded, it was an amendment to deprive the people of the right to demand a Referendum.

The Senate's reaction to this Bill and its connection with other constitutional amendments affecting the powers of the Second Chamber are dealt with in the chapter which follows.

---

[1] *Dáil Debates*, xxiv, 1740–50.

CHAPTER XIV

THE RECONSTITUTION OF THE SENATE

The Senate requests a Joint Committee to consider changes in the constitution and powers of the Second Chamber and in the method of election—Mr. De Valera's attitude—Mr. Lemass and a 'bulwark of imperialism'—The Joint Committee set up—Mr. De Valera's activities as a member of it—Abuse of the Senate by leading members of Fianna Fáil—Report of the Joint Committee—Adoption of its recommendations—Altered system of election—Minimum age and term of office reduced—Power of suspension increased—Opposition to certain of the proposed changes—Senator O'Farrell's brilliant speeches—Views of other Senators—The Second Triennial Election—Failure of the new system—Result of the election—The entry of Fianna Fáil—Influx of ex-members of the Dáil into the Senate—The work of revision summarized—Retirement of Lord Glenavy—Tributes to his conduct of the Chair—His qualities and defects—His death.

The second Triennial Election to the Senate was due to take place in the autumn of 1928. It was generally admitted that the experience of the previous election had proved that the method of election by the whole country was undesirable, but the exciting events of 1927 had left little time for a new method to be devised. There was also a feeling that some reconsideration of the composition and powers of the Second Chamber ought to be undertaken. Accordingly, the following resolution was passed by the Senate on the 15th February 1928: 'That it is expedient that a Joint Committee, consisting of five members of the Dáil and five members of the Seanad, with the Chairman of each House *ex officio*, be set up to consider and report on the changes, if any, necessary in the constitution and powers of, and methods of election to Seanad Éireann.' This resolution was adopted on the initiative of Senator O'Farrell, who proposed it in a speech which showed not only a just appreciation of the work already accomplished by the Senate but also a wide knowledge of Second Chambers in general. He made it clear that he was not personally in favour of a change in the method of election, but regarded it as a proper subject for discussion. The resolution was passed unanimously.[1]

When the appropriate message requesting concurrence came before the Dáil, Mr. De Valera explained his party's attitude in the following short speech: 'We are against the setting up of this particular Committee. We think that the proper thing to do is to end the Senate and not to attempt to mend it. It is costly, and we do not see any useful function that it really serves.'[2]

At this time the utility of the Senate to the State was at its height. Though its powers were restricted, its personnel was hardly inferior to that of any Second Chamber in Europe. The reason of the Fianna Fáil antagonism to the Senate was its hostility to the ex-Unionist section of the community, a hostility which, whilst it endures, precludes any union of hearts in the Irish Free State and makes a united Ireland a vain dream. Mr. Lemass, who followed his leader, dwelt on this aspect of the Senate. 'It is a body created, as we all know, not to improve the machinery of administration in this country, but to give political power to a certain class that could not get that power if they had to go before the people at a free election and get the people to vote them into office. The Senate was set up to put a certain section of the community into a position where they could influence the course of legislation—a section of the community that was always hostile to the interests of Irish nationalism, and that was always hostile to the Irish nation. And we think that this bulwark of imperialism should be abolished by the people's representatives on the first available opportunity that they get.'[3] On the date on which these words were spoken the number of ex-Unionists in the Senate numbered at most twenty out of a total of sixty; and nobody who knew them individually for the previous five years could believe for a moment that any single one of them was 'hostile to the Irish nation'. Many of them had proved their love of Ireland by refusing to be driven into exile by a campaign of arson directed to that end.

The Senate's proposal was agreed to by the Dáil, the whole Fianna Fáil Party voting against it; and the Joint Committee was duly set up. The purpose of the committee was, of course, to produce a better

[1] *Senate Debates*, x, 193–227.   [2] *Dáil Debates*, xxii, 140.   [3] Ibid.

and more efficient Second Chamber. Such being the case, it might have been expected that the Fianna Fáil Party, in view of their general attitude, would hold aloof from its proceedings. But Mr. De Valera himself went on the committee, taking with him his principal lieutenant, Mr. Ruttledge; and they used their position on the committee to attempt to produce, not a better Senate but a worse one. No verbatim report of the debates was published, but this fact is clearly deducible from the Journal of Proceedings. Mr. De Valera proposed that the members of the Senate be elected by the Dáil, and when an amendment was proposed that it should be elected by both Houses voting together he voted against it. This amendment having been carried, he tried, without success, to secure that outgoing Senators should not be entitled to vote. He attempted to get the numbers reduced from sixty to thirty-five, and the term of office reduced to six years. When it was proposed to increase the Senate's power of suspension to two years, he held out for nine months; and he opposed a motion that members of the Senate should not continue to be disqualified for membership of the Executive Council. In all these activities he either obtained no support at all or was supported by only one other member of the committee. Sometimes it was his colleague Mr. Ruttledge and sometimes it was a Labour Deputy. A few of Mr. De Valera's proposals were carried in the committee, but they can hardly be characterized as improvements. One of them was that the minimum age for Senators should be reduced from thirty-five years to thirty, and another was that casual vacancies should be filled by members of both Houses voting together and not, as previously, by the Senate itself.[1]

The fact that Messrs. De Valera and Ruttledge used their position on the committee to try to worsen the Senate instead of improving it is not merely a matter of deduction. It was proclaimed by Mr. Seán T. O'Kelly (who later became Vice-President) when one of the Bills to implement the committee's Report came before the Dáil. He spoke in Irish, and the following is a translation of part of what he said. 'They were not allowed to propose a motion recommending the Dáil to abolish the Senate. They did their utmost to diminish every power which the Senate had. Our Deputies on the Committee did everything they could to make the country realize that the Senate is not a useful thing, and they did their utmost to deprive the Senate of whatever authority it might have from being elected by the people.'[2] Mr. Gerald Boland, another future Minister, said: 'As we cannot abolish

[1] *Reports of Committees*, vol. ii, pp. 273-95.   [2] *Dáil Debates*, xxiv, 662.

the Senate, and as we are not going to have a referendum, we are going to make that institution as unpopular as possible.'[1]

Mr. De Valera's most perverse proposal was that the Senate should be elected solely by the Dáil. When this proposal came before the Dáil by way of an amendment to the Government's Bill, Mr. Seán Lemass, afterwards Minister for Industry and Commerce, explained its purpose to the House in the following terms: 'The purpose of such amendment is to ensure that if we must have a Senate it will be a body that will be subordinate to this House, held tight in the grip of this body and unable to wriggle unless this body so permits it. We are in favour, of course, of the abolition of the Senate, but if there is to be a Second House let it be a Second House under our thumb. Let it be a group of individuals who dare not let a squeak out of them except when we lift our fingers to give them breath to do it.'[2] Six years later, when Mr. De Valera spoke in the Dáil on the Second Reading of his Bill to abolish the Senate, he adverted to his action in proposing this particular amendment in the Joint Committee, and he explained his motives. 'I proposed that it should be election by this House. Why? Do you think I did not see that it was ultimately going to get the same political complexion as this House? I did it because I wanted to get the people to see clearly that in practice it was going to result in a Chamber practically of the same character as here, that it was going to be merely a duplication, and that the very things that are happening were bound to happen.'[3]

Let us examine what this means. Mr. De Valera was the leader of the second largest party in Parliament, and so had a considerable share in the making of his country's laws. He went, as a free agent, into a Joint Committee one of the purposes of which was to improve the personnel of the Second Chamber of the Parliament. In that committee, he resisted a proposal that the election of Senators should be from a panel selected by a nominating college and representative of agriculture, labour, education, and other interests (which might have resulted in an excellent Senate); and he proposed that the Senate should be elected by the Dáil, with the object of rendering it so worthless that its abolition would be inevitable.

The Joint Committee reported on the 16th May 1928, and all of its recommendations were duly implemented by Constitution (Amendment) Bills introduced by the Government. Such of these Bills as fall within the second Triennial Period will now be considered; the remainder, which became law in 1929 or 1930, will be dealt with in their place.

---

[1] *Dáil Debates*, xxiv, 658.   [2] Ibid., xxiv, 614.   [3] Ibid., li, 2141.

First as regards the composition of the Senate. The number of Senators remained unaltered at sixty, but the electorate was to consist of members of the Dáil and Senate voting together on principles of proportional representation (Amendment No. 6 Bill). The election was to be from a panel of candidates to be formed in manner to be prescribed by law (Amendment No. 9 Bill); and the method of forming the panel was laid down in the Seanad Electoral Bill. Before each triennial election the Dáil and Senate were each to nominate a list of as many candidates as there were members to be elected, and in the preparation of these separate lists each House was to vote on principles of proportional representation. The two lists were then to be combined in one panel, the names being arranged in alphabetical order, and the two Houses were to vote on this panel, the voting being by secret ballot and by post. Retiring Senators were not to be allowed, as of right, to have their names placed on the panel, as they had been in 1925. Thus, if there were twenty vacancies, the Senate was to prepare a list of twenty candidates and the Dáil a list of twenty candidates; and from the combined panel of forty candidates the twenty new Senators were to be elected by the secret, postal vote of all the members of the Senate and the Dáil, including the Senators who were due to retire.

The minimum age for membership of the Senate was reduced from thirty-five to thirty years (Amendment No. 8 Bill), and the period of office was altered. Under the old system (casual vacancies being disregarded), one-fourth of the House retired every three years and the new senators held office for twelve years. Now, one-third of the members were to retire every three years and their successors were to hold office for nine years (Amendment No. 7 Bill). There were some provisions of a transitory character, regarding the term of office of Senators to be elected in 1928 and 1931, so that after the election of 1931 there should be twenty Senators holding office for three years, twenty for six years and twenty for nine years, the whole Chamber being renewable in nine-year periods.

So much for the composition of the Senate. Its powers were also changed. Formerly, the Senate had had power to suspend a Bill for 270 days, on the expiry of which period, without further action by the Dáil, the Bill was to be deemed to have been passed by both Houses. We have seen that this provision had had awkward consequences in the case of the Intoxicating Liquor Bill in 1924. That Bill had not been passed by the Senate, and, at the end of the suspensory period, the Government of the day had felt constrained to have it placed on the Statute Book, although they did not then require it. A better drafted provision was now proposed (Amendment No. 13 Bill). The Senate was to be given a suspensory power of eighteen months, called the stated period. In the case of a Bill so suspended, the Dáil might, within one year of the termination of the stated period, by special resolution again send the Bill to the Senate. If it did so, the Senate was given sixty days within which to pass the Bill, either without amendment or with only such amendments as might be agreed to by the Dáil. If the Senate again proved recalcitrant, one further step was needed before the Bill could become law. On the expiry of the sixty days, it was necessary for the Dáil to pass a resolution that the Bill was deemed to have been passed by both Houses. This done, the Bill could be sent for the Royal Assent. The stated period of eighteen months was cut short by a dissolution of Parliament. In such a case, the period terminated on the date of the reassembly of Parliament following a general election.

It was thus proposed to increase the suspensory period given to the Senate from roughly nine months to roughly twenty months. As against this, it must be remembered that, at the time this Bill was being considered, there was another Bill before Parliament which had as its object the abolition of the Referendum. This was a fortuitous circumstance, but the power of three-fifths of the members of the Senate to force a Referendum on any Bill was a valuable constitutional safeguard, and, if the Senate was to agree to forgo it, the increase in its power of suspension might perhaps be regarded as a substitute. Actually, this increase had been proposed by the Joint Committee some little time before the Bill to abolish the Referendum had been introduced; and the Committee had passed a resolution recommending that, if its proposal were accepted, the right of the Senate to demand a Referendum should be confined to Bills amending the Constitution.[1]

The reception of this block of Bills in the Senate was, as might have been expected in the circumstances, very different from that accorded to them in the Dáil, where argument gave place to abuse of the Second Chamber. In the Senate they had an easy passage, with the exception of the Bill to abolish the Referendum and the Bill to alter the method of election. In the debate on the former, cognizance was taken of the fact that the Senate's power of suspension was being substantially increased, and this lessened the opposition. But if it had been known that, in a Bill which was to come the following year,

[1] *Reports of Committees*, vol. ii, p. 291.

the power of amending the Constitution by ordinary legislation was to be extended from 1930 to 1938, it seems almost certain that the Senate would have insisted on retaining the right to demand a Referendum for this class of Bill. As it was, Senators Dowdall, Linehan, Sir John Keane, and Mrs. Wyse Power voted with the Labour Party in opposition to the Government's proposals.

The protagonist for the Referendum was Senator O'Farrell, who also led the opposition to the proposed new Senate electoral system in a series of brilliant speeches on the Bill to amend the Constitution and on the Electoral Bill which implemented it. He held that the system of election by the whole country had not had a fair trial, and that the new plan was open to abuse. 'Instead of qualifying by the acquisition of useful knowledge or experience, or by a record of public service, candidates for the Senate in future will have to qualify mainly as time-servers to half a dozen Deputies. Instead of going out on the hustings and manfully looking for thousands or tens of thousands of votes from the electors for whom they propose to legislate, the candidates will now have to cadge around the lobbies of Leinster House to get the votes of the half-dozen people whose follies, or potential follies, and shortcomings it will be part of their duty to curb if elected.'[1] He castigated Mr. De Valera's followers for posing as the champions of the people's rights and at the same time denying the right of the people to vote for the members of the Second Chamber. 'The Fianna Fáil Party know that there is to be a Senate. They know that it is to have very great and very wide powers, that it is to have the power of holding up a Bill for twenty months, and that it can thwart if it wishes and can hamper the actions of a patriotic and progressive Government. In spite of all that, they say that the people are not to have any views or any effective voice in the election of members of this House. For downright, brazen hypocrisy, the action of the Fianna Fáil Party in regard to the election of the Senate is without parallel.'[2]

Senator O'Hanlon touched on the same point, and gave the reason for the attitude of the Opposition. 'They have failed to abolish this Chamber, and are likely to do so; but, inasmuch as they admit at the present that they cannot abolish this Chamber, or take the necessary steps to do so, they said, "Let us make this a weak, inane, useless institution"; and one of the preliminary steps they are adopting to make a worthless, useless institution is to remove the process of election to the Senate away from the people.'[3]

[1] *Senate Debates*, x, 955.   [2] Ibid., x, 957.   [3] Ibid., x, 970.

What seemed a sound argument against the new system was advanced by Senator Westropp Bennett, based on the experience of 1925. 'We must not overlook the fact that the last Senate was practically altogether the selection of the Dáil and the Senate, because every man who got on to the panel was put there either by a member of the Senate or by a member of the Dáil. If the members elected have proved a failure, the electorate is not responsible. Those that put them on the panel, the members of the Dáil and the Senate, are, I maintain, responsible. If you believe that the action of the Dáil and the Senate has proved to be unwise, if you believe that the opinion of the Dáil and the Senate, as expressed in the nineteen members who were returned at the last election, was bad, then I think it is not a good plan to give people who have shown their incapacity to nominate a Senate of sound views the election of them for the future.'[1]

Senator Douglas took a more generous, or perhaps a more idealistic, view of political human nature than either Senator O'Farrell or Senator Westropp Bennett. 'It seems to me that in making this experiment we are . . . trusting to the best in the respective political parties. The parties will have by Proportional Representation the power of putting men and women into this House. It will be realized that one cannot tell the exact number, but approximately one will know the number of persons which a party can elect if they put forward, as I firmly believe they will, most if not all of the persons who will be a help to their own party in public life, who will be the most prominent supporters of their party, most likely to help them in party considerations and in the councils of the party, and to cut a reasonably good figure in public life. I believe that is the type of person the parties will choose.'[2]

The weight of argument, as expressed in the debates, was against the new system, but the Bills were passed. On the Final Reading, however, Senator O'Farrell had an effective last word. He said that the system was 'open to disreputable canvassing practices which have already begun. On the last day we met Senators informed me that they had already been approached in the ante-rooms of this House and canvassed for their votes for the forthcoming election. I have myself certainly had letters asking for my support, and I heard one man proclaim joyfully and victoriously that he had devoted a week of his holidays towards securing the necessary support to enable him to be elected to the Senate for nine years to come. He was able to come back to work confident in the knowledge that already he

[1] *Senate Debates*, x, 982.   [2] Ibid., x, 966, 967.

was as good as elected. I think that is a most undesirable possibility to place within the reach of anybody who can get within speaking distance of Leinster House or who can approach sufficient Deputies and Senators outside it.'[1]

This very debatable question was soon to be put to the test of experience, as the Triennial Election was held in November 1928. There were nineteen Senators due to retire, consisting of the fifteen Senators who had originally been nominated for six years plus four others who had been elected to fill casual vacancies. Their successors were to be elected by the combined vote of 153 members of the Dáil and sixty members of the Senate—an electorate of 213. Therefore twelve first preferences would be certain to elect a Senator, and eleven or ten would be likely to do so. As a result of the general elections of June and September 1927, the smaller parties in the Dáil had all disappeared, leaving only the Government party, which, with the Farmers, had about seventy members, the Fianna Fáil Party, with fifty-seven members, and the Labour Party, with thirteen members; there being in addition about a dozen Independents. In the Senate, there was still no strict alignment of parties, with the exception of the Labour Party of five members. As the members of Fianna Fáil had been making war on the State in 1922 and had boycotted the Triennial Election of 1925, it had as yet no representation in the Senate except for two or three Senators who had joined the party after it had entered the Dáil. Apart from these and from the Labour Senators, the votes of Senators might be expected to go either to the Government candidates or to the Independent Group (most of whom were ex-Unionists) or to unattached Independents. The result might accordingly be anticipated with reasonable accuracy. The Fianna Fáil Party would be able to elect six Senators, the Labour Party two, and the remaining eleven seats would be distributed between the Government party and the Independents (including the Independent Group).

The prospects of re-election of most of the fifteen nominated Senators would have been very doubtful, and eight of them decided not to offer themselves as candidates. The four co-opted Senators, Messrs. Brady, Brown, and Hooper, and Sir Walter Nugent, all went forward again.

As there were nineteen vacancies, it was the obvious intention of the Constitution that the voting should be from a panel of thirty-eight names, compiled as to one-half by the Senate and as to the

[1] *Senate Debates*, x, 1083.

other half by the Dáil. This intention, however, was not fulfilled. The electors were to be the same people as the compilers of the panel, and it was therefore known pretty certainly in advance who would be elected and who would not. It would be foolish for any man of distinction to expose himself to the humiliation of certain defeat merely for the purpose of procuring a formal compliance with the Constitution. The Dáil portion of the panel was completed on the 7th November 1928; it contained nineteen names, but six of these were those of retiring Senators.[1] The Senate portion was completed on the 28th November; it also contained nineteen names, but no less than eleven of these were duplicated from the Dáil portion.[2] There were thus only twenty-seven candidates for the nineteen seats. Actually there were only twenty-six, as Dr. Michael Davitt, a Government candidate whose name appeared on both portions of the panel, died after nomination but before the election. The Electoral Rules had provided for an eliminating contest in each House, to reduce the number of candidates to nineteen in each case, but owing to the shortage of candidates this was not necessary.

The seven defeated candidates were:

P. J. Brady	Benjamin Haughton
R. A. Butler	Thomas Kennedy
Sir Nugent Everard, Bart.	The Earl of Wicklow
Lord Farnham	

Mr. Brady, Sir Nugent Everard, Mr. Haughton, and the Earl of Wicklow were outgoing Senators who had all been valuable members of the House. Mr. Butler, who had been chairman of the Irish Farmers' Union, was elected a Senator in 1922 but had lost his seat at the Triennial Election of 1925. Lord Farnham was a former Unionist who was a Representative Peer for Ireland. Mr. Kennedy was a Labour candidate and his unexpected defeat was due to a split in the Labour Party between the members of the Irish Transport and General Workers' Union, of which he was the nominee, and the more moderate elements of the party. He was elected a Senator in 1934.

The result of the election was as follows:

1. William Sears	4. Joseph Connolly
2. Seán Milroy	5. Séamas Robinson
3. Mrs. Kathleen Clarke	6. Joseph O'Doherty

[1] *Dáil Journal of Proceedings*, 1928, p. 471.
[2] *Senate Journal of Proceedings*, 1928, p. 178.

* 7. Rt. Hon. Andrew
     Jameson
  8. Alfred Byrne
  9. Thomas Johnson
*10. Rt. Hon. Sir Bryan
     Mahon
*11. Samuel L. Brown, K.C.
 12. Richard Wilson

*13. Dr. Oliver St. J. Gogarty
*14. John Bagwell
*15. Patrick J. Hooper
*16. Sir Walter R. Nugent, Bart.
 17. Seán E. MacEllin
 18. Michael Comyn, K.C.
 19. The McGillycuddy of the
     Reeks

The first six of these were to sit for the full term of nine years, the next eight for six years and the last five for three years. These adjustments had been made so that after the Triennial Election of 1931 exactly one-third of the House would be renewable every three years.

The Fianna Fáil Party obtained six seats: Mrs. Clarke and Messrs. Comyn, Connolly, MacEllin, O'Doherty, and Robinson. Three of the six had been members of the Dáil. Mrs. Clarke was first elected in the Sinn Féin interest in 1921; at the general election of 1922 she stood against the Treaty and was defeated; she was not a candidate in 1923; she was elected in June 1927, but lost her seat the following September; and in April 1928 she was defeated again, this time at a by-election. Mr. O'Doherty had been successful at the General Elections of 1918, 1921, 1922, and 1923, but was rejected in June 1927. Mr. Robinson was elected in 1921 but defeated in 1922, when he stood as an anti-Treaty candidate.

The Cosgrave party had four Senators: Dr. Gogarty and Messrs. Milroy, Sears, and Wilson. The first-named was an outgoing Senator, and the other three had all been members of the Dáil. Mr. Milroy had represented Cavan from 1921; he had been one of the nine members who had revolted from the Government party in November 1924 and had resigned their seats in order to found a new National Party; at a by-election in North Dublin in March 1925, caused by one of these resignations, he had stood against the Government and had been defeated; and at the general election of June 1927 he had stood for Cavan as an Independent and had again been defeated. Mr. Sears had represented Mayo continuously from 1918 to 1927, but was rejected by the electors in June of that year. Mr. Wilson had been elected as a member of the Farmers' Party in 1922 and 1923; he was a defeated candidate at both the general elections held in 1927.

The sole representative of Labour was Mr. Thomas Johnson. He had been the leader of the Opposition throughout Mr. De Valera's

* Outgoing Senator.

R

abstentionist period, from 1922 to the dissolution of August 1927; but he had lost his seat at the general election held in the following month.

The Independent Group returned four members: Messrs. Bagwell, Brown, and Jameson and the McGillycuddy of the Reeks. All but the last-named were outgoing Senators.

The list of nineteen was completed by four Independents: Messrs. Byrne and Hooper, Sir Bryan Mahon, and Sir Walter Nugent. The only newcomer to the Senate among these was Mr. Alfred Byrne, who subsequently became Lord Mayor of Dublin. At the time of his election to the Senate he was a member of the Dáil, having been a successful candidate at every general election held from 1922 onwards. He had, of course, to resign his seat in the other House, in accordance with the provision of the Constitution which prohibited dual membership.

Thus the first election held under the new system showed that Senator O'Farrell's fears and Mr. De Valera's hopes for the future of the Senate had begun to be realized; but the result would have been worse if Mr. De Valera had carried his proposal that retiring Senators should not be allowed to vote, and much worse if he had carried his other proposal that the election should be by the Dáil alone. Of the twelve new Senators, no less than eight were ex-members of the Dáil, and all but one of them had been rejected by the electors—some of them twice within a few months. It is reasonable to suppose that these were elected wholly or mainly by Dáil votes. One or two of them were undoubtedly first-class men, but the rest could scarcely be so described. In the nature of things, they were nearly all party politicians, and they were coming to a Second Chamber in which independence of thought and of action had been encouraged and where party politics had been virtually unknown.

The future of the Senate was placed by the new system in the hands of the two major political parties. One of these parties was, in the words of one of its leaders, only 'a slightly constitutional party'. It aimed at abolishing the Senate, but meanwhile 'let it be a Second House under our thumb'. It was only to be expected that a party holding these views would act accordingly in its choice of Senators; but the action of the Government party was less intelligible in sending three newcomers to the House who had all been rejected at the polls in the previous year. No criticism of the ability of any of these men individually is intended or implied; but one could not look forward without misgiving to a Senate containing increasing numbers not merely of party politicians but of party politicians who had lost their seats in the other House.

During the short period covered by this chapter the work of revision of Government Bills went quietly on, the chief Bills amended being the Currency Bill (thirty-three amendments) and the Forestry Bill (twenty-one amendments). The Currency Bill authorized the issue of a gold coinage, terminated the issue of bank notes by individual banks, and empowered the issue of such notes by a central authority styled the Currency Commission. The Forestry Bill, another of Mr. Hogan's beneficent measures, made provision for the afforestation of the country and placed restrictions on the felling of trees. These two Bills benefited considerably by the presence in the Senate of experts in banking and agriculture, and all the amendments were accepted by the Dáil. Over the whole Second Triennial Period the standard of revision set in the First Period was well maintained. About a hundred non-Money Bills were received; of these, one-third were amended, the number of amendments being roughly four hundred, all but ten of which were agreed to by the Dáil.

Lord Glenavy, who was one of the Senators due to retire, had decided not to seek re-election; and at the last meeting of the Senate before the close of the period a resolution was passed expressing deep appreciation of his services as Chairman during the six years' existence of the House. The resolution was proposed by the Vice-Chairman, Senator Westropp Bennett, who referred to Lord Glenavy's legal eminence and his undoubted ability and tact in the Chair. He continued:

'We are an assembly of men of differing views; in some cases it is hardly untrue to say that our outlook is diametrically opposed. Our Chairman is a man whose views have always been well known and forcibly and fearlessly expressed, but in this House we can say that, however opposed we may be in opinion, we are all friends. I doubt if there is in the world a House of Parliament where there is so real a sense of unity and comradeship as in this Senate, and, if there is one man to whose conduct this good will is more due than to another, it is to our Chairman.

'He came in a time of storm. When we first met, which of us knew, when he returned to his home, that he would not find that, instead of sitting at his cheerful hearth, he might warm his hands at his blazing roof tree? Which of us knew that when he retired to rest he might not wake to sounds of war and death? He leaves us in peace. He leaves us having learned that our differences can be settled by argument, and that our controversial artillery, if not infallible, is at least efficacious. But we must not forget that, in accepting the post of Chairman, Lord Glenavy not only accepted the danger in which every member of the Senate lived, but singled himself out for special attack. I am glad to say that he did not suffer in person, but he did not hesitate to run the extra danger.'

Senators O'Farrell and Douglas joined in the tribute to the retiring Chairman, and Lord Glenavy responded in a speech which expressed his pride in the Senate's work and which revealed a depth of feeling that was obviously sincere.[1]

There is no doubt that, of the sixty original members of the Senate, Lord Glenavy was easily the most suitable Chairman. He was a man of very strongly marked, and even dominating, personality, and his prestige as a former Lord Chancellor stood him in good stead. Actually, he had no special knowledge of constitutional law, and had little regard for the niceties of parliamentary procedure; and, as he had passed the allotted span at the time of his election, he could not be expected to interest himself to any great extent in the intricacies of these two subjects. But his clarity of mind and his power of expression remained in their full vigour, and in the legal examination of a case and its subsequent exposition he had no superior. He necessarily leaned to a considerable extent upon his officials, and it must be said of him that he was always ready to listen to their advice and to follow it if it commended itself to him, as it generally did. Even if he approached a problem with his mind apparently made up, he was always open to argument. If he sometimes seemed to resist, and perhaps to dismiss the matter with a caustic witticism, it was usually found later that he had been convinced. At an early stage, representations were privately made to him that there were certain matters of etiquette which would make for decorum, but which ought not to be incorporated in the Standing Orders, such as bowing to the Chair on entering and leaving the Chamber. Lord Glenavy thought them trivial, and said as much. But a few days later he asked the House to adopt them, and he always saw to it that they were obeyed.

As he had not the Standing Orders at his fingers' ends, ready to apply them instantly the occasion arose, he was necessarily a somewhat unorthodox Chairman. But he meted out substantial justice to every side, and the occasions on which the rights of a minority were infringed were very few and never wilful. He had the great gift of restoring an atmosphere of good humour to the proceedings by a

[1] *Senate Debates*, x, 1405–16.

timely quip or jest. Once a measure which had provoked some heat was followed on the Order Paper by the Wild Birds Bill. Lord Glenavy announced this item by saying in his deep bass voice, and in tones of obvious reproof, 'Wild Birds!' On another day, the sponsor of the Barbers' Registration Bill expressed the hope that it would not provoke such acrimony as the Bill which preceded it, and Lord Glenavy interjected, 'But there will be more hair flying!'

The Government's attitude towards the Senate laid upon the Chairman many of the duties that would normally fall to a Leader of the House, but it is probable that Lord Glenavy was not particularly averse from them, as they gave him scope for the exercise of his somewhat paternal manner towards the members. He always encouraged the younger men, whether Senators or officials, and he was not sparing of praise for what he thought good work, whether it was done in the Chamber or outside. He never hesitated to defend the constitutional rights of the Senate against either the Government or the Dáil; and if at times he seemed supine in other directions, it must be remembered that he was then approaching the end of a long career.

The high utility of the Senate during its first six years must be held to be due in large measure to Lord Glenavy's guidance. He did not long survive his retirement, dying on the 22nd March 1931, in his eightieth year.

PART IV

THE THIRD TRIENNIAL PERIOD
6th DECEMBER 1928 TO 5th DECEMBER 1931

'*The group of self-governing communities composed of Great Britain and the Dominions . . . are autonomous Communities within the British Empire, equal in status, in no way subordinate one to another in any aspect of their domestic or external affairs, though united by a common allegiance to the Crown, and freely associated as members of the British Commonwealth of Nations.*'

THE BALFOUR DECLARATION.

ἔχει δὲ καὶ περὶ τὴν αἵρεσιν τῶν ἀρχόντων τὸ ἐξ αἱρετῶν αἱρετοὺς ἐπικίνδυνον, εἰ γάρ τινες συστῆναι θέλουσι καὶ μέτριοι τὸ πλῆθος, ἀεὶ κατὰ τὴν τούτων αἱρεθήσονται βούλησιν.

('*The provision for the election of the rulers from among candidates chosen at a preliminary election is dangerous, for even if a moderate number of people choose to combine into a party, the elections will always go according to their wish.*')

ARISTOTLE, *Politics*, II, iii, 13.

CHAPTER XV

INTERNATIONAL DEVELOPMENT AND INTERNAL DISORDER

Growth of international status—The Briand-Kellogg Pact—Fianna Fáil opposition in both Houses—The signature of the Optional Clause —Senator Connolly's views—Election to the Council of the League of Nations—Conference on the Operation of Dominion Legislation, 1929 —The Imperial Conference, 1930—Report of the Conference approved by Senate and Dáil—The Statute of Westminster, 1931—Attitude of the Churchill group in the House of Commons—Mr. Cosgrave's caveat —Mr. Baldwin resists the amendment of the Churchill group—Result of the Statute of Westminster—The internal situation—Repeal of the Public Safety Act—Growth of extremism—Intimidation of jurors and witnesses—Murder and attempted murder—Attitude of Fianna Fáil to majority rule—A 'Dáil of usurpers'—The Juries Protection Bill, 1929 —Opposition of Fianna Fáil—The grave events of 1931—Association of Fianna Fáil with Irish Republican Army—London newspaper interview with Republican leader—Introduction of the Constitution (Amendment No. 17) Bill—Its drastic character—Opposition of Fianna Fáil— Mr. De Valera's reference to the Irish Republican Army—His theory of the continuity of British government in Ireland—His misquotation of Lord Birkenhead—The Bill becomes law—Joint Pastoral of the Hierarchy—The Irish Republican Army and other bodies declared to be unlawful associations—Establishment of the Military Tribunal.

The period from 1929 to 1931 was characterized by two principal features: on the one hand, an immense increase in the international status of the Irish Free State, and in particular in its status as a member of the British Commonwealth of Nations; and, on the other hand, a recrudescence of political unrest at home. It is somewhat of a paradox that our development to full stature as one of the free nations of the world should have been accompanied by ceaseless attacks, both verbal and physical, on the Treaty position, which was the *fons et origo* of that development.

In February 1929 the Treaty for the Renunciation of War (the so-called Briand-Kellogg Pact of Paris), which had been signed on the 27th August 1928, was approved by formal resolution of both Houses of Parliament. The debate in the Dáil was a travesty of what a debate on foreign affairs should be, and the resolution was passed in face of the strenuous opposition of Mr. De Valera's followers.[1] In the Senate the resolution was passed without a division, but Senator Connolly, the leader of the Fianna Fáil Party, took occasion to attack the United States, which at that time was engaged in safeguarding American and foreign lives and property during the guerrilla warfare in Nicaragua. He said:

'The imperial idea has been essentially developed by England and copied by Germany, and is now being pursued ruthlessly by America. It is rather extraordinary for us to sit here as a sober, intelligent people to discuss the possibility of signing a Peace Pact even with America, when we consider that at the present moment America is pursuing an absolutely cold-blooded, ruthless policy of exploitation and occupation of territory to which she is not entitled.'[2]

The Senate always provided a better forum than the Dáil for the discussion of external affairs, and in the debate on the Appropriation Bill, 1929, in a well-informed and well-argued speech, Senator Johnson raised the question of the signature of the so-called Optional Clause, that is, Article 36 of the Statute of the Permanent Court of International Justice. The signature of this Article recognized as compulsory the jurisdiction of the Court in regard to justiciable disputes between signatory States. At that time, it was rumoured that Great Britain and the other Commonwealth States would sign the Optional Clause but reserve inter-Commonwealth disputes, and Senator Johnson's purpose was to elucidate the attitude of the Government. The Minister for External Affairs (Mr. McGilligan) made that attitude clear: 'I do not see how we could possibly accept any such reservation. . . . We will take, as we have always taken, quite an independent point of view. It may happen that the result of our taking an independent point of view will be action in harmony at times with Great Britain or with a number of the Dominions of the Commonwealth, but our decision is always come to on circumstances

[1] *Dáil Debates*, xxviii, 277–320, 334–74.
[2] *Senate Debates*, xi, 335.

that are peculiar and appropriate to this State.'[1] Senator Connolly's intervention in the same debate provided a contrast to that of Senator Johnson. At that time the Irish Free State had so far progressed that it had Ministers in Washington and some of the European capitals, as well as a representative at Geneva. The leader of Mr. De Valera's party stated that he 'would like to know how far we have any influence whatever in the League of Nations' and hinted at 'international affairs in which we are involved as constituent members of this thing called the British Empire'.[2] With regard to representation abroad, it was 'absolutely essential that the individuality of this country as a State should be stressed'. He continued: 'I am not fully satisfied that that is the case. In the American activities I am afraid that we played rather a bad second fiddle to the British administration. Whether that is desirable or not I do not know. From my point of view it is anything but desirable if we have to admit that we are a subsidiary, as it were, of the British Empire and that our consulate offices and our administration, our plenipotentiary in Washington have to play second fiddle to the representative of the British Legation [sic] there.'[3] These objections were sufficiently met by the statement of Mr. McGilligan which has been quoted. As between two nations, of which one is a Great Power and the other is not, there must needs be some differentiation of function. As between the diplomatic representatives of those nations, the question of who is to play second fiddle is one that does not normally arise between intellectual equals; but this reply is hardly likely to satisfy anyone who propounds such a question.

Conformably with Mr. McGilligan's prediction, the Irish Free State signed the Optional Clause, without reservation, on the 14th September 1929 at Geneva. Great Britain and the other members of the Commonwealth signed it with a reservation as to inter-Commonwealth disputes. Resolutions of approval were passed by the Dáil on the 26th February 1930 and by the Senate on the 7th May 1930.

In September 1930 the Irish Free State was elected to a non-permanent seat on the Council of the League of Nations, in succession to Canada. In putting forward their country as a candidate, the Government stated that they did so on its merits, and not as a member of any group or combination of States. Actually, Australia was the next senior member of the Commonwealth, but it waived any claim it might have had on that ground; and, in common with the other

---

[1] *Senate Debates*, xii, 1426. [2] Ibid., xii, 1391. [3] Ibid., xii, 1389.

nations of the Commonwealth, including Great Britain, it ensured the success of the Irish candidature by its support.

Within the purely Commonwealth sphere, the advances made are almost too well known to require detailed recital. The Government's purpose was to consolidate the position achieved at the Imperial Conference of 1926, and to apply in detail the principles laid down at that Conference, with a view to the removal of even the smallest formal restriction that remained on the absolute co-equality of the other member States of the Commonwealth with Great Britain. This detailed application was the task of the Conference on the Operation of Dominion Legislation, which was held in 1929. It was attended by the Minister for External Affairs (Mr. McGilligan) and the Attorney-General (Mr. J. A. Costello, K.C.) and they gained all their objectives except a relatively minor point concerning the Colonial Stock Act. The Report of this Conference was duly approved by the Dáil, though it was opposed by the Fianna Fáil Party, who challenged a division upon it.[1] It was not submitted for the approval of the Senate.

At the full Imperial Conference of 1930 the recommendations contained in this Report were adopted almost in their entirety. By general consent one of the three or four outstanding personalities at the Conference was Mr. McGilligan; and he could claim with justifiable pride that he had placed the coping stone on the edifice that had been begun in 1926 by his friend and colleague Kevin O'Higgins. The Irish Free State emerged, in constitutional theory as well as in actual practice, as a completely autonomous nation; and the sole link between it and Great Britain was the King. But the King was to function entirely, so far as Irish affairs were concerned, at the will of the Irish Government.

Certain of the resolutions of the Imperial Conference of 1930 required to be given statutory effect by the Parliament at Westminster, at the request of the six other member States of the Commonwealth (Canada, Australia, New Zealand, South Africa, the Irish Free State, and Newfoundland). Hence the Report of the Conference was presented to the Dáil and the Senate, and a resolution was moved in each House approving the Report and recommending the Executive Council 'to take such steps as they think fit to give effect thereto'. The resolution was moved in the Dáil by Mr. McGilligan, who expounded the implications of the Report in a masterly speech. The debate was made the occasion of an attack by Fianna Fáil on Great Britain, the British Empire, and the whole Commonwealth position;

[1] *Dáil Debates*, xxxiii, 2050–167, 2195–330.

and the references to the Royal Family by one of the leaders are best left unquoted. The party divided the House on the resolution, which was carried by sixty-three votes to forty-six.[1] The debate in the Senate was, as usual, on a higher plane, and the resolution was duly approved.[2]

The Bill to implement the resolutions of the Imperial Conference was entitled the Statute of Westminster, 1931. The most important of its provisions were: (1) no law made by the Parliament of a Dominion shall be void and inoperative on the ground that it is repugnant to the law of England; and the Parliament of a Dominion shall have power to repeal or amend any existing or future Act of Parliament of the United Kingdom in so far as the same is part of the law of the Dominion; (2) the Parliament of a Dominion has full power to make laws having extra-territorial operation; (3) no future Act of Parliament of the United Kingdom shall extend to a Dominion unless it is expressly declared in that Act that the Dominion has requested and consented to its enactment. In the definition section of the Bill the Irish Free State was defined as a Dominion.

On the 20th November 1931, on the Second Reading debate in the House of Commons, Mr. Winston Churchill stated that, under the Bill, it would be open to the Dáil at any time to repudiate legally, with the full sanction of law and parliamentary procedure, every provision of the Treaty of 1921, including the Oath. Every Article of the Constitution could be likewise repealed. In such a case, the Irish Free State would have lost its foundations and have become a mere inexpressible anomaly. He expressed his intention of moving an amendment in Committee to safeguard the position from the British point of view.[3] But the sense of the House was against Mr. Churchill. Mr. Amery, who described himself as an old Unionist who had been in favour of maintaining the Union by force, said that, once Ireland had been set upon the footing of a Dominion, there was only one way to treat it, and that was like the other Dominions. In everything that he had had to do, whether as First Lord of the Admiralty or as Secretary for Dominion Affairs, he had extended to his colleagues from the Irish Free State the same complete confidence, loyalty, and whole-hearted welcome that he extended to any other statesmen of any other Dominion. 'If you give,' he added, 'you must give generously, and without looking back.'[4] This was true statesmanship,

[1] *Dáil Debates*, xxxix, 2290–332 and 2334–62.
[2] *Senate Debates*, xiv, 1599–1674.
[3] *House of Commons Debates*, cclix, 1193, 1194.   [4] Ibid., cclix, 1205.

reminiscent of Burke's pregnant saying that 'magnanimity in politics is not seldom the truest wisdom'.

The day after Mr. Churchill's Second Reading speech in the House of Commons, Mr. Cosgrave addressed a letter to the Prime Minister, in the course of which he said: 'I need scarcely impress upon you that the maintenance of the happy relations which now exist between our two countries is absolutely dependent upon the continued acceptance by each of us of the good faith of the other. This situation has been constantly present to our minds, and we have reiterated time and again that the Treaty is an agreement which can only be altered by consent. I mention this particularly, because there seems to be a mistaken view in some quarters that the solemnity of this instrument in our eyes could derive any additional strength from a parliamentary law. So far from this being the case, any attempt to erect a Statute of the British Parliament into a safeguard of the Treaty would have quite the opposite effect here, and would rather tend to give rise in the minds of our people to a doubt as to the sanctity of this instrument.'[1] This letter was read to the House of Commons, but it proved not to be necessary. Speaking on the restrictive amendment proposed by the Churchill group, Mr. Stanley Baldwin warned the Commons against thinking that they were dealing only with Ireland in these matters. The Dominions were very properly jealous of their status and jealous of each other's status. If honourable members thought they could do something which offended Ireland, and was only going to offend Ireland, they made the mistake of their lives. They were going to offend not only the Irish Free State, but every Irishman in Australia, in Canada, and in the United States of America. They would offend every Dominion, even the most British of them; and none would feel it more than Canada, which was often held up to them as an example. It was because it might go out to the world that, for all their talk, they did not trust the Dominions, and that Dominion status meant nothing to them, that he opposed the amendment.[2]

The proposed restrictive clause was defeated by the enormous majority of 360 votes against 50, and the Statute of Westminster received the Royal Assent on the 11th December 1931, six weeks before the dissolution which was the prelude to a change of government in the Irish Free State. Thus, even the possibility of British interference was removed by the action of the British themselves; and the Treaty of 1921 was invested solely with the moral sanctity of an international agreement and no longer, on any view, with the legal sanc-

---

[1] *House of Commons Debates*, cclx, 311.   [2] Ibid., cclx, 346.

tion of a British statute. No patriotic Irishman could wish it otherwise. The resultant growth of a sense of political responsibility among
all sections of the community might be slow, but it would be inevitable. Grave mistakes might be made, but in the long run they would
be rectified. There remained the problem of the partition of Ireland,
which was an inheritance from history. Henceforward, the Government and people of the Irish Free State would be completely free to
adopt the policy which best commended itself as likely to lead to an
ultimate, permanent union of Orange and Green. If one policy, even
pursued over a term of years, proved to be a failure, it could be
scrapped and another substituted for it. The closing days of 1931
thus marked the end of an epoch in Anglo-Irish affairs.

Unhappily, these triumphs (for they were no less) in the external
field were accompanied by a marked deterioration in the situation at
home. It will be recalled that, following the assassination of Kevin
O'Higgins, a stringent Public Safety Act had been passed, empowering the setting up of military courts. These courts were never, in fact,
set up, and, owing principally to the agitation conducted against it
by Fianna Fáil, the Act was repealed as from the end of 1928. The
ranks of the irreconcilables were probably swollen to some extent as
a result of the conditions brought about by the world depression,
from which Ireland had not escaped. Men of avowed communistic
principles began to emerge as leaders of the movement, and an
organization was formed called Comhairle na Poblachta (the Council
of the Republic) to co-ordinate all Republican activities. A weekly
newspaper, entitled *An Phoblacht (The Republic)*, was published, and
claimed a large circulation; it was filled with letterpress of a viru-
lence hardly to be exceeded in the propagandist sheets of Balkan
countries. The physical force necessary to all revolutionary movements was supplied in this case by the Irish Republican Army.

One of the chief activities of the irreconcilable, physical force
element was the intimidation of jurors and witnesses in criminal
cases, the result of which was that verdicts of guilty could often not
be obtained even in the clearest cases. Nor was such intimidation a
mere idle threat. In the month of August 1928 bunting was flown in
the streets of Dublin, and some business houses included the Union
Jack in the display. Organized raids were made on these premises, and
the obnoxious flag was torn down and taken away. Four young men
were charged with the larceny of a Union Jack exhibited by an insurance company. They were found guilty, but were not sentenced to
any term of imprisonment, being released immediately. One of the

officials of the company, Mr. Albert Henry Armstrong, who had been present at the time of the raid, was a witness at the trial, but his evidence was not material. On the night of the 20th February 1929 Mr. Armstrong was murdered by armed men outside his home in Dublin. None of them was apprehended.

On the 3rd December 1928 a man named Healy, who was charged with shooting at two members of the Civic Guard, on two different occasions, with intent to do grievous bodily harm, was found guilty by the unanimous verdict of twelve jurors; and he was sentenced by Mr. Justice Sullivan (now the Chief Justice) to five years' penal servitude. The names of the twelve jurors were circulated far and wide. One of them was a Mr. John White, who lived in Terenure, a suburb of Dublin. A party of armed men called at his home after dark on the 23rd January 1929 and shot him in the stomach. Fortunately, they did not succeed in murdering him; he was rushed to hospital, gravely wounded, but survived. The Government at once gave the eleven other jurymen an armed guard for their protection.

The issue of *An Phoblacht* dated the 23rd February 1929 contained two references to this attempted murder. The first is as follows: 'In Maryboro' Jail, Hogan and Con Healy are being treated as ordinary convicts. The slave-minded jurors who convicted them are responsible, and are paying for their treachery, one lying in a Dublin hospital, the others having to be protected by England's Secret Service men.' The other is a paragraph headed 'Denial of a Rumour'. 'We have heard that a brother of Mr. White, of Nevada, Terenure, who was shot last month, is spreading a rumour around town to the effect that Mr. John White was not on the jury that convicted Con Healy and sent him to penal servitude for five years. This is not a fact. He was on that jury, and well he knows it.'

In its issue of the same date another weekly newspaper, the *Nation*, which was regarded as the organ of Mr. De Valera's party at that time, contained the following in a column headed 'Prisoners' Notes', which was one of the more or less regular features of the paper: 'If anyone wants an amusing sight let him venture out on a cold, wet day and view sad and shady-looking C.I.D. men standing outside the houses and also the business premises where the jurymen live or are employed who were cowardly and misguided enough to convict of treason that Tipperary Volunteer, Con Healy, who has devoted his whole life to unselfish service of the nation, and thus handed him over to British vengeance—five years in Maryborough hell.'

This extract raises the question of the attitude of Fianna Fáil at that time towards majority rule and the legitimacy of the Parliament of the Irish Free State. Reference has been made in a previous chapter to a speech made by Mr. De Valera, in which he said that those who continued on in the organization which he and his followers had left could claim exactly the same continuity as he and his followers had claimed up to 1925. That speech was delivered less than a month after the murder of Mr. Armstrong (14th March 1929). The leader of the Labour Party (Mr. O'Connell) said that he took Mr. De Valera to mean that the legitimate government of the country were people outside the Dáil; but he invited correction by saying that he might be wrong in this conclusion. Mr. De Valera did not then correct him, however; but more than two and a half years afterwards (14th October 1931) he referred to the matter and stated that Mr. O'Connell had misinterpreted him.[1] In the circumstances, it is desirable to quote from the editorial of the *Nation* at the time (23rd March 1929), which took Mr. De Valera's speech for its subject and which interpreted it to the public.

'On the one hand, the Fianna Fáil Party had no wish to condone or to show that they condoned brutality of any sort; on the other hand, they did not wish to associate themselves with the equally brutal, inefficient, useless methods of repression adopted by the Free State Government. What had to be done was to explain these outbursts of violence, explicable (if at all) only under existing circumstances when a whole section of the community is wrongfully debarred from taking its legitimate share in the public life of the country....

'Mr. De Valera very properly seized the opportunity of explaining once more the position of Fianna Fáil in the Free State Assembly. His sincerity was patent. We entered a faked parliament which we believed in our hearts to be illegitimate and we still believe it; and we faced a junta there which we did not regard as the rightful Government of this country. We did not respect, nor do we now, such a Government or such a Parliament. . . . Our presence in the "Dáil" of usurpers is sheer expediency, nothing else. When we started a new Republican Party we did not, nor do we now, differ from Sinn Féin in principle or aim. We still respect the scruples that prevented some Sinn Féiners from walking our road. We only thought their purely negative methods too risky, not aggressive enough to save the Republican movement from threatening disaster. We have not given up our creed nor our ideals; we stand, as always, for the independence

---

[1] *Dáil Debates*, xl, 54.

S

of Ireland. The Cosgrave Government may be, and is, in spite of us, the *de facto* Government of our country; but for us it will never be the *de jure* Government. We accept the principle of majority rule and for the sake of public order we are obliged to recognize their *de facto* Government—but for what it is.'

To meet the situation caused by the threatened breakdown of the jury system, the Government introduced a Juries Protection Bill on the 1st May 1929. This measure provided for the secret empanelling of juries, majority verdicts of nine out of twelve, imprisonment for refusal to recognize the court, prohibition of the publication of jurors' names, penalties for the intimidation of jurors, and other matters. The Bill was fiercely opposed by Fianna Fáil and had to be passed under the closure. On the Second Reading Mr. De Valera said that nobody on his side of the House attempted in any way whatever to condone the two recent crimes, but his speech as a whole was devoted to the thesis that the Cosgrave Administration represented a continuation of British government in Ireland; oddly enough in these circumstances, he asserted that the Bill went 'back behind Magna Charta'.[1] Referring (presumably) to the Irish Republican Army, he said: 'Because they [the Cosgrave Government] turned their backs on what they stood for a few years ago they will not allow their prejudice to let them know that there are a few men who did not turn their backs on these principles, and who are struggling, rightly or wrongly, either supported by the majority of the people of Ireland or not supported, to secure this objective [the Republic].'[2]

The operation of the Act was limited to two years, but at the end of that time it was necessary to continue it for a like period. Indeed, the time was approaching when trial by jury for cases of alleged political crime would have to be abolished altogether. The following are among the grave events which occurred in the year 1931.

30th January. A young man named Patrick Carroll was found in a Dublin lane with his head shattered. On the 14th February *An Phoblacht* published an editorial, headed 'Executed by I.R.A.', in which murders of this type were explained and justified. Carroll was a member of the Irish Republican Army, and had been found by that organization to be giving information to the police.

20th March. Superintendent Curtin, of the Civic Guard, was shot through the heart from behind a hedge at 10.15 p.m. outside the gate leading to his home in Tipperary. He had conducted a local prosecution for illegal drilling a few days earlier. The weekly organ of the

---

[1] *Dáil Debates*, xxix, 1562.   [2] Ibid., xxix, 1576.

Fianna Fáil Party, the *Nation*, condemned this murder in the strongest terms in an editorial in its issue of the 28th March; but *An Phoblacht* of the same date contained the following, under the heading, 'Superintendent Curtin's Death—Its True Perspective': 'The shooting of Superintendent Curtin will, no doubt, be made an excuse for another attempt at the Last Conquest of Ireland, just as was the shooting of Kevin O'Higgins. . . . Like his English predecessors, O'Duffy [the Chief Commissioner of Police] has to admit that he "can see no hope for the country's future" because "murderers are being shielded by the people", who refuse "to take a bold and courageous stand in the interest of order, peace and progress" (British style!).' It also castigated the Archbishop of Cashel (Most Rev. Dr. Harty) for his 'impertinence' in condemning the murder. The reference to Kevin O'Higgins is not surprising, as the paper had described him much earlier (17th November 1928) as 'one of the most blood-guilty Irishmen in our generation'.

5th April. Approximately a hundred men were found drilling at Philipstown, King's County, under the leadership of an escaped prisoner.

23rd April. Two young undergraduates of Trinity College, Messrs. Rupert Young and George Johnson, were going for a moonlight walk in the Dublin mountains, at a spot known appropriately enough as the Hell Fire Club, when they inadvertently crossed the path of men engaged in manœuvres. They were called upon to halt but did not do so, thinking the matter was a joke. Mr. Young received a bullet through the lower part of his nose, and another grazed his body but was fortunately deflected by a button. Mr. Johnson was not hit.

10th June. A detective post which had been established near the Hell Fire Club as a result of this outrage discovered an ammunition dump in the form of a concrete chamber containing rifles, revolvers, machine-guns, and bombs, the entrance being guarded by a trap mine. *An Phoblacht*, in its issue of the 20th June, admitted the capture, but boasted that it was only one of hundreds existing throughout the thirty-two counties of Ireland. There was a by-election pending at the time, and on the day after the discovery (11th June) Mr. Daniel Buckley, then a Fianna Fáil back-bencher but afterwards His Majesty's Representative in the Irish Free State, said sarcastically: 'In view of the fact that the Hell Fire Club dump dope will not be sufficient to carry off this by-election, would it not be well to organize a few more shooting outrages?'[1]

---

[1] *Dáil Debates*, xxxix, 166.

21st June. It was the annual custom of Fianna Fáil and the Republicans to hold pilgrimages to the grave of Wolfe Tone at Bodenstown, County Kildare, each claiming to be the true inheritor of Tone's gospel. In 1931 these events took place on the date mentioned (Sunday); but it is noteworthy that the pilgrimage of the Republicans and of Mr. De Valera's followers was a combined one on this occasion. In the 'Orders for the Day' published in *An Phoblacht* for the 20th June a place in the procession was accorded to Fianna Fáil. At the request of the Government, the railway company cancelled the special trains arranged for the occasion, and military evolutions were prevented by the Civic Guards. Nevertheless, the demonstration was held, and members of Fianna Fáil marched in company with members of the Irish Republican Army and other bodies. An oration at the grave side was delivered by Mr. Peadar O'Donnell, an extremist leader, after which a wreath was laid on Tone's grave by Mr. De Valera.[1]

18th July. Warders from Mountjoy Prison were attacked, whilst off duty, by armed men, and one of them was handcuffed to an iron rail and chained by the neck and legs.

20th July. Two men, representing themselves to be detectives, called at night to the farmhouse in County Tipperary where a young farm labourer named John Ryan was sleeping. He accompanied them at their request, and his dead body was later found, riddled with bullets, at a cross roads, with a notice beside it, 'Spies and informers, beware!—I.R.A.' He had been a witness in the same drilling case as had led to the murder of Superintendent Curtin, and he had refused to commit perjury.

24th August. A long account appeared in an English daily newspaper of an interview given to its special correspondent by Mr. Frank Ryan at the offices of *An Phoblacht*, which was quoted in full by Mr. Cosgrave in the Dáil.[2] Mr. Ryan objected to the use of words like 'murder' and 'assassination' when referring to the shooting of unarmed men. 'The shootings to which you referred were not murder; they were acts of war. You must remember this, the Irish Republican Army is still at war with Britain. We regard the Free State Ministers merely as the agents of Britain.' As for Superintendent Curtin, he 'exceeded his duty. He went out of his way to persecute the I.R.A. . . . The Civic Guard have no right to interfere in matters that do not concern them. If they ask for trouble they must not be surprised if

---

[1] *Irish Independent*, 22 June 1931.
[2] *Dáil Debates*, xl, 34–6, from which the above extracts have been taken.

they get it.' John Ryan, the Tipperary farm labourer, 'gave evidence for Curtin. He was nothing else than a traitor. Then there was Carroll, the young man found dead in a County Dublin lane. This is the truth about him. He was an *agent provocateur*.'

Mr. Ryan continued: 'Military organization cannot tolerate spies or traitors. But let me tell you this—these things are not decided lightly. Decisions are made only with very, very great reluctance. Traitors must be punished, but there are fewer in our ranks than anywhere else.'

The interviewer invited Mr. Ryan to state how the Irish Republican Army proposed to overthrow the Government, and he replied: 'All I am going to say is this. One of these days there will be crowds in the street, and they will not be dispersed by baton charges. You know the old saying that England's difficulty is Ireland's opportunity. England will be engaged in another great war soon. Then she will try to take advantage of the provisions of the Treaty for garrisoning ports in Ireland. That will be the end of England's rule in Ireland.'

No government deriving its authority from the will of the people would deserve to survive if it lacked the courage to cope with the challenge disclosed by these hard facts. Trial by jury had broken down. Trial by the existing judges without a jury was impracticable; the judges had been appointed in accordance with the provisions of the Constitution, and the conditions of their appointment did not include adjudication in criminal matters on questions of fact. Mr. Cosgrave stated that, in connection with the Public Safety Act passed in 1927, he had been informed by at least two of the judges of the Supreme Court that they would require to relinquish their office if they were called upon to act as a court in such matters.[1] They were, of course, perfectly within their rights. Accordingly, the only method of trial left was that by military tribunal. Such a method must always be repugnant to the constitutionally minded; but, so far as the members of the Irish Republican Army were concerned, since they claimed to be soldiers they could not logically object to being tried by soldiers.

Immediately on the reassembly of the Dáil after the summer recess (14th October 1931) the Government introduced the Constitution (Amendment No. 17) Bill, which inserted a new Article 2A in the Constitution. Though in form Article 2A was an amendment of the Constitution, in fact it was a Public Safety Bill of a most stringent character, containing thirty-four sections and an Appendix. A military tribunal of five members was empowered to be set up, for dealing

[1] *Dáil Debates*, xl, 45.

with political crime, and the powers conferred on it (including the infliction of the death penalty) exceeded anything known in Ireland in modern times. There was no appeal from its decisions, but the Executive Council might pardon persons convicted by it and remit their punishment. The Executive Council might, by Order, declare associations to be unlawful, and the issue of such an Order was to be conclusive evidence that they were unlawful. Wide powers of arrest and detention were conferred on the police.

It was a Bill of which the introduction could be explained only by necessity and of which the operation could be justified only by the exercise of moderation. In spite of domiciliary visits, it was supported solidly by the Independent members of the Dáil and the rank and file of the Government party, as well as by two outstanding representatives of Labour (Messrs. Anthony and Morrissey), who were subsequently expelled from their party for voting for it. The Bill was strenuously opposed by Fianna Fáil, but, in view of the subsequent use made by the Fianna Fáil Government of the military tribunal set up under this constitutional amendment, the arguments they adduced have lost any force they might have had. Mr. De Valera's contribution to the debate was long and characteristic. The Government was imitating the activities of Sir Hamar Greenwood (Chief Secretary during the Black and Tan period), instead of getting to the root of the evil by abolishing the Oath. He would have been on firmer ground if he had produced some evidence that the removal of the Oath would have made any difference whatever in the attitude of the Irish Republican Army towards the institutions of the State. He stated, with obvious sincerity, that his party did not stand for crime, and made the remarkable admission that 'if there is no authority in this House to rule, then there is no authority in any part of the country to rule'.[1] But this part of his speech, which was short, was largely negatived by his reference to the long catalogue of crime read out by Mr. Cosgrave as 'incidents'.[2] He maintained that the ordinary law was quite sufficient to deal with them, ignoring the fact that the perpetrators had never been brought to justice. At a later stage, he referred to the Irish Republican Army as follows: 'These are the people who were ready to give everything that they had for Ireland, and well we know it, and now they are being deserted by the majority of their people. . . . These men are misguided, if you will, but they were brave men, anyhow; let us at least have for them the decent respect that we have for the brave. They have done terrible things

---

[1] *Dáil Debates*, xl, 54. [2] Ibid., xl, 51.

recently I admit, if they are responsible for them, and I suppose they are. Let us appeal to them and ask them in God's name not to do them.'[1]

It is perhaps permissible to point out that Messrs. Armstrong, Carroll, Curtin, Ryan, White, and Young were all shot after dark; that all of them were unarmed; and that the degree of risk incurred by their assailants is indicated by the fact that none of them was ever apprehended.

Mr. De Valera's main thesis was that the Cosgrave Government were merely the successors of the British Government, and in support of this thesis he said: 'The situation that was brought about here was thoroughly understood by the British when they forced the Treaty on us. Lord Birkenhead, in asking that that Treaty be accepted, appealed to his brothers in the House of Lords and said to them: "By all means accept this. The unruly Irish will in future be put down; they will be put down by other Irishmen with an economy of English lives. We will hand over to this new body of Irishmen who are prepared to follow our dictation and work upon the lines of our policy the task of trying to stifle those who want the complete independence of their country." '[2] The fact that these words are placed within inverted commas suggests that they are a quotation from a speech by Lord Birkenhead, in which he spoke of 'an economy of English lives'. They are, of course, a travesty of what he said, and the occasion was not one on which he was asking the House of Lords to pass the Treaty. As the occasion was important, it will be specified; the exact quotation will then be given.

In the months of February and March 1922 the British Army and police were evacuating the country, the Treaty having been accepted by the Dáil. The anti-Treaty section of the Irish Republican Army were attacking them, so as to stop the evacuation and smash the Treaty. Mr. De Valera's speeches in Munster were encouraging the Irregulars in this course. For example, on the 16th March, at Dungarvan, he said: 'The Treaty . . . barred the way to independence with the blood of fellow-Irishmen. It was only by civil war after this that they could get their independence. . . . If you don't fight to-day, you will have to fight to-morrow; and I say, when you are in a good fighting position, then fight on.'[3] A number of British officers and men were killed. In particular, on the 2nd March the Royal Irish Constabulary evacuated the police barracks at

---

[1] *Dáil Debates*, xl, 298.   [2] Ibid., xl, 54.
[3] *Irish Independent*, 17 March 1922.

Tipperary, handing them over to the authorities of the Provisional Government; they were fired upon by the Irregulars, Head Constable Davis, a man of very long service, being killed and three others being seriously wounded. Lord Carson put down a question in the House of Lords with reference to this outrage, and in his reply on the 8th March the Lord Chancellor said: 'All this, of course, is full of anxiety for every one of us, but, if I am asked for my perfectly honest opinion, it is this, that bad and anxious as the situation is, I cannot see that it is not a gain that you have in Southern Ireland men who have hitherto been organized against us now, as far as one can see, honestly attempting to carry out their duty and their responsibility, and to put down this movement in the South of Ireland. I say plainly that, having once satisfied myself that we have treated them properly, I would far rather that they were undertaking that task than that we were, and I believe that if that task is effectively and successfully carried out by them the fact that it should be done by them and not by us will have resulted in an economy of English lives, and will also in the end conduce to permanent peace in Ireland.'[1] Lord Birkenhead's motives in signing the Treaty, and in commending it to the House of Lords, are of no particular interest to Irishmen, who are concerned only with the instrument itself and with the benefits which accrued from it. But it will be seen that what he said in regard to 'an economy of English lives', and the circumstances in which he said it, are very different from what was stated by Mr. De Valera.

The Constitution (Amendment No. 17) Bill became law on the 17th October 1931, and on the same day the Executive Council promulgated the Constitution (Operation of Article 2A) Order, which brought the provisions of the Act into force. It was commonly reported that on the same night there was an exodus of the extremists from Ireland. On the following day (Sunday, 18th October), a Joint Pastoral of the archbishops and bishops of Ireland was read in all the Catholic churches. This referred to the aims of the Irish Republican Army and of Saor Éire (the Republican Communist Organization) and stated that 'it is our duty to tell our people plainly that the two organizations to which we have referred, whether separate or in alliance, are sinful and irreligious, and that no Catholic can lawfully be a member of them'. The Hierarchy also pointed out that the country had a democratic government, and that no-one had a right to seek to overthrow that government by force of arms; and they were careful to stress the fact that this was true not only of the exist-

[1] *House of Lords Debates*, xlix, 381, 382.

ing government but of any successor to it, so long as that successor secured the support of a majority of the people by constitutional means.[1] This clear and accurate statement of the moral law ought to have been sufficient to protect the archbishops and bishops from the charge that they were acting as partisans in politics on the side of Mr. Cosgrave and against Mr. De Valera. But unhappily this proved not to be the case.

On the 20th October the Government issued the Constitution (Declaration of Unlawful Associations) Order, 1931, under the powers conferred by the new Act. Twelve organizations were declared to be illegal, including the Irish Republican Army, Saor Éire, and the Friends of Soviet Russia. Persons awaiting trial were brought before the Military Tribunal, which for the most part imposed light sentences, many prisoners being released on undertaking to cease to belong to illegal organizations.

[1] *Irish Independent*, 19 October 1931.

CHAPTER XVI

PARTY POLITICS AND THE SENATE

Gradual growth of a party system—Formation of a Government party—Political alignments—Election of Chairman and Vice-Chairman—Bill to make Senators eligible for the Executive Council—Mr. Cosgrave's half-hearted advocacy—Amendment carried limiting Senate to one member of the Council—Opposition in the Dáil—Fianna Fáil abuse of the Senate—Senator O'Farrell on the Bill—Change in the method of filling casual vacancies—The Seanad Bye-Elections Bill— Period for constitutional amendments without a referendum extended from eight to sixteen years—Absence of party rigidity—The Juries Protection Bill—The Constitution (Amendment No. 17) Bill in the Senate—Its passage under the guillotine—The Chairman's position— The Third Triennial Election—Defects of the system again exemplified— Result of the election—Increasing number of Senators of a political type.

For the first six years of its existence the functions of the Senate had been discharged virtually on a non-party basis. There was a small Labour Party of five members, but they had no formal leader. The Labour movement never elected any but capable men to the Second Chamber, and one or two of them were first-class politicians in the best sense of the word. Hence the Labour Senators were not mere echoes of their colleagues in the other House, and they were a group of individuals holding similar views rather than a party. There was also an Independent Group, under the chairmanship of Senator Jameson. This was a body of Senators who habitually consulted together in regard to the measures which were to come before the House; but they were nót bound by any pledge, and they frequently voted on opposite sides in divisions. Though the majority were ex-Unionists, this group had other adherents, such as Senators Douglas and Mrs. Stopford Green. It was exclusively a Senate group, and no member of the Dáil belonged to it or attended its meetings. Lastly there was a curiously named and largely informal Progressive Party, which was no more than a loose combination of about fifteen Senators united in a tacit agreement to support the Cosgrave Government against other quarters of the House, but the individual members of which were free to vote against the Ministry on such occasions as they thought fit.

The circumstances of the Triennial Election of 1928 brought about a change, since the entry of members of Fianna Fáil into the Senate, as well as of ex-members of the Dáil on the other side, imported something like a party atmosphere into the proceedings. The change was gradual, however. Probably the great majority of Senators regarded a Senate party system with dislike, and there was still, in general, an absence of strict party ties. Moreover, the necessity for party discipline did not arise, since Fianna Fáil, even if allied with Labour, was still much too small numerically to exercise any influence in the division lobby.

There had never been a Cosgrave party, but at the beginning of this period steps were immediately taken to form one. A circular inviting adherents was sent out by Senators MacKean and Milroy, and the result was the formation of a party under the chairmanship of Senator Dr. O'Sullivan.[1] It drew most of its members from the so-called Progressive Party, which now ceased to function. The new party was not strictly regimented, and it had no leader, Dr. O'Sullivan being merely the chairman at its meetings. It is not possible to state accurately its strength at this time, but it probably numbered nineteen members.

Of the other parties or groups, the Fianna Fáil Party of six newly elected members was immediately joined by Senator Colonel Moore, who had belonged to Professor Magennis's defunct Clann Éireann; and Senator Joseph Connolly was elected leader of the party. Labour was re-inforced by Senator Johnson, formerly the chairman of the party in the Dáil, where he had been the most industrious private member and the best parliamentarian; but he joined his five Senate colleagues on an equal footing, and the Labour Party continued without a leader. The new system of election had told heavily, and would continue to tell heavily, against the Independent Group; and at the outset of this period it numbered twelve members.

The composition of the Senate might therefore be summarized as follows:

[1] *Irish Times*, 2 January 1929.

Cosgrave Party	19
Fianna Fáil	7
Independent Group	12
Independents	15
Labour Party	6
Chairman	1
	—
	60

The fifteen Independents were persons of the most diverse views, and the majority were men of distinction. They included General Sir Bryan Mahon and General Sir William Hickie, who were soldiers rather than politicians; the Earl of Granard and Sir Thomas Esmonde; Mr. Patrick Hooper, a former editor of the *Freeman's Journal*; Mr. Alfred Byrne, subsequently Lord Mayor of Dublin; Sir Walter Nugent, the chairman of the Great Southern Railways Company; and Sir John Keane, an ex-Unionist landowner. The system of election by Dáil and Senate was, of course, fatal to the future chances of such men. Four of the Independents, Senators Mrs. Wyse Power, Dowdall, Linehan, and Laurence O'Neill, voted increasingly with Fianna Fáil, and the two first-named subsequently joined that party. The other Independents in general supported the Cosgrave Party.

The Chairman and Vice-Chairman were elected at the first meeting of the Senate held after the commencement of the period (12th December 1928). Senator Westropp Bennett, the previous Vice-Chairman, was elected Chairman by 41 votes against 12 votes cast for Senator Douglas, who had been Vice-Chairman from 1922 to 1925. There were three candidates for the Vice-Chairmanship: Senator Kenny (Cosgrave party), Senator O'Farrell (Labour party), and Senator Colonel Moore (Fianna Fáil). Colonel Moore was eliminated in a preliminary poll, and in a straight vote between the two other candidates Senator Kenny was elected by 27 votes to 21. All the newly elected members of Fianna Fáil abstained from voting after their own candidate had been defeated; and the unfortunate split in the Labour Party which had cost it a seat at the Triennial Election manifested itself in the action of the two Transport Union Senators, who voted against Senator O'Farrell in both contests.[1] Senator Kenny died during the Triennial Period (22nd April 1931), and his successor in the Vice-Chair was elected on the 6th May 1931. There were again three candidates, Colonel Moore was again elimi-

[1] *Senate Debates*, xi, 8–17.

nated, and Senator P. J. Hooper (Independent) was elected by 28 votes to 18 over Senator M. F. O'Hanlon (Cosgrave Party).[1] Senator Hooper died on the following 6th September, and for the short unexpired term of the Triennial Period the vacancy in the Vice-Chairmanship was not filled.

The four remaining Bills to implement the recommendations of the Joint Committee on the constitution and powers of the Second Chamber all came before the Senate in 1929. Two of them, dealing with Money Bills and the Initiation of Bills in the Senate, are mentioned in the chapters on Money Bills and on the Formalities and Machinery of Parliament (Chapters XXXII and XXXIII). The two others are therefore all that we need consider here. One of them was concerned with the eligibility of Senators for membership of the Executive Council, and the other altered the method of filling casual vacancies.

It will be remembered that the question of opening the Executive Council to Senators had been debated at some length in 1927, but with no result. The Joint Committee which reported in May 1928 recommended that the existing disqualification of members of the Senate for the Executive Council should be removed; and the Constitution (Amendment No. 15) Bill, as introduced in the Dáil, proposed that members of both Houses should be equally eligible for the Executive, except that the President, the Vice-President, and the Minister for Finance should be members of the Dáil. But Mr. Cosgrave commended the Bill to the Dáil in a half-hearted way, and he left it to a free vote of the House. He said: 'My own view is that the Dáil might reasonably consider a Bill which would give power to have one Senator appointed as a member of the Executive Council. . . . I do not know if the particular recommendation in this case will meet with the approval of the Dáil. . . . I do not think it is at all likely within the next twenty years, even if this Bill were passed into law, that any more than one—possibly not even one—member of the Senate would be either nominated or accepted by the Dáil as a member of the Executive.'[2] On the Committee Stage Mr. Cosgrave introduced an amendment, providing that not more than one Senator might be a member of the Executive Council; and the Bill in this form was passed by the Dáil.

Even this limited and purely theoretical extension was strenuously resisted by the Opposition, and leading members of Mr. De Valera's party used the Bill as a text for the denigration of the Senate. The

[1] *Senate Debates*, xiv, 893-6.   [2] *Dáil Debates*, xxviii, 1291, 1292.

following quotations are all from the speeches of Deputies who subsequently held office in Mr. De Valera's Administration.

In his speech on the Second Reading Mr. Lemass had excepted from his strictures the six Senators who had been elected by his party, and on the Committee Stage he said:

'Is there a single member of the Senate whose inclusion in the Executive Council would justify the cost of printing this Bill? I cannot think of one. . . . Of course, I am now excluding from consideration the six just men to whom I already had occasion to make reference, like the cities in Bible history. But six just men do not redeem the Senate. I think it is extremely unlikely that the Executive Council would be thinking of any one of these six individuals as a colleague in the Executive Council. It must be some one of the remaining fifty-four, and there is not a single one of the remaining fifty-four capable, in my opinion, of acting as a member of the Dáil, much less as a member of the Executive Council, although I will admit that it is possibly easier to get members of the Executive Council than it is to get members of the Dáil; the standard of knowledge and ability is not so high, and the entrance examination is possibly easier.'[1]

Mr. MacEntee made the same point: 'I cannot see that any member of the Senate, with notable exceptions—those who, because of their own political principles, would not be included in the present Executive Council—could temper that body with wisdom, and I certainly cannot see that any Senator would vitiate it with folly, because its folly is at present all-sufficient.'[2]

Mr. Hugo Flinn carried the vituperation a stage further. He described the procedure in the Senate, and also gave a novel interpretation of the working of the British political system.

'The procedure [in the Senate] is that the bell rings for prayer. They come in, they ask what division they are to go into; then they ask what it is about, and then they legislate with their feet. It is the only part of their bodies or minds which they are accustomed to use, and they can use them in relation to a Senatorial Executive Officer in exactly the same way as they use them in relation to a non-Senatorial Executive Officer. . . . In another country where they have a House of Commons and a House of Lords, . . . those two Houses are used for certain purposes. Where a Minister has become ineffective or inefficient, he is sent to the House of Lords. That is a way of getting rid of him. Another use that is made of it—and this may become part of the machinery in this particular case—is where someone who has

[1] *Dáil Debates*, xxviii, 1811.   [2] Ibid., xxviii, 1817.

not been elected is wanted in by the existing Executive in the Parliament. Someone is persuaded to go to the House of Lords and provide a vacancy. We are improving on that machinery. We are in the position under this Constitution amendment not merely to make a Senator a member of the Executive Council, but to pick up anybody in the street we want so long as there is a majority in the Senate and the Dáil of a particular party, and put him straight into the Executive Council. All we have got to do is to arrange that one of the people whom, for one reason or another, you have sent to the local House of Lords is to cease to be a member of the local House of Lords.'[1]

These extracts have been necessary because they convey better than any mere description some idea of the attitude of Mr. De Valera's leading followers towards the Second Chamber at that time. Whether or not this attitude was the result of an inferiority complex, it is important in view of what subsequently occurred. It is clear that, if ever Mr. De Valera got into power, the Senate was doomed; and, whatever arguments might then be adduced for its abolition, the psychological factor would play a considerable part.

The value of the constitutional change effected by the Bill was justly summed up by Senator O'Farrell when the Bill reached the Senate, where it was passed unamended. He said:

'I look upon the proposal not as a privilege conferred upon the Senate so much as a constitutional concession to the Dáil. No President in the future will include in his Cabinet a member of the Senate unless he believes that by so doing he will improve his Cabinet, and even then he must have the definite approval of the other House. There is nothing very novel or very revolutionary in this. In practically all modern Parliaments, particularly in countries where the parliamentary tradition is very much more developed than it is here, and where the democratic tradition is at least as good, Governments draw on their Second Chambers for Ministers of State with very little reservation. But in actual practice, as the President was careful to remind the Dáil, the power which the Bill confers is likely to be only a very theoretical power for quite a long time to come....

'Therefore the Senate need take only a very mild interest in this amendment to the Constitution. It merely takes a short and a halting step towards bringing the constitutional theory of our Parliament into line with what is the constitutional practice in practically all modern Parliaments. Ultra-democrats need have no fear as to the

[1] *Dáil Debates*, xxviii, 1302, 1303.

result, because the protectionist policy of the Dáil will ensure that members of this House are not likely to be unduly troubled with offers of Ministerial portfolios.'[1]

The second Constitution (Amendment) Bill which it is proposed to consider here is the Amendment No. 11 Bill, which altered the method of filling casual vacancies in the Senate. The previous system had been one of co-option by the Senate itself, and it had worked extremely well. Vacancies were filled with promptitude, the type of candidate elected was uniformly good, and there had been a spirit of mutual accommodation. Thus, when a Labour Senator died or resigned, his place was filled by a member of the Labour Party; and similarly as regards the Cosgrave party and the Independent Group. The altered system emanated from the Joint Committee, in which it had been proposed by Mr. De Valera and carried by only one vote. In future, a casual vacancy was to be filled by the original electing body, that is, by the combined vote of the members of both Houses, by secret, postal ballot. This meant, of course, that the Dáil would have a preponderant voice, that the candidate would win who was put forward by the party whose combined strength was greatest, and that he would be likely to be a party politician. Of the eight Senators elected by this new method, four were former members of the Dáil; and, of the last five Senators so elected (1932–4) before the Senate was abolished, three had been in the other House up to within a few months of their election.

The machinery for the new system was provided by the Seanad Bye-Elections Bill. Under this, the conduct of the election was taken away from the Senate and placed in the control of the Government. When a vacancy occurred, the Clerk of the Senate, on the direction of the House, was to send written notice of it to the Minister for Local Government. As soon as conveniently might be thereafter, and in any case not later than six months after the receipt of the notice, the Minister was to issue a By-Election Order directing a by-election to be held, and the election was to be conducted by a returning officer appointed by him. Under the Cosgrave Government the seats were filled with reasonable expedition, but this was very far from being the case under its successor. The first vacancy was left unfilled for almost three months; the second and third for the full period of six months, and the fourth for more than seven months. This last was in breach of the statute, but the Senate had no remedy. On the date of the abolition of the House there were two vacancies, one of which

[1] *Senate Debates*, xii, 44, 45.

had existed for almost the full statutory period and the other for more than three months.

In the same year as these Bills were before Parliament (1929) there was enacted the Constitution (Amendment No. 16) Bill, which has been referred to in a previous chapter. Though it did not affect the Senate directly, it had more far-reaching consequences than any of the other Bills, and was ultimately used by Mr. De Valera to abolish the House itself and to take the King out of the Constitution. This Bill amended Article 50 of the Constitution by extending from eight to sixteen years the period within which amendments might be made to the Constitution by means of ordinary legislation, without the necessity of a referendum. The period dated from the coming into operation of the Constitution (6th December 1922); and, as the right to demand a referendum for ordinary legislation had been abolished in 1928, the result of the Bill was that constitutional changes could be made up to the 5th December 1938 by ordinary law without even the possibility of a referendum. A Bill of such importance can seldom have been enacted after less discussion. It was formally introduced in the Dáil on the 21st November 1928 and received its Second Reading on the 13th March following. Mr. Cosgrave then briefly explained its purpose in a couple of short sentences, and Mr. De Valera said: 'As it is an extension of time, and we hope to see it availed of to make changes which will make this Constitution one which will be more satisfactory to the Irish people, we will not object to it.' Mr. T. J. O'Connell, the leader of the Labour Party, expressed the prophetic fear that there would not be much of the original Constitution left at the end of the additional eight years, and there was no further discussion on the Bill.[1] The remaining stages in the Dáil (21st March) and all the stages in the Senate (10th April—9th May) were passed without debate. Thus while the Bill was passing through Parliament no explanation was given of the reason for it. But it was almost certainly due to the view held by members of the Government that it would be in the interests of the country as a whole if the Constitution were not the work solely of one administration, and that their successors in office should have an opportunity of amending it by ordinary legislation if they thought fit.

The absence of party rigidity in the Senate was exemplified by what took place during the passage of the Juries (Protection) Bill, 1929. In the successive divisions on this highly contentious measure, the combined opposition of Fianna Fáil and Labour was reinforced on

[1] *Dáil Debates*, xxviii, 1315-17.

particular points from other quarters of the House; and Sir John Griffith and the McGillycuddy of the Independent Group, Senator O'Hanlon of the Cosgrave party and Sir John Keane and Senator Hooper of the Independents all on different occasions voted against the Government. In a Second Chamber this is precisely as it should be. The Senate inserted eight amendments in the Bill, all of which were agreed to by the Dáil and of which one was specially noteworthy. In the Bill as it stood a majority verdict of nine to three sufficed for a conviction. The amendment in question provided that, whenever a jury should find a person to be guilty of a crime for which the penalty was death, the foreman of the jury should notify the judge in writing whether the verdict was or was not unanimous, and the number of dissentients (if any); and that the judge should convey this information to the Minister for Justice. In such a case, if the verdict was not unanimous it was extremely likely that the condemned man would be reprieved.

When the Bill to abolish the Senate was before Parliament in 1934 much criticism was directed against the Senate, and against its Chairman, in connection with what occurred over the Constitution (Amendment No. 17) Bill, introduced by the Cosgrave Government in the autumn of 1931. This was the Bill which established the Military Tribunal. A good deal of the criticism was ill-informed, but some of it was undoubtedly sincere. It is accordingly desirable to recall the circumstances. On Wednesday, 14th October 1931, the Bill was formally read a first time in the Dáil and a guillotine motion was passed in connection with it. On the following day (Thursday) the Second Stage and Committee Stage were disposed of under the guillotine, and by 1.45 p.m. on the next day (Friday) the remaining stages were passed, also under the guillotine, and the Bill was sent to the Senate. Only one minor amendment, which was sponsored by the Government, was inserted in the Bill during its passage through the Dáil.

On the Wednesday (the day the Bill was introduced in the Dáil), a notice of motion was handed in for the following Friday by Senators Wilson and O'Rourke, acting on behalf of the Government. This was a guillotine motion, to the effect that the Second Stage of the Bill should be begun at 4.15 p.m. on the Friday (less than three hours after the Bill was due to leave the Dáil) and that it should be allotted two and a half hours; that the Committee Stage should be taken at 8 p.m. on that day and should be concluded at 9.45 p.m.; and that the Report and Fifth Stages should be taken on the Saturday from 11

a.m. to 12 noon and from 12 noon to 1 p.m. respectively. This guillotine motion therefore enabled this momentous Bill, if the Senate so
decided, to be disposed of in two days after a total debate of five and
a quarter hours, or, including the debate on the motion itself, of six
and a half hours. The Bill passed the Dáil in three days after a total
debate of fifteen hours.[1]

Also on the Wednesday, the Vice-President (Mr. Ernest Blythe)
attended the Senate and explained to the House the Government's
reasons for desiring it to take the Bill on the Friday. Having heard the
Vice-President, the Senate decided by a large majority to meet on the
Friday, the only opposition being from Fianna Fáil and the Labour
Party.[2]

The Chairman was subsequently attacked for calling a meeting of
the House for the Friday, but this was the result of a decision of the
Senate and not of the Chairman. He was also attacked for receiving
the guillotine motion on the Wednesday, with less than the five days'
notice prescribed by the Standing Orders; but he had a discretion to
receive motions on shorter notice, and he was entitled to exercise it.
What was quite unprecedented was the fact that the motion related
to a Bill not then in possession of the Senate. If the Chairman had
refused to exercise his discretion for this reason, he would have been
within his strict rights; but such a refusal would have been, in effect,
a personal decision that a Bill was not urgent which the Government
had represented to be of the greatest urgency. On the other hand, by
accepting the motion he was not imposing a guillotine on the Senate,
but merely enabling the Senate to impose a guillotine on itself if it
saw fit. That is to say, the decision on the question of urgency, instead
of being a purely personal decision of the Chairman, would be left
to the Senate as a whole; and it should be remembered in this connection that the members of the Government party numbered about only
one-third of the House.

The action of the Chairman was justified by the event. On the two
days on which the Bill was before the Senate, there was an attendance
of fifty-seven Senators out of a possible fifty-nine, there being at that
time one unfilled casual vacancy. Neither of the two absentees (Senators Butler and MacGuinness) belonged to the Opposition. There
were thus fifty-six members entitled to vote in divisions, the Chairman being excluded. In the successive divisions on the guillotine
motion and on the Bill, the minority never exceeded fifteen, being the
combined strength of Fianna Fáil and Labour, plus Senators Dow-

[1] *Senate Debates*, xiv, 1843–5.   [2] Ibid., xiv, 1893–1916.

dall and Mrs. Wyse Power, who both subsequently joined Mr. De Valera's party. In the final division on the Bill there was an exhaustive poll, forty-one voting for the Bill and fifteen against it.

The majority contained men of the most diverse views, many of whom had frequently voted against the Government. Such of them as spoke made it clear that they felt bound, in view of the known facts, to accept the Government's assurance that the Bill was immediately necessary to deal with an armed conspiracy which otherwise would result in a continuance of political murder and ultimately destroy the State. The only effective opposition came from Senator Johnson, as Mr. De Valera's followers were but poorly equipped for a debate of this kind. Emotional references by their leader to 'Star Chamber methods to bully through legislation which is going, perhaps, to sink this country in blood'[1] read curiously in the light of after events, since the Government of which he was a member subsequently made full use of the Military Tribunal set up under this legislation for the trial, conviction, and imprisonment of members of the Irish Republican Army and others.

During this Third Triennial Period the number of non-Money Bills received by the Senate was about 120. Approximately one-quarter of these were amended, the number of amendments being roughly 170, of which practically all were agreed to by the Dáil. Among the principal Bills amended were the Landlord and Tenant Bill with thirty-six amendments, the Local Government (Dublin) Bill with thirty-seven, and the Censorship of Publications Bill with seventeen. The figures represent a considerable drop as compared with those of the previous three years, and this is probably attributable to three causes. In the first place, the number of Bills that were not susceptible of amendment was larger than previously. Secondly, the presence of Fianna Fáil as the official Opposition in the Dáil must have ensured, in some degree at least, a more careful scrutiny of Bills before they left that House. Thirdly, the new Senators, with the important exceptions of Senators Johnson and Wilson, were hardly as competent for the work of revision as those whom they had succeeded. In his speech on the Bill to abolish the Senate the Chairman of the Senate made reference to this aspect of the matter. 'When the Fianna Fáil Party were in opposition in the Dáil, numbers of amendments were moved by Fianna Fáil Senators in this House; but they generally consisted of the self-same amendments that had been moved by their Party and

1 *Senate Debates*, xiv, 1930.

rejected in the Dáil. Often, indeed, I was handed the green sheet of Dáil amendments, with the names of Fianna Fáil Deputies struck out and the names of Fianna Fáil Senators inserted. There was little evidence of independent thought.'[1]

Thus the serious work of revision continued to a large extent to be discharged by the survivors of the original Senate. Apart from this work, the reputation of the House was considerably enhanced by debates on various aspects of external affairs, occasioned by the motions for the approval of the Briand-Kellogg Pact,[2] of the adherence to the Optional Clause of the Versailles Treaty,[3] and of the Report of the Imperial Conference of 1930.[4] The speeches of Senators Johnson, Douglas, O'Farrell, and some others on these subjects had in them a quality of statesmanship not achieved in the other House except from the Ministerial bench.

The Triennial Election took place in November 1931, and the unsuitability of the system was again made manifest. There were twenty-three retiring Senators, the number being made up as follows: the twelve survivors of the fifteen Senators elected by the Dáil for nine years in 1922, one Senator elected for six years in 1925, four Senators elected for three years in 1928, and six Senators elected to fill casual vacancies during the current period. The Constitution therefore required that the election should be from a panel of forty-six names, formed as to one-half by the Senate and as to the other half by the Dáil. Arrangements were duly made for a preliminary election in each House, so as to reduce the number of candidates in each half of the panel to twenty-three. In neither case was this course necessary, however. No man of high distinction would waste his time in offering himself as a candidate at an election of which the result was practically a foregone conclusion. As in 1928 there was a dearth of candidates. The Senate nominated the twenty-three outgoing Senators as its portion of the panel. The Dáil portion contained only sixteen names instead of the twenty-three required by the Constitution, and of these sixteen no less than eleven were duplicated from the Senate portion. There were thus only twenty-eight candidates for twenty-three seats. Apart from the outgoing Senators, there were only five candidates; all of these were on the Dáil portion of the panel; four of them were followers of Mr. De Valera and one belonged to the Cosgrave party; all five were destined to be successful.

The result of the election was as follows:

[1] *Senate Debates*, xviii, 1249. [2] Ibid., xi, 321–80.
[3] Ibid., xiii, 1053–64. [4] Ibid., xiv, 1599–1674.

* 1. Laurence O'Neill
* 2. Michael Comyn, K.C.
* 3. Seán E. MacEllin
* 4. Colonel Maurice Moore
    5. Daniel H. MacParland
* 6. The McGillycuddy of the Reeks
* 7. Arthur R. Vincent
* 8. Sir John P. Griffith
* 9. James G. Douglas
*10. Thomas Farren
   11. William Quirke

*12. John J. Counihan
   13. Hugh Garahan
   14. Séamas Ryan
*15. John MacLoughlin
*16. Brian O'Rourke
   17. David L. Robinson
*18. Michael Duffy
*19. Michael Staines
*20. James MacKean
*21. Dr. William O'Sullivan
*22. Mrs. E. Costello
*23. Miss K. A. Browne

The first twenty of these were to sit for nine years, the twenty-first for six years, and the last two for three years.

The following five Senators lost their seats:

R. A. Butler
William Barrington
George Crosbie

W. J. Molloy
Sir Walter Nugent, Bart.

Sir Walter Nugent was an Independent, Mr. Barrington belonged to the Independent Group, and the remaining three were members of the Cosgrave Party. Of those who replaced them, all except Senator Garahan were members of Fianna Fáil.

In terms of parties, the result was as follows: Cosgrave party, 9; Fianna Fáil, 7; Independent Group, 4; Labour Party, 2; Independent, 1.

In connection with the 1928 election comment was made on the increasing number of Senators of a political type. Of those now elected Senator Staines had been a member of the Dáil from 1918 to 1923; Senator O'Neill was a member of the Dáil, 1922–3, and a defeated candidate in September 1927; Senator Quirke had been an unsuccessful anti-Treaty candidate at the general election of 1923; and Senator Garahan had been elected as a member of the Farmers' Party in June 1927, but had lost his seat in the following September.

* Outgoing Senator.

PART V

THE FOURTH TRIENNIAL PERIOD
6th DECEMBER 1931 TO 5th DECEMBER 1934

'*Ignorance—especially of politicians—must always be a vice, but under no circumstances can it be such a vice as when ignorant politicians set out to reform historic institutions, by neglecting experience and misrepresenting history.*'

H. W. V. TEMPERLEY, *Senates and Upper Chambers*, p. 7.

'*Being cross'd in conference by some Senators.*'

SHAKESPEARE, *Julius Caesar*, I, ii, 187.

'*What's this but libelling against the Senate?*'

SHAKESPEARE, *Titus Andronicus*, IV, iv, 17.

CHAPTER XVII

MR. DE VALERA TAKES OFFICE

Reasons for early general election—The dissolution—The election campaign—Government unpopularity—Humour and tragedy—Result of the general election of February 1932—New Chairman of the Dáil— Mr. De Valera in office—The new Administration—The Land Annuities—Quarrel with the British Government—Abortive conversations in Dublin and London—The Government defaults and the British retaliate —Beginning of the economic war—No Anglo-Irish agreement at Ottawa—The October Conference in London—Mr. De Valera's claims —Deadlock—Patrick Hogan's courageous speech—Insults to the Governor-General—His dismissal—Appointment of his successor— The internal situation—Release of the prisoners—The Military Tribunal at an end—Open drilling by the Irish Republican Army—The Wolfe Tone demonstration—Immunity of extremists—Denial of free speech—The Army Comrades Association—Boycott of British goods— Attitude of the Government—Formation of the National Centre Party —Movement for fusion with Mr. Cosgrave—The surprise dissolution.

Under an amendment of the Constitution passed in 1927[1] the life of the Dáil was fixed at 'six years or such shorter period as may be fixed by legislation'. In the original Constitution it had been four years. By the Electoral (Amendment) Act, 1927, the maximum duration was defined to be five years reckoned from the first meeting of the Dáil after the previous dissolution. After the dissolution of the 25th August 1927 the Dáil had first met on the following 11th October; the five years' period would accordingly expire on the 10th October 1932. There were, however, two compelling reasons why a general election should be held months in advance of the latest permissible date. In the week beginning the 20th June the Eucharistic

[1] Constitution (Amendment No. 4) Act, 1927.

Congress was to be held in Dublin, and with this event was to be combined the commemoration of the fifteen-hundredth anniversary of Saint Patrick's arrival in Ireland (A.D. 432). These events would attract many thousands of people to Ireland from all parts of the world, and it was desirable that the bitter storm which heralds an Irish election should be past and not impending at the time of their arrival. Further, the Imperial Economic Conference was due to be held in Ottawa from the 21st July to the 20th August, and no government could profitably attend it whose mandate might be withdrawn by the people as soon as its delegates returned. Accordingly, Parliament was dissolved by the Governor-General, on Mr. Cosgrave's advice, by Proclamation dated the 29th January 1932. The general election was fixed for the 16th February, and the date of re-assembly was the 9th March.

The Government party had little in the way of a detailed programme. They pointed, with legitimate pride, to their record in both the external and the internal field; to the co-equality formally recognized by the Statute of Westminster; to their membership of the Council of the League of Nations; to the increase in and improvement of agricultural products; to the nascent industries established under a scientific tariff; most important of all, to the restoration of order. But the party manifesto[1] contained few detailed proposals for the future and consisted mostly of warnings about the intense political agitation and unrest which would ensue if Mr. De Valera were returned to power and started to scrap the machinery of the State. This largely negative attitude was a mistake, for no government can continue successfully to rely on its past record; democracy, like the Athenians, likes to hear something new. Moreover, Mr. Cosgrave's Administration was at that time the oldest in Europe, and its ten years of office had inevitably stirred up feelings of unpopularity and resentment against it in numerous directions.

The Fianna Fáil manifesto,[2] in contrast to that of the Government, was an extremely attractive document. The parliamentary Oath was not required by the Treaty, and was to be abolished. This proposal would perhaps not excite much enthusiasm, but the same could not be said of the other items. The Land Annuities were to be retained in the State Treasury; the British were not entitled to them in law, and the farmer's title to his land would be unaffected. This meant a 'saving' of three millions sterling annually. Legal opinion was to be taken on the question of obligation to make the other

---

[1] *Irish Independent*, 8 February 1932.   [2] Ibid., 11 February 1932,

annual payments, including the pensions of the former Royal Irish Constabulary. These amounted to another two millions. Industries were to be established to meet the needs of the community in manufactured goods. Great Britain and Ireland were each other's best customer, and the machinery required for the new industries could be purchased from the British in return for a preference for Irish agricultural products. The fears of the timid were allayed by pledges that Fianna Fáil would not, if returned to power, exceed the mandate asked for in the field of international relations without again consulting the people, and that all citizens would be treated as equal before the law. From beginning to end, the Republic was not mentioned.

The manifesto of the Labour Party[1] was, as usual, well drafted, but as the party nominated only thirty-one candidates it need not be considered here. It concentrated on social rather than political issues, and was severely critical of the Cosgrave Government. It was obviously the aim of the Labour Party to put Mr. De Valera in office and to make him dependent on Labour votes.

If the Government really desired a renewal of confidence at the polls its actions immediately before the election bordered on lunacy. It announced its intention of effecting substantial reductions in the salaries of National Teachers and of making married women ineligible as teachers. The teachers are a very numerous and influential body, and their votes and those of their family connections were presumably lost to the Government. It was also proposed to reduce the pay of the Civic Guards; these have no votes, but their fathers, mothers, and wives were all on the register. Most foolish of all, a prosecution for seditious libel was instituted before the Military Tribunal against Mr. De Valera's newspaper, the *Irish Press*, and its editor Mr. Frank Gallagher, a journalist of the highest repute. The charge arose out of the alleged ill treatment of political prisoners by the C.I.D. section of the Civic Guards. Such a prosecution, if launched at all, should have been brought before the ordinary courts. The defendants pleaded justification, over fifty witnesses were examined, and for eleven days immediately prior to polling day the newspaper reports of the evidence given for the defence provided the finest possible propaganda for Fianna Fáil. Judgement was given by the Tribunal on the day after the election, and the two defendants were fined £100 each. They must have thought it cheap at the price, and in any case public opinion, irrespective of politics, was on their side.

[1] *The Watchword*, 6 February 1932.

The atmosphere of the campaign was relatively peaceful, and it was not devoid of humour. Captain Redmond, who had formerly been such a thorn in Mr. Cosgrave's side, joined the Government party, which had a virtual merger with the farmers. Fianna Fáil described these moves as 'the alliance of a dog with his fleas'. On the other side, the Government party put out an amusing poster in the form of a circus playbill, headed 'Devvy's Circus: Absolutely the Greatest Road Show in Ireland To-Day', and starring the alleged proprietor of the circus as 'The World-famous Illusionist, Oath-Swallower and Escapologist. See his Renowned Act Escaping from the Strait Jacket of the Republic!' There was also a tragedy, however. Two days before the election Mr. Patrick Reynolds, a Government Deputy who was also a candidate, was shot dead. The act was that of a demented man and had no political significance, but the facts were not known till later and the tragedy increased the tension incident to the election. The contest in the dead man's constituency (Leitrim-Sligo) had to be postponed for a fortnight; his widow took his place and was returned.

Every effort was made by Fianna Fáil to affix an imperialist label on Mr. Cosgrave, and prominence was given to the fact that his party had sought and obtained financial assistance for the campaign from the ex-Unionists. It was also pointed out that the Government had 'bribed' this element of the community by offering facilities for a War Memorial Park (which was afterwards completed under Mr. De Valera). It is true that a fund was collected by a committee of well-known persons, both ex-Unionists and ex-Nationalists, who had not joined any political party since the Treaty: and that the money so collected was used in support of candidates pledged to support the Government in the maintenance of the Constitution; but this was more than counterbalanced by the fact that the whole weight of extreme militant Republicanism was on the side of Mr. De Valera. Very shortly after the election Mr. Peadar O'Donnell wrote: 'To put Fianna Fáil in was the only way to put the Cosgrave gang out. Fianna Fáil was the flail to thrash the pious and illustrious William and Co. So Fianna Fáil goes in.'[1]

The result of the election was as follows, the party strength at the time of the dissolution being given in brackets:

---

[1] *An Phoblacht*, 12 March 1932.

Party	Candidates nominated	Members elected
Fianna Fáil (De Valera)	104	72 (56)
Cumann na nGaedheal (Cosgrave)	101	57 (66)
Independents	32	11 (13)
Labour	31	7 (10)
Farmers	9	4 (6)
Independent Labour	2	2 (2)
	279	153

The country had thus declared emphatically that it desired a change of government. On the other hand, Mr. De Valera was given only a qualified mandate. His party numbered less than half the House, and he would be obliged to depend on the support of Labour. Roughly, there would be a De Valera *bloc* of seventy-nine and a Cosgrave *bloc* of seventy-four. All the ex-Ministers were returned, but the Labour Party suffered a blow by the defeat of its chairman, Mr. T. J. O'Connell, a leader of moderation and ability. Under his successor, Mr. William Norton, Labour was destined to incline more to the Left.

When the Dáil reassembled on the 9th March 1932 Mr. Frank Fahy, a member of Fianna Fáil, was elected Chairman of the House on a purely party vote, and Mr. Michael Hayes, who had filled the office with distinction since 1922, became a private member. Mr. Fahy proved to be a capable and impartial Chairman, but the view was expressed that the occupancy of the Chair should not be determined by the varying changes of political fortune. Mr. De Valera was thereupon elected President of the Executive Council by 81 votes to 68, there being no other nomination for the office. The sitting was then suspended for a short time and, when it was resumed, the new President announced, in Irish, that his appointment had been approved by the Governor-General. The assent of the Dáil was thereupon given, without discussion and without a division, to the following members of the Executive Council:

Minister for External Affairs:	Éamon De Valera.
Vice-President and Minister for Local Government and Public Health:	Seán T. O'Kelly.
Minister for Lands and Fisheries:	Patrick J. Ruttledge.
Minister for Industry and Commerce:	Seán F. Lemass.
Minister for Finance:	Seán MacEntee.
Minister for Agriculture:	Dr. James Ryan.

Minister for Defence:	Frank Aiken.
Minister for Education:	Thomas Derrig.
Minister for Justice:	James Geoghegan, K.C.
Minister for Posts and Telegraphs:	Senator Joseph Connolly.[1]

The appointment of Senator Connolly was a surprise, in view of the determined opposition of Fianna Fáil in 1929 to the amendment of the Constitution pursuant to which this was made possible. But his nomination was not due to the fact that he was a member of the Senate.

It was only to be expected that Mr. De Valera's pre-election declarations regarding the abolition of the Oath and the retention of the Land Annuities would sooner or later lead to difficulties with the British Government; but his method of approach to the inevitable controversy can hardly be characterized as other than provocative. National dignity, as well as ordinary courtesy, would seem to have required that he should formally communicate his intentions to the British Government, with the reasons therefor, either by direct dispatch or through the medium of the High Commissioner in London. Instead, he began by intimating his proposals to numerous Press correspondents, Irish, British, and foreign, as well as by broadcasting them to the United States, leaving the British to enter a demurrer if they thought fit.

The subject of the Oath intimately concerned the Senate and is accordingly dealt with in the chapter which follows. It is no part of this history to examine the merits of the financial dispute, but it is desirable to state in general terms what the issue was. The Land Annuities are annual payments made by Irish farmers to the Irish Land Commission in repayment of sums lent to them for the purchase of their holdings under the Land Purchase Acts. So much of these Annuities as were in respect of land purchased under the Irish Land Acts, 1891–1909 (i.e. the pre-Treaty Acts), was paid over each half-year by the Cosgrave Government to the British National Debt Commissioners, to meet the service of the loans raised for that purpose. The annual amount involved was about £3,000,000. These payments were made pursuant to (a) the Financial Agreement dated the 12th February 1923, signed by Mr. Cosgrave and Major John W. Hills, the Financial Secretary to the Treasury, and (b) the Ultimate Financial Settlement, dated the 19th March 1926 and signed by Mr. Ernest

1 *Dáil Debates*, xli, 19–38.

Blythe and Mr. Winston Churchill. The 1923 Agreement was not published until after the dispute arose,[1] but the statutory authority for payment is contained in section 12 of the Land Act, 1923. The 1926 Agreement was published eight months after it had been signed. Neither was submitted to the Irish Free State Parliament for ratification.

Of the other payments involved, the principal were an annual sum of £600,000 for twenty years to the Local Loans Fund and 75 per cent of the pensions payable to former members of the Royal Irish Constabulary under the Constabulary Acts. These other payments were covered by the two Agreements specified, and they amounted in the aggregate to another £2,000,000.

The subject was first broached from the British side by the Chancellor of the Exchequer (Mr. Neville Chamberlain) in a speech at Birmingham on the 18th March. He said that any suggestion that obligations or agreements, solemnly entered into by the two countries, could be repudiated or varied by either side as though it concerned that side alone would cause the British Government the gravest concern, and, if seriously pursued, would undoubtedly revive bitterness and differences which it was hoped had been removed for ever.[2] Four days later, in response to an inquiry from the Secretary of State for Dominion Affairs (Mr. J. H. Thomas), the High Commissioner in London (Mr. J. W. Dulanty) issued a statement of his Government's intentions in regard to the Oath. It was not mandatory in the Treaty, it was a relic of medievalism, and its removal was a purely domestic matter. Mr. Thomas replied (23rd March) that the Oath was an integral part of the Treaty, and that the Irish Free State Government was bound by the most formal undertakings to pay the Land Annuities. Mr. De Valera's rejoinder (5th April) was an attack on the whole Treaty position. The Treaty gave effect to what was the will of the British Government. It was directly opposed to the will of the Irish people, and was submitted to by them only under the threat of immediate and terrible war. British maintenance parties were still in occupation of some of our principal ports. And much more to the same effect. This dispatch, of course, went far beyond the issue originally raised and made it clear that the repudiation of the whole settlement of 1921 was involved. In his reply (9th April) Mr. Thomas pointed this out; and he described the origin and nature of the Land Annuities, and the basis of the Irish liability to pay them.[3]

[1] Cmd. 4061 (1932) (vol. xiv, p. 239).   [2] *The Times*, 19 March 1932.
[3] Cmd. 4056 (1932) (vol. xiv, p. 273).

While this unhopeful correspondence was in progress, long cable-grams were received by Mr. De Valera in the first four days of April from the Prime Ministers of Australia (Mr. Lyons), South Africa (General Hertzog), and New Zealand (Mr. Forbes), expressing their concern at the turn which events were taking and hoping for a satisfactory solution. Mr. De Valera thanked them, but reiterated the points made to Mr. Thomas.[1]

Meantime, the Bill to abolish the Oath was going through the Dáil; and on the 11th May Mr. Thomas announced in the House of Commons that, as it was a direct breach of the Treaty, the British Government had decided that, if it became law, they could not be expected to negotiate further agreements in regard to tariffs with a government which repudiated existing agreements.[2] This meant no agreements at Ottawa, and such an alarming possibility seems to have decided Mr. De Valera to negotiate. At all events, Mr. Thomas told the House of Commons on the 6th June that he and the Secretary of State for War (Lord Hailsham) were crossing over to Dublin that night, in response to an invitation from Mr. De Valera, to discuss difficulties in regard to the Ottawa Conference: the conversations to be resumed in London on the 10th June.[3]

It was obvious that the British were prepared to negotiate a com-promise, and hopes ran high in Ireland. They were doomed, however, to disappointment. At the Dublin meeting, according to Mr. Thomas, Mr. De Valera pointed out that his ultimate aim was the union of the Irish Free State and Northern Ireland, and after that the recognition of a united Ireland as a republic, with some form of association with the British Commonwealth. At the moment, his Government had no mandate for this course, but it intended to abolish the Oath and re-tain the Land Annuities. On the resumption of the conversations in London, Mr. De Valera argued that the Oath was forced upon the Irish people under duress, whereupon Mr. Thomas quoted statements of Kevin O'Higgins and referred to the fact that the Oath and the Treaty had been conclusively accepted by the people at four general elections between 1922 and September 1927. As to the Land Annui-ties, Mr. De Valera asserted that they had been paid behind the backs of the people, and Mr. Thomas pointed out that the Ultimate Finan-cial Settlement had been discussed by the Dáil and that the govern-ment which concluded it had been returned at the succeeding general election. Mr. De Valera was asked to agree to submit the question

---

[1] *Irish Times*, 9 April 1932.
[2] *House of Commons Debates*, cclxv, 1914.   [3] Ibid., cclxvi, 1588–90.

of the Annuities to a Commonwealth Tribunal on the lines suggested in the Report of the Imperial Conference of 1930 (which had been approved by both Houses of the Oireachtas); but he refused, on the ground that such a Tribunal would have a natural bias against Ireland.[1] Mr. De Valera's account does not contradict that of Mr. Thomas on essential points.[2]

There followed an inconclusive correspondence (16th–22nd June), Mr. De Valera offering to agree to arbitration if the Tribunal were not restricted solely to citizens of States of the Commonwealth, and the British Government declining to accept this proposal.[3]

On the 1st July the Irish Free State defaulted over the half-yearly payment of £1,500,000 due in respect of the Land Annuities. Three days later, a Financial Resolution was passed by the House of Commons by a large majority, to enable the British Government to collect the sums in default by means of Customs duties levied on imports from the Irish Free State. This was followed up by the Irish Free State (Special Duties) Bill, which became law on the 11th July. The Irish Free State retaliated with the Emergency Imposition of Duties Bill, which was introduced in the Dáil on the 14th July and passed into law nine days later. Thus began the so-called economic war, which lasted for nearly six years, until it was ended by the Anglo-Irish Agreements signed in London on the 25th April 1938.

The Government sent a delegation to Ottawa, headed by the Vice-President of the Executive Council (Mr. Seán T. O'Kelly), and minor agreements were entered into with Canada and South Africa. No agreement was concluded with Great Britain.

By mutual arrangement, Mr. De Valera met Mr. Thomas in London on the 5th October, on his way home from Geneva, and it was agreed that the disputed payments should be made the subject of negotiation between the two countries, without prejudice to the *status quo* as regards either the withholding of the Land Annuities or the imposition of the duties on each side. The conference met in London on the 14th and 15th October. Mr. De Valera was accompanied by the Minister for Finance (Mr. MacEntee), the Minister for Justice (Mr. Geoghegan, K.C.), and the Attorney-General (Mr. Maguire, K.C.). The British delegation consisted of Mr. J. H. Thomas, Mr. Neville Chamberlain, Lord Hailsham, Sir John Simon, and Sir Thomas Inskip. On the 18th October Mr. Thomas gave an account to the House of Commons of what took place. Mr. De Valera denied that

[1] *House of Commons Debates*, cclxvii, 675–89.
[2] *Dáil Debates*, xlii, 1688–1700.   [3] Cd. 4116 (1932) (vol. xiv, p. 281).

U

any ultimate financial settlement had ever been made between the two countries, and claimed that a new settlement should be concluded, covering all financial issues. In this connection claims were put forward (a) for a sum of three hundred or four hundred million pounds for over-taxation since the Union of 1801, and (b) for an unspecified amount in respect of damage caused by Great Britain's abandonment of the Gold Standard.[1] When questioned by Mr. McGilligan in the Dáil on the following day, Mr. De Valera admitted that these claims had been made.[2] In the circumstances, it is perhaps not surprising that the negotiations broke down on the afternoon of the second day. The memoranda of the conference were afterwards published.[3] Mr. De Valera's general attitude is indicated by the following quotation: 'It is possible that if we were prepared, as they seemed to wish, to go in the role of beggars, hat in hand, asking for consideration and charity, there might be a disposition to make minor modifications and some mitigation of their claim, but simple justice they were not prepared to concede. They took their stand on the supposed inviolability of the secret documents of 1923 and 1926, and they refused to budge from that position.'[4] On the 8th November, at the annual convention of his party in Dublin, Mr. De Valera declared that, so far as his Government was concerned, the Land Annuities would never be paid;[5] and there the matter rested until the settlement of the 25th April 1938. Trade agreements of a minor character were subsequently concluded with the British Government, and the hardships inflicted upon Irish farmers were to some extent alleviated by bounties and other financial devices; but, while the economic war continued, the annual sums guaranteed to be paid by the Ultimate Financial Settlement signed by the Minister for Finance in 1926 were collected in full, and by the method most calculated to intensify ill-feeling between the two countries, namely, by means of customs duties levied at the ports.

The dispute was rendered less easy of settlement because the economic issue seemed at the time to be inextricably intertwined with the political issue. During the June negotiations it is possible that the British would not have continued to insist on an exclusively Commonwealth personnel for the proposed Arbitration Tribunal but for Mr. De Valera's proposal to abolish the Oath and his forthright intimation that his ultimate aim was the establishment of a republic. The

---

[1] *House of Commons Debates*, cclxix, 15–20.   [2] *Dáil Debates*, xliv, 138–50.
[3] Cd. 4184 (1932) (vol. xiv, p. 285).   [4] *Dáil Debates*, xliv, 141.
[5] *Irish Press*, 9 November 1932.

truth seems to be that his mind was back in 1921, and that, so far as he was concerned, the Cosgrave Government might just as well have never existed. The best comment on this unhappy position was made by the late Patrick Hogan (the former Minister for Agriculture) when speaking on the Oath Bill. The passage is from what was probably the most courageous and most statesmanlike speech ever delivered in the Dáil.[1]

'War is not the greatest of evils, but it is a terrible one. Persistent poverty, persistent unsettlement, persistent politics, persistent confusion and chaos, are worse than a decent war, far worse; worse for the man and the woman who are poor, worse for the unemployed, worse for the under-dog, worse for everybody. A war is over between two civilized countries and something is settled. What is happening here? Nothing ever begins; nothing ever ends; we are always going round in a circle, and this Bill will keep us in that position. If you ask me, there are a great number of people who call themselves patriots who want to see this country kept in this position, because they know perfectly well that politics and the Republic and all the rest of them are merely a way of avoiding work, and they know that their living, their *raison d'être*, will be gone if once you have settled conditions here. What made France and England great countries, because they are, materially, spiritually, in literature, art, and everything else? That they happened to get a fixed Constitution hundreds of years ago, due to the fact that they had great leaders, and that the citizens of these countries could forget politics, except periodically, and settle down to the really important matters, the business of life. We never could do it. It was not our fault up to 1922. We got a chance in 1922 and the President stepped in between the country and the chance that this country has been looking for for centuries. I say that the issue to-day is not whether the Treaty is good enough for us, but whether we are good enough for the Treaty. That is the real issue.'

During the months in which the Anglo-Irish discussions were in progress a series of calculated petty insults was being offered by members of the Government to His Majesty the King in the person of his Representative in the Irish Free State. The Governor-General, the late Mr. James McNeill, was a cultured Irish gentleman who had had a distinguished career in the Indian Civil Service. He had been his country's first High Commissioner in London, and since his appointment to the Governor-Generalship, in succession to Mr.

[1] *Dáil Debates*, xli, 1020-34.

T. M. Healy at the beginning of 1928, he had discharged the duties of his office with quiet courtesy and tact. On the night of Saturday, the 23rd April, a reception and dance were given at the French Legation by M. Alphand, Minister of France, who was afterwards the French Ambassador in Moscow. Among the guests were the Vice-President of the Executive Council (Mr. O'Kelly) and the Minister for Defence (Mr. Aiken). The Governor-General was also invited, and when he arrived they departed. The incident was reported in the newspapers on the following Monday, and the account in the *Irish Press*, which is the organ of the Government party, stated: 'Later the Governor-General arrived; this was a surprise, and Mr. O'Kelly and Mr. Aiken then left.' Taken in conjunction with this statement, the action of the Ministers seemed to imply that His Majesty's Ministers (for that is, of course, what they were) ought not to have been invited to a social function at which His Majesty's Representative was also a guest. For this piece of *gaucherie* the Government is said to have had to apologize to the French Minister.[1]

On the following day (26th April), the Governor-General wrote to the President of the Executive Council to protest against what was 'part of a considered policy that the Governor-General should be treated with deliberate discourtesy by members of your Council and by the newspaper which you control'. Mr. De Valera replied on the 30th April: '. . . As regards the Ministers: the incident was no less embarrassing for them than for the Governor-General, and the publicity which ensued might have seriously affected the public interest. . . . If the Governor-General's public social engagements are communicated to me in advance, such an incident will certainly not occur in the future.' In view of this unsatisfactory reply, the Governor-General addressed a further letter to Mr. De Valera, on the 2nd May, in which he said that 'an apology from you and the two Ministers concerned is due, not merely on my personal or official account, but with regard to the honour and self-respect of Irish public life'. Mr. De Valera refused to apologize, however. In his reply of the 7th May he stated that he 'regarded the whole affair as unfortunate and regrettable, and one that should not have been permitted to occur. Further than this I am unable to go.'

Before the change of government, the Governor-General, who was a Catholic, had made tentative arrangements to invite distinguished Catholics to stay with him at the Viceregal Lodge for the period of the Eucharistic Congress in June. After much delay, a verbal message

[1] *The Round Table*, September 1932, p. 768.

was conveyed to him by the Secretary of the Department of External Affairs to the effect that the issue by him of such invitations would cause embarrassment to the Government. In a letter addressed to Mr. De Valera on the 24th May, Mr. McNeill protested, and pointed out that it was then too late for him to alter his plans.

One of the features of the Eucharistic Congress was a civic reception given in the Mansion House by the Lord Mayor of Dublin, at which the Papal Legate and all the high dignitaries attending the Congress were present. For this reception the Lord Mayor requested the loan of the Army Band. The Minister for Defence had an interview with the Lord Mayor, at which he inquired whether the Governor-General would be invited. On being informed that this was so, he refused the services of the Army Band.

Another feature of the Congress was a state reception given in the historic Saint Patrick's Hall of Dublin Castle by Mr. De Valera as President of the Executive Council. The Governor-General was not invited to this function, nor did any of his guests attend it.

These incidents were detailed in a letter sent by Mr. McNeill to Mr. De Valera on the 7th July, after the Congress had ended. The letter continued:

'I never sought any public office. I am willing to return to private life when my acceptance of public duty is displeasing to a majority either of the Dáil or of the people. But I do not think I should resign any office because other office holders think I am a suitable target for ill-conditioned bad manners. I know that you have a majority in the Dáil. I know that you can have me removed.

'I have arranged that this letter and all the correspondence except your letter marked "Personal" shall be published within three days unless I receive apologies here from you and the other Ministers, who have sometimes openly and sometimes otherwise sought to behave with calculated discourtesy to the Governor-General from whom you accepted confirmation of your appointments.'

Mr. De Valera replied by return, tendering the formal advice of the Executive Council that the correspondence was not to be published. The next day (9th July) Mr. McNeill answered: '. . . In the case of affronts, however outrageous, by the President and some members of the Executive Council to the Governor-General, there is in your Council's opinion no course open to me but silent acceptance. . . . The correspondence other than your letter marked "Personal" will be published.' From that point events moved rapidly. On the afternoon of Sunday, 10th July, the correspondence was handed to the Press by the Governor-General's A.D.C. The same night high police officials visited the offices of the Dublin newspapers and warned them not to publish it. On the Monday morning the principal English newspapers printed the correspondence, and fruitless attempts were made to prevent the circulation of copies of these papers which had arrived at the ports and along the Northern Ireland border. The same afternoon the Government capitulated to the inevitable, and issued a statement that, as the correspondence had appeared in 'foreign' newspapers, publication in the Irish newspapers was authorized; and the full correspondence was printed in the Dublin press of the 12th July.

Mr. McNeill's normal term of five years would have expired in February 1933, but on the 3rd October the following announcement was issued from the Department of External Affairs: 'In accordance with the advice tendered to His Majesty by the President of the Executive Council, the King has approved of Mr. James McNeill relinquishing the office of Governor-General of the Irish Free State.' In plain language, he had been dismissed. This was followed by a further announcement from the High Commissioner's Office in London on the 26th November: 'His Majesty the King, on the advice of the Executive Council of the Irish Free State, has appointed Domhnall Ua Buachalla, Esq., to the office of Governor-General of the Irish Free State.' Domhnall Ua Buachalla, in English Daniel Buckley, was a retired country shop-keeper who had had a general store in his native town of Maynooth, less than twenty miles from Dublin. He had taken part in the Rising of 1916 and was an Irish language enthusiast. His career in politics had been chequered. He was a Sinn Féin member of the Dáil from 1918 to 1922, and a defeated anti-Treaty candidate at the general elections of 1922 and 1923. He was elected in June 1927 and defeated again in September 1927 and in 1932. He was now installed in a house taken for him in a Dublin suburb, the Viceregal Lodge being left vacant; and almost his sole duty was to affix his signature to Acts of Parliament.

The internal situation during this period must now be considered. It was the avowed intention of the new Administration to govern without coercion and they proposed to remove the Oath because, in their opinion, it involved government by coercion. The only people affected were the Republicans, and the fatal fallacy in this argument lay in the fact that the Republicans had made it clear *ad nauseam* that they had no intention of recognizing the Irish Free State even if the Oath were removed.

The Dáil met on the 9th March, the composition of the Executive Council was approved, and the Ministers received their appointments from the Governor-General. Immediately these formalities had been concluded, the Minister for Justice and the Minister for Defence proceeded straight to Arbour Hill Barracks, where the Republicans who had been sentenced by the Military Tribunal were imprisoned. The Minister for Defence spent some time in the cell of Mr. George Gilmore, who was serving a sentence of five years' penal servitude. The two men saluted each other warmly on parting, and Mr. Gilmore, who called the Minister by his Christian name, said he need not tell him that he had been glad to see him.[1] All these prisoners were released on the following day.

On the 12th March *An Phoblacht*, the weekly organ of the extremists, reappeared after having been suppressed for three months. It contained an article by Mr. Maurice Twomey, the Chief of Staff of the Irish Republican Army, in the course of which he said:

'Fianna Fáil declares its intention to chop off some of the Imperial tentacles; every such achievement is of value and will be welcomed. Notwithstanding such concessions, the Irish Republican Army must continue its work, and cannot escape its role as the vanguard of the Freedom Movement.'

On the 18th March the Government issued an Order suspending the operation of Article 2A of the Constitution. The effect of this was that the Military Tribunal came to an end, and the Order lapsed which had declared the Irish Republican Army to be an unlawful association. It was still, of course, condemned by the Church, but this fact seems to have made little difference. Drilling, and marching in military formation with military words of command, began to take place. Though the facts about this matter are not known, it seems not unlikely that the Irish Republican Army had an understanding with the Government that they would not be interfered with if they did not openly carry arms. During a debate in the Dáil on the 20th April, the Minister for Justice said: 'Military words of command necessary to prevent one of these, to my mind, wholly unnecessary processions degenerating into a mob are probably, from a practical point of view, desirable.'[2] On the same occasion, the Minister for Industry and Commerce stated that 'the title of this Dáil to legislate for this country is faulty'.[3] Mr. De Valera and his colleagues were indulging in the extremely dangerous game of playing with fire.

On the 19th June fifteen thousand men paraded in military forma-

[1] *Irish Press*, 10 March 1932. [2] *Dáil Debates*, xli, 236. [3] Ibid., xli, 217.

tion at Wolfe Tone's grave, where they were inspected by Mr. Twomey as Chief of Staff. The oration was delivered by Mr. Seán Russell, who quoted words alleged to have been used by Tone of Grattan's Parliament, 'Of all parliaments beyond all comparison the most shameful and abandoned of all sense of virtue, principle or even common decency,' and applied them to the Irish Free State Parliament. Thereupon Senator Mrs. Clarke, a member of that Parliament, in company with two others, laid a wreath on Tone's grave on behalf of the National Executive of Fianna Fáil. This last item was considered to be so important by the Government newspaper that it printed it in heavy type in its account published on the following day. The customary official parade at Tone's grave was held on the 28th June, when the Army was addressed by the Minister for Defence. In its issue of the 2nd July *An Phoblacht* denounced this parade as 'camouflage, hypocrisy and mockery'.

On the 14th July Mr. Gerald Dempsey, described by *An Phoblacht* as a captain in the Irish Republican Army, was charged at the Dublin Circuit Criminal Court with the illegal possession of a Colt revolver, an automatic pistol and ammunition. The accused refused to recognize the court and stated that the articles in question had been stolen from him. The jury returned a verdict of 'Not Guilty'. The judge, addressing the prisoner, said: 'You have heard the verdict. How you regard that verdict I don't know. Possibly you have the same contempt for it as I have.' He thereupon sentenced him to three months' imprisonment for the offence of refusing to recognize the court.[1] In its issue of the 23rd July *An Phoblacht* demanded Dempsey's release. Three days later he was unconditionally released by order of the Minister for Justice.[2]

On the 20th August the Irish Republican Army occupied Donamon Castle, County Roscommon, as a training camp for the week-end. By this time they had become so powerful that they were a serious menace to public order. Their efforts were chiefly directed to the breaking up of public meetings and the suppression of freedom of speech. As early as the month of May Mr. Cosgrave had been denied a hearing in Cork, where he had headed the poll at the general election, and the meeting ended in pandemonium.[3] This kind of activity continued throughout the summer, and as time went on the Republicans grew bolder from immunity. In successive issues of the 15th and 22nd October, *An Phoblacht* announced that 'free speech and the

---

[1] *Irish Press*, 15 July 1932. [2] Ibid., 27 July 1932.
[3] *Irish Independent*, 2 May 1932.

freedom of the press must be denied to traitors and treason-mongers';
and on the 3rd November the Government organ, the *Irish Press*,
reported a speech made by one of the Government members of the
Dáil, in which he said: 'Free speech was governed by certain conditions, one of which was that no Party advocating foreign domination
was entitled in any country to misguide the people.' Possibly encouraged by this support, Mr. Frank Ryan proclaimed at a public
meeting in Dublin on the 10th November: 'No matter what anyone
says to the contrary, while we have fists, hands and boots to use, and
guns if necessary, we will not allow free speech to traitors.'[1] And
Mr. Peadar O'Donnell said at the same meeting: 'The policeman who
put his head between Mr. Cosgrave's head and the hands of angry
Irishmen might as well keep his head at home.'[2]

The object of this intimidation, and of the suppression of free
expression of opinion (guaranteed by Article 9 of the Constitution),
was to render a free general election impossible. In the month of
August the creeping paralysis of the body politic was arrested by the
action of the Army Comrades Association, under the leadership of
Dr. T. F. O'Higgins, who possessed the courage and much of the
ability of his dead brother, Kevin O'Higgins. Originally a friendly
association of ex-officers and men of the Irish Free State Army, it
now extended its membership to all who upheld the principles of free
speech, a free Press, and a free franchise. It quickly attained a membership of some thirty thousand and it intervened effectively to prevent the breaking up of meetings. The association was not a political
body, but in the circumstances the only party which had need of its
services was the Cosgrave party. Naturally, abuse was showered upon
it by the Republicans, and the Government were seriously annoyed
by the new development, Mr. De Valera holding that the powers of
the State were adequate and were being used. Mr. E. J. Duggan, a
signatory of the Treaty, speaking of a meeting held in his own constituency, said: 'I do not admit it for one. At a meeting I was at in
Trim there were only about six Civic Guards, and were it not for the
presence of the A.C.A. we would have been run out of the town.' Mr.
Anthony (Independent Labour) added, 'A Civic Guard would be
murdered if he went to interfere.'[3]

Another activity of the Republicans was the prosecution of the
economic war on their own account, their opinion being apparently
that the Government lacked the courage to carry the fight to its logi-

[1] *Irish Press*, 11 November 1932.   [2] *Irish Independent*, 11 November 1932.
[3] *Dáil Debates*, xliv, 1573.

cal conclusion. A British Boycott Committee was formed, and the slogan 'Boycott British Goods' was taken up by *An Phoblacht*, as well as painted on dead walls throughout the country. The products of Messrs. Fry and Messrs. Cadbury were mentioned, but the principal target was Bass's ale. The committee wrote to members of the licensed trade asking them not to sell this commodity; and individual publicans were visited by young men, who requested them to dispose of their existing stocks and not to get in any more.[1] The threat as to what would happen in case of a refusal was contained in the issue of *An Phoblacht* of the 29th October. 'There was such an event as the Boston Tea Party: there might even be a Dublin Ale Party.' In a speech in the Dáil on the 7th December, Mr. Blythe said he understood that the Minister for Justice had refused to receive a deputation from the traders on the subject;[2] and it was publicly stated later that the Minister had intimated that 'there was nothing in the law to prevent people requesting them to stop selling anything, provided that intimidation was not used'. But he promised protection from 'unwarrantable interference'.[3] The Minister for Finance mentioned this promise in the Dáil, but when asked what would become of the publicans' trade he replied: 'All traders must bear in mind the consequences of flouting public opinion.'[4] On the 14th December, a Dublin Ale Party took place. A lorry containing supplies of Bass was held up on its way from the port to the stores, the ale was emptied into the roadway, and the barrels were set on fire.[5] Subsequent lorries were escorted through the streets of Dublin by members of the Army Comrades Association, at the request of the licensed trade, and there were no more ale parties.

The discontent of the Irish farmers at the dire results to them of the economic war, as well as the disgust of independently minded men at the ceaseless, barren strife over the Treaty split and the Civil War, gave rise to the formation of a new political party in the autumn of this year. Prominent in this movement were two men who had first entered the Dáil at the previous general election, Mr. Frank Mac-Dermot, who had been returned as an Independent for Roscommon, and Mr. James M. Dillon, who had been returned for Donegal, likewise as an Independent. Mr. MacDermot, who was in his middle forties, was a younger son of a very old Irish family. He had been educated in England, and had served in the British Army throughout

---

[1] *Irish Times*, 5 December 1932, and *Dáil Debates*, xlv, 998-9.
[2] *Dáil Debates*, xlv, 999.   [3] *Irish Times*, 15 December 1932.
[4] *Dáil Debates*, xlv, 1016.   [5] *Irish Times*, 15 December 1932.

the Great War, after which he had joined a firm of New York bankers. Returning home, he had contested West Belfast as a Nationalist in 1929 and had been defeated. Mr. Dillon, who was barely thirty years of age, was one of the sons of Mr. John Dillon, the Irish patriot, who had succeeded Mr. John Redmond in the leadership of the Irish Parliamentary Party on the death of the latter. A highly educated man, Mr. Dillon had been called to the Irish Bar and had extensive business interests.

On the 15th September a farmers' organization was formed at a representative meeting in Dublin, in the convening of which Mr. Patrick Belton had taken a leading part. Mr. MacDermot was unanimously elected president. He said, very sensibly, that the partition of the country could never be ended until quarrelling with England had definitely and finally stopped. He warned his audience against the current cant about the duty of good Irishmen to stand firmly behind their Government in its conflict with a 'foreign' nation, and pointed out that, whatever was to be said in favour of leaving the British Commonwealth, there was nothing to be said in favour of staying in it while suffering the disadvantages of being outside.[1]

This meeting was followed by a convention held on the 6th October, at which the political party was founded under the name of the National Farmers' and Ratepayers' League. It included among its objects the promotion of the interests of agriculture and the giving to farmers of power to mould Government policy; the restoration of markets; the obliteration of the bitterness of the Civil War; an honourable settlement of the Anglo-Irish dispute; and the removal of partition by a policy of friendliness to Northern Ireland.[2] Shortly afterwards, Mr. MacDermot secured the adherence of Mr. Dillon and the name was changed to the National Centre Party.

The new party made rapid headway, but many well-meaning people felt that the interests of the country would be better served by the dissolution of the existing opposition parties and the formation of a new, united constitutional party, having for its immediate object the re-establishment of neighbourly relations with Great Britain on an equitable basis, consonant with the national dignity of the country and its position of co-equality within the Commonwealth. This feeling received its first public expression in a letter from Senator Vincent, a member of the Independent Group in the Senate, which appeared in the Dublin newspapers on the 28th December.[3] On the following

---

[1] *Irish Times*, 16 September 1932.   [2] Ibid., 7 October 1932.
[3] Ibid., 28 December 1932.

day, at a representative meeting of professional men summoned by the Lord Mayor of Dublin, a resolution was passed to similar effect.[1] These were developments which Mr. De Valera could not afford to ignore. Four days later (2nd January 1933) the Dáil was dissolved, after a short life of less than ten months; and a fresh general election was ordered for the 24th January.

[1] *Irish Times*, 30 December 1932.

CHAPTER XVIII

THE SENATE AND THE PARLIAMENTARY OATH

Strength of parties—Absence of political animosities—Re-election of Chairman and election of Vice-Chairman—Mr. De Valera attends the Senate—His moderation and desire for friendship with Great Britain—Examination of his claim for a mandate to abolish the Oath—The Constitution (Removal of Oath) Bill—The legal and constitutional standpoint—Provisions of the Treaty and Constitution—Objects of the Bill—Mr. De Valera's election pledge—The Oath said not to be required by the Treaty—The argument on which this contention is based—Analogy with Canada—The argument from the Statute of Westminster—Reticence of the Government lawyers—Inconsistent arguments—Powers of the judiciary—Opinions of judges of the Supreme Court—The Bill in the Senate—The Senate insists on prior agreement with Great Britain—Senator Douglas and the forms common to members of the Commonwealth—Senator Connolly's views—Speeches of Senators Brown and O'Farrell—The Dáil disagrees and the Bill is suspended—The Senate's forbearance in regard to other measures—The Army Pensions Bill—The Emergency Imposition of Duties Bill—The work of revision summarized—Absence of obstructive tactics.

At the beginning of the Fourth Triennial Period the alignment of the various parties and groups in the Senate was approximately as given on page 302. The corresponding figures at the beginning of the Third Period are repeated for purposes of comparison. The two principal parties had increased their strength at the expense of the Independents and the Independent Group, the gain of Fianna Fáil being the greater because it had leeway to make up, owing to its absence from the Dáil in 1922 and its boycott of the election of 1925. Senator Alfred Byrne, the Lord Mayor of Dublin, who was an Independent, had canvassed somewhat too zealously for Mr. Laurence O'Neill, also an Independent, with the result that Mr. O'Neill was returned at the head of the poll and Mr. George Crosbie, the proprietor of the *Cork Examiner*, who was a candidate of the Cosgrave party, was defeated. The Lord Mayor very honourably resigned his seat immediately, and at the resultant by-election Mr. Crosbie was returned.

	1928	1931
Cosgrave party	19	21
Fianna Fáil	7	13
Independent Group	12	10
Independents	15	9
Labour Party	6	6
Chairman	1	1
	60	60

In view of the impending advent of Fianna Fáil to office, the alignment of parties was of more importance than previously. It will be seen that the combined strength of Fianna Fáil and the Labour Party (which was its ally in the Dáil) almost equalled that of the Cosgrave party. If a strict party system had been in force, the balance of power would have lain with the Independents and the Independent Group. Such a situation, however, seldom or never arose in practice. For one thing, the tradition of fair play and non-rigidity established between 1922 and 1928 was still very strong. For another, the Cosgrave party in the Senate, in contrast to the same party in the Dáil, contained only two men who were in active politics prior to the Treaty. The recriminations and the party spirit which so often manifested themselves in the other House were therefore totally absent from the Second Chamber. As for the members of the Independent Group, they had no alliance with the Cosgrave party, and their whole political outlook tended towards support of the duly constituted government. With regard to ordinary proposals for legislation, the Senate as a whole would discharge its function of revision with the same assiduity as before, even if the members had no great liking for the Bills concerned. On fundamental issues Mr. De Valera's Administration could hardly expect complaisance from the Upper House; but the opposition offered would be a reasoned and not a factious opposition.

At the first meeting of the Senate after the commencement of the

Triennial Period (9th December 1931) Senator Westropp Bennett was unanimously re-elected Chairman, and on the following 20th January Senator M. F. O'Hanlon was elected Vice-Chairman, also without opposition. During the first few months of the period the Senate was fully occupied with the consideration of Bills which the Cosgrave Administration wished to be enacted before the dissolution. On the 22nd March 1932, which was the first sitting day after the formation of the new Government, Mr. De Valera came to the Senate and addressed the House as President of the Executive Council. It was a courteous action on his part, as there was no business on the Order Paper which called for his attendance. He was studiously moderate in tone, and gave a general outline of his proposals. With regard to the people of Great Britain, he wanted to live on the friendliest terms with them; but he had said this so often before that one felt that, like the Queen in *Hamlet*, he was protesting too much. The main item in his legislative programme was, of course, the abolition of the Oath, for which he claimed a mandate from 'an overwhelming majority of the people'.[1] Even on the impossible assumption that everyone who voted for his party did so on this ground, the claim is not substantiated by the facts. The total number of first preferences cast for Fianna Fáil was 566,469, whereas the number cast for all other parties combined was 707,687—a balance of 141,218 against Fianna Fáil.[2] The truth is that even Mr. De Valera's remarkable powers of popular appeal had not succeeded in galvanizing the country into any enthusiasm for this particular agitation. The reason is obvious. The Oath had proved no barrier to Fianna Fáil, and as for Sinn Féin, the Irish Republican Army, and the rest of the irreconcilables, they had made it abundantly clear that the abolition of the Oath would make no difference to their view that the Dáil was an illegal body and that the Government was an imperialist, usurping junta.

In the course of his speech in the Senate Mr. De Valera answered the question why, in view of his professed friendliness to Great Britain, he was unwilling to negotiate on the question. He said: 'If representations are made to us, we are prepared to meet these representations. We feel, however, that it would be quite absurd for us, seeing that we are determined, no matter what happens, to carry out our mandate, to make representations such as have been suggested. Nothing could come of these representations.'[3] Comment on the attitude of mind revealed by this statement is needless.

---

[1] *Senate Debates*, xv, 609.   [2] *Irish Independent*, 5 March 1932.
[3] *Senate Debates*, xv, 611.

The Bill to abolish the Oath was introduced in the Dáil on the 20th April 1932 and was finally passed by that House, unamended, on the following 19th May, by the joint vote of Fianna Fáil and the Labour Party over all other parties combined. It then came before the Senate. All the previous Bills amending the Constitution had been given a serial number, but this Bill, presumably to mark its importance, was given a title indicative of its purpose, namely, the Constitution (Removal of Oath) Bill. It was, in fact, the eighteenth amendment. The action of the Senate in regard to it will presently be considered; but in view of the momentous consequences of the Bill, and of the part which the Senate's action played in leading to its own abolition, it is essential first to review the whole subject of the Oath from the legal and constitutional point of view.

The Constitution was enacted by Dáil Éireann, sitting as a constituent assembly, and by the Parliament of the United Kingdom. As passed by the Dáil, it consists of three parts, namely:

1. The Constitution Act proper, which contains the long title, a preamble, and three sections.

2. The First Schedule, which is the Constitution itself, consisting of eighty-three articles and forming the fundamental law of the Irish Free State.

3. The Second Schedule, which is the Treaty of 1921, consisting of eighteen articles and an annex.

The long title of the Constitution Act proper is: 'An Act to enact a Constitution for the Irish Free State (Saorstát Éireann) and for implementing the Treaty between Great Britain and Ireland signed at London on the 6th day of December, 1921.'

The first section of the Act states that the Constitution set forth in the First Schedule shall be the Constitution of the Irish Free State, and the third section merely gives the short title. It is the second section that is of importance from our point of view. It reads: 'The said Constitution shall be construed with reference to the Articles of Agreement for a Treaty between Great Britain and Ireland set forth in the Second Schedule hereto annexed (hereinafter referred to as "the Scheduled Treaty") which are hereby given the force of law, and if any provision of the said Constitution or of any amendment thereof or of any law made thereunder is in any respect repugnant to any of the provisions of the Scheduled Treaty, it shall, to the extent only of such repugnancy, be absolutely void and inoperative and the Parliament and the Executive Council of the Irish Free State (Saorstát Éireann) shall respectively pass such further legislation and do all such other things as may be necessary to implement the Scheduled Treaty.'

The Oath is contained in Article 4 of the Treaty, which reads as follows: 'The oath to be taken by Members of the Parliament of the Irish Free State shall be in the following form:

'I,   , do solemnly swear true faith and allegiance to the Constitution of the Irish Free State as by law established and that I will be faithful to H.M. King George V, his heirs and successors by law, in virtue of the common citizenship of Ireland with Great Britain and her adherence to and membership of the group of nations forming the British Commonwealth of Nations.'

We now turn to the Constitution itself. The relevant articles are:

1. Article 17, which gives the terms of the Oath and implements Article 4 of the Treaty by providing the machinery. The article begins thus: 'The oath to be taken by members of the Oireachtas shall be in the following form.' The terms of the Oath are then repeated verbatim from Article 4 of the Treaty, and the article concludes: 'Such oath shall be taken and subscribed by every member of the Oireachtas before taking his seat therein before the Representative of the Crown or some person authorized by him.'

2. Article 55. This article provided for the appointment of 'Extern' Ministers, and the relevant portion of it is as follows: 'Ministers who shall not be members of the Executive Council may be appointed by the Representative of the Crown and shall comply with the provisions of Article 17 of this Constitution. . . .'

3. Article 50. This confers the power of amending the Constitution. As amended during the Cosgrave Administration, the relevant portion reads: 'Amendments of this Constitution within the terms of the Scheduled Treaty may be made by the Oireachtas, but no such amendment, passed by both Houses of the Oireachtas, after the expiration of a period of sixteen years from the date of the coming into operation of this Constitution, shall become law, unless the same shall . . . have been submitted to a Referendum of the people. . . . Any such amendment may be made within the said period of sixteen years by way of ordinary legislation.'

4. Article 65. This article, which is self-explanatory, reads as follows: 'The judicial power of the High Court shall extend to the question of the validity of any law having regard to the provisions of the Constitution. In all cases in which such matters shall come into question, the High Court alone shall exercise original jurisdiction.'

X

The article which next follows (66) confers appellate jurisdiction on the Supreme Court in regard to the same matters.

So much being clear, let us see what Mr. De Valera's Bill purported to do.

First, it deleted Article 17 of the Constitution, and also the words 'and shall comply with the provisions of Article 17 of this Constitution' in Article 55 (which relates to 'Extern' Ministers).

Second, it purported to delete Section 2 of the Constitution Act itself. This is the section which gives the Treaty the force of law, and provides that any amendment of the Constitution which is repugnant to the Treaty shall be inoperative.

Third, it purported to amend Article 50 of the Constitution by deleting the words 'within the terms of the Scheduled Treaty'. This is the article which prescribes the method of amending the Constitution.

Article 4 of the Treaty, which contains the Oath but not the machinery for it, was not referred to in the Bill.

The first of the proposals mentioned above removed the Oath from the Constitution. The object of the second and third was to deprive the High Court and Supreme Court (under Articles 65 and 66) of the power to declare the Bill (when enacted) to be invalid, on the ground that it was repugnant to the Treaty.

It was claimed that the Bill containing these grave provisions (including the abrogation of the Treaty as part of the municipal law of the Irish Free State) were in pursuance of a mandate sought and obtained from the electors. It therefore becomes necessary to examine whether this is so. The Fianna Fáil Manifesto is dated the 9th February 1932, and it is signed by Mr. De Valera.[1] He subsequently stated that he had written it himself.[2] The first item for which a mandate was sought was 'to remove the Article of the Constitution which makes the signing of the Oath of Allegiance obligatory on members entering the Dáil. This Article is not required by the Treaty.' The Manifesto went on to say:

'We pledge ourselves that, if elected in a majority, we shall not in the field of international relations exceed the mandate here asked for without again consulting the people. . . .

'We ask the electors not to allow themselves to be deceived by the misrepresentations of our opponents, and we pledge ourselves not to abuse their confidence.'

In spite of this double pledge, the Bill proposed to deprive the

[1] *Irish Independent*, 11 February 1932.   [2] *Dáil Debates*, xli, 1084.

whole Treaty of the force of law and to deprive the judiciary of any power to adjudicate upon the validity of the abolition of the Oath. During the debate in the Dáil Mr. MacDermot inquired whether the Government considered the Treaty to have any validity, and, if so, just what that validity amounted to. Mr. De Valera replied: 'I am not called upon to decide that question. We are not dealing with that. We are simply putting the Treaty in its place. What that place is and what its effect may be is another question altogether.'[1] Not satisfied with this reply, Mr. MacDermot asked later whether Mr. De Valera considered the Treaty to be morally binding, and he answered: 'Whatever my own views may be about the foundation of the Treaty, as a Government here we are acting within the mandate which accepts the Treaty for the time being.' Mr. Hogan asked, 'That is what you call a straight answer?' and Mr. De Valera said 'Yes.'[2]

It will be observed that, in Mr. De Valera's manifesto, the statement was made that 'this Article is not required by the Treaty', that is to say, the Article of the Constitution which contains the Oath. During the election campaign the abolition of the Oath was not a prominent feature of Fianna Fáil speeches, attention being given to subjects more likely to attract votes, such as the retention of the Land Annuities and the proposals for the relief of unemployment. But whenever the subject was mentioned the question was argued on this basis: that the Treaty Oath was optional and not compulsory, the implication being that it was insisted upon by the Cosgrave Government for the purpose of penalizing its political opponents. Thus, Mr. De Valera said at Claremorris on the 31st January 1932: 'The removal of the oath would not mean tearing up the Treaty. It was mentioned in the Treaty, but not made obligatory.'[3] As this statement seems to be inconsistent with fact, let us examine the argument on which it is founded. The words in Article 4 of the Treaty are, 'The oath to be taken by Members of the Parliament of the Irish Free State shall be in the following form. . . .' The article does not state that 'the oath shall be taken' but merely refers to 'the oath to be taken'. Hence—so the argument runs—if the members insist on taking an oath, this must be the one they shall take; but, unless they so desire, they need take no oath at all. This extraordinary argument was resurrected from 1922, when the Bill to enact the Constitution was before the Constituent Assembly. Mr. O'Higgins then dealt with it as follows (20th September 1922):

[1] *Dáil Debates*, xli, 1132.   [2] Ibid., xli, 1179.
[3] *Irish Independent*, 1 February 1932.

'I would like that some Deputy other than myself would undertake the task of arguing that particular point across the table with British Ministers, particularly when we remember that in the last stages of the negotiations for this Treaty there was quite considerable tension about this matter of the Oath, and that eminent British lawyers and eminent British politicians racked their brains to devise some form or another that would be least objectionable to Irish sentiment by safeguarding the particular position they wished to safeguard. Finally they sat down at a table, and with considerable labour brought forth this particular form, and we are asked to believe all this trouble and racking of brains and head-scratching was about an Oath which was to be purely optional, and which a Member need only take if he had a stomach for it later. That, to my mind, is not a serious argument; it shows a finicky, irresponsible outlook which should be no part of those responsible for the government of this country to cater for.'[1]

Nevertheless, this is the argument on the faith of which Mr. De Valera obtained the mandate, such as it was, to abolish the Oath. When the Bill came before the Dáil, however, he incontinently dropped it. 'I am not making the contention, and have not made the contention at any time that I remember, that the whole question of the Oath is to be determined by the meaning of Article 4 in itself. It is not.'[2] The new argument was something quite different. The words 'to be taken' in Article 4 'might' be explicable by reference to Article 2. Article 2 provided that 'the law, practice and constitutional usage governing the relationship of the Crown or the representative of the Crown and of the Imperial Parliament to the Dominion of Canada shall govern their relationship to the Irish Free State'. But the members of the Canadian Parliament took a direct oath of allegiance to the King. A different oath was prescribed in the case of the Irish Free State. Therefore the opening words of Article 4 meant: 'The oath to be taken by Members of the Parliament of the Irish Free State shall be [not the Canadian oath, but an oath] in the following form.' But the Canadian Parliament, owing to the co-equality of status subsequently achieved, was free to repeal the Oath at any time. Therefore the Irish Free State could do the same. This is a fair summary of Mr. De Valera's new argument.[3]

It is, of course, by no means the same thing as his pre-election statements that the Oath was not required by the Treaty and was not made obligatory. He based his ability to abolish the Oath frankly on

[1] *Dáil Debates*, i, 480, 481.　　[2] Ibid., xli, 927.　　[3] Ibid., xli, 927, 928.

the Statute of Westminster,[1] but for this very reason his new argument could not have been put before the electors. The whole status of the Irish Free State had been persistently decried, belittled, and derided from the beginning. He had himself described its Parliament 'frankly as a non-sovereign, subordinate, twenty-six County institution' (1926). His party newspaper had held it up to odium as a 'faked parliament', which was 'illegitimate' (1929). The Statute of Westminster could not have applied to the Irish Free State in the absence of a resolution passed in due form by both Houses of its Parliament. But this resolution was fiercely opposed by Mr. De Valera's followers, and Mr. O'Kelly, now become Vice-President, said that the whole object was 'to nail us, to copper-fasten us, for ever to the British Empire and its King' (1931).[2] Less than twelve months later Mr. De Valera referred to 'the recognition of co-equal status which has been fully recognized by the British Parliament in the Statute of Westminster. We are, therefore, to-day quite free to do anything here without any violation of the Treaty, anything that they can do in Canada, anything that they can do in Australia or New Zealand, anything that they can do in Britain as regards relations with the Crown.'[3] This was, however, after the election. If Mr. De Valera had stated in his election manifesto that the Irish Free State Parliament was now a completely sovereign assembly, free to abolish the Oath if it wished, such a *volte face* would have been misunderstood by the electors. But a simple assertion that the Oath was not required by the Treaty was intelligible to everybody.

The Bill was piloted through the Dáil by Mr. De Valera himself. Of the two lawyers in his Cabinet, one, the Minister for Justice (now the Hon. Mr. Justice Geoghegan), took no part in the debate, though he was present in the Chamber and voted in all of the nine divisions; the other was the Attorney-General (now the Hon. Mr. Justice Maguire, President of the High Court), but his contribution was inconsiderable. It was, however, remarkable for the assertion that the proposal to delete Section 2 of the Constituent Act (designed to prevent the courts from pronouncing on the constitutionality of the abolition of the Oath) was 'necessary in order to prevent any judicial misrepresentation of the position'.[4] This must be one of the most extraordinary statements ever made by the law officer of a government.

Mr. De Valera's case was inherently weak, because it was patent that he had exceeded his mandate and that the Oath was made obli-

---

[1] *Dáil Debates*, xli, 1090, 1091.   [2] Ibid., xxxix, 2310.
[3] Ibid., xli, 1090, 1091.   [4] Ibid., xli, 1019.

gatory by the Treaty. It was accordingly obvious that, while he could legally remove the Oath under the powers given by the Statute of Westminster, he could not do so without violating the Treaty. In the circumstances, it was unfortunate for him that he had opposed to him across the floor of the House such brilliant constitutional lawyers as Mr. McGilligan and the late Mr. T. A. Finlay, K.C.; and he undoubtedly fared very badly at their hands. At times his arguments were quite bewildering. He refused to negotiate about the Oath because it was 'a domestic matter';[1] but he said a few minutes later that he would not allow the judges to review his proposals because it was 'a wrong principle to have the courts deciding an international matter'.[2] His statement that Canada could legally remove the Oath, and that the Irish Free State could therefore do the same,[3] is not in accordance with the facts. The Parliamentary Oath for Canada is contained in Section 128 of the British North America Act, 1867; and Section 7 of the Statute of Westminster states that nothing in the statute shall be deemed to apply to the repeal, amendment or alteration of the British North America Act. Canada could doubtless secede from the Commonwealth, and if she did so the Oath would go. But, apart from secession, she could abolish it only after negotiation with Great Britain and the other members of the Commonwealth. Mr. De Valera proposed neither formal secession nor negotiation.

Amid this congeries of alternative and sometimes conflicting arguments, we are constrained to the conclusion that Mr. De Valera was merely engaged in making a case for a course of action which had been predetermined; and the strength of his faith in the legality of that case may be gauged by his efforts to exclude it from the purview of the judiciary.

An amendment of the Constitution must, of course, be held to be valid unless and until it is declared by the courts to be invalid, under the power conferred by Articles 65 and 66. But in view of certain known facts, it is interesting to speculate what the result would have been if the constitutionality of the Constitution (Removal of Oath) Act had ever been tested in the courts. Article 50 states that amendments of the Constitution within the terms of the Scheduled Treaty may be made, but it gives no power to the Oireachtas to amend the Constitution Act, of which the Constitution is the First Schedule. The Constitution (Removal of Oath) Act became law on the 3rd May

---

[1] *Dáil Debates*, xli, 1182; and see *Senate Debates*, xv, 610.
[2] *Dáil Debates*, xli, 1183. [3] Ibid., xli, 928.

1933, being passed over the head of the Senate. It purported, *inter alia*, to delete Section 2 of the Constitution Act, which gives the Treaty the force of law and says that any amendment of the Constitution which is repugnant to the Treaty shall be inoperative. At that time, the Supreme Court consisted of Chief Justice Kennedy, the Hon. Mr. Justice Fitzgibbon, and the Hon. Mr. Justice Murnaghan. The composition of the court remained unchanged until the death of the Chief Justice in December 1936. In the year 1934 the question whether Article 2A (the Military Tribunal Article) was a valid amendment of the Constitution fell to be decided by the Supreme Court on appeal from the High Court, and the question was answered in the affirmative, Chief Justice Kennedy dissenting.[1] The three judgements were delivered on the 19th December 1934, and in them the power of constitutional amendment was extensively reviewed. The court was not called upon to decide whether or not the Irish Free State Parliament (Oireachtas) had power to amend the Constitution Act, but all three judges referred to the point in their several judgements.

Chief Justice Kennedy stated (page 204) that 'it is not within the power of the Oireachtas to alter, or amend or repeal' the Constitution Act; and he cited Section 2 of the Act and treated it as law.

Mr. Justice Fitzgibbon also cited Section 2, and treated it as law; and he said (page 226): 'It is further to be observed that this power to make amendments is limited to "*amendments of this Constitution*",[2] and that the Constituent Assembly did not confer upon the Oireachtas any power to amend the Constituent Act itself.'

Mr. Justice Murnaghan also cited Section 2, and treated it as law (page 241).

There thus emerges the astonishing fact that, more than a year after the enactment of the Constitution (Removal of Oath) Act, all three members of the Supreme Court ignored its most vital provision, namely, the deletion of Section 2 of the Constitution Act. The Chief Justice and Mr. Justice Fitzgibbon went further, and stated expressly that there was no power to do what had, in fact, been done; and Mr. Justice Murnaghan, whose judgement was delivered last, did not dissent from this view.

We must now revert to 1932 and consider the manner in which the Bill was dealt with by the Senate. Taken as a whole, the discussion was disappointing, and the reason is not far to seek. For a first-class

---

[1] The State (Ryan and Others) *v.* Lennon and Others, [1935] I.R. 170–245.
[2] The italics and quotation marks are in the original.

parliamentary debate the participants must be evenly matched, and in previous debates in the Second Chamber this had frequently been the case. Before 1932 the proportion of able Senators was still very high, and they often took different views; also, the Ministers who were sometimes opposed to them were for the most part capable men. The discussion on the Oath Bill revealed a change. The issue was a fundamental one, and, with very few exceptions (such as Senators Johnson and Colonel Moore), no Senator of ability was in favour of it. The result was a one-sided affair, with Mr. De Valera receiving virtually no help from his followers in meeting the arguments of Opposition speakers, such as Senator Brown, K.C. (admittedly the best authority on legal interpretation in the country) and Senators Milroy, Douglas, Miss Browne, Vincent, Sir John Keane, and numerous others.

There were two courses open to the Senate: either to reject the Bill outright or to amend it (a) by removing its most objectionable provisions such as the clause which deleted Section 2 of the Constitution Act, and (b) by inserting a new clause to provide that the Bill should not come into effect until an agreement had been reached with the other party to the Treaty of 1921. The second alternative was chosen. The Bill was given a Second Reading by 21 votes to 8, and as it emerged from the Senate it merely deleted Article 17 of the Constitution and made a consequential amendment in Article 55, with the following new clause added:

'This Act shall not come into force until an Agreement has been entered into between the Government of the Irish Free State and the British Government providing that Article 4 of the Treaty of 1921 shall cease to have effect and such Agreement has been ratified and approved by Resolution of Dáil Éireann.'

These amendments gave effect to the view, which was implicit in the original Bill, that the deletion of the Oath was a breach of the Treaty. They brought the Bill into harmony with the pledge given in Mr. De Valera's election manifesto that 'we shall not in the field of international relations exceed the mandate here asked for without again consulting the people'. Further, the new clause gave him the opportunity of acting in the spirit of the following promise contained in the same manifesto:

'We shall strive also to bring British statesmen to realize that the interests of Britain, as well as the interests of Ireland, are best secured by an understanding and settlement which will permit the people of the two islands to live side by side as independent friendly neighbours

—each respecting the rights of the other and co-operating freely in matters of common concern.'

Mr. De Valera opened the debate on the Second Reading and repeated his familiar arguments. He implied, but did not expressly state, that the Oath was not made obligatory by the Treaty. It was an imposition on the people of Ireland from outside, and it could be abolished without violating the Treaty. The nations of the Commonwealth were now co-equal; Great Britain, Canada, Australia, and South Africa could get rid of their parliamentary oath if they so wished, and therefore the Irish Free State could do the same. It was no answer to say that there might be no inclination on the part of the others to do so.[1]

Senator Douglas, who followed, pointed out that, though there had been great constitutional development since the Treaty was signed, the fundamental basis remained the same. The Irish Free State had taken a prominent part in that development, but only because they had presented their case in a friendly manner. Only five common forms remained:

1. The King as head of the Commonwealth, with his representative in each nation, nominated by the respective governments.

2. The King as an integral part of each parliament, which consists of the King and two Houses.

3. The King as nominal head of the executive, acting only on the advice of his Ministers.

4. An oath to His Majesty taken by all members of parliament in each State.

5. An obligation to consult together from time to time on all matters of general interest, and, in particular, to consult with any, or all, of the other governments on any matter which any of them may consider likely to affect their interests in any way.

It was a very proper matter for discussion how far any of the first four were essential; but the fundamental link was the absolute obligation to consult on any matter which any of the nations within the Commonwealth group believed to be of common concern.[2]

The speech of the Minister for Posts and Telegraphs (Senator Connolly) was wholly on an emotional plane, and revealed the depth of anti-British feeling among Mr. De Valera's associates. He referred to 'the so-called civilization imposed by the British Empire all over the world, that has brought about to a great extent the ruin that exists at the present time'. As for the overseas members of the Common-

---

[1] *Senate Debates*, xv, 673–85.   [2] Ibid., xv, 685–96.

wealth: 'I hold nothing is more despicable, particularly to the mind of the people of Canada, Australia, and South Africa, than pretending to feel for Britain a loyalty that they know damned well we do not believe.' Senators were threatened with what would happen if they failed to pass the Bill: 'If you people in the Senate come in here at three o'clock out of your motors, or out of First Class carriages provided for you by the State, and are not sufficiently in touch with the people to realize the mentality and spirit of the people, the sooner you are wakened up the better, because if you go on legislating in that spirit you are in for a very rude awakening. . . . We are determined that this Bill will go through and the Senate can throw it out if it will and take the consequences.'[1]

Senator Brown, who said that he had listened to Senator Connolly's speech with considerable pain, stated that, speaking as one who had spent more than forty years in the study and practice of the law, he had no doubt that the Bill was a breach of the Treaty. Mr. De Valera seemed to him to argue in an intellectual atmosphere of four dimensions, and he found it quite impossible to follow his argument. The British Commonwealth of Nations was an international partnership at will, and one of the fundamental conditions of that partnership was the duty of friendly consultation before taking any action in a matter of common concern. The refusal to negotiate was a bad case of inferiority complex—the partner who is equal in fact but is not conscious of his equality.[2]

Senator O'Farrell, who voted for the Bill out of party loyalty, made one of the most effective speeches against it.

'I look upon the introduction of lawyers at this stage to invent excuses for us as a most undignified and cowardly proceeding. A crafty lawyer may try to make crooked roads look straight, but he cannot for long deceive anybody possessed of average intelligence. Surely the Treaty debates show beyond mistaking that Deputies, both for and against the Treaty, believed the Oath to be mandatory? That was the main bone of contention, and we are now told at this stage that this is not so, and, if that is the position, are we to be told that the devastating civil war was embarked upon, that blood and treasure were dissipated, and an aftermath of bitterness created which still poisons the well-springs of every department of public life in this country in order to get rid of a test which could have been disposed of peacefully by simply omitting it from the Constitution, without in any way violating the Treaty? If that is the contention, then I say the

---

[1] *Senate Debates*, xv, 732–46.   [2] Ibid., xv, 749–54.

ghosts of the dead should haunt the waking and sleeping hours of those responsible for that terrible holocaust. Ten years after the start of the civil war, we have the legal camp-followers of Fianna Fáil called in to absolve their party from the charge of Treaty-breaking in removing the Oath. What a pity they were not called in in 1922 instead of 1932! . . .

'Failure to enter into negotiations has always presented itself to me as a sign of weakness instead of strength. It is not bravery, but bravado. The President and his party are too disposed to mistake jingoism for patriotism, and a worm's eye view for a national outlook.'[1]

The Bill was finally passed by the Senate, with the amendments indicated, on the 28th June 1932.[2] The amendments were all disagreed with by the Dáil on the following 12th July.[3] Eight days later the Senate insisted upon them.[4] On the 19th October the Government informed the Dáil that it proposed to take no further action.[5] The suspensory period was thus to be allowed to run its course. As the Bill had been received from the Dáil on the 19th May (curiously enough, exactly four years before the Senate held its final meeting before abolition), the period would expire on the 18th November 1933, unless a general election intervened. This, of course, proved to be the case.

The fact that this Bill, which contained so much explosive material, was debated by the Senate without anything approaching disorder was due partly to the restraint placed upon themselves by the majority and partly to the firm yet tactful handling by the Chairman of a difficult situation. The absence of strict regimentation among the parties manifested itself in various ways. A Labour member of the Dáil could hardly have delivered with impunity the speech made by Senator O'Farrell. The Cosgrave party had evidently decided to let the Second Reading pass without a division, yet several of its members voted against the Bill in the division which took place. Senator MacKean, who had been active in forming the Cosgrave party at the end of 1928, actually voted with Fianna Fáil in all the divisions on the Bill, but he was not expelled from the party.

The Oath Bill was the only measure suspended by the Senate during the year 1932. The principle of some of the other Bills may have been repugnant to the House as a whole, but it had no desire whatever

[1] *Senate Debates*, xv, 802–13.
[2] Ibid., xv, 1090–1101.
[3] *Dáil Debates*, xliii, 615–717.
[4] *Senate Debates*, xv, 1429–34.
[5] *Dáil Debates*, xliv, 16.

to obstruct the Government in regard to matters which, however distasteful, were not fundamental. An outstanding example was provided by the Army Pensions Bill. This Bill was sponsored by Mr. Frank Aiken, who had been Chief of Staff of the Irish Republican Army during the Civil War and was now Minister for Defence of the Irish Free State. Its object was to provide wound pensions and disability pensions for those who fought against the State as members of the Irish Republican Army and kindred organizations, up to 30th September 1923. As a measure of appeasement, there was something to be said for this proposal if it were accompanied by an assurance of finality. At the time the Bill was introduced the Irish Republican Army was still in existence, it was still armed, and its objects were the same as before Mr. Aiken had left it, namely, the destruction of the Irish Free State by force. In order to elicit, if possible, an assurance of finality, Mr. MacDermot raised the matter in the Dáil. He said : 'May I ask the Minister one question? I am exceedingly moved by the appeal for appeasement that he has made in order to justify this Bill. I should like to feel that it does not commit one to any shaking of the fundamental principles—in other words, that we can rely on the Fianna Fáil Party to accept it as their definite policy that they will always defend against armed interference the institutions accepted by the majority in this country.' Mr. Aiken gave the following answer : 'Deputy MacDermot can always rely on Fianna Fáil and the members of their party doing what they think best for Ireland and the Irish people.'[1] In spite of this ominous reply, which was quoted in the Senate, the Bill was passed through that House without amendment, no division being challenged upon it at any stage. It probably did more to reconcile the extremists to Mr. De Valera than did the Bill to abolish the Oath.

The Emergency Imposition of Duties Bill was another measure of grave import of which the passage was facilitated in every way by the Senate. This Bill was a retaliatory measure against the British for their action in imposing Customs duties to collect the amount of land annuities which were in default. It was introduced in the Dáil on Thursday, 14th July, and was passed by that House on the following day, under the closure. Before it had left the Dáil the Government requested the Chairman of the Senate to summon a meeting for the Saturday, and to accept a motion to take all stages of the Bill on that day. This was the very kind of 'indecent' haste of which Fianna Fáil had so bitterly complained when in opposition. The Chairman ex-

1 *Dáil Debates*, xliv, 254.

pressed his willingness, and Monday was agreed to as the meeting day, the notice for Saturday being impossibly short. The provisions of the Bill, and of the recommendations made to it by the Senate, will be found referred to in the chapter on Money Bills (Chapter XXXII). It is sufficient to say here that the Senate met on the Monday and complied with the Government's wishes by passing all the stages by the following Wednesday.

In his speech in defence of the Senate, the Chairman revealed an interesting fact concerning this Bill. Senators had high legal opinion to the effect that it did not come within the definition of a Money Bill contained in the Constitution. It was open to them to demand a Committee of Privileges upon it, and if they had done so the result might have been disastrous for the Government. 'The matter was privately discussed, and the leaders of the Independent Group threw their whole weight against it, on the ground that it was unfair and undemocratic to deprive the Government of a weapon which they regarded as of supreme importance in the prosecution of the so-called economic war. The proposal was thereupon dropped.'[1] These were the men who were being continuously reviled by Mr. De Valera's followers as pro-British and anti-national.

The ordinary, unobtrusive work of revision went on just as it had done under the Cosgrave Administration, but this most important function of a Second Chamber was discharged almost exclusively by the Opposition. A few amendments which represented the Government's afterthoughts were formally moved by the Minister for Posts and Telegraphs (Senator Connolly), but little attempt at independent revision was made by Fianna Fáil. The two Bills which gave most trouble were the Control of Prices Bill and the Control of Manufactures Bill, both of which were rendered necessary by the Government's new economic policy. The Senate inserted thirty-four amendments in the former, all of which were agreed to by the Dáil. In the Control of Manufactures Bill, which reached the Senate in a very faulty state, twenty-nine amendments were inserted, of which all but six were finally agreed to, and these six were not insisted upon by the Senate. During this short period of nine months, twenty-two non-Money Bills were dealt with altogether (exclusive of the Oath Bill); sixteen of these were passed unamended; in the remaining six, a total of no less than ninety-four amendments was inserted, of which all but six were agreed to by the other House.

The Senate could thus fairly claim that it had emerged from this

[1] *Senate Debates*, xviii, 1248.

difficult year with credit. The position is never easy when the Government of the day is in a minority in the Upper House, but the Senate had faithfully discharged its duty to the people. It had, it is true, suspended the Oath Bill, but this Bill went far beyond the mandate asked for and alleged to have been obtained; and the weight of argument, both on legal and on moral grounds, was overwhelmingly against it. Other Bills about which Senators had grave misgivings were passed unamended, out of a desire not to impede or obstruct the Government; and where Bills reached the Senate in an imperfect state the necessary amendments were inserted. Between Senators and those Ministers whose measures brought them frequently to the House there were symptoms of a growing cordiality which might in happier circumstances have been a hopeful augury for the future.

CHAPTER XIX

THE BLUE SHIRTS AND THE IRISH REPUBLICAN ARMY

The election campaign—Mr. De Valera's policy—Programmes of the other parties—Class issues—'No free speech for traitors'—The Army Comrades Association ensures a free election—Mr. Cosgrave's escort of military and police—Result of the general election of January 1933—Mr. De Valera's decisive victory—The figures examined—The mandate exceeded—Hope of the Government Chief Whip—Cardinal MacRory and England—Ministerial changes—The Oath Bill again sent to the Senate—Second Reading declined—The Bill becomes law—Other Bills amending the Constitution—Abolition of Privy Council appeals—Attitude of the British Government—Mr. De Valera's rejoinder in the Senate—Progress of the economic war—Plans for industrialization—The internal situation—Recruiting for the Irish Republican Army—Extremist activities—The Army Comrades Association adopts the blue shirt uniform—General O'Duffy's dismissal—The Army Comrades Association becomes the National Guard—General O'Duffy elected leader—Aims of the new organization—All firearms licences revoked—Mr. De Valera denounces the National Guard—He contrasts it with the Irish Republican Army—Mr. De Valera's virtual dictatorship—His attitude to political opponents—Banning of proposed parade of the National Guard—Recruitment into the police of ex-members of the Irish Republican Army—Sir John Keane's motion in the Senate—The National Guard proclaimed an unlawful association—The Military Tribunal re-established—Inconsistency of the Government—Formation of the United Ireland Party—The National Guard becomes the Young Ireland Association—Its policy—The Waterford farmers—The 'Boycott Bass' campaign—Outrages against the United Ireland Party—Forbearance of its members—Domiciliary visits by the police—The Young Ireland Association proclaimed an unlawful association—The Young Ireland Association becomes the League of Youth—

Legal reverses for the Government—Mr. De Valera pleads with the extremists—The Dundalk bomb affair—Rioting in Drogheda—Mr. De Valera's difficulties—Introduction of the Wearing of Uniform (Restriction) Bill—Its passage by the Dáil under the guillotine.

Mr. De Valera's decision to dissolve the Dáil took all parties by surprise, including his own. As there was an interval of only three weeks between the Proclamation and the general election, the campaign was mercifully short. It is perhaps unnecessary to state that the declaration of a republic formed no part of the Government's programme; such a proposal would have been an invitation to disaster. In his inaugural speech in Dublin on the 5th January Mr. De Valera reiterated his plans for the development of industries by protective duties and for increased tillage. The Land Annuities would be permanently retained, but the amount payable by the farmers would be reduced by half. A few days before the poll he issued a manifesto in which he stated that he desired the friendliest relations with England, but that lasting peace could be achieved only on the basis that the people of Ireland should be free to determine for themselves what their governmental institutions were to be. In the same manifesto he announced his intentions regarding Parliament in a passage which became important in the light of subsequent events: 'We propose to abolish the Senate as at present constituted and, if it be decided to retain a Second Legislative Chamber, it is our intention to reduce considerably the number of its members. We propose also to reduce substantially the number of Deputies in the Dáil.'[1] As we shall see later, this pronouncement was afterwards relied upon as conferring a mandate to establish a unicameral legislature. Any mandate received for the proposal in the second paragraph was not fulfilled. The number of Deputies was later reduced from 153 to 138, but the reduction was in accordance with Article 26 of the Constitution, which prescribed a decennial review in accordance with changes in population. Apart from this Article, the only reduction effected was by the abolition of the six university members. For this, no mandate was sought or obtained.

Mr. Cosgrave promised, if returned to power, to end the economic war in three days, to reduce the Land Annuities by half, and to suspend payment of them by the farmers for two years. He reassured manu-

[1] *Irish Press*, 21 January 1933.

facturers by undertaking to make no drastic changes in existing tariffs without due investigation, and gave a message to the electors of courage and hope instead of suffering and sacrifice.

The new National Centre Party, led by Mr. MacDermot, was outside the dissensions of the two principal parties. It stood for the honourable observance of international obligations, which alone could ensure a speedy and favourable settlement of the economic war.

The Labour Party, which had fared so disastrously in 1932, and which was now led by Mr. Norton, nominated only nineteen candidates, so that its best hope was that Mr. De Valera should be returned to power but made dependent on its votes.

Little reference was made during the campaign to the Republic and the Oath of Allegiance, and the economic war was represented as a struggle against English aggression, in which the Opposition, the National Centre Party, and the Senate were on the side of the enemy. As polling day drew nearer, greater emphasis was laid by Government spokesmen on the social side of their policy, and a direct appeal was made for the votes of the labourers and the small farmers by a promise of more relief schemes and increased bounties. It was the first general election held in Ireland in which class issues were raised, and the *Irish Press* boasted in a leading article that the Government party was the only one which considered the poor.[1]

The condition of the country by this time was such that there were serious doubts whether a free election would be possible. Grave disorder occurred at Mr. Cosgrave's meeting in Dublin on the 8th January, at which the *Irish Press* protested in the strongest manner. But it was hardly to be supposed that, after ten months' toleration, the Irish Republican Army would be amenable to mere protests, even from the Government newspaper. Attempts were made to put into effect the slogan, 'No Free Speech for Traitors', and but for the Army Comrades Association the right of public meeting would have been reduced to a farce. At a meeting of the Cosgrave party at Portarlington on the 6th January the leader of the organization, Dr. O'Higgins, prevented a fracas by telling his men, who were moving towards the interrupters, to remain where they were. He then addressed the rowdy element as follows: 'You men know, as I know, that the men behind me are the best and, if it comes to a fight, the toughest element in the country. We stand for fair play for all parties; but, if only one party is to have fair play in this election, we are going

[1] Issue of 18 January 1933.

Y

to see that all parties will be put on level terms.'[1] The same protection was given to the National Centre Party, and Mr. James Dillon told of his experience in Macroom: 'I there addressed about 700 people, and shortly after I began thirty or forty supporters of the Government came down and started to shout "Up De Valera" to prevent me from speaking. At that time the Army Comrades Association was in existence, but I had no connection with it. They stood for the right of free speech. About sixty members of the A.C.A. in Macroom went back and, in my hearing, said to those young men who had been interrupting, "Now, stop interrupting or go away, and let the speaker address the meeting." They would not do so. The man in charge of those A.C.A. looked up at me and said, "Wait a minute, Mr. Dillon." He then went back to those fifty men and wiped the square of Macroom with them, and there were no more interruptions.'[2]

Doubtless the Government did what was possible in the way of protection with the forces at their disposal. But if it is made plain that, in the Government's view, a particular statesman needs to be heavily protected from the wrath of the populace, that fact must greatly militate against the success of his party. Mr. Cosgrave, who easily headed the poll in Cork City, made this point:

'What was my experience during the late electoral contest? I was informed when I was having a meeting in Cork, going into the city, not to enter by a certain road, that there was danger of an ambush, and the information came from the Fianna Fáil headquarters. I was to approach Cork by a circuitous route, and at a later time. My meeting was held up in Cork for an hour and a half. On the following morning I was informed that I was to be escorted to Dublin by a procession, a whole pilgrimage of military and police—an armoured car, two military units and a C.I.D. car, so that anybody travelling the country could see that there was no chance of that person being elected anyhow.'[3]

The election was held on the 24th January, and the result is given opposite. The figures in brackets indicate the party strength at the dissolution on the basis of a full House. Actually, there were four by-elections pending at the time. The result was thus a decisive victory for the Government, which had gained five seats, and an even more decisive reverse for the Cosgrave party, which had lost nine. The Labour Party's first preferences were down by 19,000, but owing to the Proportional Representation system it actually gained a seat. The

---

[1] *Irish Times*, 7 January 1933.   [2] *Dáil Debates*, l, 2332.
[3] Ibid., xlviii, 2788, 2789.

National Centre Party, fighting its first general election, had done extraordinarily well, returning eleven members. In so far as Mr. De Valera's object had been to make himself independent of Labour he had not succeeded. Exclusive of the Chairman, his party numbered exactly half the House; but with Labour support he could count on a majority of sixteen.

Party	Candidates nominated	Members elected
Fianna Fáil (De Valera)	103	77 (72)
Cumann na nGaedheal (Cosgrave)	85	48 (57)
National Centre Party	26	11 [Farmers: 4]
Labour	19	8 (7)
Independents	10	8 (11)
Independent Labour	3	1 (2)
	246	153

In view of the momentous changes in the political fabric which were to take place without further appeal to the people, it is important to examine the extent to which the electors were behind Mr. De Valera at this election. This is indicated by the first preferences, which were as follows:[1]

Fianna Fáil	689,043
Cumann na nGaedheal	422,443
National Centre Party	126,771
Labour	79,224
Independents (including Independent Labour)	68,888
Total	1,386,369

Thus the Government party obtained 689,043 first preferences, or 8,283 less than all others put together (697,326). At the 1932 election a solemn personal pledge had been given by Mr. De Valera that his party would not, in the field of international relations, exceed the mandate then asked for (i.e. the removal of the Oath and the retention of the Land Annuities) without again consulting the people. No fresh mandate was asked for at the 1933 election, at which his party just failed to poll half the votes cast. And yet, without further reference to the people, the Representative of the Crown was first shorn of his functions and then abolished altogether; the King was re-

[1] *Irish Independent*, 28 January 1933.

moved from the Constitution and merely retained for external purposes in an ordinary statute, which could be repealed at any time; the Senate was abolished in order to facilitate this revolution; finally the Parliament, now consisting of a Single Chamber, passed a new Draft Constitution, which was declared to be ratified if approved by a bare majority of the electors voting at a plebiscite, and the plebiscite was held on the same day as a general election. There is here much food for thought on the method by which a virtual dictator can operate behind the façade of a parliamentary democracy.

The result of the 1933 election was hailed by Fianna Fáil and the Republicans as a triumph for Ireland over England. Mr. P. J. Little, who very shortly afterwards became Parliamentary Secretary to the President and Chief Whip of the Government party, said at Waterford on the 29th January: 'We can now say a fond farewell to England. And let us hope that we shall see the British Empire going down amidst the laughter of the Irish people.'[1] In fairness to the people of Ireland, there should be set against this and similar political outbursts the following wise words of His Eminence the Cardinal Archbishop of Armagh (Dr. MacRory), spoken a few months later on his return to Ireland after having acted as Papal Legate at the laying of the foundation stone of the Liverpool Catholic Cathedral: 'I am glad I was sent to England, when I had to go to represent the Pope, because I like England and have liked it for forty years. . . . God set these two islands together, but man has succeeded for a long time in keeping them apart. . . . The Irish people do not hate the English people, nor do the English hate the Irish. They love them.'[2]

Parliament reassembled on the 8th February, the Chairman was re-elected, and Mr. De Valera was nominated President of the Executive Council by 82 votes to 54, his proposer stating hopefully that he looked forward to proposing him on the next occasion as President of the Republic of the whole of Ireland. The Ministry was as before, with minor changes. Mr. James Geoghegan, K.C., who afterwards was elevated to the Bench, ceased to be Minister for Justice. His place was taken by Mr. Ruttledge, who handed over the portfolio of Lands to Senator Connolly, Mr. Gerald Boland succeeding to the vacant Ministry of Posts and Telegraphs.[3]

We shall first consider events in the external field. The Bill to abolish the Oath was again sent to the Senate on the 1st March 1933,

---

[1] *Waterford News*, 3 February 1933. [2] *Irish Independent*, 8 June 1933.
[3] *Dáil Debates*, xlvi, 17–30.

the Dáil passing the necessary resolution by 75 votes to 49.[1] The subsequent history of the Bill more properly belongs to the next chapter, which deals with the history of the Senate; but it is convenient to refer to it here, because of the effect which its enactment should logically have had on Mr. De Valera's attitude towards the Irish Republican Army. The Bill came before the Senate on the 15th March. Mr. De Valera stated that nothing he had heard in the debates had in the slightest degree weakened his view that the proposal was not a breach of the Treaty. The majority of Senators thought otherwise, and as a matter of principle declined to give the Bill a Second Reading. Instead, the following resolution was passed by 24 votes to 16: 'That the Senate declines further to consider the Constitution (Removal of Oath) Bill, 1933 until it has been made the subject of negotiation between the Executive Council and the British Government with a view to an amicable agreement.'[2] The Bill was thus suspended for sixty days from the 1st March. On the 3rd May the formal motion of enactment came before the Dáil. Speaking to the motion, Mr. De Valera said, 'Once this Oath is removed you will have a complete change of attitude on the part of the people of the country.' This being contrary to all reasonable expectation, he safeguarded himself by mentioning later that he did not expect a change altogether overnight.[3] The motion was passed by 76 votes to 56, and the Bill was signed by the Representative of the Crown on the same day (3rd May 1933). It remained to be seen whether Mr. De Valera would continue to tolerate the armed menace to the State constituted by the Irish Republican Army.

Three other Bills amending the Constitution were enacted during this period. The Constitution (Amendment No. 20) Bill transferred from the Governor-General to the Executive Council the power of recommending the appropriation of money; and the Constitution (Amendment No. 21) Bill abolished the Governor-General's power to withhold the King's assent to Bills and to reserve them for the signification of the King's pleasure. These powers being purely formal, the object of the two measures was clearly to assimilate the Constitution to the Republican ideal. The third Bill, the Constitution (Amendment No. 22) Bill, abolished the right of appeal to the Judicial Committee of the Privy Council. When the Cosgrave Administration was in office it had tried to achieve this by consent, and in any case it had rendered such appeal nugatory by *ad hoc* legislation on more than one occasion. Hence, so far as the individual citizen was concerned, the formal deprivation was more apparent than real.

All three Bills were introduced in the Dáil on the 9th August 1933, and they passed through their various stages in the Senate, without substantial opposition, by the end of October. The first two became law on the 2nd November and the third on the 16th November. There was an interesting sequel. On the 14th of the same month the Secretary of State for Dominion Affairs (Mr. J. H. Thomas), in reply to a Parliamentary Question in the House of Commons, stated that these Bills involved a further repudiation of the Treaty, and that by gradually eliminating the Crown from the Constitution the Irish Free State was tending to lose the advantages of Commonwealth membership.[1] The latter statement meant no more than that Mr. De Valera could not expect to have his cake and eat it, which is a truism; but the opinion on the constitutional position seems manifestly unsound, as the action taken was clearly in conformity with the Statute of Westminster. In a dispatch dated the 29th November, addressed to Mr. Thomas, Mr. De Valera requested from the British Government an unequivocal assurance that a decision of the Irish people to secede from the Commonwealth would not be treated as a cause of war or other aggressive action. In his reply, dated the 5th December, Mr. Thomas pointed out that the Treaty had been duly accepted by the elected representatives of the Irish Free State and confirmed at succeeding general elections, and stated that the British Government did 'not feel called upon to say what attitude they would adopt in circumstances which they regard as purely hypothetical'.[2]

On the 6th December the Secretary of State for War (Lord Hailsham) stated in the House of Lords that the Irish Free State could not, consistently with the Treaty, abolish the right of appeal to the Privy Council, and that its right to do so might be raised for determination by the Privy Council itself.[3] As Canada had, a short time previously, abolished this right in the case of criminal appeals, it is difficult to understand the grounds on which this opinion was based. It provided excellent propaganda for Mr. De Valera, who availed himself of it in the Senate on the very next day. The occasion was a motion approving the Report of the Imperial Economic Committee, with which the subject has no obvious connection. The

[1] *House of Commons Debates*, cclxxxi, 726–9.
[2] Full text of both Notes in *House of Commons Debates*, cclxxxiii, 1456–61.
[3] *House of Lords Debates*, xc, 325–42.

method which he adopted was peculiar but characteristic. He introduced the motion in a short, perfunctory speech. In the debate which ensued no reference was made to the Hailsham incident, but in exercising his right of replying to the debate Mr. De Valera dealt with it in detail.[1] This was a device on which the late Patrick Hogan had previously animadverted strongly in the Dáil, and one with which both Houses were to become familiar during the debates on the abolition of the Senate.

The remaining external matter which falls to be dealt with is the economic war. On the 7th March 1933 Mr. J. H. Thomas read to the House of Commons a letter from the High Commissioner of the Irish Free State, dated four days earlier, intimating his Government's decision to use for 'normal Exchequer requirements' the Land Annuities and other withheld payments, which had hitherto been retained in suspense accounts.[2] On the following day the Land (Purchase Annuities Fund) Bill was introduced in the Dáil; it was certified as a Money Bill, and became law on the 30th March. Shortly afterwards the accumulated funds were all spent. Even so, a *rapprochement* might perhaps have been effected through intermediaries at the World Economic Conference in July, but the will to negotiate was unhappily absent. Speaking on the pact of non-economic aggression, Senator Connolly, the Irish Delegate, went back over the centuries to the Cromwellian plantations as an 'historical background', and was ruled out of order by Dr. Colijn, the Prime Minister of the Netherlands, who was in the chair. He thereupon left the Chamber with his typewritten speech only half read.[3] This inability to discuss present-day problems in terms of the present day is puzzling to foreigners and distressing to ourselves.

Before the economic war Mr. De Valera had told the people that Great Britain and Ireland were each other's best customer.[4] He now said (9th August 1933) that, owing to a change in Britain's domestic policy and not because of the dispute, 'the British market is gone for ever'. 'If there is to be any hope of prosperity for this country it is by reversing that policy which made us simply the kitchen garden for supplying the British with cheap food.'[5] More than six months later he reiterated his conviction that 'the British market was gone, and gone for ever'.[6] The Minister for Lands (Senator Connolly) went further. He said, 'It had taken a hundred years to establish the cattle

[1] *Senate Debates*, xvii, 2014–20.
[2] *House of Commons Debates*, cclxxv, 983–7.
[3] *Irish Times*, 14 July 1933.   [4] *Irish Independent*, 11 February 1932.
[5] *Dáil Debates*, xlix, 1609, 1610.   [6] *Irish Independent*, 26 March 1934.

trade in this country, but with God's help it would not take a hundred years to kill it.'[1] And again: 'It was a damn good job that the English cattle market had gone, as it would make the farmers realize that they should take off their coats and till the land for production of food.'[2]

Throughout this period Mr. Lemass, who was easily the ablest member of the Government, proceeded with his plans for the industrialization of the country; but the difficulty of his task was, of course, immensely increased by the progressive deterioration of agriculture owing to the economic war. The increased unemployment due to the impoverishment of the farmers had also its effect on the internal situation, which we are now about to consider.

After Mr. De Valera's election success, to which it had in some degree contributed, the Irish Republican Army went from strength to strength and throve by immunity. In its issue of the 6th May (three days after the abolition of the Oath) its official organ, *An Phoblacht*, announced a special recruiting campaign. Recruiting posters appeared everywhere, and addresses were given in the provincial newspapers to which recruits could report. A refusal to insert these addresses would doubtless have involved severe penalties.

The Catholic Hierarchy were thoroughly alarmed, and several of the bishops uttered grave warnings. For instance, on the 29th May the Bishop of Kerry said: 'Not only are they urging boys to join, but I understand that in many cases they are administering an oath to bind their recruits. I want to tell you that any oath of that kind is not binding. It is, first of all, a grievous sin to take it, and it is a sin to keep it.'[3] Other bishops, and in particular the Bishop of Galway, impeached the Irish Republican Army and emphasized the dangers of Communistic attempts to secure a foothold in Ireland.[4] Later, Mr. De Valera stated that 'the Bishop of Galway in what he said was misled'.[5]

On the morning of Saturday, the 27th May, a band of approximately sixty men, fully armed with new rifles and two Lewis guns, arrived at the village of Ballinacarriga, County Cork, took possession of a house without the owner's consent, and indulged in military exercises throughout the week-end, to the terror of the inhabitants. The Minister for Justice admitted the facts and stated that he did not know how the new arms had got into the country.[6]

An Phoblacht of the same date contained a photograph entitled

---

[1] *Irish Independent*, 9 June 1934. [2] Ibid., 19 June 1934.
[3] *Irish Times*, 30 May 1933. [4] *Standard*, 27 May 1933.
[5] *Dáil Debates*, I, 2513. [6] Ibid., xlviii, 8, 542–3.

'Citizen Soldiers of the Republic'. It depicted a number of young men lying prone and taking aim with rifles. This issue also printed an attack on Superintendent Casserly, the head of the police in Drogheda, for prosecuting five young men who had posted up recruiting posters. He was described as 'bitterly prejudiced against Republicans'. The sequel followed on the 16th July, when, at half an hour after midnight, the Superintendent's car and residence were riddled with machine-gun bullets from close range.[1] If he had been in the car he could hardly have escaped being murdered. Questions were asked in the Dáil, but the miscreants were never brought to justice. Indeed, on the second occasion the Government appeared to resent being interrogated on the subject.[2]

Other instances could be given, but sufficient has been said to indicate the virtual anarchy which persisted long after the removal of the Oath. Indeed, conditions were so bad by the middle of July that Mr. MacDermot, the leader of the National Centre Party, who is a man of moderate speech, stated that he did 'not believe any man since Cromwell has inflicted more harm on this country' than Mr. De Valera.[3]

In face of this growing menace the Army Comrades Association had, shortly after the election, reorganized itself as a civil, unarmed organization, pledged to give disciplined service to the nation; and in the month of April 1933 it adopted the uniform of a blue shirt. The new movement was at first immensely popular and it rapidly gathered strength throughout the country. It was shortly to receive a new leader, in the following circumstances.

On the 22nd February, a fortnight after the formation of the new Government, General O'Duffy, the Commissioner of the Civic Guard, was removed from office by the Executive Council. No charge was made against him, Mr. De Valera merely stating that a change of Commissioner was desirable in the public interest and that he did not propose to give reasons or to say anything further.[4] General O'Duffy had been appointed to his post by Kevin O'Higgins shortly after the foundation of the State. Under him the Civic Guard had become one of the finest police forces in Europe, and he had earned both the confidence of the public and the affection of his men. He had been present at O'Higgins's death-bed, and it was to him that the dying Vice-President had whispered that they had done good work and to continue on the same lines. A motion of censure on the subject was

[1] *Irish Times*, 17 July 1933.   [2] *Dáil Debates*, xlix, 1628; l, 187–8.
[3] Ibid., xlviii, 2766.   [4] Ibid., xlvi, 33–5.

tabled by Mr. Cosgrave in the Dáil, and in speaking to it Mr. De Valera linked General O'Duffy's dismissal with that of Mr. McNeill. 'We say this, whether it be the Governor-General or the Chief of Police, that as long as we are responsible for public policy we will have men there in whom we have confidence.' 'Let us note that without any of the bunkum—full confidence.'[1] This argument might have had some validity if the General had been dismissed soon after Mr. De Valera's advent to power in 1932, but hardly otherwise; and the ordinary citizens could not be blind to the fact that General O'Duffy's removal had been demanded for months by *An Phoblacht*. He was offered a post of equivalent monetary value in another Department, but he rightly refused it. If he was not to be trusted as Chief of Police he was not to be trusted anywhere in the public service. The Government's ineptitude in legal matters was evidenced by the fact that in the letter of dismissal the authority relied upon was a repealed section of an Act.[2] There was legal authority to remove the Commissioner without reason stated, but it was conferred by a section of a subsequent Act.

At a meeting held in Dublin on the 20th July the name of the Army Comrades Association was changed to the National Guard and Dr. O'Higgins handed over the leadership to General O'Duffy, who was unanimously elected Director-General. The new leader announced that the aim of the National Guard would be to safeguard the national honour, the national interests, and the national culture in the widest sense. The official uniform would be the blue shirt. 'The organization will keep within the law, and illegalities will not be tolerated. Physical drill will be practised only as a means of promoting good health, character, and discipline.'[3]

From this point onwards events moved rapidly. Under the Firearms Act, 1925, thousands of persons, including bank officials, held firearms certificates entitling them to carry revolvers for their personal safety, their names being entered in a register kept by the police. All the ex-Ministers had had such certificates since the assassination of Kevin O'Higgins in 1927, and so had General O'Duffy and some other members of the National Guard. A revocation order was now issued, cancelling *all* firearms certificates, and on Saturday and Sunday, the 29th and 30th July, the police paid domiciliary visits to the holders, including the Chairman of the Senate, and collected their revolvers. Most of the ex-Ministers complied, though the sur-

[1] *Dáil Debates*, xlvi, 796–7. [2] Ibid., xlvi, 806, 807.
[3] *Irish Times*, 21 July 1933.

render placed them in jeopardy, their protective guards having been removed two months previously. Mr. Blythe refused to give up his weapon, on the ground that he was not going to allow himself to be made a defenceless target.[1]

When the matter was raised in the Dáil on the 1st August the Minister for Justice (Mr. Ruttledge) said that the matter was a simple one. The firearms certificates expired annually on the 31st July, and it was considered desirable to have a stocktaking. Mr. MacDermot said that the episode was almost too fantastic to be true and that the talk about stocktaking would not deceive a baby. He and other speakers pointed out that the Government was apparently not interested in taking stock of the arms illegitimately held. The debate proceeded on the assumption that the reason given was the real reason until the hour of the adjournment approached, when little time was left for further discussion. Mr. De Valera then denounced the National Guard. The Constitution was not good enough for General O'Duffy, who was aiming at a dictatorship, and the Government would not tolerate private armies on either side. Pressed by Mr. Dillon to state his attitude towards the Irish Republican Army, Mr. De Valera said there was no need for it, now that the Oath had been removed. It was simply a question of time until the truth had penetrated to the minds of the people, young and old. As for the National Guard, it was 'not a body which has any roots in the past, not a body which can be said to have a national objective such as the I.R.A. can be said to have'.[2]

The position, therefore, was as follows. The National Guard was a new, unarmed organization, but some of its members possessed revolvers, for which they had obtained permits from the proper authorities. They wore blue shirts and so could be readily identified if they infringed the law. Their revolvers were now to be taken from them. The Irish Republican Army was a heavily armed force, in illegal possession of large stocks of revolvers, rifles, machine-guns, ammunition, and explosives. Its members wore no uniform and they had committed many cowardly murders and outrages innumerable, usually under cover of darkness. It had been condemned by the Catholic Church. But it was a body which had roots in the past, and it could be said to have a national objective. There was now no need for its existence, but apparently no attempt was to be made to suppress it, at any rate until the truth had penetrated to young and old.

No evidence was adduced to prove that General O'Duffy was aim-

[1] *Irish Times*, 31 July 1933.　　[2] *Dáil Debates*, xlix, 1028-72.

ing at a dictatorship. On the other hand, Mr. De Valera himself was a virtual dictator. His personal domination over his party and his Cabinet was a matter of common knowledge. He had reduced the office of Governor-General to a nonentity, and during the Eucharistic Congress he had acted as the ceremonial head of the State. In a speech in the Dáil on the 7th April 1933 he had expressed his impatience of parliamentary procedure: 'One of the faults of our parliamentary institution, as it stands, is that we have to spend a great deal of time dealing with comparatively trifling things, things that in a time of emergency would not be considered at all and that we would not waste our time on. If the Executive Council is really to do good work in connection with this it will have to be given more time away from the parliamentary duties it has to attend to here. It would be a very good thing for the country to give, say, a six months' holiday to get that work done.'[1] Shortly afterwards, he departed on a Continental holiday; and, according to Reuter's correspondent, at Genoa on the 5th June 'in a statement to the Press he spoke of his great admiration for Fascism'.[2] Returning to Ireland on the 11th June, though he was only the Prime Minister, he was received with semi-regal honours, a salute of nineteen guns being fired from the battery at Dunleary as the mailboat in which he was travelling approached the harbour.[3] Such a salute had been unknown since the days of the Viceroys, and even they had received it only on ceremonial occasions.

General O'Duffy seemed to possess a quality of popular appeal second only to that of Mr. De Valera himself, and it is probable that the latter's attitude to the National Guard was due, at least in part, to a decision that he would 'bear, like the Turk, no brother near the throne'. Account must also be taken of the depth of feeling which he showed towards his political opponents at this time. This was emphasized in a startling manner on the 6th July 1933, during the debate on the Government's proposal to redeem the balance of the Irish Republican Loan, raised in the United States in 1919–21. The repayment was not due until the Irish Republic had received international recognition, and the Opposition resisted the proposal on the ground that many of the bonds had been assigned to Mr. De Valera to assist in the establishment of a newspaper. Redemption would accordingly, they said, involve the payment of thousands of pounds of the taxpayers' money to the *Irish Press*. Mr. De Valera alleged that if the ex-Ministers were in power they would abuse their office by being guilty

[1] *Dáil Debates*, xlvi, 2657. [2] *Irish Times*, 6 June 1933.
[3] Ibid., 12 June 1933.

of corruption, and he added: 'I know it is gall and wormwood to them that they are not here to do it, and that is the whole trouble. They are not here to do it, and it is the great and supreme pleasure of my life to know that they will have to digest that gall and wormwood.'[1]

During the Cosgrave régime it had been the Government's custom to hold an annual ceremony on Leinster Lawn, in front of the Parliament House, when wreaths were laid on the cross which had been erected there in memory of the dead founders of the State, Arthur Griffith, Michael Collins, and, later, Kevin O'Higgins. This ceremony had been allowed to lapse under Mr. De Valera, and General O'Duffy now announced that the National Guard would hold a parade in Merrion Square on Sunday, 13th August, marching past Leinster Lawn. As recently as the 1st June the Minister for Justice had stated: 'I do not mind what manœuvres any people in this country go through. I do not care who they are or what they are, provided that people do not go out publicly with arms or interfere in arms with people.'[2] But circumstances alter cases, and he had been thinking of the Irish Republican Army. At 12.45 a.m. on the 12th August the Government promulgated an Order bringing Article 2A of the Constitution into force, thus virtually putting the country under martial law. At the same time, and pursuant to this Article, it issued a proclamation banning the proposed parade of the National Guard. It also recruited into the Civic Guard (the new Commissioner of which was Colonel Broy) an armed auxiliary force of untrained men, who were ex-members of the Irish Republican Army and had fought against the State in the Civil War. These men were provided with rifles, machine-guns, and armoured cars. The British auxiliaries had been nicknamed the Black and Tans, after a famous Tipperary pack; the new auxiliaries received the *soubriquet* of the Broy Harriers, after the Commissioner and another well-known pack, the Bray Harriers.

General O'Duffy cancelled the parade, but announced that private parades in honour of the dead leaders would be held in each district on the 20th August. At these a message was read from him to the effect that no good could come to Ireland from the frantic squabbles of warring parties. Two days later, in a statesmanlike and sincere speech, Sir John Keane introduced a motion expressive of the opinion that the recent actions of the Government purporting to be for the preservation of public peace and order had not been justified. He was

---

[1] *Dáil Debates*, xlviii, 1861.   [2] Ibid., xlvii, 2182.

made the object of a personal attack by one of Mr. De Valera's followers, Senator Quirke, who called him the avowed spokesman of the landlord class and of the banking interests. The Minister for Justice stated that the National Guard was a heavily armed force, but he produced no evidence to justify this statement.[1] While the debate was in progress the Government issued an Order declaring the National Guard to be an unlawful association under Article 2A of the Constitution, and at the same time the Military Tribunal was set up. The personnel of the Tribunal was the same as it had been under the Cosgrave Administration.[2]

When Fianna Fáil were in opposition no measure had been attacked with such vehemence as the Constitution Amendment which empowered the establishment of the Military Tribunal. Mr. Ruttledge had described the Tribunal as a 'Star Chamber',[3] and Mr. De Valera had said: 'Anyone who gets in your path, "Squelch him, by God, squelch him," as Carlyle said of Ireland. That is the only policy apparently that the Executive Council knows how to put into operation.'[4] The Act was made an issue at the general election of 1932, and it contributed in large measure to the defeat of the Cosgrave Government. Shortly after that election, a questionnaire was submitted to Mr. De Valera by the *Irish Independent*, and the answers were published in its issue of the 27th February 1932. Among them was the following:

> *Q.* 'Will the last Constitution Amendment Act be repealed in full?'
>
> *A.* 'Yes, the Act will be repealed in full.'

It was not, however, repealed either in full or in part, and it was now brought into operation eighteen months later in order to deal with Mr. De Valera's political opponents.

It will be recalled that, at the end of December 1932, negotiations had been initiated for the fusion of the Cosgrave party and the National Centre Party, but that these had been forestalled by Mr. De Valera's action in dissolving the Dáil. Attempts to this end had since been made by various intermediaries, but without success. The creation of the National Guard under General O'Duffy now added a new factor. All three bodies were being oppressed by the Government and harried by the Irish Republican Army. Fusion was desirable if they were not to be ground between the upper and the nether

---

[1] *Senate Debates*, xvii, 1117–1220.　　[2] *Irish Times*, 23 August 1933.
[3] *Dáil Debates*, xl, 117.　　[4] Ibid., xl, 53.

millstones. Moreover, it was thought that Mr. De Valera was contemplating a fresh general election. This time the negotiations were successful; and on the 8th September conventions representing the Cosgrave party (Cumann na nGaedheal) and the National Centre Party agreed to join forces with General O'Duffy in forming a new party. The name of the new party was to be United Ireland, and its leader was to be General O'Duffy, who had no seat in Parliament. The Vice-Presidents were to be Mr. Cosgrave (who was to act as parliamentary leader) and Messrs. MacDermot and Dillon. Mr. Cosgrave has never been a man with personal ambitions, but the greatest credit is due to him for his self-abnegation in thus subordinating himself for what he believed to be the good of his country. Time unfortunately proved this not to be the case.[1] As the National Guard had been banned, it was reconstituted on strictly constitutional lines as a wing of the new party, with the title of the Young Ireland Association.

On the 11th November the United Ireland Party issued a detailed statement of its policy. This included 'the voluntary reunion of all Ireland in a single independent State as a member, without any abatement of Irish sovereignty, of the British Commonwealth in free and equal partnership'; an advantageous settlement of the economic war; the establishment of agricultural and industrial corporations with statutory powers; and the abolition of the present proportional representation system of voting.[2]

Two cases will illustrate the distinction drawn between different classes of citizens in the administration of the law at this period. On the 7th September nine respectable farmers of County Waterford were arrested and charged with unlawful association to advocate non-payment of rates and with conspiracy to compel persons to join the National Centre Party. They were not tried before the ordinary courts, but lodged in prison and in due course haled before the Military Tribunal. On the 10th October the Tribunal found them all not guilty on all the charges and they were set at liberty, after having spent a month in gaol.[3]

The 'Boycott Bass' campaign was now again in full swing. At 1 a.m. on the 12th September a dozen armed men entered a public-house in County Dublin, known, grimly enough, as 'The Dead Man's'. The proprietress had been warned a fortnight before not to sell Bass's ale. The armed men smashed the bottles of Bass and took

---

[1] *Irish Times*, 9 September 1933.   [2] Ibid., 13 November 1933.
[3] Ibid., 11 October 1933.

her brother to a lonely spot in the Dublin Mountains. He was there stripped of his clothes and a pair of drawers forced upon him, on which were painted the words, 'Boycott Bass'. In this condition he was left to make his way back to civilization. Twelve youths were arrested in connection with this outrage within the next few days. They were not brought before the Military Tribunal, but before the ordinary District Court on the 20th September. For want of evidence, all were released save one, who harangued the court in a political speech and was sentenced to two months' imprisonment in default of entering into recognisances.[1]

This man's photograph appeared in *An Phoblacht*, which also gave a 'Full Boycott League Report', showing the result of the anti-Bass campaign all over the country.[2] The previous campaign in December had been checked by the Army Comrades Association, but its successor, the Young Ireland Association, now had quite enough to do to look after itself. The autumn and winter of 1933–4 were marked by a terrible series of outrages against the members of this organization and of the United Ireland Party, of which it is possible to mention only a few. In an interview with the Press Association on the 3rd September Mr. De Valera said: 'It is up to the Government to see that opportunities for free speech are given, but the Government cannot possibly make people or causes popular.'[3] This balanced declaration was none too reassuring, and it was reminiscent of the statement of the Minister for Finance in regard to the 'Boycott Bass' campaign, made in the previous December and already referred to: protection would be given to the licensed trade, but 'all traders must bear in mind the consequences of flouting public opinion'.

21st September. Armed men fired on a member of the United Ireland Party in Dingle, County Kerry, with intent to murder him. He was seriously wounded.[4]

23rd September. Determined attempts were made to prevent a meeting of the same party in the City of Limerick. A number of people were badly hurt and motor-cars were burnt.[5]

30th September. There were similar occurrences in Cork, where the military were called out.[6]

6th October. General O'Duffy attended a meeting of the United Ireland Party in Tralee, where the mob was ready for him. He and

---

[1] *Irish Times*, 13 and 21 September 1933.
[2] *An Phoblacht*, 16 and 30 September 1933.
[3] *Irish Press*, 4 September 1933.   [4] *Irish Times*, 23 September 1933.
[5] Ibid., 25 September 1933.   [6] Ibid., 2 October 1933.

his companions had to walk down Bridge Street—a very narrow thoroughfare—where they had no police escort. General O'Duffy received several blows and was finally hit on the head with a hammer. Mr. Lynch, ex-Minister for Fisheries, was kicked. When they got to the hall there was stone-throwing, and a Mills bomb was flung on to a skylight, but some wire netting prevented it from falling into the hall and exploding.[1] According to Mr. MacDermot, the police entered the hall at the behest of the mob and brought out a delegate who was accused of carrying arms. He was searched outside and found to be unarmed.[2]

14th October. Five armed men visited the house of Joseph Hanly, Cloughjordan, County Tipperary, forcibly took him outside, and fired shots over his head, 'with a view to getting him to resign his position as Treasurer of the local branch of the United Ireland Party'.[3]

16th October. While a dance under the auspices of the same party was being held at Woodford, County Galway, miscreants fired shots through the doors and windows, wounding five people.[4]

21st October. In a paragraph headed 'Imperialist Hooligans' *An Phoblacht* stated that 'Messrs. Hugh O'Reilly and O'Leary, prominent A.C.A. supporters in Bandon, are constant visitors to the police barracks. O'Leary is the Treasurer of the Bandon Branch of the A.C.A.' Eight days later (29th October) armed and masked men visited the home of O'Leary at four o'clock in the morning, arriving in a motor-car. The door was battered in, O'Leary's father was felled with a cudgel, and the unfortunate man himself was taken out, beaten, and shot in the legs. Three-quarters of an hour later the car arrived at O'Reilly's house. His mother and sister, who tried to tear off the men's masks, were struck on the head and face with batons. O'Reilly was taken out, clad only in his trousers, and beaten all over the body. He crawled back to his house a mass of wounds, and, after hovering between life and death for two months, died on the 28th December. At the inquest his father said he was 'the same as if he had been taken out of a tub of blood' and the doctor stated that he had never seen a more terrible case.[5] The jury returned a verdict of 'Wilful Murder', but the murderers of poor O'Reilly are still at large.

The newspaper files of the period disclose no single instance of any corresponding outrage by the members of the Young Ireland Association (or Blue Shirts), nor of any act of retaliation by them against the

---

[1] *Irish Independent*, 7 and 9 October 1933.   [2] *Dáil Debates.* xlix, 2363.
[3] *Irish Independent*, 16 October 1933.   [4] Ibid., 17 October 1933.
[5] Ibid., 30 October and 30 December 1933.

Irish Republican Army. They appear to have behaved with admirable restraint in difficult circumstances. But it was clear that this state of virtual anarchy could not be allowed to continue; and at last the Government decided to take stern action. On the morning of the 30th November the police raided the offices of the United Ireland Party in Dublin, and also the homes of many hundreds of members of the party throughout the country, including those of General O'Duffy and of Mr. Ernest Blythe, the former Vice-President. On the same day, in the Dáil, the Minister for Justice read out a number of captured documents in justification of the raids. If any arms were found he did not mention the fact. The most sensational of the documents read consisted of extracts from a copy of an obviously confidential letter from one of General O'Duffy's colleagues to a Conservative Member of Parliament in England. It expressed the opinion that the Cosgrave party was finished and spoke in contemptuous, and possibly libellous, terms of Mr. MacDermot. The only object in reading it could have been to foment dissensions in the United Ireland Party.[1]

This stern action was followed up by still sterner action on the 8th December, when the Government issued an Order declaring the Young Ireland Association to be an unlawful association. No similar step was taken in respect of the Irish Republican Army. We must here interrupt the tale of outrage to consider three law cases which arose out of this Order.

The Young Ireland Association was, of course, a constituent part of the constitutional Opposition. It had been banned on the ground that it was meditating a *coup d'état*; but this seems quite incredible, as it was practically unarmed and enjoyed Mr. Cosgrave's full confidence. As it was now an unlawful association, the United Ireland Party dissolved it and formed a new organization, called the League of Youth. In order that this should not share the fate of its predecessor, they served a writ on the Attorney-General with the object of obtaining a declaration from the High Court that the League of Youth was a lawful organization. The Attorney-General moved to have the proceedings struck out as vexatious and frivolous. The Hon. Mr. Justice Johnston refused the Attorney-General's application, pointing out that the right of free speech was involved and that the plaintiffs relied on Article 9 of the Constitution, which guarantees this right. The Government thus sustained a serious legal reverse.[2]

---

[1] *Dáil Debates*, 1, 710, 711, 848–76.
[2] *Blythe and Others* v. *Attorney-General*, [1934] I.R. 266–81.

On the 17th December General O'Duffy, who was wearing a blue shirt, attempted to address a meeting at Westport, County Mayo. Amid scenes of intense excitement, he and two of his followers, similarly attired, were arrested by the police. An application for an absolute order of *habeas corpus* was at once made to the High Court. The police evidence was that the General was arrested on suspicion of being a member of an unlawful association. The Hon. Mr. Justice O'Byrne stated that he did not accept this as a true explanation. His conclusion was that General O'Duffy was arrested because he went to address a meeting attired in a blue shirt, and he was satisfied that both the arrest and the detention were illegal. He therefore ordered the immediate release of the prisoners (21st December 1933). This was another serious reverse for the Government.[1]

No sooner was General O'Duffy set at liberty than he was served with a summons to appear before the Military Tribunal on charges of (*a*) belonging to two unlawful associations, viz. the National Guard and the Young Ireland Association, and (*b*) sedition and alleged incitement to murder Mr. De Valera in a speech at Ballyshannon on 9th December. The Opposition lawyers countered this by applying to the High Court for an order prohibiting the Military Tribunal from hearing and determining the charges. A conditional order was granted, and this was later made absolute, by a majority judgement, so far as the charges of sedition and incitement to murder were concerned, but the Court held that the minor charges of belonging to unlawful associations fell properly within the jurisdiction of the Tribunal and were triable by it. It further decided that the Tribunal was a court of limited jurisdiction, which was not protected from prohibition. So far as the Government was concerned, this was the most serious reverse of all. It was, in fact, a vitally important legal decision, which safeguarded the individual from the possible tyranny of the Executive.[2]

Meanwhile, Mr. De Valera's relations with the Irish Republican Army were growing progressively more strained. Twelve members of this organization were arrested on charges of riot and unlawful assembly in connection with the affair in Tralee, when General O'Duffy had been hit on the head with a hammer and a Mills bomb had been thrown. On the 1st December they were sentenced by the Military Tribunal to terms ranging from four to six months, and they were lodged in gaol at Arbour Hill, Dublin.[3] This caused grave

[1] *In re* O'Duffy, [1934] I.R. 550–70.
[2] *The State (Eoin O'Duffy)* v. *Bennett and Others*, [1935] I.R. 70–127.
[3] *Irish Independent*, 2 December 1933.

dissatisfaction, and, on the invitation of the local branch of the Government party, Mr. De Valera went down on the 17th December to address the people of Tralee.

Mr. De Valera said, in the course of his speech, that in Arbour Hill they had a clean prison, as comfortable a one as any in which he had ever been. On the general situation, he stated that he had a long and painful list of things that had happened there within the previous few months. The only names he could honestly give to the items in that list were outrages and crimes. Houses had been fired into on several occasions, and it was a miracle that nobody had been killed. Property had been wilfully destroyed. Organized groups had taken it upon themselves to decide without any legal or moral right whatever how much liberty their fellow citizens might enjoy. Were the people going to surrender their right to decide at the ballot box what policy was best in the country's interests and what government should rule?[1]

These wholly admirable sentiments were mere echoes, in more pleading tones, of what the dead leaders, Griffith, Collins, and O'Higgins, had said when Mr. De Valera was President of a Republic in arms against a government which was based on the suffrages of the people. From the close of the Civil War to the end of 1925 he had maintained his stage title of President of that Republic. He then split the Republican Party, but still refused to recognize the Irish Free State. In 1927 he and his new party subscribed the Oath and entered the Dáil as a matter of expediency. In 1929 he said that those who continued on in the organization which he and his friends had left could claim exactly the same continuity that he and his friends had claimed up to 1925; and his newspaper, interpreting this speech in a leading article, stated that the Dáil was a faked parliament, a Dáil of usurpers. The Cosgrave Government was a junta, and would never be, for them, the *de jure* government. Since Mr. De Valera had now replaced Mr. Cosgrave as head of the Government, his complete conversion was a godsend for the country; but the failure of the Irish Republican Army to appreciate his motives was perhaps only to be expected. The outrages accordingly continued, and Mr. De Valera had increasing recourse to the Military Tribunal not only for the trial of his political opponents but for the arraignment of his former friends.

In the first week of January alone nine acts of violence were committed against members of the United Ireland Party in various parts of the country. On the 4th of that month an elderly publican of

[1] *Irish Independent*, 18 December 1933.

Dunmanway, County Cork, died as the result of sustaining a fractured skull on Christmas morning. He was a supporter of Mr. Cosgrave's and had been knocked down in the street during a tumult in which the crowd shouted, 'Up the Republic! Down with the Blue Shirts!'[1] One member stated in the Dáil that it was well known who his assailants were, and another mentioned that the names of some of them had been given to the police.[2] On the 23rd March, nine men were brought before the District Court (not before the Military Tribunal) and charged with his murder. Three days later the District Justice refused informations, on the ground that the evidence would not justify him in putting the prosecution and the defence to the expense of returning the men for trial.[3]

On the 9th January two men who were collecting for the United Ireland Party were attacked in Dundalk by a band of brigands, who kidnapped and robbed them. The following 8th February one of the two men, named McGrory, identified the robbers before the Military Tribunal, which sentenced them to imprisonment. At 8 p.m. on the following Sunday, 11th February, an immensely powerful bomb was flung into McGrory's house, which was situated in one of the most thickly populated streets in Dundalk. The house was completely demolished, and fifty windows in the street were smashed. Most of the family were absent at church, but McGrory's mother, who was over seventy, and two young boys aged about seven were terribly injured. Mrs. McGrory died from her injuries on the following 18th March.[4]

In connection with this outrage Mr. Cosgrave made what seems a very curious statement in the Dáil (16th February 1934). On the 15th September the Military Tribunal had made an order closing for six months the offices of the Army Comrades Association at 5 Parnell Square, Dublin. Nobody, therefore, had authority to enter them during that period. According to Mr. Cosgrave, police officers were in 5 Parnell Square on the day previous to the Dundalk outrage, and, with the aid of field-glasses, kept under observation another house in the square, No. 44. In this house, he said, a meeting was being held for the purpose of giving instruction in the use of a land-mine which was to be exploded on the following day. The only explosion that occurred on the following day was in Dundalk. The Minister for Justice replied that, as regards the allegation that detectives were

[1] *Irish Independent*, 5 January 1934.   [2] *Dáil Debates*, l, 883.
[3] *Irish Press*, 24 and 27 March 1934.
[4] *Irish Independent*, 12 February and 19 March 1934.

keeping watch, 'anything that was done in that way was done by the police in the exercise of their duties and in view of any information they might have had'. He further stated that the police were satisfied that there was no connection between what happened in Dundalk and anything that took place in Dublin on the previous day.[1]

Not being content with this reply, Mr. Cosgrave tabled a motion for a judicial inquiry, but this was not discussed until more than a year later (3rd April 1935). The Minister then repeated what he had said as to the lack of connection between the two events, and the motion was defeated on a party vote.[2]

Mr. Cosgrave's allegations were extraordinary enough, but they were overshadowed by what emerged later. On the 10th July 1935 five men were charged before the Military Tribunal with the murder of Mrs. McGrory. The principal witness for the State was a man named Matthew McCrystal, of Dundalk. On the 23rd March 1934 McCrystal had himself been charged before the Tribunal, and had been sentenced to three months' imprisonment, in default of recognizances, for refusing to give information in regard to his movements on the day of the outrage.[3] According to the evidence which he now gave, he was present when the infernal machine was being prepared in Dundalk, and he accompanied the accused men to the vicinity of the McGrorys' house on that night, where he remained while the bomb was thrown into it. Under cross-examination, he said that he had been a member of the Irish Republican Army and that he had himself put a few cartridges into the mine, and he admitted that he was an accomplice. In November 1934, having served his term of imprisonment, he joined the Civic Guard, which he left on the following 29th May. Counsel for the State mentioned that he was first suspended and then dismissed for refusing to answer questions put to him under Article 2A of the Constitution. The witness stated that he was then living in the Civic Guard depot.[4]

The trial ended on the 18th July. The Military Tribunal stated that they were 'not satisfied that guilt has been sufficiently brought home to the accused' and they were acquitted.[5]

The day of the Dundalk bomb outrage was also a day of terror in Drogheda. Members of the League of Youth were assailed by a furious mob with stones and bottles, to cries of 'Up De Valera! Up the Republic! Go on the murderers!' The Blue Shirts did not break

[1] *Dáil Debates*, 1, 1708, 1709, 1825. [2] Ibid., lv, 1860–84.
[3] *Irish Press*, 24 March 1934. [4] *Irish Independent*, 11 July 1935.
[5] Ibid., 19 July 1935.

their ranks or retaliate, and the mob had to be dispersed by the military, who used tear-gas bombs and fired shots over the heads of the people. When some of the rioters were subsequently brought before the District Justice, he said:

'If the Blue Shirts who came off the train had not used such self-control there might have been murder done that evening, as they might have attacked the hostile crowd and nobody could say where it would all end. . . . Any body was entitled to use the public thoroughfare as long as they did not carry arms in their hands and were not an illegal organization, and no one was entitled to molest them.'[1]

Mr. De Valera was thus faced, by the middle of February, with very serious difficulties. His toleration of the Irish Republican Army had brought into being a disciplined but unarmed organization, which was part of the constitutional Opposition and which wore the uniform of a blue shirt. The Republicans, and many of his own supporters, were continuously offering mob violence to this organization and his own efforts to suppress it had been thwarted by decisions of the High Court. On the 23rd February the Government introduced in the Dáil the Wearing of Uniform (Restriction) Bill. This extraordinary measure prohibited the wearing of uniform or badges, or the use of military titles, in support of a political party or its ancillary associations. The carrying of weapons (including sticks) at political meetings was made illegal. Heavy penalties were prescribed and an ingenious (but entirely unconstitutional) attempt was made to avoid further trouble with the judges by a provision that all offenders were to be tried before the District Court, from whose decisions there was to be no appeal, not even to the High Court.

The general purport of Mr. De Valera's speech on the Second Reading was that the Bill was essential if civil war was to be avoided. Mr. MacDermot interrupted him to point out that the Blue Shirts were not arming, but all he was able to reply was that arms were available if they wanted them, to which Mr. Dillon retorted, 'Arrest every man who has arms and we will support you.'[2] Obviously alluding to the High Court actions, he said that the Cosgrave party 'were using the machinery of the law to defeat and prevent——', but the rest of this remarkable sentence was lost in Opposition laughter. Later, however, he returned to this topic, and alleged that they were 'using the courts to hamper the Executive'.[3] Much of what he said was irrelevant to the debate; he declared his belief in democracy and

---

[1] *Irish Independent*, 12 and 24 February 1934.
[2] *Dáil Debates*, l, 2523.   [3] Ibid., l, 2524, 2525.

his abhorrence of communism, gave particulars of his parentage, and denied that there was a single drop of Jewish blood in his veins.[1] He had often wondered 'whether this country would not be better off if the whole lot of us, on the benches on both sides, were taken out and put into some foreign island, and made to live together'.[2]

The Bill was passed by the Dáil under the guillotine, after a stormy and destructive debate, on the 14th March 1933, when it was sent to the Senate.

[1] *Dáil Debates*, 1, 2514.　　　　　[2] Ibid., 1, 2503.

CHAPTER XX

TENSION BETWEEN GOVERNMENT AND SENATE

The Agricultural Produce (Cereals) Bill—Points of constitutional interest—A spate of legislation—Difficulty of revision—Cordial relations with Ministers—The Damage to Property (Compensation) Bill—Senator O'Farrell's sardonic comment—Resistance to pay-cut of Civic Guards—Bills rejected—The Local Government (Dublin) Bill—The Local Government (Extension of Franchise) Bill—Object of these measures—Their ultimate enactment—Proposed reduction of the Senate's suspensory power to three months—Mr. De Valera on the Second Chamber—His real intentions—The Senate's attitude to the Bill—Senator Douglas's able speech—Request for a Joint Committee —The request ignored—The Bill sent up again—Its rejection—Failure to enact it—Mr. De Valera's reliance on the Draft Constitutions of 1922—His error exposed by Senator Douglas—The wireless account— Elections to casual vacancies—Duly authorized visitors to the Senate refused admission by order of the Minister for Defence—His explanation—Reference to Committee of Privileges—The Committee reports a breach of privilege—The Report approved by the Senate—Amendment of the Defence Forces Bill—The Senate's action misunderstood— Attack by the Minister for Defence—An embittered atmosphere—The Wearing of Uniform (Restriction) Bill before the Senate—Arguments of the Minister for Justice—Attitude of independent Senators—The constitutional aspect—Mr. De Valera's passionate speech—Admitted impossibility of a general election—The Senate rejects the Bill—Subsequent failure to take steps for its enactment—Mr. De Valera introduces a Bill to abolish the Senate.

Immediately after the reassembly of Parliament after the general election two Bills which had already been before the Senate were sent to it again under Article 38A of the Constitution. The first, which was the Constitution (Removal of Oath) Bill, has already been referred to in the previous chapter. The second was the Agricultural Produce (Cereals) Bill, and the manner in which it was dealt with raises points of some constitutional interest.

Under Article 38A a Bill received from the Dáil which the Senate had failed to pass might be sent to it again, if the Dáil so resolved, at the end of a suspensory period. This period was normally eighteen months, but if a general election intervened it terminated on the date of reassembly. When a Bill had been sent to the Senate a second time, that House had sixty days in which to pass it, with or without amendment. After the sixty days, the Dáil could pass an enactment resolution, deeming the Bill to have been passed by both Houses and accepting such of the Senate amendments, if any, as it saw fit. When Article 38A was inserted in the Constitution in 1928 it was recognized that cases might arise in which it could not be fairly applied; and so the Article further provided that nothing in the machinery prescribed should operate to restrict the right of the Dáil to send such a Bill to the Senate otherwise than under the Article; that is to say, to allow the Senate a normal time to consider and, if necessary, to amend it. Also, the sixty-day period might be extended by agreement between the two Houses.

The Agricultural Produce (Cereals) Bill was eminently such a case. It was a complicated measure which demanded careful study, and it was not contentious in the political sense. It was received from the Dáil on the 8th December 1932, and a week later it was given a Second Reading without a division, after an informed and constructive debate which had occupied three days. In order to facilitate the Government, the Senate agreed to shorten the Christmas recess by meeting on the 11th January for the Committee Stage, although the other House had adjourned till the 1st February. Then came the surprise dissolution of the 2nd January, and on the 1st March the Bill was again sent to the Senate under Article 38A, without any extension of the sixty-day period, which was thus due to expire on the 29th April.

The Senate gave due consideration to the Bill and returned it to the Dáil on the 29th March. It had inserted forty-four amendments, of which fifteen emanated from individual Senators and the remaining twenty-nine were Government amendments—mostly to remedy defects which had been discovered in the Bill after it had been passed by the Dáil. Instead of considering the amendments at once, the Dáil made an order setting them down for the 26th April, the fifty-seventh day of the sixty-day period. Even then they were not taken, the Minister for Agriculture stating that they would be considered on the 3rd May. This was contrary to the Constitution, as it was incumbent on the Dáil to deal with the amendments before the sixty-day period had expired. The mistake was rectified later the same evening and the amendments were finally taken at 7.30 p.m. on the 27th April, the fifty-eighth day. Obviously, it was then much too late for proper consideration to be given to the revision done by the Senate. The twenty-nine Government amendments were agreed to and all the others were rejected. A message was sent requesting the Senate's concurrence, and this reached the Senate on the fifty-ninth day. The sixtieth day was a Saturday. The Senate's power to touch the Bill had therefore expired before it could consider the message. Four days later (3rd May) the enactment resolution was passed by the Dáil, precisely as if the Bill were being placed on the Statute Book over the head of a dissenting Senate. After a short interval of six months an amending Bill had to be introduced.

The Senate sat right through the summer of 1933, and, from the legislative point of view, this year was the busiest ever experienced by the House. Immense trouble was taken with Government Bills, and, to give only one example, no fewer than fifty-nine amendments were inserted in the Road Traffic Bill, all of which were agreed to by the Dáil. The work of revision was of more than ordinary difficulty, partly because of the Government's legislative inexperience and partly because its industrial and (to some extent) its agricultural policy were of necessity a process of trial and error. The number of Senators who participated in this work was growing smaller, and the members of the Government party took virtually no part in it at all, except formally to move amendments at the request of Ministers. It was becoming increasingly obvious that Senators of the type elected by the Fianna Fáil Party were either unsuitable for the work of revision or unwilling to undertake it. The relations between Senators and those Ministers who visited the House frequently, such as Dr. Ryan and Mr. Lemass, were growing increasingly cordial, and members were often thanked for their co-operation and for the improvements which they effected in the measures submitted to them. The spirit of courtesy and mutual accommodation made itself felt in the debates, and, so far as these Ministers were concerned, the legislative machine worked just as smoothly in the Senate as it had done in the days of Mr. Cosgrave.

There was a minimum of obstruction, and, as in 1932, Bills were passed without amendment which hardly commended themselves to the majority. A typical example was the Damage to Property (Compensation) Bill, which compensated persons who had fought against the State in the Civil War and whose property had been damaged, the estimated cost to the taxpayer being £350,000. There was perhaps something to be said for this proposal if it really closed the account, but another point of view was possible, and it was expressed sardonically by Senator O'Farrell:

'I hope this is really the last of the Bills we shall have regarding the payment of compensation and pensions arising out of the Civil War and the preceding war. We have had practically in every case to pay pensions and compensation to everyone engaged on either side. Now we have to pay for the damage done by both sides. Undoubtedly the principle we have adopted is a rather assuring one for those who may desire a scrap in the future. We have committed ourselves to the principle of paying everybody who engages in any fight in this country. No matter whether he wins or loses he is bound to win in the long run, so far as finances and pensions are concerned.'[1]

In the case of Bills which were amended, the Senate for the most part did not insist on amendments with which the Dáil did not agree. In fact, the only amendment over which the Senate took a stand was one exempting the Civic Guard from the salary reductions imposed by the Public Services (Temporary Economies) Bill. The amount involved was £35,000, and, unfortunately for the Government, the message conveying the Dáil's disagreement came before the Senate in the month of August, shortly after ex-members of the Irish Republican Army had been recruited into the Civic Guard and provided with arms. The debate centred on this new development, and Senator O'Rourke said: 'I voted for the cut in the pay of the Civic Guards as well as the cuts in the pay of the other services. Since then the Government have felt it necessary to spend £80,000 or £100,000 on the Broy Harriers. If they can afford to spend £80,000 or £100,000 on the Broy Harriers, the £30,000 which they are going to save by the cut in the pay of the Guards is very little, and I cannot see my way now to support that cut.'[2] The Senate insisted on the amendment, despite a warning from the Minister for Finance that the result would be the suspension of the Bill and the loss of all the proposed economies, totalling more than a quarter of a million sterling. Later, however, he changed his mind and recommended the Dáil to agree

[1] *Senate Debates*, xvii, 639.   [2] Ibid., xvii, 858.

to the amendment.[1] Had he not done so, the Labour Party would have revolted, and the Government would have been faced with almost certain defeat.

It is unfortunate, but inevitable, that the immensely valuable work of revision performed by an efficient Second Chamber attracts little attention, whereas its occasional clashes with the Government and the other House provoke wide public controversy. We are now about to consider the three Bills rejected or suspended by the Senate before the introduction of the Bill for its own abolition. The first two are, in a sense, complementary to each other and may be considered together. Both are concerned with the sphere of local government.

Early in 1924, under the Cosgrave Administration, the Dublin Corporation had been dissolved by Sealed Order of the Minister for Local Government, and from the 20th May 1924 to the 13th October 1930 the municipality was governed efficiently and well by three paid commissioners. It was never intended that this system should be permanent, and by the comprehensive Local Government (Dublin) Act, passed in 1930, the administrative area of the city was greatly extended and its government was placed under a city council in conjunction with a city manager, to whom were accorded wide powers. The council was to consist of thirty-five members, of whom thirty were to be elected by the ratepayers on the ordinary local government register and the remaining five were to be elected on a special franchise of property owners.

Under the British régime the County Councils and other local bodies, and in particular the Dublin Corporation, had provided a forum for the discussion of political questions, often to the detriment of the business for which these bodies had been created. With a native parliament now existing in the country, the Cosgrave party set its face against this custom and refused to contest the local elections, holding that the best men ought to be chosen for purely local work, irrespective of their political affiliations, if any. Mr. De Valera's party, however, took a different view and contested these elections, with the result that the Cosgrave party was forced to follow suit.

Fianna Fáil could hardly hope ever to capture the Dublin City Council while the five commercial members existed, especially if the electorate for the remaining thirty members was restricted to those who paid rates. Neither could they expect much success in the contests for the County Councils and other local bodies if the elections were left solely to the ratepayers, most of whom were large farmers

---

[1] *Dáil Debates*, xlix, 1952–54.

serving in the front trenches of the economic war. Accordingly, two Bills were introduced in the Dáil at about the same time, the Local Government (Dublin) Bill on the 26th April 1933 and the Local Government (Extension of Franchise) Bill on the following 10th May. The first purported to abolish the commercial register for the Dublin City Council, while retaining the total membership of the Council at thirty-five. The second extended the local government franchise to all persons over twenty-one years of age, irrespective of whether they were ratepayers or not. These two Bills were passed through the Dáil by the Government-Labour majority and sent to the Senate.

The Local Government (Dublin) Bill came before the Senate for Second Reading on the 14th June. The Minister for Local Government (Mr. O'Kelly) described the commercial register as 'class legislation of the worst kind' and stated that he saw 'nothing wrong in politics in local affairs'. The Senate did not agree, and rejected the Bill by 27 votes to 16.[1]

The same Minister was in charge of the Local Government (Extension of Franchise) Bill when it was discussed on the 12th July. The proposal was, of course, a revolutionary one, and the arguments for and against it need not be detailed here. Mr. O'Kelly admitted that the Government had no mandate for it, but he said that 'the Government of the day always has a mandate for any measure that it thinks will serve the country's interest'. The question of politics being raised again, he exclaimed, 'Politics means public affairs, and surely to God a local authority is entitled to discuss public affairs!' The Senate rejected the Bill by 25 votes to 13.[2]

The suspensory period of eighteen months expired in the case of the first Bill on the 6th December 1934, and in the case of the second Bill on the 27th December. By this time the political complexion of the Senate had materially altered in favour of the Government, and on the following 27th February both Bills were again sent up under Article 38A of the Constitution. Both were finally passed, without much debate, on the 28th March.

The third Bill which the Senate declined to pass was the Constitution (Amendment No. 19) Bill, the purpose of which was to curtail the Senate's power of delay from eighteen months to three months. This proposal can have had no connection with the rejection of the two Local Government Bills, as it was introduced on the 7th June 1933, before either of them had reached the Senate. It was presu-

[1] *Senate Debates*, xvi, 1770–1810.   [2] Ibid., xvii, 114–90.

mably a consequence of the Senate's refusal to pass the Removal of Oath Bill without prior negotiation with the British Government. Mr. De Valera had, of course, no mandate for thus hamstringing the Second Chamber, but it might have been supposed that it represented his considered policy regarding the Senate and that he had abandoned any intention which he might have had of abolishing it altogether. He made it clear, however, that this was not so, stating in his Second Reading speech that the Government intended to bring in proposals 'to end the present Senate, at any rate'. What had caused delay was the question whether they should substitute another for it. The Senate as at present constituted was not worth the money. It did not perform 'any function which could not as well be performed by a Committee' of the Dáil. He thought it absurd to have a Second Chamber which was 'a mere reflex' of the Dáil. If they were compelled to take action quickly, they would have to bring in a Bill for simple abolition.[1] We have seen that, in the Joint Committee of 1928, Mr. De Valera had done his best to make the Senate a still more accurate reflex of the other House by proposing that it should be elected directly by the Dáil, and that he confessed in 1934 that he had done so because he 'wanted to get the people to see clearly that in practice it was going to result in a Chamber practically of the same character as here, that it was going to be merely a duplication'. His purpose having been thus partially effected, he now contemplated the abolition of the Senate because, according to him, it served 'no really useful purpose'.

Mr. MacDermot, on behalf of the Opposition, moved a motion declining to give the Bill a Second Reading 'pending disclosure of the Government's final proposals regarding the future of the Senate'. This was defeated by the Government's mechanical majority and the Second Reading was passed. Replying to the debate, Mr. De Valera gave some hint of his real intentions. With nearly five years of power in front of him, he now said that, in his opinion, the Constitution was not 'in anything like the form it will finally be in'. A time might come, 'not very far from now, when it would be advisable to have in a wider way consideration of this so-called fundamental law.'[2] Though he did not say so, it is obvious that the changes which he contemplated in the 'so-called fundamental law' could not be effected unless the Senate were first abolished, or at the least had its power of delay reduced practically to vanishing point.

The Bill was passed by the Dáil on the 28th June and came before

[1] *Dáil Debates*, xlviii, 783, 784.   [2] Ibid., xlviii, 811.

the Senate on the 11th July, when Senator Counihan moved that the Second Reading be postponed pending the setting up of a Joint Committee of both Houses to consider the constitution and powers of the Second Chamber. The most important contribution to the debate was made by Senator Douglas. In a clear and logical speech, which eschewed rhetoric and was replete with facts, he gave chapter and verse for the misrepresentations made by Mr. De Valera in regard to the Senate and refuted them by statistics. He showed that the proposed delay of only three months was farcical, and, also by means of facts, that the considered opinion of the civilized world was in favour of bicameral legislatures. At the same time, he welcomed the proposal to set up a Joint Committee.[1] Other notable speeches followed on the same side, in particular from the Vice-Chairman (Senator O'Hanlon) and Senator O'Farrell; and the Minister for Justice, who deputized for Mr. De Valera, was not in a position to make a convincing reply. The Second Stage was postponed by 30 votes to 7, and the following resolution was then passed and incorporated in a message to the Dáil:

'That it is expedient that a Joint Committee consisting of five members of the Senate and five members of the Dáil, with the Chairman of each House *ex officio*, be set up to consider and report on the changes, if any, necessary in the constitution and powers of the Senate.'[2]

The wording of this entirely reasonable proposal was almost the same as that which had resulted in the Joint Committee of 1928; it was, however, ignored by the Government. The fact may seem incredible to those accustomed to the normal courtesies of procedure between two Houses of Parliament, but this message was printed on every Order Paper of the Dáil for almost two years. If Mr. De Valera had allowed it to be debated, and if he really was anxious for suggestions to make the Senate, in his opinion, 'worth the money', he might have found it difficult to give reasons why the proposal for a Joint Committee should not be acceded to. The suspensory period of eighteen months expired on the 27th December. Meantime, the Bill to abolish the Senate had been passed by the Dáil and rejected by the Senate.

The 27th December came and went, but Mr. De Valera made no move, and it was generally assumed that, as the Senate was shortly

---

[1] This speech, and another by Senator Douglas on the Senate Abolition Bill, were subsequently published as a pamphlet, *President De Valera and the Senate* (Eason & Sons, Dublin, 1934).

[2] *Senate Debates*, xvii, 3–112.

to be abolished in any case, he did not propose to trouble further about cutting down its power of delay to three months. Then, on the 11th April 1935, he proposed a motion in the Dáil for the purpose of sending the Bill a second time to the Senate under Article 38A of the Constitution, giving as his reason that, even if the Senate remained in existence for only a short time, the Government desired its power of delay to be restricted.[1] If that were so, it seems extremely odd that the Government had held its hand for nearly four months after the suspensory period had expired. But what was to follow was still more curious. The Bill was again considered by the Senate on the 1st May 1935; Mr. De Valera did not attend, and Senator Connolly, who took charge of the Bill in his absence, described the Senate as, among other things, 'a hand-picked, self-elected body'. The Bill was rejected by 21 votes to 20.[2] Under the Constitution, the Senate had now only sixty days within which to consider the Bill, and this period terminated on the 10th June 1935. Accordingly, at any time on or after the 11th June the Bill could have been placed on the Statute Book by the mere passage of an enactment resolution by the Dáil. But Mr. De Valera must have changed his mind again. No such resolution was proposed, and the Bill never became law.

One further matter falls to be dealt with before we leave the subject of this Bill. In his Second Reading speech in the Dáil Mr. De Valera referred to the three unpublished Draft Constitutions submitted by the Constitution Committee in 1922. He said that two of the Drafts proposed a suspensory period of 180 days for the Second Chamber, and the third a period of four months. 'In the Constitution as passed by the Dáil a period of 270 days was allowed but that was in conjunction with a referendum.'[3] When replying to the debate, he returned to the matter again. 'I ask the House to think of that and to weigh its value, that we had three Committees set up originally as Committees of experts, that had no immediate political axe to grind, that were given this task of considering what should be the Constitution . . . of the State here, and that these Committees suggested a period which is, practically, the period provided for here in this Bill.'[4] Its value was duly weighed in the Senate and found to be nil. Mr. Ruttledge, the Minister for Justice, repeated in substance what had been said by Mr. De Valera in the Dáil, but Senator Douglas gave the facts. He had been a member of the Constitution Committee and possessed copies of the three Drafts. In so far as Mr. De Valera

[1] *Dáil Debates*, lv, 2424–34.   [2] *Senate Debates*, xix, 1741–82.
[3] *Dáil Debates*, xlviii, 781.   [4] Ibid., xlviii, 807.

had implied that the delay of 180 days proposed in the first two Drafts was not in conjunction with a referendum, his statement was incorrect. These two Drafts also recommended that the Senate should be given power, after a Bill had been passed or deemed to have been passed, to suspend it for a further period of 90 days, during which it was to be submitted to a referendum. In regard to the third Draft, Mr. De Valera's statement was at complete variance with the facts. The relative provisions (of which the text has already been given in Chapter III) were quoted by Senator Douglas, and it was obvious that they would, if adopted, have conferred enormous power on the Second Chamber. What they amounted to was this: all Bills passed by the Dáil were to be submitted to the Senate for its approval. If within one month it did not express disapproval, it was to be taken to have approved. If it amended or rejected a Bill (other than a Money Bill), the Dáil was given three months within which to agree with the Senate; in the absence of agreement, the Dáil would either have to drop the Bill or else submit it to a referendum. As Senator Douglas pointed out, this proposal would have placed the Senate in a dominating position in regard to all legislation except finance. The Minister for Justice, replying to the debate, admitted that what Senator Douglas had stated was correct.[1]

On the same evening, in the News Bulletin radioed from the Dublin Broadcasting Station, the proceedings in the Senate were referred to, and the statement was made that there were three Reports from the Constitution Committee, two of which recommended six months' delay and the remaining one four months. There was no comment, except to say that the Constitution provided for nine months and that a period of three months was now proposed. Senator Douglas's detailed refutation, and the Minister's acceptance of it, were not referred to. On the following day Senator Douglas raised the matter in the House as a question of privilege. The Broadcasting Service is a branch of the Department of Posts and Telegraphs, and, on the direction of the Chairman, a letter was addressed to the responsible Minister, in which the facts were recited and a request made that a correction should be broadcast as early as possible. The correction, however, was never made, the Minister expressing the view that it 'would create a precedent which he would like to avoid, and which might involve the staff of the Broadcasting Station in future difficulties.' The correspondence was read to the House and published in the *Debates*.[2]

[1] *Senate Debates*, xvii, 21, 22, 80.　　　[2] Ibid., xvii, 289–91.

There were three by-elections during the period January 1933 to March 1934, caused respectively by the election of Senator O'Doherty (Fianna Fáil) to be a member of the Dáil in 1933 and by the deaths of Senators the Countess of Desart (Independent Group) and Séamas Ryan (Fianna Fáil). Their places were filled by three ex-members of the Dáil—Messrs. E. J. Duggan, Ernest Blythe, and R. Keyes. Mr. Duggan was a signatory of the Treaty of 1921, but had not been a prominent figure of late years in the Dáil. He had sat continuously till the dissolution of 1933, when he did not offer himself for re-election. Mr. Blythe was, of course, the former Vice-President and Minister for Finance; he had lost his seat at the 1933 general election. Mr. Keyes was a Fianna Fáil back-bencher who had been defeated at the same election. Whether the men so elected were eminent or not, they could hardly fail to import into the Senate something of the political atmosphere of the other House; and, if the Senate were to survive, one could not but view with dismay the growing habit of electing to the Second Chamber persons who had been recently rejected at the polls.

Early in 1934 the Government's hostility to the League of Youth involved it in a serious clash with the Senate, and the details of the account which follows are all taken from the published records of the House. On the 13th February Senator Miss Browne, who was a member of that organization, wrote to the Clerk of the Senate intimating that, at the next meeting of the House, she desired to introduce to the Visitors' Gallery two other members, who would be wearing the uniform of the blue shirt, and requesting the Chairman's approval. Whatever the Chairman's private opinion of the League of Youth may have been, there was no good reason for withholding permission. The courts had decided that the wearing of a blue uniform shirt was legal, and members of both Houses habitually wore it. The Chairman accordingly signified his consent, and the requisite admission tickets were issued for the meeting of the 21st February.

Miss Browne's request had brought to light the fact that for some months previously visitors to the Parliament Buildings who were so attired had been stopped at the entrance gates by the ushers. This action was taken pursuant to an instruction issued to the Superintendent by the Chairman of the Dáil at the request of the Minister for Defence. The Superintendent is an official roughly equivalent to the Sergeant-at-Arms at Westminster, except that he is responsible to both Houses. The Chairman of the Senate was not consulted regarding the instruction, which was, of course, *ultra vires* so far as the

Senate was concerned. No clash had, however, occurred, as no visitors so attired had sought admission to the Senate.

As a matter of courtesy, the Chairman of the Senate wrote to the Chairman of the Dáil to inform him that he had given instructions for the admission of the visitors. On the day of the Senate meeting the Superintendent informed the Clerk of the Dáil, in the presence of the Chairman of the Dáil, that he felt bound to obey the instructions of the Chairman of the Senate. The Clerk of the Dáil stated that the military guard would stop the visitors in any case, in pursuance of orders alleged to have been given to them by the Minister for Defence as long ago as the previous July. The Superintendent replied that, so far as he knew, the military had no such orders. The Clerk of the Dáil thereupon requested him to verify this, and, if the orders did not exist, to acquaint the Minister for Defence of all the facts. The Chairman of the Dáil concurred. The Superintendent carried out his instructions, as a result of which an order was issued by the Minister for Defence to the military guard that persons wearing blue shirts were not to be admitted to the Parliament Building. A few hours later, pursuant to this new order, the military guard refused admission to Miss Browne's two duly authorized visitors, and they went away quietly.

When the Senate met the same afternoon, the matter was raised on a question of privilege, and the Chairman deferred consideration of it pending the attendance of the Minister for Defence. The Minister did not, however, attend, but sent a communication to the Chairman which was read to the House and which the Committee of Privileges later decided was misleading. The Chairman ruled that, *prima facie*, a breach of privilege had been committed, and the appropriate motion for reference to the Committee of Privileges was set down for that day week (28th February).[1]

The Minister for Defence then attended and read to the House a typed statement, admittedly prepared after he had consulted his files. In the course of this he said:

'On 20th July 1933 it came to my knowledge that certain persons intended to seek admission to Leinster House wearing the uniform of an organization known at that time as the Army Comrades Association. I consulted the Ceann Comhairle [Chairman of the Dáil] about the matter, and afterwards, with his consent, gave instructions to the military that persons dressed in the uniform of the organization to which I have referred (other than members of the

---

[1] *Senate Debates*, xviii, 408, 409, 450–6.

Oireachtas) were to be refused admittance to Leinster House. I advised the Ceann Comhairle and the Superintendent of the Oireachtas Staff that I had issued these instructions. . . .

'Without consulting or advising me, he [the Chairman of the Senate] directed tickets to be issued, knowing they were to be used by persons wearing uniforms and whom the military guard would certainly stop at the gates unless I cancelled their previous instructions.'[1]

The motion for reference to the Committee of Privileges was passed, and on the 9th May 1934 it produced an extremely important Report, to which is appended a verbatim copy of the evidence given before the Committee by the Minister for Defence, the Superintendent (Colonel Brennan), and Senator Miss Browne.[2] The Report cites the Minister's statement quoted above, and comments on it as follows:

'The Minister, when he made these statements, must have known (1) that he did not give instructions to the military in July 1933 that persons wearing the uniform of the Army Comrades Association were to be refused admittance to Leinster House; (2) that he did not inform the Superintendent of the Oireachtas that he had issued these instructions; and (3) that the persons in respect of whom the tickets were issued by the Cathaoirleach would have been admitted but for the fact that the Minister himself, on the day on which the visitors presented themselves for admission, caused orders to be issued to the military for the first time that persons wearing blue uniform shirts were not to be admitted.

'If the House, acting on the statement read by the Minister, had considered it unnecessary to proceed with the motion for reference to the Committee on Procedure and Privileges, the actual fact, namely, that the only order of the kind given to the military guard was the order given to them about 1 p.m. on the 21st February, might not have been ascertained.'

The Report summarized the whole facts as disclosed by the evidence, and found that a breach of privilege had been committed by the Minister for Defence and by the Clerk of the Dáil. While the Committee was in session the Labour representative (Senator Johnson) had differences with the Chairman on points of procedure and resigned from the Committee. Before the Report was finally adopted, Senator Mrs. Wyse Power (Fianna Fáil) withdrew; and the only

---

[1] *Senate Debates*, xviii, 458, 460.
[2] *Reports of Committees*, vol. iv, pp. 385–428.

other member of the Government Party (Colonel Moore) was absent. The Report was adopted unanimously by the remaining members of the Committee present, the sole absentee being Senator Brown, who was abroad at the time. It was subsequently approved by the Senate, a Government party amendment to refer it back to the Committee being defeated, after an unedifying debate, by 24 votes to 12.[1] The whole episode was the most disagreeable that had ever occurred in the Senate.

Unhappily, shortly after the breach of privilege had been committed the Senate became still further embroiled with the Government, and in particular with the Minister for Defence. We have seen that ex-members of the Irish Republican Army, who had fought against the State, had been recruited into the police force. A new Volunteer Force now began to be formed as a branch of the Army, and its grey-green uniform was said to be based on that worn by Roger Casement's Irish Brigade, recruited in Germany from Irish prisoners during the Great War. Commissions in this new Force were given to other ex-members of the Irish Republican Army, and this action had given rise to considerable debate in the Dáil. On the 14th March 1934 the Defence Forces (Temporary Provisions) Bill came before the Senate for Second Reading. This was the annual Army Bill and it was necessary for it to become law by the 31st March. The existing Act was due to expire on that date, and the Bill purported to continue it for another year. The discussion centred on the method of recruitment for the new Volunteer Force, and in particular on the commissioning of the ex-members of the Irish Republican Army. Senator Blythe tabled amendments to the effect that no person should be appointed to commissioned rank unless he had had two years' training at the Irish Military College or else five years' service in the Army and one year's training at the Military College. The amendments were rightly ruled out of order by the Chairman, since no amendment may be moved to a Bill which is purely a Continuance Bill except one to extend or curtail the period for which the Principal Act is to be continued. The Principal Act was due to expire on the 31st March and the ruling was given on the 20th March; in view of the fact that the Chairman's decision had to be made without delay, he stated that he did not propose to treat his ruling as a precedent.

Senator Blythe thereupon moved an amendment limiting the operation of the Bill to the 31st July 1934 instead of to the 31st March

[1] *Senate Debates*, xviii, 1562–1628.

1935, which was the date in the Bill as passed by the Dáil. The debate on this amendment reflected the general uneasiness at the possibility of the creation of a partisan Volunteer Force and the progressive republicanization of the Forces. It cannot be said that such uneasiness was entirely groundless, and Senator Blythe's object was to gain time to consider whether the amendments which had been disallowed could, by some means, be brought before the House. The amendment was carried by 27 votes to 18, the Cosgrave party and the Independent Group combining against the Government and Labour; and the Bill was returned to the Dáil on the 20th March.[1]

It seems extremely doubtful whether the action taken by the Senate in this instance was dictated by counsels of wisdom. Whatever might be the Government's intentions in regard to the Volunteer Force, Senators could do nothing to influence its policy in the matter. It is true that all the Senate had done was to extend the duration of the Defence Forces Act by four months instead of a year, and that the only inconvenience to which the Government had been put was the necessity of introducing another short Continuance Bill and of having it passed into law before the 31st July. But previous experience had made it not unlikely that the action of the Second Chamber would be misunderstood. Five days later, at Mullingar, Mr. James Geoghegan, K.C., the former Minister for Justice (now the Hon. Mr. Justice Geoghegan, of the Supreme Court) informed his audience that the Senate 'had so mutilated the Army Bill as possibly to lead to a chaotic state of affairs if there was not a strong man at the helm of the State'.[2]

On the 21st March the Bill came before the Dáil for the consideration of the Senate's amendment, and, as the Principal Act was due to expire at the end of the month, the Minister for Defence was obliged to recommend its acceptance. In doing so, he made an attack on the Senate: 'This action on the part of the Senate is part of the obstructive tactics which have been used by elements here and in England to obstruct and sabotage the efforts of this Government to maintain and defend the rights of the people.' A fortnight previously, the Minister had been examined for a prolonged period by the Senate Committee of Privileges with reference to his Exclusion Order; and Mr. Dillon, rebuking him for what he termed his 'scurrilous attack', alleged that his 'splenetic attitude' was due to this fact.[3]

It was in this embittered atmosphere, and on the very day on which

[1] *Senate Debates*, xviii, 678–716.   [2] *Irish Independent*, 26 March 1934.
[3] *Dáil Debates*, li, 1337–42.

these speeches were delivered, that the Wearing of Uniform (Restriction) Bill came before the Senate on Second Reading. The Minister for Justice, who opened the debate, made the best of his case. He referred to laws and decrees in Belgium, Latvia, Switzerland, and the Saar Territory forbidding the wearing of political uniforms, but such references were valueless in the absence of accurate information concerning the internal situation in these countries. He quoted police reports to the effect that the presence of blue shirts at meetings was 'a source of irritation to the majority of the people'. So far as the Irish Republican Army was concerned, the Bill would deal with them or anybody else wearing uniform. The question of the amount of self-defence that is justifiable was a very dangerous one to leave in the hands of undisciplined people. The Bill was a measure that any political party should be willing to accept.

There were thus gaps in the Minister's brief. No allegation was made that the League of Youth was an armed organization, and no single instance was cited of an act of illegality committed by one of its members. When Mr. Cosgrave had introduced his Bill to set up the Military Tribunal in 1931, he had justified it by reading out a long list of outrages and murders. A similar list could have been read by the Minister for Justice, but it would not have justified his Bill, as the members of the League of Youth were the victims and not the perpetrators. The perpetrators, so far as they consisted of members of the Irish Republican Army, were to be dealt with, provided they got into uniform.

There can be no doubt that many sober-minded people were none too happy about the way in which the Blue Shirt movement seemed to be developing under General O'Duffy's leadership; but they could not close their eyes to the fact that there existed in the country a secret, heavily armed force which wore no uniform and which the Government had apparently no intention of suppressing. Interest in the Senate centred chiefly in the attitude of the Independents and the Independent Group, since the United Ireland Party would naturally vote against a Bill which proposed to outlaw its Youth Movement. One by one, those who were bound by no party ties gave their opinion on the Government's proposals. Senator Bagwell pointed out that all the time the Fianna Fáil Party had been in power they had never proclaimed the Irish Republican Army, never effectively interfered with it, and never seriously criticized it. He deduced that this army was, in effect, an ancillary association to Fianna Fáil and that the Bill was a thinly disguised attempt to suppress all effective criticism by the party in opposition. Senator Douglas stated that the Blue Shirts were unarmed and loyal not only to the State but to the principle of democratic government, and challenged anyone to deny that the Bill was an absolutely unjustifiable interference with liberty. General Sir William Hickie was of the opinion that the Bill was not a genuine attempt to suppress all private armies, and so proposed to vote against it. Senator Sir John Keane described the measure as unprecedented legislation which would bring a political party under proscription by Act of Parliament.

In the absence abroad of Senator Brown, the constitutional aspect was not touched upon; but if the Bill had ever reached the Statute Book it would probably have been challenged in the courts and might have been declared invalid. One reason has already been mentioned in the preceding chapter. Persons charged with offences under the Bill were to be tried by District Justices, and the right of appeal was taken away. But Article 64 of the Constitution invested the High Court 'with full original jurisdiction in and power to determine all matters and questions, whether of law or fact, civil or criminal'. Again, Article 9 guaranteed 'the right of free expression of opinion as well as the right to assemble peaceably and without arms and to form associations or unions for purposes not opposed to public morality'. The Bill proposed to take away these rights, and so it seemingly infringed the Constitution.

The debate proceeded for many hours, and Mr. De Valera, who had been listening to it, must soon have realized that he had no hope whatever of carrying his Bill. It was after ten o'clock when he rose to reply. His voice was vibrant with anger, and he thumped the table to emphasize his points.

In the course of this excited speech he affirmed that the changes effected in the constitution of the Blue Shirt movement were 'changes by which they might be able to advance more easily under the shelter of law and order'; and he made the following remarkable statement: 'To-morrow if we wanted to do it we would get ten shirts to your one in the country. There is not the slightest doubt about that. There will be, if necessary, a special force established to protect the country and preserve public order, under the control of the popularly elected Government of the Irish people.' What exactly he meant by this it is difficult to say, but, in view of the recruitment of ex-members of the Irish Republican Army into the Army and the Police, it sounded significant enough.

Senator Sir John Keane had said that a Bill such as this should not be passed into law without an appeal to the people at a general election. Mr. De Valera's reply was: 'Go to the country in an atmosphere like this! I will tell the Senator why not. Because if we did we would not be able to maintain order at the present time.' This was perfectly true, but it was a terrible condemnation of his Administration. His concluding words were: 'We put on you definitely the responsibility for depriving us, the elected representatives of the people, of the powers which we deem necessary to preserve public order on the one hand and the public safety on the other.'

The division was then taken, and the Bill was rejected by 30 votes to 18. The majority was made up of twenty-one members of the United Ireland Party, five members of the Independent Group, and four Independents; and the minority of twelve members of the Government party, four Labour members, and two Independents.[1]

The subsequent history of the Bill is interesting—or rather its lack of history. The suspensory period of eighteen months expired on the 13th September 1935, but the Government made no move to bring the Bill into operation. On the 19th February 1936, in the Dáil, Mr. MacDermot asked the Minister for Justice whether he intended to proceed any further with the Bill. The Minister's reply was, 'The answer is in the affirmative.'[2] It is difficult to understand why he should have given this answer, for the Bill was not sent a second time to the Senate, and it never became law.

The day after the rejection of the Bill (22nd March 1934) Mr. De Valera introduced in the Dáil a Bill to abolish the Senate.

---

[1] *Senate Debates*, xviii, 749–876.   [2] *Dáil Debates*, lx, 781.

CHAPTER XXI

THE BILL TO ABOLISH THE SENATE

Mr. De Valera's object—The Agreement with the Southern Unionists —Suggestion of a general amendment of the Constitution—Possibility of a new Constitution—Effect of the Senate Abolition Bill—Absence of safeguards—The judges and the Auditor-General—Mr. De Valera's general attitude to Second Chambers—His explanation of his mandate —Refusal of a Joint Committee—His case for the Bill—The onus placed on his opponents—The argument from experience of the existing Senate—Its alleged subservience to Mr. Cosgrave and opposition to Mr. De Valera—The argument from political theory—Methods of constituting Second Chambers impracticable or dangerous—The argument from history—Bicameralism an historical accident—Attack on Second Chambers of the United Kingdom, Canada, France—The United States—The Norwegian system—Examples from history— Attack on England—The Bill in the Senate—Mr. De Valera's brief opening—Guarantee of safeguards—The Chairman's speech—Instances of misrepresentation—The argument from history refuted—France— The United States—Citation of authoritative opinions—Detailed review of Senate's work of revision—Its exercise of the suspensory power —Comparison with Senates of Canada and South Africa—Allegation of partiality refuted by facts—Errors in the text of the Bill—Counsel's Opinion—Defence of the Independent Group—Peroration—Mr. De Valera leaves the Senate—Senator Douglas's speech—Mr. De Valera's use of J. S. Mill examined—The Norwegian system misunderstood— Omissions in regard to France—Other speeches—Mr. De Valera's reply to the debate—History jettisoned—His further reliance on J. S. Mill— His attack on the Chairman—His error in regard to the Draft Constitutions of 1922—The Senate rejects the Bill.

Viewed in retrospect, Mr. De Valera's proposal to abolish the Senate is much easier to discuss than at the time it was made. His personal ascendancy over his party, both inside and outside the Dáil, was an admitted fact; and it was alleged by his political opponents that his real object was to establish himself as a dictator behind the façade of single-chamber parliamentary government. As the world now knows, he used the single chamber, without any mandate from the people, successively to abolish the Governor-General, to take the King out of the Constitution, and finally to repeal the Constitution altogether, a new Draft being passed by the single chamber and submitted to the people for acceptance or rejection at a plebiscite held on the same day as a general election. All Mr. De Valera's prejudices against the bicameral system had by that time been overcome, and the new model provided for a Second House.

If these proposals had presented themselves to his mind as a completed plan at the time the Senate Abolition Bill was before Parliament, he did not disclose it to the Dáil. But certain statements which he then made have acquired a new significance in the light of subsequent events. It will be recalled that, when Mr. Cosgrave introduced the Constitution Bill into the Constituent Assembly in 1922 he divided it into three parts. First, there were the Articles which implemented the Treaty. The Government made these a matter of confidence; the Assembly could reject or amend them, but in such a case it would have to find a fresh government. Second, there were the Articles inserted as a result of agreement with the Southern Unionists. The Government's attitude towards these was the same. Third, there were all the remaining Articles, in regard to which the Constituent Assembly would have a free hand. The agreement with the Southern Unionists comprised (1) proportional representation in the elections for the Dáil; (2) a Second Chamber with specified powers and personnel; (3) university representation—in the Senate as originally agreed, but later transferred by consent to the Dáil. At the time the Senate Abolition Bill was going through, two other Bills, which will be referred to later (Chapter XXIV), were also before Parliament. One of these proposed to abolish university representation, and the other recast the electoral areas in such a way as to render proportional representation of little value to minorities.

When these three Bills became law there would not be much left of the agreement with the Southern Unionists. Referring to the other two classes of Articles, Mr. De Valera now said: 'This Constitution was framed originally under exceptional circumstances. There were certain Articles in the Constitution which were forced upon the people of this country. There are certain Articles which represent democratic ideals. Those that represent these ideals, in so far as a thorough examination by people who have had experience of administration goes, are consistent with practical government. These Articles ought, with all possible speed, be examined, and be made as lasting as it is possible for anything to be made lasting, in a constitutional way, without the danger of a cast-iron Constitution which, as I said, is always a temptation to revolution.' (17th May 1934.)[1]

He returned to this subject a few days later: 'If we agree in this House that a selected number of Articles guaranteeing fundamental rights are to be preserved, if we decide, for their preservation, that they cannot, for example, be changed by the Dáil except by a specified majority or on approval by the people by way of Referendum, I believe that an alteration of the Constitution embodying that will be effective. . . .

'To meet the views of those who fear that either this Dáil or a subsequent Dáil might ignore these fundamental rights in the Constitution, I propose at a later stage, when this examination shall have been completed, to indicate certain Articles and bring them in in a special measure with safeguards by which they cannot be changed by a simple majority. It will be for the Dáil to decide whether or not that course is wise and necessary. Personally, I should like to see that done, and the Government will have no objection whatever to having it done. Probably in the general interests of the country it would be a wise course.

'I would resist strongly the other Articles of the Constitution being made difficult to change, and I would resist it for the same reason that I would resist any attempt to make the present position, which we regard as a forced position, permanent.' (25th May 1934.)[2]

This proposal, which was definite, was never carried out, but the possibility of a totally new Constitution was vaguely adumbrated: 'From a legal point of view, in so far as I can presume to understand the matter, I do not know where a Constituent Assembly derives its authority from except directly from the people. If, for instance, we wanted in a short period to get this Constitution revised and a new Constitution secured, the natural way of doing it would be to get an Assembly for that purpose elected directly by the people. It is clear that the Parliament of the time would arrange for the type of Assembly and how it was to be elected.' (17th May 1934.)[3] This is, of course, a perfectly correct statement of the position from the point

[1] *Dáil Debates*, lii, 1249.   [2] Ibid., lii, 1877–8.   [3] Ibid., lii, 1219.

of view of constitutional law. But when the time was ripe Mr. De Valera did not adopt 'the natural way'.

It is in the light of these statements, made at the time, that we begin our examination of the Bill to abolish the Senate. First, it is essential to see what precisely the Bill proposed to do. It did not set up a unicameral system in the sense in which that term is usually understood, that is to say, with the safeguards against legislative tyranny which ordinarily surround such a system. It merely deleted the references to the Senate, with the result that a Constitution designed for two Houses was to have one only. This perfunctory, rule-of-thumb method is explicable by the haste in which the measure was drafted. Mr. De Valera left the Senate at 11 p.m. on the 21st March, obviously determined to abolish the Second Chamber, following its rejection of his Blue Shirt Bill. The Senate Abolition Bill was introduced in the Dáil next day, but it did not appear on the printed Order Paper, and it evidently was not ready at the usual time for the introduction of Bills, which is immediately after Questions, shortly after three o'clock. It was not, in fact, brought in by Mr. De Valera until three hours later. This precipitancy had some strange results, not the least of which was that Mr. De Valera did not entirely succeed in removing all references to the Senate from the Constitution.

On several occasions while the Bill was before the Dáil Mr. De Valera indicated that safeguards of a kind would be provided. He did not anticipate that the Senate would vote for its own demise, and the proper time to consider these was while the eighteen months' suspensory period was running. The Dáil Standing Orders could be amended so as to allow of a further careful revision of Bills after the Report Stage and before the Final Reading.[1] If these proposals had been carried out, a check would have been imposed on hasty legislation and time would have been allowed for public opinion to express itself. No action of the kind, however, was taken, and the only safeguards provided were inserted by the Government in the Bill itself, under pressure from the Opposition. These affected the Comptroller and Auditor-General and the members of the Judiciary who, under the Constitution, could be removed from office only by resolutions passed by both Houses, for stated misbehaviour or incapacity. After the disappearance of the Senate, any of them could be dismissed by a resolution passed by a bare majority of the Dáil. Two amendments provided that this majority would have to be four-sevenths of the total membership of the Dáil, exclusive of the Chairman. Mr. De Valera

---

[1] *Dáil Debates*, li, 2285, 2320, 2340; lii, 1812.

did not accept these two amendments with a good grace. He said they destroyed the symmetry of the Bill and made it unsightly.[1] Before they were passed he expressed the view that 'the best safeguard for the Judiciary is for it to establish itself soundly in the good repute of the people. There is no other way'.[2]

Virtually the whole burden of piloting the Bill through the Dáil was borne on Mr. De Valera's own shoulders. He told the House that he had given much thought to the question over a long period, and that nothing he had heard or read had changed his opinion.

'I read books on Second Chambers and their history and their value as a part of governmental machinery, and during all that time I did not hear a single good argument which would convince me that, if we were starting here a new Constitution, a Second Chamber was either necessary or fundamentally useful.

'However, I have more than once said here in the House that I believe I am a Conservative, and I thought that—as there were quite a number of Second Chambers in existence in various States—what was and what was working had something to recommend it. I kept an open mind during all these years, ready to hear from any source any suggestion as to how a Second Chamber that would be really useful might be constructed, and in all these years, with open ears and ready to receive any suggestion in an attitude favourable to the acceptance of such a suggestion, I have never been able to get, in anything I read or listened to, a suggestion that would satisfy me that it was worth while spending money on a Second Chamber.'[3]

We can now see that this was the only attitude which it was possible for Mr. De Valera to adopt if he was determined to have a period of single-chamber government for the purpose of introducing a new Constitution. He had two difficulties to surmount. The first was in connection with his mandate, based on the following pre-election declaration: 'We propose to abolish the Senate as at present constituted and, if it be decided to retain a Second Legislative Chamber, it is our intention to reduce considerably the number of its members.'

This declaration is, at best, somewhat obscure. If the intention was to set up a unicameral legislature, why should the proposal to abolish the Senate be qualified by the phrase, 'as at present constituted'? Further, who was to make the decision for or against retention of a Second Chamber? On the Second Reading, Mr, De Valera said that it was 'quite plain', but his paraphrase of it reminded one of Byron's line:

I wish he would explain his explanation.

[1] *Dáil Debates*, lii, 1866, 1867.   [2] Ibid., li, 2138.   [3] Ibid., li, 2109.

He said: 'It indicated that the present Chamber as at present constituted would, undoubtedly, go. It indicated further that if there was
to be a Second Chamber—and it left that question clearly one to be
determined, to be determined by this House, to be determined by the
Legislature and by the ordinary methods of determining it—it would
certainly be reduced in its numbers.'[1] Here again we have the phrase
'as at present constituted', and the Dáil is spoken of as the legislature.
Mr. De Valera's further reference to the matter on the Committee
stage did not clear up the obscurity. 'The principle of this Bill is to
have a one Chamber Legislature, to get rid of the Senate as at present
constituted. The intention at the present stage anyhow is to have a
one Chamber Legislature.'[2] The words 'as at present constituted'
make nonsense of the first sentence, but such passages as this served
to create a doubt as to Mr. De Valera's ultimate intentions.

This brings us to his second difficulty. He had repeatedly expressed
his willingness to consider with an open mind any workable scheme
for a Second Chamber. For nearly a year the Senate's request for a
Joint Committee on the subject had been appearing on the Dáil
Order Paper. A better method could hardly have been devised. The
most experienced men in both Houses could have been nominated to
the committee, which could have been empowered 'to send for
persons, papers and records', that is, to receive evidence from experts. The committee's labours would have been unhurried, their
findings would have commanded respect, and their report would
have provided a basis for peaceful constitutional change. But from
Mr. De Valera's point of view the proposal had the fatal defect that
there would have been no interval of single-chamber government.
When questioned by Mr. MacDermot on the point, he said that his
experience taught him that such a Joint Committee would consider
the question 'from a narrow political standpoint'. Such a committee
was not the right committee, as there ought to be other people on it.
If there was a question of determining finally the Constitution of the
country, he would strongly advocate the setting up of a commission.
Another member inquired 'Why not now?' and Mr. De Valera retorted, 'You have got a good long year, I expect, in which all these
things can be considered.'[3] He was alluding to the period for which
the Bill would be in suspension after its anticipated rejection by the
Senate; but, needless to say, nothing was done. If such a commission
had been set up shortly after the Senate had rejected the Bill on the
1st June 1934, its report would presumably have been available long

[1] *Dáil Debates*, li, 2110.   [2] Ibid., li, 2319.   [3] Ibid., li, 2140.

before the Senate was abolished on the 29th May 1936. It would then have been difficult to explain why a period of single-chamber government was necessary. Once the Senate had disappeared, no time was wasted. Eleven days later Mr. De Valera set up his Commission, which was obliged to work in extreme haste; its report was requested by the following 1st October, in view of the imminence of the new Constitution.

We now come to consider the case made by Mr. De Valera for his Bill. It is characteristic that, though his proposals affected the whole structure of the legislature, he felt under no necessity to justify them in the first instance. It was not for him to prove that he was right, but for his opponents to prove that he was wrong. In his opening speech he said: 'It is on the shoulders of those who stand for having a Second House in the Legislature must rest the responsibility for proving that such a House is necessary.'[1] And later, on the concluding Stage: 'When I introduced the Bill I said—and I repeat it—that the onus was on the Opposition to show why there should be a Second Chamber. Why should we complicate legislative machinery unnecessarily? . . . I said that it is for those who want to maintain such a check to show their reasons for it. I think that was fair. To me, it was just as if I were to have to defend the removing of hobble skirts. It is for those who say that hobble skirts, which restrict natural movement, should be worn to show why they should be worn—in other words, to show why these restrictions and this unnecessary complication in the legislative machinery should be there.'[2] However unreasonable this attitude may seem, it had certain tactical advantages. It placed the Opposition on the defensive, and it enabled Mr. De Valera to make his case at the end of the debate instead of at the beginning. His opening speech on the Second Stage fills only four columns of the *Debates*; his closing speech fills thirty-two columns, spread over two days. The Final Stage was begun by the Minister for Industry and Commerce in a speech of eight words: 'I move that the Bill do now pass.' It was closed by Mr. De Valera in a speech which, inclusive of a few interruptions, fills thirty-six columns.

Mr. De Valera's case for his Bill may be considered under three main heads:

1. The argument from experience of the existing Senate.
2. The argument from political theory.
3. The argument from history.

---

[1] *Dáil Debates*, li, 1830.   [2] Ibid., lii, 1809.

These arguments were not marshalled in orderly fashion, but they are deducible from his several speeches made during the various Stages of the Bill in the Dáil. We shall now consider them in the order mentioned.

With regard to the first argument, his points were:

(I.) The Senate, 'as at present constituted', was 'an absolute menace' to the country.[1] It was 'a real danger', and if the idea should get abroad that the will of the people, as expressed through their elected representatives, was to be thwarted by it the result would be to foster a revolutionary spirit.[2]

(II.) In rejecting the Blue Shirt Bill, the Senate had 'acted in the most partisan manner'. This was in strong contrast with the speed with which it had passed the Military Tribunal Bill in order to assist the Cosgrave Administration. By this time, Republicans were being brought in increasing numbers before the Military Tribunal, without which Mr. De Valera would not have been able to govern the country for a month. He met this point: 'We are asked, are we not using it? Yes, we are; and one of the reasons we are using it is because we know that, if we passed through this Dáil a measure that would enable us to preserve order and went to the Second Chamber, we know that in order to defeat us, and try to cripple this Administration, they would vote against us.'[3]

(III.) The Bill was introduced at that particular time because Mr. De Valera 'saw that a political game was being played in the Senate, a game which was detrimental to the interests of the country. That is the immediate and the proximate reason for bringing it in as regards time but not as regards the ultimate intention. It was due to come along in any case.'[4] And again: 'It had, in fact, been under consideration. It was kept, if you like, more or less in cold storage. It did not matter a great deal what particular time it was brought in. The Bill would get into law sometime. There was no hurry then, and no hurry up to the present, and we thought it was a suitable time to bring it in.'[5]

If the Bill had been under consideration, it is strange that it should bear so many marks of haste; and, if it was in cold storage, it is equally strange that it was not taken out of the refrigerator in time for the opening of the Dáil on the 22nd March, instead of being introduced three hours later.

(IV.) The Senate had twice rejected the Bill to abolish the Oath in spite of the declared will of the people. 'They wanted to insist that

---

[1] *Dáil Debates*, li, 1461.   [2] Ibid., li, 1831.   [3] Ibid., li, 2117, 2118.
[4] Ibid., li, 2132.   [5] Ibid., li, 2431.

they were the sovereign authority by telling us, "No, you will not get this Bill unless you go and negotiate with Britain." Of course we were able to put the Bill through in spite of them, but that attitude did not show any disposition on the part of the Senate to have any regard for the wishes of the people whose interests and will they are supposed to safeguard.'[1]

(V.) The Senate had rejected the Bill to extend the local government franchise to all persons over twenty-one years of age, irrespective of whether they were ratepayers or not. 'We wanted to get these younger people—those people to whom the people on the opposite benches are appealing—to take an interest in local and national affairs. We wanted them to have an immediate and practical interest in local as well as national affairs. The Senate stopped that Bill from becoming law.' When Mr. MacDermot pointed out that the Government had no mandate for the Bill, Mr. De Valera replied that 'no Government can possibly get mandates for everything it is called upon to do during its period of office'.[2]

(VI.) When Mr. Cosgrave was in power, the Senate was the complaisant tool of the Administration. 'There is not a single instance, when our predecessors were in office, and even when there was very good reason for believing that the legislation proposed was not in accordance with the wishes of the people, of a sustained attempt made by the Senate to stop that legislation. There is not a single instance in which the Senate did not ultimately—which meant, in that case, in a very short time—give way to the wishes of the majority party in this House.'[3] In a speech delivered in the Senate only nine months before these words were spoken Senator Douglas had given instances of the refusal by the Senate to pass Bills received from the Dáil when Mr. Cosgrave was in office.

(VII.) The Senate's attitude to the new Administration was in complete contrast to its attitude to the old: 'We have the Senate acting, as is obvious to every person in the country, in a narrow political way. They are acting as a political party and playing a political game. They are the allies of the Opposition and they are engaged in the policy which has been expressed by some members on the opposite side of putting the Government on the rocks.'[4]

(VIII.) The Senate was not a deliberative but a political assembly. 'I have not been very often in the Senate but my experience is that there is the same bitterness and the same political animosity shown

---

[1] *Dáil Debates*, li, 2118, 2119.   [2] Ibid., li, 2133.   [3] Ibid., li, 1829.
[4] Ibid., li, 2134.

there as is shown here, and that you get questions examined in precisely the same way as they would be examined here.'[1] It is unlikely that Mr. De Valera's colleagues in the Executive Council would have confirmed this opinion. His personal experience of the Second Chamber had been extremely limited. He had attended only six times in 1932, four times in 1933, and only once in 1934 up to the time these words were spoken—a total of eleven occasions out of 104 days on which the Senate had sat. Of these eleven occasions, no less than seven were concerned with matters of high controversy: six with the Bill to abolish the Oath, and the remaining one with the Bill to abolish the Blue Shirts.

We now turn to the second of Mr. De Valera's arguments, the argument from political theory.

(I.) The composition of a Second Chamber always presents two destructive alternatives. You will find that 'it is either of the same political complexion as the Lower House, in which case it is not an effective check, or that it is opposed to the majority in the Lower House, in which case it acts from political motives and, to use a phrase used in that connection long ago, is mischievous'.[2] Mr. Cosgrave ascribed the phrase to the notorious Abbé Sieyès, whom he described as 'the arch-constitution-monger of the French Revolution'.[3] Mr. De Valera did not deny the ascription, but said that Condorcet was of the same opinion.[4]

(II.) Nomination was an impracticable method. 'If you are to have a nominated Second House you will have to see how it is to be nominated. If it is to be nominated by the leaders of political parties the nominations will be of the complexion of those parties. If you are to try to get, by nomination, this venerable Senate, this wise Senate, that we have in our dreams, then I think we will wait a long time before we see our dreams realized.'[5]

(III.) The system of election was positively dangerous. 'Elect them? How are you going to elect them? Are you going to elect them directly by the people's vote? Are you going to establish another House so that it might be a rival authority—so that there will be a clash of authority between them? . . . I say, if you elect them directly you are going to have rivalry of authority, or even if you elect them indirectly. The moment you have them indirectly elected you will be up against the same difficulties.'[6]

(IV.) There was something to be said for the method of sortition.

<hr>

[1] *Dáil Debates*, lii, 1861. [2] Ibid., li, 1830. [3] Ibid., li, 1833.
[4] Ibid., li, 2112. [5] Ibid., lii, 1855. [6] Ibid., li, 2115.

'The system of lot then comes along. .... I honestly believe that, if you did want a Second House, the system of lot would be the best you could get. If you could ... have certain people who had achieved certain offices, certain positions, entered on a panel and agreement as to the type of office that would qualify for admission to the panel, and if periodically you put the names on the panel into a hat and picked them out, you would probably get a better Senate than you would get by any system of nomination.'[1]

(V.) An ideal Senate was not, however, possible. Mr. De Valera referred to the type who should be in it, 'men of probity and integrity, of sound judgment'. 'Get them for us. Show us the machinery by which they can be got, and then we will begin to see that there is a possibility of having a real Second House which will be of infinite value. The world has never been able to get that yet.'[2]

(VI.) But the failure to evolve an ideal Second Chamber was not so regrettable as it might seem. 'This world is a world of conflicts. So it seems to me at any rate, and those who are successful are the energetic and the active-minded and not those people who are, in fact, spent forces. Therefore, if we are looking to the general good of the nation as a whole, we ask ourselves this question: assuming that we could get such a Senate as we have in our minds, would it, in fact, be good for the country as a whole? I say I doubt it. I very much doubt it.'[3]

(VII.) This conclusion was supported by present-day opinion, backed by some of the great writers of the past. 'The more modern thinkers who are dealing with present-day affairs and conditions are gradually coming to the conclusion that, when all is said and done, a Single-Chamber Government is the wisest.'[4] Mr. De Valera was curiously reticent on the subject of the names of these 'more modern thinkers', but he claimed Adams, Franklin, and the third Earl Grey as champions of unicameralism. His dealings with these three authorities are examined in detail in the chapter which follows.

(VIII.) Finally, this whole question of one chamber or two chambers received far more attention than it deserved. 'After all your difficulty you will find that the object you have secured is not worth the trouble, and you will agree with what John Stuart Mill said, that all this pother about a Second Chamber is nonsense, and that if we are to have security in government we have to look for that security in the education of our people, and to the fact that the people

---

[1] *Dáil Debates*, lii, 1855.
[2] Ibid., li, 2114.
[3] Ibid., lii, 1856, 1857.
[4] Ibid., li, 2112.

will get for themselves the best class of representatives they can get, in a primary Assembly like this.'[1]

Mr. De Valera also essayed the historical method, and throughout his long speeches theory and empiricism are almost inextricably intermixed. This brings us to his third class of argument—the argument from history.

(I.) His general approach is sufficiently indicated by the following extracts.

'Historically, this idea of having a Second House in the Legislature has been the result, to a very large extent, of accident. It is not at all essential to the idea of representative government. In fact, it is, I might say, obnoxious to the idea of truly representative government.'[2]

'We have got in history the cases in which you had either hereditary chiefs or an invading force that got power by the sword, and these gradually, owing to the pressure of the people whom they ruled in their areas, allowed the people a little share of government. They had it all to themselves at the start and it has been a continual struggle over the centuries for the people to win just a little bit of their right to govern themselves from the chiefs and princes who held the power originally, and, therefore, history tells us that these Second Chambers have been a remnant, a part of the defensive armour of—I will use the word without any reference to words that have been used recently—the ascendancy class. . . . These Second Chambers, for the most part, arising from historical causes, have been due to the fact that the people did not get completely into their own. It was so in Rome, and it has been so in Britain and elsewhere.'[3]

'There are checks by these Second Chambers in all directions, but they are always checks in favour of vested interests and privilege, and they are checks against the march of the people to their rights. They never work in the opposite direction. They never work when it is a question of aggression by those who have on those who have not. They are never used then.'[4]

'Where Second Chambers exist, they exist either because of some historical reason or else they are continuing from sheer inertia.'[5]

'Having given it [the question of a Second Chamber] careful consideration, I have come to the conclusion that it is all nonsense, all prejudice, and that the whole thing is due to views current at the time when there was little experience of modern representative government and when the whole desire of the people who had influ-

---

[1] *Dáil Debates*, lii, 1865.   [2] Ibid., li, 1830.   [3] Ibid., li, 2111, 2112.
[4] Ibid., li, 2117.   [5] Ibid., lii, 1863.

ence and power was to corrupt the representatives of the plain people, to prevent them getting for the plain people the rights that were theirs, and to obtain for them the chance of getting a decent livelihood as a result of their labours.'[1]

(II.) Mr. De Valera reviewed the legislative position in different countries. He dealt with the British House of Lords. 'Why is it tolerated to-day? It is, of course, tolerated by a Conservative Government because it will never oppose them; its interests are the same. It broke the Liberal Party in Britain and prevented that Party from pursuing its ideals such as they were. The Labour Party, when it comes back to power in Britain, will be faced with the Chamber that it knows perfectly well is going to block it in its progressive measures.'[2]

(III.) The Canadian system was also criticized. 'There is in Canada, as you know, a nominated Senate. What has been the effect of it? The Senate there was nominated by the political leader of the day and it became a political body. . . . In Canada the result of this nominated Senate has been to bring it into disrepute.'[3]

(IV.) Mr. De Valera also attacked the French Senate. 'Everybody knows that at that particular time [1875] it was opposed to the sentiment of Republican France and that the Republican leader at that time [Gambetta] simply chose it because at the time he sensed a Royalist majority and it was used at that particular time simply as a means of getting the Republic through. It has persisted, but what has been its history? Its history has been that it has opposed every single progressive measure that has been brought forth. That is the history of it.'[4] And later: 'What is the history of the French Senate? It is equally bad. I think the average age of French Senators is about sixty years. What is their history? Their history is that they have been uniformly a force acting against ordinary modern social development. They opposed old-age pensions, they opposed the abolition of child labour, they opposed holidays for workers, they opposed the income-tax law, and, to this day, they have prevented the enfranchisement of women. In other words, they have been uniformly opposed to the modern conception of democratic freedom and democratic right.'[5] As we shall see presently, these animadversions on the French Senate were made the subject of a serious charge against Mr. De Valera when his Bill came before the Senate.

(V.) The United States Senate also came under notice, and Mr. De

---

[1] *Dáil Debates*, lii, 1865.   [2] Ibid., li, 2117.   [3] Ibid., lii, 1813.
[4] Ibid., lii, 1810.   [5] Ibid., lii, 1859.

Valera hazarded the opinion that 'if, to-morrow, we had the union of this country, and if there were to remain in the Six Counties a certain local Parliament and we were constituting here an all-Ireland Parliament, a very good case could be made for a Senate on somewhat similar lines'.[1] But he omitted to mention that, at the time he was speaking, every single one of the forty-eight States of the Union had bicameral legislatures.

(VI.) The remaining country mentioned by Mr. De Valera was Norway, which has a quasi-bicameral system. Immediately after each general election one-quarter of the members returned are selected, in numbers proportionate to party strength, to form an Upper House. The system seems to have had its attractions for Mr. De Valera, possibly because, as was later shown in the Senate, he had imperfectly understood it. 'With a small modification, if we want to have a modification, of the Norwegian system, we can have it here and I would propose that the moment the Senate, in its present form, would disappear the Standing Orders of the House would be changed so as to make provision of that sort.'[2] No such proposal was, of course, ever made.

(VII.) Mr. De Valera was at pains to rebut the charge that his motive in abolishing the Senate was the establishment of a dictatorship. The gravamen of the accusation against him was that, in the circumstances, single-chamber government ensured a party dictatorship which meant, in effect, his personal absolutism; and he had no difficulty in proving (for it is an obvious historical truth) that the bicameral system is no barrier to autocracy. His examples from history, were, however, unfortunate.

'Take every single dictatorship—although perhaps it is an exaggeration to speak of a single dictatorship. Take the case of Napoleon. There was a Senate to stop him. Did it stop him? Not a bit. Victor Hugo, I think, in one of his writings said of them: "The poltroons! They were bigger slaves than we wanted them to be." The same author, speaking of the experiences of a Roman Emperor, said: "The wretches! They were bigger slaves than we wanted them to be." Take the case of Louis Napoleon. Did the Senate stop him from his *coup d'état*? Not a bit of it.'[3]

Passages such as this convey better than pages of description the reason for Mr. De Valera's hold on the masses as an orator: the excited, staccato utterance, the appearance of learning, the trium-

---

[1] *Dáil Debates*, li, 2128.   [2] Ibid., li, 2143.
[3] Ibid., lii, 1810, 1811.

phant anger. But the final result is an extraordinary farrago which will not bear analysis.

(*a*) Tacitus says that the Emperor Tiberius (who always upheld the prestige of the Senate) became so disgusted at the subservience of Senators to his person that he used to mutter to himself on leaving the Curia, 'O homines ad servitutem paratos!'[1] Mr. De Valera misquotes this statement and attributes it to Hugo.

(*b*) Napoleon said of the French Senate in 1805, 'The cowards were afraid of displeasing me!' Hugo quotes it. Mr. De Valera misquotes it and attributes it to Hugo instead of to Napoleon. Incidentally, this Senate was the creation of the Abbé Sieyès, upon whom Mr. De Valera had relied as an authority.

(*c*) The source of Mr. De Valera's information was Hugo's *Napoléon le Petit*,[2] in which Hugo directs his flaming rhetoric against all who assisted in the establishment of the Second Empire. On the very next page the Chamber of Deputies is even more bitterly attacked. Such extracts are scarcely more relevant to conditions in Ireland in 1934 than something said by Tiberius nineteen hundred years ago.

(VIII.) Mr. De Valera also dealt with the case of Oliver Cromwell, and rebutted the suggestion that he 'came into existence as a dictator' as a result of the unicameral system.[3] But the case against the legislative tyranny of a single chamber can seldom have been stated so clearly as it was by Cromwell when, at a meeting of his officers, he urged the acceptance of the 'Humble Petition and Advice' as against the 'Instrument of Government'. The former prayed for the adoption of a Constitution which provided for a Second Chamber. The single-chamber Parliament established under the latter had, among other barbarities, tortured, whipped, and imprisoned James Naylor the Quaker.

'I tell you that, unless you have some such thing as a balance, we cannot be safe. Either you will encroach upon our civil liberties by excluding such as are elected to serve in Parliament—next time, for aught I know, you may exclude four hundred—or they will encroach upon our religious liberty. By the proceedings of this Parliament [i.e. the single chamber] you see they stand in need of a check or balancing power, for the case of James Naylor might happen to be your case. By the same law and reason they punished Naylor, they might punish an Independent or Anabaptist. By their judicial

---

[1] Tacitus, *Annals*, iii, 65.
[2] Victor Hugo, *Napoléon le Petit* (1852), pp. 44, 45.
[3] *Dáil Debates*, lii, 1851.

power they fall upon life and member, and doth the Instrument enable me to control it? This Instrument of Government will not do your work.'[1]

This outspoken statement from Cromwell is not very kind to Mr. De Valera's theory that bicameralism is an 'historical accident' in England.

(IX.) Mr. De Valera did make a final effort to show that the idea of a dictatorship was ridiculous while the Dáil was in existence. 'We hear talk of a dictatorship—one-man rule and so on—as if everybody in this Assembly of 153 individuals had not a voice and as if everybody here was inanimate and took no part, and played no part, in upholding the views he believed in, and the views of the people he represented.'[2]

No more impressive refutation could be placed in juxtaposition to this than an extract from the writings of Thomas Jefferson, third President of the United States. He was not one of the 'hereditary chiefs and princes' referred to by Mr. De Valera, but a man who had fought for a republic and got it. He was urging the need for a bicameral constitution for Virginia, where the existing House consisted of 173 members.

'173 despots would surely be as oppressive as one. . . . Little will it avail us that they are chosen by ourselves. An *elective despotism* was not the government we fought for, but one which should not only be founded on free principles, but in which the powers of government should be so divided and balanced among several bodies of magistracy as that no one could transcend their legal limits without being effectually checked and restrained by the others. . . . Human nature is the same on every side of the Atlantic and will be alike influenced by the same causes. The time to guard against corruption and tyranny is before they shall have gotten hold of us. It is better to keep the wolf out of the fold, than to trust to drawing his teeth and talons after he shall have entered.'[3]

Most of Mr. De Valera's historical examples were given in his reply to the debate on the Final Stage in the Dáil, when he could not be answered in that House. A number of able speeches had been made against the Bill, but Mr. De Valera's controversial method placed the speakers under a handicap; and in any case it was not to be expected that members of the Dáil would possess a detailed know-

---

[1] C. H. Firth, *The Last Years of the Protectorate* (1909), vol. i, pp. 137, 138.
[2] *Dáil Debates*, lii, 1866.
[3] Jefferson, 'Notes on Virginia' (1782) in his *Writings*, vol. iii (1894), pp. 223–5.

ledge of the work done by the Senate. The most dramatic passage of Mr. De Valera's concluding speech consisted of an attack on England. This was, of course, irrelevant to the Bill, but it was in keeping with such declarations as that of the Minister for Industry and Commerce that 'the Granards and the Jamesons and the like are no longer to be in a position to block the progress of the Irish Nation'.[1] Mr. De Valera now said that what they were doing was to undo the consequences of their defeat and win their freedom. When Mr. MacDermot inquired, 'Why not do it on the same basis as South Africa?' he replied: 'If South Africa is satisfied that is their affair. We were an ancient nation before South Africa was thought of. We are a nation as old as the British. If you want comparisons why not take the comparison that I gave with Britain? If Britain were conquered and became a subject State of the German Empire, would the people in Britain be satisfied?'[2] And a great deal more to similar effect. The Bill was finally passed by the Dáil on the 25th May 1934 by 54 votes to 38. The same evening it was announced over the wireless from the Dublin Broadcasting Station that Mr. De Valera 'tore to shreds the arguments of the Opposition'.[3]

On the 30th May the Bill came before the Senate. There was practically a full attendance of members, the public galleries were crowded, and an air of tense expectancy pervaded the Chamber as Mr. De Valera rose to open the debate. He followed the plan which he had adopted in the other House and spoke for only a few minutes, his remarks filling just two columns of the Official Report. Part of what he did say, however, is important in the light of after events and had best be quoted in full. Having stated that he did not anticipate that the Senate would pass the Bill, he proceeded:

'There will be a period in which we can take certain steps that it is intended to take, to meet a certain position that will arise when the Senate, as a constituent part of the Legislature, disappears. There are certain Articles in the Constitution guaranteeing democratic rights, and it is our intention to have these carefully examined, with the idea of putting them in a position somewhat like the position now occupied by the Comptroller and Auditor-General and the Judges with regard to their removal. There is the position in which these Articles cannot be removed by a simple majority but possibly by a majority that would be specified, by some fraction of the total membership such as four-sevenths in the case of the Comptroller and

---

[1] *Dáil Debates*, li, 1869. [2] Ibid., lii, 1869.
[3] *Irish Independent*, 28 May 1934.

Auditor-General, or, perhaps, by a simple majority provided the view of the majority of the Dáil is supported by the majority of the people in a referendum.'[1]

This is a firm undertaking that, while the suspensory period was running and before the Bill became law, action of a definite and specific character would be taken to safeguard those Articles of the Constitution which guaranteed democratic rights. That undertaking was never fulfilled.

Mr. De Valera's brief opening was followed by a surprise. The Chairman stood up and addressed the House from the Chair. He stated that in his conduct of the proceedings he had always maintained a rigid impartiality, but on the question of the abolition of the House of which he was Chairman he was not, and could not be expected to be, impartial. He had presided over the Senate for nearly half its existence and he had acquired an intimate knowledge of its work—knowledge that, in the nature of things, was open only to the occupant of the Chair. He had also learned much of the history and practice of other legislatures and had come to realize the supreme importance of the Second Chamber in our own. In view of his special knowledge, he could not in conscience remain silent; and so he had decided, on that unique occasion, to follow a precedent set up by his predecessor, Lord Glenavy, and to address Senators on the subject from the floor of the House. Having discharged what he believed to be his duty, he would resume his impartiality as between all parties and groups. He accordingly requested the Vice-Chairman to take the Chair, and he descended from the dais to the floor of the House.[2]

There followed a speech which lasted for nearly two hours, in which Mr. De Valera's arguments were reviewed by the Chairman and answered.[3]

He began by referring to the persistent misrepresentations of which the Senate had been the target. In regard to the powers of the Senate contained in one of the Draft Constitutions of 1922, Mr. De Valera had stated the exact opposite of the fact. On the day after the dissolution of January 1933 Mr. De Valera had informed a meeting of Press representatives that a hostile Senate had constantly attempted 'to harass the Government by mutilating its measures or wilfully delaying them'. A week later the Minister for Justice had told an audience

---

[1] *Senate Debates*, xviii, 1217.   [2] Ibid., xviii, 1217, 1218.
[3] Ibid., xviii, 1218–64: reprinted, with references, as a pamphlet entitled *Pro Domo Sua: being the Speech of the Chairman of the Seanad, Senator T. W. Westropp Bennett, in defence of his House of the Oireachtas against Mr. De Valera and his Government* (Dublin, 1934).

in his constituency that every Bill they had passed was being held up, particularly by the Senate. The truth, as the Chairman pointed out, was that, apart from the Oath Bill, the Senate had received twenty-two Bills, of which sixteen were passed unamended. In the six which were amended, a total of ninety-four amendments was inserted; of these, eighty-eight were agreed to by the Dáil and the remaining six were not insisted upon by the Senate. There was no unavoidable delay over any of the Bills. He quoted other statements, which he proved were equally false, and concluded:

'Of what value is a mandate given as a result of such false statements as these? Of course, it has no moral value at all. . . . It is obvious that over a long period the poison gas of calumny has been of set purpose directed against this House of the Oireachtas by Mr. De Valera and his followers. There is too much talk about liberty in this country, and too little attention paid to the things that ensure it. It is the truth that makes men free, and it is its opposite that binds them. There can be no liberty without liberty of the mind, and there can be no liberty of the mind without truth.'

The Chairman next turned to the argument from history. He quoted Mr. De Valera's statement to the effect that bicameralism was largely an historical accident, and recalled that he had challenged anyone to give him a single example of disaster following the adoption of a single chamber. Numerous instances could be given, but, as Mr. De Valera had relied on authorities from France and the United States, the Chairman would confine himself to these two countries.

As regards France, Condorcet and Sieyès had been mentioned. Condorcet was President of the National Assembly at its bloodiest epoch, and his works were on the Vatican's list of prohibited books. As a constitution-monger, Sieyès was notorious, and he had been authoritatively described as 'a byword for contemptible incompetence'. Against the advice of its own Constitution Committee, the National Assembly of the French Revolution had decided upon a single chamber by 849 votes to 89. Among those who voted for it was Mirabeau. It lasted for less than six years, was a colossal failure, and ended in complete disaster. Mirabeau was converted to the bicameral system, and remarked, 'Of all tyrannies the most insupportable is that of a single chamber.'

Turning to the United States, the Chairman cited impressive passages from Alexander Hamilton, in one of which he spoke of the danger to the people from being 'misled by the artful misrepresentations of interested men'. He said that Mr. De Valera might be interested to learn, if he did not know it already, that not one of the legislatures of the individual States consisted of a single chamber. The experiment of a single chamber had been tried in three of the States, Pennsylvania, Georgia, and Vermont. 'In each case it led to graft, dishonesty, and incompetence. In each case the experiment was soon abandoned, but not before the Single Chamber had violated a number of the principal features of the American Constitution.' But no doubt Mr. De Valera would say that these were historical accidents, and that the blame lay somewhere else.

Senator Westropp Bennett next proceeded to express his regret that, though Mr. De Valera had claimed the support of 'the more modern thinkers who are dealing with present-day affairs', he had neither disclosed their names nor quoted anything they had said. He himself cited the opinions of such representative men as Sir Henry Maine, Henry Sidgwick, and Sir John Marriott. He gave a list of the countries under single-chamber government, and asked, 'Can any sane man set this miserable list against the great and prosperous nations governed under a bicameral system?' He gave it as his opinion that single-chamber government would inevitably lead to a dictatorship of the Left, which meant revolution. 'If anyone, cleric or lay, thinks that the seeds of such a situation are not present in this country he is living in a fool's paradise.'

The Chairman then turned from theory to practical politics. He took the decennial period 1923 to 1932 and gave exact figures regarding the work of revision done in each calendar year by the Senates of Canada, South Africa, and the Irish Free State: that is to say, the number of Bills received from the other House, the number amended, the number of amendments inserted, and how many were agreed to. He then summarized the figures, which showed that the Irish Free State Senate had, in this field, done roughly three times the amount of work done by the Canadian Senate and more than ten times that done by the Senate of South Africa; and he asked what substitute could possibly be provided which would be capable of performing the function of revision in a comparable manner.

He then considered the power of delay, and gave similar figures for the same decennial period. The summary showed that no less than thirty-three Bills had been rejected by the Canadian Senate and thirteen by the Senate of South Africa. The number in the case of the Irish Free State was only three.

He examined the case of South Africa in greater detail, and contrasted General Hertzog's attitude with that of Mr. De Valera. When the former took office in 1924, he was faced with a Senate in which there was an Opposition majority. Important measures, such as the so-called Colour Bar Bill, the Precious Stones Bill, and the Iron and Steel Industries Bill, were rejected by the Upper House. Grave delay and inconvenience were thereby caused to the Government. The Prime Minister had power, under the Constitution, to procure a dissolution of the Senate, and the new Senate would undoubtedly have shown a Nationalist majority. But for six years, from 1924 to 1930, General Hertzog voluntarily left in existence a Senate in which his supporters were in a minority, 'because he is a statesman and a constitutionalist'.

One of Mr. De Valera's strongest arguments had been that the Senate had not proved to be an impartial body of men, and that its attitude towards his Government had been essentially different from its attitude towards that of Mr. Cosgrave. The Chairman now refuted this argument by giving the facts. As regards the work of revision, he gave the exact figures for the two Administrations (nine years and two and a quarter years respectively) and showed that the proportions were similar. As regards the exercise of the power of delay, two Bills had been suspended in Mr. Cosgrave's time, and under Mr. De Valera only four out of a total of 109.

'Every weapon forged by this Government for the prosecution of the so-called economic war with Great Britain has been left in their hands. Bills which effect a violent change in the country's economy, incidentally ruining the agricultural classes, a community from which many of our Senators are drawn, have even been improved here, and the improvements have been accepted by the Government and the other House. When the Government demanded haste, these Bills were passed in haste. Bills which alter the Constitution in such a way that, if they do not actually break the letter of the Treaty of 1921, they certainly violate its spirit, have been passed without a division and almost without debate. Only has the Senate interfered when it was either a matter of conscience with them to act as they did or else because they felt that their interference was necessary to protect the people from tyranny or to prevent the Government doing something cynically wrong to serve purely political ends. When Senators survey their work during the past two and a half years, they may well, like Clive, be astonished at their moderation.'

Having contrasted the circumstances of the introduction of Mr. Cosgrave's Military Tribunal Bill (which the Senate passed) with those in the case of Mr. De Valera's Blue Shirt Bill (which it rejected), the Chairman proceeded to give instances in which the Senate had facilitated the Government and refrained from obstruction. He then examined the text of the Senate Abolition Bill, and showed that, in spite of Mr. De Valera's assurance that more than ordinary care was taken over Bills to amend the Constitution, this vitally important measure contained serious errors. He had submitted the Bill to one of the most eminent constitutional lawyers in the English-speaking world, who was unconnected with our political controversies, and he had furnished an Opinion to the effect that the Bill was *ultra vires* the Constitution.

The Chairman then entered on the concluding phase of his speech. He asserted that Mr. De Valera's real object was a dictatorship, and undertook a vigorous defence of the Independent Group. 'An indecent and unmanly attempt has been made to prejudice the Senate in the eyes of the ignorant by introducing the element of religion and by stigmatizing as Unionists the members of the Independent Group in this House. . . . The rest of us have learnt to know and respect the qualities of intellect of these men, their high-mindedness, their inborn love of liberty, their genuine devotion to Ireland. . . . Unobtrusively and without advertisement, we have been realizing in our persons and in our work the ideals preached by Tone, Davis and every man who had a true conception of Irish nationality. After our twelve years' experience, I, for one, am not going to stand here and allow my friends to be calumniated. Speaking as an Irishman, to Irishmen, of Irishmen, I acclaim these men as my brothers.' He recalled the fact that Alice Stopford Green was a member of this group, and quoted passages from the message which accompanied her gift of the Casket, expressive of her ideals for the Senate and for Ireland. He then concluded this memorable speech with a striking quotation from Demosthenes: 'It is impossible, men of Athens, impossible, for one who commits injustice, breaks oaths and indulges in falsehood to acquire lasting power. Once in a way, and for a brief season, such a course of action may succeed, and, fed with hopes, make, it may be, a brave show of blossom. But time finds it out, and it falls to pieces of itself. For a house, I take it, or a ship or anything of that sort must have its main strength in its substructure; and so too in affairs of state, the principles and the foundations must be truth and justice.'[1]

Mr. De Valera left the Chamber immediately on the conclusion of the Chairman's speech, and he did not return until the third day, in time to conclude the debate. In his absence, a number of excellent

[1] *Olynthiacs*, ii, 10.

speeches were made, though the debate was, in the nature of things, one-sided. Probably the most notable, and certainly the most detailed, was the contribution of Senator Douglas.[1] Four of his points call for mention here. Mr. De Valera had claimed the support of John Stuart Mill for the view that 'all this pother about a Second Chamber is nonsense'. Senator Douglas quoted the following passage from Mill.

'A majority in a single assembly, when it has assumed a permanent character—when composed of the same persons habitually acting together, and always assured of victory in their own House—easily becomes despotic and overweening, if released from the necessity of considering whether its acts will be concurred in by another constituted authority. The same reason which induced the Romans to have two consuls makes it desirable there should be two Chambers: that neither of them may be exposed to the corrupting influence of undivided power, even for the space of a single year.'[2]

A second point dealt with the Norwegian system, by which the Second House is elected from the Primary House. Mr. De Valera had said that they could have that system 'with a small modification, if we want to have a modification'. Senator Douglas's comment was: 'It might be expected that a House so elected would always agree with the Lower House, but in fact differences do occur. The President said that these differences are settled within three days by bringing the two Houses together as one. I wonder how he calculated the three days? He omitted to mention that the two Houses in Norway do not meet together untii the Upper House has twice rejected a Bill from the Lower House and that, when they do meet together, a two-thirds majority is necessary to pass the Bill. The President also failed to tell the Dáil that even when a two-thirds majority of the two Houses sitting together passes an amendment to the Constitution, it does not become law until after the next General Election, and even then it must be passed again by a two-thirds majority of the newly-elected Parliament during the first or second ordinary Session.' This fuller information may have put an end to the proposal to adopt the Norwegian system. At all events, little more was heard of it.

The third and fourth points are concerned with France. Mr. De Valera had asserted that the bicameral system was used by Gambetta in 1875 'simply as a means of getting the Republic through'. Senator Douglas pointed out that 'he omitted to mention that afterwards Gambetta became its staunch supporter, and in 1882 declared that

---

[1] *Senate Debates*, xviii, 1278–1300.
[2] J. S. Mill, *Considerations on Representative Government* (1861), pp. 97, 98.
2C

the principle of two Chambers, "is the guiding principle of all demo-cratic government." '

The last point was more serious. Mr. De Valera had made a number of charges against the modern French Senate. Senator Douglas referred to a book published in 1919 by Professor Joseph Barthélemy, the leading French authority on political science, en-titled *Le Gouvernement de la France*, and said: 'It is a significant fact that the very charges made against the French Senate by Mr. De Valera are identical with those adduced by M. Barthélemy, and, more remarkable still, they are quoted by the President, with one excep-tion, in exactly the same order as in M. Barthélemy's book. As this can scarcely be mere coincidence, I assume that the book is the source of Mr. De Valera's information; and, if so, I am amazed that a man in his position and with his responsibility should use the criti-cisms of M. Barthélemy without at the same time giving his rebuttal of them.' Senator Douglas then set forth this rebuttal under five heads, with deadly effect, ending with M. Barthélemy's concluding words on the subject: 'The existence of a Second Chamber is the fundamental institution of all organized democracy.'

During the three days' debate only seven Senators spoke in favour of the Bill, and none of their speeches calls for special mention. Some of them were marred by personalities, and that of Senator Johnson (which was, of course, quite free from this objection) cannot have been very helpful to the Government, as he stated his opinion that a Second Chamber was needed and reprobated the tendency 'to treat a Party meeting as something very much more influential and authori-tative than the legislature itself'.[1] The case against the Bill was wound up on the third day by the Vice-Chairman (Senator O'Hanlon) in a speech delivered in the presence of Mr. De Valera, who had returned to the House in order to exercise his right of reply. In this speech the Vice-Chairman dealt with Mr. De Valera's American authorities, and what he said on this subject is fully discussed in the chapter which follows.

Mr. De Valera, whose opening speech had filled two columns of the Official Report, then took forty columns to 'reply' to a debate the greater part of which he had not heard.[2] Much of what he said was a repetition of the assertions which he had made in the Dáil. 'It is reasonable to put the onus for proving that there should be a Second Chamber, either this existing one or some other, on those who hold that it is necessary or wise.' 'There is not the slightest doubt that the

[1] *Senate Debates*, xviii, 1408.   [2] Ibid., xviii, 1485–1526.

historical existence of Second Chambers is due largely to the fact that there was a Second Chamber in existence in Great Britain.' 'If there is any lesson to be learned from the French Revolution, it is not to try by methods of coercion to stand in the way of the legitimate rights of the people.' 'If we have Senators who think that they have some divine right because they were born with a silver spoon to govern or rule—they must logically be driven back to base their rights upon power. But if they do, they will have people to dispute that.'

As all his historical arguments had been refuted, history was incontinently jettisoned: 'I submit that there is nobody here who has either the time or the opportunity or who, if he were to devote his whole life to it, could possibly fully examine this question, which means the whole question of the history of every State in the world for 150 years; and to draw conclusions simply because in the one case it failed and in another case it succeeded, without knowing all the facts, is, to my mind, proving nothing. You do not prove anything. I have not pretended to prove anything by these references to history.'[1]

Mr. De Valera chose this occasion (when no answer was possible in either House) to elaborate the allusion to John Stuart Mill. What he did was (without, however, giving his references) to quote the opening and closing sentences from the chapter on Second Chambers in Mill's *Considerations on Representative Government*. From these it was made to appear as though Mill regarded the question of one or two chambers as of secondary importance. But Mill is not a writer from whom snippets can thus be taken to buttress an argument. In his view, representative government is the best government for only a few countries. Even with them, unless minorities can be specially represented, contrary to the principle of democracy as understood by Hobbes, Locke, Rousseau, Bentham, and even Burke (who foresaw and feared the danger of tyranny from democratic majorities), it is a bad form of government, and may be the worst of all. If a form of government is truly representative (in Mill's special sense) then he considered that the question of the unicameral versus the bicameral system was relatively unimportant. Otherwise, all that he said in favour of Second Chambers is of full force and effect. But the Dáil, on Mill's canons, is very far from being truly representative. Hence his cogent reasons (one of which was quoted by Senator Douglas and is reproduced above) become applicable. Mr. De Valera must have

[1] *Senate Debates*, xviii, 1488, 1489.

been aware of those reasons, because it seems absurd to suppose that he could read the beginning and end of a chapter without noticing what was in between. Yet he seems to have been genuinely aggrieved when the Chairman asked him if he was replying to Senator Douglas, and retorted angrily, 'I beg leave to make my speech in my own way.'

This was the prelude to a number of criticisms of the Chairman, the culmination of which is described next morning by the political correspondent of one of the newspapers as follows: 'It was on a point so trivial as to be almost ludicrous that Mr. De Valera's rage finally burst all restraints. The one flaw that he could seize on in the matter of the Chairman's speech was a reference taken from himself, which he claimed had been a misquotation. Whether the President, in a Press statement with which he inaugurated his campaign at the last election, had really said that the Senate had "attempted" to hamper the Government or had been "tempted" to do so was never decided, as the President and the Chairman were each able to produce newspaper reports to support their conflicting claims. But Fianna Fáil Senators clamoured for an apology from the Chairman. It was not vouchsafed, and Mr. De Valera snapped: "I don't want an apology from Senator Bennett. I am very glad that Senator Bennett has revealed his impartiality. It is well for the country to know that they can measure the impartiality of this Senate by the speech which its Chairman has delivered." [1]

Mr. De Valera then sat down, only to be recalled to his feet immediately by a polite reminder from the Chair that he had not dealt with his misinterpretation of one of the Drafts presented by the Constitution Committee. In reply, Mr. De Valera alleged that the Chairman had accused him of wilful deceit, whereas Senator Douglas had merely said it was an error. 'This champion of unpolluted truth, who lectured us in the last paragraph of his speech about truth and made the suggestion that we were liars, does not hesitate to accuse me in that manner; does not hesitate to suggest it and to say that it was my main argument. It was not my main argument.'

The Chairman had not accused Mr. De Valera of wilful deceit in this particular matter, but of misrepresentation. The mis-statement, which was undoubtedly a grave one, was made by Mr. De Valera on the 20th June 1933. It was repeated by the Minister for Justice on the following 11th July. Senator Douglas then made the correction, but the misstatement, without the correction, was broadcast the same evening. No explanation had ever been given. Incidentally, in the

1 *Irish Times*, 2 June 1934.

same speech Senator Douglas quoted three other statements by Mr. De Valera which he not only said were untrue but proved to be untrue. He had, on the Senate Abolition Bill, spoken equally strongly of Mr. De Valera's misuse of Professor Barthélemy as an authority, but without reply.

Mr. De Valera at length came to his explanation. 'I did, as a matter of fact, make the mistake of reading "operative" for "inoperative", and the reason for my mistake was that I did not expect that those who had signed that report were likely to be more conservative in regard to the Senate than the others.' The reason given tends to prove what had been already suspected, that if what Mr. De Valera reads conflicts with his preconceived opinions he is very liable to misunderstand it.

When this explanation had been given, the division was taken, and the Bill was rejected by 33 votes to 15. As the occasion was an historic one, it is desirable to give details. The total membership of the House at the time was fifty-nine, there being one casual vacancy. Apart from the Chairman (who had only a casting vote), the maximum number of votes in the division was therefore fifty-eight. Senator Farren (Labour) was present on that day but did not take part in the division; and there were nine absentees.

The majority of thirty-three was made up as follows: United Ireland Party, 20; Independent Group, 8; Independents, 4 (Senators Sir Edward Bellingham, Sir William Hickie, Sir John Keane, and Linehan); Fianna Fáil, 1 (Colonel Moore).

The minority of fifteen consisted of: Fianna Fáil, 11; Labour 3; Independent, 1 (Senator O'Neill).

The nine absentees were:

United Ireland Party: Senators Dillon, MacGuinness, MacLoughlin, O'Rourke.

Labour: Senators Duffy and O'Farrell.

Independents: Senators Sir Thomas Esmonde and the Earl of Granard.

Independent Group: Senator Douglas.

A number of these were, of course, prevented from attending either by ill health or by absence from the country.

CHAPTER XXII

MR. DE VALERA'S HISTORICAL AUTHORITIES

Mr. De Valera's controversial method—Earl Grey's 'exact words'—Source of the quotation—Three variations of the text—Applicable solely to the Australian colonies—Rendered out of date by 1859—Dr. Temperley's warning—Mr. De Valera's reference to Adams—The Vice-Chairman's refutation as regards John Adams—His mention of Samuel Adams—Mr. De Valera's belated explanation—The explanation examined—Samuel Adams's views on bicameralism—Mr. De Valera on the duties of Members of Parliament—His reliance on Franklin—The Vice-Chairman's refutation—Inquiries instituted in Pennsylvania—The article in State Government—*Mr. De Valera's final words on Franklin—His use of the information obtained from Pennsylvania.*

It is proposed in this chapter to illustrate Mr. De Valera's controversial method by recounting, in some detail, his actions in regard to three authorities which were adduced by him as arguments for the abolition of the Senate. Though they have lost whatever polemical importance they may have derived from the immediate occasion, they are still of interest (on the principle of *ex uno disce omnes*) as showing the somewhat unusual methods which Mr. De Valera adopts to build up a case and—what is more significant—the lengths to which he is prepared to go in seeking to maintain his original position after it has been proved to be untenable.

On the Second Reading of the Abolition Bill in the Dáil Mr. De Valera followed his usual practice of reserving his arguments for his concluding speech in reply to the debate, when no answer to them was possible at that stage. In that speech, delivered on the 19th April 1934, he spoke as follows: 'The more modern thinkers who are dealing with present-day affairs and conditions are gradually coming to the conclusion that, when all is said and done, a Single

Chamber Government is the wisest. It is not only the more modern thinkers who hold that view. Take, for example, the third Earl Grey, writing in 1853. He was a man who had given considerable thought to this question. He had been a protagonist in favour of the Second Chamber, and when he writes in 1853 what does he say? I will give you his exact words: "I now consider it very doubtful, at least, whether the Single Chamber Legislature ought not under any circumstances to be preferred." [1] As Mr. De Valera professed to give Earl Grey's exact words, it would naturally be assumed that he had taken his quotation from the original. If he merely copied it from some other writer, who had in turn copied it from Grey, he could hardly make such a claim. So much being clear, let us see what Grey's exact words really are, and refer them to their context.

Mr. De Valera did not give his authority, but the quotation is taken from page 97 of volume ii of Grey's *Colonial Policy of Lord John Russell's Administration*, which was published in 1853. Here is what he wrote: 'I now consider it to be very doubtful, at least, whether the single Legislature ought not under many circumstances to be preferred.' It will be observed that, while professing to give Grey's exact words, Mr. De Valera managed in one short sentence to produce no less than three variations of his text. Two of these are of minor importance, but the third misquotation is a serious one. Mr. De Valera makes Grey say, in effect, that he thinks it doubtful whether single-chamber government is not preferable under any circumstances. What he said was that there were, in his opinion, many circumstances in which it is preferable. There is, of course, an enormous difference between these two statements, and the alteration is wholly in favour of Mr. De Valera's argument.

But that is not all. If he was quoting direct from the original, Mr. De Valera must have known that the sentence in question had reference only to the Colonies in 1852. Earl Grey was Secretary of State for War and the Colonies in Lord John Russell's Administration, 1846–52. On the defeat of the Government in the latter year he wrote a series of letters to his late chief in which he vindicated his colonial policy. These letters were published the following year, with the title *Colonial Policy of Lord John Russell's Administration*. They deal with that subject, and with nothing else.

The letter from which Mr. De Valera misquoted dealt with Australia, and is dated the 1st November 1852. Grey was considering the Constitution Act for Australia, 1850, for which he had been res-

[1] *Dáil Debates*, li, 2112, 2113.

ponsible. This Act permitted the Australian colonies, under certain limitations, to amend their Constitutions, but it provided in the first instance for a single chamber. Grey gives his personal reasons for that course—the 'many circumstances' which Mr. De Valera turned into 'any circumstances'. These reasons are summarized in an able notice of Grey's book contributed anonymously to the *Edinburgh Review* for July 1853 (page 90) by Sir Charles Adderley (afterwards Lord Norton): 'The elements for an aristocratic chamber do not exist in a young colonial community: the number of persons fitted for the duties of representation is not large, and hence their division into two houses is inexpedient; while the presence of a body of members nominated by the Governor (being a third or some other number less than half the house) serves to insure a consideration for the opinions of minorities, and to prevent an eager majority rushing at once to the attainment of their end, without due deliberation and discussion.' Earl Grey then went on to point out that the Constitution originally given to New South Wales in 1842 and extended by the Act of 1850 to the neighbouring colonies 'also makes provision, by another arrangement, for that revision of laws before they are finally passed, which it is considered one of the chief objects of the division of the Legislature into two branches to ensure'.[1] This arrangement, as he explains, was the power accorded to the governor, before giving the Assent of the Crown, to return Bills to the Parliament for reconsideration, and the power of the Crown in London to delay confirmation of colonial statutes even after they had been assented to by the governors, until the local legislatures had had an opportunity to reconsider and amend them.

Obviously, these considerations have no application in the case of a single chamber elected under universal suffrage, where no power of delay or annulment exists; or, rather, such application as they have is all in favour of a bicameral system. Yet Mr. De Valera cannot have been unaware of these facts if, as his words suggest, he was quoting from the original; for they are given in the same context as the sentence which he cited.

In his Preface Grey warns the reader that the progress of events in the times in which he lived was so rapid that a delay of even a few months had made material changes; so he took the precaution of dating each letter, and he requested that the dates be borne in mind. Actually, what he had said about the advantages of single-chamber government in the colonies was rapidly rendered out of date by the

[1] Earl Grey, *Colonial Policy of Lord John Russell's Administration*, vol. ii, p. 100.

action of the colonies themselves. The Act of 1850 permitted the Australian colonies, within certain limitations, to amend their Constitutions. They quickly took advantage of this freedom to set up bicameral legislatures: New South Wales, with its offshoots Victoria, Tasmania, and South Australia, all in 1855; and Queensland in 1859. So that what Grey had written in November 1852 was rendered completely out of date as early as 1859. Yet we find Mr. De Valera relying upon it to support his argument for the abolition of a Senate sitting in Dublin nearly eighty years later.

The third Earl Grey is not a writer whose views are considered as of serious account by students of political science, and it is some evidence of the poverty of his material that Mr. De Valera made use of him at all. If, in spite of professing to quote Grey's exact words, Mr. De Valera took them at second-hand from some other source, then there is only one work from which he could have taken them, because there is only one work in which Grey's views on Second Chambers in the Colonies have come under notice. That work is Dr. Harold Temperley's *Senates and Upper Chambers*, published in 1910. Now it is an odd circumstance that Dr. Temperley quotes (page 43) the sentence which Mr. De Valera quoted, and that the word 'many' is there misprinted as 'any'. It accordingly seems probable that Mr. De Valera was not quoting from the original, but merely from Dr. Temperley. But the change from 'many' to 'any' was far more serious in Mr. De Valera's case than in Dr. Temperley's, for the latter made no specific claim to give the exact words, nor did he found any argument upon them. On the contrary, in an addendum which Mr. De Valera can hardly have avoided reading (for attention is directed to it by a marginal note), he expressly warns the reader against accepting Grey's statement at its face value: 'It is, however, only fair to remember that Earl Grey's argument as to the Single Chamber in a Colony was based on considerations which would now be used to justify the existence of a Single Chamber only in the different States of a Federal Union. . . . In the same way, Earl Grey and his contemporaries relied on the power of the Imperial Government to retard, disallow or veto colonial statutes with a freedom which no modern English statesman would advocate' (pages 297, 298). This was written in 1910, and by 1934 the Imperial Government retained no power whatever over statutes passed in the Irish Free State, the last formal traces of such power having been removed by Mr. De Valera's own Government in the previous year, by means of an amendment to Article 41 of the Constitution.

Thus, in Grey's case, not only were the 'exact words' not given, but their strictly limited application, and the fact that they were long out of date, were both passed over in silence; though both facts should have been obvious to Mr. De Valera, from whichever of the two sources he took his quotation.

In the same speech as that in which he misquoted Earl Grey, Mr. De Valera claimed the support of American authorities for the uni-cameral system, as follows: 'It was suggested by some of the speakers on the other side that all the theorists and the practical people who have been engaged in the task of moulding Constitutions have been in favour of the Two Chamber Parliament. That is not so. America has reminded me of it. Franklin was no mean political thinker. He stood for the Single Chamber. Adams was no mean political thinker. He stood for the Single Chamber.'[1] On the Second Reading of the Abolition Bill in the Senate, the Vice-Chairman of that House (Senator O'Hanlon) dealt at length with Mr. De Valera's reliance on Adams and Franklin.[2] It is necessary that the two cases be taken separately.

In regard to Adams, Senator O'Hanlon said, quite correctly, that as John Adams, the second President of the United States, was in-comparably the most distinguished man of that surname he must be taken to be the constitution-moulder referred to by Mr. De Valera. The point is important, in view of what occurred later; but there is no need to labour it, as it is sufficiently obvious. In the case of no other Adams could the Christian name be omitted without serious risk of misunderstanding; and this is especially so when Adams is mentioned in the same breath with Franklin. In any event, any doubt that might have existed on this question of identity is dispelled by Mr. De Valera's attitude at the time. He was present in the Chamber when the Vice-Chairman delivered his speech; the latter developed his case on the assumption that John Adams was intended, and Mr. De Valera did not intervene to say that he had not referred to John Adams but to some other Adams. Nor did he make any reference to the matter in his speech, which followed immediately on that of the Vice-Chairman and which concluded the debate.

The Vice-Chairman had, of course, no difficulty in showing that, so far from Adams having 'stood for the Single Chamber', he was one of the greatest champions of the bicameral system that have ever lived. He cited passages from his *Thoughts on Government* and *Defence of the Constitutions of the United States*, such as the follow-

---

[1] *Dáil Debates*, li, 2112.   [2] *Senate Debates*, xviii, 1479–83.

ing: 'A Single Assembly possessing all powers of government would make arbitrary laws for their own interest and adjudge all controversies in their own favour.' 'I cannot think a people can be long free nor ever happy whose government is in one Assembly.' Senator O'Hanlon stated, further, that Adams's ideas on the subject were reflected in the Constitutions of Massachusetts (of which he was one of the draftsmen) and of Virginia and in the Federal Constitution of the United States; and he mentioned that Adams's exceptionally strong views on Second Chambers contributed to his defeat by Washington in the contest for the first Presidency of the United States.

The Vice-Chairman also made reference to Samuel Adams, who was associated with John Adams in the drafting of the Constitution of Massachusetts, and whom he characterized as 'relatively an unimportant person'. 'He may have in the early days of the struggle with Britain made some references in favour of a Single Chamber administration, when he was leading the Radical Opposition in the Assembly of Massachusetts against the Conservative majority in the Council. There is no proof of that whatever, but there is positive proof that when the Constitution of Massachusetts was being drafted it was submitted to a Committee of which Samuel Adams was one. They were referred to as "the brace of Adamses". The second was John Adams. The Constitution they drafted embodied a bicameral system of legislation.'

This was a damaging refutation, the more so because of Mr. De Valera's reiterated claim to have given serious study to the question of Second Chambers. He had been interested in the subject for twenty years at least. He had given thought to the matter. He had done an amount of reading and had consulted authorities; and, having given it careful consideration, he had 'come to the conclusion that it is all nonsense'.[1] The ordinary man, however, though he might experience some degree of chagrin or discomfiture at the time, would have been content to let the matter rest or, better still, to admit quite frankly that he had been mistaken. But Mr. De Valera's psychology is so unusual that a refutation of this sort assumes the aspect of an injustice not to be borne. In view of what subsequently happened, there can be very little doubt that, after Senator O'Hanlon had delivered his speech, inquiries were made by Mr. De Valera, or on his behalf, in order to discover whether *Samuel* Adams had at any time been in favour of a single chamber.

[1] *Dáil Debates*, lii, 1865, 1866.

On the 12th December 1935, more than a year and a half after Senator O'Hanlon's speech, Mr. J. M. Dillon, the Deputy Leader of the Opposition, speaking in the Dáil, recalled what John Adams had said and used words about the misuse of his name by Mr. De Valera that undoubtedly called for a reply from the latter.[1] But Mr. De Valera did not intervene to say that he had referred to Samuel Adams, and in his speech winding up the debate he was silent on the point.

On the 15th January 1936, in the Senate, the Adams question was again raised, this time by Senator Milroy. Mr. De Valera did not attend, but Senator Milroy challenged any member of the Government party to give the source upon which their leader had relied when making his statement that Adams 'stood for the Single Chamber'. There was no reply, and the speaker pointed out that the case against the Senate had been built up on misrepresentation and the falsification of evidence.[2]

The matter came up again on the 28th May 1936 in the Dáil, on the motion that the Abolition Bill be deemed to be passed by both Houses. It was two years, almost to the day, since Senator O'Hanlon had spoken on the subject, and on this occasion Mr. De Valera vouchsafed some information. When Mr. Dillon referred to one of the quotations cited from the works of John Adams by Senator O'Hanlon, Mr. De Valera interrupted him with the question, 'Are you sure I mentioned John Adams?' to which Mr. Dillon replied, 'Oh, I am never sure of anything the President says, because, if there was a possible method for the President to say anything so that it could be interpreted in six different ways, he would certainly choose that way of saying it.' To which Mr. De Valera answered, 'There happened to be a Sam Adams too.'[3]

When Mr. De Valera rose to conclude the debate, the long explanation which he gave was in striking contrast with his previous silences on the subject. He said: 'I will admit that, as there are two famous Adams, it would have been better had I mentioned Sam Adams at the time. . . . I will admit that Sam Adams was not quite so famous as John Adams, but he was Chairman of the Senate of Massachusetts. He was one of the Committee of Three which was appointed to draw up a constitution for that State. John Adams, his cousin, had a very high opinion of him, and he was at least important enough to have a "Life" written of him. In speaking of him, the author of that "Life" said that "Samuel Adams gave a tone to the

1 *Dáil Debates*, lix, 2617, 2618.   2 *Senate Debates*, xx, 1789, 1790.
3 *Dáil Debates*, lxii, 1250.

politics of America for many years ". It is true that in the Committee's report there was a recommendation for three branches: a Governor, a Senate and a Primary House. John Adams, writing of that at the time in his memoirs, said that his constituents in Boston compelled him to vote for three branches. John Adams, who was the Chairman, said that Samuel Adams concurred because of the fact that his constituents wished it. Now, I say that if I mention a man like that as "no mean political thinker", those who make a study of it will naturally think of such a man.'[1]

There is here the clearest possible suggestion, short of a categorical avowal, that when Mr. De Valera claimed that 'Adams stood for the Single Chamber' he was referring to Samuel Adams. But this cannot be the case if, as seems a reasonable deduction from his subsequent conduct, his information about Samuel Adams was sought and acquired after he had heard his name mentioned by Senator O'Hanlon.

Moreover, it will be observed that Mr. De Valera contented himself with a paraphrase of what John Adams had written. If he had given the 'exact words' the impression created would have been very different; for Samuel Adams's views on the bicameral system are of very little account (they are not even mentioned in his biography by Hosmer) and John Adams refers to his cousin's opinions on the subject in terms which are almost contemptuous. Here is the quotation: 'He very rarely spoke much in Congress, and he was perfectly unsettled in any plan to be recommended to a State, always inclining to the most democratical forms, and even to a single sovereign assembly, until his constituents afterwards in Boston compelled him to vote for three branches.'[2] The year to which the quotation refers is 1775, when the Continental Congress was in session at Philadelphia; and at that time Samuel Adams's experience of systems of government was virtually non-existent. If, instead of producing a paraphrase of second-hand evidence of Samuel Adams's views, Mr. De Valera had consulted that statesman's own writings, he would have found nothing to support his assertion that Adams 'stood for the Single Chamber'. But he would have come upon this passage, written by Samuel Adams on the 25th November 1790, after ten years' experience of the working of the Constitutions of Massachusetts and other States with bicameral legislatures:

'The American Legislatures are nicely balanced. They consist of two branches, each having a check upon the determinations of the

---

1 *Dáil Debates*, lxii, 1333, 1334.
2 *Collected Works of John Adams*, vol. iii, p. 18.

other; they sit in different Chambers, and probably often reason differently, in their respective Chambers, on the same question. If they disagree in their decisions, by a Conference their reasons and arguments are mutually communicated to each other; candid explanations tend to bring them to agreement; and then . . . the matter is laid before the first Magistrate for his revision. . . . Here is a mixture of three Powers founded in the Nature of Man; calculated . . . finally to enable them to decide, not by the impulse of passion, or party prejudice, but the calm Voice of Reason, which is the Voice of God.'[1]

Further comment on the Adams episode is unnecessary; and before we consider that of Franklin it is desirable to place on record Mr. De Valera's own conception of the duties of Members of Parliament in relation to a controversy of this kind. On the 24th May 1934, speaking on the Final Stage of the Abolition Bill in the Dáil, he said: 'It is our duty as representatives not to play the political game, in the sense of keeping back information and knowledge which ought to be used here in the Legislative Assembly for the general benefit.'[2] We have seen how wide was the gulf between his precept and his practice in the case of Grey and Adams. In the case of Franklin it was to prove even wider.

In the speech already referred to, the Vice-Chairman of the Senate dealt with Mr. De Valera's statement that Franklin 'stood for the Single Chamber'. He pointed out the well-known facts that Franklin's views on government were doctrinaire and academic, and that his practical efforts in constitution-making were singularly unsuccessful. He mentioned that the Constitution of Pennsylvania was drafted by Franklin in 1776 and embodied his two favourite ideas of a unicameral Legislature and a plural Executive; that the system was admittedly a failure; and that after an existence of only fourteen years it was abolished, being replaced in 1790 by a two-chamber system. Senator O'Hanlon further stated that, at the Convention which drew up the Federal Constitution for the United States, the motion 'that the national legislature ought to consist of two parts' was carried without a single dissentient (31st May 1787). The delegates from Franklin's own State of Pennsylvania abstained from voting, but they stated afterwards that they did so merely 'out of consideration to Dr. Franklin'.

Presumably as a result of this refutation, a communication was

---

[1] *The Writings of Samuel Adams*, vol. iv (1908), pp. 345, 346.
[2] *Dáil Debates*, lii, 1815.

sent by the Government to the Legislative Reference Bureau of Pennsylvania, in which the question was posed, 'Why did Pennsylvania abolish the unicameral system?'; and the fact of its dispatch was disclosed in an article written by Irma A. Watts and published in the issue for March 1936 of *State Government*, an American periodical which deals with matters of constitutional interest in the various State legislatures. The relevant portions of this article are as follows:

'. . . The Government of the Irish Free State recently asked the Legislative Reference Bureau of Pennsylvania, "Why did Pennsylvania abolish the unicameral system?" This provoked some interesting studies. . . .

'Under the Constitution of 1776, Pennsylvania placed the executive power of the State in the hands of a President and a Supreme Executive Council of twelve members. The law-making powers were vested in a single body known as the General Assembly of Freemen. To insure that the rights guaranteed by the Constitution would be preserved, there was created also a Council of Censors, whose duty it was to inquire whether the Constitution had been preserved inviolate in every part. This Council of Censors consisted of two persons from each city and county of the State, and was to be elected every seventh year.

'After the adoption of the Constitution of 1776 public opinion soon began to decide that the one-chamber legislature was not conducive to good government in Pennsylvania. Among the first acts of the Council of Censors was the appointment of a Committee on the Defects and Alterations of the Constitution. The Committee presented its report in 1784. . . .

'The outstanding features of the report were:

' "Your Committee, to whom it was referred to report those articles of the Constitution which are defective and the alterations and amendments, begs leave to report.

' "That by the Constitution of the State of Pennsylvania, the supreme legislative power is vested in one House of Representatives, chosen by all those who pay public taxes. Your Committee humbly conceives the said Constitution to be in this respect materially defective:

' "1. Because if it should happen that a prevailing faction in that one House was desirous of enacting unjust and tyrannical laws, there is no check upon their proceedings.

' "2. Because an uncontrolled power of legislation will always enable the body possessing it to usurp both the judicial and the executive authority, in which case no remedy would remain to the people but by a revolution."

'No immediate action resulted from this report of the Council of Censors, but it should be noted that its conclusion against the unicameral system was arrived at before the precedent of a two-House legislative body was established by the Federal Constitution.

'Four years later, at the thirteenth Session of the General Assembly of Pennsylvania, Mr. Gerardus Wynkoop, of Bucks County, made a motion to have incorporated in the minutes an address, "To the Citizens of Pennsylvania", which set forth ". . . the sentiments of the Assembly on the expediency of calling a convention for the purpose of altering the Constitution of the Commonwealth.

' ". . . To obtain and to secure that great principle of prosperity, it is indispensably requisite that caution, accuracy, order, moderation, stability and vigour should reign, in making and in executing the laws.

' "Without intending an invidious application to persons or times, we submit it to your experience and reflection, whether those qualities are to be uniformly found in a legislature consisting of a single body of men, or whether, on the contrary, precipitation and inconsistency do not often characterize the proceedings of a legislature thus formed, and restrained by no immediate control. Having recently turned your attention to the federal system, you are fully informed on this head. The government of the United States, under the late articles of confederation, consisted only of a single branch. The wisest heads and the most virtuous hearts in our nation have agreed in condemning this inefficient and dangerous arrangement. You have seen, felt, and to your never-failing honor have, with your compatriots of other States, remedied this radical imperfection. . . ."

'A resolution to call a convention to revise the Constitution was adopted four days later. That Constitution, adopted in 1790, created a General Assembly, consisting of a Senate and a House of Representatives.'

The following seem to be reasonable assumptions: (1) that the inquiry from the Irish Free State Government which provided the occasion for the above article emanated, directly or indirectly, from Mr. De Valera; (2) that a reply was sent to the inquiry; (3) that it contained, in substance, the information embodied in the article, or at all events did not contradict it in essential points; (4) that it was received by March 1936, the month of publication of the article; and (5) that it was duly seen by Mr. De Valera, or its terms communicated to him. If these assumptions are correct, Mr. De Valera had in his possession, or accessible to him, fresh information emphasizing the inherent dangers of single-chamber government before the final step was taken to abolish the Senate.

On the 28th May 1936 Mr. De Valera rose to conclude the debate in the Dáil on the motion required by the Constitution before the Abolition Bill could be passed into law. He was thus speaking for the last time on this subject. No speaker had referred during the debate either to Franklin or to Pennsylvania, and so there was no reason why Mr. De Valera should have done so either, apart from his maxim that it was the duty of representatives 'not to play the political game, in the sense of keeping back information and knowledge which ought to be used in the Legislative Assembly for the general benefit'. In the course of his speech he said:

'Franklin was a good political thinker. He had a good deal of experience. He was entrusted at that time with important missions. He was a man of the world—not a mere theorist—and he was in favour of a Single Chamber. It is said, of course, that the Legislature of Pennsylvania did not last very long, but I question whether the Single Chamber in the State of Pennsylvania was changed because it was a Single-Chamber Legislature. So far as I have been able to see it, there were, I think, other defects more fundamental even than that, and that it was because of these and the fact that the Constitution of the United States, on account of its federal character, being a Two-Chamber system, that Pennsylvania, after some fourteen years or so, adopted the Two-Chamber system.'[1]

Thus Mr. De Valera made no reference to the fact that his Government had made inquiry on the subject from Pennsylvania, and, if the reply to that inquiry was on the general lines of the article, he contradicted it in essential points, without giving any rebutting authority. He told the Dáil, in effect, that the single-chamber legislature of Pennsylvania was abolished, not because it was a single chamber, but because of other defects and because a two-chamber system had been · adopted for the Federal Constitution. The article makes no mention of any such other defects and gives no reason for the abolition other than the dangers inherent in the system. So far from the change having been made because of the adoption of a bicameral legislature for the Federation (i.e. on the 31st May 1787), we are told that 'after the adoption of the Constitution of 1776 public opinion soon began to decide that the one-chamber legislature was not conducive to good

---

[1] *Dáil Debates*, lxii, 1334, 5.

government in Pennsylvania'; and special attention is drawn by the writer of the article to the fact that the Committee of the Council of Censors, whose duty it was to report on defects in the Constitution, presented its report against the unicameral system in 1784, 'before the precedent of a two-house legislative body was established by the Federal Constitution'.

CHAPTER XXIII

DISSENSIONS ON LEFT AND RIGHT

*Schismatic tendency of Irish political parties—Placating the Re-
publicans—The Military Service Pensions Bill—The Volunteer Force
—Other factors weighing against extremism—The Vice-President
threatens physical force against the North—Republican dissensions—
Formation of the Republican Congress Party—Fracas at Wolfe Tone's
grave—Split in the Republican Congress Party—Outrages continue—
Misfortunes of the United Ireland Party—General O'Duffy's position
—The Corporate State—The Blue Shirts get out of hand—Professor
Hogan on General O'Duffy—Resignation of General O'Duffy and
split in the Blue Shirts.*

From the political point of view, the salient features of the summer
and autumn of 1934 were the increasing dissensions in the ranks of
the Irish Republican Army, and, at the other end of the scale, the
internal difficulties of the United Ireland Party. The schismatic tendency of Irish political parties was doubtless an underlying cause in
both cases, but there were other more specific reasons.

As regards the militant Republicans, the whole trend of Government activity had been in the direction of placating, and if possible
rendering innocuous, those who had fought against the State in the
Civil War of 1922-3. We have seen that some of them were given
important positions in the Volunteer Reserve and that a number of
others were recruited into a Special Armed Branch of the Civic
Guard. Those who were wounded in the Civil War had been given
pensions and those whose property had been damaged had been
compensated. On top of these measures, a Military Service Pensions
Bill was introduced in the Dáil on the 1st August 1934, the purpose
of which was to secure that those who fought on the side of the Irish
Republican Army in the Civil War should be pensioned on the same

basis as the officers and men of the Regular Army. The cost was estimated by the Minister for Defence at the enormous sum of £360,000 a year.[1] The Senate, so often accused of being reactionary, passed this Bill with celerity, and 'improved' it by inserting amendments which extended the benefits to women. All of the Senate amendments, nine in number, were agreed to by the Dáil.

It may be objected that such measures did nothing to wean from militant republicanism those who had been too young to take part in the Civil War. But for these there existed the Volunteer Force, or the Militia as it was popularly called. This was a scheme which had a very great deal to commend it, and it must have drawn off a great many potential warriors from the Irish Republican Army. Not surprisingly, it was violently attacked by the extremists, and the exhortations 'Join I.R.A. Boycott Milisha' (sic) became common on dead walls. The new Army Pensions Act was also condemned as a bribe, and on the 10th September the (Republican) Army Council issued a statement in which it was characterized as 'an attempt to buy off the hostility which exists against the rewarding and subsidising of treason'.[2]

Two other factors must have weighed against militant republicanism. The first was the change in the character of the parliamentary Opposition. In Mr. Cosgrave's time every step taken to deal with the menace from this quarter was fiercely assailed by Mr. De Valera and his followers. Now, the similar steps taken by Mr. De Valera, slow and halting though they might be, were taken in the knowledge that he had behind him a united Parliament. Moreover, he possessed, in the Military Tribunal, a weapon adequate for his purpose, with the added advantage that his abundant use of it in no way detracted from the odium incurred by his predecessor for having forged it.

The second factor was the altered character of the struggle. The previous Administration had stood upon the Treaty and the Constitution, and the issue was Irish Free State versus Republic. Its successor stood upon neither, and by this time the area comprised in the Irish Free State was as nearly a republic as makes no matter. As time went on, it was to be even more closely assimilated to that ideal. There was therefore not much left for the militant Republicans to fight about, except a republic for the whole of Ireland. Even here the Government competed with them. Mr. De Valera has stated upon occasion that the unity of Ireland can be achieved only by peaceful means, but the Administration spoke with two voices on

---

[1] *Dáil Debates*, liii, 2198.　　　[2] *An Phoblacht*, 15 September 1934.

this vital matter. Speaking in Dublin on the 26th March 1934, the Vice-President (Mr. O'Kelly) said: 'We will use every effort to re-establish a Republic for the thirty-two counties of Ireland. That is our aim, and if the gun is necessary the people have the Government to direct the Army and they have the Volunteer Force behind them again.'[1] If this was to be taken as the Government's aim, many young men might feel that they would satisfy their martial ardour, as well as their patriotic ambitions, in a more practical way by joining the Volunteer Force rather than the Irish Republican Army—and with less discomfort to themselves.

For these reasons or others, fissures began to appear early in 1934 in the ranks of the militant Republicans. The majority adhered to the Irish Republican Army, with the policy and methods of which we are familiar. They were led by Mr. Maurice Twomey, its Chief of Staff, and Mr. Seán MacBride, and they retained control of the weekly newspaper, *An Phoblacht*. The minority, headed by Mr. Michael Price and Mr. Peadar O'Donnell, formed the Republican Congress Party, its policy being the establishment of a workers' re-public through political action and by the penetration of the trades unions. At the annual pilgrimage to Bodenstown on Sunday, the 17th June, there was a clash between these two sides and something like a fracas occurred at poor Wolfe Tone's unquiet grave, the mem-bers of the Republican Congress Party being deprived of their banners.[2]

A few months later, the Republican Congress Party appears to have split again, this time, so far as can be gathered, on the question whether the ultimate aim was to be the setting up of a workers' republic or the establishment of a united front against imperialism. At a meeting of Congress held in Dublin on the 1st October, Messrs. Peadar O'Donnell, Frank Ryan, and George Gilmore were elected to the National Executive, but Mr. Michael Price, supported by the minority, refused to go forward, stating that until Congress stood for a workers' republic and the overthrow of capitalism he could not act on the executive and had but one place to turn to—the Citizen Army.[3]

It is impossible for a complete outsider to know how far, if at all, the personal element entered into these dissensions. Certainly the essential differences between all three parties do not appear to have been very great. The utterances of the Chief of Staff of the Irish

---

[1] *Irish Independent*, 28 March 1934.   [2] Ibid., 18 June 1934.
[3] *Irish Press*, 2 October 1934.

Republican Army at this time, as recorded in *An Phoblacht*, proclaim over and over again that the real enemy is the imperialist capitalist system.

The internal differences among the parties of the Left did not result in any appreciable diminution in the number of outrages and acts of intimidation, most of which went unpunished. Prominent at this time were several cases in which cinema proprietors were warned against showing pictures which did not meet with the approval of the extremists, and on the 3rd December direct action of an extremely unpleasant kind was taken against one of the largest Dublin picture houses for daring to show a film of the wedding of Princess Marina to the Duke of Kent.[1] But the principal outrages were directed against the persons and property of members of the United Ireland Party, and in particular of the League of Youth or Blue Shirts. This brings us to a consideration of the dissensions in the ranks of the official Opposition, which had long been developing and which reached their first crisis in the autumn of 1934.

It will be remembered that negotiations between Mr. Cosgrave's party and Mr. MacDermot's National Centre Party had concluded in the formation of the new United Ireland Party on the 8th September 1933, and that, to solve personal difficulties about leadership, Mr. Cosgrave had stood down in favour of General O'Duffy, who was thus brought in as a sort of *deus ex machina* to be chairman of the party. The Blue Shirts, of which he was Director-General, were constituted as a wing of United Ireland. From the very outset, the new arrangement was thoroughly unsatisfactory. Mr. Cosgrave enjoyed, and still enjoys, a personal popularity in the country far greater than that of his party as a whole or of any other member of it; and his wide experience of politics, together with his previous headship of the Government, designated him as the obvious leader of the united Opposition. General O'Duffy had none of these advantages. He had been a distinguished soldier and a first-class Chief of Police, and in the realm of athletics he had shown himself to be a capable organizer. But it quickly became apparent that he did not possess the special qualities that equip a man for leadership in political life. He had no seat in Parliament, and his numerous speeches too often indicated a lack of responsibility. Many of them, indeed, put his new colleagues in an embarrassing position.

The Blue Shirts, too, proved something of an incubus. This was a wholly admirable movement when wisely led and divorced from

[1] *Irish Press*, 4 December 1934.

politics; but a number of hot-headed young men now began to acquire an ascendancy in it, and they must have been uneasy bedfellows for the staid members of the parliamentary Opposition. Their influence made itself felt in the party's weekly newspaper, *United Ireland*, which often took on a vituperative tone that must have been distasteful to Mr. Cosgrave's better-educated followers. Some of its placards provided instances of unconscious humour, as, for instance, 'UNITED IRELAND. McGilligan Flays De Valera'.

The general feeling of uneasiness at the policy, or lack of policy, of the Opposition was not lessened by General O'Duffy's flirtation with the idea of a corporate State. Apart from thick-and-thin supporters of the Government, few people took seriously the allegation that he was aiming at a dictatorship, for he is much too genial to fill the role of a Hitler or a Mussolini. But the whole Fascist conception is repugnant to the vast majority of Irish people, who, with their strongly marked individualism and their traditional attitude towards constituted authority, are perhaps of all nations the least likely to conform to a system which demands the subordination of human personality.

Matters came to a head when, about midsummer, some of the Blue Shirts got out of hand. At this time very large numbers of farmers were defaulting over the payment of their rates and their Land Annuities. As a result, their cattle were being seized and sold by the sheriffs. By felling trees to block roads, cutting telephone wires, and other unlawful means the Blue Shirts began to impede these seizures and sales. At the first annual congress of the League of Youth, held on the 18th and 19th August and presided over by General O'Duffy, a resolution was passed calling on the farmers to refuse to pay their Land Annuities, and on the labourers to refuse to pay their rates, if the Government would neither suspend the demand for payment nor refer the question to an impartial tribunal.[1] Such a proposal cut at the root of all ordered government and could not be countenanced for a moment by any responsible parliamentary opposition. On the 31st August the National Executive of the United Ireland Party met in Dublin, and after a prolonged discussion a statement was issued that General O'Duffy had not pressed for the acceptance of the League of Youth resolution. At the same time, it was announced that Professor James Hogan had resigned.

Professor Hogan occupies the Chair of History in University College, Cork. He is a brother of the former Minister for Agriculture

[1] *United Ireland*, 25 August 1934.

and was one of the ablest men in the counsels of his party. In a statement issued to the Press he said that his resignation from the Executive was 'the strongest protest I can personally make against the general destructive and hysterical leadership of its President, General O'Duffy'. 'That Party can have no future so long as it retains at its head as leader General O'Duffy. Whatever his good qualities may be, in politics I have found him to be utterly impossible. It is about time the United Ireland Party gave up its hopeless attempt of saving General O'Duffy from his own errors.'[1]

It was obvious that such a situation could not continue, and on the 21st September it was announced from the offices of the United Ireland Party that General O'Duffy had resigned the chairmanship of the party.[2] There was then an unedifying dispute as to whether he had also resigned the post of Director-General of the League of Youth. The United Ireland Party held that he had, and appointed Commandant Cronin to fill the vacancy. Mr. Cronin was a determined young man who had originated the idea of the blue shirt uniform. A year previously he had been convicted by the Military Tribunal of membership of an unlawful association (the Blue Shirts), and, having refused to enter into recognizances, he had been sentenced to three months' imprisonment. General O'Duffy held that he himself was still Director-General, and there was a split in the ranks of the Blue Shirts, some of them following General O'Duffy and the rest following Commandant Cronin. The net result of the whole unpleasant affair was hopelessly to discredit the Blue Shirt movement and to damage the prestige of the parliamentary Opposition.

Thus by the end of 1934 the extremists on the Left were rent by dissensions, the constitutionalists on the Right had suffered the first of a series of set-backs, and Mr. De Valera was left as a *tertius gaudens*.

---

[1] *Cork Examiner*, 1 and 3 September 1934.
[2] Ibid., 22 September 1934.

CHAPTER XXIV

THE SENATE AND ELECTORAL CHANGE.
THE ARMED POLICE

Senators and General O'Duffy—Senator Douglas's Bill to restore the referendum for constitutional amendments—Passed by the Senate and ignored by the Dáil—The Defence Forces Bill—Doubtful wisdom of the Senate's action—The Bill to abolish university representation— The Vice-President's reasons—The real object—The Electoral (Revision of Constituencies) Bill—Infringement of minority rights—The two Bills in the Dáil—Attitude of the Senate—Senator Jameson's notable speech—The Senate rejects the Bill to abolish university representation —Its subsequent enactment—Amendments to the Electoral (Revision of Constituencies) Bill—The Dáil disagrees—The Chairman of the Senate gives his casting vote in favour of the Government—The Chairman's difficult position—Unrest among the farmers—The armed police —The shooting at Cork Sale Yard—Senator Wilson's motion—Retirement of the Government party from the House—The motion passed— The shooting justified by the Minister for Justice—Proceedings in the High Court—Written judgement of Mr. Justice Hanna—His Lordship's findings and conclusion—Confirmation by the Supreme Court on appeal—The Fourth Triennial Election—Analysis of the result—The defeated Senators—Increase in number of ex-members of the Dáil— The work of revision summarized.

It will be recalled that the Senate had rejected the Government's Bill to base the local government electorate on a universal adult franchise. The local elections were due to take place on the 26th June 1934, and, speaking on the 15th April as Leader of the Opposition, General O'Duffy stated that 'they were at a great disadvantage that the youth had not got a vote at these elections. It is our purpose to give the youth of this country a say, not only in national affairs,

409

but in local affairs too.'[1] In keeping with their curious belief that the majority in the Senate were the obedient tools of the Opposition, the Government attempted to initiate in the Senate, ten days later, a Bill similar to that which had already been received from the Dáil and rejected. Moving for leave to introduce it, the Minister for Lands (Senator Connolly) gave it as his opinion that this and similar statements by General O'Duffy (which he quoted) were 'an adequate reason and justification for the Senate changing its view'. Senators did not agree, and the motion was rejected by 30 votes to 17.[2] This was the only occasion in its history on which leave to introduce a Bill was refused by the Senate.

The introduction of the Senate Abolition Bill in the Dáil on the 22nd March was followed on the 9th May by the initiation in the Senate of the Constitution (Amendment No. 25) Bill. This measure was sponsored by Senators Douglas, Brown, and O'Farrell, and its purpose was to restore the referendum for constitutional amendments. Under the Constitution as it then stood, amendments to it might be made by way of ordinary legislation, and without a referendum, up to the 5th December 1938, after which a referendum became automatic for all such amendments. The effect of the Bill, if passed, would have been to make the referendum apply to all proposals to amend the Constitution by way of ordinary legislation (including, of course, the Bill to abolish the Senate), provided that it was demanded by two-fifths of the membership of the Dáil or a majority of Senators. In a very able Second Reading speech Senator Douglas showed that, under the Constitution, it was the people who were sovereign and refuted a statement made in the Dáil that that House was a sovereign assembly. He also reviewed in detail the constitutional position in various European countries and proved that, apart from the dictatorship States, there was no country in which the Constitution could be altered by a bare majority in one House. Senator Brown, who seconded, expressed the opinion that when, in 1929, Parliament extended from eight to sixteen years the period within which constitutional amendments might be made without a referendum, it had done something which it had no power to do, and that it had broken its contract with the people. He frankly admitted that the point had not occurred to him in 1929.

Senator Connolly replied for the Government. He commented on the fact that Senator Douglas had read his speech (as, in view of its importance, he was quite entitled to do by custom), and attacked both

---

[1] *Irish Press*, 16 April 1934.   [2] *Senate Debates*, xviii, 1037–46.

him and Senator Brown for their inconsistency in seeking a partial restoration of the referendum when they had supported its complete abolition in 1928. The Labour Party was in favour of the Bill, and the Second Reading was passed without a division.[1] The Final Stage was passed on the 6th June (five days after the rejection of the Senate Abolition Bill) and the Bill was sent to the Dáil.

Here its fate was similar to the Senate's earlier message requesting a Joint Committee on the constitution and powers of the Second Chamber. It was never discussed by the Dáil, and it appeared as an item on every successive Dáil Order Paper printed thenceforward for nearly two years, until the Senate was abolished on the 29th May 1936. If the Bill had been passed, most of Mr. De Valera's plans with regard to the Constitution would have been rendered difficult of execution, and possibly abortive. Even its discussion by the Dáil would have been inconvenient and dangerous; inconvenient, because Mr. De Valera would have found it hard to justify its rejection, in view of his previous attitude in 1928 and of his regard for the sovereignty of the people: dangerous, because the Labour Party might have supported it, as their colleagues had done in the Senate, in which case it would probably have been carried against the Government.

The refusal of the Senate to renew the Defence Forces Act beyond the 31st July 1934 necessitated the introduction of a fresh Continuance Bill well in advance of that date. This Bill, entitled the Defence Forces (Temporary Provisions) (No. 2) Bill, came before the Senate for Second Reading on the 6th June. The granting of commissions in the Volunteer Force to ex-members of the Irish Republican Army was again referred to, and Senator Blythe intimated his intention of again tabling amendments to provide that no person should be appointed to commissioned rank who had not undergone a period of training. This time the Chairman fortified himself by obtaining the opinion of the Committee on Procedure, which unanimously advised that the amendments were out of order, on the ground that any amendment to a Bill which merely continues the operation of a single expiring Act, other than an amendment altering the length of time of the continuance, is outside the scope of the Bill as read a second time.[2] The amendments were accordingly disallowed on this ground.

The Senate thereupon, on the initiative of Senator Blythe, inserted an amendment, by 22 votes to 12, limiting the operation of the Continuance Bill to the 30th November 1934, instead of the 31st July

[1] *Senate Debates*, xviii, 1162–94.   [2] Ibid., xviii, 1561, 1562.

1935, which was the date in the Bill as passed by the Dáil.[1] The other House disagreed with the amendment, and the Senate did not insist upon it, but altered the date to the 31st March. This was convenient, as being the end of the financial year; and the new amendment was agreed to by the Dáil.

Opinions will doubtless differ as to the wisdom or propriety of this action of the Senate with regard to the Defence Forces, following, as it did, on similar action taken only a few months previously. Those Senators who voted for the amendment on each occasion had perhaps this excuse, that the Minister for Defence, like all his predecessors in the Cosgrave Government, had promised to bring in a permanent Army Bill at an early date, to replace the existing Act which had been introduced and passed in 1923 avowedly as a temporary measure. Moreover, in addition to the question of the Volunteer Force, there was a rumour, referred to during the debate, that Major-General Brennan, whose term of office as Chief of Staff was about to expire, was to be replaced by a very prominent former Irregular leader. Even if all these facts be granted, it seems difficult to justify the action of the Senate on the second occasion in virtually holding up the Government at the pistol point with regard to the Army. Actually, the rumour concerning the Chief of Staff was falsified later. Major-General Brennan was appointed for a further term on the 16th October 1935, and he continued in office until his retirement in January 1940, his successor as Chief of Staff being a senior officer of the Regular Army.

We are now to consider two Bills which are closely connected and of which one was rejected by the Senate and the other suspended for a considerable time as a result of action taken by it. Both are concerned with the membership of the Dáil.

Under Article 26 of the Constitution the Dáil was to be composed of members representing constituencies to be determined by law. The number of members was to be fixed from time to time by Parliament, but the total (exclusive of university members) was not to be less than one for each 30,000 of the population, nor more than one for each 20,000. Parliament was charged with the duty of revising the constituencies at least once in every ten years, in accordance with changes in population as ascertained at the last preceding census.

Under Article 27, the two universities, that is to say, Dublin University (Trinity College) and the National University of Ireland, were entitled to elect three members each.

[1] *Senate Debates*, xviii, 1641–63.

The constituencies, and the number of members allotted to each, were specified in the Eighth Schedule of the Electora[1] Act, 1923, which became law on the 17th April 1923. Altogether, there were 153 members, inclusive of the six members for the universities.

The decennial revision required by the Constitution should presumably have been undertaken before the 16th April 1933, but the Government took no steps in the matter until nearly a year later, when two Bills were introduced in the Dáil on the same day (15th February 1934). One of them, the Constitution (Amendment No. 23) Bill, proposed to abolish university representation. The other was the Electoral (Revision of Constituencies) Bill,which deleted the Schedule contained in the Act of 1923 and substituted a new one, providing for a Dáil of 138 members. Under the Constitution, none of these changes could come into effect until after a dissolution.

Let us take first the Bill for the abolition of university representation. The Vice-President (Mr. O'Kelly), who introduced it, sought to justify it on three grounds: (1) the representation was out of all proportion to the number of electors concerned; (2) if a university education made a person more suitable to exercise the franchise, 'this body of intelligent voters should be distributed throughout the constituencies generally to leaven the mass'; (3) a number of the electors on the University Register were domiciled outside the country.[1] These reasons seem inadequate for depriving of the services of six educated men an Assembly which stood in great need of such services. The real object of the Bill, however, was to strengthen Mr. De Valera's hold on power. Experience of the proportional representation system, as operated up to that time, had shown how difficult it was for any single party to obtain a clear majority. At the last general election (which marked his greatest success to date) Mr. De Valera had 77 seats out of 153, or exactly half the House apart from the Chairman, who belonged to his party. If he could disfranchise some of his opponents, the position would be redressed in his favour. Normally, the three members for Dublin University voted against him on constitutional issues, especially on those connected with the maintenance of the Commonwealth connection. As regards the National University, it had been represented by three supporters of Mr. Cosgrave from September 1927 to the dissolution of 1932, one of them being the Chairman of the Dáil, whose return was automatic. From 1932 to 1933 there were two members of the Cosgrave party and one of Fianna Fáil. In 1933 the positions were reversed. By

[1] *Dáil Debates*, lii, 479–81.

abolishing university representation, therefore, Mr. De Valera stood to get rid of four or five opponents at the cost of losing one or two supporters. The Government had no mandate for this amendment of the Constitution, which, apart from its other obvious demerits, was a breach of faith with the Southern Unionist minority. Griffith and O'Higgins had promised a Senate, with university representation in that Senate. Later, this representation was transferred by consent to the Dáil. Now, both the Senate and university representation were to disappear.

The only other undertaking given to the Southern Unionists was that the rights of minorities should be respected by the adoption of proportional representation in elections for the Dáil. This undertaking was to be rendered practically valueless by the Electoral (Revision of Constituencies) Bill. It is an accepted fact that proportional representation does not afford a reasonable chance of representation for minorities in constituencies returning less than five members, and that in constituencies returning only three members a minority has virtually no chance at all of electing its candidate. A certain number of three- and four-member constituencies is, for geographical reasons, unavoidable; but the fewer they are the better the system works.

The position under the Electoral Act, 1923, was as follows:

Constituencies returning 9 members	1
Constituencies returning 8 members	3
Constituencies returning 7 members	5
Constituencies returning 5 members	9
Constituencies returning 4 members	4
Constituencies returning 3 members	6

This gives a total membership of 147, exclusive of the six members for the universities.

The new Bill made provision for a Dáil of 138 members, the reduction of nine being due to changes in population: and there was to be a startling increase in the number of constituencies having less than five members, as the following table will show.

Constituencies returning 7 members	3
Constituencies returning 5 members	8
Constituencies returning 4 members	8
Constituencies returning 3 members	15

Whereas under the existing law there were only ten constituencies having less than five members, out of a total of twenty-eight, there were now to be twenty-three out of a total of thirty-four; and the four constituencies which returned eight or nine members each were to disappear altogether. This was not all, however. Local patriotism and administrative convenience had alike been disregarded by the re-drawing of the constituencies, bits of counties being lopped off and joined on to others.

Very able speeches were made in the Dáil against both these Bills. In particular, the content and quality of those delivered by the members for the universities showed, by contrast, how much poorer intellectually the popular Chamber would be after their disappearance. Professor Thrift (now the Provost of Trinity College) said that the abolition of university representation was a breach of the agreement with the Southern Unionists. The Minister stated that no such understanding was on the records, and the Professor replied, 'There was an understanding, although whether it is on record or not I cannot say.' The Parliamentary Secretary to the Minister for Finance (Mr. Hugo Flinn) thereupon interjected, 'It is in the Lodge.' A few moments later, Professor Thrift repeated his remark, and Mr. Flinn again interjected, 'It is in the Lodge.'[1] The allusion, of course, is to Freemasonry. Professor Thrift gave the retort courteous which is appropriate in such circumstances: 'I do not pay any attention to Deputy Flinn's remarks.'

It is as well that this question of an undertaking or agreement should be cleared up. It is not disputed that university representation in the Senate was provided for in the written agreement with the Southern Unionists concluded after the Treaty.[2] When the Constitution was before the Constituent Assembly and the offer was made by Kevin O'Higgins to transfer this representation to the Dáil (4th October 1922), Professor Thrift gladly accepted it, but suggested to him 'to notify the three gentlemen who claimed to represent Southern Unionists, and see if they are satisfied with the alteration'.[3] Presumably O'Higgins did so, but the point is not very material. A fortnight later, when moving the insertion of the Article giving university representation in the Dáil, he stated that he did so, being 'anxious to make it quite clear that we did not simply enter into an agreement with certain people in London and come home and run away from it, but simply giving in place of what we removed from that agreement something considered of more value by the very people it was intended to cater for'.[4]

[1] *Dáil Debates,* lii, 599, 600.   [2] Ibid., i, 355.   [3] Ibid., i, 1153.   [4] Ibid., i, 1726.

Both Bills were passed by the Dáil by mechanical majorities and were sent to the Senate. The most notable contribution to the debate on the University Bill in that House was made by Senator Jameson. In the course of his speech he said:

'All the promises that were made by Mr. Griffith, Mr. Collins and Mr. O'Higgins are being swept away. . . . The thing of importance to this country is not that we, ex-Unionists, are being swept out of representation. Not at all. Not that the Universities are being swept out of representation, but that we are face to face with a state of affairs when the Party at present in power means to dominate the whole situation and to dictate to the whole of the Free State what it is to do. They are not merely putting out of business ex-Unionists and the members for the Universities, but their whole effort is to put the political representatives of the people in opposition to them out of business. . . . We have seen the powers of the law strained absolutely to the limit to put the representatives of the Opposition, if possible, into gaol, and anyhow to use every means that a Government could possibly use to attack them and to prevent them from getting a free method of stating their case. Let Senators think of the measures we have had here lately. We had a Bill dealing with the constituencies, so altering them as to bring in a large number of three-member constituencies, which undoubtedly will do away with the chances of Independent members, representing minorities, getting into the Dáil. Then we have a Bill at present before the House which proposes to take away representation which is also of an independent nature, University representation. Then we had a Bill which, at the end of next year, will sweep the Senate out of existence. . . .

'If the Government do favour the country with an opportunity of expressing its opinion . . . they will then have prepared the groundwork to give power to a solitary party. . . . They can make any laws they please. They can declare a Republic if they please. They can alter the laws to suit their views and to deal with their political opponents, so as generally to establish a Party dictatorship in this country. . . . This Bill about which we are now talking is only part of a great hoax. What this country will be face to face with at the end of two years is the domination of one Party, and one man at the head of that Party, with all that Party bowing in acquiescence.'[1]

The Senate rejected the Bill on the 18th July 1934, by 30 votes to 15. The suspensory period of eighteen months expired on the 4th January 1936 and the Bill was again sent up on the following 6th

[1] *Senate Debates*, xviii, 1979, 1980.

February.[1] The Senate had now only sixty days in which to consider it. The Bill was passed with an amendment providing that it should not come into operation until six months after the next dissolution.[2] This would have ensured university representation in the next Parliament, and in case of a change of government the Bill would have been dropped. On the 12th March the Dáil disagreed with the amendment.[3] Six days later the Senate insisted upon it. Finally, on the 23rd April, an enactment resolution was passed by the Dáil over the head of the Senate, and the Bill was signed by the Governor-General on the following day.[4]

We must now retrace our steps to 1934 and deal with the Electoral (Revision of Constituencies) Bill. The Second Reading was taken on the 27th June, when the Bill was subjected to detailed and informed criticism from all quarters of the House, and in particular from Senators O'Farrell and Douglas. On the Committee Stage a fortnight later a new schedule of constituencies was inserted on the initiative of Senators Brown and Douglas of the Independent Group and Senators Counihan and Wilson of the United Ireland Party. This sought to protect the rights of minorities by reducing the number of three-member constituencies while leaving the total membership unaltered at 138. This is made clear by the following table:

Constituencies returning 9 members	1
Constituencies returning 8 members	4
Constituencies returning 7 members	5
Constituencies returning 6 members	1
Constituencies returning 5 members	4
Constituencies returning 4 members	6
Constituencies returning 3 members	4

As has been said, proportional representation works fairly and effectively in constituencies which return five members or over. Under the law then existing, only thirty-four members (out of a total of 147) were returned from constituencies having fewer than five members. Under the Government's Bill, this number was to be increased to seventy-seven out of a reduced total of 138. The magnitude of the change is thus apparent. The Senate's amendment reduced the figure of seventy-seven to thirty-six. The Bill was passed with this and

---

[1] *Dáil Debates*, lx, 46–149, 225–48.
[2] *Senate Debates*, xx, 1939–2008, 2011–47.
[3] *Dáil Debates*, lx, 2122–60.   [4] Ibid., lxi, 1297–1396, 1503–28.

2E

certain consequential amendments on the 18th July and returned to the Dáil.[1]

The Dáil disagreed with the amendments on the following day;[2] and on the 22nd August the Senate took the eminently reasonable course of requesting a joint conference of five members of each House to discuss the points of disagreement.[3] This request was ignored for nearly six months until, on the 14th February 1935, the Dáil refused it.[4] Six days later the message conveying the refusal came before the Senate. By this time, owing to the Triennial Election, the composition of the House had changed, and on the question whether or not the Senate should insist on its amendment the voting was even, nineteen Senators being on each side. The Chairman thereupon gave his casting vote against the amendment and in favour of the Government, on the ground that the decennial revision of the constituencies required by the Constitution was already overdue, and that if he voted the other way the Bill might be suspended and the revision postponed still further.[5] The Bill therefore became law in its original form, with one minor amendment to rectify an error which had passed unnoticed in the Dáil.

Ever since the Chairman had delivered his striking speech in defence of the Senate from the floor of the House he had, as he had promised, resumed his rigid impartiality between all parties and groups. An instance of this has just been given, when he saved the Government from an awkward situation by giving his casting vote in their favour. But members of the Fianna Fáil Party could not forgive him for this speech, and their attitude towards the Chair underwent a change for the worse. This was exemplified in an episode which it is desirable to refer to in some detail, in view of the issues involved and of the light thrown on the methods by which the country was now being governed.

Mention has been made in the last chapter of the obstruction that was being offered to the seizure and sale of cattle owned by farmers who were in default over their Land Annuity payments. The seizure and sale, which were perfectly legal, were carried out by the sheriff under a warrant from the Land Commission, and the sale was by public auction. As the ordinary farmer would not buy cattle in such circumstances, the sales were attended by men who passed under fictitious names and who made their purchases at a gross under-

---

[1] *Senate Debates,* xviii, 1673–97, 1911–46, 2005–16.
[2] *Dáil Debates,* liii, 1764–76.   [3] *Senate Debates,* xix, 6–9.
[4] *Dáil Debates,* liv, 2051–6.   [5] *Senate Debates,* xix, 1294–1303.

value. A considerable amount of feeling was generated among the farmers, and the anonymous buyers were protected by members of the new armed police, popularly known as the Broy Harriers. On the 13th August 1934 such an auction was to be held at Marsh's Sale Yard in the City of Cork. A large crowd assembled, mainly composed of farmers, and these were kept back by a cordon of Civic Guards. A lorry filled with about fifteen men carrying sticks, but otherwise unarmed, was driven through the cordon and crashed through the closed gate of the Sale Yard, being followed into the yard by three or four persons, one of whom was a young boy named Michael Lynch. The armed police opened fire, with the result that Lynch was shot and died later the same day, and seven other people were wounded.

On the 6th September Senator Wilson brought before the Senate a motion condemning the shooting, demanding that those who took part in the fusillade be put on trial, and requesting that in future no Civic Guard be permitted to carry firearms who had not undergone the full ordinary training of members of the Force. The Minister for Lands (Senator Connolly) objected to the motion being taken at that time, on the ground that certain persons (not the police) had been arrested in connection with the affair and that the matter was *sub judice*. The Chairman, who had given consideration to the question, cited numerous exact precedents from the proceedings of the House of Commons, and concluded: 'It is clear on all the authorities that the motion is in order. It purports to condemn the action of the police, and not the action of the men who are about to be tried. So far as I am concerned, I shall do my best to ensure that nothing is said during the debate which might conceivably prejudice the fair trial of these men. A public tumult or affray is a matter of the gravest public importance, and the Oireachtas is the proper forum in which to discuss it.' Senator Connolly then made a short reply, in which he said: 'With regard to your ruling, I have no fault to find. . . . You can rule and decide within your own jurisdiction what you wish to do. That does not, at the same time, prevent us from taking any line of action that we choose to take.' He and his followers then retired from the House. Such an occurrence had never happened before in the history of the Senate, and it created a most painful impression. The motion was duly debated and carried without a division.[1]

On the following 14th November the matter was raised on the adjournment in the Dáil, and the Minister for Justice (who was res-

[1] *Senate Debates*, xix, 735–62.

ponsible for the armed police) stated that the shooting was justified, and that he was satisfied it was justified, on every ground.[1]

The whole affair had a remarkable sequel. The father of the boy who had been killed sued Chief Superintendent Fitzgerald, who was the responsible officer in charge of the Civic Guard in Cork at the time, and three of the armed police, named Moore, Condon, and Rodgers, for damages under the Fatal Accidents Act, 1846 (Lord Campbell's Act). The action was tried in the High Court by the Hon. Mr. Justice Hanna, sitting without a jury. His Lordship's written judgement, dated the 5th April 1937, is likely to become a classic on the law relating to the use of firearms by the armed forces of the State. Moreover, it seems to justify many of the actions of the Senate which incurred the hostility of the Government, such as its condemnation of the recruitment of armed police or Broy Harriers into the Civic Guard (22nd August 1933), its rejection of the Blue Shirt Bill (21st March 1934), and finally its motion of censure on the shooting in Cork (6th September 1934). In view of its importance, extensive extracts will be given from it here.[2]

His Lordship began by setting forth the nature of the claim and of the several defences, as disclosed in the pleadings. He mentioned the non-payment of Land Annuities by farmers and the steps taken by the Government for recovery, and referred more particularly to incidents alleged to have occurred at the same Cork Sale Yard on the 27th July 1934, that is to say, about a fortnight before the affray. 'At that sale it is alleged that there were three anonymous gentlemen, each of whom was known as O'Neill, one of whom was the purchaser at the sale. Until a late stage in this case everyone believed that there was only one man named O'Neill, who was referred to as either Mr. O'Neill or the man O'Neill, but an extraordinary state of affairs was alleged by the defendant Moore that these three men all passed by the name of O'Neill as a kind of trade name. How far this is true of this mysterious triumvirate I do not know, as none of these buyers was produced as a witness. It seems, however, that one man was known as "Bum" O'Neill.'

Mr. Justice Hanna referred to threats alleged to have been offered to 'Bum' O'Neill on the 27th July, but pointed out that these threats were not taken seriously at the time and that 'Chief Superintendent Fitzgerald, a sensible and experienced officer, took this view'. 'I have formed the opinion that what took place on the 27th had no impor-

---

[1] *Dáil Debates*, liv, 185–200.
[2] Lynch v. Fitzgerald and others. *Irish Law Times Reports*, vol. lxxi, pp. 212–24.

tance attached to it at the time by anyone but has been brought into
the present case now as an afterthought in an endeavour to strengthen the position of the defendants. In my opinion it only demon-
strates what the authorities already knew—that there was great
hostility and objection to the O'Neill personnel at the sales.' He believed that more importance was to be attached to the fact that the
Civic Guards in Cork became aware that there was to be a demonstration on the 13th August and took special precautions to keep the
peace on that occasion.

His Lordship next considered the position of the armed police. 'It
is necessary here to describe the protection given to the buyer or the
composite buyer when attending a sale. The buyers were protected
by members of what is known as the "S" Division of the Gárda
Síochána. Now who are they? ... From the autumn of 1933 I am of
opinion that a special body of armed men, called by courtesy
"Guards" and taking the Oath as Civic Guards, but designated
officially "S" men, was formed for the specific purpose of putting
into force the powers of the Government under Article 2A of the
Constitution, the Treasonable Offences Act and the Firearms Act;
and also, when required, to do special protection duty for individuals.
They were not given the training or discipline of the ordinary uniformed Guards, which is long and effective. For about three months
they were given instruction in these Acts of Parliament and their
duties thereunder; but I am satisfied on the evidence that these men
were selected mainly for their skill and experience with the gun. If I
am to take the seven of these men who appeared before me as typical,
they had all been members of the Irish Republican Army and admitted that they were skilled and accustomed to the use of firearms
long before joining the armed forces of the State. In the execution of
the duties detailed to them as members of the armed forces, they were
uncontrolled and left to their own undisciplined judgment in the use
of firearms. It was submitted on their behalf that, having regard to
the nature of their work, this was inevitable. While not accepting that
contention, it would seem that, even if it were so, there was all the
more necessity for careful training and severe discipline. It is necessary to make this clear inasmuch as the ordinary uniformed Civic
Guards and the crime (ordinary) detective officers undergo a prolonged training and discipline before they are released upon the
public—training which ensures judgment, prudence and self-control,
by reason of which they have never become a menace to civil liberty.

'One of these extra duties put on the "S" men was the protection of the anonymous buyers at the land annuities auctions. The defendants and some others had been at Marsh's Yard on 27th July. One of these was the defendant Moore, who, though without rank, assumed to be and was accepted as a sort of leader by the others. Between 27th July and 13th August (namely, on Thursday, the 9th) the notice of the demonstration and meeting had been issued, and on Saturday, 11th August, Moore went to Superintendent Weir, who was acting in charge of the "S" section in Dublin during the absence of Superintendent McGloin, and told him that he expected trouble in Cork on Monday, the 13th, and he would like some more men and arms beyond the usual number of seven men armed with revolvers. He was not given extra men. He was given extra arms in the form of four rifles and 200 rounds of ammunition.

'Now, I would pause here to say that, if there was a belief on the part of the authorities that a breach of the peace would occur requiring extra men or arms, the meeting should have been proclaimed under section 24 of Article 2A of the Constitution. . . . This power of proclaiming meetings is to prevent the very thing that subsequently happened—a conflict between the Guards and civilians, and to act, further, as a serious warning to those who might be inclined to take part in the meeting.

'I am satisfied that the authorities knew that this would be a big meeting and extra precautions should be taken on this occasion. The three anonymous buyers, so-called O'Neill (including "Bum" O'Neill), went from Dublin to Marsh's Yard in two cars accompanied by seven of the "S" men, each armed with revolver and ammunition, and having in each car two rifles and 100 rounds of ·303 ammunition. They said their special duty was to protect the life of O'Neill or the lives of the three O'Neills.'

Mr. Justice Hanna next proceeded to describe in detail the topography of the area adjoining the Sale Yard and of the Sale Yard itself. He then dealt with the arrangements made by the local Civic Guards in Cork to deal with any disturbance that might arise.

'In my opinion their plans were well-conceived and satisfactory from every point of view, as the result showed. Chief Superintendent Fitzgerald was in charge of the whole force from Cork. The "S" men from Dublin clearly repudiated any authority on his part to interfere with them in any way, their view being that they would not have taken orders from him, that they knew their own job and would carry it out as they thought best. I have formed the opinion that Chief Superintendent Fitzgerald, in face of this deliberate repudiation, was not quite sure of his position with regard to these men, but I am satisfied that if he had seen them doing anything wrong and had an opportunity of interfering he would have done so. The "S" men came into the Yard, parked their lorries between the covered pens and the sales ring and apparently wandered about as they liked inside the Yard.'

With regard to the number and character of the crowd outside the yard, the judge said: 'Taking what I consider the most reliable estimates, I think there must have been about 1,500 people present. They have been described as an ordinary crowd, orderly and peaceful, with no signs of arms or weapons. It was suggested that the men from the country had concealed about their persons bludgeons and sticks as if by arrangement in preparation for violence. I am not prepared to accept this, but I am equally certain that most of the farmers had sticks with them such as ashplants and the heavy sticks that are usually carried in fairs.'

His Lordship next described how the lorry drove through the cordons of police and crashed through the gate into the Sale Yard, followed by the boy Lynch and a few others. He found as a fact, which he stated to be an important fact, that the cordon at the gate was immediately re-formed and the crowd, save a few, kept out of the yard. Within fifteen or twenty seconds of the lorry's crashing through the gate the police had the outside situation under control. Once the lorry and its crew got into the Yard, they were trapped. The lorry itself was hemmed in by cattle pens and barriers, and a police cordon which was inside the gate was instantly re-formed. 'Accordingly there was no escape for the men or those who had followed them.' His Lordship found that the number of men in the lorry was between twelve and fifteen, together with the driver and one man outside, and that only three or four of the crowd followed the lorry into the yard.

'We come now to the crucial question as to the firing. The seven "S" men, without any officer or control, were at various points throughout the Yard. . . . There is no doubt in my mind that Moore started the fusillade. Coming back from the gate he heard the crash, turned, called on his comrades either to get ready or used some other words which they undoubtedly took as a command or suggestion to open fire on the crowd trapped in the lorry or about the gate. Moore fired forthwith, emptying his revolver at a distance of 15 or 20 yards. He then obtained a rifle from the cars and discharged several rifle shots. Condon emptied his revolver and then took his rifle from the car and fired with it out of the window of the sales ring. Rodgers, the other defendant, fired from his revolver and continued firing after being warned to stop by Mr. O,'Neill, T. D. [Mr. Edmond O'Neill, a member of the Cosgrave Party in the Dáil and of the Blue Shirts], and until finally stopped by Superintendent Bergin. I have no reliable evidence as to the checking of the ammunition of the "S" men and I am not satisfied as to the number of shots fired at the crowd or, as alleged, in the air. It was alleged that twenty shots were fired in the air, but I do not think any of these men would waste a shot. I believe that all of them fired to kill. . . . It is immaterial to this action that the other "S" men with the exception of O'Dowd also took part in the fusillade. . . .

'Some of the civilians, when they were seeking shelter from the fire, ran towards some tar barrels at the right of the gate. One of these was young Lynch. I think it was as he ran that he was shot in the stomach. He had got into the shelter of a barrel when Mrs. O'Neill [wife of Mr. Edmond O'Neill], with great courage, ran to help him. A remarkable fact which has impressed me very much is that on this barrel behind which Lynch crouched there were bullet marks. One was the mark of a bullet having hit the tar barrel but it did not penetrate; the second was the entrance hole and an exit, and the third was an entrance hole only. These marks were seen by the photographer for the Guards but were not photographed. They indicate to me that after the young fellow had got into some shelter, wounded as he was, some of the "S" men endeavoured to kill him. Attempted murder is the only expression in law to describe such conduct. It is unnecessary to further consider the humane treatment of Lynch by Mr. and Mrs. O'Neill and some of the uniformed Guards. He died that night from his wounds, which were undoubtedly caused by the firing. Seven other persons were wounded.'

Having stated that Chief Superintendent Fitzgerald, who was the officer in charge of the Civic Guards, 'certainly gave no order for the firing nor did he authorize or ratify it in any way whatever so as to make him liable', Mr. Justice Hanna continued:

'Mr. Black [Counsel for the defence, now the Hon. Mr. Justice Black, of the High Court], with that liberty of language which is allowed to an advocate, said it was absurd that the necessity of the occasion should be determined by an armchair strategist, meaning, with all courtesy, the Court. Fortunately or unfortunately, it is the law that a judge, hearing the evidence of both sides, is the person considered best qualified to decide such an issue. Above all, the judge has the great responsibility of standing between the civil population and the executive forces of the State and of determining whether the powers of the latter have been exceeded. Civilians have no other protection than the Judiciary, to whom accordingly absolute independence is guaranteed.

'Let us briefly summarize the facts as to the conditions outside and inside the Yard on the question of protection. Outside the Yard there were about 200 capable Guards with about a dozen armed detectives. After a few moments they held the crowd in check, save a few. Inside the Yard there were 40 Guards, including 10 ordinary detective officers armed. The lorry with its load of men had run into a veritable trap, as it was surrounded on all sides by barriers and Guards and could not make any headway. None of the men in the lorry had arms. They had sticks. The Guards inside the gate who subdued them had no arms—only batons, and none of the armed men inside or outside the Yard thought it necessary to resort to firearms except the defendants and their colleagues. The suggestion that these forces were not sufficient to protect both the "S" men and their charges against the lorry men and the few who came in following it, who had only the usual weapons of an Irish country crowd, cannot be accepted by any reasonable person. I certainly cannot hold for a moment that there was any justification for sending fusillade after fusillade of revolver and rifle shots into the men huddled in the lorry and at the three or four men running to escape.'

His Lordship then reviewed at considerable length the various legal decisions on the question of the suppression of civil disturbance by armed force, some of the cases cited being concerned with riots which had been the subject of House of Commons rulings quoted by the Chairman of the Senate. He showed that on none of the legal tests applicable to the case could the three defendants, Moore, Condon, and Rodgers, receive a favourable decision; and he continued:

'There has been disclosed a very striking and lamentable fact from the standpoint of public safety, namely, the deliberate repudiation by these armed "S" men of the authority and control of the Cork officers. This bears upon their irresponsibility. Surely it cannot be that when seven armed men of ordinary rank are sent out without a sergeant or officer in control, to do duty in a disturbed area, where there are a chief superintendent and several superintendents and inspectors, we are to be told that they are entitled to snap their fingers at those officers and be a law unto themselves. This is not a case of one man or two men protecting an individual, but of seven. The fact that Moore and Condon were made sergeants shortly after this occurrence cannot deceive anyone. It is too obvious. An ordinary Guard takes years of hard service to attain the rank of sergeant, but these two men, notwithstanding their want of training and knowledge of Guards' duties, are given (I do not say attain) that rank in about a year after joining the force. These "S" men are not real Civic Guards. They are an excrescence upon that reputable body.'

Concluding his judgement, Mr. Justice Hanna gave judgement in favour of Chief Superintendent Fitzgerald, and as regards the issues of fact raised he answered as follows:

'1. *Q*. Was it necessary in the last resort for Moore, Condon and Rodgers to fire on the lorry, and the men who came after it, in order to protect the lives of the prospective buyers, as alleged?

'*A*. No.

'2. *Q*. Did the three defendants, Moore, Condon and Rodgers, *bona fide* believe at the time that it was necessary as a last resort to fire on the lorry, and the men who came after it, in order to protect the lives of the prospective buyers?

'*A*. No.

'3. *Q*. Was it an emergency in which, having regard to all the circumstances, it was excusable or justifiable for the three defendants, Moore, Condon and Rodgers, to fire on the lorry and the men following the lorry in order to protect the lives of the prospective buyers?

'*A*. No.

'4. *Q*. Did the defendants, Moore, Condon and Rodgers, resort to unjustifiable force in firing as alleged?

'*A*. Yes.

'5. *Q*. Did the deceased boy, Lynch, receive the injuries from which he died from the wrongful act or acts of the defendants acting as a group with a common unlawful purpose?

'*A*. Yes.

'6. *Q*. Damages?

'*A*. £300.'

His Lordship then concluded as follows: 'But this case should not end with the determination of the civil liability of the defendants. The evidence disclosed a *prima facie* case of manslaughter, and it is the duty of the Court before which a *prima facie* case of a criminal offence is committed to call the attention of the Attorney-General to it and to the judge's opinion. Accordingly, it will be my duty to direct the attention of the Attorney-General to the evidence in this case and to my judgment thereon, with an expression of my opinion that the criminal liability of these three defendants against whom I have given judgment should be investigated by a jury. This investigation of the criminal liability is all the more necessary as the three defendants belonged to the armed forces of the State and there cannot be one rule for them, when their acts result in the death of a citizen, and another in the case of a motor driver who causes a death and has to stand his trial before a jury.'

An appeal was made from this judgement to the Supreme Court. On the 30th July 1937 reserved judgement was delivered by the Supreme Court, unanimously dismissing the appeal with costs.

It has been necessary to give these extensive extracts from the judgement of Mr. Justice Hanna, partly because of the intrinsic importance of the judgement itself, but also because of the light which it throws on the administration of justice at this time. The strictures passed upon the defendants may also be said to reflect upon the Government. Coming from any other source, such strictures might be disregarded as a mere *ex parte* statement of opinion; but this is not possible in the case of a judgement of the High Court, founded upon the evidence. With regard to the judge's opinion that the criminal liability of Moore, Condon, and Rodgers should be investigated by a jury, it suffices to say that no such investigation ever took place.

The fourth Triennial Election to the Senate was held in November 1934. It took place under the shadow of abolition, and it was as great a failure as its two predecessors held under the same system. As in 1931, there were twenty-three vacancies, caused by the following retirements: seven of the original fifteen Senators who had been nominated for twelve years in 1922 (all the rest having died or resigned); nine who had been elected for six years in 1928; two who had been elected for three years in 1931; and five who had been elected to fill casual vacancies in the period then current. The Constitution required that there should be a panel of forty-six names, composed as to one-half by the Senate and as to the other half by the Dáil. This requirement was not fulfilled. The Senate portion, which was formed first, consisted merely of the eighteen retiring Senators who were offering themselves for re-election. The Dáil portion contained only seventeen names, and six of these were duplicated from the Senate portion. There were thus only twenty-nine candidates for the twenty-three seats. At the time the panel was formed a by-election was in progress, the candidates being Mr. P. F. Baxter and Mr. P. Lynch, K.C. Both names were placed on the Dáil portion of the panel.

The result of the election was as follows:

* 1. T. W. Westropp Bennett.
* 2. James C. Dowdall.
* 3. Edmund J. Duggan.
* 4. Andrew Jameson.
* 5. Raphael P. Keyes.
* 6. Thomas Johnson.
* 7. Kathleen A. Browne.
* 8. Patrick Lynch, K.C.
9. Thomas Ruane.
10. Pádraic Ó Máille.
11. Thomas V. Honan.
12. Denis D. Healy.
13. James J. Boyle.
14. Séamus Fitzgerald.
*15. Jennie Wyse Power.
*16. Dr. Oliver St. John Gogarty.
17. Thomas Kennedy.
*18. Richard Wilson.
*19. Ernest Blythe.
20. Patrick F. Baxter.
*21. Samuel L. Brown.
*22. John Bagwell.
*23. Sir Edward Coey Bigger.

In view of the imminent disappearance of the Senate, the order of election was immaterial; but the first twenty Senators were to sit for nine years, the twenty-first and twenty-second for six years, and the twenty-third for three years.

In terms of parties, the result was as follows: Fianna Fáil, 10; United Ireland Party, 6; Independent Group, 4; Labour, 2; Independent, 1. The only Independent elected was Senator Westropp Bennett, and his return at the top of the poll was a merited tribute to his conduct of the Chair.

Four of the outgoing Senators had not offered themselves for re-election: the Earl of Granard, Mr. H. S. Guinness, Mr. George Crosbie, and Mr. F. MacGuinness. The two former had been members since the beginning, having been nominated in 1922; both were men of distinction, who had in every respect justified their selection. Both had suffered through their courage and public spirit in accepting nomination at that time, as their Irish residences were mined by Mr. De Valera's followers during the Civil War. Neither would have had much chance of success at the 1934 election. Messrs. Crosbie and MacGuinness both died at the end of November. Mr. Crosbie was a man of the senatorial type, and as proprietor of the *Cork Examiner* he had considerable influence in the south of Ireland. During his three years' membership he had made many useful contributions to the debates. Mr. MacGuinness had been so long prevented from attendance by ill health that his retirement made no difference other than the filling of a seat which had to all intents and purposes been vacant for six years.

* Outgoing Senator.

Of the six defeated candidates, two were newcomers—Miss K. Breen (Fianna Fáil) and Mr. M. P. Connolly (United Ireland Party) —and four were outgoing Senators—Mrs. Costello, Sir Thomas Esmonde, Sir John Keane, and Mr. James Moran. All four had been members since the beginning. Mrs. Costello had probably given the best attendance of any Senator. Sir Thomas Esmonde had been prevented by failing health from taking much part in the proceedings of late years. Mr. Moran was an extremely capable and successful man of business of a type which was by this time hardly represented in the Senate at all. The most serious loss, however, was undoubtedly that of Sir John Keane. Ever since the beginning he had proved himself to be, on the widest variety of subjects, a convincing and well-informed parliamentarian. He had originated debates probably on more occasions than any other member of the House, and he was as good a debater as he was a public speaker. Both Administrations had found in him a shrewd but not unfair critic. His great defect lay in his unwillingness to co-operate with any group or party, and his aloofness was the cause of his defeat. His natural affinity would have been with the Independent Group, led by Senator Jameson, but he did not belong to it; and by this time the members of that group and their friends in the Dáil were too weak numerically to do more than secure the return of their own four members who were going forward again—Senators Bagwell, Sir Edward Bigger, Brown, and Jameson. The case might have been different if any one of these had not been a specially suitable candidate; but all four had, over a long period of years, proved themselves in their different ways to be Senators of the highest class. As it was, three of them were placed at the bottom of the list—a sad commentary on the system of election.

The number of Senators who had been members of the Dáil was now increased by two. Senator Baxter (United Ireland Party) was defeated at the general election of 1922, elected as a Farmer in 1923 and June 1927, and lost his seat in September 1927. He stood again in 1932 and 1933 and was again defeated. Senator Ó Máille (Fianna Fáil) had been a member continuously from 1918 to 1927. He had formerly belonged to the pro-Treaty party and had been for a time Deputy Chairman of the Dáil. He had been defeated at both general elections held in 1927.

As to the work of revision done during the Triennial Period which now closed, one hundred non-Money Bills had been received, of which forty-six were amended. More than five hundred amendments were inserted, and all but forty-seven were agreed to by the Dáil.

PART VI

THE FIFTH TRIENNIAL PERIOD
6th DECEMBER 1934 TO 29th MAY 1936

'*Men must reap the things they sow,*
Force from force must ever flow.'
SHELLEY, *Lines written among the Euganean Hills.*

'*The division of the legislature into two separate and independent branches is founded on such obvious principles of good policy, and is so strongly recommended by the unequivocal language of experience, that it has obtained the general approbation of the people of this country. One great object of this separation of the legislature into two Houses, acting separately, and with co-ordinate powers, is to destroy the evil effects of sudden and strong excitement, and of precipitate measures, springing from passion, caprice, prejudice, personal influence and party intrigue, which have been found, by sad experience, to exercise a potent and dangerous sway in single assemblies.*'

JAMES KENT, *Commentaries on American Law*
(1851), vol. i, p. 228.

CHAPTER XXV

THE WHEEL COMES FULL CIRCLE

The United Ireland Party—Mr. Cosgrave elected chairman—Statistics of convictions by the Military Tribunal—The Bishop of Cork on the situation—The war in Abyssinia—Mr. De Valera's attitude at Geneva—Criticism by Opposition leaders—Resignation of Mr. Mac-Dermot—General O'Duffy's policy—Death of King George V—Resolutions in Dáil and Senate—The Irish Republican Army—Murder of Mr. Richard More O'Ferrall—Anti-Government demonstrations—Attempted interference in the Dublin tramways dispute—Ministers heavily guarded—Mr. Dillon on the extremists—The rival factions—Mêlée at Wolfe Tone's grave—The end of An Phoblacht—*Interference with Mr. De Valera's broadcast—Murder of Vice-Admiral Somerville—Condemnation by the Bishop of Ross—Murder of John Egan—Michael Conway sentenced and reprieved—The Irish Republican Army proclaimed an unlawful association—Imprisonment of its Chief of Staff—The wheel comes full circle—Mr. De Valera's regrets.*

We begin by following the fortunes, or misfortunes, of the United Ireland Party. On the 21st March 1935 Mr. Cosgrave was unanimously elected to the chairmanship, a position which had been vacant since the resignation of General O'Duffy on the previous 21st September, and Messrs. Dillon, MacDermot, Commandant Cronin and Dr. O'Higgins were elected Vice-Chairmen. The two first-named had been leaders of the National Centre Party before fusion, Dr. O'Higgins had been a prominent member of the old Cosgrave party, and Commandant Cronin was the head of that section of the Blue Shirts which had refused to follow General O'Duffy into the wilderness. Mr. Cosgrave stated on that occasion that 'membership of the Commonwealth was not only a guarantee for the maintenance of our distinct and individual nationality, but it offered us more—the guarantee of the unity and integral solidarity of our nation and people'.[1]

Throughout the summer the large farmers, who were mostly supporters of the Opposition, continued to be harassed in connection with the Land Annuities payments, and flying squads of the new armed police pursued their activities in armoured cars. Some idea of the position may be obtained from statistics officially given by the Government in the Dáil, though they cover a period prior to that which we are considering. On the 13th February 1935 Mr. Mac-Dermot was informed that the number of persons convicted by the Military Tribunal from the 1st September 1933 to the 5th February 1935 was 513. Of these, according to the best information at the Government's disposal, 375 were members of the League of Youth or its predecessor, the Young Ireland Association, and 138 were members of the Irish Republican Army—a proportion of about three to one.[2]

The situation was particularly bad in County Cork, where the farmers wrongfully took the law into their own hands and burnt the house of one of the members of the Government party in the Dáil, Mr. P. S. Murphy, a solicitor, and attempted to burn the house of another, Mr. Martin Corry. Speaking in Cork on the 5th June, the Catholic Bishop of the diocese (Most Rev. Dr. Cohalan) recalled the land war of half a century earlier and said: 'At that time "suspects" galore were arrested and lodged in gaol without trial; there were innumerable seizures; the tribe of emergency men appeared who bought at a nominal price and made a small fortune on animals that the regular buyers would not touch. They had it all back again. Do not think I am talking politics or for or against any political party. I am speaking in the interests of morals. I see the country becoming torn by political hatreds. I see class war and faction war.'[3]

The war in Abyssinia had its effect on the United Ireland Party. On the 16th September 1935 Mr. De Valera made a striking speech at the Assembly of the League of Nations at Geneva, in which he stated that his country stood by its obligations under the Covenant. The speech was received with warm applause by the other delegates.[4] The Opposition at home, however, took a somewhat different view. On the 22nd September, at Thurles, Dr. O'Higgins said that 'if their assistance was pledged without any settlement of their own quarrel

---

[1] *Irish Independent*, 22 March 1935.   [2] *Dáil Debates*, liv, 1759.
[2] *Irish Independent*, 6 June 1935.   [4] Ibid., 17 September 1935.

it was an opportunity lost which might never return'.[1] Mr. Cosgrave spoke on similar lines in Dublin on the 4th October. 'Ottawa was the first lost opportunity. The latest is Geneva.'[2]

Mr. MacDermot thereupon addressed a letter to Mr. Cosgrave, expressing his total disagreement with these sentiments and with utterances to the same effect which had been delivered by prominent members of the Opposition. He stated that Dr. O'Higgins's speech had been seen and approved by Mr. Cosgrave before it was made, and continued: 'The line of argument seems to me to offend against common sense and consistency, and to make nonsense of everything we stand for. It is one that can be renewed every time that Mr. De Valera behaves with ordinary decency in international affairs, and when it would be more becoming for us to commend him than to attack him.'[3] After this, Mr. MacDermot's resignation from the United Ireland Party was inevitable, and it was accepted on the 10th October. He made no attempt to split the Opposition, and sat in the Dáil as an Independent. The underlying cause of his break with his former colleagues probably went deeper than the occasion of it, and had its origin partly in sharp differences of temperament and partly in a fundamental difference of outlook regarding Ireland's attitude to the other members of the British Commonwealth. This episode did not end the internal troubles of the Opposition, as we shall see presently; but it lowered their prestige, weakened to some extent their debating power, and left them open to attacks from the flank as well as from the Government Front Bench.

General O'Duffy still claimed to be head of the League of Youth, but at a meeting held on the 8th June 1935 the name of his section of it was altered to the National Corporate Party. The uniform was somewhat modified, but the blue shirt was retained. General O'Duffy delivered a long address, in the course of which he said: 'We will establish a Republic *de jure* for thirty-two Counties and *de facto* for twenty-six. . . . The Empire or Commonwealth idea only appeals to those who regard themselves as British colonists.'[4] Less than nine months previously he had been chairman of the United Ireland Party, which placed first in its programme firm adherence to the Commonwealth. As regards those Blue Shirts who seceded with him, their action merely affords further proof that the tendency in Ireland is to follow persons rather than principles. Little more was heard of the National

[1] *Irish Independent*, 23 September 1935.
[2] Ibid., 5 October 1935.   [3] *Irish Times*, 8 October 1935.
[4] *Irish Independent*, 10 June 1935.

Corporate Party, for the General and his men were soon to find a fresh outlet for their energies on the far battlefields of Spain.

The rest of this chapter will be concerned with the activities of the Irish Republican Army, and with the policy of the Government in regard to that organization. But reference must first be made to the death of His Majesty the King on the 20th January 1936. On the following 5th February, at the first meeting of the Dáil held thereafter, the President of the Executive Council moved the following motion: 'That Dáil Éireann expresses its deep sympathy with his Majesty King Edward VIII, with her Majesty Queen Mary and the Royal Family, and with the people of Great Britain on the death of his late Majesty King George V.' There were no speeches, and the motion was passed in silence, the members rising in their places.[1] One week later the same motion was proposed in the Senate by the Minister for Lands (Senator Connolly), Senator Mrs. Clarke dissenting in a brief speech.[2] Those who are unaware of the facts should be slow to pass judgement on this action of Mrs. Clarke, which was quiet and dignified, and showed moral courage. She is the widow of Thomas J. Clarke, the veteran Fenian leader, who prior to his marriage had served sixteen years as a political prisoner in England. He was the first signatory of the Proclamation of the Republic issued in Easter Week, and as such, in spite of his advanced years, he was executed by order of a court martial on the 3rd May 1916. Her brother, Edward J. Daly, was executed on the following day. It is these grim legacies of the recent past that forbid any facile solution of the Irish problem.

On the 26th February, the Chairman of the Senate read to the House a message of thanks received from King Edward VIII, 'signed by His Majesty's own hand' and transmitted through the Department of External Affairs.[3] A similar message was communicated to the Dáil on the same date.[4]

We now turn our attention to the Irish Republican Army. A dispute had been in progress for a considerable time between the tenants and the owner of the Sanderson Estate, Edgeworthstown, County Longford, which had formerly belonged to the family of Maria Edgeworth, the celebrated novelist. Subsequent to the tragedy which we are about to describe, the following facts were stated in the Dáil by Mr. MacDermot and agreed to by Mr. De Valera. On the 5th November 1934 the local Town Tenants' Association passed a resolu-

---

[1] *Dáil Debates*, lx, 43.   [2] *Senate Debates*, xx, 1937.
[3] Ibid., xx, 2009.   [4] *Dáil Debates*, lx, 1145.

tion inviting the intervention of the Irish Republican Army in the dispute, and another on the 20th November, inviting the Irish Republican Army to hold a public meeting in Edgeworthstown on the 2nd December.

That meeting was duly held, and incitements to violence were uttered in the presence of Civic Guards, who duly reported to their superior officers, but no action was taken. Mr. De Valera said in mitigation of these admissions that there was nothing at the time to show that these incitements had had, or were likely to have, any inflammatory effect on public feeling; to which General MacKeon replied that one speaker had said that only one tree would be left growing on the estate, and that would be for the purpose of hanging Mr. More O'Ferrall, the agent for the property.[1] At this time, it must be remembered, numbers of farmers who were political opponents of the Government were being arrested in County Cork, haled before the Military Tribunal, and cast into gaol.

At 9 p.m. on the 9th February 1935, while Mr. More O'Ferrall was at dinner with his family in his home at Lisard, Edgeworthstown, four armed men entered the room and fired at Mr. More O'Ferrall and his son at point-blank range. The bullet glanced off the father's cigarette case, and this probably saved his life. The son, Mr. Richard More O'Ferrall, aged twenty-one and married, was not so fortunate. A bullet penetrated his stomach and lodged in his spine. The miscreants then decamped in a motor-car.[2]

Preaching in Longford Cathedral on the following Sunday, the bishop of the diocese (Most Rev. Dr. McNamee) condemned the outrage in unmeasured terms. 'There is no true liberty without law. . . . Without respect for law there can be no liberty, but only the execrable tyranny of the gunman.'[3]

The condition of young Mr. More O'Ferrall was hopeless from the beginning. He was removed to a Dublin nursing home, where he died on the 20th February. At the inquest on the following day the jury returned a verdict of 'wilful murder'.[4]

A week after the death, Mr. MacDermot asked Mr. De Valera whether, in view of recent events, the Executive Council would now consider making an Order, under Article 2A of the Constitution, declaring the Irish Republican Army to be an unlawful association. Mr. De Valera replied that it was not the opinion of the Executive Council that the necessity had arisen for the course suggested. In a

---

[1] *Dáil Debates*, lv, 342, 343.   [2] *Irish Independent*, 11 February 1935.
[3] Ibid., 18 February 1935.   [4] Ibid., 22 February 1935.

supplementary question, Mr. MacDermot asked if Mr. De Valera was aware that perhaps the greater part of the strength of such organizations was derived from the belief that in their hearts the majority of the Fianna Fáil Party approved of their existence. Mr. De Valera's answer was that such a belief, if it existed, was without any foundation.[1]

Four men were arrested in connection with the Edgeworthstown crime and charged with murder. They were not brought before the Military Tribunal, but before the Dublin Criminal Court, the case being tried before the Hon. Mr. Justice Johnston and a jury. All the accused pleaded not guilty. After lasting nearly a fortnight, the trial ended on the 12th July 1935, the foreman of the jury intimated that there was no possibility of agreement, the jury were discharged and the four accused were remanded in custody.[2] A second trial began on the 2nd December 1935, before the Hon. Mr. Justice Meredith and a fresh jury. The case for the prosecution occupied a week, and when it had concluded the foreman of the jury informed the judge that the jury wished to deliver its verdict. The judge said that 'it seemed a very serious thing that they should come to a decision before hearing the accused, who were to go into the box that morning, and before the prosecution had an opportunity of cross-examining them'. He asked if the jury had considered that aspect of the case. The foreman replied that they had, a verdict of 'not guilty' was returned in regard to all four of the prisoners, and they were released, the State entering a *nolle prosequi* in regard to certain other charges. The judge stated that 'he would like the jury to know that he quite understood the position they were in and that he agreed with their findings'.[3]

Three years afterwards, one of the discharged prisoners, J. J. Reynolds, died in remarkable circumstances. On the night of the 29th–30th November 1938 several customs huts were wrecked along the Northern Ireland border, by means of time-bombs concealed in suitcases left for deposit. On the previous evening (28th November) a cottage near the border town of Castlefin, County Donegal, was partially demolished by a terrific explosion, caused, apparently, by the premature explosion of a bomb of the same type. Three men in the cottage were killed, and one of them was J. J. Reynolds.[4]

The Laodicean attitude of the Government towards the Irish Republican Army seems to have had the effect of rousing the passions of

---

[1] *Dáil Debates*, lv, 1.   [2] *Irish Independent*, 13 July 1935.
[3] Ibid., 11 December 1935.
[4] *Irish Times*, 29 November and 1 December 1938.

the extremists without rendering them any the less dangerous. This fact was exemplified by the events of March and April 1935. Of late years the festival of Ireland's patron saint (17th March) has been made the occasion of a military display, and in this year such demonstrations took place in various places throughout the country. The march-past of the troops in College Green, Dublin, was marred by ugly scenes. A large black flag was hoisted bearing the figures '77', in allusion to the seventy-seven Irregulars executed by the Government during the Civil War of 1922–3, and pamphlets were showered on the crowd, which referred to the Army as 'England's Ally', asserted that the Free State was as detestable in 1935 as in 1922, and called for recruits for the Irish Republican Army. On the same day, in Tralee, eggs were thrown at the platform from which the Minister for Defence was taking the salute.[1]

All this may seem highly unreasonable, but it was the inevitable result of Mr. De Valera's actions and speeches from 1922 onwards, his refusal to support the Government when he was in opposition in the Dáil on the measures necessary to cope with the Irish Republican Army, and his virtual toleration of that organization since he had come into power. In particular, nothing could explain away the declaration which he made in 1929 that 'those who continued on in that organization which we have left can claim exactly the same continuity that we claimed up to 1925'. The puzzled state of mind of the average countryman is well expressed in the statement of a Kerry farmer to Professor O'Sullivan, quoted by him in the Dáil: 'One son of mine fought against the Black and Tans. The other was with Mr. De Valera in 1922 in revolt against the Treaty Party. The third took seriously Mr. De Valera's statement as to wherein lay the real authority of the country in 1929, and the fourth is also in gaol.'[2]

At midnight on the 2nd March there began a tram and omnibus strike which paralysed passenger transport in and round Dublin and lasted for seventy-six days. The hardship fell most heavily on the working classes, and from the 20th March onwards the Government placed Army lorries at their disposal, which conveyed them from the suburbs to pivotal points in the City and back again. The Irish Republican Army thereupon took a hand in the business. On the 23rd March, at midnight, two Civic Guards who were patrolling Grafton Street, Dublin, unarmed and in uniform, were shot at and wounded by men who decamped on bicycles; and about the same hour another

---

[1] *Irish Independent*, 18 March 1935.
[2] *Dáil Debates*, lvi, 417, 418.

Civic Guard was shot at close to the offices of the *Irish Press*.[1] Three days later, forty members of the Irish Republican Army and of the Republican Congress were arrested, including Mr. Michael Price, one of the leaders, and also the editor of *An Phoblacht*.[2]

On the 25th March a statement issued by the Army Council of the Irish Republican Army was published in the newspapers. It referred to the action of the Free State Government in using the Free State Army for, as it alleged, strike-breaking purposes, and said that this constituted a definite challenge to all workers. 'For these reasons,' it continued, 'the Army Council hereby expresses its willingness to assist the workers in their struggle.' The trade union leaders very wisely ignored this gratuitous offer, but the organ of the Government party, the *Irish Press*, in a leading article entitled 'Fishing in Troubled Waters', did not condemn the interference as an outrage but seemed to reason with the extremists, rebuking them for the 'thoughtlessness' with which the statement was composed.[3]

This tendency to blow hot and cold was exemplified a few days later. At Eastertide it is the custom of the Republicans to hold flag days, in which the paper emblem sold is in the form of a lily. In a leading article of the 3rd April the *Irish Press* stated: 'We understand . . . that the proceeds of the sale of Easter lilies go, at least in part, to the I.R.A., some of whose leaders have declared that they will use arms against the majority's Republican representatives.' On the following day the same newspaper published, on its front page, a large, coloured advertisement for the sale of these emblems.

By 'the majority's Republican representatives' was meant, presumably, the Government party, and it is clear that by this time Mr. De Valera and his fellow Ministers considered themselves to be in grave physical danger. Easter Sunday, which fell on the 21st April, was the next great religious festival after Saint Patrick's Day, and it also was made the occasion of a secular demonstration on a large scale. Mr. De Valera travelled in state from Portobello Military Barracks to unveil a memorial in the General Post Office commemorative of the insurrection of 1916, and the precautions taken for his safety were extraordinary. The procession did not follow the main thoroughfares, and it was alleged that the head of the Government was heavily guarded by military and police.[4]

Mr. Dillon referred in the Dáil to the protection which had to be given to Ministers. On the 3rd May 1935 he said:

[1] *Irish Independent*, 25 March 1935.   [2] Ibid., 27 March 1935.
[3] *Irish Press*, 25 March 1935.   [4] *Dáil Debates*, lvi, 307, 308.

'President De Valera is at present going round this city and country heavily guarded. There are ten or fifteen men constantly vigilant to protect him from something. The Minister for Justice is heavily guarded. The Minister for Industry and Commerce is heavily guarded. . . . Do they intend to tolerate the continued existence in this country of a body of men who they believe would murder the President of the Executive Council if he was not adequately protected by the forces of the State? . . .

'They have seen turned against themselves the very self-same methods of insolence, aggression and intimidation that they rejoiced to see turned against us in the past. . . . The humblest citizen in this State has as much right to go about his legitimate business as has the President of the Executive Council, and he ought to get the same protection. But he did not. On the contrary, the blackguard and the intimidator were clearly shown that they had the sympathy of the Government so long as they confined their activities to attacking ordinary citizens who were members of our organization.'[1]

What had happened was that the Irish Republican Army still adhered to the doctrines enunciated by Mr. De Valera in 1922, and that he was being pursued by the nemesis of his past. But the extremists now lacked the advantage, which they had enjoyed prior to 1932, of a sympathetic Opposition in the Dáil, and the repressive measures to which they were now increasingly subjected were probably rendered more effective by their own internal dissensions.

The trouble between the rival factions which had manifested itself at the annual pilgrimage to Wolfe Tone's grave in 1934 became accentuated when the anniversary came round again on the 23rd June 1935. After angry exchanges between members of the Irish Republican Army and members of the Republican Congress Party, carrying banners, there was a fierce *mêlée*. Poles marking the assembly field were pulled up, broken, and used as cudgels by the combatants. References were made to 'a Hitleritic section of the I.R.A.', and Mr. George Gilmore mentioned that he had just returned from the United States, where Republican supporters, as at home, were split into groups.[2]

The weekly newspaper of the extremists, *An Phoblacht*, was now so often suppressed that it probably seemed hardly worth while to continue its publication. Moreover, its editor was in gaol. It became at length a mere typed sheet, and its final issue, dated the 6th July 1935, breathed defiance to the last.

[1] *Dáil Debates*, lvi, 389, 391.   [2] *Irish Independent*, 24 June 1935.

'Coercion is being used against Republicans to-day because they are an embarrassment to the conspiracy for another betrayal of the Republic, based on Mr. De Valera's "external association" plan, in which Britain is to receive facilities in time of war. But Mr. De Valera can no more succeed in intimidating Republicans from defence of the Republic than Churchill or Greenwood, Collins or Cosgrave succeeded. The Republican Army will continue in its training and organization, preparing for its task of overthrowing British imperialism and native treason. That is our answer to Mr. De Valera.'

At the military parade in Dublin on Saint Patrick's Day, 1936, there was no repetition of the scenes which had taken place on the previous occasion. After the march-past, Mr. De Valera broadcast from Dublin, but the wires had been tapped and he was subjected to almost continuous interruption, which rendered his voice inaudible. At one point a man could be heard saying, 'Hello, comrades! For the past half-hour we have just witnessed a very fine display of English militarism.'[1]

And now we come to a tale of horror which will take long indeed for us to expiate. Vice-Admiral Henry Boyle Somerville, C.M.G., had had a distinguished career in the Royal Navy, and on his retirement in 1919 he had settled down with his wife in the little seaside village of Castletownsend, County Cork, where he was born. In 1936 he was seventy-two years of age, in every respect a lovable and patriotic old Irishman, whose chief interest was archaeology. His sister was Miss Edith Somerville, co-authoress of *Some Experiences of an Irish R.M.* and other books, which depict the life of the Irish countryside with much insight and sympathy. Castletownsend, like other places, was impoverished, largely through misgovernment, and the more enterprising young fellows of the neighbourhood had been accustomed to seek advice from the Admiral as to how they could join the Navy. The old man, in his kindly way, had always told them what to do and given them references. That was all.

At 9.30 p.m. on the 24th March 1936, as the Admiral was sitting with his wife, footsteps were heard on the gravel outside. He remarked that it was probably some of his boys, and he went to the hall door with a lamp in his hand. But it was four murderers who had arrived in a motor-car. The Admiral opened the door, the lamp was dashed out of his hand, and he was shot dead like a dog on his own threshold and in the presence of his wife. Beside his body was left

[1] *Irish Independent*, 18 March 1936.

a small card on which was written, 'This English Agent sent fifty-two Irishmen to the British Army in the last seven weeks.'[1]

This atrocious, cowardly crime sent a thrill of horror through the country. The Catholic bishop of the diocese (Most Rev. Dr. Casey) ordered a letter to be read in all churches on the following Sunday, in the course of which he said: 'The gospel of the present-day patriot seems to be hate, and his works murder. Let there be no mistake about it—any man, from the actual assassin down to the man who knowingly and wilfully played the least part of the tragedy, is guilty of wilful murder. Every citizen is bound to give all possible assistance to those whose duty it is to bring the miscreants to justice. It is a matter of public safety, a question as to whether we are to live as civilized people protected by law, or in fear of the secret murderer. Personally, I have long been convinced that most of the present troubles of our people are a divine judgment on past crimes. It is sad to think that we seek a remedy by plunging still deeper into iniquity.'[2]

Though the actual assassins may have come from outside the district, the crime could hardly have been committed without the assistance of persons having local knowledge. But the bishop's words fell on deaf ears, and no one was ever apprehended for it. The Government still refrained from declaring the Irish Republican Army to be an unlawful association under Article 2A of the Constitution, though the Minister for Justice, in reply to a Parliamentary Question, expressed 'the Government's sympathy with the relatives of the victim of this cowardly crime and its determination to take every possible step to bring those responsible to justice'.[3]

On the night of the 26th April 1936 four men commandeered, at the point of the revolver, a motor-car belonging to a District Justice in County Tipperary and drove in it to Dungarvan, County Waterford, where they called at the house of a young man named John Egan, aged twenty-four years. Egan was not at home, but they met him in the street about 11 p.m., beckoned him over to the car, and poured bullets into his body. He staggered as far as the priest's house, where he collapsed. The priest, hearing the firing, opened the door, and found the unfortunate man dying in a pool of his own blood. The motor-car was later found abandoned miles from the scene of the tragedy.[4]

At the inquest it transpired that Egan had at one time been a member of the Irish Republican Army. The reason for his murder is

[1] *Irish Independent*, 25 and 26 March 1936.   [2] Ibid., 30 March 1936.
[3] *Dáil Debates*, lxi, 364.   [4] *Irish Independent*, 28 April 1936.

a matter of conjecture, but he may have left, or wished to leave, that organization. Possibly he had been detailed to take part in the assassination of Vice-Admiral Somerville and had been sentenced to be executed for his refusal.

The following July, a man named Michael Conway was tried by the Military Tribunal for the murder of Egan. He refused to recognize the court or to call witnesses. On the 16th July the Tribunal held that a *prima facie* case had been made out, and it adjourned the trial for five days, in order to give the accused time to consider his position. When the court reassembled on the 21st July the position was unchanged, and Conway was found guilty of murder and sentenced to be hanged on the 12th August. On the 24th July the sentence was commuted by the Executive Council to one of penal servitude for life.[1] After serving less than two years of this sentence, Conway was unconditionally released on the 4th May 1938, the occasion of Dr. Hyde's unopposed election to the Presidency under the new Constitution.[2]

It was nearly three months after the murder of Vice-Admiral Somerville, and nearly two months after that of John Egan, that the Government took the final drastic step. On the 18th June 1936 an Order was made by the Executive Council declaring the Irish Republican Army to be an unlawful association under Article 2A of the Constitution. On the following day a meeting due to be held at Wolfe Tone's grave on the 21st June was proclaimed under the same Article; and Mr. Maurice Twomey, the Chief of Staff of the Irish Republican Army, was sentenced by the Military Tribunal to three years' penal servitude for membership of an unlawful association.

It had thus taken nearly five years for the wheel to come full circle. Let us briefly recall some of the events and utterances which have already been recorded in this book. On the 14th March 1929 Mr. De Valera said: 'The Executive have been trying to use force, and have been using it all the time. If they are going to meet force by force then they cannot expect the co-operation of citizens who wish that there should not be force.' On the 14th October 1931, when moving the Bill to insert a new Article 2A in the Constitution, Mr. Cosgrave, then the head of the Government, read out a long list of particularly atrocious and cowardly crimes attributed to members of the Irish Republican Army. On the following day, Mr. De Valera said: 'These men are misguided, if you will, but they were brave men, anyhow; let us at least have for them the decent respect that

[1] *Irish Independent*, 17, 22, 25 July 1936.   [2] Ibid., 5 May 1938.

we have for the brave.' Article 2A was inserted in the Constitution in the teeth of Mr. De Valera's opposition. On the 17th October 1931 an Order was promulgated bringing the Article into force, and three days later another Order was issued declaring the Irish Republican Army to be an unlawful association. On the 9th March 1932 Mr. De Valera was elected President of the Executive Council in succession to Mr. Cosgrave. Nine days later an Order was issued suspending Article 2A of the Constitution, and the Order which had declared the Irish Republican Army to be an unlawful association thereupon lapsed.

The outrages were resumed. On the 1st August 1933 Mr. De Valera contrasted the Blue Shirts with the Irish Republican Army, stating that the former were 'not a body which has any roots in the past, not a body which can be said to have a national objective such as the I.R.A. can be said to have'. And now, on the 18th June 1936, after many more appalling crimes, the Irish Republican Army was once more declared to be an unlawful association. Mr. De Valera was back where Mr. Cosgrave had been in 1931.

Speaking in the Dáil on the 23rd June 1936 Mr. De Valera said: 'Do I regret the policy we have adopted? If that policy has led in any way to the murder of individuals in this State I regret it. I cannot say whether it is that policy that has done it but, if it has, I must regret it.'[1] This hypothetical and characteristic expression of regret was also a fitting epitaph on his policy towards the Irish Republican Army.

[1] *Dáil Debates*, lxiii, 112.

CHAPTER XXVI

THE END OF THE SENATE

State of parties—Inroads of the party system—The Chairman re-elected by casting vote—A new Vice-Chairman—Three Bills dealing with citizenship—The Constitution (Amendment No. 26) Bill and extra-territoriality—The Irish Nationality and Citizenship Bill—Repeal of British common law and statute law relating to nationality—Mr. De Valera and cesser of status of British subject—Senator Brown's analysis of the constitutional position—Reliance on British forbearance—The position of Northern Ireland—'Nationals' and 'citizens'—The Senate's wholesale amendment of the Bill—The Aliens Bill—Definition of 'alien' —Exemption provisions—Enactment of the three Bills—The Aliens (Exemption) Order—Instances of the Senate's co-operation with the Government—The National Loan conversion operation—The imposition of sanctions against Italy—Statesmanlike attitude of Mr. De Valera—The Senate Abolition Bill again before the Dáil—Mr. De Valera and the function of revision—Absence of safeguards—His speech in reply to the debate—The period of transition—Question of a new Constitution still in doubt—The Senate's motion in regard to the Bill—Its implications examined—Mr. De Valera fails to attend the Senate—The reason given for his absence—The Chairman's explanation—Brilliant speeches against the Bill—The motion carried—Split in the Labour Party—The Senate's message ignored by the Dáil—A hand-to-mouth existence—Possible reasons why validity of abolition not challenged in the courts—Judgement of the Privy Council in Moore v. Attorney-General—Judgement of the Supreme Court in Ryan v. Lennon—Deterioration in Senate personnel—The Senate's final meeting—Disposal of the Casket—Valedictory speeches—The Senate's work summarized—The enactment motion in the Dáil—Mr. De Valera discloses his plan for a new Constitution—His speech in reply to the debate—The Senate ceases to exist.

At the outset of the Fifth Triennial Period, which was destined to last for less than half its normal term, the political complexion of the

446

Senate was as shown in the following table, the figures for the two preceding Triennial Periods being given for purposes of comparison.

	1928	1931	1934
United Ireland Party[1]	19	21	22
Fianna Fáil	7	13	19
Independent Group	12	10	7
Independents	15	9	4
Labour Party	6	6	7
Chairman	1	1	1

These figures emphasize in a striking manner the inroads made by the party system on what had been in its inception a non-political Second Chamber. The Independent Group was, as its name implies, a group of independents, since its members were in no way regimented. In 1928 this group and the unattached Independents had numbered twenty-seven, or nearly half the House; in 1931 the figure had dropped to nineteen, and now in 1934 it had dropped still further to eleven. On the other hand, Fianna Fáil had grown in six years from seven to nineteen, and the Cosgrave party showed a small increase, from nineteen to twenty-two.

The personnel of the Senate remained unchanged until its abolition. Of the original sixty Senators, twenty retained their membership continuously to the end; fifteen of these came from the half which had been elected by the Dáil, and the remaining five had originally been nominated by the President of the Executive Council. A few months before the Senate's disappearance two vacancies occurred, Senator Comyn being made a Circuit judge and Senator S. Robinson being appointed to a post under the Government. These vacancies were never filled, and the Senate ended with fifty-eight members instead of sixty.

On the 12th December 1934, at the first meeting held after the commencement of the Triennial Period, there was a test of party strength over the election of the Chairman, it being the object of the Government party to oust Senator Westropp Bennett from the office which he had held for the previous six years. Except for one member of the United Ireland Party (Senator MacKean) there was a full attendance of members, and, according to precedent, the Chair was taken by the senior elected Senator present, General Sir William Hickie, an Independent, who had headed the poll in 1925. The two candidates were the outgoing Chairman, Senator Westropp Bennett, and the

[1] Formerly Cumann na nGaedheal.

Government candidate, Senator Comyn. Neither of the candidates voted, and the number of Senators who took part in the division was therefore fifty-six. Of these, twenty-eight voted each way, those for Senator Westropp Bennett being the twenty-one members of the United Ireland Party and the seven members of the Independent Group, and those for Senator Comyn being the eighteen members of the Government party, the seven Labour members, and three Independents (Senators Sir Edward Bellingham, Linehan, and O'Neill). It therefore devolved on Sir William Hickie, as Acting Chairman, to give a casting vote, and he gave it in favour of Senator Westropp Bennett, on the ground that if he had not been in the Chair he would have voted for him. The outgoing Chairman was therefore re-elected.[1]

The outgoing Vice-Chairman (Senator O'Hanlon) was not so fortunate. The election, which took place a week later, was also contested by Senator Comyn, who defeated Senator O'Hanlon by twenty-six votes to twenty-five.[2] On the appointment of Senator Comyn to a judgeship, another member of the Government party (Senator David Robinson) was appointed to the Vice-Chair (11th March 1936). The Senate had then only a short time to run, and there was no other candidate.

Early in this Triennial Period the Senate received from the Dáil a trilogy of Bills dealing with the law relating to citizenship. These were the Constitution (Amendment No. 26) Bill, the Irish Nationality and Citizenship Bill, and the Aliens Bill. All three were sponsored by Mr. De Valera in his capacity of Minister for External Affairs.

The Constitution (Amendment No. 26) Bill was wholly uncontroversial. Article 3 of the Constitution provided that every person having the qualifications of birth, parentage, or residence therein mentioned 'is a citizen of the Irish Free State and shall within the limits of the jurisdiction of the Irish Free State enjoy the privileges and be subject to the obligations of such citizenship'. It had been contended by the Irish delegates at the Conferences of 1926, 1929, and 1930 that the Parliament of the Irish Free State was competent to give Irish Free State legislation extra-territorial operation, and Section 3 of the Statute of Westminster, 1931, declared and enacted 'that the Parliament of a Dominion has full power to make laws having extra-territorial operation'. This Bill accordingly amended Article 3 by deleting from the words quoted above the phrase 'within the limits of the jurisdiction of the Irish Free State'.

Article 3 had also stipulated that 'the conditions governing the

---

[1] *Senate Debates*, xix, 765–70.   [2] Ibid., xix, 833, 834.

future acquisition and termination of citizenship in the Irish Free
State shall be determined by law'. The enactment of a law relating
to citizenship was therefore long overdue, and the omission was now
rectified by the Irish Nationality and Citizenship Bill. If this measure
had merely been drafted on the general lines of similar Acts promulgated by some of the other members of the Commonwealth it also
would have been uncontroversial. But Mr. De Valera continued his
policy of piecemeal republicanism by the insertion in the Bill of a
clause in the following form:

'(1) The British Nationality and Status of Aliens Act, 1914, and
the British Nationality and Status of Aliens Act, 1918, if and so far
as they respectively are or ever were in force in Saorstát Éireann, are
hereby repealed.

'(2) The common law relating to British nationality, if and so far
as it is or ever was, either wholly or in part, in force in Saorstát
Éireann, shall cease to have effect.

'(3) The facts or events by reason of which a person is at any time
a natural-born citizen of Saorstát Éireann, shall not of themselves
operate to confer on such person any other citizenship or nationality.'

This clause, with its qualificatory phrases, affords a good example
of Mr. De Valera's reluctance to face facts which he does not like.
Article 73 of the Constitution provided that the laws in force in the
Irish Free State at the date when the Constitution came into operation (6th December, 1922) should, to the extent to which they were
not inconsistent therewith, continue to be of full force and effect until
repealed. Accordingly, there never was any doubt that the common
law, and also the Acts of 1914 and 1918, were part of the substantive
law of the country.

The matter, however, went further than that. Without any mandate from the people, Mr. De Valera was attempting to deprive Irish
men and women of their right to be regarded as British subjects. The
language which he used in the Dáil left no doubt on the point. 'We
are not able to take Acts off the British Statute Book. We are not
able to prevent the British from calling our citizens British subjects.
. . . When this Bill becomes law it would be an impertinence if they
were to claim as citizens of their country people who are obviously
citizens of another country. . . . Under Irish law, no Irish citizen
will be a British subject when this Act is passed. . . . I want to say
that not a single line of this Bill need be altered if a Republic were
declared in Ireland to-morrow.'[1]

[1] *Dáil Debates*, liv, 410.

As usual, these provocative declarations were made, not in Mr. De Valera's opening speech on the Second Reading in the Dáil, but in his concluding speech. Mr. MacDermot interrupted him to express his regret that they had not been made earlier, so that the discussion might have taken note of them; and he recalled the fact that, in the debates on the Oath Bill, Mr. De Valera himself had been careful to point out that the mere abolition of the Oath did not alter the fact of allegiance. Mr. De Valera's reply now was: 'Well, it does not matter. What I say is that the Oath of Allegiance is a different thing altogether. That does not say that I accepted the matter of allegiance any more than the oath.'[1]

On the 17th January 1935, in the debate in the Senate, this question was dealt with by Senator Brown in a speech which revealed all his familiar clarity of thought and of expression and which, because of its importance, he read from a manuscript. He said that Mr. De Valera's assumption that he could get rid of the status of British subject within the Irish Free State was due to a misconception of the nature of that status as applied to members of the British Commonwealth, and a misconception of the power of any one member of the Commonwealth to discard that status without the consent of all the other members of the Commonwealth. He referred to Mr. De Valera's assertion in the Dáil that any benefits which come to us as British subjects come, not from allegiance, but from 'the fact of association', and from nothing else. Senator Brown traversed this statement and asked, 'What creates the association, for it is not in the air?' He answered this question by quoting the famous Balfour Declaration contained in the Report of the Imperial Conference of 1926 and also that part of the preamble of the Statute of Westminster, 1931, which states that 'the Crown is the symbol of the free association of the members of the British Commonwealth of Nations, and as they are united by a common allegiance to the Crown. . . .' Senator Brown asked, 'What language could be plainer than that?' and continued: 'Now this new common allegiance to the King of the United Kingdom as the sovereign head of the British Commonwealth of Nations involves a common status which is still called "British subject" but which differs from the status of British subject when applied to the citizens of Great Britain and Northern Ireland. The difference would seem to be this: the citizen of the United Kingdom as a British subject not only owes allegiance to the King as King of the United Kingdom, but is also bound to perform all the obligations arising

[1] *Dáil Debates*, liv, 413–14.

from his allegiance to his own King, and to observe all the laws of his own country. The citizens of each of the other members of the British Commonwealth of Nations owe allegiance to the King in his capacity as sovereign head of the Commonwealth and in no other capacity. They have no other obligations to the King, except allegiance, and they are not bound, while outside the United Kingdom, to obey any law of the Parliament of Great Britain. There is surely nothing derogatory to the dignity of any of the Dominions in this common status of British subject; and it carries with it, not only the right to appeal as a British subject for protection all over the world, but also to claim in the United Kingdom the rights and privileges which are open to British subjects coming from the Dominions.'

Senator Brown referred further to the preamble of the Statute of Westminster, which he described as 'a solemn statement of the fact of the agreed constitutional position of all the members of the Commonwealth with reference to the Crown'. He pointed out that it had been accepted by Mr. De Valera himself as—in his own words—a 'declaration solemnly made' when speaking in the Senate on the Bill to abolish the Oath. He concluded: 'If I am right in this as a conclusion of Constitutional Law, then section 30 of this Bill, in so far as it seeks to put an end to the status of British subject as applicable to the Irish Free State, is inoperative not only in the United Kingdom and in the other Dominions, but also within the Irish Free State itself.'[1]

This exposition of the constitutional position seems to be sound: but in any case the fact is undeniable that by such actions as these Mr. De Valera has placed his country in an inferior position as regards Great Britain. He could ask for a clear mandate to secede from the Commonwealth and, in the unlikely event of his receiving that mandate, he could exercise it. Instead, membership of the Commonwealth is continued and steps are taken which are plainly inconsistent with membership. Though the truth may not be admitted, reliance is placed on British forbearance—a course which hardly redounds to the national dignity. Moreover, the Irish who live or travel in the United Kingdom or abroad and who require for their purposes the recognition of their status as British subjects are compelled expressly or by implication to repudiate the views of the head of their Government. In the recent past many Irish people have, as British subjects, been removed from the theatres of conflict in China and Spain by ships of the Royal Navy, some of the officers and men of which were also doubtless of Irish nationality. It is unlikely that

[1] *Senate Debates*, xix, 1034–40.

either rescuers or rescued were unduly troubled by the fact that this humanitarian work proceeded on an assumption which the head of the Irish Free State Government had characterized as an impertinence.

Senator Brown's speech on this question of status was ably reinforced by another from Senator Milroy, but no attempt was made to delete this particular section in committee. If such an amendment had been proposed, it is unlikely that it would have been carried, in view of the changed political complexion of the House. Mr. De Valera was involved in difficulties of another kind by his desire so to frame his Citizenship Bill that not a line of it need be changed in the event of a republic being declared for the whole of Ireland. In the Bill as it left the Dáil persons in Northern Ireland who desired registration would have been obliged to have their names entered in the Foreign Births Register. Attention was drawn to this peculiarity when the Bill came before the Senate, and provision was made for a Northern Ireland Register, necessitating voluminous amendments.

Another difficulty was not solved because it is insoluble. Article 3 of the Constitution states that citizens of the Irish Free State, as therein defined, shall enjoy the privileges and be subject to the obligations of citizenship. A curious legal point arises under this Article, the territory for citizenship purposes being the area of the jurisdiction of the Irish Free State at the time of the coming into operation of the Constitution, i.e. the 6th December 1922. But on that date the area of the Irish Free State was co-terminous with the whole of Ireland, since Northern Ireland did not exercise the right, granted to it under the Treaty of 1921, to opt out until the following day (the earliest date at which it could have done so). It would seem, therefore, that the bulk of the inhabitants of Northern Ireland are, in law, citizens of the Irish Free State by virtue of Article 3 of the Constitution. The point is, of course, purely academic, since the Irish Free State Government had no power to impose any obligations on them, and it had long ago made it clear that it was not prepared to accord them any privileges. The very first Budget of the Fianna Fáil Administration, in 1932, had discriminated against the tobacco factory established in Dublin two years previously by Messrs. Gallaher of Belfast, with the result that the factory had to be closed down and three hundred Dublin workers were thrown out of employment.[1] The term 'national' had been defined in numerous statutes, such as the Control of Imports Act, the Agricultural Produce (Cereals) Act, the

[1] *Dáil Debates*, xlii, 601–12.

Moneylenders Act, and the Control of Manufactures Acts, but the definition had always been such as to exclude an inhabitant of Northern Ireland. This was perhaps inevitable, but it was odd that the Irish Nationality and Citizenship Bill took no account whatever of these 'nationals'. When the Bill became law the anomaly would exist of persons who would be 'nationals' for the purpose, for example, of holding shares in companies, but who would not necessarily be 'citizens', and of 'citizens' who, if they were on the Northern Ireland Register, would not be 'nationals' for such a purpose. Senator Douglas drew attention to what he termed an absurdity, and suggested the introduction of a short Bill to codify and clarify the law on the subject of 'nationals' as opposed to 'citizens'. This course, however, has not been taken.

Altogether, no less than thirty amendments, covering six pages of the Order Paper, were inserted in the Bill by the Senate. Most of them were to remedy defects which had passed unnoticed during the period of six months which had elapsed between its introduction in the Dáil and its arrival in the Senate. The majority were sponsored by the Government, but, even so, it was necessary for the Chairman to draw Mr. De Valera's attention to errors in some of them. The whole experience may perhaps have helped to convince him of the necessity for a revising Chamber.

The third Bill of the trilogy was the Aliens Bill. This followed closely the existing British legislation, and it was complementary to the measure which we have been discussing. The Senate inserted six amendments in the Bill, all of which improved it and were accepted by the Dáil. The word 'alien' was defined to mean a person who is not a citizen, thereby making aliens of all citizens, subjects, or nationals of the other member States of the British Commonwealth of Nations. But, by a characteristic piece of drafting, the resultant chaos was avoided by the following clause: 'The Executive Council may by order exempt from the application of any provision or provisions of this Act, or of any aliens order, the citizens, subjects or nationals of any country in respect of which the Executive Council are satisfied that, having regard to all the circumstances and in particular the laws of such country in relation to immigrants, it is proper that the exemption mentioned in such order should be granted.' Power was given to the Executive Council to revoke such an order at any time.

The passage of the three Bills through Parliament was so regulated that they became law at or about the same time, the Constitution

(Amendment No. 26) Bill on the 5th April, 1935, and the other two on the 10th April. On the 12th April the Aliens (Exemption) Order was promulgated by the Executive Council, exempting from the provisions of the Aliens Act the citizens, subjects, or nationals of the countries named in the Schedule to the Order. The countries named in the Schedule were: the United Kingdom, Canada, Australia, New Zealand, South Africa, Newfoundland, and India. Make-believe could scarcely go further, but it is significant that the citizens, subjects or nationals of the other countries forming the British Commonwealth are aliens under the municipal law of the Irish Free State and are saved from the consequences of alien status only by an Executive Order which the Government is free to revoke whenever it sees fit to do so.

Much of the other business dealt with during the year 1935 has already been referred to in previous chapters, consisting as it did of several Bills which had been rejected or otherwise held up by the Senate and were now sent up again after the expiration of the suspensory period. In addition, there was a succession of measures designed to cope with the situation arising out of the economic war; these were subjected to the same critical but not unfriendly scrutiny as previous Bills of the same kind. It is pleasant to be able to record two notable instances of the cordial co-operation extended by the Senate to the Government at this time. In the autumn of 1935 the Minister for Finance (Mr. MacEntee) was carrying through a large-scale conversion operation in connection with the First National Loan, and the appropriate Bill came before the Senate on the 6th November. The Minister's introductory statement was immediately followed by a cordial speech from his predecessor as Minister for Finance, Senator Blythe, who congratulated Mr. MacEntee on the success of the conversion operation. Senator Jameson, the chairman of the Independent Group, next added his tribute, and his recommendation of the loan to investors was all the more valuable as coming from a Director and former Governor of the Bank of Ireland. The Minister acknowledged the reception given to the Bill in a graceful reply.[1]

The second occasion arose over the League of Nations (Obligations of Membership) Bill, which was necessary to enable the country's obligations to be carried out under the League Covenant for the imposition of sanctions against Italy. As Minister for External Affairs, Mr. De Valera was in charge of the Bill, and he had the experience, unusual for him, of hearing speeches from all quarters of the House in

[1] *Senate Debates*, xx, 1085–93.

support of his proposals. With a few unimportant exceptions, the members of the United Ireland Party declined to follow that section of the Opposition in the Dáil which held that the Italo-Abyssinian war ought to have been made the occasion of an attempted bargain with Great Britain, and the Second Reading of the Bill was carried with only one dissentient. Mr. De Valera made a long speech in reply to the debate, and it was a model of what such a speech should be. It was moderate and statesmanlike, and lacked qualifications or parentheses. He deplored the fact that sanctions were necessary, but maintained that they were unavoidable if obligations entered into for the good of humanity were to be kept. He took note of the doubt felt in some quarters regarding the sincerity of some members of the League but said that it was a healthy doubt. 'If the same state of mind existed in every country that exists here, I do not think it would be harmful, provided only that people were not led, because of that doubt, to deny the aid which is necessary to maintain the League. If you withhold your service, if you do not give your aid properly and loyally, then you are doing your part to bring about the wrong results which you fear may be brought about by the action of others. While there may be doubts of this kind, these doubts should not lead us to withhold the aid we should give as loyal members of the League in order to make the League successful.'[1] Speeches such as this conveyed the impression that the reputation gained by Mr. De Valera through his occasional speeches at the League Assembly was fully deserved.

The period for which the Senate Abolition Bill had been suspended expired on the 24th November 1935, and on the following 12th December Mr. De Valera proposed in the Dáil a motion to send the Bill again to the Senate under Article 38A of the Constitution. Such a momentous occasion undoubtedly demanded a long speech from the head of the Government. By that time he had had eighteen months within which to consider the arguments advanced by the Chairman of the Senate, the Vice-Chairman, Senator Douglas, and others, and this was the appropriate time to deal with them if he was able to do so. Furthermore, it was his plain duty to take the Dáil and the country into his confidence with regard to his future intentions touching the legislature and the Constitution, since nobody knew for certain whether or not he proposed to have an entirely new Constitution and, if so, whether it would provide for one House of Parliament or two.

[1] *Senate Debates*, xx, 1142.

Mr. De Valera spoke for two or three minutes, his speech filling just one column of the *Debates*. But his few short sentences made it clear that a longer oration would have been superfluous. About half of his speech consisted of the following passage: 'There is, perhaps, only one matter that would merit attention at this stage, and that is that certain work which was performed in the Senate in regard to trimming up Bills gave an opportunity, as all Deputies know, to the Minister after the Report Stage had been passed to examine the Bill as a whole and to consult with the draftsman as regards the full effect of any amendments that might have been introduced. When the Senate goes I think some provision must be made for a Stage here in the Dáil which would enable that general review of a Bill as a whole to be undertaken and give to the Minister in charge of the Bill an opportunity, such as was afforded him in the past in the Senate, to make any small amendments which might be necessary to make the Bill a completely consistent whole and an artistic whole, if you like, from the draftsman's point of view.'[1] Such was his conception of the function of revision as exercised by the Senate for thirteen years. Even in this declaration he could not avoid a blunder. After the Report Stage of a Bill had been passed in the Senate, no further amendment was possible, save purely verbal amendments to rectify errors of grammar and the like.

It will be recalled that, when the Senate Abolition Bill was before the Dáil for the first time, the Opposition had objected that safeguards against hasty legislation ought to be provided. Mr. De Valera had replied that he did not expect that the Senate would vote for its own demise, and that there was therefore plenty of time in which all these things could be considered. On one occasion he had said that the Norwegian system might perhaps be adopted, and on another he had suggested that the Standing Orders of the Dáil might be amended so as to allow of a further revision of Bills. The eighteen months' period had expired, but nothing had been done.

The debate on the motion served to emphasize Mr. De Valera's ascendancy over his party. The discussion lasted for five hours, but no other member spoke from the Government side, except to interrupt, and Mr. De Valera's only supporter in the debate was the leader of the Labour Party, Mr. Norton. Several brilliant speeches were delivered against the Bill, and it was obvious that members had profited by a study of the facts and statistics which had been given in the Senate.

[1] *Dáil Debates*, lix, 2553, 2554.

Mr. De Valera's reply to the debate traversed the whole wearisome ground again and showed, if it was sincere, that all the previous discussions had passed completely over his head. He said that 'nobody has brought forward on the opposite side a single argument except this so-called appeal to the common practice and the common experience of mankind', and asserted, without going into details, that the origins of the bicameral system 'were largely the result of a fear of the people'. He again reviewed the possible methods of constituting a Second Chamber—direct election, indirect election, nomination—and found them all to be objectionable or impracticable. It was *Athanasius contra mundum*. His views could not be disregarded as unworthy of respect merely on the ground that they were based on insufficient study and experience, for he informed the Dáil that he had been dealing with the question 'much more than fourteen or fifteen years ago ... longer, probably, than anybody in this House'.

What was required by the country was a lucid statement of his intentions regarding the legislature and the Constitution. This, however, was not forthcoming. He said: 'The Senate is to be removed. This, for a time, at any rate, is going to be a single-Chamber Legislature.' Here we have the qualificatory phrases which are so characteristic of Mr. De Valera's utterances. Later he returned to the point, but left the issue still in doubt. 'During this period, as far as we are concerned, we are going to try what can be done by a single Chamber and, notwithstanding these prognostications to which we have listened to-night, I, for one, am perfectly certain that our experience will not be one which will make us in too great anxiety to change it. However, if anyone can indicate to us how to set up a Second Chamber which will serve us and will not be a definite barrier to progress or be simply a reproduction of the conditions in this House, I shall still keep simply an open mind.'

Mr. De Valera approached the conclusion of his speech without having made a single reference to his project for a new Constitution, though it must by this time have evolved from the nebulous stage, since he had announced in Ennis so long ago as the 29th June 1935 that 'before the present Government left office they would have an Irish Constitution from top to bottom'.[1] Mr. MacDermot inquired whether Mr. De Valera would appoint an outside body to consider the question of a Second Chamber, in view of his statement that a Joint Parliamentary Committee, such as had been suggested by the Senate itself, was unsuitable for the purpose. Mr. De Valera res-

[1] *Irish Press*, 1 July 1935.

ponded by giving the following paraphrase of what he had said on the 20th April 1934: 'I said that, if we did come to frame a permanent Constitution for this country, then certainly the body that should examine it should be an independent body. I think he [Mr. MacDermot] will find that I referred to this whole period as a necessary period of transition. What the necessary period will be will be different.' The natural conclusion to be drawn from this statement is that on the date it was made (12th December 1935) the question whether there was to be a new Constitution or not was still undecided.

Shortly afterwards Mr. De Valera concluded his speech, the division was taken, and the motion was passed by 76 votes to 57.[1] The Senate had then sixty days in which to consider the Bill, that is to say, until the 10th February 1936. There was no special urgency, since the Senate was powerless further to delay the Bill, and on the 18th December an order was made to take it on the 15th January, together with a motion which had been tabled by Senator Douglas in regard to it. This motion was as follows:

'That consideration of the Second Stage of the Constitution (Amendment No. 24) Bill, 1935, be postponed until a later date to enable the following Message to be sent to the Dáil:—

' "That inasmuch as the Senate is willing to pass the Constitution (Amendment No. 24) Bill, 1935, provided that an amendment is inserted therein to the effect that the Bill shall not come into operation until a Constitution Amendment Bill has been passed by the Dáil establishing a Second Chamber in substitution for Seanad Éireann, the Senate proposes a Conference between members representing both Houses of the Oireachtas for the purpose of considering an amendment of the character suggested and such other amendments providing for the period of transition or otherwise as may be found desirable:

' "That the Senate be represented at such Conference by seven Senators."

'That a Message be sent to the Dáil accordingly.'

Let us examine the implications of this proposal. First, every Senator who assented to it would assent to his own political extinction as a member of the existing Second Chamber and few would have any feeling of assurance as regards their membership of the new one. Accordingly, those who voted for the motion could not be charged with having been actuated by motives of self-interest. Second, it kept Mr. De Valera within the terms of his alleged mandate, which

[1] *Dáil Debates*, lix, 2657–68.

was for the abolition of the Senate 'as at present constituted', not for the establishment of a unicameral legislature. Third, it afforded a conclusive test of Mr. De Valera's sincerity. As long ago as the 11th July 1933 the Senate had proposed a Joint Committee on the constitution and powers of the Second Chamber; this proposal had been ignored and, by implication, the motion accepted the view that the investigation should not be conducted by a Joint Committee but by an outside body. The original proposal was not renewed, but a conference was requested with a view to devising an amendment which would ensure that the Senate should not be abolished until provision for a new Second Chamber had been made by the Dáil. Mr. De Valera had said that there was to be a necessary period of transition. This also was accepted, and the motion asked that the conference should insert the safeguards which he had promised but which had not so far been forthcoming.

When the House met on the 15th January the Chairman pointed out that, as Senator Douglas's motion took precedence of the motion for the Second Reading of the Bill, the President of the Executive Council was precluded from opening the debate. In the circumstances, he suggested that Mr. De Valera might speak as soon as Senator Douglas's motion had been seconded, and stated that he would be allowed to speak again before Senator Douglas rose to conclude. To the general astonishment, Mr. De Valera was not present, however. Not even Senator Connolly, the Minister for Lands, was in his place. The whole debate had accordingly to proceed on the assumption that the Government was determined on the establishment of a single chamber without safeguards and did not intend to make any reply to the motion before the House.

It was not until the discussion had been in progress for more than two hours that a member of the Government party, Senator Quirke, gave what he stated was the real reason for Mr. De Valera's failure to attend. It appears that the Legal Adviser to the Department of External Affairs had entered the Chamber at the beginning of the proceedings, and had occupied one of the seats reserved for officials attendant on Ministers. The Assistant Clerk asked him whether the President was coming, this inquiry having been made, as the Chairman subsequently explained, out of consideration for Mr. De Valera and also for the official concerned, so that he should not be disturbed if Mr. De Valera was momentarily expected, even though it was not strictly in accordance with practice for him to be allowed to remain. The Legal Adviser stated that he did not know whether Mr. De Valera was coming or not, whereupon he was informed that he could not remain where he was, but that a seat would be found for him in the front row of the Distinguished Strangers' Gallery. The official replied, 'Tell him to communicate that to me in the proper way.' The Chairman thereupon prepared and signed a minute, framed in courteous language, but by this time the official had left the Chamber. Senator Quirke, who had been in conversation with Mr. De Valera, gave his version of the incident, stated that the action taken was premeditated and vindictive, and asked, 'Could the President, under those conditions, come here to-day?' He omitted, however, the vital fact that when the Legal Adviser was asked whether Mr. De Valera would be present he had stated that he did not know. Senator Quirke had mentioned that Mr. De Valera was 'in the House', meaning presumably either the Parliament Building or the Chamber of the Dáil. The Dáil was in session on that day, but Mr. De Valera took no part in its proceedings except to vote in a division held long after the Senate had adjourned; and no explanation was ever given as to why he was not present in the Senate when the debate opened on Senator Douglas's motion.

In reply to Senator Quirke, the Chairman informed the House of what had really occurred, and also addressed a letter to the President of the Executive Council, setting forth in polite and dignified language the whole facts of the case and the practice hitherto observed in regard to the officials attendant on Ministers. This letter was read to the Senate at the beginning of the proceedings on the following day. It ended: 'In conclusion, I should like to add that nothing was further from my mind than to offer any discourtesy to you or to one of your officials. It had not occurred to me that any intention you may have had to be present at the debate yesterday would have been affected by the place accorded to your Legal Adviser pending your arrival.'[1]

The debate continued for two days, but neither Mr. De Valera nor Senator Connolly attended on the second day, though their presence cannot have been required in the Dáil, as it was not meeting. In the absence of any spokesman of the Government, the whole discussion had an air of unreality. It was characterized, however, by a number of speeches of outstanding merit, including those of the mover of the motion. The only argument from history which had not been dealt with was that which concerned the Senate of Canada, mentioned by Mr. De Valera in his concluding speech in the Dáil,

[1] *Senate Debates*, xx, 1780–3, 1811–13.

when he could not be answered. Senator Milroy took up this argument and replied to it in a convincing speech. Senator Sir John Griffith, then in his eighty-eighth year, made a moving plea against the Bill, stating that he believed that it would lead to the permanent partition of Ireland. Senator Blythe gave a statesmanlike contribution, in which he spoke of the value of the Senate from the point of view of his long experience as Minister for Finance. Senator O'Farrell's long speech, filled with argument and showing a robust sense of realities, made it obvious that, if Ireland could only rid itself of demagogy, he would be an outstanding figure in political life. The misgivings of certain members of the Government party regarding single-chamber government were voiced by Senators Dowdall and MacEllin, the speech of the latter being one of the most thoughtful and intelligent delivered by a Fianna Fáil Senator, other than the members who had been in the House before that party was formed. Few speeches were made against Senator Douglas's motion, and it is best to extend to most of them the charity of silence.

The motion was carried by 30 votes to 20, the only feature of interest about the division being the split in the Labour Party. Three of the members (Senators Farren, Johnson, and O'Farrell) voted for the motion and four others (Senators Cummins, Duffy, Foran, and Kennedy) voted against it.[1]

The appropriate resolution was then sent to the Dáil in the form of a message (16th January 1936). Parliamentary courtesy demanded that it should be considered and a reply sent, accepting or rejecting the proposals of the Senate. It was, however, completely ignored. Any more humiliating position for a House of Parliament could scarcely be conceived. The constitutional position was that at any time on or after the 11th February the Dáil could procure the abolition of the Senate by the mere passage of a simple resolution, the only limitation being that such action would have to be taken within twelve months. The 11th February came and went, and from that time forward the Senate lived a hand-to-mouth existence. Bills were sent up to it as usual and were dealt with in the same way as before: and, as time went on, doubts began to arise as to the intentions of the Government. With a view to elucidating the position, Mr. MacDermot put a Parliamentary Question in the Dáil on the 4th March. He asked whether it was proposed to fill the two casual vacancies then existing, and for how long and for what purpose it was intended to retain the Senate. The Vice-President's reply left the issue

1 *Senate Debates*, xx, 1813–1936.

still obscure. He said that it was not intended to fill the vacancies and that he was 'not at the moment in a position to give an exact answer to the second part of the question'.[1] The Government were bound under the Constitution to fill the first vacancy before the 11th June 1936, so that all that could be deduced from this reply was that it was intended to abolish the Senate before that date.

We may pause here to consider some of the possible reasons why the validity of the abolition of the Senate was never tested in the courts. Though these are, of course, purely speculative, they are none the less important. Mention has already been made of the statement made by the Chairman that he had obtained counsel's opinion from a distinguished authority on constitutional law, who had stated his view (a) that the amendment made to the Constitution in 1929, extending the period from eight to sixteen years within which constitutional amendments might be effected by ordinary legislation without a referendum, was invalid, and (b) that the Bill to abolish the Senate was not an amendment of the Constitution within the meaning of the Constitution. Since that opinion was given, there had been two notable judicial decisions bearing on the subject.

First in order of time was the judgement of the Judicial Committee of the Privy Council in the case of Moore and Others v. the Attorney-General of the Irish Free State and Others. The question at issue was the validity of the Constitution (Amendment No. 22) Act, 1933, which amended Article 66 of the Constitution by terminating the right of appeal to His Majesty in Council, that is, of course, to the Judicial Committee of the Privy Council. The Attorney-General did not appear before the Committee and the other respondents were not represented. The judgement of the Committee (the Lord Chancellor and Lord Atkin, Lord Tomlin, Lord Macmillan, and Lord Wright) was delivered on the 6th June 1935.[2] In it the Committee stated that Counsel for the appellants had rightly conceded the validity of the Constitution (Amendment No. 16) Act, that is, the extension from eight to sixteen years. They also held that, under Section 2 of the Statute of Westminster, 1931, the Irish Free State had power to abolish the right of appeal to the Privy Council, and that the Constitution (Amendment No. 22) Act was therefore valid. The judgement contains the following significant passage: 'It would be out of place to criticize the legislation enacted by the Irish Free State Legislature. But the Board desired to add that they were expressing no

---

[1] *Dáil Debates*, lx, 1538.
[2] *The Times*, 7 June 1935.

opinion on any contractual obligation under which, regard being had to the terms of the Treaty, the Irish Free State lay. The simplest way of stating the situation was to say that the Statute of Westminster gave to the Irish Free State a power under which they could abrogate the Treaty, and that, as a matter of law, they had availed themselves of that power.'

The importance of this judgement is far-reaching, and it has an obvious bearing on the abolition of the Senate. It did not, of course, bind the Supreme Court of the Irish Free State, but it made it clear that the extension from eight to sixteen years was a valid amendment of the Constitution, and that any argument against the validity of the Senate Abolition Bill which was based upon the provisions of the Treaty could not safely be relied upon.

The second judgement is that of the Supreme Court in the case of the State (Ryan and Others) *v.* Lennon and Others.[1] There were in fact three judgements, all delivered on the 19th December 1934, and some of the *obiter dicta* have already been cited in connection with the Bill to abolish the Oath. The question which fell to be decided was whether the insertion of Article 2A (the Military Tribunal Article) was a valid amendment of the Constitution, and the Supreme Court decided, Chief Justice Kennedy dissenting, (*a*) that the extension from eight to sixteen years was a valid amendment, (*b*) that the power of amendment of the Constitution (as distinct from the Constitution Act) conferred by Article 50 was unrestricted, and (*c*) that the power of amendment included the power of repeal.

This decision disposed of some, but not all, of the arguments which could have been adduced if the validity of the Senate Abolition Bill had been tested in the courts. But other reasons, unconnected with law, may perhaps have decided those who might have taken the initiative to stay their hand. Ever since the system of election had been altered in 1928 there had been a progressive deterioration in the personnel of the Second Chamber and a progressive increase in its political character. Since that date, out of thirty-five newcomers to the Senate no less than fourteen were former members of the Dáil, most of whom imported something of a political atmosphere into the discussions. The result of each Triennial Election could be predicted with fair certainty, and, on the assumption that no substantial change took place in the Dáil, the composition of the Senate after the 6th December 1937 would have been as follows:

[1] [1935] I.R., 170–245.

Fianna Fáil	27
United Ireland Party	18
Independent Group	7
Labour Party	6
Independent	1
Chairman	1
	—
	60
	—

Thus the Government party would have dominated the House. It would probably have been composed of men few of whom would have opposed Mr. De Valera on any major issue. The members who had made the Senate tradition were growing older, and their period of useful parliamentary work was coming to an end. In all the circumstances, even passionate believers in the value of such a Second Chamber as the Senate had been might well have been excused for taking the view that it was hardly worth while to challenge the validity of the Abolition Bill.

At length the formal motion of enactment, which was the final step necessary for the abolition of the Senate, was set down in the Dáil for Tuesday, 19th May. The Chairman of the Senate immediately summoned the House for that day, and the benches and public galleries were crowded for what all present knew would be its final meeting. The time for controversy was overpast, and those who spoke on this last day desired only to recall the good that had been done and to express their hope for the future. First, the Senate completed the few items of ordinary business which had remained outstanding, so that neither the Dáil nor the Government should be embarrassed by its omission to do so. Senator Brown thereupon moved the following motion: 'That it is hereby resolved that, in the event of the existence of Seanad Éireann as a constituent House of the Oireachtas being terminated by the enactment of the Constitution (Amendment No. 24) Bill, 1934, the Cathaoirleach be directed to offer the Casket presented to Seanad Éireann by the late Senator Mrs. Alice Stopford Green, together with the contents thereof, as a gift for preservation to the Council of the Royal Irish Academy.' Senator Brown spoke of the great beauty of the Casket, and recalled the fact that in November 1924 it had fallen to his lot to present it to the Senate on behalf of Alice Stopford Green. It had been his great privilege, he said, to be admitted to her intimate friendship. She was an historian of great authority, imbued with an intense love of her own land. Her purpose had been, in her own words, that the Casket should be placed on the table at the beginning of each meeting of the Senate as 'a perpetual memorial of the foundation of this body, and a witness in later times of its increasing service to the country'. Senator Brown then remarked sadly: 'To-day, after less than twelve short years, it falls to my lot to propose a resolution which provides for the perpetual safe-keeping in other hands of this gift to a Senate which will cease to exist within the next few days.' He expressed the hope, however, that within a short time the House would have a successor, 'truly representative of the various interests of our people, and chosen without regard to party politics'. The motion was spoken to by Senators Dr. Gogarty, Robinson, Douglas, and Dowdall and was carried without dissent.

Next, Senator O'Farrell moved a motion appreciative of the manner in which the Clerk and Assistant Clerk of the Senate had discharged their duties. Having paid a graceful tribute to these officials, he referred in moving terms to the impending abolition.

'Representatives of every aspect of Irish social and economic life have had their place in this Assembly and made a contribution to its deliberations. I believe personally that there have been no enemies of this land on the membership roll of this House. I believe that at heart each member was passionately devoted to his country, proud of its traditions, its history and its storied past. After all, different people have different methods of working for the same ideal, and patriotic speeches replete with fiery national sentiments are not the only means by which one can serve his country.

'The battle for the life of this Assembly has been fought and lost. We must probably leave to other days and other men to say who has taken the right course and who has taken the reverse. At all events, I hope that every member of the Assembly voted for the course which he or she considered the best calculated to serve the nation's interest. That being the case, we, individually at least, accept the result without complaint and without asperity, although, perhaps, not without a little anxiety as to the future. We met originally almost as strangers. We part to-day as colleagues and friends.'

A number of Senators associated themselves with the motion, which was passed. Senator MacLoughlin, who had proposed the late Lord Glenavy for the Chairmanship in 1922, then rose to express the indebtedness of himself and his colleagues to Senator Westropp Bennett for his 'dignified, courteous and impartial conduct' of the Chair during the preceding seven and a half years. It was a fitting

2H

tribute to a man who had striven to be fair almost to the point of scrupulosity, and whose only crime had been that when his House of Parliament had stood in need of defence he had had the courage to defend it.

The last word lay with the Chairman. '. . . So now we come to the end. No recriminations may or should be allowed. All I ask leave to do is to express the hope that we who have striven for the upbuilding of this State will continue to uphold this State so far as we can. If I might venture to express a hope, it would be that my voice, addressed from this Chair for the last time, would go out over our heads to the country at large in an appeal for respect for the law. The law is being made by our representatives for all of us. There is no safeguard for democracy but in the keeping of the law. I hope it will be kept. If we, who are in the sere and yellow leaf, are approached for our counsel, I hope we shall say, "Work for the law, by the law and with the law." Thus only will democracy be preserved and strengthened. . . .

'I thank you all. We shall remember the contacts we made here. We shall remember our friends of different creeds, of different politics, of different ideals, animated by one desire—the advancement of this State. So far as God gave us light, we fulfilled our duty.'

He then declared the Senate adjourned *sine die* and vacated the Chair. The Casket was removed, and the members filed slowly through the doors of the Chamber. An historic occasion had passed into history.[1]

The Senators whose membership was of long standing could certainly look back upon a record of work of which any Second Chamber might well be proud. That record will be found given in detail in the Appendices. In its short life of thirteen years and a half the Senate had received 489 Bills from the Dáil (other than Money Bills) and 182 had been amended. The number of amendments reached the enormous total of 1,831, and practically all of these had been accepted by the other House, for the most part without modification. The power of suspension had been exercised in only eight cases (apart from the Senate Abolition Bill) and in two of these the Government refrained from passing the Bills into law when the period of suspension had expired. Even in the closing eighteen months, since the beginning of the Fifth Triennial Period, the revision done was considerable; of the fifty-five Bills received, thirteen had been amended, the number of amendments being 170, of which 160 were accepted by the Dáil.

The motion of enactment was not taken in the Dáil until the 28th

---

[1] *Senate Debates*, xx, 2418–36.

May. Mr. De Valera's opening speech was longer than usual, and he went over the ground again. 'We must try, if we are to be practical, not merely to argue in generalities, not merely to say, "Oh, the common experience of the world has been in favour of a Second Chamber" without any analysis of the conditions in the various places. . . . In unitary States, has their origin been examined to see how far these Second Chambers have been adopted without examination, simply because they were used in other countries?' And again: 'Shall I say once more that it is the duty of those who believe that a Second Chamber is necessary, and can work, to show us how they would constitute it, and what powers they would give it, instead of simply saying "Oh, the experience of the world has been in favour of two Chambers." That is all nonsense. The experience has got to be examined in detail.'

The only part of his speech worthy of particular attention was this passage: 'I hope that in the autumn we will have a measure here outlining a new Constitution. Whether that Constitution is to be based on the principle of a single Chamber or two will depend upon whether it is possible to devise a Second Chamber which can be of value and not a danger. I have not myself—I have told the House my own view on the matter—been able to devise any really satisfactory Second Chamber, one that I think would be worth while putting into the Constitution. I have had many suggestions put before me and many of them examined and the challenge which I issued still holds. If it can be shown how we can constitute a Senate which, practically, will be of value then certainly we will give such a proposition most careful consideration. If it cannot, then the Constitution will be introduced with a Single-Chamber Legislature. I have indicated, as far as I am concerned, that I have had a hankering after a Second Chamber, which most of us had, mainly because we visualized an ideal Senate which cannot be attained in practice and which, in my opinion, has not so far even been approximated to.'

Speaking later in the debate, Mr. MacDermot described the promise of a new Constitution in the autumn as an 'interesting revelation'. But it was much more than that. It supplied the clue to much that had been formerly obscure concerning Mr. De Valera's attitude towards the Senate. In the debate on the Bill in the previous December, he had got no further than to say that 'if we did come to frame a permanent Constitution for this country' the question of a Second Chamber might be examined by an independent Commission. If at that time he had felt able to make the definite announcement that a new Constitution was to be promulgated, it is hard to imagine any convincing reason why that commission should not then have been set up, why a period of single-chamber government was necessary, and why he proposed to abolish the Senate altogether instead of the Senate 'as at present constituted'. But on the assumption that he was ridding himself of the Senate because he knew that it would reject his new quasi-republican Constitution (for which he had no mandate from the people) his conduct becomes readily intelligible. On this basis also it is possible to explain his refusal to consider the Senate's offer of a Joint Committee on the subject (July 1933), its Bill to restore the referendum for constitutional amendments (June 1934), and, finally, its offer to consent to its own abolition provided that another Second Chamber were substituted for it (January 1936).

The debate followed the familiar lines, statesmanlike, and sometimes brilliant, speeches being delivered by such members as Professor O'Sullivan, Dr. Rowlette, and Messrs. Dillon, Anthony, and McGilligan, and no fresh argument being evoked from the other side. The speech which Mr. De Valera made in reply to the discussion was the last that could be made by anybody in either House on the subject of the Bill. He opened by saying: 'On a previous occasion I did not think it worth while, when concluding, to justify the statements that I had made in the Dáil on that occasion. The suggestion is that what I had said was "torn to shreds" in the Senate. I think that subsequent events have proved that some of the *ex cathedra* statements of the Chairman of that body have been proved to be absolutely absurd.' Unfortunately, he did not specify what these subsequent events were. He then dealt at considerable length with his references to Adams and Franklin, but his explanations have already been examined in a previous chapter. After some more constitutional theory, he turned to the future and expressed the view that it would be in the general interest to associate all parties in working out the new Constitution; and he accepted a suggestion thrown out by Mr. MacDermot that a commission should be set up to examine the question of a Second Chamber, though he could promise nothing more than that he would consult his colleagues in the Executive Council on the proposal. Finally, with only a few moments available before the hour of adjournment, he could not resist two further quotations, with the object of proving that the whole question of one or two Chambers was not at all vital. One was, word for word, the passage from J. S. Mill which he had already cited in the Senate and which has already been examined in its proper perspective. The other was from Sir John Marriott; and it is curious to recall that when, in the original debate in 1934, Professor O'Sullivan had apparently relied upon some of Sir John Marriott's material, Mr. De Valera had rebuked him for, as he alleged, 'taking something as an accepted fact from some conservative writer without any attempt whatever to examine it for himself'.[1] It was a fitting ending to an inglorious but tragic episode in the history of Ireland.

The division was then taken, and the motion was carried by 74 votes to 52.[2] The Constitution (Amendment No. 24) Bill, 1934, was signed by the Governor-General on the following day, Friday, 29th May 1936. The Senate had ceased to exist.

---

[1] *Dáil Debates*, lii, 1809, 1810.   [2] Ibid., 1195–1348.

PART VII

SINGLE CHAMBER GOVERNMENT

αἴτιοι δ'εἰσὶ τοῦ εἶναι τὰ ψηφίσματα κύρια ἀλλὰ μὴ τοὺς νόμους οὗτοι, πάντα ἀνάγοντες εἰς τὸν δῆμον· συμβαίνει γὰρ αὐτοῖς γίνεσθαι μεγάλοις διὰ τὸ τὸν μὲν δῆμον πάντων εἶναι κύριον τῆς δὲ τοῦ δήμου δόξης τούτους, πείθεται γὰρ τὸ πλῆθος τούτοις.

(*These men cause the resolutions of the people to be supreme and not the laws, by referring all things to the people; for they owe their rise to greatness to the fact that the people is sovereign over all things while they are sovereign over the opinion of the people, for the multitude listens to them.*)

ARISTOTLE, *Politics*, IV, iv, 6.

'*Temporary feelings and excitements, popular prejudices, an ardent love of theory, an enthusiastic temperament, inexperience and ignorance, as well as preconceived opinions, operate wonderfully to blind the judgment and seduce the understanding.*'

JOSEPH STORY, *Commentaries on the Constitution of the United States* (1851), vol. I, p. 376.

'*A single legislature is calculated to unite in it all the pernicious qualities of the different extremes of bad government. It produces general weakness, inactivity and confusion; and these are intermixed with sudden and violent fits of despotism, injustice and cruelty.*'

JAMES WILSON, (Justice of the Supreme Court of the United States),

Law Lectures, 393.

CHAPTER XXVII

THE ABDICATION AND 'EXTERNAL ASSOCIATION'

Death of Patrick Hogan—His statesmanlike qualities—Dissensions in the United Ireland Party—Split in the League of Youth—The end of the Blue Shirts—General O'Duffy in Spain—The Irish Christian Front —Irish Republicans also in Spain—The Government adheres to non-intervention—Return of General O'Duffy and his volunteers—Mr. De Valera's defence policy—The Vice-President and partition—Constitutional changes—The interview in the Philadelphia Record—*The election pledge in 1932—The clearing of the ground—The abdication of King Edward VIII—The constitutional position—Action taken in the several overseas Dominions—The British Act—Mr. De Valera's true alternatives—Special meeting of the Dáil—The Constitution (Amendment No. 27) Bill—Elimination of the Crown—Communication with the British Government—Criticism by the Opposition—Errors in the Bill—The guillotine falls—The Executive Authority (External Relations) Bill—'External association'—Views of the ex-Attorney-General —Enactment of the Bill—The electors not consulted.*

On the 14th July 1936 the United Ireland Party suffered a severe loss by the death in a motor accident of Mr. Patrick Hogan, the former Minister for Agriculture. Of late years his attendance in the Dáil had been infrequent, partly because he was a solicitor in large practice in the west of Ireland, but more because he was sick at heart and thoroughly disillusioned. Hogan was a realist, who consistently preached the value and necessity of hard work, and he disdained to flatter the multitude. As a nation-builder upon the basis of the Treaty his niche in history is secure.

The internal dissensions of the Opposition continued. In September 1934 General O'Duffy had resigned, taking with him a number of the Blue Shirts. Those who remained still kept the title of the League of Youth, and the new Director-General was Commandant Cronin, who was one of the Vice-Chairmen of the United Ireland Party. In October 1935 Mr. MacDermot had resigned. In the summer of 1936 there were grave differences between Commandant Cronin and his colleagues, and the trouble came to a head on the 9th October, when, by a majority, the Standing Committee of the party decided to terminate the system of 'an autonomous self-directed political organization within another political organization'. The Committee thereupon took over direct responsibility for the League of Youth.[1] Commandant Cronin decided to maintain the League of Youth as an independent organization, and so he departed, taking with him some more of the Blue Shirts. This was apparently the end of the Youth Movement under any leader. At all events, the blue uniform shirt has disappeared.

Thus the ill-starred union, on the 8th September 1933, of Mr. Cosgrave's party, Mr. MacDermot's National Centre Party, and General O'Duffy's Blue Shirts had, after three unhappy years, resulted in the disappearance for all practical purposes of two of its three components. It is true that Mr. Cosgrave had obtained from the National Centre Party an able and energetic lieutenant in the person of Mr. James M. Dillon. But with this important exception there was no new blood, and the men of influence in the Opposition were still the ex-Ministers. The party was, in all essentials, the old Cumann na nGaedheal (League of Gaels). Even the title of United Ireland Party had long ago been supplanted, in ordinary use, by Fine Gael, which means Tribe of Gaels, though the one cannot, by any stretch of the imagination, be regarded as the equivalent of the other. New Fine Gael was but old Cumann na nGaedheal writ small.

The outbreak of the Spanish Civil War in July 1936 had its influence on Irish affairs. General O'Duffy, who is a devout Catholic, at once announced his intention of going to fight for the insurgents. Numbers of Irishmen followed his lead, and, after a due interval of preparation, they made their way to Spain, where they fought in the front trenches, as a separate unit, under the command of General O'Duffy. Mr. Pembroke Stephens, the war correspondent of the *Daily Telegraph* (who was later killed in China) described the Irish as the best of Franco's foreign troops and his only genuine volunteers.

About the same time a new movement began, called the Irish Christian Front. Its chief leader was Mr. Patrick Belton, a man of

[1] *Irish Independent*, 10 October 1936.

energetic personality who had fought in the insurrection of Easter Week, 1916, and had since had a varied parliamentary career. He had been a member of Mr. De Valera's party before it entered the Dáil, but had taken the Oath a fortnight before his leader decided to do so. He had then sat as an Independent, and subsequently he had had some connection with the formation of the National Centre Party, which, as we have seen, became merged in the United Ireland Party. At the time of the split he had sided with General O'Duffy and had resumed his independence. The Irish Christian Front now collected very large sums of money for the provision of ambulances and medical supplies for the insurgents, and also came to the aid of General O'Duffy's volunteers. Little is now heard of the movement, presumably because its mission has been fulfilled. It is fortunate that it did not develop into a political party, for few things could be more disastrous for Ireland than anything in the nature of a clerical party, having as its inevitable concomitant an anti-clerical party.

Mr. Frank Ryan and a band of Republicans, small in number compared with General O'Duffy's men, also travelled to the Peninsula, where they fought with great bravery on the Government side. It is tragic that Irishmen should thus have been engaged on opposite sides on a foreign field in a quarrel which was not their own.

The Irish Free State Government officially adhered to the policy of non-intervention, and the passage into law on the 26th February 1937 of the Spanish Civil War (Non-Intervention) Act was probably the principal factor in General O'Duffy's decision to return home with his volunteers. Thenceforward he could obtain no further drafts, and the ranks were depleted by death, wounds, and sickness. It is known, however, that the men under his leadership were a prey to grave dissensions. Since his return home, on the 21st June 1937, General O'Duffy has taken no part in politics.

The Government Bill for non-intervention was strenuously opposed not only by Mr. Belton but also by the official Opposition, though, as Mr. De Valera pointed out, Mr. Cosgrave had explicitly stated as recently as the previous 27th November that he agreed with that policy. The Opposition now, however, wished to make non-intervention conditional on the severance of diplomatic relations with the Valencia Government. The Bill was carried by a comfortable majority.[1]

The tense political situation in Europe during the summer of 1936 gave rise to two speeches, one by the President of the Executive

[1] *Dáil Debates*, lxiv, 1197, and lxv, 597–1024.

Council and the other by the Vice-President. It will be remembered that, under Article 7 of the Treaty of 1921, the British were entitled, for defence purposes, to certain facilities at Berehaven, Queenstown, and Lough Swilly; and also, 'in time of war or of strained relations with a Foreign Power, such harbour and other facilities as the British Government may require for the purposes of such defence as aforesaid'. Article 7 was deleted by the Anglo-Irish Agreement of the 25th April 1938, but the extract about to be quoted is still important, as giving the point of view of the Head of the Government at the time.

In the course of a speech in the Dáil on the 18th June 1936, Mr. De Valera said:

'Any Government at the present time would have seriously to consider the question of the defences of the country. Our position is particularly complicated. If we held the whole of our territory, there is no doubt whatever that our attitude would be . . . that we have no aggressive designs against any other people. We would strengthen ourselves so as to maintain our neutrality. . . . But we are in this position, that some of our ports are occupied, and, although we cannot be actively committed in any way, the occupation of those ports will give to any foreign country that may desire a pretext an opportunity of ignoring our neutrality. . . .

'The first thing that any Government here must try to secure is that no part of our territory will be occupied by any forces except the forces that are immediately responsible to the Government here. I have tried to indicate on many occasions that that is our desire, and that it would work out to the advantage of Britain as well as to our own advantage. I think Britain . . . wants to feel that they are not going to be attacked through foreign States that might attempt to use this country as a base. We are prepared, and any Government with which I have been associated has always been prepared, to give guarantees, so far as guarantees can be given, that that will not happen. We are prepared to meet the necessary expense, and to make the necessary provision to see that the full strength of this nation will be used to resist any attempt by any foreign power to abuse our neutrality by using any portion of our territory as a base. If that situation were realized, then of course the Government here would have a definite task. All the uncertain elements of the present situation would disappear. We would know what to expect; in the main, we would know what to provide against. But in the present uncertain position it is very difficult to have any adequate scheme of defence, or to take any adequate measures which would safeguard us against the risks which we have got to face, now that our territory is within reaching distance of aeroplanes from the Continent, and that we are liable, on account of the occupation of certain parts of our territory, to attack by any enemy of Great Britain.'[1]

This appears to be an offer of neutrality provided that (as has since happened) the three ports in question were evacuated by British forces. But the Administration seemed to speak with two voices in this matter, for, in a speech delivered a month later at Milford, County Donegal, the Vice-President is reported to have said:

'There will be no cessation of the fight until the people of Ireland are satisfied that Irish independence and Irish unity have been achieved and won to their satisfaction. In other words, until partition was ended there would not be peace in Ireland, and difficulties might come for England again.

'It was not so many weeks ago since England found herself in very big international difficulties, and these things would recur again, and then England would be looking around to see where were her friends and her enemies.

'It will be well for her to realize that she has Ireland to reckon with, and that Ireland will not be there as a friend so long as England countenances partition in this country.'[2]

We are now about to consider the changes made in the constitutional position after the abolition of the Senate. Early in 1930 Mr. De Valera was in the United States, being at that time Leader of the Opposition in the Dáil. According to an account published in the *Philadelphia Record* of the 6th January 1930, he stated in an interview: 'There's got to be an election before 1932, according to the Constitution, and we'll get a majority. Once we have our majority, we're going to make our bid for real freedom. With control of the Assembly, we'll be able to overthrow the Constitution. . . .'[3] The time of the election arrived, but this design was concealed from the people. The Fianna Fáil Election Manifesto was written and signed by Mr. De Valera. He asked for a mandate to abolish the parliamentary Oath (which he said was not required by the Treaty) and to retain the Land Annuities. For the rest:

'We pledge ourselves that, if elected in a majority, we shall not in the field of international relations exceed the mandate here asked for without again consulting the people. . . .

---

[1] *Dáil Debates*, lxii, 2659, 2660.   [2] *Weekly Irish Times*, 25 July 1936.
[3] Quoted in the *Irish Independent*, 10 February 1930.

'We ask the electors not to allow themselves to be deceived by the misrepresentations of our opponents, and we pledge ourselves not to abuse their confidence.'[1]

On this basis Mr. De Valera obtained the confidence of the people. Though there was another election within twelve months, no fresh mandate was asked for in the field of international relations. The Oath had been abolished, the Land Annuities had been retained, and there had been no further election. The position in 1936 was, therefore, that the mandate was exhausted and that Mr. De Valera had given a pledge, by which he was still bound, not to exceed it.

If Mr. De Valera was correctly reported as having said that 'with control of the Assembly, we'll be able to overthrow the Constitution' his statement was inaccurate. He would need first to abolish the Senate. The Senate was abolished on the 29th May 1936.

Still the way was barred to some extent against hasty legislation of a revolutionary character by Mr. De Valera's own half-promises, made during the progress of the Senate Abolition Bill, that the Standing Orders of the Dáil would be amended so as to provide safeguards. On the 3rd June 1936 the Dáil Committee on Procedure presented a Report recommending numerous amendments to the Standing Orders as a result of the abolition of the Senate. The Report was formally adopted two days later. The amendments were all strictly consequential on the disappearance of the Second Chamber. There were no safeguards.[2]

On the 27th November 1936 the Dáil adjourned until the 3rd February 1937. On the morning of the 10th December 1936 His Majesty King Edward VIII executed an Instrument of Abdication, whereby he abdicated the throne. A constitutional crisis of the first magnitude thus arose. Before stating the nature of the action taken as a result of it, it is desirable to suggest the course which the situation actually demanded; and this in turn can be understood only by reference to constitutional law. A short exposition on the subject is all the more desirable because it does not so far appear to have been discussed with special reference to the Irish Free State.

Canada, Australia, New Zealand, South Africa, the Irish Free State, and Newfoundland had severally requested and consented to the enactment by the Parliament of the United Kingdom of the Statute of Westminster, 1931. In Section 1 of the Statute these countries are defined to be Dominions, and it is recited in the

---

[1] *Irish Independent*, 11 February 1932.
[2] *Dáil Debates*, lxii, 1871.

Preamble to the Statute that 'it would be in accord with the established constitutional position of all the members of the Commonwealth in relation to one another that any alteration in the law touching the Succession to the Throne or the Royal Styles and Titles shall hereafter require the assent as well of the Parliaments of all the Dominions as of the Parliament of the United Kingdom'. The Preamble further recites that 'it is in accord with the established constitutional position that no law hereafter made by the Parliament of the United Kingdom shall extend to any of the said Dominions as part of the law of that Dominion otherwise than at the request and with the consent of that Dominion'. Preambles to Acts of Parliament have not, of course, in general the force of law, but the Preamble to this Statute has a peculiar sanctity in view of the origin of the Statute itself. The second quotation is, moreover, reinforced by Section 4 of the Statute: 'No Act of Parliament of the United Kingdom passed after the commencement of this Act shall extend, or be deemed to extend, to a Dominion as part of the law of that Dominion, unless it is expressly declared in that Act that that Dominion has requested, and consented to, the enactment thereof.'

It is a permissible legal view that the signature by King Edward VIII of the Instrument of Abdication had, *per se*, brought about a demise of the Crown. Such was the opinion of the Government of South Africa, as we shall see in a moment. Had it been universally held, no legislative action would have been necessary, as the Duke of York would have succeeded to the Throne automatically. The British Government, however, was of the opinion that King Edward wore the Crown by virtue of the Act of Settlement of 1700 and could not properly lay it aside until another Act of Parliament confirmed his intention to do so. But before such an Act could be passed it was necessary to consult the governments of the countries named in the Statute of Westminster, except Newfoundland, which has temporarily lost its Dominion status. We shall now consider the action taken by the overseas Dominions, and then return to the British Act.

Canada. At the time of the Abdication, Parliament had stood prorogued to the 14th January 1937. The 'request and consent' referred to in Section 4 of the Statute of Westminster were made and given by the Executive by means of an Order-in-Council dated the 10th December. At the beginning of the new Session a Bill confirmatory of the British Act was introduced and passed into law on the 20th January, though opinions were expressed in both Houses that it was unnecessary.

Australia. The position of Australia was peculiar. Under Section 10 of the Statute of Westminster Section 4 did not apply to it unless it was adopted by the Australian Parliament. The 'request and consent' did not, therefore, apply. But Section 9 stated that, in the application of the Act to Australia, the 'request and consent' mentioned in Section 4 should mean the request and consent of the Parliament and Government of the Commonwealth. To meet this somewhat anomalous situation, both Houses were kept in being during the constitutional crisis, and on the 11th December they passed parallel resolutions, giving, not the 'request and consent' mentioned in Section 4, but the 'assent' mentioned in the Preamble.

New Zealand. This Dominion was also excluded from the operation of Section 4 until its Parliament should adopt it. Parliament had been prorogued from the 3rd November 1936 to the 12th August 1937. The 'assent' mentioned in the Preamble was given by Order-in-Council dated the 10th December 1937.

South Africa. The situation in the Union was exceptional. In 1934 the South African Parliament had passed the Status of the Union Act, which declared South Africa to be a sovereign, independent State and incorporated as part of its municipal law the Preamble and Section 4 of the Statute of Westminster. Speaking in the House of Assembly on the 25th January 1937, the Prime Minister (General Hertzog) stated that the British Government had suggested that the Union Government should 'request and consent' under Section 4 of the Statute. To this the Union Government could not and would not accede, being precluded from doing so under Section 2 of the Status of the Union Act. But it was prepared to give, and did actually give, its 'assent'. Furthermore, the Union Government had disagreed from the very beginning with the view that an Act of Parliament was necessary to give effect to the King's Abdication. But, as other members of the Commonwealth took a different view, the matter was put beyond doubt by a declaratory enactment, and His Majesty King Edward the Eighth's Abdication Act became law on the 10th February 1937. It fixes the date of the Accession of King George VI as the 10th December 1936—the date of the execution of the Instrument of Abdication.

We are now in a position to return to the British Act, entitled His Majesty's Declaration of Abdication Act. It recites in its Preamble that Canada had requested and consented to the enactment of the Act, pursuant to Section 4 of the Statute of Westminster, and that Australia, New Zealand, and South Africa had assented thereto. The reason for this distinction will now be appreciated. The Irish Free State was nowhere mentioned, and the Prime Minister (Mr. Baldwin), speaking on the Second Reading, stated that he had received a message from Mr. De Valera saying that he proposed to call his Parliament together to pass legislation to deal with the situation.[1] We may perhaps assume from this that the British Government had asked for a 'request and consent' under Section 4 and had been refused. The British Act became law on the 11th December, so that the Accession of King George VI dates from that day so far as the British Empire, Canada, Australia, and New Zealand are concerned.

This review of the constitutional position, and of the decisions taken in the light of it, makes certain matters clear that might otherwise be obscure or in doubt. In the first place, there was obviously no need whatever for the Dáil to be summoned in the middle of the recess for the purpose of enacting emergency legislation to deal with the situation. The only Dominion Parliament which met during the crisis was that of Australia, and this course was necessitated by its peculiar position under the Statute of Westminster. The Irish Free State was in exactly the same position as Canada. Both came under Section 4 of the Statute and there was no complicating factor in either case, such as the Status of the Union Act in South Africa.

In the second place, we can see what Mr. De Valera's true alternatives were, due allowance being made for his Republican tendencies and regard being had to his solemn personal pledge that he would not exceed his mandate without again consulting the people.

1. To inform the British Government that, in the view of his Government, the signature of the Instrument of Abdication had caused a demise of the Crown; that the succession had already passed to the Duke of York and his heirs; that an Act of Parliament was therefore unnecessary; and that the Irish Free State would not be a party to such an Act.

2. To have given the 'request and consent' mentioned in Section 4 of the Statute of Westminster, and to have declined further legislation.

3. To have given the bare 'assent' referred to in the Preamble.

The political advantage to Mr. De Valera of any of these courses would have been that the crisis could have been surmounted by a mere act of the Executive. When the Dáil reassembled in the normal course on the 3rd February the affair would have blown over, and it is unlikely that the Opposition would have attempted to make

[1] *House of Commons Debates,* cccxviii, 2203.

political capital out of the painful circumstances surrounding the Abdication. It is right, however, to point out that the third course might not have been regarded as practicable, since the 'assent' required by the Preamble is that of the Parliament. But this fact did not prove to be a barrier in the case of New Zealand.

What actually happened was very different. It is, indeed, likely to be cited in future text-books on political science as a classic instance of the exercise of power by a single chamber. On Thursday, 10th December, the date of Abdication, Members of the Dáil were summoned by telegram to meet at 3 p.m. on the following day. Professor O'Sullivan, who lives in Dublin, stated that he received the summons at 7 p.m. and that on the following morning he received by post the two Bills to be dealt with. Members residing at a distance from the capital would have had to leave home before the Bills arrived, and many doubtless saw them for the first time when they entered the Chamber. Members who happened to be away from home might not have received the summons at all. The authority to print a Bill is usually taken to be conferred by the Dáil when leave is given to introduce it. No such leave had been given in respect of these two Bills. Professor O'Sullivan protested that 'the great bulk of the people have no knowledge whatsoever of what we are called together for here to-day'. One of Mr. De Valera's followers interjected, 'They will know it to-morrow'—that is to say, when the Bills had been passed into law.[1]

The business for the first day, Friday, 11th December, was the formal introduction of the two Bills, followed by a guillotine motion of a most drastic character, whereby all Stages of the first Bill would have to be concluded before 11 p.m. the same night, and all Stages of the second Bill would have to be completed between 10.30 a.m. and 10.30 p.m. on the following day, Saturday, 12th December. The Parliamentary Secretary to the President, who moved the guillotine, did not say a single word in justification of it, and the motion was carried, under the closure, by 71 votes to 55.

The first Bill was entitled the Constitution (Amendment No. 27) Bill, 1936, and its long title was: 'An Act to effect certain amendments of the Constitution in relation to the executive authority and power and in relation to the performance of certain executive functions.' Its general purpose was to remove the King from the Constitution and to abolish the Representative of the Crown. Article 1 of the Constitution was left untouched: 'The Irish Free

[1] *Dáil Debates*, lxiv, 1238–40.

State is a co-equal member of the Community of Nations forming the British Commonwealth of Nations.' Otherwise the King disappeared, and the Governor-General was stripped of his functions. The Royal Assent to Bills was at an end, and in future they were to become law on the signature of the Chairman of the Dáil. This official was also to summon and dissolve Parliament on the direction of the Executive Council. The successive changes in Article 12 illustrate the constitutional progress. In its original form this Article stated that the legislature 'shall consist of the King and two Houses'. After the abolition of the Senate, it was to 'consist of the King and one House'. Now it was to 'consist of one House'.

For external purposes, however, some use was found for the Crown, which was referred to anonymously and in defective English in the following proviso added to Article 51: 'Provided that it shall be lawful for the Executive Council, to the extent and subject to any conditions which may be determined by law to avail, for the purposes of the appointment of diplomatic and consular agents and the conclusion of international agreements of any organ used as a constitutional organ for the like purposes by any of the nations referred to in Article 1 of this Constitution.'

It will be apparent that these proposals have no logical connection whatever with the Abdication and that there was accordingly no urgency about them from a constitutional standpoint. But they became law in eight hours. Speaking on the First Stage of the Bill, Mr. De Valera referred to his new Constitution, which was then being drafted, and said that he had indicated quite clearly to the British Government that the King would not appear in it. He added: 'Of course, it was only indicated informally, and as a matter of courtesy because, again, they have no right to interfere.' The following extract from the Official Report will illustrate the fog which surrounded the Government Benches during the debate. It is offered without further comment.

'Mr. Cosgrave: May I ask the President, Sir, if the Dáil will get the correspondence to which reference has been made by the President in connection with the informal notification between all the members of the British Commonwealth?

'The President: I did not say that it was done informally.

'Mr. Cosgrave: Was it done by correspondence?

'The President: No, I do not think so.

'Professor O'Sullivan: The President does not know?

'The President: I do not know that it was done by correspondence.

It was probably word of mouth; by the High Commissioner, possibly.

'General Mulcahy: Was it done at all?

'The President: I think so.'[1]

The discussion on the measure, was, as usual, thoroughly one-sided. Brilliant searchlights were thrown on the Bill and its implications by such masters of their subject as Professor O'Sullivan, Mr. McGilligan, and Messrs. Costello, K.C., Lavery, K.C., and Fitz-gerald-Kenney, K.C.; but they failed to penetrate the fog on the other side. Mr. MacDermot approached the matter from a different angle. Referring to the new proviso to Article 51, in which the King is alluded to as an organ, he said: 'How do we know that this Bill is not going to subject this House and country to a resounding humiliation? How would it be if the new King said—as I would if I were in his shoes—"Go and be damned; I am not interested in acting as your deputy for certain purposes while I am not recognized as King of the country"?'[2] If His Majesty had adopted this attitude, the whole scheme of legislation would, of course, have collapsed.

As usual, the Government's haste gave rise to blunders. Following constitutional forms, Article 51 declared the executive authority to be vested in the King, exercisable by the Governor-General on the advice of the Executive Council. The references to the King and the Governor-General were now to be deleted, and the executive authority was to be exercised by the Executive Council. It was nowhere stated, however, in whom such authority was vested. Mr. McGilligan raised the point, and the Attorney-General (Mr. James Geoghegan, K.C.) gave it as his opinion that the executive authority would be vested in the people.[3]

Shortly before the guillotine was due to fall, Mr. Lavery adverted to the provision that the Dáil should in future be summoned and dissolved by the Chairman of the Dáil. He pointed out that, when the Dáil had been dissolved, there would be no Chairman of the Dáil, and, therefore, no person to summon it. The disclosure of this ludicrous error seems to have caused perturbation on the Government Front Bench, and the Attorney-General asked leave to move an amendment. But the Opposition objected, as it was now 10.30 p.m., the hour fixed by the Government for the closure. The objection was upheld by the Chair and the Bill went through unamended, the Final Stage being passed by 79 votes to 54.[4]

---

[1] *Dáil Debates*, lxiv, 1233–5.
[3] Ibid., lxiv, 1378.

[2] Ibid., lxiv, 1263.
[4] Ibid., lxiv, 1379–84.

The second measure was the Executive Authority (External Relations) Bill. This was begun at 10.30 a.m. on the next day (Saturday, 12th December), and it was finished less than seven hours later. The long title was: 'An Act to make provision, in accordance with the Constitution, for the exercise of the executive authority of Saorstát Éireann in relation to certain matters in the domain of external relations and for other matters connected with the matters aforesaid.' Thus, reference to the Abdication of King Edward was avoided in both the long and the short titles. Indeed, the Instrument of Abdication itself was not to be found in the original Bill, but was added as an afterthought, in the form of a Schedule, by means of a Government amendment inserted in Committee. The main section of the Bill had also to be redrafted. Sections 1 and 2 of the Bill in its final form provided that the State's diplomatic and consular representatives should be appointed, and its international agreements concluded, on the authority of the Executive Council. Section 3, which is the main section, is in two parts. The first sub-section reads as follows: 'It is hereby declared and enacted that, so long as Saorstát Eireann is associated with the following nations, that is to say, Australia, Canada, Great Britain, New Zealand and South Africa, and so long as the king recognized by those nations as the symbol of their co-operation continues to act on behalf of each of those nations (on the advice of the several Governments thereof) for the purposes of the appointment of diplomatic and consular representatives and the conclusion of international agreements, the king so recognized may, and is hereby authorized to, act on behalf of Saorstát Éireann for the like purposes as and when advised by the Executive Council so to do.' This sub-section was riddled by the arguments of Messrs. Costello and McGilligan, who had both taken an active part in the Imperial Conferences which led up to the Statute of Westminster. Referring to the phrase 'the king recognized by those nations as the symbol of their co-operation', Mr. Costello proved conclusively in a long and cogent argument that it is true neither in law nor in fact. It is as well here to recall the definition of the nations of the Commonwealth adopted in the Report of the Imperial Conference of 1926, to which the Irish Free State was a party. 'They are autonomous communities within the British Empire, equal in status, in no way subordinate one to another in any aspect of their domestic or external affairs, though united by a common allegiance to the Crown, and freely associated as members of the British Commonwealth of Nations.' Mr. Costello moved an amendment to delete the words 'their co-operation' and to substitute the words 'the free association of the members of the British Commonwealth of Nations'. Mr. De Valera was prepared to accept 'association' for 'co-operation', but he hesitated at the word 'free', though, by the terms of the sub-section, it applied to the association of the other members and not to that of the Irish Free State. After a good deal of fencing, he said, 'I am not certain that in all cases it is free.'[1] The amendment was rejected.

The second sub-section of Section 3 reads: 'Immediately upon the passing of this Act, the instrument of abdication executed by His Majesty King Edward the Eighth on the 10th day of December, 1936 (a copy whereof is set out in the Schedule to this Act) shall have effect according to the tenor thereof and His said Majesty shall, for the purposes of the foregoing sub-section of this section and all other (if any) purposes, cease to be king, and the king for those purposes shall henceforth be the person who, if His said Majesty had died on the 10th day of December, 1936, unmarried, would for the time being be his successor under the law of Saorstát Éireann.' Thus His Majesty King George VI was again referred to anonymously. In Friday's Bill he was an organ; in Saturday's, a person.

Section 4 of the Bill gave the short title, and the Schedule, as already stated, consisted of the Instrument of Abdication.

The Final Stage was passed by 81 votes to 5, the Opposition voting for it and the minority consisting of Labour members. The Bill was enacted on the day on which it was passed, 12th December 1936; and, by its terms, King Edward then ceased to be king, not, as in the United Kingdom, on the previous day.

The Executive Authority (External Relations) Act, 1936, is in no way affected by Mr. De Valera's new Constitution, and so it is still the law. From the statutory point of view, it is the sole remaining link with the Crown and with the British Commonwealth of Nations; and, as it is merely an ordinary Act of Parliament, it can be repealed at any time. Speaking in Dublin on the 23rd April 1939, Mr. De Valera hinted that it may be repealed 'if it became clear that that was not the way to secure unity'.[2]

The passage of these two Bills in the space of slightly over twenty-four hours fully justified the allegations made against Mr. De Valera, at the time the Senate Abolition Bill was before Parliament, that his real aim was a personal dictatorship to be exercised through his mechanical majority in the single chamber. His 'external association'

---

[1] *Dáil Debates*, lxiv, 1487.   [2] *Irish Times*, 24 April 1939.

policy was put into force, not only in direct violation of his pledge to the electors, but so quickly that public opinion could not have time to express itself. Henceforward, the institution of monarchy, which has existed in Ireland since the dawn of history, is, like an embrocation, to be used for external application only—'Not to be taken internally.'

As Mr. De Valera's new Constitution was so nearly ready, it may be asked why he did not wait until its introduction before effecting the change. The answer is that the Abdication provided him with an opportunity of putting 'external association' into force without consulting the people. Otherwise, the issue at the plebiscite would have been the old Constitution based on the Treaty versus the new Constitution based on 'external association'. His action ensured that 'external association' would not be a factor at the plebiscite; but, even so, his new Constitution secured only a small majority, as we shall see presently.

CHAPTER XXVIII

THE END OF THE IRISH FREE STATE

Mr. De Valera's attitude to the Coronation—No representation at the Imperial Conference—The Executive Powers (Consequential Provisions) Bill—The Governor-Generalship abolished—Compensation of the last holder of the office—Introduction of the Draft Constitution—The Second Chamber Commission—Its personnel and Report—Mr. De Valera discloses his reason for abolishing the Senate—Unique features of the Draft Constitution—Character of the State not designated—The position of Northern Ireland—The President—Mr. Pádraic Colum's criticism—The Council of State—The Parliament—Composition and powers of the Second Chamber—The referendum—'External association'—Power to establish Special Courts—Declarations of a homiletic character—Religion—Divorce—Mr. MacDermot and recognition of membership of the British Commonwealth—Attitude of the Opposition —Method of enacting the new Constitution—Submission to a plebiscite —Mr. De Valera's reasons for the procedure—The sovereignty of the people—Reason for no Constituent Assembly—Reason for plebiscite on same day as general election—The general election of July 1937— Analysis of the result—Virtual elimination of Independents—Result of the plebiscite—Slender majority for the new Constitution—The plebiscite considered on an all-Ireland basis—The end of the Irish Free State.

There was considerable curiosity as to whether the Government would be officially represented at the Coronation (12th May 1937) and at the Imperial Conference which followed it. On the 24th February 1937 Mr. De Valera informed the Dáil that he had been kept informed of the changes to be made in the Coronation Oath in view of the altered status of the Dominions. He added: 'I had made it clear that our attitude towards the whole Coronation ceremony must be one of detachment and protest while our country was

partitioned and while the Coronation Service implied discrimination
—as it still does—against the religion to which the majority of our
people belong.'[1] A few days later it was announced from the Vatican
that the Pope was to send a Papal Legate to London for the occasion.
The Coronation ceremonies were in the charge of the Earl Marshal
(His Grace the Duke of Norfolk), who is, of course, a Catholic. The
Prime Minister of Australia (the late Rt. Hon. J. A. Lyons, M.P.), a
Catholic of Irish descent, was present in Westminster Abbey, as were
hundreds of other Catholics from all over the British Commonwealth,
including a large number from Ireland.

Between the 17th February and the 8th April Mr. James M. Dillon
made four unsuccessful attempts, by means of Parliamentary Questions, to elicit the Government's attitude towards the Imperial
Conference. On the 27th April his pertinacity was rewarded. At first,
Mr. De Valera merely referred him to the previous answer. Mr.
Dillon then asked if he was to understand that the Executive Council
had not yet made up its mind whether it was to be represented or not.
Mr. De Valera replied: 'I think the Deputy is going a little too far in
that. The question is that the necessity for a decision would only
arise in case the circumstances were such that the interests of the
State would be served by going there.' After this typically cryptic
reply had been repeated with variations, Mr. Dillon inquired further,
'So we will not be represented at the Imperial Conference?' Mr. De
Valera replied, 'No', and Mr. Dillon said, 'Now we have it at last.
We very much regret that decision.'[2]

The Republican extremists warned the film renters that the
Coronation film was not to be shown, and it was not shown. Enterprising cinema proprietors in Belfast and Newry advertised special
performances in the Dublin newspapers, the Great Northern Railway Company ran special trains, and thousands of persons crossed
the border into Northern Ireland for the purpose of seeing the film.

The Constitution Amendment Act passed on the day after the
King's Abdication had not, apparently, completely got rid of the
Governor-General; and so, on the 11th May 1937, the Executive
Powers (Consequential Provisions) Bill was introduced. By this
measure his surviving powers and functions were distributed and the
Governor-General's Salary and Establishment Act, 1923, was re-
pealed. But the proposal which attracted most public attention was
the provision made for the last holder of the office, Mr. Daniel
Buckley. He had been appointed on the 26th November 1932, after

the virtual dismissal of Mr. James McNeill, so that his normal term of five years had almost expired. Under Article 60 of the Constitution, the salary of the Representative of the Crown was to be the same as that of the Governor-General of Australia, that is, £10,000 a year. This salary had been paid to Mr. Buckley's predecessors, but they had lived in the Viceregal Lodge, had entertained on a large scale, and had discharged all the customary duties of their high office. Mr. Buckley had been accommodated in a house in the suburbs, and, on the Second Reading of the Bill, the Minister for Justice revealed the fact that he had been in receipt of £2,000 a year and an allowance. So far as the general public is aware, the only substantial service he rendered in return for this large stipend was to affix his signature to Bills. Mr. De Valera said that he 'voluntarily surrendered' the £10,000 'without any bond or anything of that sort'.[1] Such a bond would, of course, have been *ultra vires* the Constitution, and therefore unenforceable. The Bill now conferred on Mr. Buckley, within a few months of his normal term, a gratuity of £2,000, and a pension of £500 a year for life. In spite of protests, it became law on the 8th June 1937.

The new Draft Constitution was formally introduced in the Dáil on the 10th March 1937. As it contained provisions for a Senate, it is necessary to state in this place that on the 9th June 1936 (less than a fortnight after the enactment of the Senate Abolition Bill) a Commission was set up by the Executive Council with the following terms of reference: 'To consider and make recommendations as to what should be the functions and powers of the Second Chamber of the Legislature in the event of its being decided to make provision in the Constitution for such Second Chamber and, further, to consider and make recommendations as to how in that event such Chamber should be constituted as regards number of members, their qualifications, method of selection and period of office, and what allowances (if any) should be made to such members.' The personnel of the Commission consisted of the Chief Justice (chairman), the Attorney-General (vice-chairman), seven members of the Dáil, five ex-Senators, four university professors, two Civil Servants, and three others—twenty-three members in all. The Parliamentary Opposition was not represented, as it had refused to co-operate on the ground that there was no undertaking that a Second Chamber would, in fact, be established.

The Commission was requested to report by the 1st October, and

[1] *Dáil Debates*, lxvii, 591–664.

it did so, the Report being subsequently published. The time allowed was obviously insufficient for a due consideration of the issues involved, and no witnesses were called. The Report is a curious document. It consists of (1) the 'Report of the Commission', which is in the nature of a narrative and is signed by the chairman, though he disagreed with most of its recommendations; (2) five separate reservations; (3) an additional Report embodying the chairman's own views; (4) a Minority Report; (5) reservations to the Minority Report; (6) a Report from one member.

An extraordinary feature about this Commission was the appointment to it of two serving Civil Servants—or rather three, for ex-Senator Connolly, who was a member of it, had been made Chairman of the Commissioners of Public Works. The other two were respectively the Secretary to the Executive Council and the Legal Adviser to the Department of External Affairs. The proper function of such Civil Servants is to advise the Government, and it was disturbing to find them nominated to a Commission which was to report on the character of the Legislature under which they might have to work. The fact that these three particular officials were appointed to the Commission was, however, taken as an indication that there was to be a Senate under the new Constitution. Either Mr. De Valera had rapidly changed his mind on the subject of Second Chambers or he had merely abolished the Senate to suit his own purposes. On the 2nd December 1937, long after those purposes had been effected, he admitted in a singularly candid passage that the latter alternative was correct. He said: 'In the constitutional circumstances in which we were, with the national objectives which we had in front of us, I wanted to get rid of a Second House, and particularly I wanted to get rid of the previous Second House whilst a certain piece of constitutional work was being done. Fortunately for the country, it was not there at the time that a certain piece of important constitutional work had to be done.'[1]

The Draft Constitution was published, in Irish and English, on the 30th April 1937. To emphasize the patriotic character of the document, the Irish text was printed in Gaelic type, which had long ago been superseded by Roman type so far as parliamentary publications were concerned. A detailed analysis of the new Draft does not fall within the scope of this book, but it is of such importance that some reference to its main provisions is called for. In at least three respects it is unique among the Constitutions of the world:

[1] *Dáil Debates*, lxix, 1608.

1. The character of the State—whether monarchy or republic—is not designated. Article 5 states that 'Ireland is a sovereign, independent, democratic State', but this does not answer the question. South Africa is described in similar terms in the Status of the Union Act, 1934; and South Africa is a monarchy.

2. Virtually no reference is made to external affairs.

3. The language of the basic text (Irish) is one that the vast majority of members of Parliament, Bench and Bar, and of the population generally, can neither read, write, speak, nor understand.

So far as nomenclature goes, the Irish Free State is abolished, and it is declared that 'the name of the State is Éire, or, in the English language, Ireland'. Further, 'the national territory consists of the whole island of Ireland, its islands and the territorial seas'. 'Éire' is the name for Ireland in the Irish language. It is so often mispronounced that it is as well to mention that it rhymes, approximately, with 'Sarah'.

The *de facto* position with regard to Northern Ireland is recognized by Article 3, which reads: 'Pending the re-integration of the national territory, and without prejudice to the right of the Parliament and Government established by this Constitution to exercise jurisdiction over the whole of that territory, the laws enacted by that Parliament shall have the like area and extent of application as the laws of Saorstát Éireann and the like extra-territorial effect.'

There is a President of Ireland, popularly elected by all citizens eligible to vote at Dáil elections. His term of office is seven years, and he is eligible once for re-election. His powers and functions are largely, but not wholly, formal. He is to take precedence over all other persons in the State, but is not designated as its head. The following views of Mr. Pádraic Colum, published in the American *Commonweal*,[1] are interesting as being those of a distinguished Irish man of letters, unconnected with politics, who resides outside his own country.

'President De Valera has been careful not to name the Head of the State—and a State has to have a Head. Neither the President nor the Prime Minister is so designated. . . . This evasiveness on fundamental issues, this deliberate veiling of essential situations, is bound to create a bad moral atmosphere in the country. The Irish people either see through it or make up their minds that they do not want to see through it, and in either case the result is morally bad: it makes for either cynicism or pretence. After all, it should be the main pur-

[1] Issue of 16 July 1937, pp. 297–9.

pose of legislators to make a people upright and self-reliant; a Constitution that does other than this has the gravest, possible defect.'

A Council of State is set up 'to aid and counsel the President'. It is very roughly analogous to the Privy Council.

The Parliament is to consist of the President and two Houses. The provisions with regard to the Dáil are not substantially altered. As to the new Senate, when speaking in the Dáil on the enactment motion which abolished the old Senate (28th May 1936) Mr. De Valera referred to the system of nomination and said that a nominated Senate could not be a real safeguard, and that it was open to attack from many directions. As to a Senate based on vocational representation, he said, quite truly: 'I have found, first of all, that we are not organized in that sense here in a way that would enable us satisfactorily to choose such a Second Chamber; and, secondly, that I certainly could not fulfil the second part of the election pledge we gave if I were to attempt to form one. I do not think you can get really satisfactory vocational representation with a number as small as the number that I had in mind.'[1] The part of the election pledge alluded to is that in which he promised to reduce considerably the number of members of the Senate. The new Senate is to be composed of sixty members, the same number as the old. Of these, eleven are to be nominated by the Prime Minister; three each are to be elected by the two universities; and the remaining forty-three are to be elected on a basis of vocational representation. All the Senators are to go out of office together, a general election for the Senate taking place not later than ninety days after a dissolution of the Dáil. The method of election is to be determined by law.

The power of the Senate over Money Bills is roughly the same as before, the period of twenty-one days being retained. The definition of a Money Bill is also retained, save for slight changes in the phraseology, the reason for which is not obvious. In regard to Bills other than Money Bills, the Senate has a suspensory power of only ninety days, and machinery is provided for abridging this period in cases of urgency or emergency. But a Bill in respect of which the period has been abridged shall remain in force for no longer than ninety days unless both Houses agree to extend the date of its expiry. Bills are to be signed and promulgated by the President.

Provision is made for a referendum, and a distinction is drawn between Constitution Amendment Bills and other Bills. Bills of the

[1] *Dáil Debates*, lxii, 1197, 1200, 1201.

former class must be submitted to a referendum, and are held to have been approved by the people if a majority of the votes cast is in favour. (The Constitution may, however, be amended by ordinary legislation, without a referendum, for a period of three years reckoned from the date on which the first President enters upon his office.) In regard to every other Bill, a majority of the Senate and one-third of the Dáil may present a joint petition to the President not to sign and promulgate it, on the ground that it contains a proposal of such national importance that the will of the people ought to be ascertained. The President, after consultation with the Council of State, may accede or decline. If he accedes, either (a) a referendum takes place, and the Bill is held to have been vetoed if a majority of the votes cast is against it *and* if the votes cast against it amount to not less than one-third of the total voters on the register: or (b) the Dáil may pass a resolution, after a dissolution and reassembly within eighteen months of the petition, approving the Bill, in which case it must be signed and promulgated. The effect of alternative (a) might well prove extraordinary. If, at the time of a referendum, the number on the register was, for example, the same as at the 1937 plebiscite, viz., 1,775,055, then the Bill would be deemed to *pass* if the voting was, For, 200: Against, 590,000, because the number against would be less than one-third of the total voters on the register.

The provisions regarding the Executive are not greatly altered, except that the term 'Government' replaces 'Executive Council' in the English text. Two Ministers may be members of the Senate. In the section of the Constitution devoted to the Government there is reproduced, in substance, the provision made at the time of the Abdication for the use of an organ for external affairs; but by this time it had become much more vague. The organ had then been designated as that used by the British Commonwealth of Nations. The new provision is: 'For the purpose of the exercise of any executive function of the State in or in connection with its external relations, the Government may to such extent and subject to such conditions, if any, as may be determined by law, avail of or adopt any organ, instrument or method of procedure used or adopted for the like purpose by the members of any group or league of nations with which the State is or becomes associated for the purpose of international co-operation in matters of common concern.'

The provisions with regard to the Courts of Justice call for no particular comment, except to say that 'special courts' may be established to deal with cases for which the ordinary courts are inadequate.

This is a belated recognition by Mr. De Valera of the necessity for some such tribunal as that set up by Article 2A of the old Constitution.

Large sections of the new Constitution consist of declarations of a homiletic character concerning personal rights, the family, education, private property, religion, and directive principles of social policy. Many of these are so vague that they could not possibly be impleaded in the courts, and it is difficult to see what purpose they serve in such a document. Dr. Rowlette criticized the Constitution from this aspect as follows: 'A Constitution is essentially a legal document and should be declaratory of the structure of the State. . . . Above everything else, it should be declaratory of the rights of the individual citizen. This draft document that we are considering contains phrases directive rather than declaratory. It consists largely of a moral homily in which various directions are given as to the lines on which the State should work in future. Where general principles appear, one finds that almost every one of them is qualified by following phrases, so that when attempting to interpret them one does not know what meaning is conveyed. That occurs over and over again. Instead of a clear statement as to the structure of the State and the right of individual citizens, we have a vague, indeterminate series of statements and sentences which to a great extent are opposed to each other and are almost contradictory.'[1]

In the section on religion, the following paragraph occurs: 'The State recognizes the special position of the Holy Catholic Apostolic and Roman Church as the guardian of the Faith professed by the great majority of the citizens.' But, read in conjunction with the rest of the section, this appears to amount to no more than a statement of the fact, universally known, that all but a small percentage of people living in the area heretofore known as the Irish Free State are Catholics. For the section goes on to declare that the State also recognizes the Church of Ireland, the Presbyterian Church, the Methodist Church, the Religious Society of Friends, the Jewish Congregations, 'and the other religious denominations existing in Ireland at the date of the coming into operation of this Constitution'. The Catholic Church obtains no 'special position', as freedom of conscience and the free profession and practice of religion are guaranteed, and the State guarantees not to endow any religion. Further, no disabilities may be imposed nor discrimination made on account of religious belief or status.

[1] *Dáil Debates*, lviii, 386, 387.

In these general sections of the Constitution, the only other provision which calls for notice here is the following:

'No law shall be enacted providing for the grant of a dissolution of marriage.

'No person whose marriage has been dissolved under the civil law of any other State but is a subsisting valid marriage under the law for the time being in force within the jurisdiction of the Government and Parliament established by this Constitution shall be capable of contracting a valid marriage within that jurisdiction during the lifetime of the other party to the marriage so dissolved.'

This prohibition of divorce and re-marriage within the jurisdiction gives constitutional recognition to what has been the *de facto* position since the beginning.

The new Constitution was not the result of the labours of jurists and other experts. So far as is known, its author is Mr. De Valera himself, aided, no doubt, by Civil Servants and others whose duty it is to advise him and his Government. As it embodies his own policy of 'external association', he can hardly have been surprised by the fact that his appeal to the Opposition for co-operation in its enactment fell on deaf ears. The Labour Party also was hostile to and suspicious of a number of its provisions. The net result was that Mr. De Valera was on the defensive most of the time that the Draft was passing through the Dáil; and the general apathy of the single chamber is shown by the fact that on several occasions the proceedings were interrupted for want of a quorum.

Of the numerous amendments offered on the Committee Stage one is specially noteworthy. Mr. MacDermot proposed a new article as follows: 'The Irish nation hereby declares its free and equal membership as a sovereign State of the British Commonwealth of Nations, and so long as such membership continues recognizes King George VI and each of his successors at law as King of Ireland.' Mr. MacDermot developed his arguments in a reasoned speech, and reinforced them by quotations showing the attitude to the Crown of Wolfe Tone, Thomas Davis, and Parnell. He also said that it was only by making the Crown an integral part of the Constitution that a beginning could be made with reconciliation with the North of Ireland. The amendment received no support from the United Ireland Party, and it was defeated by 56 votes to 3, the minority consisting of Mr. MacDermot himself, Professor Alton (Independent, Dublin University), and Mr. John Good (Independent, County Dublin).[1] Subse-

1 *Dáil Debates*, lxvii, 953–68.

quently, Mr. James Dillon, who is a vice-chairman of the United Ireland Party, gave his opinion on the question: 'Personally, I take the view that the last place you ought to put a definition of our constitutional position *vis-à-vis* the Commonwealth is in the Constitution, and I want to say why. I want to make it the easiest thing in the world to declare a republic in this country. I believe that, the easier you make it to declare a republic, the more certain it is that our people will not do it.'[1] From this time forward, very large numbers of people took the view that there was now no substantial difference between the two principal political parties in their attitude towards the Crown.

The method adopted for the enactment of the new Constitution is of very great constitutional importance. The existing Constitution was, of course, the fundamental law of the Irish Free State, and Article 50 provided the method whereby it could be changed. As amended by successive Constitution (Amendment) Acts, this Article read as follows:

'Amendments of this Constitution may be made by the Oireachtas but no such amendment, passed by Dáil Éireann after the expiration of a period of sixteen years from the date of the coming into operation of this Constitution shall become law [i.e. after the 5th December 1938] unless the same shall, after it has been passed by Dáil Éireann, have been submitted to a Referendum of the people, and unless a majority of the voters on the register shall have recorded their votes on such Referendum and either the votes of a majority of the voters on the register, or two-thirds of the votes recorded, shall have been cast in favour of such amendment. Any such amendment may be made within the said period of sixteen years by way of ordinary legislation.'

On the 17th May 1934, nearly three years before the new Draft Constitution was published, Mr. De Valera had suggested another possible method. 'From a legal point of view, in so far as I can presume to understand the matter, I do not know where a Constituent Assembly derives its authority from except directly from the people. If, for instance, we wanted in a short period to get this Constitution revised and a new Constitution secured, the natural way of doing it would be to get an Assembly for that purpose elected directly by the people. It is clear that the Parliament of the time would arrange for the type of Assembly and how it was to be elected, and I cannot see how, if it so chose, you could prevent any Parlia-

---

[1] *Dáil Debates*, lxviii, 367, 368.

2K

ment from constituting itself, if need be, into a Constituent Assembly.'[1]

None of these courses was followed. The new Constitution did not profess to operate as an amendment of the old under Article 50; a Constituent Assembly was not elected, and no resolution was passed by the Dáil constituting itself a Constituent Assembly. The Draft Constitution was treated in all essential respects like an ordinary Bill. Between the beginning of the Second Reading on the 11th May and the completion of the Final Stage on the 14th June it occupied part of eleven days, ordinary legislation and other parliamentary business being proceeded with at the same time. At the end of the debate on the Final Stage, instead of the usual question, 'That the Bill do now pass', the form of the motion was 'That the Draft Constitution, 1937, be and is hereby approved by Dáil Éireann'—that is, approved for submission to the people.

Twelve days previously (2nd June 1937) a Plebiscite (Draft Constitution) Act was passed. This provided that the Draft Constitution should be submitted to a plebiscite, and that the plebiscite should be held on the same day as the next general election for the Dáil. The corresponding provision in the Draft Constitution is contained in Article 62, which reads as follows:

'This Constitution shall come into operation

'i. on the day following the expiration of a period of one hundred and eighty days after its approval by the people signified by a majority of the votes cast at a plebiscite thereon held in accordance with law, or

'ii. on such earlier day after such approval as may be fixed by a resolution of Dáil Éireann elected at the general election the polling for which shall have taken place on the same day as the said plebiscite.'

Thus, all that was required for the enactment of the Constitution was a bare majority of those voting, irrespective of the proportion which the number voting bore to the total on the register; and provision was made for the eventuality of Mr. De Valera's winning the plebiscite but losing the general election. He said: 'If the new Dáil passes a resolution that this Constitution is to come into operation, then before six months it comes into operation. If the new Dáil neglect their duty, even whether they like it or not, it becomes law within six months from the date of the plebiscite.'[2]

Under Article 48, as from the date of the coming into operation of

---

[1] *Dáil Debates*, lii, 1219.   [2] Ibid., lxvii, 74.

the new Constitution, the old Constitution was repealed, as was also the Constitution Act of 1922, 'in so far as that Act or any provision thereof is then in force'. This Act consisted of the Act proper and two Schedules, one of which was the Constitution and the other was the Treaty.

We shall now give, in Mr. De Valera's own words, the reasons for the procedure adopted. Mr. J. A. Costello, K.C., the former Attorney-General, had given it as his opinion that the new Constitution could legally operate only as an amendment of the existing Constitution within the meaning of Article 50 thereof. Mr. De Valera said that he was mistaken. 'Deputy Costello would be telling us that he would have a grand time going to the Supreme Court asking them to say that the Constitution was *ultra vires*. But neither Deputy Costello nor anybody else can tell us that this Draft Constitution is *ultra vires* for it is the people themselves who will enact it. They are the authority. The people have power to determine from time to time who their rulers will be and also what their Government will be. The Government can go back to the people and the people can effect that revolution and change their form as long as it is referred to themselves. In this case they will be doing that and I would like to see the lawyers who would stand in their way. This Draft Constitution, if passed at all, is going to be passed by the sovereign people who are above the lawyers and above the Government and all others. . . . Therefore it is that in this case we are not bothering very much about what the lawyers think or say about this Constitution. I know, however, that the lawyers would have a lot to say about it if it were brought in as an amendment of the old Constitution.'[1] And again: 'The Courts here have expressed certain opinions in dealing with certain cases and made certain suggestions as to their views about the powers here to pass Acts in relation to the terms of the Treaty. We were not going to risk a Constitution like this, even though it was the right way to judge a Constitution like this, being enacted here and being operated with such possible views held by the Courts. What we are doing is, we are going back to the sovereign authority, to the Irish people, or that section of the Irish people whom we can consult on the matter. We go back to them and ask them to enact it. It is they who will enact it and, as I said in my introductory speech, when they enact it there is a provision that any judge, or anybody else, who is not prepared to function under it can resign and get out.'[2]

The reference to certain cases, certain suggestions, and certain opin-

---

[1] *Dáil Debates*, lxvii, 74, 75.   [2] Ibid., lxvii, 416.

ions is doubtless an allusion to the unanimous view of the Supreme Court, expressed in the judgement in the State (Ryan and Others) *v.* Lennon and Others, that the Oireachtas had no power to amend or repeal the Constitution Act. It is pertinent here to recall that Mr. De Valera assured the electors that the Oath was not required by the Treaty; that the Bill to abolish the Oath was drafted in such a way as to forestall, if possible, a decision of the courts on this question; and that the Attorney-General stated that this was 'necessary in order to prevent any judicial misrepresentation of the position'.

On the question why a Constituent Assembly was not set up to frame the Constitution (as he had said three years earlier was 'the natural way') Mr. De Valera said: 'Were we to have a new Constituent Assembly called? I claim that such a Constituent Assembly could not possibly do the work if the Dáil set itself out to do it properly. If it did not set itself out to do it properly, then the blame is not on these benches but on the opposite benches'[1] [for withholding their co-operation]. A Constituent Assembly elected *ad hoc* by the people might conceivably have contained a majority against the Government, in which case the whole plan would have miscarried.

The only other matter which calls for explanation is why the plebiscite should be held on the same day as the general election. Mr. De Valera would have preferred it otherwise. He said: 'From my own point of view, I should prefer to see this Constitution voted on at a time when there is no election—voted on at a time in which the matter, probably, would get more consideration and, if I might say so, a less biassed consideration—but this being the first time our people will have a referendum, and there being the danger that it might be difficult to get them out to vote in a referendum on the first occasion, it is about the best method of doing it. There is always just that danger in a referendum at the start.'[2] The method adopted also had the advantage that two campaigns could be conducted at the same time.

On the day on which the Draft Constitution was finally approved (Monday, 14th June) the Dáil was dissolved, and the general election and the plebiscite were held on the 1st July. One of the points stressed by the Government Party in favour of the new instrument was that it made provision for a Second Chamber. 'It [the Constitution] establishes the BICAMERAL SYSTEM of Parliamentary Government in this country upon a firm basis. . . . If you are not against a Second House or Senate, can you find any good reason why you should

[1] *Dáil Debates*, lxviii, 414.   [2] Ibid., lxviii, 287, 288.

vote against the Constitution? Then you *must* vote for the Constitution!'[1]

The annual pilgrimage of the Republicans to Wolfe Tone's grave occurred during the campaign (Sunday, 20th June). In 1936 this meeting had been proclaimed. This year the demonstrators were not interfered with.[2] On the previous day the Parliamentary Secretary to the Minister for Local Government (Dr. Ward) made a speech in his constituency, in the course of which he is reported to have said: 'If Fianna Fáil were going to be impeded in national progress there was only one other method left. If an Imperialist Party was elected in this country it would not be long until there was bloodshed, because there were still men in Ireland who would never allow the British to dominate the country.'[3]

The result of the general election was as shown below. The party strength at the dissolution is given in brackets, on the basis of a full House. There were, however, three vacant seats at the time.

Party	Candidates nominated	Members elected
Fianna Fáil (De Valera)	100	69 (80)
United Ireland Party (Cosgrave)	95	48 (53)
Labour	23	13 (8)
Independents	36	8 (12)
	254	138 (153)

The comparatively large number of Independent candidates is partially explained by the reduction of the total membership from 153 to 138. Room could not be found for all the former members, and some of those who were not officially adopted went forward as Independents, most of them being unsuccessful. Among other defeated Independents were Commandant Cronin, formerly of the United Ireland Party, and Mr. Frank Ryan, the Republican leader who had fought in Spain. Mr. Frank MacDermot did not offer himself for re-election. The Administration was virtually unchanged.

The large increase in the number of three-member constituencies had its expected result in the virtual elimination of members who were not tied to party. Only eight Independents were successful: Mr. R. S. Anthony (Independent Labour, Cork City); Mr. T. J.

[1] Fianna Fáil advertisement in the *Irish Times*, 1 July 1937.
[2] *Irish Times*, 21 June 1937.   [3] *Sunday Independent*, 20 June 1937.

Burke (Farmer, Clare); Rt. Hon. Alfred Byrne, Lord Mayor of Dublin (Dublin, North-East); Mr. James Larkin, the veteran Labour leader (Dublin, North-East); Mr. Alfred Byrne, junior (Dublin, North-West); Mr. J. J. Cole (Cavan); Dr. J. Hannigan (Dublin, South); and Major S. Myles (Donegal, East). Mr. Cole and Major Myles come from the border counties, and might be described as ex-Unionists. The latter headed the poll in his constituency, but Mr. Cole only just managed to secure election. It is significant that, of the seven constituencies which returned Independents, all except one have more than three members. The exception is North-East Dublin, where the Lord Mayor's deserved popularity gave him thousands more votes than any other candidate; but General Richard Mulcahy was defeated in the same constituency, and so the Opposition Front Bench lost one of its ablest and most experienced members.

The result of the general election was a great disappointment for the Government party. It had now only sixty-nine members out of 138, or exactly half the House; excluding the Chairman, it was in a minority of one. The United Ireland Party, with forty-eight seats, had more or less maintained its position; and the principal gainer was Labour, which, in a smaller Dáil, had actually increased its representation from 8 to 13. This result was probably due in large measure to the fact that the Labour Party's opportunist policy of pseudo-republicanism attracted extremist support. The total first preferences were:

> For the Government Party   603,172
> Against the Government Party   720,892[1]

Mr. De Valera was thus back to the 1932 position, when his Government was able to carry on only on Labour sufferance.

Nor can Mr. De Valera have regarded the result of the plebiscite with considerable satisfaction. The official figures are:

> For the Constitution   685,105
> Against the Constitution   526,945[2]
> Majority in favour   158,160

Under Article 62 of the instrument only a bare majority of those actually voting was required, and so the new Constitution had been enacted by the people. But if the conditions laid down in Article 50 of the old Constitution had been incorporated in Article 62 it would have been decisively rejected. Article 50 required, for a valid amendment of the Constitution, either a majority of the total voters on the

---

[1] *Irish Times*, 7 July 1937.   [2] *Iris Oifigiúil* (Official Gazette), 16 July 1937.

register or two-thirds of the votes recorded. The total number of voters on the register was 1,775,055.[1] A simple calculation shows that the votes in favour of the new Constitution fell short by 202,423 of a majority of the total votes on the register; and they fell short by 122,928 of two-thirds of the votes actually recorded. In terms of percentages, and to the nearest integer, 39 per cent voted for the new Constitution, 30 per cent voted against it, and 31 per cent did not vote at all. Five of the thirty-four constituencies showed adverse majorities, viz. Dublin County, Dublin Townships, West Cork, Sligo, and Wicklow.

As the Constitution is so framed as to apply to the whole of Ireland when partition has been ended, it is of some interest to state the result of the plebiscite on an all-Ireland basis, without, however, drawing any conclusions on the subject. The plebiscite did not, of course, apply to Northern Ireland, but on the register which came into operation on the 15th December 1937 (which is sufficiently close to the date of the plebiscite for purposes of computation) the electors in that area numbered 822,860.[2] The total electorate for the entire country was therefore 2,597,915; and, on the figures given above, the following are the percentages:

	per cent
For the Constitution	26
Against the Constitution	20
Eligible to vote but did not note	22
Ineligible to vote	32
	100

No steps were taken by the new Dáil to bring the new Constitution into operation by means of a resolution passed under Article 62; and so, under the same Article, it came into existence automatically one hundred and eighty days after its approval by the people, that is to say, on Wednesday, 29th December 1937. After a short life of fifteen years, the Irish Free State was at an end.

[1] *Report of the Department of Local Government and Public Health*, 1937–8, p. 13.
[2] *Ulster Year Book*, 1938, p. 308.

PART VIII

CHAPTERS ON SPECIAL SUBJECTS

'*No one who is not blind to the political development of our time can have failed to perceive that parliamentary government has* . . . *become the chief problem in the science of public law—in the theory and practice of politics. Nor can there be any doubt that the central element of the problem* . . . *is the manner in which a parliament is to discharge the function of enabling the State to perform its regular* work.'

JOSEF REDLICH, *The Procedure of the House of Commons*,
Introduction, p. xxiii.

'*The action of our Acts of Parliament grows more and more dependent upon subsidiary legislation. More than half our modern Acts are to this extent incomplete statements of law.*'

C. T. CARR, *apud* SIR JOHN A. R. MARRIOTT: *The Mechanism of the Modern State*, vol. II, p. 207.

CHAPTER XXIX

ATTENDANCE AND PAYMENT OF MEMBERS

Constitutional provisions for payment of members—Resolution of the Provisional Parliament—Resolutions of Senate and Dáil—The Oireachtas (Payment of Members) Act, 1923—The Amending Acts— Proposals to reduce remuneration of Chairman and Vice-Chairman of Senate—Report of Select Committee—New scales adopted—Salaries of members of the Government—Professor Thrift's Bill to reduce remuneration of Senators—Joint Committee set up with extended terms of reference—The Committee's Report—No action taken—Rejection of Professor Thrift's Bill by the Dáil—Attendance of members of the two Houses compared—Their different responsibilities—Average number of sitting days of Senate and duration of sitting—Average attendance—Indifferent individual records—Abortive proposals of Joint Committee—Improvement after 1928 accompanied by deterioration in personnel—Connection of payment of members with bad attendance— Problem of the impecunious candidate—Inappropriateness of comparison with overseas Dominions—Non-payment no barrier to Labour Senators—The door closed to no legitimate interest.

As the question of attendance is intimately connected with that of the payment of members, it is appropriate that these two subjects should be dealt with in the same chapter. For the sake of completeness, it will be desirable to treat also of the payment of members of the Dáil and to make some reference to the remuneration of the Chairman and Vice-Chairman of each House and of members of the Executive Council.

Under Article 21 of the Constitution it was the duty and privilege of each House to prescribe, *inter alia*, the remuneration of the Chairman and Vice-Chairman of that House; and it was provided by Article 23 that the Oireachtas should make provision for the pay-

507

ment of its members, and might, in addition, provide them with free travelling facilities in any part of Ireland.

Prior to the coming into operation of the Constitution, the Provisional Parliament, on the 20th September 1922, had passed a resolution adopting the report of a Committee which recommended that the Chairman and the Deputy Chairman of the Dáil should be paid salaries of £1,700 and £1,000 a year respectively, that members of the Dáil (other than Ministers and the Chairman and Deputy Chairman) should be paid an allowance of £30 a month towards expenses, and that free first-class railway travelling facilities should be provided for all members between Dublin and their respective constituencies. The salaries to be paid to Ministers were stipulated in the same resolution. On the 10th January 1923 the Senate resolved that the remuneration payable to members of the Senate, and to the Chairman and Vice-Chairman of that House, should be the same as that fixed in the case of the Dáil, and also that first-class railway travel should be provided for Senators between Dublin and their homes. On the 24th January 1923 the Dáil passed a resolution in similar terms to that passed by the Provisional Parliament and referred to above.

These resolutions of Dáil and Senate were given statutory effect, so far as allowances and travelling facilities were concerned, by the Oireachtas (Payment of Members) Act, 1923, passed on the 18th June 1923. The salary paid to the Chairman and Vice-Chairman of each House, to the President of the Executive Council, and to Ministers was to be deemed to be inclusive of the allowance, and the allowance and travelling facilities were to commence from the day on which the Oath was taken under Article 17 of the Constitution. The remuneration of the Chairman and Vice-Chairman of each House depended on the original resolutions and did not need confirmation by statute; the amounts were included in the annual Estimates and the money was duly appropriated by successive Appropriation Acts. Under the Ministers and Secretaries Act, 1924, the remuneration of the President was fixed at 'an annual sum by way of salary not exceeding £2,500' and the maxima of other Ministers, and of Parliamentary Secretaries set up under the Act were fixed in similar terms at £1,700 and £1,200 respectively.

The original Act of 1923 was amended by three other Oireachtas (Payment of Members) Acts, passed respectively in 1925, 1928, and 1933. Doubts having arisen as to whether the allowance of £30 a month was liable to income-tax and super-tax, the Act of 1925 was passed to give statutory effect to the original intention that it was not to be so liable. The Act of 1928 extended the travelling facilities to travel by omnibus or other public conveyance, and provided for the repayment of expenses incurred by members using their own motor-cars. The Act of 1933 removed the provision about the taking of the Oath, which had been deleted from the Constitution by an Act passed earlier in the same year.

As the duties of the Chairman and Vice-Chairman of the Senate proved in practice to be much less onerous than those of the corresponding officers of the Dáil, there was little to be said in favour of continuing to remunerate them at the same rates, namely £1,700 and £1,000 a year respectively. But it is invidious to reduce the salary of an office during the tenure of the holder of it, and the one post could hardly be dealt with without the other. Hence during the six years' Chairmanship of Lord Glenavy no attempt at revision was made. At the beginning of the Third Triennial Period, however, and before the election of Lord Glenavy's successor, Senator Jameson sought to have the question referred to a committee of the Senate; but he was unable to have the motion debated before the elections had been held. These resulted in the appointment of Senator T. W. Westropp Bennett as Chairman and of Senator P. W. Kenny as Vice-Chairman. Senator Jameson's motion was then discussed, but the opinion of the majority was unfavourable to it, and, on a division, it was adjourned *sine die*.[1]

The question was not allowed to remain in that indeterminate condition. Six days later Senator Joseph Connolly, the leader of the De Valera party in the Senate, tabled a motion to fix the remuneration of the Chairman at £750 a year and of the Vice-Chairman at £400 a year. The debate upon the motion took place on the 20th February 1929, but the reductions proposed were so drastic that it commanded no support, and an amendment was carried referring the matter to a Select Committee.[2] The Report of this Committee, which was unanimous, stated that the Committee had taken into account the duties of the two offices and had considered the salaries paid to the Speakers or Chairmen in the parliaments of the overseas members of the Commonwealth; and it recommended that the remuneration of the Chairman of the Senate should be fixed for the future at £1,200 a year and of the Vice-Chairman at £750 a year.[3] The Report was adopted by the Senate, without debate, on the 9th May 1929, and the new rates were made operative as from the 1st June following.

---

[1] *Senate Debates*, xi, 54–90. [2] Ibid., **xi**, 294–310.
[3] *Reports of Committees*, vol. iii, p. 873.

Before we proceed to consider the question of allowances to Senators it is desirable to complete our reference to the remuneration of officers of the other House and of members of the Government. Shortly after Mr. De Valera's advent to power in 1932 the salaries of the following officers were voluntarily reduced to the extent shown (the previous figures are given in brackets):

President of the Executive Council (£2,500) £1,500
Ministers (£1,700) £1,000
Parliamentary Secretaries (£1,200) £900
Attorney-General (£2,500) £1,500
Chairman of the Dáil (£1,700) £1,000
Deputy Chairman of the Dáil (£1,000) £750.

The only Senator affected by this self-denying ordinance was Senator Connolly, who held ministerial office under Mr. De Valera until the House was abolished. The reductions were by no means so substantial as they appear on paper, as the reduced salaries were all free of income-tax. The position so remained until the Estimates for the financial year 1937–8, when the former amounts were restored; and these are the amounts stipulated by the Ministerial and Parliamentary Offices Act, 1938, passed on the 22nd December 1938. The same Act fixes the salaries of the Chairman and Vice-Chairman of the new Senate at £1,200 and £750 respectively, as before. In addition, provision is made for the payment of annual allowances of £800 and £500 to the leaders of the two principal opposition parties in the Dáil.

An attempt was made, on the ground of economy, to reduce Senators' allowances from £360 to £200 a year by means of a Bill entitled the Oireachtas (Payment of Members) (No. 2) Bill, 1928, introduced on the 30th November 1928 by Professor Thrift, acting on behalf of the Independent Group in the Dáil. After a tedious Second Reading debate which lasted over three days, an amendment was carried postponing consideration until the question should have been considered by a Joint Committee of both Houses, or for three months, whichever period should be the shorter. The Senate extended the terms of reference of the Joint Committee so as to cover the general question of the remuneration of Ministers and the allowances paid to members of the Dáil as well as the Senate. The Dáil concurred and the Committee, which was presided over by Senator P. J. Hooper, reported on the 4th December 1929.[1]

With regard to the Ministers, the Committee recommended that their salaries should remain unaltered, but that a scheme of special

[1] *Reports of Committees*, vol. iii, p. 819.

allowances for ex-Ministers should be introduced, such allowances to continue for a period not exceeding five years after retirement from office.

With regard to the question of allowances to members of the Senate and the Dáil, the Committee reported as follows:

'The Committee does not feel justified in recommending any reduction in the present scale of allowances paid to members of the Oireachtas. In arriving at this conclusion the Committee was influenced by two main considerations:

(*a*) that, in a democratic State, membership of either House of the Legislature should be open to citizens of every rank without undue sacrifice of private interests, and

(*b*) that, having regard to the actual interference with such interests and to the expenses inevitably incidental to their position as members of the Oireachtas, Senators and Deputies who discharge their duties conscientiously give full value to the State for the allowances now paid to them. A minority contended that the allowances to Senators should be reduced, because the parliamentary duties and public activities which Senators are required to undertake are not so extensive as in the case of Deputies. This contention was not accepted by the majority, which held that the existing allowance rate should be regarded as a minimum for members of either House, that there should be an increase in the amount of work entrusted to Senators, and that if any financial change were to be made it should take the form of an increase in the allowance to Deputies.

The methods of payment of members in different countries were considered, and it is agreed unanimously that the present system of payment at a fixed rate is the most satisfactory arrangement. It is held that a person who becomes a member of either House of the Oireachtas, whether his attendance at the House or at Parliamentary Committees be required frequently or not, must be prepared to devote much of his time and attention to parliamentary business in general, and that attendance at sittings would provide a false basis on which to assess the actual amount of work he is expected to perform.'

No action was taken by either House on foot of this Report; and the recommendations for allowances to ex-Ministers, and for increasing the amount of work entrusted to the Senate, were not implemented. But the Ministerial and Parliamentary Offices Act, 1938, already referred to, now makes provision for pensions to the former holders of ministerial and other offices.

Before we deal with the Joint Committee's findings on the subject of Senators' allowances it will be as well to follow the history of Professor Thrift's Bill to its conclusion. After the Report of the Committee had been received, the Second Reading was resumed; and, when the discussion had extended over four separate days, the Bill was finally rejected on the 12th March 1930. The standard of discussion throughout is an exhibition of democracy at its worst.[1] Serious argument was hardly attempted by anybody. Unhumorous puns were made on Professor Thrift's surname and on that of Deputy Hugh Law by a member who is now one of Mr. De Valera's Parliamentary Secretaries, and who also aspersed the motives of the promoters of the Bill and indulged in personalities at the expense of members of the Labour Party on account of their attitude towards it. Allegations and counter-allegations were made by members of the two principal political parties with regard to each other's party funds. A Deputy who was later to become one of Mr. De Valera's Ministers asserted that 'the Senate meets on an average about forty days in the year and meets for the purpose of watching the Clerk stamp Government Bills and of discussing the advisability of adjourning for tea'. As this idle and unprofitable talk fills not far short of two hundred columns of the Dáil *Debates*, occupying in the aggregate some nine or ten hours of parliamentary time, there was a touch of comedy in the statement of this future Minister that 'the view of Deputies on these benches is that if we want . . . work done well it should not be entrusted to Senators, but if it is of an unimportant nature which would be likely merely to waste the time of the Dáil, it might safely be entrusted to the Second Chamber'. Professor Thrift must have heaved a sigh of relief when the rejection of his Bill by two votes put an end to the possibility of further scurrility on this topic.

It is difficult to appreciate the point of view of the majority of the Joint Committee that there should be no differentiation between the two Houses in respect of the allowances paid. The Dáil sat much more frequently than the Senate, and the average duration of the sitting was much longer. Let us take, as a specimen, the year 1933, which is the year most favourable to the Senate, because the number of days sat and the total time were greater than in any other year.[2] In 1933 the Senate sat on fifty-one days, the total time was 199 hours 40 minutes, and the average duration of each sitting was 3 hours 50

[1] *Dáil Debates*, xxviii, 375–400, 548–77, 792–8; xxxiii, 764–832, 1376-1412, 1623–40, 1767–72.
[2] The statistics for each calendar year are given in Appendix H.

minutes. The Dáil sat on eighty days, the total time was 549 hours 5 minutes, and the average duration was 6 hours 50 minutes. The time spent in Joint, Select, and Special Committees did nothing to redress the balance. In this same year (1933) the time occupied by Senators in committee work of this kind was considerably less than twenty hours, and of course the Senators who sat on such committees were few.

If we have regard to the demand on extra-parliamentary time, and to the calls on the individual purse, a comparison is still unfavourable to the Senate. Each member of the Dáil represented a constituency, and that constituency (except in the case of the university members) was very large and very populous. In every constituency there were numbers of electors with posts to seek or grievances to be redressed; and each member of the Dáil was a conduit-pipe through which such grievances or requests were conveyed to the appropriate Government Department, or given publicity by means of a Parliamentary Question. Requests for posts, even from the ill-qualified, had to be dealt with, and grievances, whether real or imaginary, had to be heard with a sympathetic ear; for indifference, or seeming indifference, might easily spell disaster for a Gallio at a succeeding general election. Hence much time was spent by Deputies in personal interviews, their correspondence was voluminous, and their postage bill a heavy one. Moreover, constituencies have to be nursed, an attention which costs time and money; and when general elections occur (sometimes, as in 1927 and 1932–33, twice within twelve months) the drain upon the financial resources of retiring members must be heavy. None of these considerations applied to Senators. They represented no constituency, no Parliamentary Questions were allowed, and their correspondence, *qua* Senators, was either small or non-existent. In 1925, when they were elected by the country as a whole, their election expenses can have amounted to little more than the cost of a small amount of advertising in the newspapers. Subsequently, after the system was changed to election by members of both Houses, the total electorate numbered only 213, and nothing was needed beyond personal contacts and canvassing, involving no expenditure.

The sole valid argument why the rate of allowance should be the same for the Senate as for the Dáil was that the work done by the average Senator, while occupying a much shorter time, was more valuable than that done by the average Deputy, and was accordingly remunerated, proportionately to time, at a higher rate. But we can come to a just conclusion on the subject only after considering

2L

two factors: first, the calls upon the time of Senators, and, second, the way in which those calls were answered—that is to say, the average attendance. Attendance at committees was, as has been indicated, a negligible factor; and the view of the Joint Committee that 'attendance at sittings would provide a false basis on which to assess the actual amount of work' members are 'expected to perform' is not one that carries conviction. The word 'expected' seems to suggest that the basis for the committee's conclusions was theoretical and not empirical.

Commencing on the 30th May 1923 a record of the attendance at each meeting of the Senate was taken by the Clerks at the Table and printed in the *Journal of the Proceedings* of the House.[1] The statistics show that the Senate sat, on an average, for forty days a year, and that the average duration of the sitting was 3 hours 10 minutes. Actually the latter figure does not quite do the Senate justice. In all Second Chambers a number of formal meetings are necessitated from time to time, and the business transacted at them is quickly disposed of. It seems fair to treat any sitting of half an hour or less as a formal sitting, and during the life of the Senate there were thirty-two such sittings, which lasted in some cases for as short a period as ten minutes. If these be disregarded, the average duration would be nearer three hours and a half. We shall therefore not be far wrong in saying that if a member of the Senate did his full duty he might expect to have to attend for about forty days a year and to give something under four hours of his time on each of those forty days.

As this demand was not very great, it might have been expected that the percentage of attendance would be fairly high. Actually, it was quite reasonably high—forty-one out of sixty over the whole period: probably forty-three if we disregard the formal sittings, at which it was sufficient if a mere quorum was present for the transaction of non-contentious business. But there was no spread-over of this average over the whole personnel of the Senate. Some Senators attended on almost every possible occasion; the attendance of most of the others was reasonably satisfactory; the attendance of a few was indifferent.

During the first two Triennial Periods, 1922–8, the bad attendance of certain Senators was a grave scandal, which was the subject of frequent animadversion in the Senate. The worst offenders were to be found among the nominated half of the House—some of them former Southern Unionists, the protection of whose interests had

[1] The average attendance for each calendar year is shown in Appendix I.

been one of the factors which led to the establishment of the Second Chamber. (In fairness to them it should be remembered that a number of them lived in England, their Irish homes having been burnt or otherwise destroyed by Mr. De Valera's followers.) From the date on which the attendance began to be officially recorded (30th May 1923) to the end of the second Triennial Period (5th December 1928) the Senate met on 220 occasions. During this period one Senator, who lived near Dublin, attended only twice: so that, if he drew his 'allowance towards expenses' of £30 a month, as presumably he did, he received from the State the sum of £2,160, free of income-tax, for virtually no return. Another Senator attended only twenty-six times, a third only thirty-seven times, a fourth only fifty-one times, and a fifth only sixty-five times. These five Senators were all nominated and sat for six years; and when their term of office expired they did not offer themselves for re-election. It is right to say that the two whose attendance was poorest, both of whom are now dead, were not Southern Unionists.

This laxity in attendance was considered by the Joint Committee, though it seems doubtful if they were aware of its extent. Their Report deals with the matter as follows: 'It was brought to the notice of the Committee that occasionally there have been members of the Dáil and Senate who by lax attendance at sittings have shown disregard for their obligations as legislators. These, however, are exceptional cases, and in the opinion of the Committee should be the subject of special provision. The Committee is not satisfied as to the feasibility of any general scheme involving automatic diminution of allowance on account of non-attendance, but thinks that the law should be amended to permit of each House establishing a procedure for dealing with special cases of protracted absence or irregular attendance of its members. The Committee recommends that such procedure should make provision for the summoning by the House of the member to attend, failure to comply with this summons, without adequate explanation, to be followed by withdrawal of his allowance, either wholly or in part, for a specified period.'

No attempt was made to procure the requisite changes in the law, either on the lines recommended by the Committee or in some other way. So far as the Senate was concerned, from the beginning of the third Triennial Period (6th December 1928) until the date of abolition there was a marked improvement in the attendance, as reference to Appendix I will show. A number of Senators whose attendance had been poor had either died, resigned, or not offered themselves for re-election, and their successors attended more frequently. Unfortunately, this improvement was accompanied by a deterioration in personnel. But the chief reason for the upward trend in the attendance figures was the introduction of party politics, rendered inevitable by the advent of Mr. De Valera's followers. Their general attitude towards the Senate and its functions was completely at variance with the traditions which had been built up during the preceding six years. One of their number was quite frank about it. 'I say for myself, and I think I can say for every member of this Party, that we came into it [the Senate] on the invitation of the Party. When I came in here, I came in on the definite understanding that when the time arose I was to be here to do my bit to wreck this House. I am here to-day to see that wrecking, and I make no apologies for that. When this House is abolished I will feel that I will have done a good day's work for my country.'[1] When the members of a political party have this outlook, the atmosphere of reasoned discussion must inevitably give place to the arbitrament of the division lobby, and something in the nature of a party system becomes a necessity. In 1928 there were only fourteen divisions; the following year there were fifty. If the policy of 'wrecking' was not to prevail, it was essential that there should be a substantial attendance of those who were opposed to the wreckers.

The scandal of individual bad attendance, however, continued until the end. In the last complete Triennial Period (1931–4) there were 132 meetings of the Senate. One Senator, who is now dead, *never attended at all* and therefore gave no return whatever for the £30 a month which he received during those three years. (This same Senator had, in the previous three years, attended only eighteen times out of a possible 109, and so in six years he was paid more than £2,000 for virtually nothing.) Another Senator attended only eighteen times out of 132, and a third only twenty-eight times; and there were others whose attendance was nearly as bad. This third Senator was not elected until the 6th December 1931, and from that date until the Senate was abolished he attended on only thirty-nine occasions out of a possible 185.

Unreasonably low attendance on the part of a few of its members thus characterized the Senate from the beginning until the end. It would, of course, have been possible so to amend the electoral laws as automatically to vacâte the seat of any Senator who, without just or sufficient cause, gave less than a prescribed minimum of attendance in any period of twelve consecutive months; and, in the case

[1] *Senate Debates*, xx, 1895.

of Senators offering themselves as candidates for re-election, the example might well have been followed of certain learned societies which, in the elections to their governing bodies, print on the ballot paper, against the name of each such candidate, figures giving his attendance during his period of office, with the possible maximum shown in brackets. But no such experiments were tried, and it must be confessed that they would have been only palliatives. They would not have gone to the root of the evil, which was directly traceable to the fact that Senators were paid.

The fact well exemplifies the truth of the Horatian maxim, *Naturam expellas furca, tamen usque recurret.* One cannot change human nature, and it is natural that, in a country in which dependence on government is, through no fault of the people, something of a tradition, the position of a Senator should be coveted by many largely on account of the emoluments attached to it. Nobody who is familiar with the intimate history of the Senate can be unaware of the fact that, at every election from 1922 onwards, there were some candidates who had little claim to be qualified to share in the making of their country's laws, and who would not have been candidates but for the fact that a seat in the Senate carried with it a salary. A few of these candidates were successful at every election, and this must always be the case when the electorate is small, because of the greater activity in canvassing of those whose pecuniary need is pressing. Though the sum of £360 a year was expressed to be an 'allowance towards expenses', it was in actual fact the greater part of the income of some Senators of this type. Such men contributed little or nothing of value to the deliberations of the House, their attendance was often indifferent, and when they were ill for prolonged periods they could not face the loss of income which resignation would entail.

If Senators (other than the Chairman and the Vice-Chairman) had not been paid, or had received merely their out-of-pocket expenses, the attendance scandal might have been minimized and the personnel of the Senate would undoubtedly have been improved. Comparison with such countries as South Africa and Australia is beside the point, because of the vast distances that have to be travelled in those countries. In time of session Senators who live in, say, Maritzburg or Freemantle must be prepared to reside continuously in Cape Town or Canberra, as the case may be; but Irish Senators could, in nearly every instance, attend a sitting in Dublin and be at home the same night, or, at latest, by noon on the following day. In the State of New South Wales, where the Senate is exactly framed on the Dublin model, the members are unpaid, and the result has been admirable.

The statement of the Joint Committee that 'in a democratic State, membership of either House of the Legislature should be open to citizens of every rank without undue sacrifice of private interests' is excellent as a general principle; but, as in the case of so many general principles, the difficulty lies in its practical application. The idea which found expression in some quarters that the Second Chamber should be open to working men has not a great deal to be said for it. If, by the time a working man had reached the mature age desirable for the revision of legislation, he had acquired sufficient ability to engage successfully in the task of such revision, he would also assuredly have acquired sufficient ability so to establish himself in his chosen sphere as to be independent of a stipend as a Senator. It was sometimes also asserted that non-payment of Senators would have debarred members of the Labour Party. This, however, is very far from being the case. Labour members such as Senators O'Farrell, Johnson, and others were among the best legislators that the Senate ever had; but they would have been in the Senate irrespective of payment, partly from a sense of public duty and partly because it was vitally important for the powerful Labour organizations that their point of view should find expression in the most cogent way possible, in the Second Chamber, by men who were of the hierarchy of Labour. The place for Labour politicians of a different type, who belonged to the rank and file, was not in the Senate but in the Popular House.

In short, non-payment of members would have closed the Senate's doors to no legitimate interest; it would have solved the problem of the impecunious candidate and so have procured a superior personnel, and, probably, a better attendance; and it would have set an example of the dignity and honour of service in the legislature which could not but have enhanced the general prestige of the Second Chamber and of its individual members.

For the sake of completeness, it is desirable to add a note on the changes which have taken place since the Constitution of 1937 was promulgated. The Oireachtas (Allowances to Members) Act, 1938, passed on the 21st December 1938, consolidates the law on the subject, the four existing statutes being repealed. The allowance to members of the Dáil is fixed at £40 a month, and members of the new Senate receive an allowance of £30 a month—the same as was paid to members of the old.

CHAPTER XXX

THE INITIATION OF LEGISLATION[1]

Co-equal right of the Senate under the Constitution—Two ways in which this right normally exercised elsewhere—Complex Government Bills of a non-controversial type—Private Members' Bills—No Government Bills initiated in the Senate—Resultant clogging of the legislative machine—Reasons for the Government's attitude—The Industrial and Commercial Property (Protection) Bill—No Parliamentary Draftsman—No power to pay witnesses' expenses—Fate of Senate Bills in Dáil—The Bill to restore the referendum ignored—The Town Planning Bill—Its careful preparation—No consideration in Dáil— Similar treatment of other Bills—Peculiar effect of Article 39 of the Constitution illustrated by history of the Wild Birds Protection Bill.

Under Article 39 of the Constitution the Senate possessed the right, co-equally with the Dáil, of initiating legislation. In other bicameral legislatures, where this right is general, it is normally exercised in two ways. First the Government, which is represented in the Upper House by one or more Ministers, relieves the congestion in the Popular Chamber by introducing in the Senate a number of Bills, which are often of an administrative rather than of a political character. In the case of Bills of any complexity this procedure has manifest advantages; for, since the members of a Second Chamber may be presumed to possess, in general, a somewhat higher level of ability, a wider horizon and perhaps greater leisure than their colleagues in the other House, a Second Chamber is an excellent place for such Bills to be 'licked into shape', as the phrase goes, before they are presented to the Lower House. The second way in which this right is exercised is by the introduction of Private Members' Bills, which are often of such a character that, while desirable in themselves, they are

[1] A complete list of Bills initiated in the Senate is printed in Appendix G.

not normally included in any Government's programme because their electoral appeal is small. In this category are Bills which deal with humanitarian and cultural matters and those of which the scope is sectional rather than national.

Bills of the former class, namely Government measures of an administrative, non-political, and complex type, were never initiated in the Senate. A few days before the dissolution of the 9th August 1923 the Government relieved the congestion in the Dáil by initiating in the Senate three short Bills which called for no amendment. These were the Dyestuffs (Import Regulation) Repeal Bill, the League of Nations (Guarantee) Bill, and the Valuation (Postponement of Revision) Bill. As there was no Minister in the Upper House, two of these were introduced by the Vice-Chairman and one by a private Senator; and they were passed unamended by both Houses. From first to last, this was the full extent of the Government's use of the Senate in the matter of initiating legislation. Periodically, the Dáil was working at high pressure while the Senate was idle; and then, usually just before the summer or Christmas recess, the Senate was confronted with a mass of Bills, often ill-digested, which the Government required to be passed into law within a few weeks. On such occasions protests were made, and suggestions thrown out that better use could be made of the Second Chamber as part of the legislative machine. On one occasion indeed (21st May 1924) Mr. Cosgrave stated that it was the intention to initiate Government Bills in the Senate, and there is little doubt that, left to himself, he would have carried this out. But it is a fact, familiar to all who were connected with the growth of our parliamentary institutions, that the general attitude of the Government towards the Second Chamber, and still more the attitude of the Dáil, was one of detachment, dislike, and distrust; and its function in the legislative sphere was to be the minimum accorded to it by the Constitution. By the time the De Valera Administration took office in March 1932 the position had become stabilized; but in any case the extreme hostility of the new President and his Ministers towards the Upper House made any change out of the question.

How much was lost by this policy of non-co-operation may be judged by the part played by members of the Senate in framing our law relating to patents and copyright. In the spring of 1925 the Government introduced a Bill entitled the Industrial and Commercial Property (Protection) Bill in the Lower House, where it duly received a Second Reading. This was a very complex measure of almost two hundred clauses, and it seems to have been recognized that it could not be adequately dealt with at that stage without the expert assistance available in the Senate. However that may be, the Dáil took the unusual course, never afterwards repeated, of requesting the Senate to nominate members to a Joint Committee to consider the Bill before it was proceeded with further in the Dáil. The Senate concurred, and among the Senate members of the Committee were Sir John Purser Griffith, the *doyen* of Irish engineers, Mr. W. B. Yeats, the poet, whose position as an author of international reputation qualified him to speak with authority on the subject of copyright, and Mr. S. L. Brown, K.C., admittedly the foremost expert in the country on Patent Law. After months of work, the Committee, under the chairmanship of Senator Brown, produced a voluminous report of such a character as necessitated the recasting of the entire Bill.[1] The original Bill was withdrawn and a new one substituted for it; but even when this had been passed by the Dáil it was still so susceptible of improvement that no less than seventy amendments were inserted in it by the Senate, all of them being accepted by the other House. One cannot but regret that the Government did not profit by this experience by subjecting Bills of a similar character and complexity to the same process, or, preferably, by initiating them in the Senate.

We now come to the second class of Bills, namely, those introduced by individual Senators on their own responsibility. Here there were certain difficulties. The Senate had not the services of a parliamentary draftsman, and this was, of course, a serious disadvantage. But it was offset to some extent by the fact that the House possessed in Senator S. L. Brown possibly the profoundest Irish lawyer of his time, and certainly the greatest authority on interpretation. He drafted the Bills of which he was the introducer, or in which he was otherwise interested, and his assistance was at all times freely available to his fellow members.

When a Bill initiated in the Senate had passed its Second Reading, the normal procedure, unless the Bill was of a very simple character, was to refer it to a Select Committee of the House entitled, as the phrase has it, 'to send for persons, papers and records', that is to say, to take sworn evidence. This course was followed in such cases as the Coroners (Amendment) Bill, 1926, and the Slaughter of Animals Bill, 1933. Here another difficulty arose. The Senate had no control over its own finances, and it was in the humiliating position

[1] *Reports of Committees*, vol. ii, p. 125.

of being unable to defray even the out-of-pocket expenses of persons willing to give evidence. Nevertheless, owing to the public spirit of those concerned, valuable evidence was tendered and the results were incorporated in the respective Bills.

When a Bill initiated in the Senate had passed through all its Stages, it was duly certified and sent to the Dáil, with a request for the concurrence of that House. But its further progress to the Statute Book was problematical. There was, in fact, no guarantee that it would even be considered. The appropriate Standing Order of the Dáil provided that a Bill initiated in the Senate should be deemed to have passed its First Stage in the Dáil and should be placed on the Order Paper for its Second Stage; but that, if no motion for its Second Reading were proposed on the day it first appeared on the Order Paper, it was to disappear from the Order Paper and could not be further proceeded with except by leave of the Dáil. Though this Standing Order was not strictly enforced, the history of Bills initiated in the Senate is not encouraging reading. A glance at the Table (Appendix G) will show that, if we exclude the three small Government Bills already referred to, and also the Oireachtas Witnesses Oaths Bill, 1924 and the Private Bills Costs Bill, 1924, which were purely machinery Bills, a total of fourteen Bills were initiated in and passed by the Senate and sent to the Dáil. Of these, only one-half reached the Statute Book in any form; three were rejected, and four were not even considered. Four were passed unamended and three were passed with amendments. Of the four which were ignored, one was quite a short measure, but it raised a point of outstanding importance. This was the Constitution (Amendment No. 25) Bill, 1934, introduced by Senator Douglas and sent to the Dáil on the 6th June 1934. This sought to reinsert the referendum in the Constitution in the case of constitutional amendments. Obviously such a Bill was unwelcome to the De Valera Administration, because, if it had become law, the abolition of the Senate, and of university representation in the Dáil, could not have been achieved without a direct mandate from the electorate. Nevertheless, it might have been expected that the Government would have allowed the Bill to be considered by the Dáil and that Ministers would have been prepared to give reasons why it should be rejected. The more prudent course was taken of ignoring it altogether, and it finally lapsed two years later with the abolition of the Senate.

The other three Bills which were not considered were all skilfully drafted measures on which much time and trouble had been spent. The first of them in point of time was the Town Planning and Rural Amenities Bill, 1929. This was introduced by Senator Johnson, who enlisted the services of the leading experts on the subject. Their help, together with his own skill and the work done on the Bill during the period of close on a year when it was before the Senate, resulted in an eminently satisfactory measure. At the least, it was a Bill which ought to have been acceptable when amended by the Dáil in accordance with the advice of the Government's own experts. It was sent to the Dáil on the 12th March 1930, it was never considered, and it was killed by the dissolution nearly two years later (29th January 1932). Mr. De Valera took office, and in the course of time his Government produced a Bill on the same subject, and this was duly passed into law more than four years after Senator Johnson's Bill had left the Senate.

The fate of Senator O'Farrell's Slaughter of Animals Bill was similar. Here also was a well-conceived and competently drafted measure, designed to render more humane the slaughter of animals for food. It was amended in Select Committee in accordance with evidence given by the best available experts on the subject;[1] and it was sent to the Dáil on the 23rd February 1934. No action was taken upon it, and more than a year and a half later the Government produced its own Bill on the same subject. This was duly passed into law.

The third Bill was the Nurses' and Midwives' Pensions Bill, 1935, the title of which sufficiently explains the scope of the measure. This was introduced by Senator J. C. Dowdall, a member of the Government party, though the actual work of piloting it through the House was undertaken by Senator Sir Edward Coey Bigger, the chairman of the Central Midwives Board. The Bill was sent to the Dáil on the 5th December 1935, it was ignored, and it lapsed with the abolition of the Senate.

The conclusion is irresistible that, whatever government was in power, few Bills of any importance initiated in the Senate were acceptable to the Dáil, even as a basis on which, by means of amendment, to erect a statute.

It is desirable to close this chapter by drawing attention to the peculiar, and even ludicrous, effect of Article 39 of the Constitution on Bills initiated in the Senate and amended by the Dáil. The Article in question provided that a Bill so amended should be considered as a Bill initiated in the Dáil. The effect of this provision is best illustrated by an example. Senator Brown's admirable Wild Birds Protec-

[1] *Reports of Committees*, vol. iv, p. 481.

tion Bill, 1929, which codified the law on the subject, was sent down to the Dáil and passed by that House with some seventeen amendments. These were for the most part of a trifling character, such as the deletion from or addition to a Schedule of the name of a particular bird. But the whole Bill, as amended, was reprinted by the Dáil, the amendments being nowhere indicated by italics or otherwise; and a certified copy was sent to the Senate, with a request that that House should pass it. To render the proceedings intelligible to Senators, it was necessary for Senator Brown, as the sponsor of the original Bill, to explain to the House, in detail, in what respects the new Bill differed from the old. The Bill was then put through its different Stages in the Senate, and a message sent to the Dáil stating that the Senate had agreed to it. There seems to have been no sound reason for the provision in the Constitution which gave rise to this unusual procedure, which Senator Brown characterized as 'a clumsy way of carrying on legislation'.[1] If the Senate should refuse to agree to an amendment made in one of its own Bills by the Dáil, and a deadlock should ensue, it is difficult to see how the Lower House could be damnified by the loss of a Bill which it had not originated. Nevertheless, the provision is reproduced in the Constitution of 1937 (Article 20).

[1] *Senate Debates*, xiii, 1346.

CHAPTER XXXI

DELEGATED LEGISLATION

Meaning of the term—Remarkable growth of delegated legislation—Statistics for the whole period—Bureaucratic invasion of parliamentary rights—Often no retention of ultimate control—Four main classes in which control retained—The First Class—The power of annulment—Variations of the common form—Sub-division of the First Class—Watchfulness of the Senate—Examples—The Censorship of Publications Bill—The Unemployment Assistance Bill—Attempts to exclude the Senate from control—Incuriosity of legislators—Little attempted use of power of annulment—The Second Class—A positive resolution of approval required—The Courts of Justice Bill, 1923—Struggle over the Rules of Court—Lord Glenavy's ridicule—Senator Brown's amendment—Government's attempt to secure hasty approval of the Rules—The Senate's Refusal—Disagreement with the Government over procedure—Anomalous position of the District Court Rules—The Rules of the Circuit Court—The first set withdrawn—The second set also withdrawn—The third set approved after five years—Advantages of positive resolutions—Sub-divisions of the Second Class—The State Lands Act—The Control of Imports Act—Quota Orders—High level of debates in Senate—The Third Class—Confirmation by statute—The Emergency Imposition of Duties Act—Number of Orders thereunder—The Fourth Class—Senate given a power of recommendation only—False analogy with Money Bills—A point of constitutional interest—Sharp controversy with the Government—Acceptance of the Senate amendments—Subsequent rejection of the Senate point of view.

By the term 'delegated legislation', as used in this chapter, is meant that body of law which is made administratively by means of rules, orders, and regulations framed and promulgated by a Minister of State, or by the Executive Council collectively, in pursuance of a power conferred on such Minister or Council by an Act of Parliament. The term seems preferable to 'administrative law', as it avoids any suggestion of an exact analogy with *droit administratif.*

The growth of this delegated legislation in the post-war period, representing, as it does, an enlargement of the bureaucracy at the expense of Parliament, is a phenomenon which has excited apprehension in Great Britain and other States of the British Commonwealth among those who have a proper regard for democratic institutions. The abuses inseparable from it have been trenchantly exposed by the present Lord Chief Justice of England (Lord Hewart) in his book *The New Despotism* (1929), and the matter has been the subject of an inquiry by a Select Committee of the House of Commons, which reported in 1932.[1] But it is improbable that delegated legislation has attained in these other countries the remarkable dimensions which it has achieved in the Irish Free State, where its sinister growth (especially in recent years under Mr. De Valera's Administration) has passed almost unnoticed. The following Table shows the number of Acts passed by Parliament and the number of Statutory Rules and Orders promulgated by the Executive (or by an Executive Minister) during each of the thirteen completed years of the Senate's existence.

Year	Number of Acts	Number of Statutory Rules and Orders
1923	50	24
1924	62	36
1925	42	67
1926	45	83
1927	40	110
1928	38	82
1929	42	73
1930	36	98
1931	56	89
1932	34	119
1933	53	190
1934	47	389
1935	47	684
TOTAL	592	2,044

It must be conceded that these are striking figures. Over the whole period of thirteen years the number of items of delegated legislation

[1] *Report of the Committee on Ministers' Powers, 1931–32*, Cmd. 4060 (1932), vol. xii, p. 341.

exceeds the number of statutes by more than three to one, but in the final year (1935) the proportion has become nearly fifteen to one. In this one year alone Mr. De Valera's Government promulgated more Statutory Rules and Orders than were issued during the whole nine years when Mr. Cosgrave was in power (684 against 662). This alarming situation is so much taken for granted that two members of the Bar (one of whom is now a judge) could write as follows in the Introduction to *A Register of Administrative Law in Saorstát Éireann*, which covers the period down to the end of 1933 and which was compiled by them and published under Government auspices in 1935:

'The Oireachtas, accepting the view that its laws should in the main be statements of principle, has shown a notable tendency to delegate the detailed elaboration and the practical application of its enactments. Legislation over a very wide area of civic activities has accordingly been reinforced by administrative directions of the most varied kinds and an extensive range of subsidiary law has grown up in the twelve years under review, far greater in volume than the body of law directly enacted by the Oireachtas.'

The assertion that the Oireachtas has accepted 'the view that its laws should in the main be statements of principle' is a matter of opinion with which it is possible to disagree. There certainly was never any conscious acceptance of such a view; and it would doubtless be more correct to say that this delegated legislation has grown to such an extent because members of both the Senate and the Dáil were insufficiently on their guard against the invasion by the bureaucracy of the rights of Parliament. What happened in practice was very much as has been described by Sir Lynden Macassey, K.C., writing of the Parliament at Westminster:

'Government Bills are forced through Parliament under the pressure of the Government Whips; there is little time for discussion of their provisions either in the House or in Committee; legislation is passed in the most general terms and left to some Government department to apply as it thinks fit under machinery or rules to be made by it; the Cabinet is therefore in a position, through its member at the head of a Government department, to embark on a particular policy which has never in any detail been discussed in Parliament or communicated to the public. If the action of the department is challenged in the House, the Government can say, as has been done, that the action of the department is fully within the powers conferred upon it by the Legislature.'[1]

[1] *Journal of Comparative Legislation and International Law*, vol. v, part i, p. 73.

In the great majority of cases, Parliament retained no power of ultimate control over this delegated legislation, and the bulk of it was not even brought to the notice of the Senate and the Dáil by being formally laid on the table of each House. In 1935, for example, there were 684 Statutory Rules and Orders, but only 474 papers laid on the table of the Senate; and of these 474 papers a large number, amounting possibly to as much as one-half, consisted of documents other than Statutory Rules and Orders, such as statistics and reports of various kinds.

The cases in which some form of ultimate control, positive or negative, was retained are reducible, so far as the Senate was concerned, to four main classes. In all cases, the document was required by statute to be laid on the table of each House.

The first, and by far the commonest, class was that in which the Act which delegated the power of making rules, orders, or regulations reserved to Parliament the power of annulment, by means of a section or sub-section in the following form: 'Every regulation made under this section shall be laid before each House of the Oireachtas as soon as may be after it is made, and if a resolution is passed by either such House within the next subsequent twenty-one days on which such House has sat after such regulation is laid before it annulling such regulation, such regulation shall be annulled accordingly, but without prejudice to the validity of anything previously done under such regulation.' This clause, or a variant of it, appeared possibly a hundred times in the Acts passed during the thirteen and a half years' existence of the Senate, sometimes more than once in the same statute. Some of the variations were probably due to inadvertence. Thus, under the Censorship of Films Act, 1923 (Section 12), and the Electoral Act, 1923 (Section 64), the appropriate resolution had to be passed within twenty-one days on which *either* House had sat. Under the Land Act, 1923 (Section 76), the period of twenty-one days signified ordinary days, not sitting days; under the Industrial and Commercial Property (Protection) Act, 1927 (Section 153), the period was not twenty-one days but forty days, and under the Cement Act, 1933 (Section 9), it was ten days.

A sub-division of this first class is provided by those statutes, few in number, under which a resolution of *both* Houses was necessary for annulment, viz., the Army Pensions Act, 1923 (Section 15), the Damage to Property (Compensation) Act, 1923 (Section 13), the Local Government (Temporary Provisions) Act, 1923 (Sections 4, 5, and 20), the Local Government (Collection of Rates) Act, 1924

(Section 7), and the Civil Service Regulation Act, 1924 (Section 9). In the case of the last-mentioned Act, the Senate passed an amendment deleting the words 'both Houses' and substituting the words 'either House'. This was rejected by the Dáil at the instance of the Government, but the principle (if any) on which the distinction was made between these cases and the others was not made clear during the discussion.[1]

The Senate had, in general, much more regard than had the Dáil to the necessity of preserving the ultimate control of Parliament over this delegated legislation. On numerous occasions Bills reached the Senate from the other House in which Ministers were empowered to make regulations or orders but containing no provision that such regulations or orders should be laid before Parliament, nor, of course, any power of annulment. Amendments were moved and carried in the Senate to remedy these omissions, often against the wishes of the Government, and they were subsequently accepted by the Dáil. Two examples will suffice—one from each Administration.

In 1928 a Censorship of Publications Bill was introduced by Mr. Cosgrave's Government and passed by the Dáil. This was a highly contentious measure, which provided for a censorship of books and for the restriction of reports of certain classes of judicial proceedings; and the Minister for Justice was empowered by order to make regulations covering the whole subject-matter of the Bill, with, however, no provision that such regulations should be brought to the notice of Parliament, and no provision for annulment. An amendment to make good these defects, couched in the usual form, was moved by Senator Hooper, a former editor of the *Freeman's Journal*; and it was resisted by the Minister for Justice (Mr. Fitzgerald-Kenney, K.C.), who spoke as follows:

'I suggest that the Senate ought not to accept this amendment. The laying of rules, which are merely rules of procedure, before the Dáil and the Senate sometimes leads to a great deal of trouble and difficulty. . . . I suggest that the proper procedure would be that the rules would be made. The Minister who makes the rules is responsible. If anybody objects to any particular rule, then a motion of censure can be put down, and the rule objected to can be discussed in that way. It appears to me that, except in very rare cases, the whole method of laying rules of procedure on the Table of the Dáil or Senate, or both together, is not a desirable form of procedure. It is troublesome, slow and quite unnecessary.'[2]

[1] *Dáil Debates*, vi, 1451–64.   [2] *Senate Debates*, xii, 608, 609.

2M

This, of course, was the voice of bureaucracy. Senators were un-
convinced, and they passed Senator Hooper's amendment, which
was subsequently accepted by the Dáil.

Some years later, after the change of government, a far-reaching
Unemployment Assistance Bill was brought forward, the Minister
in charge of it being Mr. Seán Lemass, Minister for Industry and
Commerce in Mr. De Valera's Administration. This Bill, which was
one of great complexity, made provision, as its title indicates, for the
financial relief of unemployed persons. In spite of its length, it would
not be unfair to say that the Bill was to some extent a skeleton, which
required to be filled in by regulations which the Minister was duly
empowered to make; but the provisions for tabling and annulment
were lacking as before. Senator Brown, K.C., accordingly proposed
an amendment, embodying these provisions in the common form.

'I think', he said, 'there never was a Bill about which we have so
little idea as to how it is going to work or how much it is going to
cost. . . . On the Second Reading of the Bill the Minister himself I
think rather vaguely suggested, but still did suggest, that the figure
was quite likely to be over £1,000,000 a year. . . . The whole thing is
a leap in the dark, but it is a leap which we have got to take. . . . I
respectfully submit that the regulations made by the Minister are of
such vital importance to the due and proper administration of the
Act that they should be laid on the Table of the House, so that the
House will have an opportunity of seeing the steps that are taken to
provide for the due and proper administration of the Act, about which
we can know so little and about which we can only fear so much.'[1]

The Minister opposed the amendment: 'One cannot conceive any
Minister administering an Act of this kind with any expedition if the
regulations that he makes are to be subject to revision or annulment
within a specified time which may run to three or four months. . . .
So far as this Act is concerned, it is in a sense taking a leap in the
dark. We are going to make regulations under the Act. We are going
to change those regulations and possibly change them again before
we will be able to build up the code of regulations which will satisfy
our requirements and give us the type of administration that we
desire. But Ministers are only human beings. If they make regulations, and can amend them as occasion requires, they will do so, but
if they have to come to the Dáil and Senate and table amending
regulations in order to remove mistakes in earlier regulations, then
they will be much slower in making regulations at all. . . .

[1] *Senate Debates*, xvii, 1702, 1703.

'If we want to bring the Act into operation speedily we must be given a certain amount of discretion in the matter of making regulations. If Senators want to take away from us that discretion: to ensure that all these administrative acts will come under the review of both the Dáil and the Senate and in that way be subject to annulment or amendment, then we are going to go more slowly and not leave ourselves open to the criticism that we made mistakes that we could have avoided by going more slowly.'[1]

Here, again, was the voice of bureaucracy, but the Senate was not convinced. It passed Senator Brown's amendment, which was accepted by the Dáil and is now incorporated in the Act.

During Mr. De Valera's Administration attempts were occasionally made by the Government to exclude this delegated legislation from the purview of the Senate by limiting the tabling and the power of annulment to the Dáil. This happened, for example, in the cases of the Dairy Produce (Price Stabilization) Bill, 1932 (Section 42), and the Control of Manufactures Bill, 1934 (Section 16). In each case, the co-equal power of the Senate was restored by means of amendments carried in that House and accepted by the Dáil. The power of annulment was, of course, theoretically a greater safeguard for the people in the case of the Senate than in the case of the other House; for, as the Government is responsible to the Dáil, an annulment motion in that House might be treated as a matter of confidence. If so, the Party Whips would ensure that it would be rejected. These considerations did not apply to the Senate.

This, however, is mere theory. It is a curious psychological fact, and one doubtless of much comfort to a bureaucracy, that even the most conscientious public representative will scarcely be at the pains to read a document formally laid on the table of the House unless his attention is specially directed to it or unless he is personally interested in the subject-matter of it. The 'table', of course, is a fiction, since no table could be found large enough to accommodate the vast quantity of documents presented so that each could be adequately displayed. Copies were not circulated to Senators in the same way as Bills, and Senators knew that they would not normally be called upon to discuss their contents in the House. All that happened in practice was that the titles of such documents as were received were printed on the Order Paper next prepared after receipt, under the general heading of 'Papers on the Table'. This was a sufficient intimation to the curious that copies might be consulted in the Parlia-

[1] *Senate Debates*, xvii, 1706–8.

mentary Library; but, as there were sometimes large numbers on a single Order Paper (on one occasion in 1935 there were no less than 119), any individual item was liable to be overlooked.

Doubtless for these reasons, the power of annulment was virtually a dead letter in both Houses. A motion to annul a Ministerial order or Ministerial regulations was proposed in the Senate on only five occasions: three times by Senator Sir John Keane and twice by Senator Johnson. Sir John Keane's motions were put down for the purpose of discussion, and were withdrawn by him when that purpose had been served. Senator Johnson's motions were pressed to a division and lost.

Hitherto we have been considering delegated legislation of the first class, in which Parliament reserved to itself a negative control by means of a power of annulment. We now come to the cases of the second class, in which the *vis inertiae* lay the other way: that is to say, a positive resolution of both Houses was required before the orders, rules, or regulations became of statutory effect. The number of cases in this class was extremely small; and, while it is not claimed that the following list is complete, it probably is complete or nearly so.

1. Courts of Justice Act, 1924 (Section 101). Approval of Rules of Court.

2. Gárda Síochána Act, 1924 (Section 8). Regulations as to Pensions of Members of the Police Force.

3. Police Forces Amalgamation Act, 1925 (Section 13). Ditto.

4. Summer Time Act, 1925 (Section 3). Alteration by Order of statutory period of Summer Time.

5. Local Government (Dublin) Act, 1930 (Section 103). Abrogation by Order of Private Acts and Orders relating to the City of Dublin.

6. Teachers' Superannuation Act, 1928 (Section 5). Confirmation of Pension Schemes of Secondary Teachers.

Incomparably the most important of these cases is the Courts of Justice Act, 1924. The Bill was introduced in the Dáil in the autumn of 1923, and it recast the whole judicial system of the country. In the days before the Treaty the system had consisted principally of Petty Sessions Courts, presided over by unpaid magistrates assisted by a paid resident magistrate: County Courts, one for each county: the Supreme Court of Judicature, consisting of the High Court of Justice and the Court of Appeal: and the Court of Crown Cases Reserved, the only Court of Criminal Appeal. On the 27th January 1923, a Judiciary Committee was set up, under the chairmanship of Lord

Glenavy, to advise the Executive Council as to the establishment of a new system, under Article 64 of the Constitution. The Courts of Justice Bill was largely based on the recommendations of this Committee. It provided for District Courts, to replace the old Petty Sessions Courts, presided over by paid District Justices, with an enlarged jurisdiction: eight Circuit Courts, grouped by counties, replacing the County Courts, and with a greatly enlarged jurisdiction: a High Court of six judges, one of whom was to preside, with the title of President of the High Court: a Supreme Court of three judges, one of whom was to be Chief Justice (the prefix 'Lord' being dropped): and a Court of Criminal Appeal. Matters formerly under the jurisdiction of the Lord Chancellor were placed under the special jurisdiction of the Chief Justice.

Under the old régime the Rules of Court, which might be described as the machinery whereby justice is dispensed, were made by the judges under the Judicature Act, the signature of the Lord-Lieutenant being appended as a mere formality. Under the provisions of the new Bill, the Rules of the High Court and Supreme Court were to be made by the Minister for Home Affairs, with the concurrence of a committee consisting of the judges and certain practising lawyers. The provisions regarding the Rules of the Circuit Court and District Court were similar. Thus the manner in which the jurisdiction vested in the new courts, as regards pleading, practice, and procedure, and even as regards the dress to be worn by Bench and Bar, was to be decided by Rules of Court to be made by an Executive Minister; and though these Rules were admitted by the Attorney-General (the late Hugh Kennedy, K.C.) to be delegated legislation, the only power purported to be accorded by the Bill to Parliament was the negative power of annulment within one month.

A strenuous campaign of opposition to these innovations was conducted in the Senate. Ridicule is always a potent weapon in Ireland, and the proposal about dress was a promising target for it. It was known that the Attorney-General was determined, if possible, to abolish the traditional wig and gown and had been making inquiries about the special costume, if any, worn by the Irish brehons (judges) centuries ago. Lord Glenavy fixed upon this proposal as a butt for the display of his old forensic power of derision.

'Remember, this is a thing that can be altered and re-altered by each successive Minister for Home Affairs. The present Minister for Home Affairs might prefer a kilt. His successor might be a sporting man, and he might prefer a jockey's costume. The next successor might have clerical tendencies, and he might prefer to see the judges robed in clerical costume. Where is this thing to end?'[1]

In the face of ridicule of this kind, and of the united opposition of Bench and Bar, any idea of abolishing the wig and gown had perforce to be dropped. The legal and constitutional arguments against the transfer to the Minister of the rule-making authority were expounded with consummate ability by Senator S. L. Brown, K.C.[2] Though he failed to carry the Senate with him in his amendments to the rule-making sections, he did secure that Parliament's negative power of annulment within one month should be altered to a positive power of approval without limit of time. This section finally read as follows: 'No rules of court made under this Act shall come into operation unless and until they have been laid before each House of the Oireachtas and have been approved by resolution of each such House.'

Senator Brown's successful championship of the constitutional rights of Parliament proved to be amply justified by the event. Irrespective of the political party in office, the bureaucracy is always in favour of haste at the expense of discussion. On the 7th July 1926, when the Rules of Court had not been formally made by the Minister for Justice (Kevin O'Higgins), though the drafts had been circulated, he attended the Senate with the request that they should pass resolutions of approval of the three sets of rules, viz. Rules of the High Court and Supreme Court, Rules of the Circuit Court, and District Court Rules, two days later (9th July), being the day on which he proposed to sign them. The Senate very properly refused to accede to this request, but on the 8th July it appointed a Select Committee to consider the Rules, and agreed to take the motions for approval on the 22nd July. Actually, when the Senate appointed this Committee it was not in possession of the Rules, for they were not formally laid before the House until the 14th July. The Select Committee reported that the Rules of the High Court and Supreme Court should be approved *in toto*, but recommended that the other two sets of Rules should be approved with certain exceptions, stating their reasons for these exceptions.[3]

On the 22nd July 1926 the Senate met to consider motions which had been handed in pursuant to the Report of the Select Committee. The Rules of the High Court and Supreme Court were formally approved, after amendments had been discussed and rejected, dealing

---

[1] *Senate Debates*, ii, 416.　　[2] Ibid., ii, 418, 631–59, 856–63, 883, 951, 1154.
[3] *Reports of Committees*, vol. i, p. 541.

with the status of the Irish language in the courts and the robes to be worn by the judges, Senator W. B. Yeats making an earnest but fruitless plea for a new judicial costume designed by Sir Charles Shannon, R.A.

The District Court Rules were then formally approved, with eight exceptions. The eight rules which were not approved were severally put to the House, and the motion 'That the Rule be not approved' was carried in each case, after debate. Mr. O'Higgins stated that it was his view, and that of the Attorney-General, that the rules must be approved or rejected as a whole, and that the rejection of even one rule rendered the whole corpus of rules inoperative. Lord Glenavy did not accept this view, and in ruling against it he was fortified by an opinion obtained, in anticipation of the situation which actually arose, from the late Sir Lonsdale Webster, Clerk of the House of Commons and editor of Sir Erskine May's standard work on parliamentary procedure. Lord Glenavy read this opinion to the House.

'The question he was asked was: "Whether in accordance with British practice a motion to approve the Rules of Court, pursuant to Section 101 of the Courts of Justice Act, 1924, would be open to amendment by way of leaving out a specified Rule or Rules, or whether it would be incumbent on the Senate to pass such Rules *in globo*?"

'This is his answer: "My answer . . . would be that a motion to approve a set of Rules would be open to amendment by way of leaving out a specified Rule or Rules. The effect of an amendment or amendments being agreed to would be that the final question would be for approval of the Rules, other than those omitted by amendment or amendments." '[1]

The District Court Rules were approved *in globo* by the Dáil on the 21st July 1926, the Chairman of that House having ruled that the motion of approval was not open to amendment by omitting a specified rule or rules. The Government then took a step which it is difficult to understand on any view of procedure. They published the District Court Rules as signed by the Minister, with an asterisk directing attention to a footnote in which it was stated that Rules 20, 24, 36, 93, 95, 151, 171, and 180 had not been approved by the Senate. If Lord Glenavy was right, these eight rules should have been omitted, as they were inoperative. If the Minister for Justice and the Attorney-General were right, then the whole corpus of rules was

[1] *Senate Debates*, vii, 1101, 1102.

rendered inoperative by the Senate's action in refusing to approve eight of them, and the rules should not have been published at all.

The Rules of the Circuit Court had a chequered history. They were made on the 13th July 1926 by the Minister for Justice, laid on the table of the Senate on the following day, and laid on the table of the Dáil on the 20th July. In order to rush them through before Parliament adjourned for the summer recess, a motion to approve the Rules was taken in the Dáil on the very day that they had been tabled in that House; but they met with such hostile criticism from all quarters of the House that the Minister withdrew the motion on the following day. The parallel motion in the Senate was likewise postponed (22nd July 1926).

It is pertinent to point out that, but for the fight put up by Senator Brown which resulted in his amendment to the Courts of Justice Bill, these Rules would pretty certainly have come into force, in spite of their imperfections. Under the Bill as it left the Dáil, the two Houses were merely given a power of annulment, and that power had to be exercised within one month. The Rules were tabled at the end of July, when both Houses were on the point of adjourning for the summer; and they did not reassemble until the following November.

Nearly two years later, on the 25th April 1928, a second set of Rules of the Circuit Court was laid on the table of both Houses. This second set was referred to a Joint Committee of both Houses, consisting of six lawyers (drawn from both branches of the profession), three business men, and one member of the Labour Party. This Committee produced a long and unanimous Report, dated the 26th June 1928, and signed by Lord Glenavy as chairman. The Report was completely hostile to the rules. The Committee was 'satisfied that if these Rules are approved they will so materially increase the duties of the Judge, the County Registrar and the official staff as to make a substantial increase in their number inevitable, while the added complication, expense and delay will be practically prohibitive for poorer litigants' (paragraph 4). The Committee concluded that 'the difficulties and defects which had already developed [in the working of the new Circuit Court system] would be materially aggravated by the adoption of these Rules' (paragraph 13).[1]

In the face of this Report, the Government made no attempt to secure the approval of Parliament for this second set of Circuit Court Rules. The Joint Committee, not content with mere negation, had suggested lines on which the rules should be framed, based largely

[1] *Reports of Committees,* vol. ii, p. 251.

on the County Court Rules of pre-Treaty days, which were actually being used by the Circuit Courts, *mutatis mutandis*, in default of rules of their own. In the course of time, yet a third set of rules was produced, drafted in conformity with the suggestions of the Joint Committee. These rules were laid before the Dáil on the 27th February 1930, and before the Senate on the 12th March following. The Minister for Justice (Mr. Fitzgerald-Kenney, K.C.) moved the motion of approval on that day in the Dáil; but it happened that a Joint Committee was at that time considering the whole operation of the Courts of Justice Act, 1924, and it was objected from all quarters of the House that these rules ought not to be promulgated until that Committee had presented its Report. The Minister was accordingly obliged to withdraw his motion. The Committee in question reported on the 6th November 1930;[1] and the long-delayed Rules of the Circuit Court were formally approved by resolution of the Dáil on the 22nd October 1931, and of the Senate on the 4th November 1931—more than five years after the Government's abortive effort to obtain parliamentary approval for the first set of rules within a few days of their being signed.

The parliamentary history of the Rules of Court has been recounted at some length because of its importance in connection with this subject of delegated legislation. It shows that, if Parliament insists on reserving to itself the ultimate power of control by means of positive resolution, that power can and will be used in cases where the public interest justifies its exercise. The fact that such power was available in the case of the Rules of Court was due to the Senate, and in particular to Senator Brown, whose efforts in this connection were perhaps not the least of the services of that remarkable man to the Irish people.

Hitherto we have been considering what we have designated as the second class of delegated legislation, namely, that in which a positive resolution of approval is necessary for ratification. A curious sub-division of this class is provided by the State Lands Act, 1924, and the State Lands (Workhouses) Act, 1930; in these cases a positive resolution was possible, but not necessary. Under Article 11 of the Constitution all the former Crown Lands were vested in the State, and these two Acts enabled leases or licences to be granted in respect of such lands. The Act of 1924 (Section 2) provided that a statement of every proposed lease or licence should be laid before each House, and then proceeded as follows:

[1] *Reports of Committees*, vol. iii, p. 181.

'No lease or licence shall be made or granted under this Act until either—

'(a) each House of the Oireachtas has by resolution authorized the making or granting of such lease or licence either with or without modification of any of the proposed provisions of such lease or licence, or

'(b) the expiration of whichever of the following periods shall be the longer, that is to say:

'(i) twenty-one days after the first day on which either House of the Oireachtas shall sit next after the statement in accordance with this section shall have been laid before the Houses of the Oireachtas, or

'(ii) twelve days on which either House of the Oireachtas shall have sat after the said statement shall have been so laid before the Houses.'

The provisions in the Act of 1930 (Section 4) were somewhat similar. The statements of these proposed leases or licences were periodically laid on the table in batches, and they must have amounted in the aggregate to thousands. But no positive resolution was ever moved under paragraph (a). Few can have read this singularly involved clause a sufficient number of times to discover what it really meant.

Another variant in this second class of delegated legislation is provided by the Control of Imports Act, 1934. This was an Act designed to further the industrial policy of Mr. De Valera's Administration, by enabling the Executive Council, by means of orders termed quota orders, to prohibit or restrict the importation of any classes of goods. The Bill as passed by the Dáil contained two very bad defects, which were remedied in the Senate at the instance of Senators Counihan, Johnson, Douglas, and others. There was a provision (Section 4) that every quota order should cease to have effect at the end of six months from its having been made, unless approved by resolution of the Dáil within the six months, the Senate being omitted; and the section was so drafted as to make it possible for the Government (in the not very likely event of their wishing so to do) to dispense with parliamentary approval by making a fresh quota order, dealing with the same class of goods, shortly before the original order was due to expire, and so causing a fresh six months' period to run. By means of amendments carried in the Senate and agreed to by the Dáil, the co-equal rights of the Senate in regard to this delegated legislation were restored, and the section was made water-tight against possible abuse.

In the twenty-six months which elapsed between the passage of the Control of Imports Act and the abolition of the Senate, no less than 155 quota orders were promulgated by the Executive—an average of six a month. In view of the allegation so often made by the ill-informed that the Senate adopted an obstructive attitude towards the Government's general policy, it is as well to place the fact on record that in no single instance was the appropriate motion of approval refused, or even seriously opposed, in that House. The debates on these motions in the Senate were on a level generally higher than the corresponding debates in the Dáil; they provided the occasion for a public interchange of views between the Minister for Industry and Commerce on the one hand and Senator Douglas and other business men on the other; and they had their value in contributing to an informed public opinion on the industrial policy of the Government.

The third class of delegated legislation consists of cases in which the Executive Council, or a Minister of State, is empowered by statute to make Orders, but all such Orders require to be confirmed by Act of Parliament. The main sphere of this class of legislation lies in matters of local or specialized interest, such as piers, harbours, and pilotage. A number of such Orders were made during the existence of the Senate, and subsequently ratified by statutes termed Provisional Order Confirmation Acts. The only case of general importance is the Emergency Imposition of Duties Act, 1932, enacted on the 23rd July 1932 by Mr. De Valera's Government and designed to serve as a weapon in the so-called 'economic war' with Great Britain. Under that Act the Executive Council were accorded the widest powers to impose customs and excise duties by Order, and the saving provision was as follows: 'Every Order made by the Executive Council under this section shall have statutory effect upon the making thereof and, unless such Order either is confirmed by Act of the Oireachtas within eight months after the making thereof or is an Order merely revoking wholly an Order previously made under this section, such Order shall cease to have statutory effect at the expiration of such eight months but without prejudice to the validity of anything previously done thereunder.' In all, 106 Emergency Imposition of Duties Orders were made under this Act up to the time of the abolition of the Senate. As the Bills by which they were confirmed were all certified as Money Bills, the theoretical power of the Senate in regard to these Orders was much less than it was in the case of the Quota Orders under the Control of Imports Act already referred to.

The fourth and last class of delegated legislation is partly akin to the first and partly to the second, in that, of the four statutes in the class, two provide for a negative power of annulment and two for a positive power of approval; but the class as a whole must be regarded as a separate one because of the restricted power accorded to the Senate. The statutes in question are: Dáil Éireann Loans and Funds Act, 1924; Gárda Síochána (Temporary Provisions) Act, 1923; Superannuation and Pensions Acts, 1923 and 1929. All of these, except the second, had been, before enactment, certified Money Bills, and the three which were passed in 1923 and 1924 were rushed through the Senate without adequate discussion.

In the case of the Dáil Éireann Loans and Funds Act, 1924 (Section 2), and the Gárda Síochána (Temporary Provisions) Act, 1923 (Section 8), there is an annulment clause, which is couched in the following terms: 'Every Order made under this section shall be laid before each House of the Oireachtas as soon as may be after it is made, and if a resolution is passed by Dáil Éireann within the next subsequent twenty-one days on which Dáil Éireann has sat annulling such Order, such Order shall be annulled accordingly, but without prejudice to the validity of anything previously done under such Order, and any recommendation in respect of such Order which shall be made by Seanad Éireann within such twenty-one days shall be duly considered by Dáil Éireann.' The Orders referred to in these two Acts dealt respectively with the disposal of the Republican Loan raised prior to the Treaty of 1921 and with the pay and allowances of the newly established Police Force or Civic Guard; they were thus concerned exclusively with money matters.

The Superannuation and Pensions Act, 1923 (Section 5), provided for the grant, by Ministerial Order, of pensions to certain members of the former Royal Irish Constabulary who had resigned or been dismissed in stated circumstances. The amending Act of 1929 (Section 3) made similar provision for the widows of such persons. In both cases, a positive resolution of approval by the Dáil was necessary, the clause being in the following terms: 'No Order made under this section shall come into operation unless and until it has been laid before each House of the Oireachtas, and approved by resolution of Dáil Éireann, and when considering any such resolution Dáil Éireann shall duly consider any recommendation which shall have been previously made by Seanad Éireann in respect of such Order.' There was a similar clause (Section 9) in the Gárda Síochána (Temporary Provisions) Act, 1923, already referred to, with respect to regulations as to the pensions of the newly established Civic Guard.

The point of constitutional interest in the cases of this fourth class is, how far was it justifiable to import into the statutory safeguards, positive or negative, surrounding this delegated legislation the provisions of the Constitution regarding Money Bills, whereby the legislative authority lay with the Dáil and the Senate was confined to the making of recommendations? As has been indicated, the point passed unnoticed in the three Acts mentioned which were passed in 1923 and 1924, but in the latter year the Government sent up to the Senate a Bill to establish the Civic Guard on a permanent basis (Gárda Síochána Bill, 1924). It was not, of course, certified as a Money Bill. Section 7 of the Bill provided that the Minister for Justice, with the sanction of the Minister for Finance, might by order regulate the pay and allowances of the said new Force, *including the conditions applicable thereto*; and the section went on: 'Every Order made under this section shall be laid before each House of the Oireachtas as soon as may be after it is made and if a resolution is passed by Dáil Éireann within the next subsequent twenty-one days on which Dáil Éireann has sat annulling such Order, such Order shall be annulled accordingly, but without prejudice to the validity of anything previously done under such Order, and any recommendations in respect of such Order which shall be made by Seanad Éireann within the said twenty-one days shall be duly considered by Dáil Éireann.' In Select Committee of the Senate (11th June 1924) this was altered to the common form, whereby each House had the right to annul.[1] On the Report Stage of the Bill in the House itself the point was argued at considerable length between the Minister for Justice (Kevin O'Higgins) on the one hand and Lord Glenavy, Senator O'Farrell (for the Labour Party), Senator Brown, and other Senators on the other.[2] Lord Glenavy examined the matter at great length from the legal aspect, and showed that this particular proposal had no warrant in the Constitution and was, in fact, an invasion of the legislative authority of the Senate. The reluctance of the Government to concede full legislative co-equality to the Upper House was very perceptible in Mr. O'Higgins's reply. He stressed the non-representative character of the Senate, hinted that the spirit of the Constitution was being broken by the amendment, and said that, if such regulations as these were unreasonably annulled by the Senate, the Government would embody the subject-matter of them in a Bill, which would, he con-

[1] *Reports of Committees*, vol. i, p. 401.   [2] *Senate Debates*, iii, 276–294.

tended, inevitably be certified as a Money Bill. To this argument Senator Guinness retorted, very sensibly, 'But in that case you would be acting quite regularly: in this case it would be irregular.'

Senator Brown stated that his objection was that the proposal of the Government introduced 'into what I might call delegated legislation, that is, legislation through an Order of the Minister, a limit to the power of the Senate that would not exist if it were a Bill that had to pass from this House. With great respect, I do not agree with the Minister that the regulations, which under section 7 may contain conditions of service as well as mere rates of pay, would possibly be considered or certified as a Money Bill.'[1]

No member of the Senate supported Mr. O'Higgins's view in the debate, and the Bill was returned to the Dáil with the clause as amended by the Select Committee of the Senate. A similar amendment was made to Section 8 (dealing with the pensions of the Force), but in this case a resolution of *both* Houses was necessary for annulment.

When the Bill came before the Dáil for consideration of the Senate's amendments, they were accepted on the motion of Mr. O'Higgins. He stated that he took this course solely because the temporary Act was about to expire, and if the permanent measure was not passed into law the Civic Guard would cease to exist. He reiterated his opinion that the Senate had, by its action, contravened the spirit of the Constitution, but no member of the Dáil supported him in this view. On the contrary, two of the ablest members of that House, Mr. Thomas Johnson (the Leader of the Opposition) and Mr. Darrell Figgis, expressed the contrary view, and expressed it with considerable force.[2]

In later years, when Mr. De Valera's followers used as an argument for the abolition of the Senate the allegation that Senators had always shown subservience during Mr. Cosgrave's Administration, those who had been associated with the Senate when Mr. De Valera was in the wilderness recalled such sharp conflicts as this.

The question did not arise again until it occurred in connection with the Superannuation and Pensions Bill, 1929. This was a certified Money Bill, which purported to amend the Act with the same title passed in 1923. The relative clause in this Bill has already been quoted above. A recommendation to restore the common form was adopted on the motion of Senator Johnson, who was thus quite consistent in maintaining his previous attitude when Leader of the

---

[1] *Senate Debates*, iii, 286, 287.   [2] *Dáil Debates*, viii, 475–85.

Opposition in the other House.[1] This recommendation, however, was rejected by the Dáil on the following day without debate.[2] It is interesting to note, in conclusion, that this was the only recommendation made by the Senate to a Money Bill and rejected by the Dáil during the whole course of Mr. Cosgrave's Administration.

[1] *Senate Debates*, xii, 461–70.   [2] *Dáil Debates*, xxix, 1780.

CHAPTER XXXII

MONEY BILLS

Constitutional provisions regarding Money Bills—Indifferent drafting of Article 38—The Senate's interpretation of its functions—Form of recommendations and procedure adopted—Beneficial results— Educative Second Reading debates—The Finance Bill—The Appropriation Bill—Three-day period for demanding a Committee of Privileges found to be too short—Increase of the period to seven days— Other constitutional changes—Total number of Money Bills—Statistics of recommendations—Failure to pass the Dáil Supreme Court (Pensions) Bill—Government's use of Senate's power of recommendation— Other examples of its value to the Government—Special experience of Senators—Co-operation with the Dáil—A Senate recommendation accepted by the Dáil against the Government—Effect of the change of Government—The Import Duties Bill—Safeguards proposed by the Senate—A Committee of Privileges demanded only once—Requisition by Dáil members—The Land Purchase (Guarantee Fund) Bill—Difficulties of procedure—The Chairman's three alternatives—His decision —Mr. De Valera's accusation—The decision challenged by the Government party—The ruling approved by the Senate Committee of Procedure—The Committee's Report approved by the House—The Dáil requisition for a Committee of Privileges—Representative character of the signatories—Mr. De Valera's attitude—The Dáil nominations to the Committee—The Senate nominations—The case made by Senator Douglas—The Committee's decision—A considered judgement not required by the Constitution—The Second Reading in the Senate— Senator Brown's views—Recommendations made—Tactics of the Government party—Constitutional requirements—The Bill returned to the Dáil—The recommendations rejected—An unpleasant episode.

The provisions regarding Money Bills as contained in the Constitution before it was amended are to be found in Articles 35 and 38. It

544

is accordingly necessary to quote the former in full and also the relevant portion of the latter.

'Article 35. Dáil Éireann shall in relation to the subject matter of Money Bills as hereinafter defined have legislative authority exclusive of Seanad Éireann.

'A Money Bill means a Bill which contains only provisions dealing with all or any of the following subjects, namely, the imposition, repeal, remission, alteration or regulation of taxation; the imposition for the payment of debt or other financial purposes of charges on public moneys or the variation or repeal of any such charges; supply; the appropriation, receipt, custody, issue or audit of accounts of public money; the raising or guarantee of any loan or the repayment thereof; subordinate matters incidental to those subjects or any of them. In this definition the expressions "taxation", "public money" and "loan" respectively do not include any taxation, money or loan raised by local authorities or bodies for local purposes.

'The Chairman of Dáil Éireann shall certify any Bill which in his opinion is a Money Bill to be a Money Bill, but, if within three days after a Bill has been passed by Dáil Éireann two-fifths of the members of either House by notice in writing addressed to the Chairman of the House of which they are members so require, the question whether the Bill is or is not a Money Bill shall be referred to a Committee of Privileges consisting of three members elected by each House with a Chairman who shall be the senior Judge of the Supreme Court able and willing to act, and who, in the case of an equality of votes, but not otherwise, shall be entitled to vote. The decision of the Committee on the question shall be final and conclusive.'

'Article 38. Every Bill initiated in and passed by Dáil Éireann shall be sent to Seanad Éireann and may, unless it be a Money Bill, be amended in Seanad Éireann and Dáil Éireann shall consider any such amendment; . . . every Money Bill shall be sent to Seanad Éireann for its recommendations and at a period not longer than twenty-one days after it shall have been sent to Seanad Éireann, it shall be returned to Dáil Éireann, which may pass it, accepting or rejecting all or any of the recommendations of Seanad Éireann, and as so passed or if not returned within such period of twenty-one days shall be deemed to have been passed by both Houses. . . .'

It is unfortunate that Article 38 was so indifferently drafted as to leave the precise functions of the Senate in regard to Money Bills without positive definition. Article 35 states that the Dáil is to have legislative authority exclusive of the Senate in relation to Money

2N

Bills, and, taken by itself, seems not to contemplate the sending of Money Bills to the Senate for any purpose. Article 38, however, goes on to provide that a Money Bill, after it has been passed by the Dáil, is to be sent to the Senate; the Senate may not amend the Bill, but may make recommendations in regard to it; and the Bill must be returned to the Dáil within twenty-one days. After the Bill has been returned, the Dáil 'may' pass it; so that the Article prescribes a procedure that can hardly have been intended, namely, that a Money Bill is to be passed by the Dáil twice: once before it has been sent to the Senate and again after it has been received back from the Senate, and after, possibly, all the recommendations made by that House have been rejected. The Article nowhere states, in terms, that the function of the Senate is confined to the making of recommendations, or that Money Bills are not to be passed by that House. But this is left to be inferred from the phrase 'and as so passed or if not returned within such period of twenty-one days shall be deemed to have been passed by both Houses'. This seems to imply that the Senate can do nothing with a Money Bill except make recommendations to it. When the Bill has been returned, the Dáil may pass it a second time. If it does so, the Bill is 'deemed to have been passed by both Houses'; similarly if the Senate fails to return the Bill within the prescribed period.

The Attorney-General (Hugh Kennedy, K.C., afterwards Chief Justice) was of opinion that the functions of the Upper House in regard to Money Bills were strictly limited to the making of recommendations. But the Senate drew up its Standing Orders in accordance with the view that Money Bills should be dealt with, so far as possible, on the same basis as other Bills. Every Money Bill was given a Second Reading, when a general discussion might take place upon it; a Third (Committee) Stage and a Fourth (Report) Stage, when recommendations (instead of amendments) might be proposed; and a Fifth Stage, when the Bill was finally passed. It was then duly certified and returned, within twenty-one days, to the Dáil, with a list of the recommendations (if any) that had been made in regard to it, or a certificate that no recommendations had been made. The recommendations might be of a general character, such as: 'The Senate recommends that the provisions of section 9 of the Bill [the Finance Bill, 1923] regarding the exemption of Charities be extended so as to apply the exemption to income derived by Charities from land and house property.' More usually, however, they took the form of suggesting the addition or deletion of specific words or figures. The Dáil, for its part, ignored the constitutional provision regarding the second passing of the Bill. It considered the recommendations and accepted or rejected them. If an accepted recommendation was of a general character, such as that quoted above, an amendment was drafted in accordance with it. The recommendations that had been accepted were made the subject of substantive amendments, which were inserted in the Bill. A message was dispatched to the Senate stating which recommendations had been accepted and which rejected, and the Bill was sent for the Royal Assent.

The procedure laid down by the Senate proved, in the light of experience, to be beneficial alike to the House itself, to the Government, and to the public at large. It would have been impracticable to propose recommendations of value in the absence of a Second Reading debate, in which these could be first adumbrated and the sense of the House taken on them in a general way, after the views of the Minister in charge of the Bill had been heard. Moreover, a number of Money Bills reached the Senate annually which, irrespective of whether any recommendations might be proposed, almost invariably provided the occasion for a first-class debate which had its value in moulding public opinion. For example, the Senate was precluded from discussing the annual Budget, but the Budget was subsequently embodied in the Finance Bill, and this always gave rise to an extended Second Reading debate, in which the whole financial and fiscal policy of the Government was passed in review. These debates were frequently on a higher plane than those on the same subject in the Dáil, and points of view were sometimes put forward which, in the other House, had found expression either imperfectly or not at all. As a direct result of the discussion on Second Reading, recommendations were not infrequently proposed, either with the consent or on the direct initiative of the Government; and the results were subsequently embodied in the Bill.

The case of the annual Appropriation Bill was similar. This was a type of Bill which rarely permitted of any recommendations being proposed in regard to it; but the Second Reading debate on it in the Senate ranged over the whole field of governmental administration. The result was a satisfactory ventilation of opinion on matters of general interest and importance.

Before some further considerations are dealt with on this subject of Money Bills, it is desirable to make some reference to a change made in Article 35 by way of constitutional amendment. It will be recalled that, under the third paragraph of that Article, two-fifths of

the members of either House might require the question whether a
Bill which had been certified as a Money Bill was in fact a Money
Bill to be referred to a Committee of Privileges; but that this action
had to be taken within three days after the Bill had been passed by
the Dáil. Experience showed that this was an inconveniently short
period. The Chairman of the Dáil did not issue his certificate until
the Bill had been finally passed by the Dáil, because of course it was
not possible to state with certainty that the Bill came within the
definition of a Money Bill until the possibility of amendment was at
an end. But such a Bill might be (and very often was) passed at a
time when the Senate was not sitting, or on a Friday, when the period
of grace would be Saturday, Sunday and Monday. In such circumstances it would obviously not be feasible, if the occasion arose, for
the requisite action to be taken within the period prescribed.

The point was considered by the Joint Committee of both Houses
set up in 1928 to review the constitution and powers of the Senate;[1]
and, as a result of one of their recommendations, Article 35 was
amended by the Constitution (Amendment No. 12) Act, 1930, passed
on the 24th March 1930. Under the Article as so amended the period
of three days was increased to seven, with the important proviso that,
if the Bill was returned by the Senate to the Dáil within the seven
days, the right of members of either House to demand a Committee
of Privileges upon it was thereby terminated. The Committee of
Privileges might be required by two-fifths of the members of either
House by notice in writing as before; but the Senate was given the
additional power of demanding it by a formal resolution of the House,
passed by a majority of the members present and voting at a sitting
at which not less than thirty members were present. If a Committee
of Privileges, duly set up, failed to report its decision within twenty-
one days of the Bill having been sent to the Senate, the decision of
the Chairman of the Dáil was to become final.

During the thirteen and a half years' existence of the Senate it received from the Dáil 110 Money Bills and 489 non-Money Bills:[2]
that is to say, Money Bills were about one-fifth of the total. This may
seem rather a large proportion, but it must be remembered that in
every year at least one Appropriation Bill, Finance Bill, and Central
Fund Bill were sent up—sometimes more than one—and these were
all necessarily Money Bills. Alterations in Customs duties, supple-

[1] *Reports of Committees*, vol. ii, p. 273.
[2] Statistical tables with regard to Money Bills will be found in Appendices
D and E.

mentary to the annual Budget, had to be the subject of separate Bills, and others dealing with such matters as superannuation and pensions were of frequent occurrence. Mr. Cosgrave's Administration, which lasted nine years, was responsible for sixty-five Money Bills, an average of seven a year; and from the date of Mr. De Valera's advent to power until the abolition of the Senate (four and a half years) there were forty-five such Bills, an average of ten a year. The higher average in the latter case is principally due to the fact that the tariff policy of Mr. De Valera's Administration necessitated a succession of Bills dealing with import duties.

Of Mr. Cosgrave's sixty-five Money Bills, recommendations were made to nine. The total number of recommendations was eighteen, of which all but one were accepted. Recommendations were made to ten of Mr. De Valera's forty-five Bills, and the total number of recommendations was thirty-eight. Of these, eighteen were accepted and twenty rejected. The difference in the figures of the respective Administrations is a reflection of the political conditions of the times.

In only one case throughout the whole period did the Senate fail to pass a Money Bill. This was the Dáil Supreme Court (Pensions) Bill, 1925, which gave pensions to the Republican Judges of the Supreme Court which had functioned under the authority of the Dáil prior to the Treaty. The Bill was given a Second Reading, without discussion, on the 7th April 1925. The Chairman (Lord Glenavy) pointed out that, if no further steps were taken, the Bill would become law automatically after twenty-one days, and remarked that that might 'not be a great catastrophe'. No order was made for the Committee Stage, and the Bill became law after the prescribed period.

In view of the provision in the Constitution that the Dáil should have exclusive legislative authority in relation to Money Bills, there is an element of humour in the fact that, upon occasion, the Government of the day used the Senate's power of recommendation in order to get the Senate to 'recommend' to the Dáil the rectification of mistakes which had escaped notice during the successive stages of the Bill in the Lower House. This happened, for example, in the case of the Appropriation Bill of 1923, the Army Pensions Bill of the same year, and the Land Bond Bill of 1933.

The Senate's consideration of Money Bills proved useful to the Government and to the Dáil in other and equally unexpected ways. It sometimes happened that an important amendment moved to a Finance Bill in the Dáil had to be refused by the Minister as a matter of caution, because his advisers had not had time to examine it in all its implications. But when the Bill came before the Senate, the Minister welcomed a recommendation in the same terms as the amendment, so that the Bill might be returned to the Dáil and the matter be reconsidered there. A case in point arose in connection with the Finance Bill, 1928, when Mr. Blythe, the Minister for Finance, speaking in the Senate said: 'I am very frequently in the position of opposing amendments in the Senate, and when they are carried, recommending the Dáil to pass them. I am in the opposite position now. I opposed this particular amendment in the Dáil and secured its defeat. I am asking the Senate to pass it and to let the Dáil have an opportunity of reconsidering the matter.'[1]

Two similar instances occurred in connection with the Finance Bill, 1929, when two important recommendations, which had been refused by the Government when put forward as amendments in the Dáil, were accepted by that House on the motion of the Minister, who had by that time been able to give further thought to the subject-matter.[2]

There were also occasions when the special experience of Senators in banking, finance, and administration enabled them to raise points which had not been adverted to in the other House. If the points were ones of substance and the arguments adduced in their favour commended themselves to the Minister, he introduced appropriate recommendations in the Senate on the Report Stage, and got them accepted by the Dáil. This happened, for example, in the case of the Finance Bill, 1926 (Mr. Blythe), and the Industrial Credit Bill, 1933 (Mr. MacEntee). On other occasions, a point of relatively minor importance which passed unnoticed in the Dáil, but which affected adversely a small group or class of the community, was brought up in the Senate and the hardship removed. Thus, the Finance Bill, 1925, imposed an excise duty of ten shillings on dogs; a recommendation was proposed in the Senate, and accepted, exempting from this duty dogs owned and kept by the blind or purblind for the purpose of acting as guides.

On the whole, it would be true to say that during Mr. Cosgrave's Administration the co-operation of the Senate was welcomed by the Dáil in regard to Money Bills. An incident in connection with the Finance Bill of 1924 is noteworthy as showing the independence of the Dáil at that time in relation to the Government. Under the then existing law persons who owned the houses in which they lived were allowed to deduct one-sixth of the income-tax payable, in order to

[1] *Senate Debates*, x, 926, 927.   [2] *Dáil Debates*, xxxi, 971–4.

meet the cost of repairs. The Bill proposed to abolish this relief. A recommendation made by the Senate sought to restore it. When the Bill was returned to the Dáil, in spite of the strong opposition of Mr. Cosgrave (who was both President and Minister for Finance), the Dáil accepted the recommendation, which was advocated by such prominent supporters of the Government as General Mulcahy. Mr. Cosgrave at once accepted the position and proposed an amendment to give effect to the Dáil's decision.[1]

In the case of Mr. De Valera's Administration, it is necessary to draw a distinction. In the numerous Bills which implemented the Government's industrial policy, the Minister for Finance and the Minister for Industry and Commerce showed a creditable willingness to discuss with Senator Jameson, Senator Douglas, and other industrialists across the floor of the House the incidence of the proposed new taxation over the wide range of commodities involved, and, so far as possible, to meet their points of view. In regard to the more highly controversial legislation the same spirit of accommodation was hardly to be expected; but even here the Senate was able to procure safeguards and effect improvements. A case in point is the Emergency Imposition of Duties Bill, 1932. Mr. De Valera had withheld payment of the Land Annuities; the British Government had imposed special import duties to enable it to collect the money; and this Bill purported to give the Irish Free State Government power to take reprisals. It was the first shot on the Irish side in the so-called economic war. The powers sought were frankly dictatorial, since the Executive Council was accorded the widest authority to impose tariffs by Order; every such Order was given immediate statutory effect, and remained in force for a period of eight months without requiring to be confirmed by Act of Parliament. By passing the Bill in the form in which it left the Dáil, that House had virtually surrendered to the Executive its constitutional power of fiscal control. Before the eight months' period had expired the original Order could be revoked and a new one substituted, from the date of which a fresh eight months' period would start to run; or an amending Order could be made, again with a fresh period. The Senate saved the Dáil from itself by proposing, on the motion of Senator Brown, recommendations which provided adequate safeguards against possible abuses of this kind; and another which stipulated that if, when any such Order was made, the Dáil stood adjourned for more than ten days, it should be summoned by the Chairman on receipt of a requisi-

[1] *Dáil Debates*, viii, 1576–1602.

tion to that effect signed by a majority of the members. These recommendations were accepted by the Government and the Dáil, but two others were refused; and the Dáil debate on the Senate's recommendations extended over a period of nearly nine hours, during which the closure was applied.

It was not until towards the close of the Senate's life that a Committee of Privileges was demanded under Article 35 of the Constitution, and the requisition came, not from the Senate but from the Dáil. The circumstances were so extraordinary as to merit exposition in some detail. The Land Purchase (Guarantee Fund) Bill, 1935, was passed by the Dáil after 10 p.m. on Wednesday, 11th December 1935, the Senate having adjourned until next day some hours earlier. Immediately after the Bill had been passed, the Chairman of the Dáil, whose ability, experience, and impartiality were unquestioned, certified it to be a Money Bill, and it was forthwith sent to the Senate. The Senate Standing Orders provided for a minimum interval of three days between the receipt of a Bill from the Dáil and its appearance on the Order Paper, but this provision did not apply to Money Bills. The Bill was accordingly placed on the printed Order Paper for the following day for its Second Reading, together with the text of a motion which had been received from the Government Whip, the purpose of which was to enable the remaining Stages to be taken and and the Bill passed into law on that day.

It is as well here to recall the provisions of Article 35 of the Constitution, as amended in 1930, so far as they are relevant to the present case. A Committee of Privileges might be set up on the written requisition of two-fifths of the members of either House, made within seven days of the Bill being sent to the Senate; but if the Senate returned the Bill to the Dáil within the seven days, the power to demand a Committee of Privileges was at an end. Under the Dáil Standing Orders the members of that House were given only three days, instead of seven, within which to present a requisition.

As soon as the Bill had been certified, steps were taken in the Dáil to prepare such a requisition. The fact quickly became known throughout the Parliament Building, and it was reported in the three Dublin morning newspapers the next day. Of course, the obtaining of the signatures of sixty-two members at a time when the Dáil was not sitting was not a matter which could be done quickly; and some time necessarily had to elapse before the requisition could be presented. But until it had been presented the Chairman of the Senate could have no official knowledge of it.

It had not been so presented when the Senate met the day after the Bill had left the Dáil, and the Chairman had to deal with an Order Paper on which the first item was the Second Stage of the Bill and the second item was a Government motion to enable the Bill to be passed into law forthwith. He had three courses open to him:

(a) To allow the Second Stage and the motion to take the remaining Stages to be taken, if the House so decided. The objection to this course was that it would have been theoretically possible for the Bill to have been passed by the Senate and returned to the Dáil the same day, before a requisition could be presented by members of the Dáil. In that case, the Dáil Standing Order which allowed three days for such presentation would have been rendered nugatory, and the spirit of Article 35 of the Constitution would have been violated.

(b) To allow the Second Stage to be taken, but to disallow the motion for the remaining Stages. In such a case, it would have been within the power of the Senate to reject the Bill on Second Reading. But any Committee of Privileges that might be set up would find its responsibility gravely increased by the knowledge that a decision that the Bill was not a Money Bill would result in its being suspended for eighteen months.

(c) To rule that the Second Stage could not be taken until the three days had expired within which a requisition for a Committee of Privileges could be demanded by members of the Dáil. This would mean merely a few days' postponement, which could not possibly prejudice either the Government or the Opposition.

The third course was the only one which was open to no objection, and it was the one adopted by the Chairman. He conveyed his ruling to the House at the opening of the sitting in a long statement which set forth clearly the reasons for his decision. But, notwithstanding the fact that he had safeguarded the undoubted constitutional right of the minority in the Dáil, Mr. De Valera, speaking in the Dáil the same evening, accused the Chairman of the Senate of being actuated by party motives.[1]

Mr. De Valera's followers in the Senate resorted to a Standing Order which provided that the Chairman's ruling in such a case as this might be referred to the Committee of Procedure on the requisition of fifteen Senators, and they handed in the necessary requisition before the close of the sitting. It occasioned some surprise to find that among the signatories were the three Government members of this Committee, who were thus to sit in judgement on a case brought by

[1] *Dáil Debates*, lix, 2658.

themselves. One of them was the Vice-Chairman of the Senate, who had been in office for only twelve months. The Committee had no difficulty in approving the Chairman's ruling, the three Government members dissenting. As the majority was composed of representatives of all the other parties in the Senate, it was impossible for it to be impugned on the ground of partisanship. The Report of the Committee, which is dated the 31st December 1935,[1] was approved by the Senate on the 14th January 1936 without a division.[2] The only point made by the minority was that the Chairman had no right to act except on an official intimation. But Senator O'Farrell, with robust common sense, retorted that the case was as if the parliamentary buildings were on fire and the conflagration were approaching the Chamber: the Chairman was aware of the fact, but only unofficially, and while he was awaiting an official intimation from the Captain of the Guard the members were roasted alive.

On the evening of the day on which the Chairman of the Senate delivered his ruling, the requisition for a Committee of Privileges was duly presented by two-fifths of the members of the Dáil. It was signed by sixty-two Deputies, of whom about fifty were members of the Opposition and the remainder were Independents of various kinds. The signatories were accordingly representative of the whole of the minority in the Dáil except the Labour Party, with which the Government party was at that time in alliance. On the following day (13th December) Mr. De Valera asked the Dáil to approve a motion appointing three Deputies to the Committee of Privileges, and the three names he put forward were the Attorney-General (Mr. Conor Maguire, K.C.), the ex-Minister for Justice (Mr. James Geoghegan, K.C.), and the Leader of the Labour Party (Mr. William Norton). The Bill was undoubtedly a border-line case, which turned upon the interpretation of Irish Land Law—a very complex subject; and it was very desirable that there should be a legal member of the Committee who could adequately expound the minority point of view. Hence the name of Mr. J. A. Costello, K.C., a former Attorney-General, was proposed in substitution for that of Mr. Geoghegan. But Mr. De Valera used his majority to secure the rejection of this proposal. The two Government lawyers, he said, were 'to meet any case that may be put up', and he thought it sufficient to say that he had read the Bill over and over again to see whether he could find any grounds for the minority point of view, and he had been unable to find them. He accordingly concluded that the exercise by the

[1] *Reports of Committees*, vol. iv, p. 465.   [2] *Senate Debates*, xx, 1661–90.

minority of their constitutional right was a party manœuvre. Professor Thrift, of Trinity College, interrupted him with a dignified repudiation on behalf of those for whom he spoke, but the result was a foregone conclusion.

The levity which members of the Government party in the Dáil occasionally brought to the discussion of matters of serious import is well illustrated by the contribution to this debate made by Mr. Hugo Flinn, who holds the responsible position of Parliamentary Secretary to the Minister for Finance. Alluding to the approaching demise of the Senate, he said: 'I must say this is the most cheerful funeral I have been at for a long time. I have heard of funerals in Ireland called sod picnics. There was a sod picnic on one occasion when a very charming young lady went to the funeral. When she came home her mother said, "Mary, how did you enjoy the funeral?" She replied, "Mother, it was lovely. I sat in the car forninst the husband of the corpse, and he squeezed my hand and said, 'Mary, you are the belle of the funeral.'" That is very much the spirit in which we here are celebrating the wake of the half dead.'[1]

The matter came before the Senate on the 18th December for the nomination of three Senators to act on the Committee of Privileges. Senators Milroy, Douglas, and Brown, speaking for the majority, expressed their regret that the Dáil had seen fit to exclude any representative of the minority in the other House, and the names of Senators Blythe, Douglas, and O'Hanlon were proposed, being two representatives of the Cosgrave party and one Independent. This procedure was forced upon the Senate by the action of the Dáil, and was necessary if the decision was to be left to the casting vote of the Chief Justice. But Mr. De Valera's followers were not satisfied. The Vice-Chairman (Senator Comyn, K.C.) proposed, as an amendment, that three members of his own party be appointed. This amendment, if carried, would have reduced the proceedings to a farce, for the Committee of Privileges would have consisted of six members all taking Mr. De Valera's view, together with the Chief Justice. The amendment was pressed to a division, but defeated.

The Committee of Privileges met in the Parliament Building on the 19th December, under the Chairmanship of the Chief Justice (the late Mr. Hugh Kennedy, K.C.). The points developed on both sides were of an extreme technicality, and need not be detailed here.[2] The discussion lasted for over three hours, the case that the Bill was not a

[1] *Dáil Debates*, lix, 2715, 2716.
[2] The published Report contains a verbatim account of the proceedings.

Money Bill being put at great length by Senator Douglas, who is not a lawyer, but who marshalled his arguments with such consummate ability as to evoke tributes from the two lawyers on the other side. The question at last came to a vote and, as was expected, the three Senators voted on one side and the three Deputies on the other. The Chairman then spoke as follows: 'There is an even division of voting. I do not want to state reasons. I want to say that I have been a good deal shaken by a number of the arguments by Senator Douglas; but having weighed it all up—it is a decision of very great importance—I am of opinion that this is a Money Bill.'

This was at once too much and too little. Under the Constitution, it was not incumbent on the Chairman, when giving his casting vote, to state the reasons for his decision. But, since he confessed that he had been 'a good deal shaken' by Senator Douglas's arguments, it is to be regretted that he omitted to explain why they failed to carry conviction to his mind, or why he held any arguments adduced on the other side to be of greater cogency. A considered judgement might have afforded valuable guidance for the future; but a mere casting vote, without stated reasons, rendered of little value the precedent established by this decision.

The experience of this case showed that the period of twenty-one days prescribed by Article 35 of the Constitution was inconveniently short, and that a period of a month would have been preferable. The Report of the Committee of Privileges, duly signed by the Chief Justice, was presented to the Chairman of each House on the 20th December. The intervention of the Christmas holidays prevented the Senate from meeting earlier than the 31st December, and on that day the Bill appeared on the Order Paper for its Second Stage, followed by a motion in the name of the Government Whip to enable the remaining Stages of the Bill to be taken on that day. After a prolonged debate, the Second Reading was passed, with two dissentients—the Vice-Chairman of the Senate and one other Government supporter; and it was then found that the Government Whip was not in his place to move his motion. It is possible that the action of the Vice-Chairman and the absence of the Government Whip were due to the fact that Mr. De Valera's supporters had supposed that the twenty-one-day period would expire on that day, in which case the failure of the Government Whip to move his motion would have deprived Senators of the power to move recommendations. Actually, the period did not expire till midnight on the following day.

The House accordingly adjourned until next day (New Year's Day,

1936), when the Committee Stage of the Bill appeared on the Order Paper, together with a motion enabling the remaining Stages to be taken—this time in the name of a Senator belonging to the Cosgrave party. Senator Brown, K.C., whose aloofness from anything that savoured of party politics was as unquestioned as his eminence in the legal profession, spoke as follows: 'This is the most objectionable retrospective legislation that we have had, so far, in this country. It is the first case in which the Government, by retrospective legislation, has made it, or intends to make it, practically impossible for a Court to decide against the Government in a case in which the Government itself is the defendant.'[1] Three recommendations, designed to remove these retrospective provisions, were moved on the Committee Stage. These were opposed by the supporters of the Government and members of the Labour Party, and a division was challenged on each. There was an equality of votes in each case, the Chairman gave his casting vote in favour, and the recommendations were declared carried. The Committee Stage was then concluded.

It now became the object of Mr. De Valera's supporters to prevent the Bill, with the three recommendations, from being returned to the Dáil. With this purpose in view they opposed the motion to enable the remaining Stages to be taken on that day (which was the last of the twenty-one days allowed to the Senate under the Constitution). The voting on the motion was again equal, the Chairman gave his casting vote in its favour, and it was declared carried. The climax of this humiliating situation was then reached. After a debate on the Fifth Stage, the Chairman put the final question, 'That the Bill do now pass,' and the Government supporters of this Government Bill opposed it. The Opposition rightly refused to participate in what had degenerated into an undignified game of party tactics; they declined to vote for a Bill with which they thoroughly disagreed; no division was challenged, and the question was declared lost.

The tactics of the Government party had been based on a misconception of the constitutional position. Under Article 38 of the Constitution it was mandatory on the Senate to return the Bill to the Dáil. Accordingly, the Bill was returned the same evening, together with a message specifying the three recommendations made by the Senate. The Government presumably took the view (which was unquestionably correct) that the Dáil was obliged to consider the Senate's recommendations, in spite of the failure of that House to pass the Final Reading; for they requested the Chairman of the Dáil to summon a

---

[1] *Senate Debates*, xx, 1607.

special meeting for that purpose. This meeting was held on the 15th January and the recommendations were rejected, on a party vote, after a debate which lasted more than six hours.

It has seemed desirable, because of their unprecedented nature, to recount at some length the circumstances surrounding the passage into law of this Bill. It was the only Bill in respect of which the constitutional provisions regarding a Committee of Privileges were operated. The requisition for the Committee came, not from the Senate, but from the minority in the Dáil. Every effort was made by Mr. De Valera and his followers in both Houses to frustrate that minority in the exercise of their undoubted constitutional right. It was demonstrated at the Committee, and in effect admitted by the Chief Justice, that there were arguments of substance to support the view that the Bill was not a Money Bill. The efforts of the Government party to pack the Committee having failed, its members in the Senate strove first to prevent that House from making any recommendations, and then to prevent the recommendations, when made, from being considered by the Dáil. During the progress of the Bill a ruling of the Chairman of the Senate, honestly given and subsequently ratified, was challenged by Mr. De Valera's followers, and the Chairman's good faith was publicly impugned by Mr. De Valera himself.

Coming, as it did, towards the close of the Senate's life, this episode did something to reconcile many of those associated with the Senate from the beginning to the severance from public life which the abolition of that House entailed for them. They had built up a Second Chamber in which political bitterness and party tactics of the baser sort were almost unknown. Within its four walls a spirit of good humour, mutual accommodation, and respect for the opposite point of view had created an atmosphere of co-operation between the various classes which might in time have leavened the Dáil and the country at large, and without which no ordered system of society is possible. And they had seen these wholesome things first threatened and then gradually brought to ruin.

CHAPTER XXXIII

FORMALITIES AND MACHINERY
OF PARLIAMENT

Centrifugal tendency of the Irish Free State—Divergencies of procedure as compared with the overseas Dominions—The practice elsewhere—Summoning, prorogation and dissolution of Parliament—Parliamentary sessions—Advantages of the procedure—Constitutional requirements of Article 24—The Governor-General's Address to both Houses, December 1922 and October 1923—The Governor-General never again visits Parliament—Unfortunate practical results—No Debate on the Address—Absence of sessions—Consent of Senate to conclusion of session first sought and then disregarded—Constitutional amendments—No robes worn by the Chairman—Method of administering parliamentary Oath—Necessity for procedure in Dáil—Procedure in Senate—The Dáil, not the Parliament, enumerated—Language provisions—No formal intimation of Royal Assent to Bills—The Casket —The opening prayer.

In this chapter it is proposed to group together certain matters of some general interest which are not specially technical in character. Most of them serve to emphasize the centrifugal tendency, as regards the British Commonwealth, of the Irish Free State from the beginning, and the divergencies of procedure in its Parliament as compared with Parliaments of the other Dominions. No criticism is offered of these facts, which are attributable to a number of causes that need not be examined here; but it would be unhistorical to ignore them.

The overseas Dominions follow fairly closely the practice of Westminster in the matter of summoning, prorogation, and dissolution of Parliament, these formal acts being effected by Proclamation of the Governor-General in the name of the King. After a general election, the new Parliament is opened in state by the Governor-General, who delivers a speech, in which the country's position, internal and international, is passed in review and the Government's proposals for legislation are outlined. Each Parliament is divided into sessions by prorogation and each session is normally opened by the Governor-General, whose speech indicates the Bills likely to be submitted in that session.

Disregarding for the moment the special considerations that might be held to apply in Ireland, we can see that this procedure is founded in good sense. The pomp which surrounds the opening of Parliament, and of each session of Parliament, is no mere idle show, but serves to invest the whole system of parliamentary government with a certain dignity. As such, it is calculated to impress on the members of both Houses a sense of their responsibility as legislators and on the public at large a feeling of respect for the country's laws.

Again, the speech of the Governor-General has the great practical advantage of communicating to Parliament and to the nation an outline of the measures proposed to be enacted in a particular session. These are very thoroughly discussed by both Houses in what is usually called the Debate on the Address, by which the Government is kept in touch with public opinion and as a result of which its proposals are not infrequently modified. As this procedure occurs at least once a year, Parliament is closely associated with the function of government, a degree of precision is maintained in regard to its work, and the encroachments of the bureaucracy are resisted.

Moreover, the system of yearly sessions makes for the businesslike dispatch of the affairs of the nation. There is a definite beginning and a definite end. Certain months become recognized as months of session: in South Africa from January to July, in New Zealand from July to October, and so on. Members thus know beforehand what demands are likely to be made on their time by their parliamentary duties.

It is clear that the Constitution intended that this procedure should apply to the Irish Free State. Article 24 reads as follows: 'The Oireachtas shall hold at least one session each year. The Oireachtas shall be summoned and dissolved by the Representative of the Crown in the name of the King and subject as aforesaid Dáil Éireann shall fix the date of reassembly of the Oireachtas and the date of the conclusion of the session of each House: Provided that the sessions of Seanad Éireann shall not be concluded without its own consent.'

On the 6th December 1922 the Constitution came into force by Royal Proclamation. The Dáil sat on that day, and the Senate met for the first time five days later. On the 12th December members of both Houses assembled in the Chamber of the Dáil to hear an address from the Governor-General, the Chairman of the Dáil being in the Chair. There was a minimum of ceremonial. The Governor-General (the late Mr. T. M. Healy, K.C.) drove to the Parliament Building from the Viceregal Lodge in a motor-car, accompanied by two aides-de-camp. He was met by a military guard of honour, a bugle sounded the salute, and he entered the precincts. Addressing the members, he read a Message from the King, and then delivered a speech, in which he referred to the historic occasion and detailed the legislative proposals of the Government. The Labour Party officially boycotted the Joint Sitting.[1] Subsequently, there was a Debate on the Address in both Houses.

On the 9th August 1923 Parliament was dissolved by Proclamation of the Governor-General in the name of the King and was summoned to meet again on the following 19th September, subsequent to the general election. On the 3rd October the Governor-General again addressed a Joint Sitting of both Houses, the procedure being exactly as before. He reviewed the work of the Parliament that had been dissolved and outlined the Bills to be submitted in 'the present session'. There was again a boycott by Labour, and Debates took place on the Address.[2]

This was the last occasion on which the Governor-General visited Parliament. The discontinuance of the procedure is doubtless to be explained by the Government's desire to keep the Representative of the Crown in the background so far as possible and, while observing the strict letter of the Treaty and the Constitution, to eschew the forms and ceremonies associated with parliamentary usage in the British Commonwealth. This was in some degree part of the Government's policy in countering Mr. De Valera's anti-Treaty propaganda, but it would be idle to deny that it was also to a large extent the result of the repugnance felt at that time in Government circles to what were regarded as British symbols.

There is room for legitimate difference of opinion as to whether or not this policy was commendable, but that its practical results were unfortunate seems undeniable. Parliamentary sessions ceased to exist in the ordinary sense, and became co-terminous with Parliaments. The opening of each new Parliament was marked by no formality whatever, beyond the reading of the Proclamation in each House.

[1] *Irish Times*, 13 December 1922, and *Senate Debates*, i, Appendix.
[2] Ibid., 4 October 1923, and *Senate Debates*, ii, Appendix.
20

The occasion was therefore drab and uninspiring. As there was no Governor-General's Address, the only indication of the legislative intentions of the Government lay in their pre-election promises, which sometimes proved an unreliable guide. In the other countries of the Commonwealth the Debate on the Address generally occupies a considerable time, during which the parliamentary draftsman, in conjunction with the several Departments of State, is able to prepare the necessary Bills. In the Irish Free State, after the first formal meeting pursuant to the Proclamation, the Houses often found themselves with nothing much to do and had to adjourn.

The absence of sessions meant that there were no well-recognized months during which Parliament would sit. The Government drove members as hard as it dared, and almost every year there was an inconclusive wrangle as to when the summer recess should begin, with the date getting gradually pushed further back. But the fact that there was no prorogation had another and much more sinister aspect. Within a year or so of a general election those of the Government's election pledges which it intends to respect have usually been fulfilled. From that point onwards, no occasion arose for the communication to Parliament of the Government's proposals for the future. What happened was (and this applies more particularly to Mr. De Valera's Administration) that these proposals were first disclosed to a party meeting behind closed doors, or else to the annual convention of the Government party. This pernicious practice is the very negation of parliamentary democratic government and leads inevitably to the suspicion that the Government is acting primarily in the interests of its supporters rather than in the interests of the country as a whole.

The stipulation in Article 24 of the Constitution that the sessions of the Senate should not be concluded without its own consent was first obeyed and then disregarded. Before the dissolution of August 1923 the Dáil sent a message to the Senate requesting its consent to the conclusion of the session, and this was given by formal resolution passed on the 9th August. A similar resolution, in reply to a similar message, was passed on the 20th May 1927, the dissolution following three days later. No such message was received as regards the sessions which were terminated by the dissolutions of August 1927, January 1932, and January 1933.

The word 'session' appeared elsewhere in the Constitution. Article 39 provided that a Bill initiated in the Senate should be introduced in the Dáil, but if rejected by the Dáil 'it shall not be introduced again in the same session'. The word having become meaningless, the sentence containing it was deleted by the Constitution (Amendment No. 14) Act, 1929.

The word also occurred in Article 37, which ran as follows: 'Money shall not be appropriated by vote, resolution or law, unless the purpose of the appropriation has in the same session been recommended by a message from the Representative of the Crown acting on the advice of the Executive Council.' Though this article was amended by the Constitution (Amendment No. 20) Act, 1933 (the Representative of the Crown being deprived of this formal function), Mr. De Valera seems to have overlooked the desirability of dealing with the word 'session'.

The anxiety to avoid any resemblance to the procedure at Westminster and in the Parliaments of the overseas Dominions probably accounted for the fact that the Chairmen of both Houses and the Clerks at the Table wore neither wig and gown nor robes of any sort. These things inculcate respect for the Chair, and therefore make for dignity and decorum. Incidentally, they are not confined to the nations of the British Commonwealth.

The method of administering the parliamentary Oath was also peculiar. Article 17 of the Constitution provided that it should be taken and subscribed by every member, before taking his seat, before the Representative of the Crown, or some person authorized by him. When the Dáil met on the 6th December 1922, Mr. Michael Hayes, who had been Chairman of the Constituent Assembly, announced that he had been authorized by the Governor-General to administer the Oath, and he did so in public in the Dáil Chamber. But this procedure involved risks of disorder. At the first meeting of the Constituent Assembly on the previous 9th September the late Mr. Laurence Ginnell had created a scene and in the end had had to be forcibly ejected because he refused to sign the Roll as required by the Standing Orders (there was, of course, no Oath at that time). If the Oath had continued to be administered in public there would have been no power to debar Mr. De Valera and his followers from access to the Dáil Chamber, and there might have been demonstrations. Accordingly, the Dáil Standing Orders were altered, and arrangements were made by the Clerk of the Dáil for the Oath to be taken on a day or days prior to the first meeting day of a new Parliament.

The Senate was in no such difficulty, since there were no abstentionist Senators. When it met on the 11th December 1922 the Oath was administered by Mr. E. J. Duggan, Minister without portfolio, being the person authorized by the Governor-General. After the election of Lord Glenavy as Chairman, he was authorized to administer it, and he did so, in public in the Senate Chamber, during the whole period of his Chairmanship. On the 28th November 1928, immediately before the commencement of the Third Triennial Period (which saw the advent of Fianna Fáil to the Senate), the procedure was changed by an amendment of the Standing Orders, and the practice of the Dáil was followed thereafter. It is not easy to understand the reason for the change, unless it was desired to assimilate the Senate's procedure to that of the Dáil. The abstentionist policy had by that time been abandoned for more than a year.

Another striking difference lies in the method of denoting particular parliaments. Australia numbers hers from the date of federation, South Africa from the date of the Union, and so on. Thus reference is made, for example, to the Second Session of the Fourteenth Parliament of the Commonwealth of Australia. But the Irish Free State considered its parliamentary history to date, not from the foundation of the Irish Free State on the 6th December 1922, but from the Declaration of Independence on the 21st January 1919. The Dáil, not the Parliament, was numbered, the Senate being treated as an appanage of the Dáil. The series therefore is: First Dáil, 21st January 1919 to 10th May 1921; Second Dáil, 16th August 1921 to 27th May 1922 (this was the Dáil which approved the Treaty); Third Dáil, 9th September 1922 to 9th August 1923 (this was the Dáil which began as a single Constituent Assembly under the Provisional Government and subsequently became one of the two Houses of Parliament of the Irish Free State); Fourth Dáil, 19th September 1923 to 23rd May 1927; Fifth Dáil, 23rd June 1927 to 25th August 1927; Sixth Dail, 11th October 1927 to 29th January 1932; Seventh Dáil, 9th March 1932 to 2nd January 1933; Eighth Dáil, 8th February 1933 to 14th June 1937. The First, Second, and Third Dáil are statutorily defined in the Interpretation Act, 1923 (Section 2). It was the Eighth Dáil that abolished the Senate.

Article 4 of the Constitution stated that 'the national language of the Irish Free State is the Irish language but the English language shall be equally recognized as an official language'. Matters were so arranged, however, that the question of versional discrepancies in Bills never arose, as it does in countries like Canada and South Africa. Of the 153 members of the Dáil probably not more than half a dozen at the very outside would have been able to carry on a debate in Irish, and only two or three could be said to be more at home in Irish than in English. Bills were therefore invariably introduced and passed in English. Article 42 provided that, as soon as a Bill had received the King's Assent, two copies were to be prepared, one in Irish and one in English. One was to be signed by the Representative of the Crown and enrolled for record, and in case of conflict between the two copies that signed by the Representative of the Crown was to prevail. He invariably signed the English copy, and no case of conflict ever occurred.

The ceremony of intimating, in either House or both, the Royal Assent to Acts was dispensed with. The fact of Assent was published in the *Iris Oifigiúil* (the successor of the *Dublin Gazette*) and in the Dáil *Journal of Proceedings*.

Reference has already been made to the Casket presented to the Senate by Alice Stopford Green, which was laid on the table at the commencement of the sitting. The only other formality was a prayer, which, on and after the 28th November 1923, was read by the Clerk of the House, in Irish and English, before the opening of the proceedings. This prayer ran: 'O Almighty and Eternal God, Ruler of all things and of all men, we, Thy servants here assembled, most humbly beseech Thee to grant us Thy Divine Guidance in our deliberations, that Peace, Justice, Truth, Religion and Piety may reign in our Country, to the Honour and Glory of Thy Name. Through Jesus Christ Our Lord. Amen.' This is a beautiful invocation, and the credit for its adoption so early in the Senate's history must be given to Senator the Earl of Wicklow, a man of deep religious feeling. With considerable energy and tact, he personally interviewed both the Catholic and the Protestant Archbishops of Dublin, and, fortified by their approval, he had no difficulty in persuading the Senate to adopt it.[1] It was many years before the Dáil followed suit, and it was not until the 19th October 1932 that the proceedings of that House were opened by prayer.

[1] *Senate Debates*, ii, 85–91.

PART IX

EPILOGUE

'There is no constitutional hybrid between a republic and a monarchy.'

KEVIN O'HIGGINS, in the Dáil, 18th September 1922.

EPILOGUE

It remains to chronicle the principal events from the promulgation of the new Constitution up to the outbreak of the present European war. It will be realized, however, that in dealing with events of such recent date it is not easy for them to be viewed in their proper perspective.

On the date on which the new Constitution came into operation (29th December 1937) the following statement was issued by the British Government:

'His Majesty's Government in the United Kingdom has considered the position created by the new Constitution, which was approved by the Parliament of the Irish Free State in June 1937, and came into force on December 29.

'They are prepared to treat the new Constitution as not effecting a fundamental alteration in the position of the Irish Free State, in future to be described under the new Constitution as "Éire" or "Ireland", as a member of the British Commonwealth of Nations.

'His Majesty's Government in the United Kingdom have ascertained that His Majesty's Governments in Canada, the Commonwealth of Australia, New Zealand, and the Union of South Africa are also prepared so to treat the new Constitution.

'His Majesty's Government in the United Kingdom take note of Articles 2, 3 and 4 of the new Constitution.

'They cannot recognize that the adoption of the name "Éire" or "Ireland", or any other provision of those Articles, involves any right to territory or jurisdiction over territory forming part of the United Kingdom of Great Britain and Northern Ireland, or affects in any way the position of Northern Ireland as an integral part of the United Kingdom of Great Britain and Northern Ireland.

'They, therefore, regard the use of the name "Éire" or "Ireland" in this connection as relating only to that area which has hitherto been known as the Irish Free State.'[1]

Thus the other five member-States of the Commonwealth proposed to continue to treat the Irish Free State, under its new designation, as a full member of the Commonwealth, with the rights and duties appertaining to such membership. As 'external association', if recognized, would undoubtedly effect 'a fundamental alteration' in the status of the Irish Free State, it follows from this communication that they do not recognize it. In addition, the British Government does not recognize the claim to *de jure* jurisdiction over Northern Ireland.

We shall next consider the manner in which the Constitution was implemented in regard to the formation of a Senate and the election of a President of Ireland.

The Constitution provides that, out of a Senate of 60 members, 11 shall be nominated by the Prime Minister and the remaining 49 shall be elected—3 from each of the two universities and 43 from five vocational panels, representing cultural and professional interests, agriculture, labour, industry and commerce, and public administration. The Seanad Electoral (Panel Members) Act, 1937, provides the

[1] *Irish Times*, 30 December 1937.

machinery for the election of these 43 members. The electorate consists of the Dáil (138 members), plus 7 representatives from each of the 31 county councils, making an electoral college of 355 members in all. The five panels of candidates are constituted (a) by nominations made by bodies whose claims to nominate are admitted by the statutory Returning Officer, and (b) by nominations made by members of the Dáil. The necessity was overlooked of making provision for casual vacancies caused by the death or resignation of any of the forty-three senators so elected.

Thus, against all experience, the principle was retained of constituting members of the Dáil as both nominators and electors; and the result of the first election held under this extremely cumbrous system was in accordance with informed expectation.

First, the 217 electors of the county councils had to be elected. Then the Returning Officer published the register containing the names of the bodies whose claims he had admitted to exercise the right of nomination to each of the five vocational panels. As the country is not organized on a vocational basis, this must have presented some difficult problems. For instance, the claim to nominate to the labour panel was admitted in the case of an obscure society known as the Ballingarry Cottage Tenants' and Rural Workers' Association. The Returning Officer had no option in the matter, in view of the loose wording of the Constitution, which merely specifies 'labour, whether organized or unorganized'; and in any case his decision was confirmed by the statutory Appeal Committee of the Dáil. But to give to a society established in a Limerick village of less than 500 inhabitants co-equal nominating power with the whole trade union movement was a manifest absurdity. The Trade Union Congress protested strongly, alleging that the Ballingarry Association had been defunct for some time and was now specially revived for the purpose of the election; that it had no rules and no staff; and that its total income during the past two years of its existence was only eleven pounds. The protest being unavailing, the Labour Party boycotted the election, nominating no candidates and returning no members.

The five panels of candidates, as finally constituted, contained 132 names, of which 92 were on the nominating bodies' sub-panel and 40 were on the Dáil sub-panel. The Act specifies that 21 senators shall be elected from the former and 22 from the latter, the election being held on principles of proportional representation. This remarkable election resulted in a triumph for the politicians and a rout for those who had allowed their names to go forward in the belief that a vocational second chamber would eventuate. Of the 43 successful candidates, 19 were former members of either Dáil or Senate. No fewer than 95 separate counts were required before the result was arrived at, but long before the race was over most of the distinguished representatives of law, medicine, agriculture, commerce, and the professions generally were out of the running. A good many of them, indeed, may be said to have fallen at the first fence, since they did not receive a single first preference vote. Some men of proved ability were, however, returned, such as Mr. Michael Hayes, the former Chairman of the Dáil, General Mulcahy (who had lost his seat in the Dáil at the previous general election), and ex-Senator Douglas.

Of the six candidates on the cultural panel who are specially identified with the Irish language, only one was successful—the headmaster of a secondary school where teaching is conducted through Irish, in one of the Irish-speaking districts. The President of the Gaelic League, the Director of the Irish Folk-Lore Commission, and three distinguished workers in the academic field were all defeated.

The six university members did something to improve the personnel. The National University returned Mrs. Helena Concannon, Professor Michael Tierney, and Surgeon Barniville. Professor Tierney was a particularly valuable acquisition. He had represented his university in the Dáil from 1927 to 1932, during which period he had shown that detachment, independence of mind, and power of expression which one expects of a profound classical scholar; and his qualities later received recognition by his appointment as Vice-Chairman of the new Senate (30th November 1938). Dublin University (Trinity College) elected two of its former representatives in the Dáil, Professor Alton and Dr. Rowlette, and a newcomer in Mr. Joseph Johnston, an expert in economics, who is also a Fellow of the college. All three were of the senatorial type.

The Senate was completed by the eleven members nominated by Mr. De Valera as Prime Minister. His nominees included Sir John Keane and Mr. Frank MacDermot, neither of whom could fairly be regarded as his political supporter, and Dr. Douglas Hyde, who has never been connected with politics; but otherwise his list was not particularly distinguished, and, taken as a whole, it showed none of the breadth of outlook which characterized Mr. Cosgrave's nominations in 1922. His selection did little to increase the vocational character of the Second Chamber. On the contrary, indeed, it seems to have increased its political complexion.

The result of the first Senate election had disclosed an undoubted flaw in the Constitution in providing for a vocational second chamber in a country which is not organized vocationally. In the preparation for the election of a President another defect was made manifest. The Constitution provides that the President shall be elected by direct vote of the people, from among candidates nominated either by (a) not less than twenty members of the Dáil or Senate, or (b) not less than four county councils. The machinery was supplied by a voluminous Presidential Elections Act, 1937. It was generally understood that the Deputy Prime Minister, Mr. Seán T. O'Kelly, was a possible candidate, and the Rt. Hon. Alfred Byrne, Lord Mayor of Dublin, made it clear that in that event he would go forward also. There might have been other candidates as well. Thus, what seemed likely to happen was exactly what is contemplated by the Constitution, namely, that two or more prominent public men should engage in a nation-wide contest for the office of President. No sooner was this fact realized than there was general agreement that an election must at all costs be avoided. Such an event would only have aroused undesirable contention concerning a position which should be removed from the arena of party politics. If Messrs. Byrne and O'Kelly had been the sole candidates, the country would have been rent by dissension, the victor would probably have had only a narrow majority, and it is to be feared that some of the minority would not have accorded to him the respect due to his office.

To prevent such an untoward result a conference was arranged between two members of the Government and two members of the Opposition Front Bench. They met on the 21st April 1938, and it was agreed, after some discussion, that Dr. Douglas Hyde should be requested to accept nomination. The Labour Party signified its approval, Dr. Hyde agreed, and there was no other candidate. He was therefore declared elected, unopposed, on the 4th May 1938.

No happier choice could well be imagined. For a period of half a century Douglas Hyde, avoiding all political entanglements, has steadily pursued with single-minded endeavour his self-appointed task of rescuing the Irish language from oblivion. If anyone is deserving of the highest honour the State can bestow, it is he. Moreover, he is no scholarly recluse, but a genial man of the world whom it is easy to love and impossible to dislike; and, as is the case with most educated men who know the Irish language thoroughly, his devotion to it has never made him intolerant. There is the added fact that, as Dr. Hyde is not of the faith of the majority, his unopposed election

to the Presidency afforded a salutary object-lesson in religious toleration.

The 25th June 1938 was the date fixed for the inauguration of the
President. On the morning of that day the Prime Minister and the
Catholic members of Parliament attended a solemn Votive Mass in
St. Mary's Pro-Cathedral and the President-elect and the Protestant
members attended a special Divine Service in St. Patrick's Cathedral.
Thereupon the simple yet dignified ceremony of installation took
place in the historic St. Patrick's Hall of Dublin Castle. Dr. Hyde
took and subscribed the declaration of fealty prescribed by the Constitution, in the presence of the judges, members of the Oireachtas,
and other public personages, and entered on his office as first President of Ireland. Addressing the new President on this occasion, Mr.
De Valera said, with hyperbole pardonable in the circumstances, 'In
you we greet the successor of our rightful princes.'[1] In practice, however, the manner of the President's appointment proved to be not so
very dissimilar from that of the Governors-General. Notionally, the
Governor-General was appointed by the Crown; actually, he was
appointed by the Irish Government. Notionally, the President was
elected by the people; actually, his appointment was due to an arrangement between the Government and the Opposition, owing to
the desirability of avoiding the bitterness of a contested election.
The point is of some importance, because it is hardly to be expected
that on future occasions an agreed candidate of the outstanding
merit of Douglas Hyde will be easy to find.

We now turn our attention to Anglo-Irish relations. On the 11th
January 1938 Mr. De Valera informed the Dáil that a meeting was
to be held in London on the 17th January between representatives of
the two Governments, for the purpose of discussing outstanding
questions. Asked by journalists the same evening whether the partition issue would be raised, Mr. De Valera replied, 'Inevitably.' On
the following day Lord Craigavon, anxious as ever to put a spoke in
Mr. De Valera's wheel, announced a general election for Northern
Ireland.

Besides partition, the main questions were the occupation by
British forces of the three Treaty ports and a settlement of the economic war. The Irish delegation was headed by Mr. De Valera, who
was accompanied by three of his Ministers, and the British delegation consisted of Mr. Neville Chamberlain and three members of his
Cabinet. On the 19th January it was officially announced that, while

[1] *Irish Independent*, 27 June 1938.

no agreement had been reached, the preliminary negotiations had proceeded far enough to justify a more detailed examination of a number of points by officials of both Governments.

On the 10th February, while this examination was in progress, the general election was held in Northern Ireland. The result was as follows, the number of members returned unopposed being given in brackets:

Unionists	39 (14)
Nationalists	8 (6)
Independent Unionists	2
Labour	2 (1)
Independent	1
	52 (21)

The result shows the political stagnation in the Six-County area. In nearly half the constituencies (exclusive of the university, which returns four members) there was no contest at all, since opinions are so fixed that the result would have been a foregone conclusion. Although Belfast and, to a less extent, Derry are heavily industrialized areas, the Labour Party could return only two members. Since the Nationalists comprise more than one-third of the population, they could normally return more than one-third of the membership—in other words, double their present strength. But a number of factors render this impossible: the abolition of proportional representation in 1928; the gerrymandering of the constituencies; and the Nationalists' own internal dissensions, coupled with their reliance on Dublin for nonexistent leadership instead of seeking leaders of their own. However, the Nationalists were unopposed in five of the border constituencies —Mid-Derry, Derry City, South Fermanagh, Mid-Tyrone, and West Tyrone—as well as in Belfast Central; and they contested and won two other seats—East Tyrone (also a border constituency) and the Falls division of Belfast.

The election, in fact, proved nothing that was not well known already. Northern Ireland contains six of the nine counties of the province of Ulster. In four of these counties, taken as a whole (Antrim, Derry, Down, and Armagh), there is a large majority in favour of the continuance of partition. In the two remaining counties (Tyrone and Fermanagh) there is a much smaller majority, but still a majority, in favour of reunion with the rest of Ireland.

Lord Craigavon hailed the result as a great victory, as, from his point of view, he was quite entitled to do. 'I am deeply gratified by the overwhelming response to my appeal for a renewal of your confidence and at the magnificent reply you have given to the latest demand from Southern Ireland for the surrender of Ulster. Mr. De Valera has again presumed to dictate his terms to the Imperial Government for the severance of Ulster from the United Kingdom. That question, however, was not for him, but for the people of Ulster to decide.'[1]

It will be observed that the Prime Minister of Northern Ireland uses the term 'Ulster', though his authority extends to only six of its nine counties, and, morally, he can speak for only four. He also employs the offensive and non-existent term 'Southern Ireland', in regard to which it is sufficient to point out that the area to which he refers contains the most northerly county in Ireland (Donegal) and that in Derry, which is the most northerly city in the country, the Unionists did not even put up a candidate in one of its two constituencies.

Mr. De Valera delivered a pungent reply. 'Lord Craigavon makes a mistake. So long as this nation endures, the recovery of that part of the province of Ulster which has been wrongfully torn away will be the first item on the agenda in every conference between the representatives of Ireland and Britain until that item is finally wiped off in the only way in which it can be wiped off, by the restoration of Ireland's natural unity.'[2]

On the 19th February the Irish delegates crossed over to London again, but the resumption of the discussions was held up for four days on account of Mr. Chamberlain's preoccupation with the international situation, owing to the menacing attitude of Germany to the Austrian Government. Returning to Dublin on the 26th February, Mr. De Valera informed the press that 'a comprehensive settlement —the only one that would have world significance—now seems almost unattainable'.[3] By this he meant that his attempt to end partition had met with no success; but he seems to have decided, very sensibly, that an agreement on the other issues was preferable to no agreement at all. On the 2nd March the delegation returned to London, and by the 12th March the talks had so far progressed that Mr. De Valera and his colleagues came home for consultation with the Cabinet as a whole. The 12th March was a black-letter day in the annals of Europe, for it was on that day that Hitler marched into

---

[1] *Irish Independent*, 11 February 1938.   [2] Ibid., 11 February 1938.
[3] Ibid., 28 February 1938.

Austria; and it is possible that the growing threat from Nazi Germany was a factor in inducing the British Government to go as far as it could in the way of establishing a friendly Ireland on the western flank of Great Britain.

Finally, on the 25th April 1938, three separate Agreements of outstanding importance were signed in London.[1] The signatories were, on the Irish side, the Prime Minister (Mr. De Valera), Mr. Lemass, Mr. MacEntee, and Dr. Ryan, and, on the British side, the Prime Minister (Mr. Neville Chamberlain), Sir John Simon, Sir Samuel Hoare, and Mr. Malcolm MacDonald. In addition, Sir Thomas Inskip signed the first Agreement and Mr. W. S. Morrison the third. The preamble to the Agreements stated that the two Governments were 'desirous of promoting relations of friendship and good understanding between the two countries, of reaching a final settlement of all outstanding financial claims of either of the two Governments against the other, and of facilitating trade and commerce between the two countries'.

The first Agreement annulled the provisions of Articles 6 and 7 of the Anglo-Irish Treaty of 1921 and of the Annex thereto. Article 6 provided that 'until an arrangement has been made between the British and Irish Governments whereby the Irish Free State undertakes her own coastal defence, the defence by sea of Great Britain and Ireland shall be undertaken by His Majesty's Imperial Forces'. Article 7 provided that the Irish Free State Government should afford to the said Forces (*a*) the harbour and other facilities indicated in the Annex, namely, the Admiralty property and harbour defences at Cove (Queenstown), Berehaven, and Lough Swilly, and (*b*) 'in time of war or of strained relations with a Foreign Power such harbour and other facilities as the British Government may require for the purposes of such defence as aforesaid'. In addition to deleting these provisions of the Treaty, the new Agreement provided that these three ports, 'now occupied by care and maintenance parties furnished by the United Kingdom', should be transferred to the Government of Éire, and that the transfer should take place not later than the 31st December 1938. Actually, Cove was handed over on the 11th July, Berehaven on the 29th September, and Lough Swilly on the 3rd October—the last two during and after the Munich crisis.

The form of this Agreement is of some constitutional interest. Since it provides that certain portions of the Treaty of 1921 'shall cease to have effect', there is an implicit acknowledgement by the

[1] Cmd. 5728 (1938) (xxx, p. 1001).

signatories that the Treaty, as amended by mutual agreement, although no longer part of our municipal law, is still a subsisting international instrument of full validity. And Article 1 of the Treaty provides that 'Ireland shall have the same constitutional status in the Community of Nations known as the British Empire, as the Dominion of Canada, the Commonwealth of Australia, the Dominion of New Zealand, and the Union of South Africa'.

The second Agreement was a financial agreement. The Government of Éire agreed to pay to the Government of the United Kingdom the sum of £10,000,000, and this was to 'constitute a final settlement of all financial claims of either of the two Governments against the other'. In other words, the Land Annuities and other periodical payments specified in the repudiated Ultimate Financial Settlement of 1926 were compounded for this amount. The only exception of substance was an annual sum of £250,000 which the Cosgrave Administration had undertaken to pay in respect of damage to property under the Agreement of the 3rd December 1925. This Agreement had been ratified by the Dáil, and the liability under it had never been in dispute. As a corollary to the new Agreement, both Governments undertook to abolish the penal duties which had been in force since 1932. Thus, after nearly six years, the economic war was brought to an end, after having cost the Irish people, according to one expert estimate, the colossal sum of forty-eight millions sterling.[1]

The third Agreement was a trade agreement of an extremely comprehensive character, comprising nineteen articles and six schedules. It was to remain in force for three years, and, broadly speaking, one might describe it as the kind of agreement that might have been expected to result from the Ottawa Conference of 1932 if the British Government had not then declined to negotiate an agreement with the Irish delegates. In general, Irish goods were to be admitted free of customs duties into the British market, with certain provisions concerning the quantitative regulation of imports of agricultural products. Reciprocally, the Irish Government guaranteed the right of free entry for certain classes of British goods which were not subject to duty at the date of the Agreement, and it undertook to remove or to modify the duties on certain other classes of British goods. The method adopted was that the existing protective duties should be reviewed by the (Irish) Prices Commission, with a view to giving United Kingdom producers and manufacturers full opportunity of reasonable competition, while affording adequate protection to Irish

[1] *Irish Independent*, 26 April 1938.

industries; and British producers and manufacturers were granted the right of audience before the Commission. The chief benefit to both sides of this mutually advantageous commercial treaty has been the improvement in the trade of agricultural products—a trade which is the economic mainstay of Ireland and is, under war conditions, almost equally important to Great Britain.

These three Agreements reflect the greatest credit on the good sense of both sides, and particularly on Mr. De Valera and Mr. Neville Chamberlain. They were duly ratified by the United Kingdom Parliament by the Éire (Confirmation of Agreements) Act, which received the Royal Assent on the 17th May.[1] On the Irish side, although the preamble to the Agreements states that they are to be 'subject to Parliamentary confirmation', a simple resolution of the Dáil was deemed sufficient, no parallel resolution being submitted to the Senate. The Dáil resolution was passed, without a division, on the 29th April, after three days' debate.[2] The agreement to accept transfer of the ports incurred some criticism, both from the Opposition Front Bench and from the Labour Party. Mr. Cosgrave disclosed the fact that his Government had been requested to take over the ports, but had declined to do so on account of the cost; and this statement was later confirmed in the Senate by Mr. Desmond Fitzgerald, who was Minister for Defence in 1928 when the request was made.[3] The Leader of the Labour Party inquired whether there was any understanding that the British Navy would be allowed the use of the ports as bases. Any such understanding was denied by Mr. De Valera, and it has been proved by subsequent events to have been non-existent. But some colour was given to this suggestion by Mr. De Valera's announcement that the harbour defences of Cove, Berehaven, and Lough Swilly would not be allowed to become derelict, but would be maintained and modernized. As these bases are useless for purposes of defence except in conjunction with a fleet, the decision to spend money on them is difficult to understand. The British Navy is not to be allowed to use them. Ireland has no navy and cannot afford to build one.

This is a subject on which there has been a good deal of muddled thinking. In stipulating that the defence by sea of Great Britain and Ireland should be undertaken by the British Navy, the Treaty of 1921 recognized the strategic unity which, in a predatory world, is im-

[1] *House of Commons Debates*, cccxxxv, 1071–1184; *House of Lords Debates*, cix, 2–22.
[2] *Dáil Debates*, lxxi, 32–60, 163–304, 306–456.
[3] *Senate Debates*, xxiii, 171.

posed on the two islands by the facts of geography. During the war of 1914–18 the ports in question were bases of the highest importance, from which the navy was enabled to defend the western approaches to what was then the United Kingdom. Hence the provision in the Treaty that the harbour defences should remain in charge of British care and maintenance parties and that the British Admiralty should be accorded facilities thereat. But Ireland's national dignity, and her co-equality as a member of the Commonwealth, were safeguarded by a proviso in Article 6 that she should undertake her own coastal defence after a period of five years.

In offering to transfer the ports in 1928, the British Government probably contemplated a similar agreement to that concluded with South Africa in 1922 with regard to Simonstown, whereby the Union makes itself responsible for the maintenance and manning of the forts and guarantees that Simonstown will at all times be in a position to serve as a British naval base. An Anglo-Irish agreement on these lines might have been a practicable proposition in 1928, and, while recognizing existing realities, it would have been no more derogatory to our national status than the Simonstown Agreement is to that of South Africa. But it would have gravely compromised our right to neutrality in war, and with Mr. De Valera's advent to office in 1932 any such solution became out of the question. For he held— and it is, of course, a permissible point of view—that the continued occupation by the British of these ports was an outrage on national sentiment, just as General Hertzog holds that the British Navy's right to use Simonstown is 'a national servitude'. Nevertheless, it is clear that, whether Ireland is at war or is at peace, her only defence against aggression is provided by the British Navy. During the debate on the Agreement Mr. De Valera repeated, with obvious sincerity, his assurance that his Government would not allow their territory to be used as a base of attack against Great Britain. But a moment's reflection will show that his decision to maintain and modernize the three former naval bases does little to enable him to implement that assurance. If the British Navy, even temporarily, lost command of the sea to an enemy which then decided to invade Ireland, it is hardly to be supposed that he would attempt to effect a landing at the three fortified positions instead of at one of the countless other practicable landing-places round the Irish coast, which must remain undefended because they cannot be effectively defended.

Not long after the conclusion of the London Agreements, the Parliamentary Opposition presented Mr. De Valera with an opportunity of capitalizing the popularity which he had obtained by the termination of the economic war and the transfer of the ports. On the 25th May 1938, in the Dáil, a motion relating to the claim by Civil Servants for an independent Arbitration Board was pressed to a division and carried against the Government by 52 votes to 51, the United Ireland Party and the Labour Party joining forces.[1] Two days later the Dáil was dissolved, and, in the course of a statement issued the same evening, Mr. De Valera said:

'During the past six years the Government has been severely handicapped, and the national interest has suffered, by the fact that the Government's parliamentary position was deemed insecure. On two occasions I appealed to the people to set this right. Unfortunately, owing to the system of proportional representation, my appeal on these occasions proved to be ineffective. I now appeal once more.'[2]

However that may be, there can be no doubt that the defeat of the Government on a major issue justified Mr. De Valera in seeking a renewal of confidence at the polls.

Owing, possibly, to the suddenness of the dissolution, the campaign was one of the quietest on record. In the absence of any clear-cut distinction between the policies of the two major parties, the attitude of the Labour Party must have been worth a good many votes to Fianna Fáil. For Labour nominated only thirty candidates, and its manifesto made it clear that, if the party again secured the balance of power, its aim would be to secure a forty-hour week, holidays with pay for all workers, and increases in all the social services.[3] Numbers of people who viewed with alarm the deteriorating financial position of the country, and who felt that the Government party would probably be returned in any case, must have voted for that party in the hope of making the new Administration independent of Labour.

The campaign was notable for two speeches. Speaking in Dublin on the 8th June, the Deputy Prime Minister (Mr. O'Kelly), who, it will be remembered, had been seriously mentioned a short time previously as a possible candidate for the office of President, referred to the London Agreements and said:

'I think that no one will doubt that England and the British Empire is a very powerful—if not the most powerful—political force in the world to-day, and in the last six years look how we whipped John Bull every time. Look at the last agreement we made with her. We

[1] *Dáil Debates*, lxxi, 1865–8. [2] *Irish Independent*, 28 May 1938.
[3] Ibid., 7 June 1938.

won all round us; we wiped her right, left and centre, and, with God's help, we shall do the same again.'[1]

Two days later General Mulcahy administered a dignified rebuke to Mr. O'Kelly for this puerile outburst and stressed the importance of a strong Britain if spiritual values are to be maintained in the modern world.

'If there was one Power in Europe whose strength was important to the maintenance of Christianity, it was Great Britain, with the new rising nationalities of Canada, Australia, South Africa, and New Zealand, and the great English-speaking people of the United States of America. If Great Britain were injured, not alone European civilization, but Christianity itself would be struck a blow from which it would be difficult to recover. Providence would look after Christianity, but it might be many years before civilization as we knew it would recover.'[2]

The general election was held on the 17th June 1938, and the result was as follows, the party strength at the dissolution being given in brackets:

Party	Candidates nominated	Members elected
Fianna Fáil (De Valera)	92	77 (69)
United Ireland Party (Cosgrave)	74	45 (48)
Labour	30	9 (13)
Independents	11	7 (8)
	207	138

Thus, as compared with the election held less than twelve months earlier, Mr. De Valera greatly improved his position, gaining three seats from the Cosgrave Party, four from the Labour Party, and one from the Independents, and having a clear majority of fifteen (exclusive of the Chairman of the Dáil) over all other parties combined. General Mulcahy returned to the House after a year's absence, but Mr. Cecil Lavery, K.C., a member of the Cosgrave Party, lost his seat, and so the Dáil was deprived of the services of one of the most brilliant lawyers in the country. The personnel of the new Administration was unchanged.

Under the new Constitution an election for the Senate must take place not later than ninety days after a dissolution of the Dáil. Hence

---

[1] *Irish Times*, 9 June 1938.   [2] Ibid., 11 June 1938.

the forty-three senators elected on the 31st March had been given a very short run for their money, having met on only ten occasions. The election was completed on the 18th August, and twenty out of the forty-three were newcomers. The changes were largely due to the fact that the Labour Party did not again boycott the proceedings, and to the increased Fianna Fáil representation in the Dáil. Distinguished professional candidates were worsted as before, and Mr. De Valera's nominees were unchanged, as was the membership of the two universities. The result was a political second chamber of the same complexion as the Dáil, more than half the Senators being former members of the Dáil or of the old Senate before it was abolished.

On the 8th August, not long after the general election, the Government published the Report of the Banking Commission, a document of enormous length and of transcendent importance. The Commission was appointed on the 20th November 1934 by the Minister for Finance (Mr. MacEntee), with very wide terms of reference. It was to examine and report on the system of currency, banking, credit, public borrowing and lending, and the pledging of State credit on behalf of agriculture, industry, and the social services, and to consider and report what changes, if any, were necessary or desirable to promote the social and economic welfare of the community and the interests of agriculture and industry. The Commission consisted of twenty-one members, the Chairman being Mr. Joseph Brennan, the Chairman of the Currency Commission; and among its other members were three university Professors of Economics, the Secretary of the Department of Finance and other prominent Civil Servants, a number of bank directors, representatives of Labour, and two outside experts —Professor T. E. Gregory and Mr. Per Jacobsson of the Bank for International Settlements. The Committee reported on the 23rd March 1938, and, as the majority report is signed by no less than sixteen of the twenty-one members, it carries very great authority. A detailed examination of its contents does not fall within the scope of this book, but it has been desirable to refer to it because it consists of an expert survey of the whole economic life of the country. In general it is severely critical of the policy of economic self-sufficiency pursued by Mr. De Valera's Administration since 1932.

The Munich crisis of September 1938 found Ireland unprepared. Speaking in the Dáil on the previous 13th July, Mr. De Valera was unable to give any clear indication of his policy on defence, except that the Government had no commitments in the event of war and would avoid being involved if it could. He agreed, however, that owing to the withdrawal of the British garrisons from our harbours we were 'in a position to approach this whole question from a new angle'.[1] On the 12th September Mr. De Valera was elected President of the League Assembly, and he was therefore absent in Geneva during these anxious days. On the 27th, when war seemed inevitable, he sent a telegram of encouragement to Mr. Chamberlain, imploring him to let nothing daunt him or deflect him in his efforts to secure peace.[2] Nobody, of course, knew whether, in the event of hostilities, Germany would respect Ireland's neutrality, or for how long; and the settlement reached on the last day of September was greeted with almost as much relief in Dublin as in London, though it was tempered by a profound feeling of sympathy with Czechoslovakia, a country with which Ireland has always had much in common. The general indignation at the country's lack of preparedness was expressed in a letter to the press by Dr. O'Higgins, a member of the Opposition Front Bench, when the crisis was over.

'We had no policy, no plan, no aeroplanes, no defence equipment, no gas masks. . . . In the absence of a policy or a plan we sent officers and Civil Servants rushing over to London to hammer on the Admiralty and War Office doors in a panicky endeavour to purchase hundreds of thousands of pounds' worth of aeroplanes, anti-aircraft guns, gas masks, etc., just on the eve of the outbreak, when every nation required all such supplies for themselves.'[3]

Both before the Munich crisis and subsequently Mr. De Valera has continued to keep the partition issue in the forefront of Irish politics. As this difficult problem is dealt with at some length in the Introduction to this book, it will suffice here to give some specimen quotations.

On the 14th June 1938, in an election speech at Dunleary, he is reported to have spoken as follows:

'For twenty years he had said they wanted to be good neighbours with the neighbouring peoples, particularly with the nearest neighbour. Now Britain had realized that, and he was certain that when they got a majority in the North for unity there would be no outside interference.'[4]

This is a very important statement, but it appears to be very largely negatived by other utterances of the same speaker. Thus, on the 22nd November 1938 Mr. De Valera referred to his conversations with British Ministers during the London negotiations in the previous spring, and he continued:

---

[1] *Dáil Debates*, lxxii, 639–716.　　[2] *Irish Press*, 28 September 1938.
[3] *Irish Independent*, 8 October 1938.　　[4] *Irish Times*, 15 June 1938.

'We were told that nothing could be done without the consent of the people of the North, and there are some people who say that Britain could wash her hands of it. The Irish people throughout the world will, nevertheless, hold Britain responsible for creating partition and for continuing it, because they know perfectly well that partition could not continue if the support which it is getting was withdrawn.'[1]

The nearest approach that Mr. De Valera has made to a detailed plan for the ending of partition is that contained in an interview which he gave to a special correspondent of the London *Evening Standard*. This was published on the 17th October 1938 and reproduced in full by the Dublin morning newspapers on the following day. The part of the interview which contains his concrete proposals is as follows:

'Taking into account the prevailing sentiment of the present majority in the Six Counties and bearing in mind also the sentiment of the minority there and the majority in the whole island, here is what I propose. If I could have my own way, I would have immediately a single All-Ireland Parliament, elected on a system of proportional representation so as to be fair to minorities—this might entail a different form of executive. But what I propose, in the existing situation, is not that. I would say to Belfast: "Keep all your present powers. We ask only one thing of you. We think the area you control is not the area which in justice you could claim, even for a local parliament, but we make the concession if you guarantee fair play for the minority and consent to the transfer to an All-Ireland Parliament of the powers now reserved to the Parliament at Westminster."

'I want to make it as easy as possible for Northern Ireland to join us, because it is my fixed belief that, once we are working together and prejudices eliminated, the North would speedily find it more economical and satisfactory to surrender their local parliament altogether and come into a single All-Ireland Parliament.'

Interviewed on the evening that this proposal was published, Lord Craigavon said, 'I can only reiterate the old battle-cry of Northern Ireland—"No Surrender!"'[2]

The controversy about partition was rendered more acute by the conscription issue which arose in the spring of 1939. On the 16th March Nazi Germany completed the destruction of Czechoslovakia, and this act seems to have convinced the British Government that Hitler's word could not be relied on and that war was probably inevi-

[1] *Irish Press*, 23 November 1938.   [2] *Irish Independent*, 18 October 1938.

table. On the 26th April, in the House of Commons, the Prime Minister announced the Government's decision to introduce compulsory military service.[1] Mr. De Valera was due to sail for the United States on the 28th, to open the Irish Pavilion at the New York World's Fair and to undertake a tour in furtherance of his campaign against partition. But the day after Mr. Chamberlain's announcement he informed the Dáil that 'certain grave events which occurred yesterday' had caused the postponement of his mission.[2] Everybody knew that the allusion was to the effect on Northern Ireland of the British Government's decision.

This is a subject which demands clear thinking and plain speech. Conscription is the legal right to compel male citizens of military age to take up arms in defence of their country. In the ultimate, it implies physical force, and therefore it can be resisted only by physical force. Ordinarily, the question of resistance does not arise, since the obligations of citizenship are co-extensive with the rights which it confers. The situation in Northern Ireland is, however, exceptional. The Catholic Nationalists, forming more than one-third of the total population, are condemned to be in a perpetual minority so far as governmental functions are concerned. Notionally, no doubt, they have full citizenship rights equally with the majority, but Lord Craigavon has himself boasted (he used that word) that Northern Ireland has a Protestant Parliament and is a Protestant State.[3]

However that may be, it is not disputable that any attempt to enforce conscription in Northern Ireland would have met with physical resistance on the part of the minority, and the Belfast Government can hardly have been unaware of this fact. The British Government also, one might have supposed, should have profited by its fruitless attempt to impose conscription on the whole of Ireland in April 1918. The results would have been negligible from a military point of view, the German Fuehrer would have been presented with an inestimable piece of propaganda against England, and British prestige would have been lowered throughout the world. As for the majority in the Six Counties, compulsion was presumably unnecessary, since, if the professions of their leaders are to be believed, their 'loyalty' would have rallied them to the colours as one man under the voluntary system.

On the 1st May the six Catholic bishops whose dioceses lie within

---

[1] *House of Commons Debates*, cccxlvi, 1150–4.
[2] *Dáil Debates*, lxxv, 1155.
[3] *House of Commons Debates* (*Northern Ireland*), xvi, 1095 and xvii, 73.

the Six-County area, headed by Cardinal MacRory, issued a statement declaring that they were convinced that any attempt to impose conscription in Northern Ireland would be disastrous and that the British Government stood to lose rather than gain by such an attempt. They also described it as 'an outrage on the national feeling and an aggression upon our national rights'.[1] On the following day Lord Craigavon crossed over to London at the request of the British Government, and, with full knowledge of what the result would be, he pressed for the enforcement of conscription.

Also on the 2nd May, Mr. De Valera stated in the Dáil that his Government had 'protested to the British Government in the strongest terms against the threatened imposition of conscription in that part of our country'; and he later characterized the proposal as 'an act of aggression'.[2] The Dáil, irrespective of party, supported this attitude, and it became obvious that the British Government, by giving heed to Lord Craigavon's reckless importunacy, had allowed a very serious situation to develop. Fortunately, they withdrew in time; for, two days later, when moving the Second Reading of the Military Training Bill, Mr. Chamberlain stated that it had been decided that the Bill should not extend to Northern Ireland. Referring to Lord Craigavon's visit, he said that 'the people of Northern Ireland are above all loyal to the Crown and to the connection with the rest of the United Kingdom, and nothing would cause so much resentment in Ulster (sic) as the suggestion that they should in any way be relieved of burdens or of sacrifices which were being borne by their fellow citizens over here. When I saw Lord Craigavon on this matter, he vehemently asserted that position.' Lord Craigavon stated, however, 'that he would desire to leave the ultimate decision of what should be done in the hands of His Majesty's Government. We warmly welcome this attitude on the part of Lord Craigavon and his Government, an attitude which is inspired by the purest kind of patriotism.'[3] One might comment that, if patriotism of this type were more widespread, there would soon not be much left of the British Commonwealth of Nations.

The question of conscription for Irishmen came up again later, but the principle involved was entirely different. The Military Training Act having become law on the 26th May, Mr. De Valera protested to the British Government against the inclusion of any Irish citizens in the category of British subjects liable for military service. This time,

---

[1] *Irish Independent*, 1 May 1939.
[2] *Dáil Debates*, lxxv, 1415, 1429.
[3] *House of Commons Debates*, cccxlvi, 2103–5.

however, his protest was unavailing.[1] Indeed, it does not appear to be well founded either in equity or in common sense. In spite of Article 1 of the Treaty, Mr. De Valera regards Éire as an independent State (the character of which, whether monarchy or republic, is not designated), in 'external association' with the British Commonwealth. Great Britain and the other members of the Commonwealth regard Éire as a full member of the Commonwealth. Hence Irishmen who choose to go to live in England are not liable to any of the restrictions imposed on aliens. They are clothed with the full legal status of British subjects, on exactly the same footing as Englishmen, Scotsmen, and Welshmen. In these circumstances they can hardly expect to enjoy all the privileges of their status and to repudiate its obligations. To do them justice, the overwhelming majority of them have never attempted to do so. Speaking in the Dáil on the 14th June 1939, Mr. De Valera made it clear that, in his opinion, such people cannot expect to have it both ways, and that his protest was based on the fact that they are treated as British subjects.[2] This is only one of the many contradictions into which he is led by his policy of 'external association'. Actually, the British Government has behaved in a very fair manner as regards Irishmen living in Great Britain. The Act fixes a period of two years as a sufficient indication to reside permanently in Great Britain; moreover, if Irish citizens can show that, even though their period of residence exceeds two years, it has a temporary or exclusively educational purpose, they are not liable to serve. On the 27th September 1939 Mr. De Valera informed the Dáil that, since the outbreak of war, no obstacle had been put in the way of large numbers of Irish citizens with a much longer period of residence than two years returning to this country.[3]

Since Mr. De Valera's anti-partition campaign represented partition as a continuing act of aggression on the part of Great Britain, it was to be expected that it would have repercussions, not only upon the delicate international situation (one of his speeches was quoted by Hitler), but also among the extremists at home. Indeed, the experience of 1932 must have shown him how readily his verbal attacks are supplemented by unofficial physical attacks. During the greater part of 1938 the Irish Republican Army remained comparatively quiescent, their only spectacular exploit being the burning of a number of customs huts along the border on the night of the 29th November. But on the 8th December a body of seven persons (six men and one

---

[1] *Dáil Debates*, lxxvi, 311, 312.   [2] Ibid., lxxvi, 973–4.
[3] Ibid., lxxvii, 192–4.

woman) styling themselves the 'Executive Council of Dáil Éireann, Government of the Republic' issued a Proclamation, which was quoted in full by the Minister for Justice (Mr. Ruttledge) in the Dáil[1] and of which the first paragraph is as follows:

'Dáil Éireann: In consequence of armed opposition ordered and sustained by England, and the defection of elected representatives of the people over the periods since the Republican Proclamation of Easter, 1916, was ratified, three years later, by the newly inaugurated Government of the Irish Republic, we hereby delegate the authority reposed in us to the Army Council, in the spirit of the decision taken by Dáil Éireann in the Spring of 1921, and later endorsed by the Second Dáil.'

This calls for some recapitulation. The Second Dáil was the one which approved the Treaty (7th January 1922). The seven signatories of this Proclamation were all members of this Dáil and voted against the Treaty. After the approval of the Treaty had been overwhelmingly ratified by the people at a general election, the dissident minority appointed a 'President of the Republic', nominated a 'Government' (25th October 1922), and, a few days later, purported to rescind the Dáil resolution approving the Treaty. They could have quoted the authority of their leader at that time for the rescission of the Dáil resolution ('The majority have no right to do wrong'), for their rejection of the will of the people expressed at an election which they had contested ('The people have never a right to do wrong'), and for their reliance on the force supplied by the Irish Republican Army ('Republicans maintain . . . that there are rights which a minority may justly uphold, even by arms, against a majority'). On the 14th November 1925 the 'Army' repudiated the 'Government'. And now, in 1938, this pitiful remnant of a remnant of the Second Dáil, still claiming to be the lawful Government of the Republic of the whole of Ireland, purported afresh to delegate its functions to the Irish Republican Army.

Invested with this spurious authority, the Irish Republican Army, on the 15th January 1939, issued a Proclamation, signed by six signatories, 'on behalf of the Republican Government and the Army Council of the Irish Republican Army'. It was posted up in public places throughout the country, and it was also quoted in full by the Minister for Justice in the Dáil.[2] The concluding paragraph runs:

'We call upon England to withdraw her armed forces, her civilian officials and institutions, and representatives of all kinds from every

[1] *Dáil Debates*, lxxiv, 1285-6.   [2] Ibid., lxxiv, 1288.

part of Ireland as an essential preliminary to arrangements for peace
and friendship between the two countries; and we call upon the people
of all Ireland, at home and in exile, to assist us in the effort we are
about to make, in God's name, to compel that evacuation and to en-
throne the Republic of Ireland.'

At the same time an ultimatum was served on the British Foreign
Secretary (Lord Halifax). According to a statement made by the
Home Secretary in the House of Commons, this ultimatum demanded
an instant withdrawal of British troops from Northern Ireland, giving
a time limit of four days for their departure and threatening England
with reprisals if the ultimatum was not accepted.[1]

Shortly afterwards the Irish Republican Army began its campaign
against England, but not against Scotland or Wales, with which countries it does not, apparently, consider itself to be at war. The technique
has become familiar. Time-bombs are placed in postal packages and
carrier-bicycles, or concealed in suit-cases deposited in railway left-
luggage offices, and there has been a certain amount of sabotage.

It was imperative for Mr. De Valera's Government to meet this
challenge to its authority within the area of its jurisdiction: but the
powers contained in Article 2A of the old Constitution were not reproduced in the new Constitution. Fresh legislation was accordingly
necessary, and on the 8th February 1939 two Bills were introduced in
the Dáil. The first, a Treason Bill, provides for the infliction of the
death penalty for acts of treason as defined in the Constitution. The
other, entitled the Offences Against the State Bill, is roughly analogous to the old Article 2A. It is designed to prevent the usurpation of
the authority of the State, empowers the Government to declare any
particular organization to be unlawful, and authorizes the establishment of special criminal courts. These measures were duly passed by
both Houses and became law, the Treason Bill on the 30th May and
the Offences Against the State Bill on the 14th June.

On the 23rd June, in virtue of the new powers, the Government
issued the Unlawful Organization (Suppression) Order, declaring the
Irish Republican Army to be an unlawful organization; and, on the
same day, the Commissioner of the Civic Guard banned the customary demonstration at Wolfe Tone's grave, which had been arranged
for the following Sunday.[2]

On the final stage of the Offences Against the State Bill in the
Senate, Senator Desmond Fitzgerald, who had been successively
Minister for External Affairs and for Defence in the Cosgrave Ad-

[1] *House of Commons Debates*, cccl, 1047.　[2] *Irish Independent*, 24 June 1939.

ministration, said that, for the well-being and the good name of Ireland, the Government should include in the Bill adequate powers to
deal with men who sheltered behind the security which they found
they had at home to order unfortunate dupes in England to embark
on a career of crime. Senator Sir John Keane followed on the same
lines, but the Minister for Justice merely said in reply that he did not
know but that there might be certain cases *sub judice*, and he thought
it would be most improper for him to go into the merits, or anything
else, of those cases.[1] This reply is the more difficult to understand as
the Minister, being a solicitor, is presumably aware that the fact that
certain cases were *sub judice* need not have prevented him from condemning, on moral grounds, the general results of a campaign undertaken in pursuance of a Proclamation which he himself had read to
the Dáil.

In a further effort to elicit the attitude of the Government, Senators MacDermot and Professor Tierney tabled the following motion
in the Senate:

'That, in the opinion of the Senate, the country is entitled to an
explicit statement from the Government as to the justifiability and the
expediency of bombing activities in Great Britain by Irish citizens.'

Speaking in the debate on the 26th July, Mr. De Valera made a
long speech, in which he expressed surprise at the motion, since he
thought that the Government had made its attitude quite clear.
He referred to the iniquity of partition, the necessity for obedience to
majority rule under the new Constitution, and the injury done to his
own anti-partition policy by the activities of the extremists. But he
nowhere pronounced a forthright condemnation of the bombing outrages on moral grounds.[2] We have indeed travelled far from the day
in March 1924 when the Dáil adjourned, on the motion of Mr.
Cosgrave, 'as an evidence to the British nation and to the civilized
world of the regret and humiliation' felt by the Irish nation over the
shooting by members of the Irish Republican Army of unarmed
British soldiers at Cove.

On the 19th July the Prevention of Violence (Temporary Provisions) Bill was introduced in the House of Commons, 'to prevent the
commission in Great Britain of further acts of violence designed to
influence public opinion or Government policy with respect to Irish
affairs'. It received the Royal Assent on the 28th July, and, under the
powers conferred by it, a number of suspected persons have since
been deported to Ireland.

[1] *Senate Debates*, xxii, 2164–6.   [2] Ibid., xxiii, 998–1006.

The outrages in England continued, and on the 22nd August Mr. De Valera's Government issued two Proclamations, bringing into force Parts V and VI of the Offences Against the State Act. This enabled suspects to be interned without trial, and a special criminal court to be set up. On the 24th August the Special Criminal Court was established, consisting of the five army officers who had formed the Military Tribunal under the old Constitution. The following day there was a terrific bomb explosion in Coventry, which killed five people, wounded about seventy others, and did thousands of pounds' worth of damage.

On the 14th December, at Birmingham Assizes, two Irishmen were convicted of the murder of one of the victims of the Coventry explosion and sentenced to death. On the 22nd January their appeal was dismissed by the Court of Criminal Appeal, and the execution was fixed for the 7th February. The 4th February was the Sunday before Lent, and several of the bishops, in their Lenten Pastorals, renewed the formal condemnation of the Irish Republican Army which had been pronounced by the united Hierarchy some years before and which still stands. As the date of execution approached there was a crescendo of excitement in Ireland. The most strenuous efforts were made to secure a reprieve, and persons of all shades of political opinion and of religious belief participated in them. Mr. De Valera took the question up with the British Government, and the High Commissioner (Mr. Dulanty) interviewed both the Dominions Secretary and the Prime Minister. The efforts were unavailing, the two men were duly executed, and the day of execution was treated almost as a day of national mourning in Ireland. Flags were flown at half-mast, and the Dublin theatres were closed. The closing of shops, however, was to some extent due to the fact that the day in question was Ash Wednesday.

The proscription of the Irish Republican Army in Ireland and the Coventry outrage in England occurred during the fateful closing days of August 1939. The German-Soviet pact of non-aggression was published on the 24th. Next day Great Britain and Poland concluded an agreement for mutual assistance. On the last day of the month the German Minister in Dublin (Dr. Eduard Hempel) called on Mr. De Valera 'to find out what was likely to be the attitude of the Government in the event of a European War'. 'The Minister said that the German attitude towards our country in case of war would be peaceful and that it would respect our neutrality. I replied that, as far as we were concerned, we wished to be at peace with Germany as well as with other States.'[1] On the 1st September, without any declaration of war, the German hordes invaded Poland and began to batter down that historic bulwark of Catholicism and of European civilization against eastern barbarism.

A European war being thus rendered inevitable, the Dáil and Senate met on the 2nd September to enact two Bills which postulated neutrality. The first was designed to remedy a defect in the Constitution, which enabled emergency legislation to be passed for the purpose of securing the public safety in time of war but made no such provision in the case of neutrality during a general war. The Bill extended the phrase 'time of war' to mean a time when there is taking place an armed conflict in which the State is not a participant. The second Bill contained the emergency legislation. As no political party was opposed to the policy of neutrality, both Bills were passed without a division; but one or two speakers referred to the possible effect of that policy on the ultimate unity of Ireland.

Introducing the first Bill, Mr. De Valera said that it was only natural that, as individual human beings, they should sympathize with one side or the other. He knew that there were very strong sympathies in regard to the present issues, but he did not think that anybody, no matter what his feelings might be, would suggest that the official policy of the State should be other than what the Government would suggest. He continued:

'We, of all nations, know what force used by a stronger nation against a weaker one means. We have known what invasion and partition mean; we are not forgetful of our own history, and, as long as our own country, or any part of it, is subject to force, the application of force, by a stronger nation, it is only natural that our people, whatever sympathies they might have in a conflict like the present, should look at their own country first and should, accordingly, in looking at their own country, consider what its interests should be and what its interests are.'[2]

On the 3rd September war was declared on Germany by Great Britain and France, and the British declaration, of course, involved Northern Ireland in belligerency. The remaining member-States of the Commonwealth—Australia, New Zealand, South Africa, and Canada—in the exercise of their constitutional right as free nations, successively ranged themselves on the side of Great Britain. And so began a conflict from the results of which Ireland cannot remain immune, and of which as yet no man can see the end.

[1] *Senate Debates*, xxiii, 1051.   [2] *Dáil Debates*, lxxvii, 1–8.

2Q

APPENDICES

PERSONNEL OF THE SENATE

The personnel of the Senate throughout its existence will be found exhibited in the following lists. The figure in brackets after the name of each Senator indicates his period of office in years, dating from the beginning of the appropriate Triennial Period. The Triennial Periods commenced on the 6th December 1922, the 6th December 1925, and so on.

FIRST TRIENNIAL PERIOD—1922–5

John Bagwell (6)
Dr. Henry L. Barniville (3)
William Barrington (9)
T. W. Westropp Bennett (3)
Rt. Hon. H. G. Burgess (6)
Richard A. Butler (3)
Mrs. E. Costello (9)
John J. Counihan (3)
Peter De Loughry (3)
Ellen, Countess of Desart (12)
James G. Douglas (9)
James C. Dowdall (12)
Michael Duffy (9)
The Earl of Dunraven (12)
Sir T. Grattan Esmonde, Bart. (12)
Sir Nugent Everard, Bart. (6)
Edmund W. Eyre (6)
Thomas Farren (9)
Martin Fitzgerald (12)
Baron Glenavy (6)
Dr. Oliver St. J. Gogarty (6)

James P. Goodbody (6)
The Earl of Granard (12)
Mrs. Alice Stopford Green (9)
Captain J. H. Greer (6)[1]
Sir John Purser Griffith (9)
Henry S. Guinness (12)
Benjamin Haughton (6)
The Marquess of Headfort (6)
Cornelius J. Irwin (3)
Arthur Jackson (6)
Rt. Hon. Andrew Jameson (6)
Sir John Keane, Bart. (12)
Patrick W. Kenny (9)
The Earl of Kerry (12)[2]
Thomas Linehan (3)
Joseph C. Love (3)
Edward MacEvoy (3)
James MacKean (9)
John MacLoughlin (9)
Edward MacLysaght (3)
Thomas MacPartlin (9)
Rt. Hon. Sir Bryan Mahon (6)

[1] Afterwards Sir Henry Greer.
[2] Afterwards the Marquess of Lansdowne.

Edward Mansfield (3)
The Earl of Mayo (12)
William J. Molloy (9)
Colonel Maurice Moore (9)
James Moran (12)
George Nesbitt (3)
Michael O'Dea (3)
John T. O'Farrell (3)
Brian O'Rourke (9)

Dr. William O'Sullivan (9)
James J. Parkinson (3)
Sir Horace Plunkett (12)
Sir W. Hutcheson Poë, Bart. (12)
Mrs. J. Wyse Power (12)
Dr. George Sigerson (12)
The Earl of Wicklow (6)
William Butler Yeats (6)

Senator Lord Glenavy and Senator Douglas were elected respectively Chairman and Vice-Chairman.

The following vacancies occurred during the First Triennial Period:

Edward Mansfield (resigned 12th December 1922, without having taken his seat)
Thomas MacPartlin (died 20th October 1923)
Sir Horace Plunkett (resigned 28th November 1923)
Sir William Hutcheson Poë, Bart. (resigned 9th December 1924)
Dr. George Sigerson (died 17th February 1925)

The following were elected to fill these vacancies respectively:

William Cummins (21st February 1923)
Thomas Foran (28th November 1923)
Samuel L. Brown, K.C. (12th December 1923)
Dr. Douglas Hyde (4th February 1925)
John O'Neill (5th March 1925)

At the Triennial Election, 1925, the following eleven outgoing Senators failed to secure re-election:

Samuel L. Brown, K.C.
Richard A. Butler
Peter De Loughry
Dr. Douglas Hyde
Cornelius J. Irwin
Joseph C. Love

Edward MacEvoy
Edward MacLysaght
George Nesbitt
Michael O'Dea
John O'Neill

SECOND TRIENNIAL PERIOD—1925-8

John Bagwell (3)
Dr. Henry L. Barniville (12)
William Barrington (6)
Sir Edward Bellingham, Bart. (12)

T. W. Westropp Bennett (9)
Sir Edward Coey Bigger (9)
Rt. Hon. H. G. Burgess (3)
Mrs. E. Costello (6)

John J. Counihan (6)
William Cummins (12)
Ellen, Countess of Desart (9)
James Dillon (12)
James G. Douglas (6)
James C. Dowdall (9)
Michael Duffy (6)
The Earl of Dunraven (9)
Sir T. Grattan Esmonde, Bart. (9)
Sir Nugent Everard, Bart. (3)
Edmund W. Eyre (3)
Michael Fanning (12)
Thomas Farren (6)
Martin Fitzgerald (9)
Thomas Foran (12)
Baron Glenavy (3)
Dr. Oliver St. J. Gogarty (3)
James P. Goodbody (3)
The Earl of Granard (9)
Mrs. Alice Stopford Green (6)
Sir Henry Greer (3)
Sir John Purser Griffith (6)
Henry S. Guinness (9)
Benjamin Haughton (3)
The Marquess of Headfort (3)
Sir William B. Hickie (12)

Arthur Jackson (3)
Rt. Hon. Andrew Jameson (3)
Sir John Keane, Bart. (9)
Cornelius Kennedy (12)
Patrick W. Kenny (6)
The Earl of Kerry (9)
Thomas Linehan (12)
Francis MacGuinness (9)
James MacKean (6)
John MacLoughlin (6)
Rt. Hon. Sir Bryan Mahon (3)
The Earl of Mayo (9)
William J. Molloy (6)
Colonel Maurice Moore (6)
James Moran (9)
Joseph O'Connor (12)
John T. O'Farrell (12)
Michael F. O'Hanlon (12)
Stephen O'Mara (12)
Brian O'Rourke (6)
Dr. William O'Sullivan (6)
James J. Parkinson (12)
Mrs. J. Wyse Power (9)
Thomas Toal (12)
The Earl of Wicklow (3)
William Butler Yeats (3)

Senator Lord Glenavy and Senator T. W. Westropp Bennett were elected respectively Chairman and Vice-Chairman.

The following vacancies occurred during the Second Triennial Period:

The Earl of Dunraven (resigned 27th January 1926)
Stephen O'Mara (died 26th July 1926)
Martin Fitzgerald (died 9th March 1927)
The Earl of Mayo (died 31st December 1927)

The following were elected to fill these vacancies respectively:

Samuel L. Brown, K.C. (10th February 1926)
Patrick J. Brady (26th January 1927)
Patrick J. Hooper (23rd March 1927)
Sir Walter Nugent, Bart. (1st March 1928)

At the Triennal Election, 1928, the following four outgoing Senators failed to secure re-election:

Patrick J. Brady
Sir Nugent Everard, Bart.
Benjamin Haughton
The Earl of Wicklow

The following eight outgoing Senators did not seek re-election:

Rt. Hon. H. G. Burgess   Sir Henry Greer
Edmund W. Eyre   The Marquess of Headfort
Baron Glenavy   Arthur Jackson
James P. Goodbody   William Butler Yeats

THIRD TRIENNIAL PERIOD—1928–31

John Bagwell (6)
Dr. Henry L. Barniville (9)
William Barrington (3)
Sir Edward Bellingham, Bart. (9)
T. W. Westropp Bennett (6)
Sir Edward Coey Bigger (6)
Samuel L. Brown, K.C. (6)
Alfred Byrne (6)
Mrs. Kathleen Clarke (9)
Michael Comyn, K.C. (3)
Joseph Connolly (9)
Mrs. E. Costello (3)
John J. Counihan (3)
William Cummins (9)
Ellen, Countess of Desart (6)
James Dillon (9)
James G. Douglas (3)
James C. Dowdall (6)
Michael Duffy (3)
Sir T. Grattan Esmonde, Bart. (6)
Michael Fanning (9)
Thomas Farren (3)
Thomas Foran (9)
Dr. Oliver St. J. Gogarty (6)
The Earl of Granard (6)
Mrs. Alice Stopford Green (3)
Sir John Purser Griffith (3)

Henry S. Guinness (6)
Sir William B. Hickie (9)
Patrick J. Hooper (3)
Rt. Hon. Andrew Jameson (6)
Thomas Johnson (6)
Sir John Keane, Bart. (6)
Cornelius Kennedy (9)
Patrick W. Kenny (3)
The Marquess of Lansdowne (6)
Thomas Linehan (9)
Seán E. MacEllin (3)
The McGillycuddy of the Reeks (3)
Francis MacGuinness (6)
James MacKean (3)
John MacLoughlin (3)
Rt. Hon. Sir Bryan Mahon (6)
Seán Milroy (9)
William J. Molloy (3)
Colonel Maurice Moore (3)
James Moran (6)
Sir Walter Nugent, Bart. (3)
Joseph O'Connor (9)
Joseph O'Doherty (9)
John T. O'Farrell (9)
Michael F. O'Hanlon (9)
Brian O'Rourke (3)
Dr. William O'Sullivan (3)

James J. Parkinson (9)   William Sears (9)
Mrs. J. Wyse Power (6)   Thomas Toal (9)
Seumas Robinson (9)   Richard Wilson (6)

Senator T. W. Westropp Bennett and Senator Patrick W. Kenny were elected respectively Chairman and Vice-Chairman. On the death of Senator Kenny, Senator Patrick J. Hooper was elected Vice-Chairman.

The following vacancies occurred during the Third Triennial Period:

William Sears (died 23rd March 1929)
Mrs. Alice Stopford Green (died 28th May 1929)
The Marquess of Lansdowne (resigned 5th June 1929)
Sir Nugent Everard, Bart. (died 12th July 1929)
Sir Bryan Mahon (died 24th September 1930)
Patrick W. Kenny (died 22nd April 1931)
Patrick J. Hooper (died 6th September 1931)

The following were elected to fill these vacancies respectively:

Sir Nugent Everard, Bart. (10th April 1929)
Miss Kathleen Browne (20th June 1929)
Laurence O'Neill (20th June 1929)
Richard A. Butler (23rd October 1929)
Michael Staines (12th December 1930)
Arthur R. Vincent (28th May 1931)
George Crosbie (5th November 1931)

At the Triennial Election, 1931, the following five outgoing Senators failed to secure re-election:

William Barrington
Richard A. Butler
George Crosbie
William J. Molloy
Sir Walter Nugent, Bart.

FOURTH TRIENNIAL PERIOD—1931–4

John Bagwell (3)   Miss Kathleen Browne (3)
Dr. Henry L. Barniville (6)   Rt. Hon. Alfred Byrne (3)
Sir Edward Bellingham, Bart. (6) Mrs. Kathleen Clarke (6)
T. W. Westropp Bennett (3)   Michael Comyn, K.C. (9)
Sir Edward Coey Bigger (3)   Joseph Connolly (6)
Samuel L. Brown, K.C. (3)   John J. Counihan (9)

Mrs. E. Costello (3)
William Cummins (6)
Ellen, Countess of Desart (3)
James Dillon (6)
James G. Douglas (9)
James C. Dowdall (3)
Michael Duffy (9)
Sir T. Grattan Esmonde, Bart. (3)
Michael Fanning (6)
Thomas Farren (9)
Thomas Foran (6)
Hugh Garahan (9)
Dr. Oliver St. J. Gogarty (3)
The Earl of Granard (3)
Sir John Purser Griffith (9)
Henry S. Guinness (3)
Sir William B. Hickie (6)
Rt. Hon. Andrew Jameson (3)
Thomas Johnson (3)
Sir John Keane, Bart. (3)
Cornelius Kennedy (6)
Thomas Linehan (6)
Seán E. MacEllin (9)
The McGillycuddy of the Reeks (9)

Francis MacGuinness (3)
James MacKean (9)
John MacLoughlin (9)
Daniel H. MacParland (9)
Seán Milroy (6)
Colonel Maurice Moore (9)
James Moran (3)
Joseph O'Connor (6)
Joseph O'Doherty (6)
John T. O'Farrell (6)
Michael F. O'Hanlon (6)
Laurence O'Neill (9)
Brian O'Rourke (9)
Dr. William O'Sullivan (6)
James J. Parkinson (6)
Mrs. J. Wyse Power (3)
William Quirke (9)
David L. Robinson (9)
Seumas Robinson (6)
Seumas Ryan (9)
Michael Staines (9)
Thomas Toal (6)
Arthur R. Vincent (9)
Richard Wilson (3)

Senator T. W. Westropp Bennett and Senator M. F. O'Hanlon were elected respectively Chairman and Vice-Chairman.

The following vacancies occurred during the Fourth Triennial Period:

The Rt. Hon. Alfred Byrne (resigned 10th December 1931)
Joseph O'Doherty (deemed to have vacated his seat, 24th January 1933, on being elected a member of the Dáil)
The Countess of Desart (died 29th June 1933)
Seumas Ryan (died 30th June 1933)
Arthur R. Vincent (resigned 21st February 1934)
George Crosbie (died 28th November 1934)
Francis MacGuinness (died 30th November 1934)

The following were elected to fill the first five of these vacancies respectively:

George Crosbie (2nd January 1932)
Edmund J. Duggan (19th April 1933)

Ernest Blythe (2nd January 1934)
Raphael P. Keyes (2nd January 1934)
Patrick Lynch, K.C. (28th September 1934)

No by-elections were rendered necessary by the deaths of Senator George Crosbie and Senator Francis MacGuinness. Both these Senators were due to retire at the end of the current Triennial Period. Neither had offered himself for re-election and at the time of their deaths the Triennial Election was in progress.

At the Triennial Election, 1934, the following four outgoing Senators failed to secure re-election:

Mrs. E. Costello
Sir T. Grattan Esmonde, Bart.
Sir John Keane, Bart.
James Moran

The following four outgoing Senators did not seek re-election:

George Crosbie
The Earl of Granard
Henry S. Guinness
Francis MacGuinness

FIFTH TRIENNIAL PERIOD—1934–6

(The Senate was abolished by the enactment on the 29th May 1936 of the Constitution (Amendment No. 24) Act, 1936)

John Bagwell (6)
Dr. Henry L. Barniville (3)
Patrick F. Baxter (9)
Sir Edward Bellingham, Bart. (3)
T. W. Westropp Bennett (9)
Sir Edward Coey Bigger (3)
Ernest Blythe (9)
James J. Boyle (9)
Samuel L. Brown, K.C. (6)
Miss Kathleen Browne (9)
Mrs. Kathleen Clarke (3)
Michael Comyn, K.C. (6)
Joseph Connolly (3)
John J. Counihan (6)
William Cummins (3)
James Dillon (3)

James G. Douglas (6)
James C. Dowdall (9)
Michael Duffy (6)
Edmund J. Duggan (9)
Michael Fanning (3)
Thomas Farren (6)
Seumas Fitzgerald (9)
Thomas Foran (3)
Hugh Garahan (6)
Dr. Oliver St. J. Gogarty (9)
Sir John Purser Griffith (6)
Denis D. Healy (9)
Sir William B. Hickie (3)
Thomas V. Honan (9)
Rt. Hon. Andrew Jameson (9)
Thomas Johnson (9)

Cornelius Kennedy (3)

Thomas Kennedy (9)

Raphael P. Keyes (9)

Thomas Linehan (3)

Patrick Lynch, K.C. (9)

Seán E. MacEllin (6)

The McGillycuddy of the Reeks (6)

James MacKean (6)

John MacLoughlin (6)

Daniel H. MacParland (6)

Seán Milroy (3)

Colonel Maurice Moore (6)

Joseph O'Connor (3)

John T. O'Farrell (3)

Michael F. O'Hanlon (3)

Pádraic Ó Máille (9)

Laurence O'Neill (6)

Brian O'Rourke (6)

Dr. William O'Sullivan (3)

James J. Parkinson (3)

Mrs. J. Wyse Power (9)

William Quirke (6)

David L. Robinson (6)

Seumas Robinson (3)

Thomas Ruane (9)

Michael Staines (6)

Thomas Toal (3)

Richard Wilson (9)

Senator T. W. Westropp Bennett and Senator Michael Comyn, K.C., were elected respectively Chairman and Vice-Chairman. On the resignation of Senator Comyn, Senator David L. Robinson was elected Vice-Chairman.

The following vacancies occurred after the commencement of the Fifth Triennial Period:

Seumas Robinson (resigned 11th December 1935)

Michael Comyn, K.C. (deemed to have vacated his seat, 24th February 1936, on being appointed a Circuit Judge)

Owing to the abolition of the Senate, these two vacancies were not filled.

APPENDIX B

TABULAR STATEMENT OF BILLS (OTHER THAN MONEY BILLS) RECEIVED FROM THE DAIL

1 Year	2 Number of Bills received	3 Number of Bills amended	4 Number of amendments	5 Agreed to by Dáil	6 Agreed to as amended by Dáil, Senate concurring	7 Not agreed to by Dáil, but amendment made by Dáil in lieu, Senate concurring	8 Not agreed to by Dáil and not insisted on by Senate	9 Not agreed to by Dáil. Bills passed under Article 38a of Constitution	10 Further amendments made by Senate and agreed to by Dáil	11 Consequential amendments made by Dáil, Senate concurring
1922	3	1	1	1						
1923	47	22	171	156	6	2	7		2	1
1924	48	19	291	278	6		7			1
1925	41	15	71	68			3			
1926	36	14	139	137		1	1			
1927	24	11	196	191	2		3		3	
1928	39	11	85	79			6			
1929	36	13	77	74	1		2			
1930	27	10	94	88	3	1	2			
1931	36	6	21	21						
1932	23	8	142	115	2		6	19	2	
1933	47	22	254	233	1	1	19		1	
1934	44	26	230	223			7			
1935	31	4	59	55			4			
1936	7									
Total	489	182	1,831	1,719	21	5	67	19	8	2

APPENDIX C

LIST OF BILLS AMENDED BY THE SENATE

Year	Title of Bill	Number of amendments inserted	Agreement or otherwise by Dáil, etc.
1922	Adaptation of Enactments Bill	1	Agreed to.
1923	Censorship of Films Bill	1	Not agreed to. Dáil made an amendment in lieu and a consequential amendment. Amendment in lieu and consequential amendment agreed to by Senate, and further amendment inserted. Further amendment agreed to by Dáil.
	Civic Guard (Acquisition of Premises) Bill	1	Agreed to.
	Civic Guard (Temporary Provisions) Bill	3	Agreed to.
	Civil Service Regulation (No. 2) Bill	7	5 agreed to; 2 not agreed to and not insisted on by Senate.
	Coroners (Qualification) Bill	1	Agreed to.
	Courts of Justice Bill	44	41 agreed to; 1 agreed to as amended by Dáil; 1 not agreed to; and 1 not agreed to but amendment made by Dáil in lieu. Senate agreed to the amendment as amended by Dáil and to the amendment in lieu, and did not insist on the amendment not agreed to.

Bill	No.	Disposition
Damage to Property (Compensation) Bill	16	12 agreed to; 4 agreed to as amended by Dáil. Senate agreed to the amendments as amended by Dáil, and inserted 1 further amendment. Further amendment agreed to by Dáil.
District Justices (Temporary Provisions) Bill	5	Agreed to.
Electoral Bill	15	14 agreed to; 1 agreed to as amended by Dáil. Senate agreed to the amendment as amended by Dáil.
Enforcement of Law (Occasional Powers) Bill	7	Agreed to.
Fisheries Bill	1	Not agreed to; amended by Senate and again not agreed to. Senate did not insist.
Land Bill	27	Agreed to.
Land Law (Commission) Bill	2	Agreed to.
Local Government (Collection of Rates) Bill	6	5 agreed to; 1 not agreed to. Senate did not insist.
Local Government Electors Registration Bill	1	Not agreed to. Senate did not insist.
Local Government (Temporary Provisions) Bill	4	Agreed to.
Ministers and Secretaries Bill	10	Agreed to.
National Health Insurance Bill	1	Not agreed to. Senate did not insist.
Prevention of Electoral Abuses Bill	3	Agreed to.
Public Safety (Emergency Powers) Bill	13	Agreed to.

Year	Title of Bill	Number of amendments inserted	Agreement or otherwise by Dáil, etc.
1923	Public Safety (Powers of Arrest and Detention) Temporary Bill	2	Agreed to.
	Unemployment Insurance Bill	1	Agreed to.
1924	Agricultural Produce (Eggs) Bill	12	Agreed to.
	Criminal Justice (Administration) Bill	8	Agreed to.
	Dáil Eireann Courts Winding-up Act, 1923, Amendment Bill	1	Agreed to.
	Dairy Produce Bill	43	42 agreed to; 1 agreed to as amended by Dáil, which made a consequential amendment. Senate agreed to the amendment as amended by Dáil and to the consequential amendment.
	Dublin Port and Docks Bill	11	Agreed to.
	Dublin Reconstruction (Emergency Provisions) Bill	13	Agreed to.
	Enforcement of Law (Occasional Powers) Bill	4	Agreed to.
	Gárda Síochána Bill	6	Agreed to.
	Housing (Building Facilities) Bill	5	Agreed to.
	Intoxicating Liquor (General) Bill	12	9 agreed to; 3 not agreed to. After conference, Dáil agreed to 2 and disagreed with remaining 1. Senate did not insist.

	Bill		
	Juries (Amendment) Bill	3	Agreed to.
	Live Stock Breeding Bill	19	Agreed to.
	Local Government Bill	109	98 agreed to; 5 agreed to as amended by Dáil; 6 not agreed to. Senate agreed to the amendments as amended by Dáil and did not insist on the amendments not agreed to.
	Medical Bill	1	Agreed to.
	National Health Insurance Bill	4	Agreed to.
	Old Age Pensions Bill	3	Agreed to.
	Police Forces Amalgamation Bill	1	Agreed to.
	Public Safety (Punishment of Offences) Temporary Bill	8	Agreed to.
	Railways Bill	28	Agreed to.
1925	Acquisition of Land (Allotments) Bill	1	Agreed to.
	Arterial Drainage Bill	4	Agreed to.
	Censorship of Films (Amendment) Bill	2	Agreed to.
	Constitution (Amendment No. 1) Bill	2	Agreed to.
	Electricity Supply (Special Powers) Bill	1	Agreed to.
	Firearms Bill	1	Agreed to.
	Fisheries Bill	15	13 agreed to; 2 not agreed to. Senate did not insist.
	Local Authorities (Combined Purchasing) Bill	7	6 agreed to; 1 not agreed to. Senate did not insist.

Year	Title of Bill	Number of amendments inserted	Agreement or otherwise by Dáil, etc.
1925	Oil in Navigable Waters Bill	1	Agreed to.
	Prisons (Visiting Committees) Bill	1	Agreed to.
	School Attendance Bill	1	Agreed to.
	Shannon Electricity Bill	9	Agreed to.
	Statistics Bill	11	Agreed to.
	Street Trading Bill	4	Agreed to.
	Treasonable Offences Bill	11	Agreed to.
1926	Betting Bill	4	Agreed to.
	Constitution (Amendment No. 2) Bill	2	Agreed to.
	Court Officers Bill	24	Agreed to.
	Enforcement of Court Orders Bill	7	Agreed to.
	Immature Spirits (Restriction) Bill	2	Agreed to.
	Increase of Rent and Mortgage Interest (Restrictions) Bill	7	Agreed to.
	Industrial and Commercial Property (Protection) Bill	70	Agreed to.
	Juries (Dublin) Bill	1	Agreed to.
	Local Authorities (Officers and Employees) Bill	3	Agreed to.
	Local Government Bill	9	8 agreed to; 1 not agreed to. Senate did not insist.

	Bill	No.	Outcome
	Railways (Existing Officers and Servants) Bill	1	Agreed to.
	Shop Hours (Drapery Trades, Dublin and Districts) Bill	2	Both disagreed with. After conference, 1 insisted on by Senate and agreed to by Dáil; 1 amended by Senate and agreed to by Dáil.
	Tariff Commission Bill	3	2 agreed to; 1 not agreed to but amendment made by Dáil in lieu. Senate agreed to amendment in lieu.
1927	Wireless Telegraphy Bill	4	Agreed to.
	Agricultural Credit Bill	32	Agreed to.
	Barrow Drainage Bill	10	Agreed to.
	Circuit Court Appeals Bill	1	Agreed to.
	Currency Bill	33	Agreed to.
	Dentists Bill	8	4 agreed to by Dáil; 1 agreed to as amended by Dáil; 3 not agreed to. Senate agreed to the amendment as amended by Dáil, did not insist on the 3 amendments with which the Dáil had disagreed, and inserted 3 further amendments. These were agreed to by Dáil.
	Electricity (Supply) Bill	54	Agreed to.
	Intoxicating Liquor Bill	28	Agreed to.
	Juries Bill	13	12 agreed to; 1 agreed to as amended by Dáil. Senate agreed to the amendment as amended by Dáil.

Year	Title of Bill	Number of amendments inserted	Agreement or otherwise by Dáil, etc.
1927	Land Bill	13	Agreed to.
	Medical Practitioners Bill	1	Agreed to.
	Railways (Road Motor Services) Bill	3	Agreed to.
1928	Arterial Drainage (Minor Schemes) Bill	15	10 agreed to; 5 not agreed to. Senate did not insist.
	Censorship of Publications Bill	17	Agreed to.
	Constitution (Amendment No. 12) Bill	4	Agreed to.
	Cork City Management Bill	4	Agreed to.
	Courts of Justice Bill	1	Agreed to.
	Creamery Bill	6	Agreed to.
	Forestry Bill	21	Agreed to.
	Gas Regulation Bill	3	2 agreed to; 1 not agreed to. Senate did not insist.
	Legal Practitioners (Qualification) Bill	4	Agreed to.
	Local Government (Rates on Small Dwellings) Bill	8	Agreed to.
	Slaughtered Animals (Compensation) Bill	2	Agreed to.
1929	Agricultural Produce (Fresh Meat) Bill	6	Agreed to.
	Game Preservation Bill	7	6 agreed to; 1 agreed to as amended by Dáil. Senate insisted on amendment in its original form. After conference, Senate agreed to the amendment as amended by Dáil.

Bill	No.	Result
Housing Bill	1	Agreed to.
Illegitimate Children (Affiliation Orders) Bill	2	Agreed to.
Industrial and Commercial Property (Protection) (Amendment) Bill	1	Agreed to.
Intoxicating Liquor (Amendment) (No. 2) Bill	2	Agreed to.
Juries (Protection) Bill	8	Agreed to.
Legitimacy Bill	1	Agreed to.
Local Government (Dublin) Bill	37	Agreed to.
National Monuments Bill	6	4 agreed to; 2 not agreed to. Senate did not insist.
Public Charitable Hospitals (Temporary Provisions) Bill	2	Agreed to.
Seanad Bye-Elections Bill	1	Agreed to.
Totalisator Bill	3	Agreed to.
1930 Agriculture Bill	1	Agreed to.
Apprenticeship Bill	8	Agreed to.
Betting Bill	9	Agreed to.
Currency (Amendment) Bill	4	Agreed to.
Electoral (Dublin Commercial) Bill	6	Agreed to.
Land Bill	7	Agreed to.
Sea Fisheries Bill	1	Agreed to.

Year	Title of Bill	Number of amendments inserted	Agreement or otherwise by Dáil, etc.
1930	Town Tenants Bill	36	32 agreed to; 3 agreed to as amended by Dáil; 1 not agreed to but amendment made by Dáil in lieu. Senate agreed to the amendments as amended by Dáil and to the amendment in lieu.
	Veterinary Surgeons Bill	3	1 agreed to; 2 not agreed to. Senate did not insist.
1931	Vocational Education Bill	19	Agreed to.
	Agricultural Produce (Potatoes) Bill	2	Agreed to.
	Housing (Miscellaneous Provisions) Bill	12	Agreed to.
	Merchandise Marks Bill	2	Agreed to.
	Public Charitable Hospitals (Amendment) (No. 2) Bill	2	Agreed to.
	Railways (Valuation for Rating) Bill	1	Agreed to.
	Tourist Traffic Development Bill	2	Agreed to.
1932	Agricultural Produce (Cereals) Bill	44	29 agreed to; 15 not agreed to. Bill passed (with the 29 agreed amendments) under Article 38A of the Constitution.
	Constitution (Removal of Oath) Bill	4	Not agreed to. Bill passed under Article 38A of the Constitution.

Bill	No.	Notes
Control of Manufactures Bill	29	21 agreed to; 8 not agreed to; 1 consequential amendment made by Dáil. Senate did not insist on 6 of the 8 amendments not agreed to by Dáil, but insisted on 2. Senate did not agree to consequential amendment made by Dáil, but inserted an amendment in lieu and a further consequential amendment. Amendment in lieu and further consequential amendment agreed to by Dáil; 2 amendments on which Senate had insisted also agreed to by Dáil, with amendments. Senate agreed to the amendments as amended by Dáil.
Control of Prices Bill	34	Agreed to.
Dairy Produce (Price Stabilisation) Bill	15	Agreed to.
Eucharistic Congress (Miscellaneous Provisions) Bill	3	Agreed to.
Housing (Financial and Miscellaneous Provisions) Bill	12	Agreed to.
Therapeutic Substances Bill	1	Agreed to.
1933		
Agricultural Products (Regulation of Export) Bill	6	Agreed to.
Approved Investments Bill	1	Agreed to.
Cement (No. 2) Bill	7	6 agreed to; 1 not agreed to. Senate did not insist.

Year	Title of Bill	Number of amendments inserted	Agreement or otherwise by Dáil, etc.
1933	Constitution (Amendment No. 22) Bill	1	Agreed to.
	Cork Tramways (Employees' Compensation) Bill	1	Agreed to.
	Damage to Property (Compensation) (Amendment) (No. 2) Bill	1	Agreed to.
	Dangerous Drugs Bill	2	Agreed to.
	Harbours (Regulation of Rates) Bill	9	Agreed to.
	Horse Breeding Bill	5	Agreed to.
	Land Bill	31	18 agreed to; 13 not agreed to. Senate did not insist, but inserted an amendment in lieu of 1 of those not agreed to. Dáil agreed to amendment in lieu.
	Local Services (Temporary Economies) (No. 2) Bill	9	Agreed to.
	Moneylenders (No. 2) Bill	16	Agreed to.
	Musk Rats Bill	3	Agreed to.
	National Health Insurance Bill	7	Agreed to.
	Public Hospitals Bill	7	3 agreed to; 4 not agreed to. Senate did not insist.
	Public Services (Temporary Economies) Bill	4	1 agreed to; 2 not agreed to; 1 not agreed to but amendment made by Dáil in lieu. Senate agreed to the amendment in lieu and insisted on the 2 others not agreed to. Dáil agreed.

Bill	No.	Status
Railways Bill	19	18 agreed to; 1 not agreed to. Senate did not insist.
Road Traffic Bill	59	Agreed to.
Road Transport Bill	11	Agreed to.
Town and Regional Planning Bill	27	Agreed to.
Unemployment Assistance Bill	4	Agreed to.
Workmen's Compensation Bill	24	22 agreed to; 1 agreed to as amended by Dáil; 1 not agreed to. Senate agreed to the amendment as amended by Dáil and did not insist on the amendment not agreed to.
1934		
Acquisition of Land (Allotments) (Amendment) Bill	4	Agreed to.
Agricultural Co-operative Societies (Debentures) Bill	7	Agreed to.
Agricultural Produce (Cereals) Bill	16	Agreed to.
Aliens Bill	6	Agreed to.
Children Bill	3	Agreed to.
Control of Imports Bill	11	Agreed to.
Control of Manufactures Bill	12	Agreed to.
Criminal Law Amendment Bill	1	Not agreed to. Senate did not insist.
Defence Forces (Temporary Provisions) Bill	1	Agreed to.
Defence Forces (Temporary Provisions) (No. 2) Bill	1	Not agreed to. Senate did not insist but made an amendment in lieu. Amendment in lieu agreed to by Dáil.

Year	Title of Bill	Number of amendments inserted	Agreement or otherwise by Dáil, etc.
1934	Electoral (Revision of Constituencies) Bill	4	Not agreed to. Senate did not insist but made 1 further amendment. Further amendment agreed to by Dáil.
	Electricity (Supply) (Amendment No. 2) Bill	2	Agreed to.
	Industrial Alcohol Bill	2	Agreed to.
	Irish Nationality and Citizenship Bill	30	Agreed to.
	Military Service Pensions Bill	9	Agreed to.
	Milk and Dairies Bill	16	15 agreed to; 1 not agreed to. Senate did not insist.
	Pigs and Bacon Bill	46	Agreed to.
	Public Assistance (Acquisition of Land) Bill	2	1 agreed to; 1 not agreed to. Senate did not insist, but inserted an amendment in lieu. Amendment in lieu not agreed to by Dáil. Senate did not insist.
	Public Dance Halls Bill	2	Agreed to.
	Registration of Maternity Homes Bill	1	Agreed to.
	Road Transport Bill	2	Agreed to.
	Sale of Food and Drugs (Milk) Bill	1	Agreed to.
	Shannon Fisheries Bill	5	Agreed to.
	Sheepskin (Control of Export) Bill	1	Agreed to.
	Slaughter of Cattle and Sheep Bill	43	Agreed to.

1935	Tobacco Bill	2	Agreed to.
	Conditions of Employment Bill	32	29 agreed to; 3 not agreed to. Senate did not insist.
	Dairy Produce (Price Stabilisation) Bill	17	Agreed to.
	Road Transport Bill	1	Agreed to.
	Widows' and Orphans' Pensions Bill	9	8 agreed to; 1 not agreed to. Senate did not insist.

APPENDIX D

MONEY BILLS RECEIVED BY THE SENATE

Year	Number of Bills	Number of Bills to which recom- mendations made	Number of recommendations	Accepted by Dáil	Rejected by Dáil
1922	1				
1923	11	3	9	9	
1924	5	1	2	2	
1925	7	1	1	1	
1926	5	1	1	1	
1927	6				
1928	6	1	1	1	
1929	8	2	4	3	
1930	3				1
1931	13				
1932	10	4	24	12	12
1933	12	3	5	5	
1934	11	1	5	1	
1935	8	2	4		4
1936	4				4
Total	110	19	56	35	21

620

APPENDIX E

LIST OF MONEY BILLS TO WHICH RECOMMENDATIONS MADE BY THE SENATE

Year	Title of Bill	Number of recommendations made	Number accepted by Dáil	Number rejected by Dáil
1923	Appropriation Bill	3	3	
	Army Pensions Bill	4	4	
1924	Finance Bill	2	2	
1925	Finance Bill	2	2	
1926	Finance Bill	1	1	
1928	Finance Bill	1	1	
1929	Finance Bill	1	1	
	Finance Bill	2	2	
	Superannuation and Pensions Bill	2	1	1
1932	Emergency Imposition of Duties Bill	5	3	2
	Finance Bill	13	6	7
	Finance Bill	3		3
	Finance (Customs Duties) (No. 2) Bill	3	3	
	Finance (Customs Duties) (No. 4) Bill	1	1	
1933	Gárda Síochána (Pensions) Bill	2	2	
	Industrial Credit Bill	2	2	
	Land Bond Bill	5	1	4
1934	Finance Bill	1		1
1935	Finance Bill	3		3
	Land Purchase (Guarantee Fund) Bill			
	Total (1922–36)	56	35	21

APPENDIX F

BILLS IN RESPECT OF WHICH THE SUSPENSORY POWER WAS EXERCISED BY THE SENATE

Title of Bill	Short Subject Matter	Remarks
Intoxicating Liquor Bill, 1923.	Extension of prohibited hours for sale of intoxicating liquor.	Second Stage postponed, 8th August 1923. Signed by the Governor-General, 23rd July 1924. (*Text, pp.* 125–6, 235–6.)
Dáil Supreme Court (Pensions) Bill, 1925.	Conferment of pensions on judges of the former Dáil (Republican) Supreme Court.	A Money Bill. Second Stage passed, 7th April 1925, but no further action taken and Bill not returned to Dáil. Signed by the Governor-General, 27th April 1925. (*Text, p.* 549.)
Civil Service Regulation (Amendment) Bill, 1925.	Enabling Civil Service posts to be confined to persons of one sex.	Rejected on Second Stage, 17th December 1925. Signed by the Governor-General, 22nd September 1926. (*Text, p.* 208.)
Constitution (Removal of Oath) Bill, 1932.	Removal of Oath from Constitution.	Passed, 28th June 1932, with amendments with which the Dáil refused to agree. Sent again to Senate, 1st March 1933. Amendment carried on Second Stage, declining further considera-

		tion until Bill made subject of negotiation with British Government, 15th March 1933. Enactment resolution passed by Dáil, 3rd May 1933. Signed by the Governor-General, 3rd May 1933. (*Text, pp.* 304–15, 324–5.)
Agricultural Produce (Cereals) Bill, 1932.	Control and regulation of milling.	Second Stage passed, 15th December 1932. Parliament dissolved, 2nd January 1933. Sent again to Senate, 1st March 1933. Bill passed with 44 amendments, 29th March 1933. Message sent by Dáil agreeing with 29 amendments and disagreeing with remaining 15, 27th April 1933. Enactment resolution passed by Dáil, 3rd May 1933 (before Dáil message could be considered by Senate). Signed by the Governor-General, 4th May 1933. (*Text, pp.* 346–7.)
Local Government (Dublin) Bill, 1933.	Abolition of the Commercial Register, which elected five members to the Corporation of Dublin on a special franchise.	Rejected on Second Stage, 14th June 1933. Sent again to Senate, 27th February 1935. Passed by Senate, 28th March 1935. Signed by the Governor-General, 29th March 1935. (*Text, p.* 350.)

Title of Bill	Short Subject Matter	Remarks
Constitution (Amendment No. 19) Bill, 1933.	Reduction of Senate's suspensory power to three months.	Second Stage postponed and Joint Committee requested on constitution and powers of Senate, 11th July 1933. Sent again to Senate, 11th April 1935. Rejected on Second Stage, 1st May 1935. No further action taken by Dáil, and Bill never became law. (*Text*, *pp.* 350–3.)
Local Government (Extension of Franchise) Bill, 1933.	Extension of local government franchise to all persons over twenty-one years of age.	Rejected on Second Stage, 12th July 1933. Sent again to Senate, 27th February 1935. Passed by Senate, 28th March 1935. Signed by the Governor-General, 29th March 1935. (*Text*, *p.* 350.)
Wearing of Uniform (Restriction) Bill, 1934.	Prohibition of wearing of political uniforms.	Rejected on Second Stage, 21st March 1934. No further action taken by Dáil, and Bill never became law. (*Text, pp.* 343–4, 360–2.)
Constitution (Amendment No. 23) Bill, 1934.	Abolition of university representation in the Dáil.	Rejected on Second Stage, 18th July 1934. Sent again to Senate, 6th February 1936. Passed by Senate with 2 amendments, 26th February 1936. Dáil disagreed with amendments, 12th March 1936. Senate insisted, 18th March

		1936. Enactment resolution passed by Dáil, 23rd April 1936. Signed by the Governor-General, 24th April 1936. (*Text, pp.* 413–17.)
Constitution (Amendment No. 24) Bill, 1934.	Abolition of the Senate.	Rejected on Second Stage, 1st June 1934. Sent again to Senate, 12th December 1935. Second Stage postponed and conference requested, 16th January 1936. Enactment resolution passed by Dáil, 29th May 1936. Signed by the Governor-General, 29th May 1936. (*Text, pp.* 363–402, 455–69.)

BILLS INITIATED IN THE SENATE

Title of Bill	Name of Introducer	Remarks
Public Holidays Bill, 1923	Edward MacLysaght	Remaining Stages not proceeded with.
Dyestuffs (Import Regulation) Repeal Bill, 1923	James G. Douglas	Passed unamended by the Dáil.
League of Nations (Guarantee) Bill, 1923	James G. Douglas	Passed unamended by the Dáil.
Valuation (Postponement of Revision) Bill, 1923	Thomas Linehan	Passed unamended by the Dáil.
Oireachtas Witnesses Oaths Bill, 1924	James G. Douglas	Passed unamended by the Dáil.
Private Bill Costs Bill, 1924	James G. Douglas	Passed unamended by the Dáil.
Coroners Bill, 1925	Peter De Loughry	Withdrawn after consideration by Select Committee; used as basis for Coroners (Amendment) Bill, 1926 (q.v.).
Land Bill, 1925	Richard A. Butler	Withdrawn after Second Stage.
Shop Hours (Barbers and Hairdressers, Dublin and Districts) Bill, 1925	Thomas Farren	Rejected on Second Stage.
Shop Hours (Drapery Trades, Dublin and Districts) Bill, 1925	James G. Douglas	Passed unamended by the Dáil.

Title of Bill	Name of Introducer	Remarks
Coroners (Amendment) Bill, 1926	Samuel L. Brown, K.C.	Passed by the Dáil with eleven amendments.
Registered Accountants Bill, 1927	James G. Douglas	Rejected on Second Stage.
Wild Birds Protection (Amendment) Bill, 1927	Samuel L. Brown, K.C.	Rejected by the Dáil.
Bodies Corporate (Executors and Administrators) Bill, 1928	James G. Douglas	Passed unamended by the Dáil.
Children Bill, 1928	Patrick J. Brady	Passed by the Dáil with one amendment.
Dublin City and County (Relief of the Poor) Bill, 1929	Thomas Johnson	Rejected by the Dáil.
Intoxicating Liquor (Amendment) Bill, 1929	Patrick J. Hooper	Passed unamended by the Dáil.
Town Planning and Rural Amenities Bill, 1929	Thomas Johnson	Not considered by the Dáil and killed by the dissolution on the 19th January 1932.
Wild Birds Protection Bill, 1929	Samuel L. Brown, K.C.	Passed by the Dáil with seventeen amendments.
Shop Hours (Drapery Trades, Dublin and Districts) Bill, 1930	James G. Douglas	Rejected by the Dáil.
Trustee Bill, 1931	Samuel L. Brown, K.C.	Passed unamended by the Dáil.
Animals (Anæsthetics) (Amendment) Bill, 1933	John J. Counihan	Rejected on Second Stage.
Slaughter of Animals Bill, 1933	John T. O'Farrell	Not considered by the Dáil.

Title of Bill	Name of Introducer	Remarks
Constitution (Amendment No. 25) Bill, 1934	James G. Douglas	Not considered by the Dáil and lapsed by abolition of the Senate.
Local Government (Extension of Franchise) Bill, 1934	Joseph Connolly	Leave to introduce Bill refused.
Nurses' and Mid-wives' Pensions Bill, 1935	James C. Dowdall	Not considered by the Dáil and lapsed by abolition of the Senate.

NUMBER OF SITTING DAYS
AND DURATION OF SITTING

Year	Number of sitting days	Total time[1]		Average duration of sitting[1]	
		h.	m.	h.	m.
1922	5	6	50	1	20
1923	45	144		3	10
1924	46	128	20	2	50
1925	41	119	10	2	50
1926	32	90	10	2	50
1927	44	113	10	2	30
1928	32	77		2	20
1929	41	132	50	3	10
1930	30	104	20	3	30
1931	39	132	50	3	20
1932	36	117	40	3	20
1933	51	199	40	3	50
1934	43	154	50	3	40
1935	37	136	40	3	40
1936	13	47	20	3	40
Total	535	1704	50	3	10 (over whole period)

Average number of sitting days per year for the thirteen completed years 1923–35: 40.

[1] To nearest ten minutes.

AVERAGE ATTENDANCE
IN EACH CALENDAR YEAR

Year	Average attendance	Percentage
1923	37	62
1924	35	58
1925	37	62
1926	38	63
1927	37	62
1928	41	68
1929	43	72
1930	43	72
1931	45	75
1932	44	73
1933	40	67
1934	42	70
1935	43	72
1936	46	77
Average over whole period	41	68

Note.—The total membership occasionally fell below 60, on account of the existence of one or more casual vacancies. Due regard has been had to this fact in the compilation of the above table, the figures being adjusted to a notional total of 60.

INDEX

INDEX

2T

O'Donnell, Peadar—*continued*
Wolfe Tone's grave, 260; (*1932*) on extremist support for Fianna Fáil, 284; on policemen and Mr. Cosgrave, 297; (*1934*) a founder and member of Executive of Republican Congress Party, 405
O'Duffy, General Eoin: (*1924*) Commissioner of Civic Guard, appointed to deal with Army mutiny, 141; (*1927*) at death-bed of Kevin O'Higgins, confidence of O'Higgins in, 196, 329; (*1931*) reference of Republican journal to, 259; (*1933*) dismissal from office, 11, 329–30; Director-General of National Guard, 330; Mr. De Valera's attitude to, 331–2; cancels parade of National Guard, 333; leader of United Ireland Party, 335; assaulted in Tralee, 336–7; domiciliary visit by police, 338; arrest of, and release by *habeas corpus*, 339; High Court order of prohibition to Military Tribunal re certain charges against, 339; (*1934*) on extension of local government electorate, 409–10; resignation from United Ireland Party, 11, 406–8; (*1935*) founds ational Corporate Party, policy of all-Ireland republic, 435; (*1936–7*) commands Irish volunteers in Spanish Civil War, 474–5
Farrell, John T.: (*1922*) interview with Mr. De Valera prior to Civil War, 59; elected to Senate, 94, 95; (*1923*) supports amendment to Public Safety Bill, 127; (*1924*) amendment to Courts of Justice Bill, 151; resists attempt to restrict Senate's power over delegated legislation, 541; (*1925*) speech in divorce debate, 168; sequel to attitude in divorce debate, 171; re-elected, 155; opposes Boundary Agreement, 198; (*1926*) on hasty legislation, 201; (*1928*) proposes motion re changes in constitution and powers of Senate, 231–2; opposes abolition of referendum and altered Senate electoral system, 237; on canvassing for election to Senate, 238–9; tribute to Lord Glenavy on retirement, 244; defeated in contest for Vice-Chair, 268; (*1929*) on ministerial representation in Senate, 271–2; (*1929–30*) speeches on external affairs, 277; (*1932*) speech on Removal of Oath Bill, 314–15; (*1933*) initiates Slaughter of Animals Bill, 523; on compensation

and pensions to ex-members of I.R.A., 348; on Bill to reduce Senate's suspensory power, 352; (*1934*) sponsors Bill to restore referendum for constitutional amendments, 410; criticism of Revision of Constituencies Bill, 417; (*1935*) on Fianna Fáil challenge to Chairman's ruling re Land Purchase Bill, 554; (*1936*) speech on Senate Abolition Bill, votes for motion thereon, 461; speech at final meeting of Senate, 465. Reference to (payment of members), 518
O'Hanlon, Michael F.: (*1925*) elected to Senate, 155; (*1927*) resigns from Farmers' Party, 191; (*1928*) on Fianna Fáil attitude to Senate, 237; member of Cosgrave Party, 274; defeated in contest for Vice-Chair, 269; (*1929*) votes against Government on Juries Bill, 274; (*1932*) elected Vice-Chairman, 303; (*1933*) on Bill to reduce Senate's suspensory power, 352; (*1934*) on Senate Abolition Bill, 386, 394–5, 398; defeated in contest for Vice-Chair, 448; (*1935*) elected to Committee of Privileges, 555
O'Hegarty, P. S.: quoted, 43, 50
O'Higgins, Kevin, T.D., Vice-President of Executive Council, 1922–7, Minister for Home Affairs, 1922–4, Minister for Justice, 1924–7, Minister for External Affairs, 1927: (*1922*) member of Dáil Cabinet and Provisional Government, 55; negotiations with British Government re Draft Constitution, 72; enumerates Constitution Articles of Treaty obligation, 72; description of agreed Draft, 73; on character of Southern Unionist negotiators, 75; takes part in formal negotiations with Southern Unionists, 76, 78; attitude to Unionist minority, 77; statements in Dáil on negotiations, 77, 78; on character of agreement reached, 78, 79, 414, 415; on effect of Civil War on post-Treaty negotiations, 81–2; pilots Constitution Bill through Dáil, 84–6; 'no constitutional hybrid' between republic and monarchy, 568; on claim that Oath in Treaty not obligatory, 307–8; on execution of Irregular leaders, 101; (*1923*) murder of father, 100; opposes Senate amendments to Public Safety Bill, 127, 129; refusal to tolerate two governments and two armies, 137; on Mr. De Valera's

WORLD AFFAIRS: National and International Viewpoints
An Arno Press Collection

Angell, Norman. **The Great Illusion, 1933.** 1933.

Benes, Eduard. **Memoirs:** From Munich to New War and New Victory. 1954.

[Carrington, Charles Edmund] (Edmonds, Charles, pseud.) **A Subaltern's War.** 1930. New preface by Charles Edmund Carrington.

Cassel, Gustav. **Money and Foreign Exchange After 1914.** 1922.

Chambers, Frank P. **The War Behind the War, 1914-1918.** 1939.

Dedijer, Vladimir. **Tito.** 1953.

Dickinson, Edwin DeWitt. **The Equality of States in International Law.** 1920.

Douhet, Giulio. **The Command of the Air.** 1942.

Edib, Halidé. **Memoirs.** 1926.

Ferrero, Guglielmo. **The Principles of Power.** 1942.

Grew, Joseph C. **Ten Years in Japan.** 1944.

Hayden, Joseph Ralston. **The Philippines.** 1942.

Hudson, Manley O. **The Permanent Court of International Justice, 1920-1942.** 1943.

Huntington, Ellsworth. **Mainsprings of Civilization.** 1945.

Jacks, G. V. and R. O. Whyte. **Vanishing Lands:** A World Survey of Soil Erosion. 1939.

Mason, Edward S. **Controlling World Trade.** 1946.

Menon, V. P. **The Story of the Integration of the Indian States.** 1956.

Moore, Wilbert E. **Economic Demography of Eastern and Southern Europe.** 1945.

[Ohlin, Bertil]. **The Course and Phases of the World Economic Depression.** 1931.

Oliveira, A. Ramos. **Politics, Economics and Men of Modern Spain, 1808-1946.** 1946.

O'Sullivan, Donal. **The Irish Free State and Its Senate.** 1940.

Peffer, Nathaniel. **The White Man's Dilemma.** 1927.

Philby, H. St. John. **Sa'udi Arabia.** 1955.

Rappard, William E. **International Relations as Viewed From Geneva.** 1925.

Rauschning, Hermann. **The Revolution of Nihilism.** 1939.

Reshetar, John S., Jr. **The Ukrainian Revolution, 1917-1920.** 1952.

Richmond, Admiral Sir Herbert. **Sea Power in the Modern World.** 1934.

Robbins, Lionel. **Economic Planning and International Order.** 1937. New preface by Lionel Robbins.

Russell, Bertrand. **Bolshevism:** Practice and Theory. 1920.

Russell, Frank M. **Theories of International Relations.** 1936.

Schwarz, Solomon M. **The Jews in the Soviet Union.** 1951.

Siegfried, André. **Canada:** An International Power. [1947].

Souvarine, Boris. **Stalin.** 1939.

Spaulding, Oliver Lyman, Jr., Hoffman Nickerson, and John Womack Wright. **Warfare.** 1925.

Storrs, Sir Ronald. **Memoirs.** 1937.

Strausz-Hupé, Robert. **Geopolitics:** The Struggle for Space and Power. 1942.

Swinton, Sir Ernest D. **Eyewitness.** 1933.

Timasheff, Nicholas S. **The Great Retreat.** 1946.

Welles, Sumner. **Naboth's Vineyard:** The Dominican Republic, 1844-1924. 1928. Two volumes in one.

Whittlesey, Derwent. **The Earth and the State.** 1939.

Wilcox, Clair. **A Charter for World Trade.** 1949.